Impacts of AI on Students and Teachers in Education 5.0

Froilan Delute Mobo
Philippine Merchant Marine Academy, Philippines

IGI Global
Scientific Publishing
Publishing Tomorrow's Research Today

Vice President of Editorial	Melissa Wagner
Managing Editor of Acquisitions	Mikaela Felty
Managing Editor of Book Development	Jocelynn Hessler
Production Manager	Mike Brehm
Cover Design	Phillip Shickler

Published in the United States of America by
    IGI Global Scientific Publishing
    701 East Chocolate Avenue
    Hershey, PA, 17033, USA
    Tel: 717-533-8845
    Fax: 717-533-8661
    Website: https://www.igi-global.com E-mail: cust@igi-global.com

Library of Congress Cataloging-in-Publication Data

Names: Mobo, Froilan Delute, 1979- editor.
Title: Impacts of AI on students and teachers in education 5.0 / Edited by
    Froilan Mobo.
Description: Hershey, PA : IGI Global Scientific Publishing, [2025] |
    Includes bibliographical references and index. | Summary: "This book
    explores the transformative effects of artificial intelligence (AI)
    within the context of Education 5.0, a concept that emphasizes a
    human-centered approach to education, leveraging advanced technologies
    to enhance learning experiences"-- Provided by publisher.
Identifiers: LCCN 2024054508 (print) | LCCN 2024054509 (ebook) | ISBN
    9798369381915 (hardcover) | ISBN 9798369381922 (paperback) | ISBN
    9798369381939 (ebook)
Subjects: LCSH: Artificial intelligence--Educational applications. |
    Education--Effect of technological innovations on. | Student-centered
    learning.
Classification: LCC LB1028.43 .I475 2025 (print) | LCC LB1028.43 (ebook)
    | DDC 370.285/63--dc23/eng/20240115
LC record available at https://lccn.loc.gov/2024054508
LC ebook record available at https://lccn.loc.gov/2024054509

British Cataloguing in Publication Data
A Cataloguing in Publication record for this book is available from the British Library.

Table of Contents

Detailed Table of Contents

Chapter 1
D. Rajalakshmi, SASTRA University, India
G. Revathy, SASTRA University, India
T. Priyanka, SASTRA University, India
M. Martinaa, SASTRA University, India

Many times in our daily routines, we face challenging decisions that require careful consideration and analysis due to their complexity and significance. Achieving the most effective solution often involves weighing multiple factors relevant to the situation. This study aims to apply a structured decision-making process by analogizing a community issue to a student scenario, illustrating a methodical approach to resolve complex problems using fuzzy soft sets. The same dataset has been applied to Machine learning models such as Random forest, Support vector machine and Naive Bayes. Out of which Random forest achieves the highest accuracy exactly matching the Fuzzy soft set results. Hence forth by using Fuzzy soft sets and ML based models we can predict the student dismissal rate and provide suggestions and improvements in reducing the dismissal and increasing the retention rate.

Chapter 2
Satyabrata Pandit, Brainware University, India
Saptarshi Kumar Sarkar, Brainware University, India
Sreya Barik, Brainware University, India
Sutapa Sahu, Brainware University, India

Thus, the chapter aims to unravel the role of AI in skill enhancement with reference to critical thinking ability, problem-solving skills, and digital skills. With AI technologies gradually progressing to redefine employment situations in different parts of the world today, it has become essential to train the learners for the arising complex employment scenario. The first part of the chapter explores how critical thinking and problem solving can be improved by AI, such as using adaptive learning systems, simulation, and data analysis. It then goes further to illustrate how the use of AI tools in the teaching of digital literacy is conducted, with a focus on how the use of AI in learning makes it possible for a learner to be taught based on his/her specific needs and the acquisition of the fundamental skills needed in the digital competency. The last part looks at the ways of teaching education to prepare students for jobs with artificial intelligence, balancing between technical and humanities, ethics, and retraining.

Chapter 3

Snehasis Dey, College of Engineering Bhubaneswar, BPUT University, India

Barsha Baishali Sahoo, College of Engineering Bhubaneswar, BPUT University, India

Education 5.0 is still in its infancy. After covid-19, the education sector has propelled a milestone by integrating virtual means of education. Though it was not completely successful in the covid era but impact of virtual education has opened a new dimension to the reality of integrating the most successful technology into its field. AI is the new research topic in every field. AI integration to the education sector will enhance the productivity and effectiveness amongst learner and educator. Different AI enabled services may be integrated in the education so that the challenges in providing a sustainable environment towards education will definitely be achieved. As education is diversified to learner and educator or student and teacher so the technological implementations may be done from grass roots level. This chapter dives into the education 5.0 basics and the means of AI integration to Education 5.0. It also provides a design structure of AI integrated education, it's possible challenges and research scope for future ahead.

Chapter 4

Sucheta Yambal, Dr. Babasaheb Ambedkar Marathwada University, India

Yashwant Arjunrao Waykar, Dr. Babasaheb Ambedkar Marathwada University, India

AI is revolutionizing education, especially classroom management. AI-driven technologies boost productivity, student engagement, and personalized instruction. AI's role in classroom management is examined in this research. It analyzes how AI technologies like intelligent tutoring systems, behavior analysis tools, and adaptive learning platforms may reduce administrative tasks, enhance interactive learning environments, and provide quick student performance insights. The report also addresses ethical problems including data protection, algorithmic bias, and transparency, which are crucial to AI inclusion in education. This research explores the pros and cons of AI-driven classroom management to demonstrate how AI may be utilized ethically and effectively. This talk underlines the need of properly employing AI technology to balance operational efficiency with fair and transparent processes, making education more effective and engaging.

Chapter 5

Myla Arcinas, De La Salle University, Philippines

This chapter investigates the integration of artificial intelligence (AI) in higher education peace programs, examining its effects on student outcomes, engagement, and critical thinking. Employing a concurrent mixed-methods approach, the study collected data from 500 survey respondents and 50 interviewees across five institutions. Quantitative findings reveal significant improvements in learning outcomes, particularly in knowledge acquisition ($d = 0.82$) and critical thinking ($d = 0.70$), with increased student engagement ($d = 0.46$–0.61). AI integration emerged as the strongest predictor of learning outcomes ($\beta = 0.41$, $p < .001$). Qualitative analysis highlights AI's potential for enhancing engagement, personalization, and critical thinking, while also identifying implementation challenges and ethical concerns. The study concludes by recommending gradual AI integration, emphasizing personalized learning, and developing ethical guidelines, addressing issues such as technology overload and equitable access in AI-enhanced peace education.

Chapter 6

Mansi Trivedi, Amity Law School, Amity University, Noida, India
Shantanu Bindewari, IILM University, India

A lot of industries, including education, are fast changing due to artificial intelligence (AI). Artificial Intelligence (AI) is evolving into a potent tool for meeting a variety of educational needs because to its ability to handle enormous volumes of data, recognize patterns, and carry out difficult tasks. One of its most exciting uses is the assistance it gives visually impaired pupils, giving them more chances to study, be involved, and be independent. Traditional teaching strategies and resources can provide serious difficulties for pupils who are visually impaired. A heavy emphasis on visual materials—like textbooks, whiteboards, and computer screens—can make it difficult for students to learn and participate.

The incorporation of Artificial Intelligence in modern education has revolutionized the learning experience, but it also raises concerns about widening existing gaps in education, particularly in terms of gender and geographical location. This research delves into the effects of AI on students and educators, with a focus on the unequal access to digital technologies and its consequences for education. Our findings indicate notable differences in AI performance based on gender and location, with male students and urban areas performing better than their female and rural counterparts. We investigate how AI can both reduce and amplify existing disparities, and suggest approaches to ensure that the benefits of AI are shared fairly.

The digital divide hinders Indigenous empowerment by restricting access to services and economic opportunities, thereby affecting cultural preservation. This chapter emphasises culturally appropriate and sustainable strategies. It examines historical and contemporary factors, such as infrastructure limitations and systemic inequalities, using frameworks such as the diffusion of innovations and digital citizenship to promote Indigenous self-determination in the digital age. Lessons from national and international initiatives advocate increased infrastructure investment and tailored digital literacy programs. Sustainable initiatives have been proposed to empower Indigenous communities to control their digital futures, highlighting the importance of partnerships among Indigenous organisations, governments, and technology companies for long-term support and capacity building. This approach aimed to bridge the digital gap and create an inclusive digital world for Indigenous communities.

   Yakkala B. V. L. Pratyusha, Infelearn, India
   Bindi Varghese, Christ University, India

The chapter focuses on concepts of Education 5.0 and its competence in shaping future learning environments. It emphasises on learners social and personal growth by improving quality of life standards with the help of current technologies and digitalisation. (Shabir Ahmad, 2023) To deliver humanised approach by the application of new technologies is the primary use of Education 5.0. However, usage of new age technology in education doesn't mean giving laptop and tablet to each and every child and the usage of digital mediums for teaching and learning. After covid-19, digitisation becomes the integral part of our life, education is no exception for that. (Shabir Ahmad, 2023) Beyond digitalisation pandemic also remained us the importance of human hardships to social transformation with emotional intelligence driving technology as a tool. In short education 5.0. (SYDLE.com, 2023) referring to the significance of human, social and emotional abilities to enhance wellbeing of an individual by using technology advancement as a tool.

   Minh Tung Tran, FPT School of Business and Technology, FPT
      University, Vietnam

This research proposes an innovative AI-driven educational psychology model, the AI-EcoCollaborative Educational Psychology Model, to foster pro-environmental behaviors in Education 5.0. By integrating AI technologies with educational psychology principles, the model aims to create personalized, engaging, and interactive learning experiences that promote environmental awareness and action. The model incorporates various components, including personalized interventions, virtual reality simulations, and ethical considerations, to ensure effective and responsible implementation. Through case studies and future directions, the research explores the potential of AI-driven educational psychology in shaping a sustainable future.

Kalyani Nakul Satone, St. Vincent Pallotti College of Engineering and
    Technology, India
Pranjali B. Ulhe, School of Allied Sciences, Datta Meghe Institute of
    Higher Education and Research, India
Anushree Sandeep Deshmukh, Rajiv Gandhi Institute of Technology,
    India
Leena Mandurkar, St. Vincent Pallotti College of Engineering and
    Technology, India

Artificial intelligence (AI) is transforming education by being essential to the growth
of students' digital literacy, critical thinking, and problem-solving abilities as well
as their readiness for the quickly changing AI-driven labor markets. This abstract
explores the multidimensional impact of AI on skill development in education.
In order to prepare the complexity of the modern world, Students must be able to
think critically and solve problems in order to be prepared for the complexity of
the modern world. To develop skills, it gets achieved through adaptive assessments,
real-world simulations, and tailored learning experiences. Through the use of AI,
teachers may customize course materials to each student's unique learning style and
speed, improving comprehension and student engagement. The ability to effectively
and ethically acquire, assess, and use information in digital environments is referred
to as digital literacy.

Dhruv Sabharwal, Sharda University, India
Archan Mitra, Presidency University, Bangalore, India

The role of Artificial Intelligence (AI) in Education 5. 0 is changing the paradigm of
the student learning process and the teaching process as well. This chapter discusses
the effects of AI on students and teachers for personalisation, student motivation
and teacher practice. With the help of AI technologies, one gets better and more
efficient educational process by providing better learning conditions and thus –
making education more flexible. Teachers have less work load to handle or to be
more precise the work load that teachers handle is now more intelligent, AI provides
data, teachers use this data to imply a better teaching strategy. As Education 5. 0
narrative emerges, a conceptual balance of the role of AI can strengthen of learning
spaces, enable innovation and preserve humanistic ideals. Thus, this chapter emphasis
each of the four themes regarding the need for the responsible development and
implementation of AI in order to create a future for education that will be inclusive,
equitable and adaptable.

Chapter 13

*Debasis Pani, Gandhi Institute of Advanced Computer and Research,
India*
*Narayana Maharana, Gayatri Vidya Parishad College of Engineering,
India*
Sunil Kumar Pradhan, Berhampur University, India
Saumendra Das, GIET University, Gunupur, India

Education 5.0 emphasises not only the integration of technology in education but also a humanitarian approach by incorporating artificial intelligence. This approach focuses on the emotional, social, and intellectual growth of students, aiming to enhance their overall learning experience and foster sustainable learning outcomes for holistic societal development. AR and VR play a crucial role in this transformation, offering immersive and interactive learning environments. Despite their significant benefits, AR and VR technologies are still evolving, presenting new challenges for educators and students as they advance. This chapter explores the transformative potential of AR and VR in enhancing learning outcomes within self-directed learning programs. It examines how these immersive technologies can create interactive and engaging experiences that promote better retention and application of knowledge. This chapter bridges theory and practice, providing educators, designers, and policymakers with better insights on using AR and VR to enhance self-directed learning.

Chapter 14

Sakshi Saxena, Garden City University, Bangalore, India
Swetha Appaji Parivara, Presidency College, Bangalore, India

In the wake of the COVID-19 pandemic, educational institutions globally face unprecedented challenges, with data analytics emerging as a vital tool to bridge learning gaps across K-12 and higher education. This chapter explores how data analytics can transform education by personalizing learning, optimizing instructional strategies, and assessing academic progress. With access to vast amounts of data, institutions can make informed, data-driven decisions in curriculum design and resource allocation. By utilizing data sources such as demographics, engagement metrics, and performance data, educators gain insights into learning trends and outcomes. The chapter discusses practical applications, including adaptive learning tools and predictive analytics for early interventions to improve student retention. It also addresses challenges related to data privacy, equity, and ethical use. By embracing emerging technologies like AI, blockchain, and VR, educational institutions can foster a culture of continuous improvement, enhancing resilience and educational outcomes on a global scale.

Chapter 15
Perception About Usage of GAI Tools in Teaching and Research by Teachers and Students in Higher Education Institutions 381
Chinna Suresh, SASTRA University, India
Sunkesula Mahammad Ali, AP Model School and Jr. College,
Amarapuram, India
V. Devaki, SASTRA University, India

In recent days, due to the evolution of Artificial Intelligence, education and research are in the process of rapid development. The AI, particularly GAI tools such as individualized learning and intelligent tutoring systems, are recreating traditional pedagogies and research methodologies. Consequently, in this chapter, global practices of AI in higher education are explored together with their applications in Journal publications. Surveys on AI acceptance reveal mixed perceptions among students and faculty. While students value AI's individualized learning experiences and self-paced study options, faculty acknowledge its ability to automate tasks but are worried about data privacy and students' ethical use of AI. Therefore, this chapter underlines a balanced method for AI integration, advocating for technical advancements that advocate educational values. To this end, recommendations and guidelines for adopting AI tools in higher education are provided with special emphasis on the role of educators to be aware and committed to conform with Institutional AI policies.

Chapter 16
Predictive Model for Enhancing Learning Skill Through Biometric Integration: A Review 413
Surekha Yashodharan, Government Engineering College, A.P.J. Abdul
Kalam Technological University, India
K. S. Vijayanand, A.P.J. Abdul Kalam Technological University, India

In the field of education, early identification of students who require additional support due to learning difficulties is paramount importance. This paper offers a pioneering approach to revolutionize education by harnessing biometric data for personalized and effective learning experiences. This research provides a foundation for further exploration in the field of adaptive learning technologies and their potential to transform the way we educate and acquire knowledge. This study proposes the development of a predictive model that leverages biometric information, such as physiological and behavioural data, to provide real-time insights into the learning process. The predictive model is designed to adapt and personalize learning experiences based on the individual's biometric responses. By continuously monitoring and analyzing biometric data, the system can dynamically adjust the difficulty level of educational content, provide timely interventions, and optimize learning strategies.

Chapter 17

Myla Arcinas, De La Salle University, Philippines

This study explores the transformative potential of e-learning technologies in indigenous education, addressing persistent educational disparities. Through comprehensive literature analysis and international case studies, it investigates how digital resources and innovative educational strategies can overcome geographical barriers, preserve indigenous languages and foster culturally responsive education. The paper critically analyzes successful digital learning initiatives and identifies best practices in implementation. It concludes with actionable recommendations for researchers, educators, and policymakers, advocating for indigenous leadership, investment in digital infrastructure, and the respectful integration of indigenous and Western knowledge systems. By navigating these complexities, the study posits that e-learning is a powerful tool for creating global equitable, culturally affirming and effective educational experiences for indigenous learners.

Chapter 18

Robertas Damaševičius, Vytautas Magnus University, Lithuania

This chapter introduces a pioneering educational paradigm that integrates the principles of quantum computing to redefine teaching and learning. Quantum Pedagogy leverages quantum mechanics concepts such as superposition, entanglement, and quantum tunneling to create highly personalized, adaptive, and immersive learning environments. By harnessing the unprecedented computational power of quantum computing, this framework offers innovative solutions for real-time curriculum adjustment, individualized tutoring, and predictive analytics for student success. The chapter explores the transformative potential of Quantum Pedagogy through key themes including quantum-adaptive learning systems, quantum-enhanced collaborative platforms, and quantum data analytics. Case studies demonstrate the practical applications and benefits of this framework, while addressing the challenges and ethical considerations inherent in its implementation.

Artificial Intelligence (AI) is a technology slowly gaining traction in the Philippine educational landscape. This chapter intends to investigate and share the different perspectives and insights of higher education institutions in the country regarding the use of AI in faculty and students' teaching and learning experiences. Given that the Philippines is a developing country with numerous educational issues and problems, the impact of the previous COVID-19 pandemic has led to the emergence of additional challenges. The abrupt transition from face-to-face to online learning paved the way for students and faculty to use AI as a helpful tool to adapt to the changes in the education spectrum. The authors argued that there were essential mechanisms that higher education institutions must look over before embracing AI in the curriculum. The institutions must first weigh the benefits and risks to arrive at a sound policy regulating AI within the educational system.

This chapter analyses recommended journal articles to explore the impact of AI in Education 5.0. These reviews indicated that the establishment of intelligent tutoring systems, personalized learning, curriculum development and evaluation, research support, learning analytics, and gamification of learning were the main uses of artificial intelligence in Education 5.0. The key findings from the chapter are the transformative role that artificial intelligence has played in education by creating a more independent, student-centred and student-directed learning environment that enables learners to demonstrate their innovative skills. The main obstacles to the adoption of Education 5.0 were concerns about ethics, security, and finances as well as legislation. The chapter went on to suggest investments in infrastructure development, user training, and policy initiatives.

Preface

On the cusp of Education 5.0, it is AI that is assuming an increasingly dominant position in reshaping the learning space in incredible ways. This new era aims at integrating the rationality of advanced technology with the humane reason for learning tailored to the learner, for effective thinking, the future-equipped character. As such, my chapter will endeavor to unravel these deep effects, illustrating how learning agendas are not only augmented by but fundamentally transformed by AI in addition to the shifting identities of students and educators.

In fact, Education 5.0 is built upon the principles of flexibility and proactivity to respond to the new requirements of education for the multicultural and global student audience. This goal is well aligned with what AI can provide: guidance for individual learning processes, efficient management of administrative burdens in educational practice, and concrete information for effective learning process management to allow educators to concentrate on the tasks of guiding learners rather than administrative routines. However, as these advances are infinitely promising, so are the arising practical difficulties and complications.

Teachers are now called upon to redesign their approaches to teaching, use AI innovation in harmony with interpersonal aptitudes, as well as consider ethical problems concerning data protection and AI prejudice in tools. This chapter reviews these dynamics, with emphasis on the latest research the author and other researchers have conducted and case studies to show how and where AI is being implemented in various global classrooms. Ranging from adaptive learning technologies that help to tailor the learning materials to the specific needs of a student to AI platforms that assist a teacher in real time, each example is a proof of the potential AI found in the learning process that can help make it more inclusive and efficient. Furthermore, the chapter discusses how educators, as facilitators in learning experiences, help the learners appreciate the potentials and pitfalls of AI as well as be responsible consumers of technology while keeping as the driving force human compassion and logic. As you will begin this journey to understand the impact of AI in Education 5.0, let me look at the razor's edge we are riding—balance between science and spirituality. Thus, we are able to provide a better picture of how AI can be adaptive, constructive, and supportive, which can turn into an enabler rather than disrupting the most valuable part of human interaction—education.

Froilan Delute Mobo

Philippine Merchant Marine Academy, Philippines

Chapter 1
Advanced Techniques in Predicting Student Dismissal Fuzzy Soft Sets vs. Machine Learning

D. Rajalakshmi
https://orcid.org/0000-0003-4851-7685
SASTRA University, India

G. Revathy
https://orcid.org/0000-0002-0691-1687
SASTRA University, India

T. Priyanka
SASTRA University, India

M. Martinaa
SASTRA University, India

ABSTRACT

Many times in our daily routines, we face challenging decisions that require careful consideration and analysis due to their complexity and significance. Achieving the most effective solution often involves weighing multiple factors relevant to the situation. This study aims to apply a structured decision-making process by analogizing a community issue to a student scenario, illustrating a methodical approach to resolve complex problems using fuzzy soft sets. The same dataset has been applied to Machine learning models such as Random forest, Support vector machine and Naive Bayes. Out of which Random forest achieves the highest accuracy exactly

DOI: 10.4018/979-8-3693-8191-5.ch001

matching the Fuzzy soft set results. Hence forth by using Fuzzy soft sets and ML based models we can predict the student dismissal rate and provide suggestions and improvements in reducing the dismissal and increasing the retention rate.

INTRODUCTION

Set theory was introduced in 1874 by German mathematician George Cantor. Set theory is the branch of mathematics concerned with the properties of well-defined collections of things (known as sets). Set theory is commonly utilized in science and math subjects such as physics, biology, and chemistry, as well as electrical engineering and computer engineering. When uncertainty came into existence, set theory is unsuitable for solving any problems, as it requires a strong understanding of logic and mathematical reasoning. In 1962, Zadeh introduced Fuzzy set theory, to overcome uncertainity and also had a number of applications (Zadeh, 1965).

The fuzzy set theory gets enhanced by its membership function,

$$FY : Y \rightarrow [0, 1] \text{ (Eq 1)}$$

Using the membership function we can determine to what extent an element belongs to the set. The difficulty is that how its differs in particular case. Molodtsov initiated the concept of soft theory as a different model for solving complicated problems. Soft set theory can be seen as generalization of fuzzy set theory, a soft set is a parameterized family of sets, this is named soft as the boundary of the set depends on its parameters (Molodtsov, 1999). Maji et al. in the year 2002 further investigated both fuzzy set theory and soft set theory to introduce a new theory called fuzzy soft sets. They further confirmed that soft sets can be applied for decision making.

Maji et al. (2003) investigated the relationship between fuzzy set theory and soft set theory and proposed the concept of the fuzzy soft set, which contains a subset, a superset of a soft set, equality of soft sets, and operations on soft sets such as union, intersection, AND, and OR. They also explored and analyzed the fundamental features over these operations, as well as various applications of soft set theory to decision-making (Maji, Biswas, & Roy, 2003). Pei and Maio gave an alternate definition for the subset and intersection of a soft set in 2005, improving on the work of Maji, Roy, & Biswas (2002; 2003). Chaudhuri, De & Chatterjee (2013) focused on soft relations and fuzzy soft relations, which they implemented to find a solution to several decision-making problems.

Majumdar and Samanta provided several similarity measures between soft sets and used them to tackle decision-making problems in 2008 Majumdar & Samanta, (2008), and Kharal and Ahmad (2009) defined updated definitions and uses for the similarity measure between soft sets. Majumdar and Samanta introduced general-ized fuzzy soft sets theory in 2010 and investigated its qualities and applications in decision-making challenges and medical diagnosis methods (Majumdar & Samanta, 2010).

In 2011, Shabir and Naz (2011) introduced and the concept of soft topological spaces, also defined and investigated many different soft properties as generaliza-tion of the classical ones. In 2020 Renukadevi and Sangeetha defined certainty and coverage of a parameter as a concept related to the soft set and they established a different approach using the certainty of a parameter to determine a decision-making problem over the soft universe (Vellapandi & Gunasekaran, 2020).

In 2021, Debnath in his work, introduced a fuzzy hypersoft set as a combination of fuzzy set and hypersoft set. The adaptability of new idea is to deal with parame-terized complexities of instability as more as compared to a fuzzy soft set.

In 2021, Phaengtan et al. studied partial averages of fuzzy soft sets and devel-oped an algorithm for solving a variety of decision-making problems depending on partial averages. Moreover, they proved that this algorithm is precise for addressing decision-making.

Mockor and Hurtik (2021) studied fuzzy soft relations and explained the fuzzy soft approximation of fuzzy soft sets related to this relation. They applied fuzzy soft approximations in selective colour segmentation problems, where trustworthy and fully automated methods are yet to exist. The soft set theory gives a general mathematical tool for handling uncertainity, fuzzy, and other problems where are the objects are not clearly defined.

LITERATURE SURVEY

Fuzzy set theory, launched by Zadeh (1965), provides a mathematical framework for representing and reasoning with uncertainty and vagueness. Fuzzy sets generalize classical sets by allowing elements to have partial membership rather than just binary membership. Numerous researchers have extended and applied fuzzy set theory in various fields such as control systems, decision-making, pattern recognition, and artificial intelligence.

Zadeh's (1965) paper "Fuzzy sets" in Information and Control is a seminal work that introduced fuzzy set theory. It provides the foundational concepts for repre-senting and reasoning with uncertainty using fuzzy sets, which allow elements to have partial membership. This paper laid the groundwork for subsequent research in fuzzy logic and its applications across various fields

The book authored by Klir, and Yuan (1996) titled "Fuzzy Sets and Fuzzy Logic Theory and Applications," serves as a comprehensive resource on fuzzy set theory and its related applications. It encloses the theoretical foundations of fuzzy sets, fuzzy logic, and their applications in a variety of fields such as control systems, decision-making, and pattern recognition. This book is widely regarded as a fundamental reference for anyone interested in understanding and applying fuzzy logic concepts.

Molodtsov in 1999, by introducing the soft set theory he gave a mathematical framework to deal with uncertainty and he cleared the vagueness in data analysis & decision-making processes. Soft set theory provides a flexible approach that can handle imprecise, uncertain, and incomplete information. Several researchers applied soft set theory in different fields such as decision-making, pattern recognition, image processing, and data mining.

Some keynote references for soft set theory are

The introductory paper named" Soft set theory—first results," is the foundational work that introduced soft set theory to the academic community. In this paper, Molodtsov proposes a novel mathematical framework to handle uncertainty and vagueness in decision-making and data analysis processes. He defines all basic concepts of soft sets and establishes fundamental operations within the theory. Molodtsov's paper forms the groundwork for subsequent research in soft set theory and its applications in various domains. Maji, Biswas, and Roy (2003) in their paper titled "Soft set theory," build upon Molodtsov's foundational work on soft set theory, this paper further develops the theory by introducing the notion of a soft set as a pair of sets, namely a parameter set and a decision set, along with the operations of union, intersection, and complementation. The authors also explore the relationships between soft sets and classical sets, fuzzy sets, and rough sets, highlighting the versatility and applicability of soft set theory in handling with uncertainty and vagueness in decision-making problems.

Ali et al. (2009) in their paper "On some new operations in soft set theory," introduced additional operations to soft set theory, expanding its applicability in decision-making and data analysis. These new operations include Cartesian product, power set, and composition, enhancing the theory's versatility.

Preliminaries

Definition 3.1

Let X be the universal set. A fuzzy set is defined as follows.

$$F = \{(x, \mu_{F(x)}) \mid x \in X\}$$

where $\mu_{F(x)}$ denotes the membership function. The Membership function maps each element of X to a membership value between 0 and 1. In general a fuzzy set F is the function, F: $X \rightarrow [0, 1]$

Definition 3.2

The union of two fuzzy sets M and N with respect to the universal set X is defined by the equation,

$(M \cup N)(x) = max[M(x), N(x)]$,

where max denotes the maximum operator.

Definition 3.3

The standard intersection of two fuzzy sets M and N over the set X is defined by the equation,

$(M \cap N)(x) = min[M(x), N(x)]$,

where min denotes the minimum operator.

Definition 3.4

The complement M' of fuzzy set M over the set X is defined for by the equation,

$M'(x) = 1-M(x)$.

Remark:
1. Element of X for which $M(x) = M'$ are equilibrium points of M.
2. For standard complement, the membership values of equilibrium points are 0.5.

Definition 3.5

Let X denote initial universe set and E be a set of parameter with respect to U. Let P(U) denote the power set of U and $R \subseteq E$.
A pair (F, R) is said a soft set over U where F is a mapping given by,

$F_R: R \rightarrow P(U)$

Example 3.5

Let U be the set of toys and Let G be the set of parameters. $U=\{t_1,t_2,t_3,t_4,t_5\}$ and $G=\{$beautiful, costly, modern, cheap$\}=\{g_1,g_2,g_3,g_4\}$

Suppose (F, G) is a soft set of the attractiveness of the toys, $F(g_1)=\{t_1\}$

$F(g_2)=\{t_3,t_4\}$

$F(g_3)=\{t_1,t_2,t_5\}$

Then (F, G) is a soft set of $\{F(g_i): i=1,2,3$

i.e., $(F, G)=\{\{t_1\}, \{t_3 , t_4\}, \{t_1, t_2, t_5\}\}$

Definition 3.6

let two soft sets be defined as (P, A) and (Q, B) over a common universe U, we say that (P, A) is a soft subset of (Q, B) if,

(i) $P \subseteq Q$

(ii) $\forall p \in P$, P(p) and Q(p) are identical approximation. we write $(P,A) \subset (Q, B)$

(P, A) is said to be a soft super set of (Q, B) if (Q, B) is a soft subset of (P, A). We denote it by, $(P, A) \supset (Q, B)$

Definition 3.7

Two soft sets (P, A) and (Q, B) over a common universe U is said to be soft equal if (P, A) is a soft subset of (Q, B) and (Q, B) is a soft subset of (P, A).

Definition 3.8

A soft set (P, A) over U is considered a NULL if $\forall p \in P$ then $F(p)=\emptyset$.

Definition 3.9

A soft set (P, A) over U is said to be an absolute soft set if $\forall p \in P$ then $F(p)=U$.

Definition 3.10

The identity soft set function I on a soft set (P, A) is defined by,

I:(P, A) → (P, A) as I(P(p))=P(p), ∀P(p) in (P, A).

Definition 3.11

If (P, A) and (Q, B) are two soft sets then "(P, A) AND (Q, B)" denoted by (P, A) ∧ (Q, B)=(R, A × B), where R((α), (β))=P((α)) ∩ Q((β)),

∀((α), (β)) ∈ A × B.

Definition 3.12

If (P, A) and (Q, B) are two soft sets then "(P, A) OR (Q, B)"
denoted by (P, A) ∨ (Q, B) is defined by (P, A) ∨ (Q, B) = (R, A × B) where,
$R(\alpha,\beta) = P(\alpha) \cup Q(\beta)$, ∀ (α, β) ∈ A × B.

Definition 3.13

Union of two soft sets of (P, A) and (Q, B) over the common universe U is the soft set (R, C), where C = A ∩B,∀ e ∈ C

$$H(p) = \begin{cases} F(p) \; if\, p \; \in \; A - B \\ G(p) \; if\, p \; \in \; B - A \\ F(p) \cup G(p) \; if\, p \; \in \; A \cap B \end{cases}$$

i.e (P, A) ∪ (Q, B) = (R, C).

Definition 3.14

The intersection of two soft sets of (P, A) and (Q, B) over the common universe U is the soft set (R, C), where C = A ∩ B, where ∀ p ∈ C and R(p)=P(p) or Q(p).

$(P, A) \cap (Q,B) = (R, C)$.

METHODOLOGY

In this work, we make use of symbols Stochastic processes as "Stochastic", Finite Automata as"Finite", and Mathematical Statistics as"Statistic"
Find the average value of "Stochastic", "Finite", and "Statistics" for all students using a program.

We make use of the marks of 52 students from the maths department - Sastra University, Kumbakonam. To find the average value of marks in "Stochastic", "Finite" and "Statistics" for all student using a program, a sample data is shown in the below table 1.

Table 1. Sample Data

X	Stochastic	Finite	Statistic
x_1	0	4	52
x_2	68	70	86
x_3	40	6	50
x_4	82	84	94
x_5	50	32	52
x_6	56	50	62
x_7	46	38	76
x_8	54	30	62
x_9	20	2	58
x_{10}	36	8	60
x_{11}	62	28	76
x_{12}	74	80	86
x_{13}	9	9	40
x_{14}	82	44	82
x_{15}	80	42	78
x_{16}	52	50	76
x_{17}	76	60	84
x_{18}	80	32	72
x_{19}	50	20	70
x_{20}	64	32	72
x_{21}	56	24	50
x_{22}	56	18	74
x_{23}	56	10	50
x_{24}	54	32	70
x_{25}	32	4	68
x_{26}	76	54	80
x_{27}	68	34	60
x_{28}	76	12	78

Definition 4.1

We fuzzificate (Dombi, 1990) the details of students into Low "L", Middle "M", High"H", and Very high "VH".

$$F_{(L,\,A)} = \begin{cases} 1, & if\ a \le 60, \\ \frac{70-a}{10}, & if\ 60 < a < 70 \\ 0, & if\ a \ge 70 \end{cases}$$

$$F_{(M,\,A)} = \begin{cases} 1, & if\ a \le 60, \\ \frac{a-60}{10}, & if\ 60 < a < 70 \\ \frac{80-a}{10}, & if\ 70 < a < 80 \\ 0, & if\ a \ge 80 \end{cases}$$

$$F_{(H,\,A)} = \begin{cases} 1, & if\ a \le 70, \\ \frac{a-70}{10}, & if\ 70 < a < 80 \\ \frac{90-a}{10}, & if\ 80 < a < 90 \\ 0, & if\ a \ge 90 \end{cases}$$

$$F_{(L,\,A)} = \begin{cases} 1, & if\ a \le 80, \\ \frac{70-a}{10}, & if\ 80 < a < 90 \\ 0, & if\ a \ge 90 \end{cases}$$

we identify the membership grades of the student from the equations (Omar Adil, 2015) as shown in the figure 1,

Figure 1. Membership grades from the students

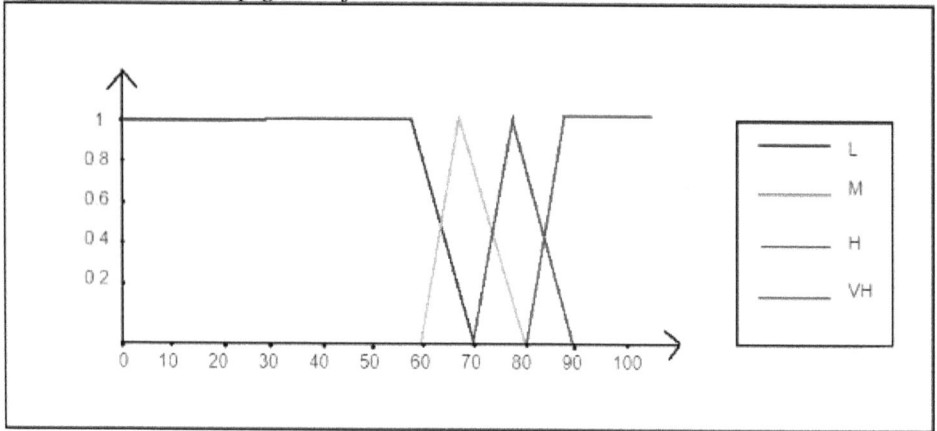

The above diagram is based on the Triangular and trapezoidal membership functions (Barua, Mudunuri, & Kosheleva, 2013).

By using the above membership function for the average value of arks of the student, we fuzzify the data (Rasmani & Shen, 2006).

4.1 Obtaining Soft Sets

Aktas and Cagman (2007) showed that every fuzzy set can be treated a soft set, so that we can transform student information what we have obtained in the previous section into smooth sets as follows,

$X = \{x_1, x_2, x_3, ..., x_{52}\},$

$E = \{0, 0.2, 0.4, 0.6, 0.8, 1\}$

4.1.1 Stochastic Processes

$(F_{Stochastic.L}; E) = \{0 = \{\emptyset\}; 0.2 = \{x_2, x_{27}, x_{37}\}; 0.4 = \{\emptyset\}; 0.6 = \{x_{20}\}; 0.8 = \{x_{11}, x_{38}\};$

$1 = \{x_1, x_3, x_5, x_6, x_7, x_8, x_9, x_{10}, x_{13}, x_{16}, x_{19}, x_{21}, x_{22}, x_{23}, x_{24}, x_{25}, x_{29}, x_{30}, x_{32}, x_{33}, x_{34}, x_{36}, x_{39}, x_{40}, x_{41}, x_{42}, x_{43}, x_{44}, x_{45}, x_{46}, x_{47}, x_{48}, x_{49}, x_{50}, x_{51}\}.$

$(F_{Stochastic.M}; E) = \{0 = \{x_1, x_3, x_5, x_6, x_7, x_8, x_9, x_{10}, x_{13}, x_{16}, x_{19}, x_{21}, x_{22}, x_{23}, x_{24}, x_{25}, x_{29}, x_{30}, x_{32}, x_{33}, x_{34}, x_{36}, x_{39}, x_{40}, x_{41}, x_{42}, x_{43}, x_{44}, x_{45}, x_{46}, x_{47}, x_{48}, x_{49}, x_{50}, x_{51}\};$
$0.2 = \{x_{11}, x_{31}, x_{38}\};$

$0.4=\{x_{17}, x_{20}, x_{26}, x_{28}\}$; $0.6=\{x_{12}\}$; $0.8=\{x_2, x_{27}, x_{37}\}$; $1=\{\varnothing\}\}$.

$(F_{Stochastic.H}; E)=\{0=\{\varnothing\}; 0.2=\{\varnothing\}; 0.4=\{x_{12}\}; 0.6=\{x_{17}, x_{26}, x_{28}\}; 0.8=\{x_4, x_{14}, x_{35}, x_{52}\}; 1=\{x_{18}\}\}$.

$(F_{Stochastic.VH}; E)=\{0=\{x_{15}, x_{18}\}; 0.2 = \{x_4, x_{14}, x_{35}, x_{52}\}; 0.4=\{\varnothing\}; 0.6=\{\varnothing\}; 0.8=\{\varnothing\}; 1=\{\varnothing\}\}$.

4.1.2 Finite Automata

$(F_{Finite.L}; E)=\{0=\{x_2\}; 0.2=\{\varnothing\}; 0.4=\{\varnothing\}; 0.6=\{\varnothing\}; 0.8=\{\varnothing\};$

$1=\{x_1, x_3, x_5, x_6, x_7, x_8, x_9, x_{10}, x_{11}, x_{13}, x_{14}, x_{15}, x_{16}, x_{17}, x_{18}, x_{19}, x_{20}, x_{21}, x_{22}, x_{23}, x_{24}, x_{25}, x_{26}, x_{27}, x_{28}, x_{29}, x_{30}, x_{31}, x_{32}, x_{33}, x_{34}, x_{35}, x_{36}, x_{37}, x_{38}, x_{39}, x_{40}, x_{41}, x_{42}, x_{43}, x_{44}, x_{45}, x_{46}, x_{47}, x_{48}, x_{49}, x_{50}, x_{51}, x_{52}\}\}$.

$F_{Finite.M}; E)=\{0=\{x_1, x_3, x_5, x_6, x_7, x_8, x_9, x_{10}, x_{11}, x_{13}, x_{14}, x_{15}, x_{16}, x_{17}, x_{18}, x_{19}, x_{20}, x_{21}, x_{22}, x_{23}, x_{24}, x_{25}, x_{26}, x_{27}, x_{28}, x_{29}, x_{30}, x_{31}, x_{32}, x_{33}, x_{34}, x_{35}, x_{36}, x_{37}, x_{38}, x_{39}, x_{40}, x_{41}, x_{42}, x_{43}, x_{44}, x_{45}, x_{46}, x_{47}, x_{48}, x_{49}, x_{50}, x_{51}, x_{52}\}; 0.2=\{\varnothing\}; 0.4=\{\varnothing\}; 0.6=\{\varnothing\}; 0.8=\{\varnothing\}; 1=\{x_2\}\}$.

$(F_{Finite.H}; E)=\{0=\{\varnothing\}; 0.2=\varnothing\}; 0.4=\{\varnothing\}; 0.6=\{\varnothing\}; 0.8=\{\varnothing\}; 1=\{x_{12}\}\}$.

$(F_{Finite.VH}; E)=\{0=\{x_{12}\}; 0.2=\varnothing\}; 0.4=\{x_4\}; 0.6=\{\varnothing\}; 0.8=\{\varnothing\}; 1=\{\varnothing\}\}$.

4.1.3 Statistics

$(F_{Statistics.L}; E)=\{0=\{x_{19}, x_{24}, x_{37}\}; 0.2=\{x_{25}\}; 0.4=\{\varnothing\}; 0.6=\{\varnothing\}; 0.8=\{x_6, x_{50}, x_{52}\};$

$1=\{x_1, x_3, x_5, x_9, x_{10}, x_{13}, x_{21}, x_{23}, x_{27}, x_{29}, x_{30}, x_{31}, x_{34}, x_{36}, x_{38}, x_{39}, x_{40}, x_{41}, x_{42}, x_{43}, x_{44}, x_{45}, x_{46}, x_{47}, x_{48}, x_{49}, x_{51}\}\}$.

$(F_{Statistics.M}; E)=\{0=\{x_3, x_5, x_9, x_{10}, x_{13}, x_{21}, x_{23}, x_{27}, x_{29}, x_{30}, x_{32}, x_{34}, x_{36}, x_{38}, x_{39}, x_{40}, x_{41}, x_{42}, x_{43}, x_{44}, x_{45}, x_{46}, x_{47}, x_{48}, x_{49}, x_{50}, x_{51}x_{52}\}; 0.2=\{x_6, x_8, x_{15}, x_{28}\}; 0.4=\{x_7, x_{11}, x_{16}\};$

$0.6=\{x_{22}, x_{31}\}; 0.8=\{x_{18}, x_{20}, x_{25}\}; 1=\{x_{19}, x_{23}, x_{37}\}\}$.

$(F_{\text{Statistics.H}}; E)=\{0=\{x_4, x_{35}\}; 0.2=\{x_{18}, x_{20}\}; 0.4=\{x_2, x_{12}, x_{22}, x_{31}\};$

$0.6=\{x_{17}, x_{11}, x_{16}\}; 0.8=\{x_{28}, x_{14}, \}; 1=\{x_{26}, x_{33}, x_{36}\}\}.$

$(F_{\text{Statistics.VH}}; E)=\{0=\{x_{26}\}; 0.2=\{x_{14}, x_{20}, \}; 0.4=\{x_{17}, x_{22}, x_{31}\}; 0.6=\{x_2, x_{12}\};$
$0.8=\{\varnothing\}; 1=\{x_4, x_{35}\}\}.$

4.2 Results

Now, we define some results by using $\wedge$ operation (Sezgin & Atagün, 2011) on student's details

$^{(1)}{}^{F}\text{Stochastic.M}^{(0)} \wedge {}^{F}\text{Finite.M}^{(0)} \wedge {}^{F}\text{Statistics.M}^{(0)} =$

$\{\{x_1, x_3, x_5, x_6, x_7, x_8, x_9, x_{10}, x_{13}, x_{16}, x_{19}, x_{21}, x_{22}, x_{23}, x_{24}, x_{25}, x_{29}, x_{30}, x_{32}, x_{33}, x_{34}, x_{36}, x_{39}, x_{40}, x_{41}, x_{42}, x_{43}, x_{44}, x_{45}, x_{46}, x_{47}, x_{48}, x_{49}, x_{50}, x_{51}\} \wedge$
$\{x_1, x_3, x_5, x_6, x_7, x_8, x_9, x_{10}, x_{11}, x_{13}, x_{14}, x_{15}, x_{16}, x_{17}, x_{18}, x_{19}, x_{20}, x_{21}, x_{22}, x_{23}, x_{24}, x_{25}, x_{26}, x_{27}, x_{28}, x_{29}, x_{30}, x_{31}, x_{32}, x_{33}, x_{34}, x_{35}, x_{36}, x_{37}, x_{38}, x_{39}, x_{40}, x_{41}, x_{42}, x_{43}, x_{44}, x_{45}, x_{46}, x_{47}, x_{48}, x_{49},$
$x_{50}, x_{51}, x_{52}\} \wedge \{x_3, x_5, x_9, x_{10}, x_{13}, x_{21}, x_{23}, x_{27}, x_{29}, x_{30}, x_{32}, x_{34}, x_{36}, x_{38}, x_{39}, x_{40}, x_{41}, x_{42}, x_{43}, x_{44}, x_{45}, x_{46}, x_{47}, x_{48}, x_{49}, x_{50}, x_{51}, x_{52}\}\}.$

Then, $^{F}\text{Stochastic.M}^{(0)} \wedge {}^{F}\text{Finite.M}^{(0)} \wedge {}^{F}\text{Statistics.M}^{(0)} =$

$\{x_3, x_5, x_9, x_{10}, x_{13}, x_{16}, x_{19}, x_{21}, x_{23}, x_{29}, x_{30}, x_{32}, x_{34}, x_{36}, x_{39}, x_{40}, x_{41}, x_{42}, x_{43}, x_{44}, x_{45}, x_{46}, x_{47}, x_{48}, x_{49}, x_{50}, x_{51}\}.$

$^{(2)}{}^{F}\text{Stochastic.L}^{(1)} \wedge {}^{F}\text{Finite.L}^{(1)} \wedge {}^{F}\text{Statistics.L}^{(0.8)} =$

$\{\{x_1, x_3, x_5, x_6, x_7, x_8, x_9, x_{10}, x_{13}, x_{16}, x_{19}, x_{21}, x_{22}, x_{23}, x_{24}, x_{25}, x_{29}, x_{30}, x_{32}, x_{33}, x_{34}, x_{36}, x_{39}, x_{40}, x_{41}, x_{42}, x_{43}, x_{44}, x_{45}, x_{46}, x_{47}, x_{48}, x_{49}, x_{50}, x_{51}\} \wedge$
$\{x_1, x_3, x_5, x_6, x_7, x_8, x_9, x_{10}, x_{11}, x_{13}, x_{14}, x_{15}, x_{16}, x_{17}, x_{18}, x_{19}, x_{20}, x_{21}, x_{22}, x_{23}, x_{24}, x_{25}, x_{26}, x_{27}, x_{28}, x_{29}, x_{30}, x_{31}, x_{32}, x_{33}, x_{34}, x_{35}, x_{36}, x_{37}, x_{38}, x_{39}, x_{40}, x_{41}, x_{42}, x_{43}, x_{44}, x_{45}, x_{46}, x_{47}, x_{48}, x_{49}, x_{50}, x_{51}, x_{52}\} \wedge \{x_6, x_{50}, x_{52}\}\}=\{x_6, x_{50}\}.$

(3) $\text{FStochastic.M}(0.4) \wedge F_{\text{Finite.M}}(0) \wedge \text{FStatistics.M}(0.8) = \{\{x_{17}, x_{20}, x_{26}, x_{28}\} \wedge$

$\{x_1, x_3, x_5, x_6, x_7, x_8, x_9, x_{10}, x_{11}, x_{13}, x_{14}, x_{15}, x_{16}, x_{17}, x_{18}, x_{19}, x_{20}, x_{21}, x_{22}, x_{23}, x_{24}, x_{25}, x_{26}, x_{27}, x_{28}, x_{29}, x_{30}, x_{31}, x_{32}, x_{33}, x_{34}, x_{35}, x_{36}, x_{37}, x_{38}, x_{39}, x_{40}, x_{41}, x_{42}, x_{43}, x_{44}, x_{45}, x_{46}, x_{47}, x_{48}, x_{49}, x_{50}, x_{51}, x_{52}\} \wedge \{x_{18}, x_{20}, x_{25}\}\}=\{x_{20}\}.$

(4) $\text{FStochastic.M}(0.6) \wedge F_{\text{Finite.VH}}(0) \wedge \text{FStatistics.H}(0.4) = \{\{x_{12}\} \wedge \{\{x_{12}\} \wedge$
$\{x_2, x_{12}, x_{22}, x_{31}\}\}=\{x_{12}\}.$

(5) $\text{FStochastic.M}(0.4) \wedge F_{\text{Finite.M}}(0) \wedge \text{FStatistics.H}(0.2)=\{\{x_{17}, x_{20}, x_{26}, x_{28}\} \wedge$

$\{x_1, x_3, x_5, x_6, x_7, x_8, x_9, x_{10}, x_{11}, x_{13}, x_{14}, x_{15}, x_{16}, x_{17}, x_{18}, x_{19}, x_{20}, x_{21}, x_{22}, x_{23},$
$x_{24}, x_{25}, x_{26}, x_{27}, x_{28}, x_{29}, x_{30}, x_{31}, x_{32}, x_{33}, x_{34}, x_{35}, x_{36}, x_{37}, x_{38}, x_{39}, x_{40}, x_{41}, x_{42},$
$x_{43}, x_{44}, x_{45}, x_{46}, x_{47}, x_{48}, x_{49}, x_{50}, x_{51}, x_{52}\} \wedge \{x_{18}, x_{20}\}\} = \{x_{20}\}.$

(6) ^{F}Stochastic.M$^{(0)} \wedge {}^F$Finite.M$^{(0)} \wedge {}^F$Statistics.L$^{(1)} =$

$\{\{x_1, x_3, x_5, x_6, x_7, x_8, x_9, x_{10}, x_{13}, x_{16}, x_{19}, x_{21}, x_{22}, x_{23}, x_{24}, x_{25}, x_{29}, x_{30}, x_{32}, x_{33},$
$x_{34}, x_{36}, x_{39}, x_{40}, x_{41}, x_{42}, x_{43}, x_{44}, x_{45}, x_{46}, x_{47}, x_{48}, x_{49}, x_{50}, x_{51}\} \wedge$
$\{x_1, x_3, x_5, x_6, x_7, x_8, x_9, x_{10}, x_{11}, x_{13}, x_{14}, x_{15}, x_{16}, x_{17}, x_{18}, x_{19}, x_{20}, x_{21}, x_{22}, x_{23},$
$x_{24}, x_{25}, x_{26}, x_{27}, x_{28}, x_{29}, x_{30}, x_{31}, x_{32}, x_{33}, x_{34}, x_{35}, x_{36}, x_{37}, x_{38}, x_{39}, x_{40}, x_{41}, x_{42},$
$x_{43}, x_{44}, x_{45}, x_{46}, x_{47}, x_{48}, x_{49},$
$x_{50}, x_{51}, x_{52}\} \wedge \{x_1, x_3, x_5, x_9, x_{10}, x_{13}, x_{21}, x_{23}, x_{27}, x_{29}, x_{30}, x_{31}, x_{34}, x_{36}, x_{38}, x_{39},$
$x_{40}, x_{41}, x_{42}, x_{43}, x_{44}, x_{45}, x_{46}, x_{47}, x_{48}, x_{49}, x_{50}, x_{51},\}\}.$

Then, ^{F}Stochastic.M$^{(0)} \wedge {}^F$Finite.M$^{(0)} \wedge {}^F$Statistics.L$^{(1)} =$

$\{x_1, x_3, x_5, x_9, x_{10}, x_{13}, x_{21}, x_{23}, x_{27}, x_{29}, x_{30}, x_{32}, x_{34}, x_{36}, x_{38}, x_{39}, x_{40}, x_{41}, x_{42}, x_{43},$
$x_{44}, x_{45}, x_{46}, x_{47}, x_{48}, x_{49}, x_{50}, x_{51}\}.$

(7) ^{F}Stochastic.L$^{(1)} \wedge {}^F$Finite.M$^{(0)} \wedge {}^F$Statistics.M$^{(0)} =$

$\{\{x_1, x_3, x_5, x_6, x_7, x_8, x_9, x_{10}, x_{13}, x_{16}, x_{19}, x_{21}, x_{22}, x_{23}, x_{24}, x_{25}, x_{29}, x_{30}, x_{32}, x_{33},$
$x_{34}, x_{36}, x_{39}, x_{40}, x_{41}, x_{42}, x_{43}, x_{44}, x_{45}, x_{46}, x_{47}, x_{48}, x_{49}, x_{50}, x_{51}\} \wedge$
$\{x_1, x_3, x_5, x_6, x_7, x_8, x_9, x_{10}, x_{11}, x_{13}, x_{14}, x_{15}, x_{16}, x_{17}, x_{18}, x_{19}, x_{20}, x_{21}, x_{22}, x_{23},$
$x_{24}, x_{25}, x_{26}, x_{27}, x_{28}, x_{29}, x_{30}, x_{31}, x_{32}, x_{33}, x_{34}, x_{35}, x_{36}, x_{37}, x_{38}, x_{39}, x_{40}, x_{41}, x_{42},$
$x_{43}, x_{44}, x_{45}, x_{46}, x_{47}, x_{48}, x_{49},$
$x_{50}, x_{51}, x_{52}\} \wedge \{x_3, x_5, x_9, x_{10}, x_{13}, x_{21}, x_{23}, x_{27}, x_{29}, x_{30}, x_{32}, x_{34}, x_{36}, x_{38}, x_{39}, x_{40},$
$x_{41}, x_{42}, x_{43}, x_{44}, x_{45}, x_{46}, x_{47}, x_{48}, x_{49}, x_{50}, x_{51}, x_{52}\}\}.$

Then, ^{F}Stochastic.L$^{(1)} \wedge {}^F$Finite.M$^{(0)} \wedge {}^F$Statistics.M$^{(0)} =$

$\{x_3, x_5, x_9, x_{10}, x_{13}, x_{21}, x_{23}, x_{27}, x_{29}, x_{30}, x_{32}, x_{34}, x_{36}, x_{38}, x_{39}, x_{40}, x_{41}, x_{42}, x_{43}, x_{44},$
$x_{45}, x_{46}, x_{47}, x_{48}, x_{49}, x_{50}, x_{51}\}.$

(8) FStochastic.VH(0.2) $\wedge$ F$_{Finite.L}$(1) $\wedge$ FStatistics.H(0.8) $= \{\{x_4, x_{14}, x_{35}, x_{52}\}$
$\wedge$
$\{x_1, x_3, x_5, x_6, x_7, x_8, x_9, x_{10}, x_{11}, x_{13}, x_{14}, x_{15}, x_{16}, x_{17}, x_{18}, x_{19}, x_{20}, x_{21}, x_{22}, x_{23},$
$x_{24}, x_{25}, x_{26}, x_{27}, x_{28}, x_{29}, x_{30}, x_{31}, x_{32}, x_{33}, x_{34}, x_{35}, x_{36}, x_{37}, x_{38}, x_{39}, x_{40}, x_{41}, x_{42},$
$x_{43}, x_{44}, x_{45}, x_{46}, x_{47}, x_{48}, x_{49}, x_{50}, x_{51}, x_{52}\} \wedge \{x_{28}, x_{14}\}\}.$

Then, ^{F}Stochastic.VH$^{(0.2)} \wedge {}^F$Finite.L$^{(1)} \wedge {}^F$Statistics.H$^{(0.8)} = \{x_{14}\}.$

(9) ^{F}Stochastic.H$^{(0.6)} \wedge {}^F$Finite.M$^{(0)} \wedge {}^F$Statistics.VH$^{(0.4)} = \{\{x_{17}, x_{26}, x_{28}\} \wedge$

$\{x_1, x_3, x_5, x_6, x_7, x_8, x_9, x_{10}, x_{11}, x_{13}, x_{14}, x_{15}, x_{16}, x_{17}, x_{18}, x_{19}, x_{20}, x_{21}, x_{22}, x_{23}, x_{24}, x_{25}, x_{26}, x_{27}, x_{28}, x_{29}, x_{30}, x_{31}, x_{32}, x_{33}, x_{34}, x_{35}, x_{36}, x_{37}, x_{38}, x_{39}, x_{40}, x_{41}, x_{42}, x_{43}, x_{44}, x_{45}, x_{46}, x_{47}, x_{48}, x_{49}, x_{50}, x_{51}, x_{52}\} \wedge \{x_{17}, x_{22}, x_{31}\}\}.$

Then, ^{F}Stochastic.H$^{(0.6)} \wedge {}^F$Finite.M$^{(0)} \wedge {}^F$Statistics.VH$^{(0.4)} = \{x_{17}\}$.

(10) ^{F}Stochastic.L$^{(1)} \wedge {}^F$Finite.M$^{(0)} \wedge {}^F$Statistics.M$^{(0.2)} =$

$\{\{x_1, x_3, x_5, x_6, x_7, x_8, x_9, x_{10}, x_{13}, x_{16}, x_{19}, x_{21}, x_{22}, x_{23}, x_{24}, x_{25}, x_{29}, x_{30}, x_{32}, x_{33}, x_{34}, x_{36}, x_{39}, x_{40}, x_{41}, x_{42}, x_{43}, x_{44}, x_{45}, x_{46}, x_{47}, x_{48}, x_{49}, x_{50}, x_{51}\} \wedge$
$\{x_1, x_3, x_5, x_6, x_7, x_8, x_9, x_{10}, x_{11}, x_{13}, x_{14}, x_{15}, x_{16}, x_{17}, x_{18}, x_{19}, x_{20}, x_{21}, x_{22}, x_{23}, x_{24}, x_{25}, x_{26}, x_{27}, x_{28}, x_{29}, x_{30}, x_{31}, x_{32}, x_{33}, x_{34}, x_{35}, x_{36}, x_{37}, x_{38}, x_{39}, x_{40}, x_{41}, x_{42}, x_{43}, x_{44}, x_{45}, x_{46}, x_{47}, x_{48}, x_{49}, x_{50}, x_{51}, x_{52}\} \wedge \{x_6, x_8, x_{15}, x_{28}\}\}.$

Then, ^{F}Stochastic.L$^{(1)} \wedge {}^F$Finite.M$^{(0)} \wedge {}^F$Statistics.M$^{(0.2)} = \{x_6, x_8\}$.

(11) ^{F}Stochastic.M$^{(0)} \wedge {}^F$Finite.L$^{(1)} \wedge {}^F$Statistics.M$^{(1)} =$

$\{x_1, x_3, x_5, x_6, x_7, x_8, x_9, x_{10}, x_{13}, x_{16}, x_{19}, x_{21}, x_{22}, x_{23}, x_{24}, x_{25}, x_{29}, x_{30}, x_{32}, x_{33}, x_{34}, x_{36}, x_{39}, x_{40}, x_{41}, x_{42}, x_{43}, x_{44}, x_{45}, x_{46}, x_{47}, x_{48}, x_{49}, x_{50}, x_{51}\} \wedge$
$\{x_1, x_3, x_5, x_6, x_7, x_8, x_9, x_{10}, x_{11}, x_{13}, x_{14}, x_{15}, x_{16}, x_{17}, x_{18}, x_{19}, x_{20}, x_{21}, x_{22}, x_{23}, x_{24}, x_{25}, x_{26}, x_{27}, x_{28}, x_{29}, x_{30}, x_{31}, x_{32}, x_{33}, x_{34}, x_{35}, x_{36}, x_{37}, x_{38}, x_{39}, x_{40}, x_{41}, x_{42}, x_{43}, x_{44}, x_{45}, x_{46}, x_{47}, x_{48}, x_{49}, x_{50}, x_{51}, x_{52}\} \wedge \{x_{19}, x_{23}, x_{37}\}\}.$

Then, ^{F}Stochastic.M$^{(0)} \wedge {}^F$Finite.L$^{(1)} \wedge {}^F$Statistics.M$^{(1)} = \{x_{19}, x_{23}, x_{37}\}$.

(12) ^{F}Stochastic.L$^{(1)} \wedge {}^F$Finite.M$^{(0)} \wedge {}^F$Statistics.L$^{(0)} =$

$\{\{x_1, x_3, x_5, x_6, x_7, x_8, x_9, x_{10}, x_{13}, x_{16}, x_{19}, x_{21}, x_{22}, x_{23}, x_{24}, x_{25}, x_{29}, x_{30}, x_{32}, x_{33}, x_{34}, x_{36}, x_{39}, x_{40}, x_{41}, x_{42}, x_{43}, x_{44}, x_{45}, x_{46}, x_{47}, x_{48}, x_{49}, x_{50}, x_{51}\} \wedge$
$\{x_1, x_3, x_5, x_6, x_7, x_8, x_9, x_{10}, x_{11}, x_{13}, x_{14}, x_{15}, x_{16}, x_{17}, x_{18}, x_{19}, x_{20}, x_{21}, x_{22}, x_{23}, x_{24}, x_{25}, x_{26}, x_{27}, x_{28}, x_{29}, x_{30}, x_{31}, x_{32}, x_{33}, x_{34}, x_{35}, x_{36}, x_{37}, x_{38}, x_{39}, x_{40}, x_{41}, x_{42}, x_{43}, x_{44}, x_{45}, x_{46}, x_{47}, x_{48}, x_{49}, x_{50}, x_{51}, x_{52}\} \wedge \{x_{19}, x_{24}, x_{37}\}\}.$

Then, ^{F}Stochastic.L$^{(1)} \wedge {}^F$Finite.M$^{(0)} \wedge {}^F$Statistics.L$^{(0)} = \{x_{19}, x_{24}\}$.
A similar approach can be made to derive a variety of rules.

RESULTS AND DISCUSSION

Now, for a student who applies his information with Result (1), the dismissed risk is 55% .similarly, we can find the percentage of the risk of dismissed students in different cases:

We can easily find the dismissed risk percentage of each result, we obtained above (Khattack et al., 2017).

Now, we explain the method of determining the risk percentage (Zou & Xiao, 2008) of the vResult(1).

^{F}Stochastic.$M^{(0)}$ $^\wedge$ ^{F}Finite.$M^{(0)}$ $^\wedge$ ^{F}Statistics.$M^{(0)}$ =

$\{x_3, x_5, x_9, x_{10}, x_{13}, x_{16}, x_{19}, x_{21}, x_{23}, x_{29}, x_{30}, x_{32}, x_{34}, x_{36}, x_{39}, x_{40}, x_{41}, x_{42}, x_{43}, x_{44}, x_{45}, x_{46}, x_{47}, x_{48}, x_{49}, x_{50}, x_{51}\}$.

27 students are applying to the condition of the Result(1) including 11 furlough students. Hence

Dismissed risk of result(1) = (15/27) x 100 = 55.5%

It can be said that for the student who applies his information with Result v(1), the dismissed risk is 55% .

In the same way, we can find the percentage of the dismissed risk of students in different cases:

Rule 1

^{F}Stochastic.$M^{(0)}$ $^\wedge$ ^{F}Finite.$M^{(0)}$ $^\wedge$ ^{F}Statistics.$M^{(0)}$ =

$\{x_3, x_5, x_9, x_{10}, x_{13}, x_{16}, x_{19}, x_{21}, x_{23}, x_{29}, x_{30}, x_{32}, x_{34}, x_{36}, x_{39}, x_{40}, x_{41}, x_{42}, x_{43}, x_{44}, x_{45}, x_{46}, x_{47}, x_{48}, x_{49}, x_{50}, x_{51}\}$,

Dismissed risk of result(1) = (15/27) x 100 = 55.5%

This implies that the dismissed rate is 55.5%

Rule 2

^{F}Stochastic.$L^{(1)}$ $^\wedge$ ^{F}Finite.$L^{(1)}$ $^\wedge$ ^{F}Statistics.$L^{(0.8)=\{x6,x50\}}$,

Dismissed risk of result(2) = (2/2) x 100 = 100%

This implies that the dismissed rate is 100%

Rule 3

^{F}Stochastic.$M^{(0.4)}$ $^\wedge$ ^{F}Finite.$M^{(0)}$ $^\wedge$ ^{F}Statistics.$M^{(0.8)=\{x20\}}$,

Dismissed risk of result(3) = (1/1) x 100 = 100%

This implies that the dismissed rate is 100%

Rule 4

^{F}Stochastic.$M^{(0.6)} \wedge {}^F$Finite.$VH^{(0)} \wedge {}^F$Statistics.$H^{(0.4)}=\{x12\}$,
Dismissed risk of result(4) = (1/1) x 100 = 100%
This implies that the dismissed rate is 100%

Rule 5

^{F}Stochastic.$M^{(0.4)} \wedge {}^F$Finite.$M^{(0)} \wedge {}^F$Statistics.$H^{(0.2)}=\{x20\}$,
Dismissed risk of result(5) = (1/1) x 100 = 100%
This implies that the dismissed rate is 100%

Rule 6

^{F}Stochastic.$M^{(0)} \wedge {}^F$Finite.$M^{(0)} \wedge {}^F$Statistics.$L^{(1)}=$
$\{x_1, x_3, x_5, x_9, x_{10}, x_{13}, x_{21}, x_{23}, x_{27}, x_{29}, x_{30}, x_{32}, x_{34}, x_{36}, x_{38}, x_{39}, x_{40}, x_{41}, x_{42}, x_{43}, x_{44}, x_{45}, x_{46}, x_{47}, x_{48}, x_{49}, x_{50}, x_{51}\}$,
Dismissed risk of result(6) = (16/27) x 100 = 59.2%
This implies that the dismissed rate is 59.2%

Rule 7

^{F}Stochastic.$L^{(1)} \wedge {}^F$Finite.$M^{(0)} \wedge {}^F$Statistics.$M^{(0)}=$
$\{x_3, x_5, x_9, x_{10}, x_{13}, x_{21}, x_{23}, x_{27}, x_{29}, x_{30}, x_{32}, x_{34}, x_{36}, x_{38}, x_{39}, x_{40}, x_{41}, x_{42}, x_{43}, x_{44}, x_{45}, x_{46}, x_{47}, x_{48}, x_{49}, x_{50}, x_{51}\}$,
Dismissed risk of result(7) = (15/27) x 100 = 55.5%
This implies that the dismissed rate is 55.5%

Rule 8

^{F}Stochastic.$VH^{(0.2)} \wedge {}^F$Finite.$L^{(1)} \wedge {}^F$Statistics.$H^{(0.8)}=\{x14\}$,
Dismissed risk of result(8) = (1/1) x 100 = 100%
This implies that the dismissed rate is 100%

Rule 9

^{F}Stochastic.$H^{(0.6)} \wedge {}^F$Finite.$M^{(0)} \wedge {}^F$Statistics.$VH^{(0.4)}=\{x17\}$,
Dismissed risk of result(9) = (1/1) x 100 = 100%

This implies that the dismissed rate is 100%

Rule 10

^{F}Stochastic.L$^{(1)}$ ∧ ^{F}Finite.M $^{(0)}$ ∧ ^{F}Statistics.M$^{(0.2)}$ = {^{x}6,^{x}8},
Dismissed risk of result(10) = (1/2) x 100 = 50%
This implies that the dismissed rate is 50%

Rule 11

^{F}Stochastic.M$^{(0)}$ ∧ ^{F}Finite.L$^{(1)}$ ∧ ^{F}Statistics.M$^{(1)}$ = {^{x}19,^{x}23,^{x}37},
Dismissed risk of result(11) = (1/3) x 100 = 33.3%
This implies that the dismissed rate is 33.3%

Rule 12

^{F}Stochastic.L$^{(1)}$ ∧ ^{F}Finite.M $^{(0)}$ ∧ ^{F}Statistics.L$^{(0)}$ = {^{x}19,^{x}24},
Dismissed risk of result(12) = (1/2) x 100 = 50%
This implies that the dismissed rate is 50%.

COMPARISON OF RESULTS WITH ML MODELS

The Table 1 data is been applied to Machine learning models such as Support Vector Machine, Naïve Bayes and Random Forest model with means of Orange Data mining tool.

The model when applied with SVM predicts the result in accuracy of 98%, Naïve Bayes 80% and Random forest 100%.

Figure 2. Sample result with SVM

	SVM	error	RESULT	Stochastics	maths	Finite Automata
1	0.04 : 0.96 → Y	0.041	Y	0	0	2
2	0.43 : 0.57 → Y	0.569	N	34	68	35
3	0.04 : 0.96 → Y	0.039	Y	20	40	3
4	0.93 : 0.07 → N	0.070	N	41	82	42
5	0.02 : 0.98 → Y	0.016	Y	25	50	16
6	0.02 : 0.98 → Y	0.017	Y	28	56	25
7	0.02 : 0.98 → Y	0.021	Y	23	46	19
8	0.01 : 0.99 → Y	0.013	Y	27	54	15

Figure 3. SVM classification accuracy results

Model	AUC	CA	F1	Prec	Recall	MCC
SVM	1.000	0.981	0.979	0.981	0.981	0.808

Figure 4. Result analysis with naïve bayes

Predictions (2) - Orange

how probabilities for Classes in data ∨ ☑ Show classification errors

	Naive Bayes	error	RESULT	Stochastics	maths	Finite Automata
1	0.06 : 0.94 → Y	0.058	Y	0	0	2
2	0.87 : 0.13 → N	0.127	N	34	68	35
3	0.06 : 0.94 → Y	0.058	Y	20	40	3
4	0.87 : 0.13 → N	0.127	N	41	82	42
5	0.05 : 0.95 → Y	0.054	Y	25	50	16
6	0.21 : 0.79 → Y	0.210	Y	28	56	25
7	0.21 : 0.79 → Y	0.210	Y	23	46	19
8	0.05 : 0.95 → Y	0.054	Y	27	54	15

Figure 5. Naïve bayes classification accuracy

Model	AUC	CA	F1	Prec	Recall	MCC
Naive Bayes	0.929	0.808	0.857	0.956	0.808	0.429

Figure 6. Result analysis with random forest

	Random Forest	error	RESULT	Stochastics	maths	Finite Automata
1	0.00 : 1.00 → Y	0.000	Y	0	0	2
2	0.35 : 0.65 → Y	0.650	N	34	68	35
3	0.00 : 1.00 → Y	0.000	Y	20	40	3
4	0.42 : 0.58 → Y	0.580	N	41	82	42
5	0.00 : 1.00 → Y	0.000	Y	25	50	16
6	0.00 : 1.00 → Y	0.000	Y	28	56	25
7	0.00 : 1.00 → Y	0.000	Y	23	46	19
8	0.00 : 1.00 → Y	0.000	Y	27	54	15

Figure 7. RF classification accuracy results

Model	AUC	CA	F1	Prec	Recall	MCC
Random Forest	1.000	0.962	0.952	0.963	0.962	0.566

CONCLUSION

This study examined two methods for predicting student dismissal: machine learning models and fuzzy soft sets. Because fuzzy soft sets were easily interpretable, machine learning models demonstrated higher predicted accuracy and efficiency. According to the findings, a hybrid strategy that combines the two approaches may be able to produce accurate predictions and insightful information for focused actions. Better educational outcomes could result from this dual method, which could also increase student retention.

REFERENCES

Aktaş, H., & Çağman, N. (2007). Hacı Akta¸ s and Naim C¸ a˘gman. Soft sets and soft groups. *Information Sciences*, 177(13), 2726–2735. DOI: 10.1016/j.ins.2006.12.008

Ali, M. I., Feng, F., Liu, X., Min, W. K., & Shabir, M. (2009). On some new operations in soft set theory. *Computers & Mathematics with Applications (Oxford, England)*, 57(9), 1547–1553. DOI: 10.1016/j.camwa.2008.11.009

Barua, A., Mudunuri, L. S., & Kosheleva, O. (2013). Why trapezoidal and triangular membership functions work so well: Towards a theoretical explanation.

Chaudhuri, A., De, K., & Chatterjee, D. (2013). Solution of the decision making problems using fuzzy soft relations. arXiv preprint arXiv:1304.7238.

Debnath, S. (2021). Fuzzy hypersoft sets and its weightage operator for decision making. *Journal of Fuzzy Extension and Applications*, 2(2), 163–170.

Dombi, J. (1990). Membership function as an evaluation. *Fuzzy Sets and Systems*, 35(1), 1–21. DOI: 10.1016/0165-0114(90)90014-W

Feng, F., Li, C., Davvaz, B., & Irfan Ali, M. (2010). Soft sets combined with fuzzy sets and rough sets: A tentative approach. *Soft Computing*, 14(9), 899–911. DOI: 10.1007/s00500-009-0465-6

Kharal, A., & Ahmad, B. (2009). Mappings on fuzzy soft classes. *Advances in Fuzzy Systems*, 2009(1), 1–6. DOI: 10.1155/2009/407890

Khattak, A. M., Khan, G. A., Ishfaq, M., & Jamal, F. (2017). Characterization of soft α-separation axioms and soft β-separation axioms in soft single point spaces and in soft ordinary spaces. *Journal of New Theory*, (19), 63–81.

Klir, G. J., & Yuan, B. (1996). Fuzzy sets and fuzzy logic: Theory and applications. *Possibility Theory versus Probab.Theory*, 32(2), 207–208.

Lotfi, A. (1965). Zadeh. Fuzzy sets. *Information and Control*, 8(3), 338–353. DOI: 10.1016/S0019-9958(65)90241-X

Maji, P. K., Biswas, R., & Ranjan Roy, A. (2003). Soft set theory. *Computers & Mathematics with Applications (Oxford, England)*, 45(4-5), 555–562. DOI: 10.1016/S0898-1221(03)00016-6

Maji, P. K., Roy, A. R., & Biswas, R. (2002). Akhil Ranjan Roy, and Ranjit Biswas. An application of soft sets in a decision making problem. *Computers & Mathematics with Applications (Oxford, England)*, 44(8-9), 1077–1083. DOI: 10.1016/S0898-1221(02)00216-X

Majumdar, P., & Samanta, S. K. (2008). Similarity measure of soft sets. *New Mathematics and Natural Computation.*, 4, 1–12.

Majumdar, P., & Samanta, S. K. (2010). Generalised fuzzy soft sets. *Computers & Mathematics with Applications (Oxford, England)*, 59(4), 1425–1432. DOI: 10.1016/j.camwa.2009.12.006

Močkoř, J., & Hurtík, P. (2021). Jiˇ rˊı Moˇckoˇ r and Petr Hurtˊık. Approximations of fuzzy soft sets by fuzzy soft relations with image processing application. *Soft Computing*, 25(10), 6915–6925. DOI: 10.1007/s00500-021-05769-3

Molodtsov, D. (1999). Soft set theory—First results. *Computers & Mathematics with Applications (Oxford, England)*, 37(4-5), 19–31. DOI: 10.1016/S0898-1221(99)00056-5

Omar Adil, M. (2015). Ali, Aous Y Ali, and Balasem Salem Sumait. Comparison between the effects of different types of membership functions on fuzzy logic controller performance. *International Journal (Toronto, Ont.)*, 76, 76–83.

Phaengtan, K., Aimcharoen, N., & Suebsan, P. (2021). Partial averages of fuzzy soft sets in decision-making problems. *Journal of Interdisciplinary Mathematics*, 24(4), 1035–1052. DOI: 10.1080/09720502.2021.1881223

Rasmani, K. A., & Shen, Q. (2006). Data-driven fuzzy rule generation and its application for student academic performance evaluation. *Applied Intelligence*, 25(3), 305–319. DOI: 10.1007/s10489-006-0109-9

Sezgin, A., & Atagün, A. O. (2011). On operations of soft sets. *Computers & Mathematics with Applications (Oxford, England)*, 61(5), 1457–1467. DOI: 10.1016/j.camwa.2011.01.018

Shabir, M., & Naz, M. (2011). On soft topological spaces. *Computers & Mathematics with Applications (Oxford, England)*, 61(7), 1786–1799. DOI: 10.1016/j.camwa.2011.02.006

Vellapandi, R., & Gunasekaran, S. (2020). A new decision making approach for winning strategy based on muti soft set logic. Journal of fuzzy extension and applications, 1(2), 112-121.

Zou, Y., & Xiao, Z. (2008). Data analysis approaches of soft sets under incomplete information. *Knowledge-Based Systems*, 21(8), 941–945. DOI: 10.1016/j.knosys.2008.04.004

Chapter 2
AI in Skill Development, Critical Thinking, Digital Literacy, and AI–Driven Job Preparation

Satyabrata Pandit
https://orcid.org/0009-0008-2404-4207
Brainware University, India

Saptarshi Kumar Sarkar
https://orcid.org/0009-0004-1786-8284
Brainware University, India

Sreya Barik
Brainware University, India

Sutapa Sahu
Brainware University, India

ABSTRACT

Thus, the chapter aims to unravel the role of AI in skill enhancement with reference to critical thinking ability, problem-solving skills, and digital skills. With AI technologies gradually progressing to redefine employment situations in different parts of the world today, it has become essential to train the learners for the arising complex employment scenario. The first part of the chapter explores how critical thinking and problem solving can be improved by AI, such as using adaptive learning systems, simulation, and data analysis. It then goes further to illustrate how the use of AI tools in the teaching of digital literacy is conducted, with a focus on how the

DOI: 10.4018/979-8-3693-8191-5.ch002

use of AI in learning makes it possible for a learner to be taught based on his/her specific needs and the acquisition of the fundamental skills needed in the digital competency. The last part looks at the ways of teaching education to prepare students for jobs with artificial intelligence, balancing between technical and humanities, ethics, and retraining.

1. INTRODUCTION

1.1 Background of the Study

AI is gaining its unobtrusive yet permanent place in civilizational development and thus is introducing a new paradigm, which reshuffles the economy, segments of industries, and even individual lives. AI is set to rapidly grow and invade nearly every sector, be it the medical field, the fiscal, the manufacturing or the learning sector. AI is comprised of machine learning, NLP, CV, and robots. With the development of these technologies, the process of executing tasks is changed altogether, and therefore employees need to develop new skills and knowledge. Education systems throughout the world are challenged with ensuring comparable transitions by facilitating students to learn new skills to conform to these changes and to match the skill demands of AI-based employment markets (Brynjolfsson & McAfee, 2017).

This has brought into question a more flexible and elastic learning model which is going against the traditional education model that has more or less been focused to rote learning and information memorization. It is in such methods that the higher order thinking skills of creativity, problem solving, critical thinking have to be accorded the highest priority given the fact that these cognitive skills are not only relevant but critical in a world that is increasingly being dominated by Artificial Intelligence. Also, due to the rapid trend in digitalization of the ways and means of communication and information, there is need to imbibe good digital intelligence in order to effectively manage the digital tools and information. The instructing approaches preparing the students to get prepared for work in the future concerning need to transform according to the nature of work as AI emerges. This means that all these above vital abilities are essential in the future where AI will be more than just a technology in the preparation of personal and career needs (Schwab, 2016).

1.2 Importance of Skill Development in the AI Era

Thanks to AI, the focus on skills training has shifted in parallel, from less valuable hard skills and muscle memory to the higher, abstract skills that are challenging to program. Nevertheless, the use of AI systems is still limited to domains where creative skills, empathy, and critical judgment are involved, although these systems are highly effective for all tasks that involve big data analysis, pattern matching, and repetitive tasks. Therefore, it gets increasingly important to learn skills that fortify AI as opposed to negating it. In particular, critical thinking as well as problem solving seems to be indispensable for contemporary industry. These qualities are highly valued in a world where artificial intelligence (AI) takes over routine work because let people evaluate complex circumstances, make reasonable decisions, and think of unusual solutions (Shute & Becker, 2010).

1.2.1 Critical Thinking and Problem-Solving Skills

Critical thinking is the ability to reason and think for one's self and is one of the important skills needed in the twenty-first century. It involves information gathering, screening of the evidence, recognition of bias, and rational decision making. According to the scope of the work, there are problem identification, problem analysis and problem solving as other components that have a established tie with critical thinking. These are critically important in the conditions of organisational uncertainty and in the conditions when fast decision-making is possible.

Thinking critically and solving problems are activities that receive a different meaning in the given context of application of artificial intelligence. To these procedures, the AI system might be useful by providing information and better options or by performing recurrent decision-making tasks. Nevertheless, the professional decision making implies prioritizing the role of humans in decision making as they have to assess the outcomes generated by an AI system, assess the ethical implications and make the final judgments.

1.2.2 Digital Literacy

The single unification of knowledge in the contemporary world is digital literacy, which in the present moment may be defined as the ability to work with digital technologies in learning, critical analysis, search for, and sharing of information. They incorporate a wide range of skills from the ability to engage with technologies, software and the internet, and use it, understand it and deal with the information found on it. Also, digital literacy in the context of the use of AI involves conducting falsification, managing personal data on the internet, and understanding the moral angle of the use of technology.

There is a great role for AI to contribute to enhance the digital literacy. Artificial intelligent solutions can deliver learning experience that are personalized due to the unique needs of the learner which it can provide resources and feedback (Ng, 2012).

1.3 Objectives of the Study

This research's purpose is to explore the way through which AI can be utilized in enhancing students' critical thinking and problem solving, promoting and preparing them for the emergence of job automation through the application of AI. The purpose of the project is to provide awareness of how such developments may augment these fundamental learning domains so that learners can graduate with the adequate competencies for a career in a world governed by AI. The study's specific objectives are to:The study's specific objectives are to:

> **Examine the impact of AI tools on the development of critical thinking and problem-solving skills:** This research attempt to find out how in detail these essential skills might be supported by AI by reviewing a number of applications in the educational settings.
>
> **Evaluate the effectiveness of AI in promoting digital literacy:** This project will assess the way that AI-based interventions and curricula may enhance technological literacy for students and the manner that specific forms of AI can meet individual students' needs.
>
> **Analyze how AI prepares students for AI-driven job markets:** It will examine the current practices of the industry and the approaches in education, determine what skills will be required in the future workplace, and estimate the extent to which AI can assist in enhancing them.
>
> **Provide practical recommendations for educators and policymakers:** The practicable recommendations for inputting of AI into educational institutions for enhancing skill development, and the preparing and equipping of students for the future workforce, will be attained from the discovery.

1.4 Theoretical Framework

Taking into account the broad framework of the learning theories that regard learning as a construct that occurs through experience, interaction, and reflection this study is grounded in the so-called constructivism. The principles of constructivism centre on learner's interactions, problem solving and thinking skills in the learning process. Vygotsky's (1978) and Piaget's (1970) theories are good samples of theories developed to explain the process of learning. To these beliefs are associated with the contention that students engage the new content, synthesizing it with prior knowledge to form new constructs. Constructivist theories are suitable implicitly for using in AI technologies since such technologies presuppose individual approach and est [...] These technologies enable learners to experiment and also work in complex learning environments.

This sort of research employs constructivism and also the concept of what is referred to as the 21stand century skills, a set of skills that is essential in the current employment market. Some of these skills include; critical thinking and Problem Solving, Computer literacy skills, Interpersonal/Teamwork/Social skills, Oral/Written communication skills, and adaptability. The skills required for learning in the 21 st century identifies the role to prepare students for the world characterized by globalization and technology improvements that bring shift in capabilities required in learning. AI has the capability in helping enhance the development through providing students with an array of complex tasks that require complicated and specific thinking as well as diverse learning.

The research also considers the contribution of social constructivism particularly the ideas of Vygotsky; aspects such as social interaction and working in groups or teams for learning was noted as important by this theory. In Vygotsky's Zone of Proximal Development the studetn who is helped by the professor or fellow student with greater abilities can learn and grasp at a level above the current one. AI can be an effective and a knowledgable other through providing learners with instructions on how to solve tasks, helping with specific problems and facilitating co learning among them (Vygotsky, 1978).

1.5 Significance of the Study

Thus, on the following grounds, this research is important: First, it addresses the growing pressure to provide effective training for improvement of skills in the context of AI, providing insights on how the AI can help to achieve cognitive, problem solving and digital literacy skills. Apprehending ways of critical analysis, handling challenging problems, and navigating through digital spaces will be even more valuable as AI encroaches upon sectors and labor markets. By studying how AI contributes to the development of these proficiencies, this study contributes to the existing literature on how educational systems may need to evolve in the twenty-first century (Piaget, J. et al., 2016).

Second, differing from other works that consider AI as a potential threat to learning abilities, the study presents real-life outcomes of the impact of AI technologies on the development of learners' skills. However, as the amount of research on potential benefits of AI in education increases, the detailed studies that speak to how exactly can bring more value to learning process, and therefore contributes to better learning outcomes, are still lacking. As the audience for this knowledge gap, this research aims to provide comprehensive assessments of AI systems and the impact they have on learning environments ; moreover, due attention is paid to the strengths in development of digital literacy, problem solving, and critical thinking skills (Holmes et al., 2019).

Third, the study provides practical recommendations to educators and policy-makers, which allow them to implement AI-based learning program and projects. There is a pressing need for strategies that have research backing to guide the optimal employment of AI given that it is increasingly being adopted in learning institutions. The purpose of this study is to ensure that new policies and practices leading to environmental enhancement of learning as well as improvement of the learners in the work market place are developed by having an insight of the possibility of AI in education and its challenges (Ng, 2012).

Finally, because it considers how or in what way educational institutions might assist in the development of a workforce capable of performing in a job environment that might be shaped by advanced AI deployment, then this study has implications that are broader in terms of society. Three of these skills are problem-solving, critical thinking, digital literacy, all of which are seen as vital for success in personal and public life. Education systems may ensure that there are people with the skills of facing the opportunities and challenges of the twenty-first century for the creation of economic development, social cohesion and competitiveness on a global level by enhancing such skills (Schwab, 2016).

1.6 Overview of the Study

rganisation of sections in this study paper is as follows: The background of the study to explore the nature and work of artificial intelligence (AI) for education, the advance of critical thinking and problem solving skills, the deliverance of digital literacy and the preparedness for the AI integrated jobs markets is described in the literature review section. One of the advantages of the literature review is to present common trends and to specify lack of knowledge, when using data from several researches. This section provides an overview of the research methodology used in the study as well as the data gathering techniques and data analysis techniques used in the study. Details regarding the selection of participants, information collection and analysis tools, and processes are provided in this part in detail.

The results of the main study are described and given are the implications in the results and discussion section. The next part is dedicated to the evaluation of data studies that demonstrate the use of artificial intelligence (AI) in enhancing the level of digital competence, problem-solving, and critical thinking skills. Other implications that accord to these findings are also presented, with consideration of how they will apply to subsequent research, policy, and education. In the conclusion of the study we are drawing the findings of the study, the recommendation for further research and application. At the end of this section, useful recommendations to educators, legislative body, or anyone with an interest in the study is provided and how this study adds value to the information existing in different repositories. It also outline how the research could be progressed in the future.

2. LITERATURE REVIEW

2.1 Overview of Existing Research on AI in Education

2.1.1 The Evolution of AI in Education

Artificial intelligence (AI) has gained tremendous traction and applied in education system starting from the initial computer based instruction programs to smart instruction delivery system. The first area of the application of AI in education focused on ITSs which provided customized education and feedback to the learners (Woolf, 2010).

Education-wise, the enhacement of AI technologies in learning has emerged side by side with the type of technology. The contemporary AI-based educational technologies employ NLP and data analytics as well as employ machine learning algorithms to provide highly personalized flexible learning experience. Such tools enable the trainer to deliver training that meets specific needs of each student due to the big data, which makes it possible to determine trends on students' behavior, learning preferences, and performance (Piaget, J. et al., 2016)

2.1.2 AI's Role in Personalizing Learning

One of the most significant fields in the AI research of education is individualization of training, which means its customization to meet the needs and preferences of each learner. The following are some indications of how it has impacted learners: Personalized learning has been associated with improvement in learners' motivation, participation and performance in class (Pane et al., 2015).

For instance, Knewton is an adaptive learning platform that uses data regarding the interactions students have with course content to adjust student interactions as well as task complexity and feedback. Research done on Knewton and other learning applications has explained how well they are when it comes to enhancing learning outcomes especially for those who have difficulties with traditional learning techniques (Baker, 2016).

However, there is a list of challenges that prevent AI from achieving its objectives of effective delivery of personalized learning. The issue of data collection and privacy generate a lot of ethical concerns. People's data is needed in significant amount for AI technologies to perform effectively, and thus, there are issues involving the collection, storage, and use of such information. Experts have urged for enhancement of ethical norms as standards of AI use in education as well as concerns for students' privacy and ensuring equitable utilization of context AI (Holmes et al., 2019).

2.1.3 The Impact of AI on Educational Equity

While AI holds the promise of boosting the students' accomplishments, it remains unclear whether it has the abilities of exercising the equality in education. This current progress of AI can help to narrow down achievement gap between high achievers and non achievers in the following ways. For instance, using of AI in tutoring can assist low-performing students to learn with better performing learners by availing learning support to them (Zawacki-Richter et al., 2019).

However, prejudice might still be present and be used in algorithms that are used in the Ai systems. In education, these prejudices are similar, and AI systems can strengthen or even amplify said prejudices if they are trained on biased data; As such, uneven outcomes for different student groups will occur (Noble, 2018).

2.1.4 AI and Teacher Professional Development

That is why another area of considerable interest is the application of AI in enhancing teacher professional learning. Professional learning can be provided to the teachers in a more customized form and fashion, by AI-based systems and platforms where materials and feedbacks as well as professional support can be provided according to the needs and goals of the teachers. These tools can also be used to enable educators to share, thus be able to get knowledge from their colleagues (Hwang et al., 2020).

In the literature study of how artificial intelligence is implemented in the teacher professional development, some promising studies were identified. For instance, the use of AI-based coaching solutions allows analyzing the interactions occurred in the classroom and offering teachers applicable tips on how to enhance their approach. With its help, the teachers will be able to focus on the aspects of improvement and employ the evidence-based strategies in the classroom process supported by the real-time feedback (Kim et al., 2019).

2.2 Studies on Critical Thinking and Problem-Solving Skills Development

2.2.1 The Importance of Critical Thinking and Problem-Solving in Education

As it has been stated in many discourses and writings, critical and creative thinking skills and problem solving skills are required for success in the twenty first century. It skills allow individuals to evaluate the data, evaluate complex situations, imagine novel and effective approach as to problems, generate sound decisions. Well, it is even more important to be able to reason and solve problems in the world that is turning increasingly complex anddynamic (Shute & Becker, 2010).

Many researchers and theorists in child education have time and again called for the development of these skills in children. Broadly, Bloom's Taxonomy – a commonly used process of categorising learning outcomes – positions problem-solving and critical thinking skills at the uppermost end of knowledge acquisition process (Bloom et al., 1956).

Likewise, the Partnership for 21st Century Skills (P21) has grouped problem solving and critical thinking as two of the 'four Cs', or skills that students need in order to be successful in the current economy (P21, 2019).

As for the fact that their importance is accepted in general, there is a constant debate on the most effective approach to training for these skills. Traditional approaches to teaching that often involve the passing of knowledge and facts and reinforcement rote knowledge in particular are not effective fordevelopment of critical thinking skills. While, teachers adopted controlling and directive approach, researchers encourage students engage themselves in incidents of control and be active learners (Hmelo-Silver, 2004).

2.2.2 AI's Role in Developing Critical Thinking and Problem-Solving Skills

Actually AI could significantly facilitate the growth of critical thinking as well as problem solving skills. Automatic learning resources help students get an opportunity to practice on complicated practical problems that require higher order skills. For example, machine learning/based interventions such as game-based simulations for self-learning might present student with certain challenging scenarios where they have to reason in order to emerge as winners (Gee, 2003).

There is another area, in which the use of the ITS for teaching critical thinking and problem solving is possible to show potential of AI. When students are solving problems ITS may provide them tutoring and guidance, thus helping them learn these skills in a safe environment. This is how effectively ITS have been described in different studies and how they successfully assist learners in improving their performance on such assignments as arithmetic (VanLehn, 2011).

Another advancements of AI in this field includes applying NLP to support the enhancement of reasoning and argumentation skills. The current NLP-based technologies can assess oral presentations and writings of students depending on the cohesiveness, coherence as well as the logical construction of the arguments presented. These resources can be useful when students need to peer review each other and engage in group projects will allow students to collaborate with others in applying knowledge that they have acquired to shape their ideas and productive discussion (Woolf, 2010).

2.2.3 Challenges in Using AI for Skill Development

Several opportunities open by AI, the Matter of enhancing immunity to critical-thinking and problem-solving nutrients exists large barriers to consider. This may seem like a paradox, but the crux of the matter lies in the first part of the statement: designing assets that will eventually serve as the basis for AI systems capable of representing and helping these complex thought processes is perhaps the biggest challenge. People are fit to perform critical thinking and problem solving which also covers cognitive rationality, innovation, insti nct, and discretion. Using the current state of AI it becomes challenging to make the system to understand such fine details (Dreyfus, 2001).

That is, AI has been seen to pose the following challenges; The first one is that AI might reinforce more of a formulaic cognitive style than intended. AI systems if not designed rightly may lead to the students focusing only on 'finding the right answer' instead of engaging in the critical thinking process of questioning and exploration. As for this, researchers emphasize the importance of cognitive diver-sification of AI systems, different perspectives, and the ability to assess different outcomes (Kim et al., 2019).

The final topic is always about making such technologies equal and accessible for everyone. The institutions' socio-economic status and technical support are two factors that have been mentioned earlier that are likely to hinder uptake of AI in education. If these hindrances are not addressed, the potential benefits that can be derived from applying artificial intelligence in enhancing thinking skills as well as solving problems may not be achieved as they can widen the existing gaps in education (Noble, 2018).

2.3 Research on Digital Literacy and Its Importance

2.3.1 Defining Digital Literacy

Digital literacy is a rather vast concept which encompasses different skills and competencies related to the effective utilization of computerized tools. One of the most widely used definitions points to the ability to find, evaluate, create and disseminate information through the use of technology; nevertheless, there isn't a definition of digital literacy that is universally accepted (Ng, 2012).

Digital literacy has now become crucial for participation in the contemporary world since digital technology has become part of people's lives. Hence, for the students to succeed in a technologically enhanced learning environment that requires the use of technology in finding information, working in teams and creating knowledge, the students must be technically competent (Bawden, 2008).

2.3.2 The Role of AI in Teaching Digital Literacy

In the following points, it is demonstrated that AI has many facades that would prove beneficial to the teaching of digital literacy. Harnessing the help of artificial intelligence means may help students develop the necessary knowledge and skills for functioning in the digital environment by focusing on individual learning. For example, AI, coupled with technology, could present learning activities and content and deliver them in line with the learners' individual needs and learning styles and in the process help them build their digital competency under safe conditions (Holmes et al., 2019).

An inspiring example of applying AI to this field is the utilization of tests which would help to determine a person's level of digital competence. Many researchers use simple tests of basic computing skills or questionnaires completed by participants that are generally not a accurate way of assessing digital literacy. On the other hand, it can be possible to assess in use how the pupils use the digital equipment in actual sense by the AI driven tests to offer a clear picture of their aptness in digital literacy skills (Ng, 2012).

AI can be of assistance in the process of improving digital literacy with help of adaptive learning. Intelligent adaptive learning solutions change the level of the learning activities' complexity and the content presented based on the student's needs determined through AI analysis of learning data collected from students. With the help of this approach, the students can learn new digital literacy skills at one's own pace and establish a strong foundation to the skills necessary for effective digital literacy (Piaget, J. et al., 2016).

2.3.3 Digital Literacy and Critical Thinking

You are right for linking critical thinking and digital literacy, to an extent, because both skills involve the ability to evaluate information. Perhaps that is why it is important today more than ever to possess the skills that would enable one to question the comparability and reliability of the content in the digital age when a mountain of information can be obtained in a few minutes. Through providing pupils with the tools to decide on the accuracy and quality of the data that they come across, AI supports one of the crucial aspects of media literacy (Bawden, 2008).

For instance, the use of fact check technologies implemented via artificial intelligence can support students in identifying fake or misleading content on the internet, thus developing media literacy and critical thinking skills. These technologies are capable of processing digital text, photo, and video messages and look for biases, contradictions or mistakes in the information. Some of the tools that may be observed are: Teachers might help students learn main elements needed to navigate the complex information space of digital age by explaining how to use those tools (Holmes et al., 2019).

2.3.4 Challenges in Teaching Digital Literacy with AI

While we are now showing AI has promising prospects regarding the teaching of digital literacy, one should note its disadvantages. One of the major problems is that of a rapid pace of delivering technologies, which might be a problem for AI-driven products to adapt, for instance, to the newest breakthroughs in the application of digital technologies. Often, an AI system may become useless in the context of digital literacy since this field is fluid and changes with time (Ng, 2012).

The conflict that exists in the fact that AI can potentially amplify or increase already existing inequity in access to the digital technology is another problem. socioeconomic status and availability of technical resources are some of the widespread factors revealed earlier which can hinder people's engagement with AI-based educational content. If these barriers are not addressed, it may be that the benefits of AI in DL instruction will be felt inequitably which will augment pursuing such imbalances in education (Noble, 2018).

The final challenge is how to ensure that the use of technology, with explicit references to AI-based technologies, is ethical and promotes proper use of digital technologies. While technical know-how is one part of being digitally literate other parts include ethical sensitivity, reason, and the ability to safely and appropriately use technology. This means that to complement these larger aspects of digital literacy, AI systems should also be designed, to enable students to be capable of rightfully handling the digital world (Bawden, 2008).

2.4 Preparing for AI-Driven Job Markets

2.4.1 The Changing Nature of Work

The use of automation and artificial intelligence (AI) for working is altering the face of employment and hence is bringing a drastic shift to the competencies and skills that are in demand. Some jobs may become obsolete due to automation, but that will create new opportunities in such areas as Data Science, Digital Marketing, and AI Industry (Brynjolfsson & McAfee, 2017).

Expanding literature on the future of work has shown the need of developing a diverse range of skills most likely to be useful in a job market administered by Artificial Intelligence. This includes skill areas such as interpersonal skills like, Problem solving, creativity, and interpersonal skills inter alia, and technical skills such as computer programming, statistical analysis among others (Binkley et al., 2012).

2.4.2 AI's Role in Preparing Students for the Workforce

AI can help student to get prepared for job through career planning as well as other support. Machined learning systems are capable of analysis of student data regarding interests, aptitudes and accomplishments to recommend relevant skills, career paths and education. Moreover, these platforms may help students to acquire the required knowledge and gain the necessary experience in finding a mentor, an internship or employment to successful compete in the industry (Piaget, J. et al., 2016).

There is one field where the use of AI-based simulations and virtual reality training, and others are interested: professional training. From these resources, the student may stand the chance of getting a feel of what awaits him/her in the job market in terms of experience and disciplines to undertake. For instance, there is use of AI-based simulations, where students within specific industries such as engineering, finance, or health are trained, as the use of an actual environment comes with risk and regulation (Holmes et al., 2019).

2.4.3 The Importance of Lifelong Learning

This concern is particularly important because there is an increased awareness of the importance of learning that occurs throughout one's working years due to the dynamism in the type of employment. In order to cope with conditions of an AI-type economy the consumer will be forced to update knowledge and skills from time to time in order to fit the requirements of the employment market. AI enhance the ability of lifelong learning by providing flexible forms of learning that would cover students' needs and goals at distinct stages of their profession (Binkley et al., 2012).

AI based platforms can offer a lot of knowledge in different forms including simple online courses and micro credentials which will let people develop new skills and knowledge quite easily. Also, the almost limitless available repositories of information provided by these platforms also give these applications the power of recommending the kind of learning experience that is relevant to the skills set that the user seeks to acquire in order to get the right job (Ng, 2012).

2.4.4 Challenges in Preparing for an AI-Driven Workforce

There are challenges which hinder the preparation of pupils for a workforce that will be dominated by Artificial Intelligence. Another major challenge lies in ensuring that educational institutions one is good enough to cope with the higher speeded technological advancement. In most LM contexts, the emergence of AI products and platforms implies that such products and platforms need to be frequently upgraded to be relevant (Brynjolfsson & McAfee, 2017).

Another challenge because of the use of AI remains in the ethic implication in the workplace setting. There have been questions regarding how automation is threatening employment and there is further fear that AI may cause job loss to become worse with accrued technology being the factor considering its increasing incorporation into the society. To prepare a workforce for opportunities and challenges in the AI economy it is vital to make sure that AI is used as a tool towards justice and equal opportunity in the job market (Schwab, 2016).

The final issue is to ensure that all learners get necessary tools and support they may need to function in economy dominated by artificial intelligence. As pointed out earlier, socioeconomic status and technical access are core issues that limit populance's ability to access AI-delivery education. These challenges must be addressed to ensure that every learner gets an opportunity to develop those attributes and knowledge that they need to succeed in an age of artificial intelligence (Noble, 2018).

3. DEVELOPMENT OF CRITICAL THINKING AND PROBLEM-SOLVING SKILLS

Analytical and problem solving skills are most relevant in today's world of dynamic changes to cope with the complex reality of the modern world. They enable individuals to evaluate situations, identify challenges and develop viable strategies. All these abilities are assuming increasing significance as society increasingly depend on technology. Artificial intelligence (AI) is gradually gaining recognition as a strong tool, which may enhance the development of analytical and problem-solving abilities. In this part, the definition and importance of these abilities, how AI can enhance them, AI exemplars, AI integration into the training process advantages and challenges will be also highlighted.

3.1 Definition and Importance of Critical Thinking and Problem-Solving

3.1.1 Critical Thinking

Critical thinking requires the efforts to analyze, assess, and integrate information that is acquired through studying and analyzing data and facts. That is, it requires asking questions to assumptions, recognizing bias, and taking into consideration other perspectives (Ennis, 2011).

Most importantly one cannot overemphasise the importance of critical thinking. Having the ability to analyse information with a certain degree of scepticism is necessary in today's world as everyone gets access to a lot of data. Critical thinking skills enable individuals to solve severe issues, reason decidedly and clearly differentiate between facts and myths. Critical thinking correlates with academic performance as well as the ability to learn throughout one's educational process (Facione, 2011).

3.1.2 Problem-Solving

It could be defined as an ability of a person to ascertain, assess and respond to a situation in the best way possible. This involves a countless of processes involving identification of such an issue, generating potential solutions, evaluation of the solutions, and lastly, implementation of the best solution (Jonassen, 2011).

Problem solving skills is another complex skills that are relevant both in our private and working life. It enables individuals to move beyond barriers, achieve goals and adapt to change. The applicability of problem solving in the organizational environment is normally associated with creativity and productivity because the problem solvers are favorable to the growth of their firms (Kurtz, 2015).

3.2 How AI Tools Can Enhance Critical Thinking and Problem-Solving Skills

3.2.1 Personalized Learning Experiences

That is why AI can help to revolutionize the education system as it allows the learning process to be individualized according to each learner's needs and preferred learning styles. As a result of evaluation of students' outcome data, it is possible to identify students' strengths and difficulties and provide them with tools and practice tasks that promote critical thinking (Piaget, J. et al., 2016).

The ability to increase or decrease the difficulty of the content based on students' performance is one of the precursors of using AI technologies in developing the personalized learning process. AI features are capable of constantly assessing the learner when completing the tasks and adjusting the task's level of complexity. This ensures that pupils are always challenged, hence the development of their skills for analysis and for solving problems at their own pace.

3.2.2 Simulation and Scenario-Based Learning

cenario approach and simulations assist in the development of thinking and solving skills among the learners. There is no doubt that AI-supported exercises can create realistic environments in which students can get more experience in applying their knowledge and skills. they may include; engineering students can use AI to develop and build models in a simulated environment or medical students can use the same to practice diagnosing patients and prescribing appropriate treatment..

As such, it makes it possible for the students to test all the options that are available for handling certain issues while receiving immediate results concerning the alternatives they have chosen. Thus, the consideration of the attitudes towards pupils and the fostering of the logical thinking as well as the ability to adapt strategies are developed in result of such approach. Also, real-life challenges can be recreated in the AI models, and this provides learners with the best opportunity of addressing ambiguity in real life situations (De Jong & Joolingen, 1998).

3.2.3 Data-Driven Insights and Analytics

AI technologies can provide the teachers with information and analysis that will help them to be more effective in enlightening their children and as well understand their progress in critical thinking and problem solving skills. Even in situations where the analysis of the students' demographics is not possible, the AI systems can identify patterns and trends that may be indicative of domains where the students may require further assistance based on how the students interact with teaching materials (Baker & Siemens, 2014).

By using such knowledge, teachers are able to make changes in their lesson plan to correspond to the individual learning styles of students and provide enhanced services that support the development of students' problem solving skills. Also, teachers can enhance existing methods for helping learners by analyzing the effectiveness of the specific teaching approaches with the help of analytics based on AI (Siemens & Long, 2011).

3.2.4 Collaborative Learning and AI

AI may help in the development of abilities in critical thinking and problem-solving in other models such as collaborating learning. With the help of AI, students can be grouped in a systematic way with other of like mind, or of similar skills in relation to what is being offered. One example of an AI system may involve grouping students together based on the performance of the group members in different areas thus giving them partners to work with in areas that may require brainstorming and problem solving (Dillenbourg, 1999).

Group learning is also another mode which can be applied in the student context through the use of AI peers or virtual agents that dialog with the students. These virtual assistants can ask meaningful questions that can make initial contributory discussions within the group thought-provoking, give feedback that makes the students think about their contributions to the group analytically and provide samples of how problems can be solved efficiently (Rosé & Fischer, 2013).

3.3 Case Studies or Examples of AI Applications in Skill Development

3.3.1 Case Study 1: AI in Medical Education

AI implementation is increasingly observed in medical education, as it plays an important role to foster students' critical and problem-solving thinking. One example is their use in a medical education program which involves the use of simulations led by artificial intelligence. These simulators can mimic the patients and the students can learn how to diagnose and treat a number of medical illness in a simulated environment.

Some of the examples of using AI include the virtual patient simulator known as "Harvey" to teach medical students performance diagnostic of heart problems. Harvey can mimic a range of cardiovascular disorders; thus, the trainees gets an opportunity to diagnose a non-existent patient before touching real patients.

3.3.2 Case Study 2: AI in Engineering Education

It might be noted that the usages of artificial intelligence techniques have been made in engineering education with the view to enhancing the problem-solving ability of students. One example is implementation of artificial intelligence in design software that allows students to build and experiment with engineering designs virtually. This program, which is based on AI algorithms and tries to mimic various circumstances that can be met in realistic simulations, can assist the students to determine how efficient their design strategies are in this or that situation.

A notable example of the use of AI is the "Design by Number" program at the Stanford University where students design as well as optimise buildings and bridges with the help of AI techniques. The AI system means that students' designs are assessed, and alterations as well as advice on weaknesses and strength are provided. Regarding the iterative process, students' problem-solving skills are sharp-ened since this empowers they to modify their designs according to the outcomes suggested by the AI (Smith & Stone, 2018).

3.3.3 Case Study 3: AI in Business Education

In business education this element is also applied in the development of cognition fundamentals accompanied by critical thinking and problem-solving skills. Virtual simulations like "CapSim" give the business students the opportunity to engage in actual-looking business challenges enhanced by AI. In these simulations, students have to make business decisions differently ranging from the marketing strategies, financing, operation, and hiring while bearing in mind the overall success of the business.

Students participating in CapSim simulations for example would be assigned the role of operating an organization in which they would have to allocate resources, evaluate the market and respond to pressure from competitors. This format appears more effective as students can see the outcome of the activities that they engage in and change their plan since the AI system offers feedback on the choices made. This practice work enables the students enhance on their thought process as they work to accomplish the tasks at hand (Anderson & Lawton, 2009).

3.4 Challenges and Opportunities in Using AI to Develop Critical Thinking and Problem-Solving Skills Challenges

3.4.1 Access and Equity

The last hurdle is making sure that all students have equal chances of using AI to help him or her to improve on aspects like critical thinking and problem solving abilities. But indeed, Liben and her colleagues also pointed out that while AI has an optimistic role in education, not all the population will benefit from equally. For some of the student this could become a problem due to limited funding or inability to get to resources for example students coming from disadvantaged background (Noble, 2018).

To tackle this problem it is imperative to create strategies that promote digital equity in classrooms, so that all students could have equal chances and opportunities towards achievement. This might mean investing in the technology setup of under-privileged communities, training educators as to how to utilize AI tools effectively and benefiting a wider population by offering a choice of AI solutions, either in the form of free or open source.

3.4.2 Data Privacy and Ethics

The subject of confidentiality is another problem when it comes to the application of the use of the AI system in education. Privacy concerns are brought up by the fact that most AI-based edtech apps rely on large datasets for achieving personalization of learning processes. Student data that is collected can be misused by those individuals or accessed by the wrong people which may lead to a violation of the students' privacy (Holmes et al., 2019).

The following are some of the ways through which the dangers mentioned above could be negated as well as ensure that data is collected and processed appropriately This is why it is important to have strict standards and policies that guide the use of AI in education. This may require the addition of high levels of data protection, student and their families' consent, and AI solutions to communicate their operation.

3.4.3 Over-Reliance on AI

Also, students may become idle, and rely on the automation tools thus reducing their performance during reality and comprehension tests and assignments in class. Despite this, it cannot be overemphasized that students have to practice these skills on their own without relying much on AI (Kim et al., 2019).

Hence, the teachers should balance between assisting the students improve their learning through use of AI while at the same time enable them solve problems on their own and think critically. It could include developing learners' embrace of the concept of the Protestant work ethic, providing the learners with an opportunity to apply their skills in practice, and integrating the regular traditional with the modern AI-based approaches to learning.

3.5 Opportunities

3.5.1 Enhancing Personalized Learning

In spite of that, it is crucial to understand that there are many advantages of applying AI when it comes to improving the individuals' thinking and problem-solving skills. Among the most promising possibilities, the opportunities for implementing the individual learning experiences, which are relevant to the particular learners, are given. Resources based on artificial intelligence technology permit real-time adaptive learning support for the students and valuable feedback and encouragement to further develop these skills (Piaget, J. et al., 2016).

Other more sophisticated personalized learning paradigms that will assist the learners in achieving deeper thought processes in problem solving and critical thinking skills may be achieved as AI technology evolves. A prototype of such AI-driven platforms is also amenable to having natural language processing integrated into it so that students can be engaged in complex discussions. This would promote critical thinking on major aspects and give feedback based on the outcome depending on the students' inputs.

3.5.2 Fostering Collaboration and Communication

Technologies powered by AI also provide students an opportunity to interact or maybe even communicate with fellow learners something that is very vital in critical thinking and solving problematic tasks. Technology may also assist students in developing their interpersonal skills and which will include how better to interact with other members of the group in order to exchange ideas and to solve problems collaboratively.

It may be possible with the progress in AI technology to be provided with more advanced tailored learning environment and or learning experiences which may assist in helping the students in mastering knowledge and skills in critical thinking and problem-solving at a much deeper level. It is possible to utilize AI-based platforms giving them the ability to use natural language processing, to engage students in complex discussions. This would provide the basis on which students could be challenged on different fronts and given feedback based on the answers that they gave.

3.5.3 Preparing Students for the Future

AI technologies also enable students to interact with one another, something that is very essential in critical thinking and problem solving. AI can facilitate students to learn working together, sharing ideas and solving problems in group context through possibilities for collaborative learning.

Use of AI in classrooms can also prepare the learners with actual feel of AI technology which will put them in a better vantage point compared to others in the job market. Applying AI tools in learning may improve students' understanding of AI principles and apps; critical thinking and problem solving; they may be more attractive to employers in tech industries.

4. ROLE OF AI IN TEACHING DIGITAL LITERACY

Digital Literacy has now evolved into a major aspect of people's lives within the contemporary society as means by which people are able to glance, operate, and communicate with technologies in the society. This paper therefore concludes that digital literacy is paramount for social and economic activities as well as individual emancipation as societies technological apparatus expands. AI is therefore enhancing more use of digital literacy education since it has the capability of handling big volumes of data, task customization, emulation of real life situations. This section will identify the nature of digital literacy, the components of digital literacy, how AI can support the promotion of digital literacy, the tools and programs that can be used in teaching digital literacy and the effectiveness and success of these AI-based crusades.

4.1 Definition and Components of Digital Literacy

4.1.1 Digital Literacy: An Overview

Digital literacy is a rather broad concept that implies a set of skills and information required to use digital devices and to interact in the social media and access the Internet. It goes beyond using the software and operating the computer; it also requires the knowledge of how the digital technologies work, the ability to evaluate content found on the internet and computer and the skills of creating information on the computer most appropriately.

The European Commission (2006) has described digital literacy as the 'effective and appropriate utilisation of Information Society Technology (IST) in learning, work, leisure and interpersonal communications It involves both technical and analytical skills augmented with sensitivity of the moral and social implications of digital media. Due to the fact, that digital literacy allows users to successfully function in new digital environments, it is a form of lifelong learning.

4.2 Components of Digital Literacy

4.2.1 Technical Skills

These include performers' use of cellphones, laptops and software programs in the performance. It also prescribes an introduction to basic logical problem-solving approaches as well as how to take care of digital devices (Bawden, 2008).

4.2.2 Information Literacy

It relates to locating, evaluating as well as applying information effectively. It involves managing information electronically, assessing the credibility of sources from the World Wide Web and understanding the principles of search engines (Webber & Johnston, 2000).

4.2.3 Media Literacy

Curation and recommendation of content is another method AI helps with digital literacy education. Large volumes of digital content may be analyzed by AI algorithms, which can then suggest appropriate resources to students depending on their interests, learning objectives, and skill levels. In addition to saving teachers and students time, this guarantees that students are exposed to pertinent, high-quality content (Livingstone, 2004).

4.2.4 Communication Skills

Real communication competence, as a part of digital competence, also includes the ability to communicate effectively in the Web, in social networks, by e-mail and other use of technologies. It also involves knowing how to protect such identities and understanding digital manners as well (Hobbs, 2010).

4.2.5 Ethical and Social Awareness

Ethical considerations of technological advancement including in security, privacy, and digital citizenship knowledge is needed for this component. It also means having the ability of functioning appropriately in the cyber world and understanding how informational technologies impact culture (Ribble, 2011).

4.2.6 Creative and Critical Thinking Skills

Other elements which are considered to be the part of digital literacy include the ability to leverage technology meaningfully to create, and the ability to reason about content. This has posed new challenges to the learners and educators, requiring creativity, problem solving and flexibility to operate in new digitalised milieu (Belshaw, 2012).

4.3 AI as a Facilitator in Teaching Digital Literacy

4.3.1 Personalized Learning Experiences

Because it is capable of providing differentiated instruction, which adapts to the student's learning needs, it is possible that AI will revolutionize the manner in which digital literacy is taught. Learning environments that are powered by artificial intelligence are capable of evaluating students' performance and adapting the material offered so that it will be challenging yet helpful to learners (Piaget, J. et al., 2016).

Learning management systems that are operated using artificial intelligence, for example, may observe the learners' preference for and interactions with data in a digital environment, identify possible issues, and provide the learners with tools that may prevent those problems from arising. As such by posing a high relevance to each of the students' needs, this approach enhances not only learning achievement but also student's interest (Pane et al., 2015).

4.3.2 AI-Driven Content Curation and Recommendation

The last means through which the AI aids in the education of digital literacy is through curation and recommendation of content. Lots of information are available which can be processed by AI and based on students' preferences, academic goals and abilities select the necessary resources. Apart from this, it will save the time of teachers as well as students and at the same time ensures that students are exposed to relevant and quality material (Rose & McKinley, 2018).

For example, artificial intelligence systems applied in "Coursera" and "edX" use machine learning to recommend the courses and materials according to the learner's preferences and the skills of the learner. Furthermore, these platforms can also provide specific learning type pathways that take the students through a set of classes that is designed to build up the digital literacy skills in a systematic and sequential manner (Kizilcec et al., 2017).

4.3.3 AI-Powered Simulations and Virtual Environments

AI learning environments and simulations help learners establish a safe, regulated setting in which to perfect their use of the media. These demonstrations allow students to select from different forms of approaches as a concern of solving numerous issues and arriving at numerous decisions in a real life like setup (VanLehn, 2011).

For example, AI-based cybersecurity training can help students study how to avoid threats, such as viruses and phishing attempts, by practically trying to navigate through them. In these simulations, there are certain digital literacy skills students might get a chance to develop, such as identifying a scam email, understanding about encryptions and protecting oneself from privacy invasion on the World Wide Web (Bada et al., 2019).

4.3.4 Automated Feedback and Assessment

AI can also be used to present assessment and feedback which are useful in teaching digital literacy. Some forms of AI-based interventions could assess how comprehensively students complete digital literacy tasks and provide feedback in real-time that not only inform the students' weaknesses, but also teaches them. This kind of close feedback is critical for increasing learning and ensuring that students attain the appropriate skills for functioning in the digital world (Shute & Wang, 2016).

Some of the Artificial intelligence-based writing tools like "Grammarly" may help students get feedback instantly on their writing and improve communication skills and the understanding of the digital citizenship principles crucial in students' writing, for instance correct citation and referencing, and checking for plagiarism.

Similarly, the AI-based evaluation systems are capable of grading the digital literacy assignments and inform the teachers about the students' progress and future potentialities (Nye, 2015).

4.4 Programs and Tools Designed to Improve Digital Literacy through AI

4.4.1 AI-Powered Educational Platforms

There are a lot of AI-based learning solutions introduced to improve digital competence by providing personal tutoring, assessment, and valuable resources. These platforms are designed for users of all skill levels and of all ages, from junior to senior users.

4.4.2 Khan Academy

Thus, the usage of AI in Khan Academy customized students' learning experiences. The subjects offered via the course include information literacy, computer studies, and programming, and the course offers them in a large variety. AIS also observe the progress of pupils and provide recommendations of what extra classes they may need (Murphy et al., 2014).

4.4.3 Duolingo

Although Duolingo is known as a language learning application it applies AI in promoting digital literacy as well. As an example, with the help of artificial intelligence technologies of adaptive learning, the platform offers courses in the sphere of digital competencies, for example, in communication on the internet and in creating content (Settles & Meeder, 2016).

4.4.4 Coursera

Thus, the educational technology company Coursera offers programs in different fields connected to digital competence. The mode of utilization of the platform is that depending on the interests of the learners as well as their ability, use artificial intelligence to recommend appropriate courses and other learning resources. There are also Specialized Digital Literacy Courses on Coursera to help learners master this. One of them is the "Google IT Support Professional Certificate" that contains information management and cybersecurity (Kizilcec et al., 2017).

4.4.5 AI-Driven Tools for Digital Literacy

There is also several AI-based technologies that have also been designed exclusively for teaching and learning of digital literacy, other than education solutions.

4.4.6 Grammarly

Grammarly is an application which uses artificial intelligence in an effort to improve a users writing by providing them with instant suggestions related to grammar and spelling as well as general writing style. It can strongly be considered the tool is practically beneficial for training digital communication skills since it gives suggestions on how to improve tone and clarity, too (O'Neill & Russell, 2019).

4.4.7 Turnitin

Turnitin is a Plagiarism Checker which applies artificial intelligence in attempt to help the learners address the importance of correct referencing and honesty in academic work. Assigned as a writing tool, Turnitin assists students in preventing different forms of plagiarism such as self-plagiarism and failure to acknowledge references appropriately by determining the similarity index of the text (Martin, 2011).

4.4.8 Code.org

A non-profit company which is called Code. org provides learners of any age the opportunity to attend free tutorial in computer science. This one exploits an artificial intelligence to give feedback to students on their code as well as to adapt coding classes. The courses taught by Code. org focus that is to help students develop the digital literacy skills, such as problem solving, computational thinking, and digital content creation (Partovi, 2014).

4.4.9 CyberPatriot

CyberPatriot is a program for promoting cybersecurity and which involve using artificial intelligence to simulate real-life situations in terms of cybersecurity. The program provides learners with the practical aspects such as cybersecurity attack simulations that helps them to practice and learn from live threats. It is important to note that CyberPatriot's aim is to enhance students' awareness of cybersecurity and to help them get ready for jobs in this industry (Bada et al., 2019).

4.5 Analysis of Effectiveness and Impact

4.5.1 Evaluating the Effectiveness of AI in Teaching Digital Literacy

The extent to which AI in teaching digital literacy can be assessed may be subjective or measured by certain yardsticks like, students' involvement, lessons learned, and ultimately, or mainly, imparting of digital literacy. In terms of students' digital literacy some of the major findings are that education-based AI platform and tools enhance students digital literacy through intelligent recommendations and feedbacks, and through access to high-quality digital resources (Piaget, J. et al., 2016; Shute & Wang, 2016).

For example, the study of Pane et al. (2015) has revealed that students who were engaged in AI-based personalized learning applications achieved considerably higher levels of digitally related competencies in comparison with students studied with the help of traditional methods. The study also pointed out that the use of AI plat forms led to improvement of student engagement since the information supplied was customized to what the learner wanted to learn.

Likewise, studies that have explored the use of writing assistants that employ AI – like Grammarly – have found out that students benefit from these tools by enhancing their digital literacy skills through feedback the software offers whenever the learners are typing (O'Neill & Russell, 2019).

4.5.2 Challenges and Considerations

Despite the fact that AI can be helpful for the teaching of digital literacy, certain difficulties and questions need to be discussed to consider their efficiency and outcomes. These are concern that pertain to access and equity, data privacy, and dependency on AI-based tools.

4.5.3 Access and Equity

The first difficulty when using AI to teach material that involves digital literacy is to make sure that all of the students have access to AI- based tools and interfaces. If certain students do not have the necessary resources to take advantage of artificial intelligence in learning then chances are that this technique in education will only serve to reinforce inequalities present in society.

4.5.4 Data Privacy

Most of the educational platforms based on artificial intelligence involve gathering and analyzing significant amounts of information about the students in order to deliver individualized learning experience. This creates a problem regarding data privacy and also have doubts on how student's information may be exploited. This means that teachers and decision-makers must prioritize protecting the students' data especially when implementing the use of AI in teaching digital citizenship lessons.

4.5.5 Over-Reliance on AI

One concern is the dependency that may arise in terms of students and educators using AI related tools in the near future and may reduce the development of effective student's and teachers' digital competencies. That is why, it is crucial to make certain that students should practice these skills on their own, without constant reliance on AI assistants.

4.6 Future Directions

Looking at the opportunities that have been provided by AI technology, there are several areas which could be further explored when it comes to the education of digital literacy. This should be done in future research where the effects of the use of the AI tools on the digital literacy skills will be investigated, as well as the efficiency of the AI in imparting different elements of digital literacy including media literacy and ethical learning.

At the same time, there is an opportunity to create even more complex AI educational applications that will allow creating even more individual and engaging lessons. For instance, through AI-enabled immersive environments, a number of training activities within the context of virtual reality may enable the learners to engage in proactivity and hone on their digital literacy effectively (Bailenson, 2018).

5. PREPARING STUDENTS FOR AI-DRIVEN JOB MARKETS

5.1 Overview of AI-Driven Job Markets and Required Skills

5.1.1 The Impact of AI on Job Markets

There is evidence that shows that AI has begun to revolutionalise both business-es and employees as it alters the model of work markets across globe. In the year 2025, use of automobiles and AI, 85 million has predicted for reduction in the job while 97 million for new jobs that have been revealed by a World Economic Forum of 2020. These new positions will require different sets of skills especially in the use of Artificial Intelligence (AI), machine learning and data analysis, and skills in new digital technologies

Further, it is not simply restricted to those markets which directly relate to tech-nology such as employment in health service industries or in finance industries or manufacturing industries or the retail sector or education employment sector; and many others. For example, it is used in the healthcare system to enhance patient satisfaction, provide personalised treatment therapies and facilitate better diagnostic. It is now applied in finance where chatbots are used to provide customer services, Automated trading, and detection of froud activities. One of the trends that are ex-pected to grow in the future is the use of many more 'AI-related' talents owing to growing incorporation of Artificial intelligence in various occupations (McKinsey Global Institute, 2017).

5.1.2 Key Skills for AI-Driven Job Markets

Consequently, undergraduate and graduate students need to develop ones technical for data processing, analytical and soft skills in order to be successful in employment markets dominated by artificial intelligence. Among the essential abilities that will be in demand are the following: Among the essential abilities that will be in demand are the following:

5.1.3 AI and Machine Learning

Hence, students must comprehend the basis of machine learning and artificial intelligence so that they can join employment areas dominated by artificial intel-ligence. This indents to include understanding of deep learning techniques, neural network, data structures and algorithms (Russell & Norvig, 2016).

5.1.4 Data Science and Analytics

Skills in data science and analytics are important due to current, continuous reliance on data in the execution of organization's operations. Apart from computer programs such as Python and R, the students should be fluent in data collection, analyzing, visualizing, and interpreting the data (Provost & Fawcett, 2013).

5.1.5 Digital Literacy

Digital competencies cannot be present in the absence of the capacity to effectively apply digital resources and technologies. Digital literacy in today's labor market with AI involves an understanding of how to interface, work and operate AI across different work fields (Eshet-Alkalai, 2004).

5.1.6 Problem-Solving and Critical Thinking

AI powered job markets seek for people who are intelligent with strong aptitude in solving problems. Today's pupils must be armed with knowledge that can make them recognize a particular situation, identify concerns and learn how to develop novel ideas with the help of AI technologies (Jonassen, 2011).

5.1.7 Adaptability and Lifelong Learning

Due to this, the student should be willing to change and adapt to new knowledge as a result of admitting the fact that technology is very dynamic. This means that one has to acquire new skills on a continuous basis and be conversant with developments in AI (Lifelong Learning Platform, 2018).

5.1.8 Collaboration and Communication

Identity and management competency will also be critical working in artificial intelligence employment sectors where collaboration and communication shall be critical. Pupils should be able to reason sufficiently and learn to communicate with students of other origin: orally as well as in writing when giving out complex information (Trilling & Fadel, 2009).

5.1.9 Ethical and Social Awareness

Here, the students must be ready to face the ethical and social question in reference to the AI technologies. This means that there must be an understanding of the ethical implication arising from artificial intelligence (Floridi et al., 2018).

5.2 Curriculum Changes to Integrate AI-Related Skills

5.2.1 The Need for Curriculum Transformation

If students are to be prepared for radically different employment markets sooner rather than later, then curriculum shifts have to be made significantly in education systems. Modern education which traditional pedagogy which often reduces learning to memorization and rote learning is inadequate to prepare young people for an AI led economy. On the contrary curriculum should be reshaped to focus on critical thinking, interdisciplinary and learning of skills pertaining to artificial intelligence (Piaget, J. et al., 2017).

The need to shift the goals and purposes of learning means that a more integrated approach is needed to add new topical AI skills into the curricula. This means providing the students with opportunities to practice what they have learnt in real contexts or situations and promoting an openness to learning in search of solutions (OECD, 2018).

5.3 Key Curriculum Changes

5.3.1 Incorporating AI and Machine Learning into STEM Education

AI and Machine Learning should be incorporated in STEM education as a curriculum improvement that is needed. These objectives can be achieved through an introduction of AI concepts and tools into children's curriculum at a tender age for instance, through the arduous robotic operations, data science programs, and coding sessions (Wing 2006). With this in mind, there is also a need to introduce AI into the STEM related areas that are already existent which include computer science and mathematics for maximum impact on the pupils (NRC, 2011).

5.3.2 Interdisciplinary Learning and Project-Based Education

The future AI job markets require individuals who can easily work with different fields and apply what they know in tackling difficult problems. Project based learning approaches should be integrated into curricula because they enable the students to harness technology to solve problems in groups hence encouraging Interdisciplinary learning (Barron & Darling-Hammond, 2008).

5.3.3 Developing Digital and Data Literacy

Knowledge and skills concerning data, and digital information specifically, are the key requirements for employment markets based on artificial intelligence. Tutors should ensure that they teach their students lessons on how to use technology, how to analyze data and how to interpret results among others. This could include possible projects related to data supported activities, training in data presentation techniques or actual application of data analysis tools (Davies et al., 2011).

5.3.4 Fostering Critical Thinking and Problem-Solving Skills

Creativity and critical thinking skills are crucial competencies required especially in the realms of artificial intelligence in the employment domain. Curriculum that promote Skill -based learning that engage the students in posing questions and answering for difficult questions promotes these skills (Jonassen, 2011).

5.3.5 Ethics and Social Implications of AI

To note, curriculum must also address the causal relation that arises with the application of these technologies along the ethical implications that arise with the different consequences that the societal advocates for. This could include such exercises which ask students to reflect on the impact of AI on society as well as AI-related lectures on ethical, privacy, and bias issues (Floridi et al., 2018).

5.3.6 Lifelong Learning and Continuous Skill Development

Due to rapid development of the technology, children should be prepared for it and develop lifelong learning. It is necessary to explain the importance of continuous learning of IT skill and provide the instruments and opportunities to the students to update their knowledge regularly in terms of AI (Lifelong Learning Platform, 2018).

5.4 Role of AI in Personalized Learning and Career Guidance

5.4.1 Personalized Learning with AI

The ability of a computer to deliver material in the way least stressful to the learner makes it one of the major contributions of the technology in the field of education. AI EduTech platforms are capable of identifying each students' learning style, strengths, and gaps and with that come up with individual learning paths that will be customized for the students' understanding. (Piaget, J. et al., 2016).

Web-based technologies of learning are employed by AI-based systems including "Knewton" and "Smart Sparrow" to provide students with equally unique feedback and material content depending on the results obtained. For students to be able to improve their outcome of tasks in AI-related areas, these platforms can adjust the level of the problems, provide related links and feedback immediately (Pane et al., 2015).

5.4.2 AI-Powered Career Guidance

Thus, AI may also find its application as a tool that can complement career counseling in addition to facilitating individualized learning paths by guiding students through various types of careers and helping them identify the appropriate opportunities which would fit their profile. With the help of AI advanced career guidance systems are capable of assessing the students' participation in co curricular activities, academic performance, and preferences in order to recommend suitable careers and the relevant skill set for a certain job (Riva et al., 2020).

Other examples include 'Pymetrics', which recruits student's employers based on his/her character from cognitive and emotional tests based on artificial intelligence and neuroscience. Furthermore, these platforms can provide students with specific goals for job development along with certification, internship, and other courses to achieve that goal depending on student's goal and preferences (Chamorro-Premuzic et al., 2016).

To meet the need of students for the AI-based job markets, the concept of AI-based career counselling will help the students in making wise decisions in selection of their future profession. With the help of AI, students may gain the tools for the job market with the subsequent professional advancement and develop themselves as highly demanded specialists.

5.5 Industry Partnerships and Real-World Training

5.5.1 The Importance of Industry Partnerships

The education systems require strong partnerships with business leaders to ensure that students being prepared for employment anticipating artificial intelligence filled environments are adequately prepared for the challenge. Such collaborations may provide a student with a chance to have actual experience in AI technology and essential information regarding the needs of the modern world (Bailey et al., 2003).

Industry engagement can occur in various formats example these comprises of research partnerships or projects, training and guiding partnerships, work-place training, and training schemes. Such programs can provide students with actual experience, and thereby help the students apply their AI-related knowledge in practice and acquire a more profound understanding of the opportunities and challenges in the AI-oriented industries.

5.5.2 Real-World Training and Experiential Learning

Apart from industry partnership real-world training and experience learning are effective approaches since they prepare students for the job markets that are increasingly characterized by innovations in artificial intelligence. Examples of experiential learning include project based learning, co-op, internship and others. In this way it can help students understand the working place better, establish contacts and work on their skills (Kolb, 1984).

For instance, to innovate more number of colleges have established innovation hubs and labs on artificial intelligence (AI), where student can work with business partners on projects. These labs also allow students to engage in projects that address the existing challenges and also, exposes them to advanced AI implements and hardware (Piaget, J. et al., 2017).

Virtual simulations and thus AI also have value in enhancing the experience-based learning. By using these technologies, the students can endeavour to hone these skills in an offline environment that is duplicated in the real setting while practicing in safe environments (Bailenson, 2018).

6. METHODOLOGY

In every research study one will find the methodology section that gives the methodical approach used in data collection as well as analysis. The method to be used in this project along the theme: 'Preparing Students for the Job Markets with

Artificial Intelligence Integration' will include: Sample selection Data collection techniques Data analysis frameworks Ethical issues The aim of this part is to provide a clear understanding of the framework which has validity and reliability of the study findings across different settings.

6.1 Research Design and Approach

6.1.1 Research Design

As the guideline to the overall method and framework of the investigation, the research design is a key aspect of the technique. Integrated approach or a concurrent mixed method design was adopted in this study due to the theoretical rationale that posited it as appropriate for organisational research that transcends the possibility of a single method. However, the mixed-methods approach allows for the combining of the strengths of both research paradigms and enables the exploration of the subject in greater detail while providing a better understanding of how students may be sufficiently prepared for employment markets driven by Artificial Intelligence.

From tracking of EmIS, quantitative research methodologies will be used for the collection of statistical data on educational outcomes, skill deficiencies and student preparedness. Due to conducting sturctured surveys and using standards to analysis the data that is going to be collected, the researcher will be able to identify trends and patterns in a large sample . Another advantage that comes with the use of the quantitative technique is that results can be generalized to a greater population (Creswell & Plano Clark, 2017).

On the other hand, interview, questionnaires, and focus group discussion will be used to assess the students', teachers', and business expertise's experiences, perceptions, and behavior. Such insights will be gained with semi structured interviews, focus groups and case studies and will give further insight into the contextual factors which inform students' readiness. The nature of phenomena which cannot be measured quantitatively or the comparison between how AI influences career plans or how good or bad certain methods of teaching are are all made probative through the use of the qualitative method.

6.1.2 Research Approach

This research incorporates deductive and inductive approaches of research. Part of the deductive approach are validation of prior givens or hypotheses about student preparedness and job markets that are powered by AI. For instance, the study could ask whether teaching curriculum with skills aligned in AI increases the student's performance in AI-infused tasks. This involves the use of means, ANOVA, t-test among others to test specific hypothesis in order arrive at conclusions which will fit into the quantitative part of the study.

The opposite of it is the inductive technique as it is based on creating new hypotheses or ideas in view of the obtained data. It is particularly relevant to the qualitative part of the research, which is an attempt to explore variables that influence students' readiness for employment markets enabled with the help of artificial intelligence. The researcher will retrieve reoccurring themes and patterns that will help in the development of new ideas through Thematic analysis of focus group talks and interview transcripts (Glaser & Strauss, 2017).

The investigation aims at providing a comprehensive study which goes beyond merely verifying the existing theories while also contributing to the existing body of knowledge in the area of AI education by employing a combination of deductive and inductive approaches.

6.2 Data Collection Methods

6.2.1 Surveys

The survey is one of the major instruments that are used in this study for the purposes of collecting data. Thus, the quantitative data about several aspects of students' preparedness for AI-driven employment markets will be collected The survey will be designed as a structured one. To acquire quantitative data for analysis, Likert scale and close ended questions and answers will be employed.

A fairly large group of students, teachers, and other business people from different schools and universities will be given the survey. Data collection on the following important areas is the goal: Data collection on the following important areas is the goal:

6.2.2 Current AI-Related Skills and Knowledge Among Students

In this area, students' self-assessed competence in relation to AI skills & knowledge in addition to their recognition of AI concepts, technologies, and overall applications will be assessed.

6.2.3 Perceptions of AI-Driven Job Markets

In this section, attention will be paid to how AI affects the employment rate, and what participants expect today's employees, and in the future, to be significant for the job market.

6.2.4 Educational Practices and Curriculum Design

In this section, information about how much of AI-associated content is integrated into curricula and to what extent various pedagogical approaches would aid prepare students for jobs that are guided by AI will be obtained.

6.2.5 Barriers and Challenges to AI Education

The fundamental challenges which will impede successful implementation of AI teaching will be outlined in the present section that comprises of resource deficiency, inadequate teacher training, and issues regarding students' engagement.

Both the descriptive and the inferential statistics will aid in the analysis of the survey data in a bid to determine specific patterns, association, or unique differences in result among different groups (e.g., students vs. educators, different educational institutions).

6.2.6 Interviews

Some of the topics of the study will be explored through a limited number of moderating, semi-structured interviews with students, teachers and business executives. The rationale of carrying out these interviews is to gather qualitative data that provides richer insights regarding the factors that affect the students' preparedness to participating in employment domains with AI integration.

Semi-structured interviewing is flexible in terms of the interviewing process where the interviewer is able to go deeper into certain areas of focus while at the same time ensuring that there is some sort of standardization in all the interviews. The following important topics will be covered by the interview questions .

The following important topics will be covered by the interview questions:

6.2.7 Experiences with AI Education

The particular experiences of the participants that will be invited will be experiences in relation to AI-related projects, courses or other related activities. This will help in understanding the challenges faced by the students as well as the educators and also the effectiveness of various instructions methods.

6.2.8 Perceptions of AI-Driven Job Markets

Specific questions in relation to the participants' perception about the place of AI in career prospects as well as skills they deem relevant in the current job market will be asked.

6.2.9 Barriers to AI Education

Participants will be required to enumerate the factors that hinder the delivery/ receipt of AI education including; For participants providing the education; Students' engagement challenges, lack of support from institutions, and scarcity of resources to support the education, inadequate students to support the AI education etc.

6.2.10 Recommendations for Improving AI Education

To ascertain participants' perception on how to enhance AI education with an aim of preparing the students for job market needs, participants will be asked questions. This could entail recommendations on changes that could be made on the curriculum, how lessons delivered and who could be partner with in business ventures.

6.2.11 Case Studies

Specific case studies of certain educational programs or institutions that have managed to integrate AI-related competencies into their curricula will be presented in the form of case studies. Due to the case study approach, an important understanding of the aspects that contribute to the success of such programs, partnerships with industries, approaches to learning, and institutional support, is achieved.

A number of interviews, document analysis, and observations will be conducted during the case studies with key stakeholders such as administrators, teachers and students. The aim is therefore to search for such practices and learning points that other educational institutions might wish to apply in improving their AI education programs.

6.3 Sample Selection and Description

6.3.1 Sample Selection

Both purposive and random sampling methods are also going to be employed in selecting the sample of the study. The purposeful sampling will be used to select participants with expertise in AI education and employment markets, including educators, business entities and student enrolled in AI programs. By so doing, the sample ensures that there are people who have adequate information that can help in offering the required perceptions on the subject the study embraces (Patton, 2015).

For the purpose of selecting a greater number of instructors and students from different learning institutions, random sampling will be used. This allows the acquisition of data which represents a larger demographic thus increasing the relevancy of the conclusions (Bryman, 2016).

6.3.2 Sample Description

The sample for this study will include the following groups:

6.3.3 Students

The students sample will include people taking graduate and undergraduate programs in different universities. Meanwhile, priority will be given to students, who are studying AI-related curriculums more (like computer science, data science, engineering, etc.) or students, who are from other fields of professions. The goal is to gather data on students' readiness for employment from the perspective of AI-based markets across different fields of study.

6.3.4 Educators

The participants will be selected from a pool of current educators such as professors, instructors and curriculum developer who implement or design AI content into courses or teach courses related to AI. Control of variables The teachers in the study will be selected randomly from different types of schools and they will be from technical as well as non technical background (e.g., universities, community colleges, vocational schools).

6.3.5 Industry Professionals

Industry professional sample will include persons working in the industries such as manufacturing, technology, finance, and healthcare industries that adopt AI to serve their clients' needs. Employees of all types from those that are relatively new to the workforce to those who are at the managerial level will feature in the sample. The aim is to obtain data regarding the employers' requirements and the skills and expertise required in artificial intelligence orientated labor markets.

6.3.6 Institutional Representatives

Officials and administrators of educational institutions as well as policymakers who are mandated with the responsibilities of formulation and implementation of AI education policies shall form the sample. These people will provide insights into the institutional factors influencing the efficiency of AI education programmes.

To select the overall sample size, the principle of data saturation whereby the data collection stops when new themes or pattern are no longer found will be employed. However, it is expected that the sample will comprise of 200- 300 people and it will be equally distributed across the mentioned groups.

6.4 Data Analysis Techniques

6.4.1 Quantitative Data Analysis

In analyzing the quantitative data that will be collected from the two state surveys, both the descriptive and inferential statistics shall be used at the same time. Mean and median together with variability will be a part of the descriptive statistics that will be used for data synthesis and presentation of the main conclusions (e.g., standard deviation) (Field, 2013).

They are used to make relationships between variables and test hypotheses while inferential statistical analysis is aimed at generalizing results. This could include regression analysis, Analysis of variance and t-tests among other statistical tests depending with the type of data analyzed and the research questions being addressed. For instance, the application of regression analysis can help examine the relationship between the students' level of preparedness for AI jobs and the AI skills (Pallant, 2020).

6.4.2 Qualitative Data Analysis

In this study, focus will be focused on employing of the thematic analysis of data gotten from focus groups, cases and interviews. When it comes to systematic and iterative process of identifying, analyzing and reporting patterns (themes) within the given qualitative data, the process is referred to as thematic analysis.

6.4.3 Familiarization

The transcripts will be read in their whole and again by the researcher to familiarise with the data..

6.4.4 Coding

After that, the investigator will systematically sort the obtained information, and single out the text fragments that are connected, for instance, with certain topics or concepts. Other software that will be used to code comprises the NVivo qualitative data analysis software that is used in effectively sorting, organizing and analyzing large volumes of qualitative data.

6.4.5 Theme Development

The main themes will be derived from the data by doing further coding to pool the related codes into broader categories. In other to ensure that these themes fit the data and help to meet the study objectives, the researcher will refine them.

6.4.6 Theme Definition and Naming

As for every theme, the researcher will define it and provide a brief and comprehensible description of the value of each of them.

6.4.7 Reporting

Assigning the final breakdown is the last producing platform whereby the author devises at writing up the findings and presenting the impact of each topic under a particular research question.

The researcher shall go back to the data and modify the themes if necessary while going through the analytical process of assessing the qualitative data. In this way, their understanding of the factors influencing students' preparedness for AI-centered occupations can be multifaceted and elaborate.

6.5 Ethical Considerations

It is true that in this research human subjects are used hence, presenting high level of ethical concern. The research procedure shall be conducted with adherence to the following ethical principles:The research procedure shall be conducted with adherence to the following ethical principles:

6.5.1 Informed Consent

All the volunteers will be provided with detailed information concerning the aim of the study, the procedures which are going to be implemented, any weaknesses of the study, and the strengths. Inadverte al Etiology Participant consent will be sought prior beginning the study to establish that they understand and full well the dangers involved and their seuh willful consent will be sought.

6.5.2 Confidentiality and Anonymity

Particularly, participants' anonymity and their information will be safeguarded throughout the study process. All collected data will be de-identified without possibility to recover identity of any User involved in the study. To enhance the security of the data collected the information will be safely stored in a manner that only other members of the research team will be able to access the data. The participants will be informed of such precautions and be assured that their personal information shall not reach any third party.

6.5.3 Right to Withdraw

Another concern for the study is preserving the participants' rights where they would be allowed to quit the study at any time of their convenience without any judgment or consequences. In the first instance, at the start of the study, they will be informed of their right to do so and this will be provided in the informed consent form. Participants will also have a choice to opt out of the study if that is what they want and they will also have the capacity to have their data expunged from the study.

6.5.4 Avoidance of Harm

It is noteworthy that all possible attempts will be made towards minimizing participant risk on the identified research design. This includes social loss such as loss of reputation if the case reveal the company's omissions or mistakes and other forms of psychological damage such as stress or discomfort when making comments in focus groups or making an interview as a respondent. To ensure that participants are comfortable to share their experiences the researcher will ensure that they adhere to necessary measures that will make participants feel safe and comfortable to talk about issues affecting them though the researcher will be sensitive to any sign of discomfort shown by the participants.

6.5.5 Ethical Approval

The study will be strictly confined to the ethical guidelines provided from the different professional and scholars' associations. Somewhat prior to data collection, the permission to conduct the research will be sought from the researcher's institution's ethical review committee, or the Institutional Review Board (IRB), as the case will be. This permission shall ensure that the rights of the participants and their welfare are protected as well as ensure that the research is conducted ethically.

7. RESULTS AND DISCUSSION

There must always be a section with the label "Results and Discussion" in any research report because the section offers the findings of the study and discusses their significance. Finally, this section discusses the findings' implications for educators, politicians, and other industry players and compare them with the existing literature. The implications and further analysis of the study as well as the possibilities of training students for employment in AI-centered economies are discussed in the following material.

7.1 Presentation of Research Findings

Self-generated questionnaires, interviews, and case studies formed the basis of this study and therefore informed the conclusions. These are arranged in a number of relevant domains, including the students' familiarity with AI and what they consider AI's abilities and deficiencies when approaching markets, learning, and employment, barriers to AI education, as well as their potential recommendations toward AI education improvement.

7.1.2 AI-Related Skills and Knowledge Among Students

Self-generated questionnaires, interviews, and case studies formed the basis of this study and therefore informed the conclusions. These are arranged in a number of relevant domains, including the students' familiarity with AI and what they consider AI's abilities and deficiencies when approaching markets, learning, and employment, barriers to AI education, as well as their potential recommendations toward AI education improvement.

Additionally, analysis revealed that as compared with students from non technical field, the students of technical background, including computer science and engineering students, are more likely to perceive that they possess higher level of

AI competence and awareness. For instance, while only 15% of students from non-computing background said that they were proficient in programming languages such as Python and R, 75% of the respondents who were computer science students.

These findings of the study of enhanced and non-enhanced AI courses give more credence to the fact that there is a chief lacuna when it comes to equipping technical and non-technical students to the demands of learners across diverse fields for AI education. Also, it extends doubt over some areas in the existing curriculum that hampers the non-technical students from preparing for jobs in AI-driven industries.

7.1.3 Perceptions of AI-Driven Job Markets

Therefore, from the opinions given from the poll and face to face interviews, there is a controversy whether AI led job markets are good, bad or ugly depending on the sample of the respondents. But here was some confusion concerning the explicit know-how and skill sets required to perform on those markets while 70% of participants agreed the AI is getting more and more important across a wide range of businesses.

The survey also revealed that forty percent of the students were worried that AI would lead to emergence of robots in their respective fields of here. Concerns which were raised by students concerning the effects of AI on the availability of jobs were expressed. However, half of the students felt that AI will create new jobs such as data analyst, software developers and specialists in artificial intelligence.

Apart from narrowly technical skills related to AI, individuals connected to education and business emphasised such soft competencies as critical thinking, problem-solving, and flexibility. As these competencies would be required by students in the employment markets created by AI, where learning and technology literacy is of paramount importance, they underscored their importance.

7.1.4 Educational Practices and Curriculum Design

The findings show that schools are getting increasingly aware of the urgency of infusing information on AI in their settings. Yet these efforts were uneven across schools and the impact of the initiatives also differed across schools.

51% of educators said that they had seen AI related modules or courses in their schools especially in technical faculties. Normally, these courses covered issues or topics such as data science, Machine Learning and AI ethics. Nevertheless, only thirty percent of educators claimed that fields of business, humanities, and social sciences had included an AI-related course.

From interviews and case studies, some of the universities have adopted innovative approaches in training of AI, such as cross cutting streams that combines technical and non technical or collaboration with the industry partners. Overall, it was believed that the aforementioned methods would enable students to find jobs in AI-centered sectors, when the methods in questions enabled practical application of AI tools and technology.

But at the same time a large portion of educators spoke about problems they faced in implementing AI education – the problem of financing, preparation of teachers, and a weak institutional framework. These hardships are more evident in small or the poorly funded universities as the introduction of content linked to the application of artificial intelligence was often regarded as relatively insignificant.

7.1.5 Barriers to AI Education

Several challenges to quality AI education were identified which might hinder students' preparedness for the employment domains with often prevalent AI applications. Among these obstacles are:

Resource Constraints: Several instructors reported a scarcity of resources, financial, AI tools & technology, and institutional support system. Some of these challenges proved to be a challenge particularly to less endowed schools or schools which could not afford to invest in the basics of education let alone incorporate technology such as ai into their curriculum.

Instructor Training: The information showed a sizable void in the preparation of teachers for teaching AI. About half of educators—especially those from non-technical fields—said they felt unprepared to teach material connected to artificial intelligence. One of the main obstacles to the successful integration of AI into the curriculum was thought to be this lack of training.

Student Engagement: It revealed a rather significant gap in the preparation of teachers to teach AI in their classrooms. Educators who had their background in non-technical disciplines reported that half of them felt ready to teach something related to Artificial intelligence. This absence of training was believed to be one of the significant challenges towards the adoption of using the AI in the curriculum.

Curriculum Design: Some of the social issues that came up when students engage with artificial intelligence included inputs from educators and business people. Some of the students, particularly those who had poor backgrounds in computer programming and technology, did not have as much desire to learn AI as the did, while there were still others who had a lot of zeal in the field of artificial intelligence. This was often attributed to the students' beliefs over the complexity of the AI related subjects and their lack of knowledge of how they could be applied in fields outside of computing.

7.1.6 Recommendations for Improving AI Education

Curriculum Design: The findings the studies have suggested that there is still a shortfall as far as educational curriculum is concerned when it comes to fulfilling the requirements of the current labor markets defined by the capabilities of AI. More courses with technical and non technical components are required as it; Increased emphasis on soft skills such as critical thinking and problem solving capacity is also required.

Interdisciplinary Courses: The results led to the identification of a number of recommendations for enhancing AI education and better prepare students for employment markets powered by AI:The results led to the identification of a number of recommendations for enhancing AI education and better prepare students for employment markets powered by AI:

Hands-On Experience: The possibilities for the practical use of AI tools and technology in the learning process of the students should be higher. This could be implementing business projects in collaboration with business partners, internships or incorporating AI tools and solutions in learning.

Instructor Training: In order to ensure that teachers are prepared for teaching content related to artificial intelligence particularly those who have teaching background in other fields institutions should provide funding for training. This could involve going out for more information from professionals and practitioners in the field, carrying out workshops or even enrolling for online courses.

Student Engagement: More efforts should be made to attract more of the students in non-CS disciplines to get interested in AI-related content. This may involve making people understand the importance of artificial intelligence (AI) in their preferred fields and possibly providing them with everything they require to overcome any barrier that they may come across while studying the technology.

Curriculum Alignment: Designing curriculum should incorporate what is required in job markets by artificial intelligence stressing less on technical skills and more on flexible skills such as adaptability, problem-solving, and critical reasoning. This means that, in addition to providing to updating and relevant AI education programs, the academic institutions should also maintain close industry relationships.

7.2 Analysis and Interpretation of Results

The findings of the study offers insights about what kind of state education in Artificial intelligence is at present and how students can be prepared to get a job in industries where AI is dominant. The findings show that while the importance of AI education is slowly gaining more acceptance the there are still many challenges gaps that need to be addressed.

7.2.1 Disparities in AI-Related Skills and Knowledge

The variation of knowledge and skills in AI between students from technical and non-technical backgrounds is among the study findings. This divergence poses a worry given the fact that a significant number of students would be graduating to an environment that they can hardly succeed in any field related to artificial intelligence.

This is a finding that is consistent with the previous studies, which stress the need to improve the AI education that should encompass the needs of learners with diverse learning abilities (West, 2018).

Some of the studies have pointed the fact that this divergence may be due to the segregation of technical and non-technical subjects in the higher education system that could hinder cross-disciplinary integration and synergy (Li et al., 2020).

This means that more Md courses should be developed, which offers both technical and non-technical content; more effort should be made to introduce information about AI in fields that are not closely related to computing. This could well assist ensure that all students of a specific academic background are set adequately for AI driven employment markets that are likely to emerge in future.

7.2.2 Uncertainty About AI-Driven Job Markets

Surprisingly the survey also showed that there is a significant level of misperception among educators, experts, and students about what knowledge and skills help one be ready for the AI-driven labor markets. It is quite clear that AI will remain a valued aspect; however, it is still uncertain which skills will be most valuable in the future job market.

This result synchronizes with the past research where similar fluctuation is observed in the situations where the technology is developed rapidly like artificial intelligence.

Possible causes stated in the literature include the fast pace of AI technologies' advancement which often makes it hard to predict needs and demands in the labor market in the future (Bessen, 2019).

According to the findings of the research, increased education Sector collaboration with industry players is suggested so that the institutions can help in reducing uncertainty in the job markets that will result from artificial intelligence). This may include coming up with course content which will reflect what market demands, and sessions to inform the learners of the benefits and detriments of artificial intelligence.

7.2.3 Importance of Soft Skills

The conclusions drawn in the study also highlight the necessity of soft skills in with traditional AI-related technical skills such as critical thinking, problem-solving and flexibility. In line with literature, soft skills are seen as important in AI based employment markets characterized by rapid changes with periodic shifts in demand for different skills.

The literature study shows that while IT skills are fundamental, they are inadequate to ensure success in artificial intelligence-driven industries. Instead, individuals are boom waking up to the fact that soft skills are most going to be crucial in assisting individuals manage the problems ensuing from the use of technologies in the future such as artificial intelligence.

This paper suggests that in their AI education programmes, academic institutions should pay more attention to the enhancement of soft skills. This may refer to implementing and urging students to consider extra courses involving AI through cross-disciplinary paradigms to comprehend its consequences, besides including critical thinking and problem-solving exercises in classes regarding to AI.

7.2.4 Barriers to AI Education

It was also observed that a number of barriers to effective delivery of AI to students include shortage of equipment, poorly prepared teachers, low student interest, and unstructured curriculum. These challenges relate with other findings done in other studies that have also shown similar challenges in technology enhanced learning .

The literature suggests that some of these challenges might be as a result of the fast pace at which technology is growing making it difficult for educational institutions to keep abreast with modern developments in areas such as artificial intelligence among others.

In addition, there are many insufficiencies in institutions which do not have proper tools and resources to support AI education which can result in critical issues for both instructors and learners.

Based on the results of this study, it is evident that there is a need for enhancement of funding for AI education mainly in the areas of curriculum development, professional development of instructors, and assets. This could help in negations of the impediments this study established and ensure every learner gets an opportunity to attain the necessary skills and knowledge necessary for success in AI employment domains.

7.3 Implications for Educators, Policymakers, and Industry Stakeholders

As a result, the findings of this study have implications to educators, legislators and business stakeholders who have roles to play in preparing pupils for employment markets defined by AI.

8. CONCLUSION

The study investigated a multi-faceted issue of preparing the students for the employment markets that are driven by artificial intelligence, and it thus requires a comprehensive approach that involves intellectual, interpersonal, and technical perspectives. The following is the conclusion of the observations made in the study. Profound differences in the knowledge and skills that are related to artificial intelligence were evident in the students from different backgrounds. More specifically, Group 2 comprising of students from non-information technology disciplines showed less confidence and experience in the AI instruments and ideas and significantly lower knowledge in likened tools and ideas than Group 1 students, who were from computer science and engineering disciplines. This raises the question of a more comprehensive approach to the inclusion of AI within the curriculum, as well as providing for education which will support learners from a wide range of background. From the survey, cross-sections of educators, professionals, and students show low appreciation of the specific competency requirements when entering job markets associated with AI. That artificial intelligence will be paramount cannot be in doubt, as to which sub-set of AI-related skills will be most sought after in the workforce of the future, remains a mystery at this point. This uncertainty needs to be addressed to provide students with more accurate career guidance since today's paradigms require rethinking of educational models to target the requirements set by the modern labor market. The study brought out the importance of soft skills in relation to AI such as critical thinking skill, problem solving and change management skills in addition to technical skills in relation to AI. These skills are important when it comes to the extent and management of AI and other innovative technologies' relevance, thus, the awareness of such skills is growing. It has been observed that several challenges hamper the quality of AI education which include poor fund, poor trainings for the faculty, poor student interest and misalignment of the program. These difficulties are seen most acutely in smaller or poorly-resourced institutions where sheer practical limitations might preclude the development of AI-related content. The findings suggest that awareness funding be provided to AI education to fund curriculum development and instructors as well as their resources. It therefore has implications for academics, legislators and business professionals among other people. Therefore, it is suggested that educators should design a number of cross-discipline courses combined with technical and art classes; students should be provided with hands-on training in utilizing AI technologies in their projects; and soft skills should be the main focus of educators' attention. States' representatives are invited to support AI educational initiatives, including through funding.

REFERENCES

Aleandri, G. (2021). lifelong, lifewide y lifedeeP learning. análisis y PersPectivas Pedagógicas. EXPERIENCIAS Y APRENDIzAJES A LO LARGO DE LA VIDA, 19.

Bailey, T. R., Hughes, K. L., & Moore, D. T. (2003). *Working knowledge: Work-based learning and education reform*. Routledge. DOI: 10.4324/9780203463956

Barron, B., & Darling-Hammond, L. (2008). *Teaching for Meaningful Learning: A Review of Research on Inquiry-Based and Cooperative Learning*. Book Excerpt. George Lucas Educational Foundation.

Bawden, D. (2008). Origins and Concepts of Digital Literacy. In Lankshear, C., & Knobel, M. (Eds.), *Digital Literacies: Concepts*. Policies, and Practices.

Bloom, B. S. (1956). *Taxonomy of educational objectives: the classification of educational goals*. Susan Fauer Company.

Brynjolfsson, E. (2014). The second machine age: Work, progress, and prosperity in a time of brilliant technologies.

Chadwick, A., & Howard, P. N. (Eds.). (2009). *Routledge handbook of Internet politics*. Routledge.

Chamorro-Premuzic, T., Akhtar, R., Winsborough, D., & Sherman, R. A. (2017). The datafication of talent: How technology is advancing the science of human potential at work. *Current Opinion in Behavioral Sciences*, 18, 13–16. DOI: 10.1016/j.cobeha.2017.04.007

Davies, R. S., Dean, D. L., & Ball, N. (2013). Flipping the classroom and instructional technology integration in a college-level information systems spreadsheet course. *Educational Technology Research and Development*, 61(4), 563–580. DOI: 10.1007/s11423-013-9305-6

Dillenbourg, P. (1999). What do you mean by collaborative learning?. Collaborative-learning: Cognitive and computational approaches., 1-19.

Ennis, R. H. (2011). The nature of critical thinking: An outline of critical thinking dispositions and abilities. *University of Illinois*, 2(4), 1–8.

Facione, P. A. (2011). Critical thinking: What it is and why it counts. Insight assessment, 1(1), 1-23.

Floridi, L., Cowls, J., Beltrametti, M., Chatila, R., Chazerand, P., Dignum, V., Luetge, C., Madelin, R., Pagallo, U., Rossi, F., Schafer, B., Valcke, P., & Vayena, E. (2018). AI4People—an ethical framework for a good AI society: Opportunities, risks, principles, and recommendations. *Minds and Machines*, 28(4), 689–707. DOI: 10.1007/s11023-018-9482-5 PMID: 30930541

Gačić, M. (2009). Recommendation of the European Parliament and of the Council of 18 December 2006 on key competences for lifelong learning.

Gee, J. P. (2003). What video games have to teach us about learning and literacy. Computers in entertainment (CIE), 1(1), 20-20.

Hobbs, R. (2010). Digital and Media Literacy: A Plan of Action. A White Paper on the Digital and Media Literacy Recommendations of the Knight Commission on the Information Needs of Communities in a Democracy. Aspen Institute. 1 Dupont Circle NW Suite 700, Washington, DC 20036.

Holmes, W., Bialik, M., & Fadel, C. (2019). *Artificial intelligence in education promises and implications for teaching and learning*. Center for Curriculum Redesign.

Illanes, P., Lund, S., Mourshed, M., Rutherford, S., & Tyreman, M. (2018). Retraining and reskilling workers in the age of automation. *McKinsey Global Institute*, 8(1), 1–8.

Jonassen, D. H. (2010). *Learning to solve problems: A handbook for designing problem-solving learning environments*. Routledge. DOI: 10.4324/9780203847527

Kizilcec, R. F., Piech, C., & Schneider, E. (2013, April). Deconstructing disengagement: analyzing learner subpopulations in massive open online courses. In *Proceedings of the third international conference on learning analytics and knowledge* (pp. 170-179). DOI: 10.1145/2460296.2460330

Kolb, D. A. (2014). Experiential learning: Experience as the source of learning and development. FT press.

Meyer, A., Rose, D. H., & Gordon, D. (2014). *Universal design for learning: Theory and practice*. No Title.

Nisha, N. B., & Varghese, R. R. (2021). Literature on information literacy: A review. *DESIDOC Journal of Library and Information Technology*, 41(4).

Noble, S. U. (2018). Algorithms of oppression: How search engines reinforce racism. In *Algorithms of oppression*. New York university press.

O'Lawrence, H. (2017). The workforce for the 21st century. *International Journal of Vocational Education & Training*, 24(1).

Piaget, J. (1970). *Piaget's theory* (Vol. 1). Wiley.

Ribble, M. (2015). *Digital citizenship in schools: Nine elements all students should know*. International Society for Technology in Education.

Roberts, T. S. (2008). Student plagiarism in an online world: An introduction. In *Student plagiarism in an online world: Problems and solutions* (pp. 1–9). IGI Global. DOI: 10.4018/978-1-59904-801-7.ch001

Settles, B., & Meeder, B. (2016, August). A trainable spaced repetition model for language learning. In *Proceedings of the 54th annual meeting of the association for computational linguistics* (volume 1: long papers) (pp. 1848-1858). DOI: 10.18653/v1/P16-1174

Shute, V., & Wang, L. (2016). Assessing and supporting hard-to-measure constructs in video games. The Wiley Handbook of Cognition and Assessment: Frameworks, Methodologies, and Applications, 535-562. DOI: 10.1002/9781118956588.ch22

Vygotsky, L. S. (1978). *Mind in society: The development of higher psychological processes* (Vol. 86). Harvard university press.

Woolf, B. P. (2010). *Building intelligent interactive tutors: Student-centered strategies for revolutionizing e-learning*. Morgan Kaufmann.

Chapter 3
AI Integration in Education 5.0:
Design, Challenges, and Future Prospects

Snehasis Dey

https://orcid.org/0000-0002-0490-8628

College of Engineering Bhubaneswar, BPUT University, India

Barsha Baishali Sahoo

College of Engineering Bhubaneswar, BPUT University, India

ABSTRACT

Education 5.0 is still in its infancy. After covid-19, the education sector has propelled a milestone by integrating virtual means of education. Though it was not completely successful in the covid era but impact of virtual education has opened a new dimension to the reality of integrating the most successful technology into its field.AI is the new research topic in every field. AI integration to the education sector will enhance the productivity and effectiveness amongst learner and educator. Different AI enabled services may be integrated in the education so that the challenges in providing a sustainable environment towards education will definitely be achieved. As education is diversified to learner and educator or student and teacher so the technological implementations may be done from grass roots level. This chapter dives into the education 5.0 basics and the means of AI integration to Education 5.0. It also provides a design structure of AI integrated education, it's possible challenges and research scope for future ahead.

DOI: 10.4018/979-8-3693-8191-5.ch003

INTRODUCTION

Education 5.0 is the fifth industrial revolution in the field of education by leveraging digital and smart technologies. Different barriers in learning can be eradicated by the implementations of current technologies like artificial intelligence and machine learning in education. The new paradigm of education has created a revolution in teaching and learning methodologies by inculcating the AI technology with education. The concept of education has been redefined after covid-19 because of the rise of internet of things (IoT) and information communication technology (ICT). The amalgamation of sensor technologies and the frequent analysis of data through smart technology like artificial intelligence (AI) and machine learning has facilitated the emergence of state-of-the-art educational systems. The domain of education is intrinsically connected to the industrial revolutions, with the fourth industrial revolution showcasing significant advancements towards the implementation of Education 4.0, aimed at enriching the educational experience through the integration of Information and Communication Technology (ICT) and Internet of Things (IoT) innovations. Nevertheless, in spite of its numerous enhancements relative to traditional educational paradigms, the escalating necessity for customized tutoring and educational frameworks, as well as game-based learning, has heralded the inception of a fifth revolution in the field of education.

Education 5.0 has prioritized the different learning schemes to become the most perfect education system. This includes the frequent using of ICT tools, data analytics procedures and different IoT tools. Education system has travelled a long distance from education 1.0 to education 5.0. Education 1.0 generally based on class room teaching and root learning whereas education 5.0 is totally focused on adaptive learning, focused learning, technology-based learning and AI integrated learning.

Figure 1. Evolution of education industry

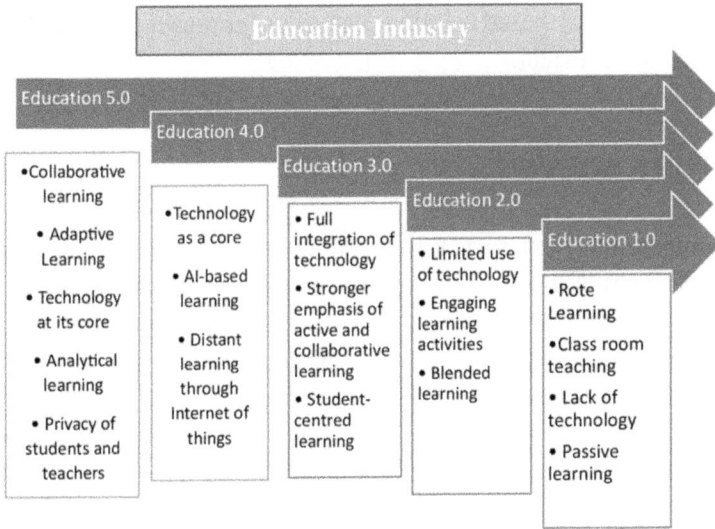

With the advent of Education 5.0, the educational paradigm is articulated through the convergence of innovative technologies like artificial intelligence (AI), the Internet of Things (IoT), advanced data analytics, and cloud computing. AI, in particular, serves as a pivotal force for educational reform, presenting the opportunity to tailor learning experiences in accordance with the distinct needs and preferences of individual learners. The incorporation of AI not only promotes personalized learning trajectories but also facilitates adaptive systems that responsively adjust to the learner's developmental progress, thereby enhancing the overall efficiency and effectiveness of the educational process. The evolution from education 4.0 to the nascent education 5.0 reflects an intensified dedication to personalized learning experiences. Education 5.0 anticipates a future wherein the synergistic interplay between human cognition and AI optimally enhances the augmentation of learners' intellectual capacities. Recent scholarly investigations and technological advancements have facilitated the incorporation of artificial intelligence (AI) and machine learning (ML) within the educational sphere. AI and ML possess the capacity to customize the educational experience through the examination of student data, thereby modifying the instructional content and tempo to align with the unique requirements and competencies of each learner.

Figure 1 describes the evolution of education sphere from education 1.0 to education 5.0. The conventional classroom teaching has been evolved to personal learning and technology-based learning. The AI integration has assured the learning modalities to a great extent.

LITERATURE SURVEY

The complete literature survey shows how the education system transformed from various stages of the critical learning and education industry revolution.

Raj and Renumol (2022) reviewed and suggested a systematic analysis on learning content recommenders in adaptive and personalized learning environments. It mentioned different attributes of learning environments and recommended a few techniques like cognitive metrics, evaluation metrics and diverse techniques etc.

Major et al. (2021) presented the innovative digital technology through which accessing the personalized education learning. This can be very crucial for low- and middle-income country where quality education and personalized education is far from reality. The meta-analysis examined the use of technology and its ground reality.

Lampropoulos et al. (2022) highlighted the use of augmented reality and gamification in the educational process. It personified the concept of more engagement and satisfied learning environment instead of conventional learning after covid-19.

Zhang and Aslan (2021) in his article described AI integration in modern education system through the AIEd technologies. It specified some innovation AI tools that can manifest the education environment into a great extent through technological advancement. AIEd technology or artificial intelligence integrated education technologies are proven to be game changer for current personalized learning schemes and these includes machine learning, chatbots, and intelligent tutors.

Li and Heng (2021) used different personalized learning scenarios to draw the conclusion of blended learning environment which would be making the educational advancement in a systematic way. In his study he concluded that mobile learning can also be treated as personal learning.

Green et al. (2020) studied different digital technology for education and its future advancement. This perhaps provided the adequate platform to accommodate future generation education and growth simultaneously.

Mageira et al. (2022) proposed educational chatbots for content and language integrated learning. Using advanced artificial intelligence this paper described the user cases of educational chatbots for integrated learning for high school students and different scale of language learning's.

The above studies have unique ways of describing AI integrated education that is education 5.0 but there is a huge scope in the studies that will definitely can add to the above field. These are listed as follows:

- Identification of AI technologies for education 5.0.
- Leveraging the AI tools for education 5.0.
- Creating a specific expert system for teaching and learning program.
- Uses of machine learning for computation of large-scale student data base.
- Proper implementations of e-learning environment.
- Creating proper visualization and virtual learning environment in education 5.0.
- Promoting the customized services like materials and guidance through intelligent agents.
- Factors that influence the adoption of Industry 5.0 technologies in education.

The above-mentioned scope will engage huge research opportunities in the field of AI integrated education 5.0 field that will revolutionize the upcoming education system in society.

State of Art Requirements in Education 5.0

Education 5.0 definitely integrates the advantages of AI and the computational skills of machine learning for huge student data base. For the same purpose there is huge demand of some specific sectors which are basic requirements in education 5.0. These are shown in figure below.

1.Personalized Learning

Education 5.0 emphasizes the provision of customized educational experiences that are responsive to the distinct needs and capabilities of each student. This objective can be realized through the implementation of artificial intelligence and machine learning technologies to formulate individualized learning plans and to modify instructional methodologies in real-time, contingent on the progression of the student. Personalized Learning is a crucial component of Education 5.0, designed to customize the learning experience to meet the unique needs and abilities of each student. The success of personalized learning can be evaluated by criteria such as student engagement, motivation, academic achievement, and the educator's capacity to adjust to the individual requirements and skills of each learner.

Figure 2. State of art requirements of Education 5.0(Ed 5.0)

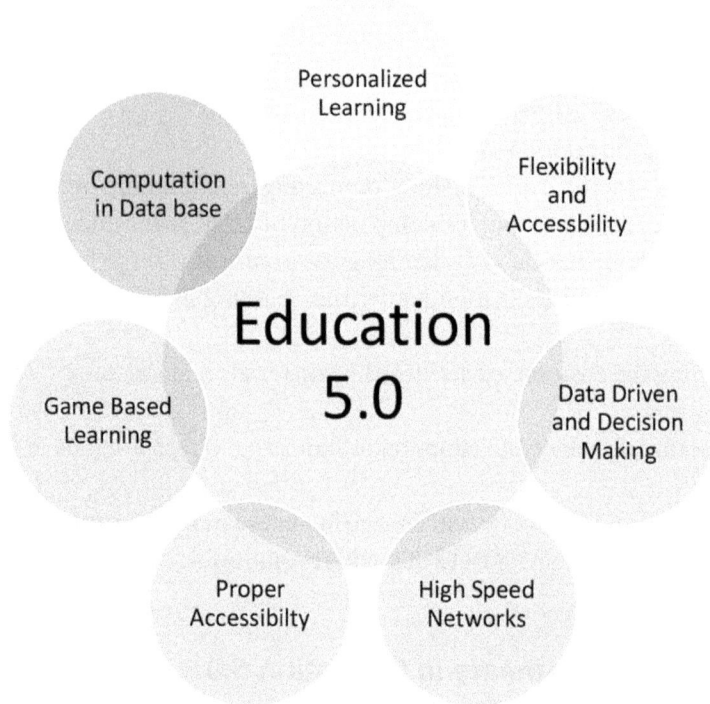

2. Flexibility and Accessibility

Education 5.0 endeavors to enhance the flexibility and accessibility of educational opportunities by eliminating obstacles to education, including geographical and financial limitations. This goal can be realized through the deployment of technological progressions such as cloud computing, which allows students to access digital resources and materials from virtually any location and at any time. The characteristics of flexibility and accessibility are pivotal within Education 5.0, which pertains to the incorporation of technology in educational settings to improve the overall learning experience. Flexibility in educational contexts signifies the capacity to accommodate diverse learning styles and individual needs. A widely utilized metric to evaluate the adaptability of an educational program is the Learner Satisfaction Index (LSI), which measures students' contentment with the program's flexibility. The LSI may be assessed through surveys or interviews conducted with students, thereby serving as a tool for identifying potential areas for enhancement within the program. The concept of educational accessibility involves making learning opportunities available to every learner, irrespective of their physical, cognitive, or financial limitations. A frequently employed metric for evaluating the accessibility of an educational program is the Universal Design for Learning (UDL) framework.

3. Data-Driven Decision Making

Education 5. 0 relies on data-based decision making. Evaluating the success of data-driven decision making (DDDM) in Education 5. 0 involves using a variety of metrics to evaluate student outcomes, learning analytics, technology adoption, user satisfaction and refunds.

4.High Speed Networks

The role of high-speed networks is pivotal in Education 5.0, as they support the immediate distribution of digital resources and educational content to students and teachers alike. The incorporation of high-speed networks within the educational framework facilitates uninterrupted communication and collaborative efforts among students, educators, and academic institutions. Furthermore, high-speed networks guarantee that students have the capability to access educational resources remotely. To assess the efficacy of high-speed networks in the educational sector, various metrics may be employed, including network reliability (NR), network capacity (NC), and network latency (NL).

5.Proper Accessibility

Education 5.0 seeks to eliminate obstacles to education and to enhance the accessibility of educational opportunities for all individuals across all the possible way. Achieving this objective necessitates the implementation of advanced technologies, including 5G networks and cloud computing, which can accommodate the substantial bandwidth demands of numerous contemporary educational technologies, thereby rendering education more adaptable and reachable. The assessment of the accessibility of Education 5.0 is paramount in determining its efficacy. Accessibility is defined as the extent to which educational resources and opportunities are accessible to individuals, irrespective of their geographical location or socio-economic standing and along the line of digital divide. To effectively appraise the accessibility of initiatives associated with Education 5.0, it is imperative to take into account various evaluative metrics. One such metric worthy of consideration is the availability of educational resources, encompassing online courses, textbooks, and instructional materials.

6.Game Based Learning

Game-based learning is an important requirement for Education 5.0 because it can engage students in ways that traditional classroom instruction cannot. Game-based learning can increase motivation, engagement and learning outcomes. Evaluating the effectiveness of gamification in education is important to determine its impact on student learning outcomes. Several criteria can be used to evaluate the effectiveness of game-based learning. One of the important criteria is student participation, which refers to students' motivation, interest and participation in learning activities.

7.Computation in Database

Computation in database is a measure of the computation done in student huge databases like student information, category, standard and types. These databases can be managed and computed by the implementation of proper machine learning tools like different learning algorithms may be supervised, unsupervised or reinforced type depending upon user requirements. It deals with metrics like student volume and size.

Depending upon the state of art requirements and evaluation metrices the below table can be formed by considering the below relation.

If requirements are a basic need for the construction of Education 5.0 scenario, then the evaluation metrics holds the key of evaluating it by proposing a full score of "1 else it is 0". So, we can write here,

Requirements = R and Evaluation metrics = E

Such that R E then the condition is true and holds 1.

Else the condition is false and it is 0

Here R1, R2, R3, R4, R5, R6, R7 are respective state of art requirements and E1, E2, E3, E4, E5 are evaluation metrices.

Figure 3. Requirements and evaluation metrics mapping

R ────▶ E		E1	E2	E3	E4	E5
R1	Personalized learning. (Student Engagement/Motivation)	1	0	0	0	0
R2	Flexibility & Accessibility/Learner Satisfaction Index (LSI)	0	1	0	0	0
R3	DDDM/Student outcomes, Learning analytics, Technology adoption	0	0	1	0	0
R4	High speed n/w/NR, NC, NL	0	0	0	1	0
R5	Proper Accessibility/Educational resources	0	0	0	0	1
R6	Game based learning/Student Participation	1	0	0	0	0
R7	Computation in database/Student volume and size.	1	0	0	0	0

The above figure describes the state of art requirements and evaluation metrics mapping where the first five requirements R1, R2, R3, R4, R5 and evaluation E1, E2, E3, E4, E5 mapping gives a diagonal matrix where the last two R6 and R7 mapping with E1 provides a fruitful setting. This provides the strongest evaluation and requirement performance sheet for constructing the Education 5.0 building blocks. Here each evaluation is based on the relation of R and E such that there will be a "1" value for a successful mapping between R and E and a "0" value for unsuccessful mapping. For example, E1 and R1 mapping case we got "1" and E2 with R1 case it is "0".

Algorithm:

{

Step1: Start

Step 2:   Take the value of requirements = R.
Step 3:   Take the value of evaluation = E.
Step 4:   Define each requirement and evaluation mapping.
Step 5:   Design the mapping set of (E, R)
Step 6:   Build the matrix by assigning 1 and 0 value.

Step 7:   (E, R) gives value of 1 for each successful mapping.

and 0 for unsuccessful mapping.

Step 8: The matrix can be designed such that there will be

at least a successful mapping.

Step 9: Terminate the steps when condition satisfied.
Step 10:   Stop

}

Identification of AI Tools and Leveraging Them into Education 5.0

Different technological enhancement and their successful inclusion with education system will create a holistic environment for learning. Technologies like artificial intelligence (AI), machine learning (ML), internet of things (IoT), big data analytics, block chain, VR and AR will boost up the education system efficiently. Artificial Intelligence-driven instruments possess the capacity to tailor educational experiences, furnish instantaneous feedback, and support educators in evaluating students' advancement; Virtual Reality and Augmented Reality have the potential to deliver deeply immersive and interactive pedagogical experiences, thereby enabling learners to investigate novel environments and disciplines in a more captivating manner.

The Internet of Things (IoT) connects various devices and sensors to the internet, which in turn supports the instant observation and assessment of student engagement and academic performance; alternatively, cloud computing grants the ability to obtain digital resources and educational content from virtually any location at any time, enriching the adaptability and accessibility of learning. Moreover, the utilization of big data and analytics facilitates the monitoring and assessment of student development, identifies educational shortcomings, and caters instructional methods to meet distinct learning requirements, while blockchain technology can be utilized to provide safe storing of student data. Ultimately, 5G networks possess the capacity to accommodate the high bandwidth demands of numerous contemporary educational technologies, including virtual reality, and contribute to the provision of a seamless educational experience. Thus, identifying these AI tools and technological tools are very crucial in education 5.0. The use of IoT devices in education can facilitate the implementation of personalized and collaborative learning, resulting in a more effective and efficient learning experience for students. Frequent use of technologies like AR, VR and XR can revolutionize the way student interact and learn in education 5.0 by providing it more interactive and engaging for students.

- Artificial Intelligence for Decision making in education 5.0.
- Machine learning for computation of student database.
- Gamification for healthy collaborations.
- Big data analytics for data modification and correct decision making in education 5.0.
- Block chain technology for security and privacy of data in education 5.0.
- IoT for flexibility and accessibility.
- VR and AR for personalized learning.

Figure 4. Different technological requirements of Education 5.0.

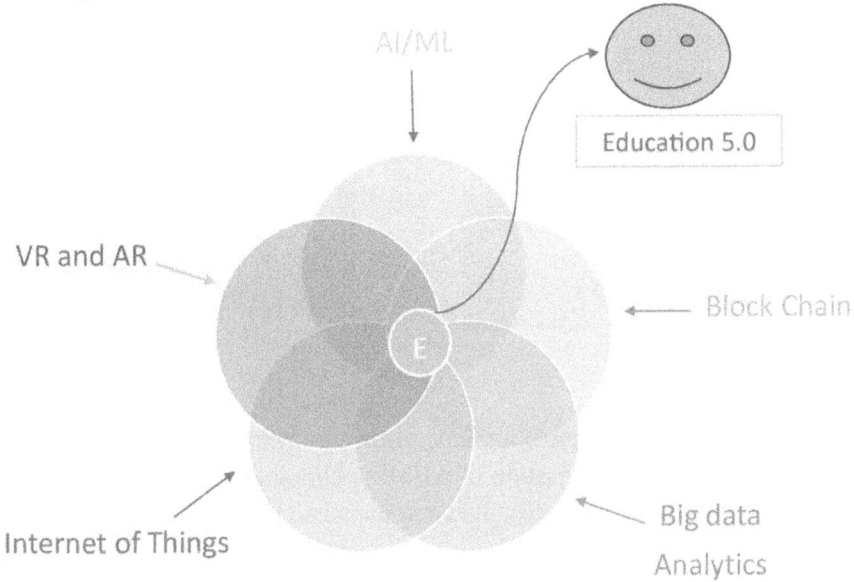

As figure 4 shown above, different enabling technologies have made education 5.0 very realistic and effective one. Big data analysis refers to the use of advanced data processing and analysis techniques to extract important insights from large and complex datasets. Data analysis for academic performance and decision-making processes in areas such as academic success, teacher effectiveness, organizational development and technology are being revolutionized by big data. Block chain technology helps in managing and controlling safe data base for the education 5.0 system. AI integrated education system will definitely foster the data mining and data analytics capability of this technology to enhance its effectiveness and robustness. To strengthen administrative processes and safeguard those, big data analytics will streamline administrative processes, such as student enrollment, scheduling, and data management etc. Gamification will cater to the entertainment part of learning like student engagement and interactive sessions through reward based or feedback based. For this utilization of algorithms like reinforced learning is quite effective one.

Figure 5. AI/ML integrated Education 5.0 for next generation

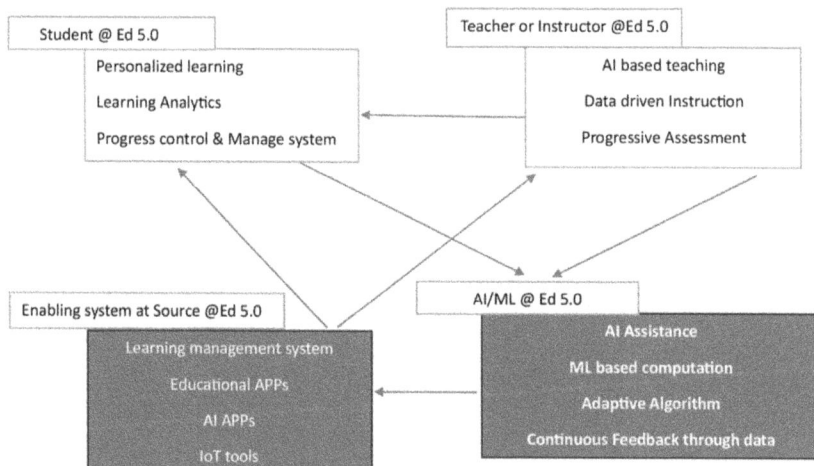

Figure 5 describes a typical architecture where next generation education system is designed by the integration of AI/ML technologies and algorithms. All the constituted stake holders are designed and managed through the AI technologies.

Typical AI role in Education 5.0

A brief summary has been provided here that describes the role of AI in education 5.0. These are the building blocks of the education 5.0.

- Personalized and adaptive learning
- Intelligent learning system
- Predictive Analysis
- Constant Assessment
- Gamification and simulated learning

- Ethical AI and integrated education
- Decision driven system
- Feedback and reward system
- Automated administrative work
- Virtual classes and monitoring

Future Prospect and Challenges in Education 5.0

- The advent of quantum computing possesses the potential to fundamentally transform the capabilities of artificial intelligence within the educational sector, addressing intricate challenges at unparalleled velocities, thereby facilitating customized learning experiences and sophisticated research endeavours.
- The amalgamation of Brain-Computer Interface technology with Artificial Intelligence within the educational sphere has the potential to facilitate unmediated communication between the human cerebral cortex and computational systems, thereby promoting more intuitive and immersive pedagogical experiences.
- The integration of Artificial Intelligence in Education 5.0 has the potential to enhance global collaboration by linking students and educators across the globe via virtual classrooms, thereby fostering a multifaceted and enriching educational atmosphere.
- Future iterations may concentrate on the integration of emotional intelligence algorithms within artificial intelligence frameworks in educational contexts, facilitating an understanding of and appropriate responses to students' emotional conditions, thereby augmenting overall well-being through tailored support mechanisms.
- The partnership among educators, technologists, policymakers, and industry stakeholders is crucial for the formulation and execution of effective AI-integrated educational frameworks. Collaborative interdisciplinary efforts can facilitate the development of pioneering methodologies and instruments for utilizing AI to enhance pedagogical and learning results while simultaneously addressing ethical, social, and cultural implications.
- The biggest challenge is to bring all these stake holders into one platform for efficient education system.

CONCLUSION

The integration of Artificial Intelligence (AI) into the field of education signifies a profound transition from traditional pedagogical methods to the realms of Education 5.0.AI integration will foster the progressive learning in education system by integrating the AI/ML technologies into the conventional methodologies of education system. This chapter caters to the diversity field of AI integrated education system and studies various designing algorithms involved in it. Some very interesting future research must be considered while integrating AI in education 5.0 like quantum computing in education, global collaboration through AI integration and brain computer interface etc. Future of education 5.0 holds the key in bringing faster technologies that are suitable for all stake holders of education systems.

REFERENCES

Al-Samarraie, H., Shamsuddin, A., & Alzahrani, A. I. (2020). A flipped classroom model in higher education: A review of the evidence across disciplines. *Educational Technology Research and Development*, 68(3), 1017–1051. DOI: 10.1007/s11423-019-09718-8

Anggriani, A., Sarwi, S., & Masturi, M. (2020). The effectiveness of guided discovery in distance learning to improve scientific literacy competencies of primary school students. *Journal of Primary Education*, 9(5), 454–462.

Blau, I., Shamir-Inbal, T., & Avdiel, O. (2020). How does the pedagogical design of a technology-enhanced collaborative academic course promote digital literacies, self-regulation, and perceived learning of students? *The Internet and Higher Education*, 45, 100722. DOI: 10.1016/j.iheduc.2019.100722

Chen, Z., & Demmans, C. (2020). *Csclrec: Personalized recommendation of forum posts to support socio-collaborative learning*. International Educational Data Mining Society.

Dey, S. (2022). Phenomenon of Excess of Artificial Intelligence: Quantifying the Native AI, Its Leverages in 5G/6G and beyond. In *Radar and RF Front End System Designs for Wireless Systems* (pp. 245–274). IGI Global.

Dimitriadou, E., & Lanitis, A. (2023). A critical evaluation, challenges, and future perspectives of using artificial intelligence and emerging technologies in smart classrooms. *Smart Learning Environments*, 10(1), 1–26. DOI: 10.1186/s40561-023-00231-3

Lampropoulos, G., Keramopoulos, E., Diamantaras, K., & Evangelidis, G. (2022). Augmented reality and gamification in education: A systematic literature review of research, applications, and empirical studies. *applied sciences, 12*(13), 6809.

Li, X., & Heng, Q. *"Design of mobile learning resources based on new blended learning: a case study of superstar learning app,"* in 2021 IEEE 3rd International Conference on Computer Science and Educational Informatization (CSEI). IEEE, 2021, pp. 333–338. DOI: 10.1109/CSEI51395.2021.9477709

Mageira, K., Pittou, D., Papasalouros, A., Kotis, K., Zangogianni, P., & Daradoumis, A. (2022). Educational AI chatbots for content and language integrated learning. *Applied Sciences (Basel, Switzerland)*, 12(7), 3239. DOI: 10.3390/app12073239

Major, L., Francis, G. A., & Tsapali, M. (2021). The effectiveness of technology-supported personalised learning in low-and middle-income countries: A meta-analysis. *British Journal of Educational Technology*, 52(5), 1935–1964. DOI: 10.1111/bjet.13116

Nguyen, A., Gardner, L., & Sheridan, D. (2020). Data analytics in higher education: An integrated view. *Journal of Information Systems Education*, 31(1), 61.

Ofosu-Ampong, K. (2020). The shift to gamification in education: A review on dominant issues. *Journal of Educational Technology Systems*, 49(1), 113–137. DOI: 10.1177/0047239520917629

Tapalova, O., & Zhiyenbayeva, N. (2022). Artificial intelligence in education: Aied for personalised learning pathways. *Electronic Journal of e-Learning*, 20(5), 639–653. DOI: 10.34190/ejel.20.5.2597

Van Leeuwen, A., & Janssen, J. (2019). A systematic review of teacher guidance during collaborative learning in primary and secondary education. *Educational Research Review*, 27, 71–89. DOI: 10.1016/j.edurev.2019.02.001

Xie, H., Chu, H.-C., Hwang, G.-J., & Wang, C.-C. (2019). *"Trends and development in technology-enhanced adaptive/personalized learning:"* A systematic review of journal publications from 2007 to 2017. *Computers & Education*, 140, 103599. DOI: 10.1016/j.compedu.2019.103599

Yurtseven Avci, Z., Ergulec, F., Misirli, O., & Sural, I. (2022). Flipped learning in information technology courses: Benefits and challenges. *Journal of Further and Higher Education*, 46(5), 636–650. DOI: 10.1080/0309877X.2021.1986623

Zhang, K., & Aslan, A. B. (2021). AI technologies for education: Recent research & future directions. *Computers and Education: Artificial Intelligence*, 2, 100025. DOI: 10.1016/j.caeai.2021.100025

Chapter 4
AI–Driven Classroom Management:
Balancing Efficiency, Engagement, and Ethics

Sucheta Yambal

Dr. Babasaheb Ambedkar Marathwada University, India

Yashwant Arjunrao Waykar
https://orcid.org/0000-0002-9693-9738

Dr. Babasaheb Ambedkar Marathwada University, India

ABSTRACT

AI is revolutionizing education, especially classroom management. AI-driven technologies boost productivity, student engagement, and personalized instruction. AI's role in classroom management is examined in this research. It analyzes how AI technologies like intelligent tutoring systems, behavior analysis tools, and adaptive learning platforms may reduce administrative tasks, enhance interactive learning environments, and provide quick student performance insights. The report also addresses ethical problems including data protection, algorithmic bias, and transparency, which are crucial to AI inclusion in education. This research explores the pros and cons of AI-driven classroom management to demonstrate how AI may be utilized ethically and effectively. This talk underlines the need of properly employing AI technology to balance operational efficiency with fair and transparent processes, making education more effective and engaging.

DOI: 10.4018/979-8-3693-8191-5.ch004

INTRODUCTION

As technology continues to evolve, its integration into educational settings has become increasingly sophisticated, transforming traditional teaching practices. Among the most notable advancements is the application of artificial intelligence (AI) in classroom management. AI-driven tools are poised to revolutionize how educators approach teaching by enhancing operational efficiency, boosting student engagement, and creating more personalized learning experiences. From automating administrative tasks to providing real-time feedback and insights, AI offers substantial benefits for managing classroom dynamics. However, the implementation of AI in education also raises critical ethical considerations, including concerns about data privacy, fairness, and transparency. Balancing these elements is essential for leveraging AI's potential while ensuring that its use aligns with educational values and practices. This overview explores the multifaceted impact of AI-driven classroom management, highlighting the opportunities and challenges associated with its integration into modern educational environments.

Attendance Tracking

Facial Recognition Systems: Automatically track student attendance using facial recognition technology. Facial recognition technology has evolved significantly over the past decade, making its way into various domains, including education. One of the most promising applications of this technology is in automating student attendance. Facial recognition systems offer a modern solution to traditional attendance tracking methods, addressing challenges such as accuracy, efficiency, and administrative burden. This write-up explores how facial recognition systems streamline the attendance process, reduce administrative tasks, and ensure accurate records.

UNDERSTANDING FACIAL RECOGNITION TECHNOLOGY

"Facial recognition systems streamline the attendance process, reducing administrative burdens on teachers and ensuring accurate records. These systems can identify students as they enter the classroom, allowing for real-time attendance updates." Facial recognition technology involves identifying and verifying individuals based on their facial features. The technology operates through several stages, including detection, alignment, feature extraction, and recognition. Initially, the system detects a face within an image or video stream. It then aligns the face to a standard pose, extracts unique facial features, and compares these features against a database to identify the individual.

Modern facial recognition systems leverage advanced algorithms and machine learning models to enhance accuracy and efficiency. Deep learning techniques, particularly convolutional neural networks (CNNs), have significantly improved the system's ability to recognize faces in various conditions, including different lighting, angles, and expressions.

Streamlining the Attendance Process

Traditionally, tracking student attendance has involved manual processes such as roll call, sign-in sheets, or biometric systems like fingerprint scanning. These methods can be time-consuming, prone to errors, and cumbersome for both teachers and students. Facial recognition technology offers a streamlined approach by automating the attendance process.

1. **Automatic Detection and Recording**: Facial recognition systems can automatically detect and record student attendance as they enter the classroom. Cameras positioned at entry points or within the classroom capture images of students' faces, which are then analyzed and matched against a pre-existing database of enrolled students. This automation eliminates the need for manual roll call and reduces the chances of errors associated with manual entry(Khong, Tan, & Ng, 2024).
2. **Real-Time Updates**: The integration of facial recognition technology allows for real-time updates on attendance records. As students' faces are recognized, their attendance status is immediately updated in the system. This provides teachers and administrative staff with up-to-date information on student attendance without delay.
3. **Reduced Administrative Burden**: By automating attendance tracking, facial recognition systems alleviate the administrative burden on teachers. Teachers no longer need to spend time managing attendance records manually or dealing with discrepancies. Instead, they can focus on teaching and engaging with students, enhancing the overall educational experience.

Figure 1. AI driven classroom management

Accuracy and Reliability

One of the key advantages of facial recognition systems is their accuracy. Traditional attendance methods can be prone to inaccuracies, such as students being marked absent when they are present or vice versa. Facial recognition technology reduces these errors by providing a reliable and consistent method for identifying students(Devender et al., 2023).

1. **Minimizing Errors**: Facial recognition systems use sophisticated algorithms to accurately match students' faces with their profiles. This reduces the likelihood of false positives (incorrectly identifying someone as a student) and false negatives (failing to recognize a student who is present). The technology's ability to handle variations in lighting, angles, and expressions further enhances its accuracy.
2. **Tamper-Proof System**: Unlike manual methods where students might falsely mark their attendance or use proxies, facial recognition systems are designed to be tamper-proof. The system's reliance on unique facial features makes it difficult for individuals to manipulate or bypass the attendance process.
3. **Consistency**: Facial recognition systems provide consistent and objective attendance records. This consistency helps in maintaining reliable attendance data, which is crucial for tracking academic progress, compliance with regulations, and addressing any discrepancies.

Enhancing Security and Privacy

While facial recognition technology offers numerous benefits, it also raises concerns regarding security and privacy. Addressing these concerns is essential to ensure the ethical use of facial recognition systems in educational settings.

1. **Data Security**: Educational institutions must implement robust security measures to protect facial recognition data. This includes encrypting data during transmission and storage, as well as implementing access controls to prevent unauthorized access. Regular security audits and updates are also necessary to safeguard against potential vulnerabilities.
2. **Privacy Considerations**: Privacy is a significant concern when using facial recognition technology. Institutions must ensure that students' facial data is collected, stored, and used in compliance with relevant privacy regulations. Clear consent procedures should be in place, and students and parents should be informed about how their data will be used and protected.
3. **Ethical Use**: The ethical use of facial recognition technology involves transparency and accountability. Institutions should establish guidelines for the use of facial recognition systems and ensure that they are used solely for the intended purpose of attendance tracking. Regular reviews and audits of the system's usage can help maintain ethical standards.

Future Directions

The use of facial recognition technology in education is likely to continue evolving, with potential advancements and innovations on the horizon. Future developments may include:

1. **Integration with Learning Management Systems (LMS)**: Facial recognition systems could be integrated with LMS platforms to provide a seamless experience for tracking attendance and accessing course materials. This integration could enhance the overall efficiency of administrative tasks and provide a more comprehensive view of student engagement.
2. **Enhanced Accuracy and Adaptability**: Ongoing advancements in artificial intelligence and machine learning may further improve the accuracy and adaptability of facial recognition systems. Enhanced algorithms could better handle challenging conditions, such as variations in student appearances or diverse classroom environments.

3. **Broader Applications**: Beyond attendance tracking, facial recognition technology may find applications in other areas of education, such as monitoring student behavior, ensuring secure access to facilities, and providing personalized learning experiences(Aneesh, 2023).

The crux says it all by mentioning that Facial recognition systems represent a significant advancement in the automation of student attendance tracking. By streamlining the attendance process, reducing administrative burdens, and ensuring accurate records, these systems offer numerous benefits for educational institutions(Wilmar & Norberto, 2024). However, it is essential to address security and privacy concerns to ensure the ethical and responsible use of this technology. As facial recognition technology continues to evolve, its potential applications in education will likely expand, further enhancing the efficiency and effectiveness of administrative tasks.

ENHANCING ENGAGEMENT THROUGH EMOTION DETECTION SOFTWARE

"Emotion detection software leverages computer vision and machine learning to interpret facial expressions, providing insights into student engagement levels. This allows teachers to adjust their methods and address any signs of distress or disengagement promptly." In the evolving landscape of education, the integration of advanced technologies into the classroom has opened new avenues for understanding and improving student engagement. Among these innovations, emotion detection software stands out as a powerful tool that leverages computer vision and machine learning to interpret facial expressions. This technology offers valuable insights into students' emotional states, enabling educators to tailor their instructional methods and address signs of distress or disengagement promptly. This essay explores the role of emotion detection software in behavioral analysis within educational settings, its benefits, challenges, and potential impact on teaching and learning.

The Fundamentals of Emotion Detection Software

Emotion detection software utilizes a combination of computer vision and machine learning techniques to analyze facial expressions and infer emotional states. At its core, the software relies on high-resolution cameras to capture images of students' faces. These images are then processed using algorithms that detect and interpret various facial features and expressions, such as smiles, frowns, and raised eyebrows (Pantic & Rothkrantz, 2003). Machine learning models are trained on large datasets to recognize and classify these expressions into distinct emotional categories, such as happiness, sadness, anger, or confusion (Mollahosseini et al., 2017).

The software typically involves several key steps:

1. **Image Acquisition**: Cameras positioned in the classroom capture real-time images or video streams of students' faces.
2. **Feature Extraction**: Algorithms analyze facial features such as the position and movement of facial muscles to identify specific expressions.
3. **Emotion Classification**: Machine learning models classify these expressions into emotional categories based on pre-trained data.
4. **Data Interpretation**: The software provides insights into students' emotional states, which can be used to gauge engagement and identify areas of concern.

Enhancing Engagement Through Real-Time Insights

One of the primary benefits of emotion detection software is its ability to provide real-time insights into student engagement levels. By continuously monitoring facial expressions, the software can detect changes in students' emotional states throughout a lesson. This capability allows teachers to assess engagement and understanding dynamically, rather than relying solely on traditional methods such as quizzes or feedback forms (D'Mello et al., 2011).

For instance, if the software detects signs of confusion or frustration in a student's expression, the teacher can intervene promptly to offer clarification or adjust the teaching approach. This immediate feedback loop helps ensure that students receive the support they need to stay engaged and succeed academically (Baker et al., 2010). Additionally, recognizing positive emotions such as interest or enthusiasm can help teachers identify and reinforce effective teaching strategies, further enhancing the learning experience.

Addressing Distress and Disengagement

Emotion detection software also plays a crucial role in identifying and addressing signs of distress or disengagement. Emotional states such as anxiety, boredom, or sadness can significantly impact a student's ability to learn and participate in class. Traditional methods of detecting these issues often rely on verbal communication or observable behavioral changes, which may not always be timely or accurate (Picard et al., 2001).

By leveraging emotion detection software, educators can gain a more nuanced understanding of students' emotional well-being. For example, if the software detects a pattern of negative emotions in a student over several sessions, it may indicate underlying issues that require attention, such as academic difficulties or personal challenges. Teachers can then take appropriate steps, such as offering additional support or referring the student to counseling services, to address these issues effectively (Mayer et al., 2008).

Benefits of Emotion Detection Software

1. **Personalized Learning**: Emotion detection software enables personalized learning experiences by providing insights into individual students' emotional states. Teachers can tailor their instructional methods to better meet the needs of each student, fostering a more inclusive and supportive learning environment (Liu et al., 2020).
2. **Enhanced Teacher-Student Interaction**: By understanding students' emotional responses, teachers can engage in more meaningful interactions with their students. This increased awareness can help build stronger teacher-student relationships and improve overall classroom dynamics (Baker et al., 2011).
3. **Early Detection of Issues**: The ability to detect signs of distress or disengagement early allows educators to intervene before problems escalate. This proactive approach can help prevent academic failure and promote student well-being (Koedinger et al., 2015).
4. **Data-Driven Insights**: Emotion detection software provides valuable data that can inform instructional decisions and educational research. Analyzing patterns in student emotions can help educators and researchers identify trends, evaluate the effectiveness of teaching strategies, and develop new approaches to enhance learning outcomes (Conati & Maclaren, 2009).

Challenges and Considerations

Despite its potential benefits, emotion detection software also faces several challenges and considerations:

1. **Privacy and Ethical Concerns**: The use of emotion detection software raises important privacy and ethical questions. The collection and analysis of students' facial expressions involve sensitive personal data, and institutions must ensure that they comply with privacy regulations and obtain informed consent (Harris & Rea, 2018).
2. **Accuracy and Reliability**: The accuracy of emotion detection software can be influenced by factors such as lighting conditions, camera quality, and individual differences in facial expressions. Ensuring the reliability of the software across

diverse settings and populations is essential for its effective implementation (Seneff & Wang, 2019).

3. **Cultural and Individual Differences**: Facial expressions of emotion can vary across different cultures and individuals, which may impact the software's ability to accurately interpret emotions (Ekman & Friesen, 1971). Adapting the software to account for these variations is crucial for its success in diverse educational environments.

4. **Potential for Misuse**: The use of emotion detection software must be carefully managed to prevent potential misuse. For example, there is a risk that the technology could be used to monitor or evaluate students in ways that may be perceived as intrusive or punitive (Hollis et al., 2020).

Emotion detection software represents a significant advancement in the field of behavioral analysis and has the potential to transform educational practices by providing deeper insights into student engagement and emotional well-being. By leveraging computer vision and machine learning, educators can gain real-time feedback on students' emotional states, allowing for more personalized and responsive teaching. However, the successful implementation of this technology requires careful consideration of privacy, accuracy, and ethical issues. As emotion detection software continues to evolve, its integration into educational settings offers the promise of a more empathetic and effective approach to teaching and learning.

CLASS PARTICIPATION: ENHANCING ENGAGEMENT THROUGH VOICE RECOGNITION AND ANALYSIS

Voice Recognition and Analysis: Monitor and analyze student participation through speech recognition. Class participation is a fundamental aspect of the learning process, fostering student engagement, critical thinking, and communication skills. Effective participation not only enriches the classroom experience but also provides educators with valuable insights into student understanding and involvement. In recent years, voice recognition technology has emerged as a powerful tool for monitoring and analyzing student participation in class discussions. By leveraging speech recognition capabilities, educators can track how often students contribute, ensure equitable participation, and identify those who may need additional encouragement to engage more actively(Mohammed et al., 2023).

Understanding Voice Recognition Technology

Voice recognition technology, also known as speech recognition, involves the conversion of spoken language into text by analyzing audio signals. This technology utilizes algorithms and machine learning models to process and interpret human speech(Krupa et al., 2024). In educational settings, voice recognition systems can capture and transcribe classroom discussions, enabling educators to monitor and analyze student participation in real-time.

The technology works through several key components:

1. **Audio Capture**: Microphones placed in the classroom capture audio from student interactions and discussions. These microphones can be part of a larger network of devices or integrated into individual student devices.
2. **Speech Processing**: The captured audio is processed by speech recognition algorithms that identify and transcribe spoken words. Advanced systems can distinguish between different speakers and understand various accents and speech patterns.
3. **Text Analysis**: The transcribed text is analyzed to determine participation metrics, such as the frequency and content of student contributions. Natural language processing (NLP) techniques can be used to assess the relevance and quality of the contributions.
4. **Data Integration**: The analyzed data is integrated into a system that provides educators with insights into student participation levels. This data can be visualized through dashboards or reports to facilitate decision-making and intervention.

Figure 2. Voice recognition technology

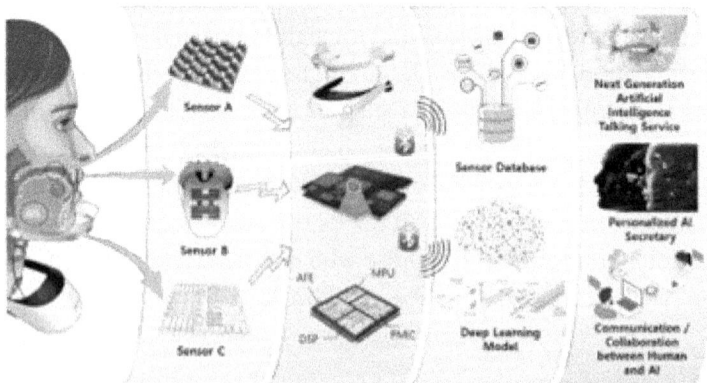

Benefits of Voice Recognition for Class Participation

1. **Tracking Participation Levels**: Voice recognition technology allows educators to track how often each student participates in class discussions. By analyzing the frequency of contributions, educators can ensure that all students have the opportunity to engage. This tracking helps identify students who may be less vocal and provides insights into overall class dynamics (Zhou et al., 2020).
2. **Ensuring Equitable Engagement**: One of the challenges in classroom discussions is ensuring that all students are equally engaged. Voice recognition technology can help identify patterns of participation, such as whether certain students dominate the discussion or if others are consistently quiet. This information enables educators to implement strategies to balance participation, such as calling on quieter students or facilitating group discussions to encourage more inclusive engagement (Zhou et al., 2021).
3. **Providing Targeted Feedback**: By analyzing the content of student contributions, voice recognition systems can provide valuable feedback on the quality of participation. Educators can assess whether students are making relevant points, asking insightful questions, or demonstrating understanding of the material. This feedback can guide students in improving their contributions and enhancing their overall participation skills (Choi et al., 2019).
4. **Identifying Students in Need of Support**: Voice recognition technology can help identify students who may need additional support or encouragement to participate more actively. For example, students who frequently speak hesitantly or contribute infrequently may benefit from targeted interventions, such as one-on-one support or confidence-building activities. Early identification of these needs allows educators to address potential barriers to participation (Smith et al., 2018).
5. **Enhancing Classroom Dynamics**: Real-time monitoring of student participation can contribute to a more dynamic and interactive classroom environment. By using voice recognition data to guide discussions and adjust teaching strategies, educators can create a more engaging and responsive learning experience. This approach helps maintain student interest and fosters a collaborative learning atmosphere (Miller et al., 2020).

Challenges and Considerations

1. **Privacy and Consent**: The use of voice recognition technology in the classroom raises important privacy and consent issues. Recording and analyzing students' speech requires careful consideration of privacy regulations and ethical guidelines. Educators must ensure that students and their families are informed about

the use of voice recognition technology and obtain appropriate consent (Liu et al., 2021).

2. **Accuracy and Limitations**: Voice recognition systems are not infallible and may face challenges related to accuracy and speech interpretation. Factors such as background noise, overlapping speech, and variations in accents can affect the system's performance. Educators must be aware of these limitations and complement voice recognition data with other forms of assessment and observation (Miller et al., 2020).

3. **Implementation Costs**: Implementing voice recognition technology involves costs related to hardware, software, and system integration. Educational institutions must consider these costs and plan accordingly to ensure that the benefits of the technology outweigh the expenses. Additionally, ongoing maintenance and updates may be required to keep the system functioning effectively (Smith et al., 2018).

4. **Potential Biases**: Voice recognition systems may exhibit biases related to gender, accent, or speech patterns. These biases can impact the accuracy of participation tracking and may lead to unequal treatment of students. Institutions must work to address these biases and ensure that the technology is used fairly and inclusively (Choi et al., 2019).

Voice recognition technology offers significant potential for enhancing classroom participation by providing real-time insights into student engagement. By tracking and analyzing speech, educators can ensure equitable participation, provide targeted feedback, and support students who may need additional encouragement. However, the successful implementation of voice recognition systems requires careful consideration of privacy, accuracy, costs, and potential biases. As technology continues to advance, integrating voice recognition into educational settings has the potential to transform classroom dynamics and improve the learning experience for all students.

CLASSROOM ENVIRONMENT MONITORING- ENHANCING LEARNING THROUGH IOT DEVICES AND SENSORS

IoT Devices and Sensors: Use sensors to monitor environmental factors such as noise levels, temperature, and air quality. IoT devices equipped with various sensors can help maintain an optimal learning environment by providing real-time data on factors like noise levels, temperature, and air quality. This information can help teachers create a more conducive learning atmosphere.

The classroom environment plays a crucial role in influencing student learning and overall well-being. Factors such as noise levels, temperature, and air quality can significantly impact student concentration, comfort, and academic performance. Recent advancements in technology, particularly in the realm of the Internet of Things (IoT), have introduced innovative solutions for monitoring and managing these environmental factors. IoT devices equipped with various sensors provide real-time data that can help create and maintain an optimal learning environment. This write-up explores how these technologies function and their benefits in enhancing the classroom atmosphere.

Figure 3. Classroom Environment Monitoring- IoT Devices and Sensors

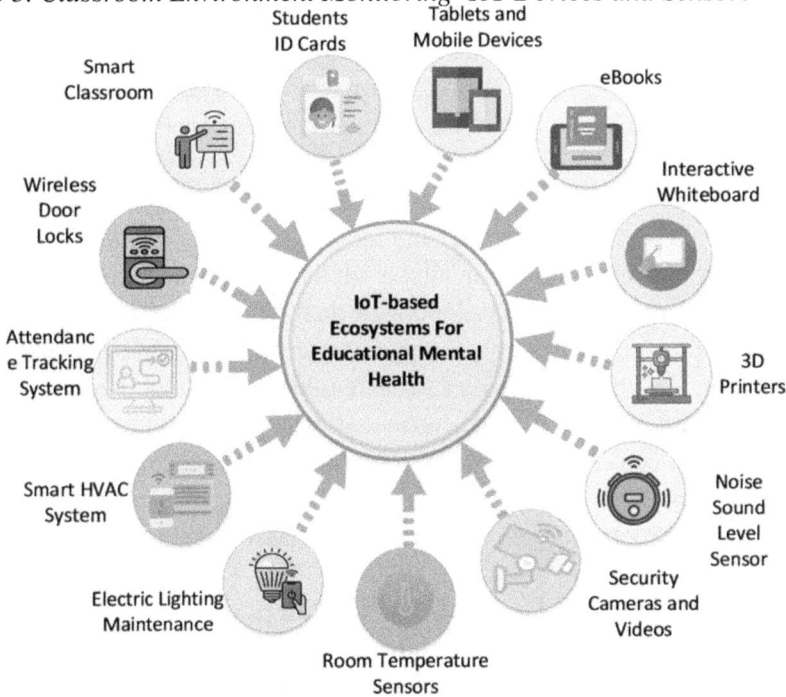

The Role of IoT Devices in Classroom Monitoring

IoT devices refer to interconnected sensors and smart devices that collect and exchange data through the internet. In the context of classroom environment monitoring, these devices are equipped with sensors that measure various environmental parameters. The data collected is transmitted to a central system, where it can be analyzed to assess and manage classroom conditions effectively(Saru, Maheshwari, & Sharma, 2024).

1. **Noise Level Monitoring**: Noise levels in the classroom can affect students' ability to concentrate and absorb information. Excessive noise can be distracting and may hinder effective learning. IoT devices equipped with sound level meters can continuously monitor ambient noise levels. These sensors detect decibel levels and provide real-time feedback on classroom acoustics. By analyzing this data, educators can make adjustments to reduce noise, such as implementing noise-cancellation measures or addressing sources of disruption (Harrison et al., 2017).

2. **Temperature Regulation**: Temperature control is vital for maintaining a comfortable learning environment. Extreme temperatures, whether too hot or too cold, can lead to discomfort and distract students from their studies. IoT devices equipped with temperature sensors can provide continuous readings of classroom temperatures. This data allows for precise control of heating, ventilation, and air conditioning (HVAC) systems. Teachers and facility managers can use this information to ensure that the classroom remains within an optimal temperature range, enhancing student comfort and focus (Zhao et al., 2016).

3. **Air Quality Monitoring**: Air quality is another critical factor affecting student health and concentration. Poor indoor air quality, characterized by high levels of carbon dioxide (CO_2), volatile organic compounds (VOCs), or particulate matter, can lead to health issues and decreased cognitive function. IoT devices with air quality sensors measure concentrations of these pollutants and monitor ventilation effectiveness. Real-time air quality data enables educators to take timely actions, such as improving ventilation or using air purifiers, to ensure a healthier classroom environment (Dora et al., 2020).

Benefits of Using IoT Devices for Classroom Environment Monitoring

1. **Enhanced Learning Conditions**: By providing real-time data on environmental factors, IoT devices help maintain an optimal learning environment. For example, monitoring noise levels can help educators address issues related to classroom acoustics, while temperature and air quality control ensure that students remain comfortable and focused. These improvements contribute to a more conducive learning atmosphere and can positively impact student performance (Harrison et al., 2017).

2. **Proactive Management**: IoT devices enable proactive management of classroom conditions by providing continuous monitoring and data analysis. Instead of reacting to environmental issues after they arise, educators and facility managers can use real-time data to anticipate and address potential problems before they affect students. This proactive approach helps prevent disruptions and maintains a stable learning environment (Zhao et al., 2016).
3. **Data-Driven Decision Making**: The data collected by IoT devices provides valuable insights into classroom conditions. Educators and administrators can use this data to make informed decisions about classroom management and environmental adjustments. For instance, patterns in noise levels or temperature fluctuations can inform decisions about the placement of furniture or the scheduling of HVAC maintenance (Dora et al., 2020).
4. **Improved Student Well-Being**: Monitoring and managing environmental factors such as noise, temperature, and air quality contribute to students' overall well-being. A comfortable and healthy classroom environment can reduce stress and discomfort, leading to improved focus, engagement, and academic outcomes. Ensuring that students are in a conducive learning environment supports their physical and cognitive development (Harrison et al., 2017).

Challenges and Considerations

While IoT devices offer significant benefits for classroom environment monitoring, there are challenges and considerations associated with their implementation:

1. **Privacy and Security**: The use of IoT devices involves the collection and transmission of data, which raises privacy and security concerns. Ensuring that data collected from classroom sensors is securely stored and transmitted is essential to protect sensitive information. Educational institutions must implement robust cybersecurity measures to safeguard data and comply with relevant privacy regulations (Yang et al., 2021).
2. **Cost and Maintenance**: The deployment of IoT devices and sensors can involve substantial initial costs, including purchasing equipment and installing necessary infrastructure. Additionally, ongoing maintenance and calibration of devices are required to ensure accurate readings. Institutions must consider these factors and plan accordingly to manage costs and maintain the effectiveness of the monitoring system (Zhao et al., 2016).
3. **Integration with Existing Systems**: Integrating IoT devices with existing classroom management systems and infrastructure can be complex. Compatibility issues may arise, and careful planning is needed to ensure seamless integration and functionality. Institutions should work with technology providers to address

integration challenges and ensure that the monitoring system operates effectively within the existing environment (Dora et al., 2020).

4. **Data Interpretation and Action**: The data collected by IoT devices must be interpreted and acted upon effectively. Simply having access to real-time data is not enough; educators and facility managers must have the skills and resources to analyze the data and implement appropriate actions based on the findings. Training and support are necessary to ensure that the data is used effectively to enhance classroom conditions (Harrison et al., 2017).

IoT devices and sensors represent a significant advancement in classroom environment monitoring, offering real-time data on noise levels, temperature, and air quality. By leveraging these technologies, educators and facility managers can create and maintain an optimal learning environment that supports student comfort, concentration, and overall well-being. While there are challenges associated with implementing and managing IoT devices, the benefits of enhanced learning conditions, proactive management, and data-driven decision-making make them a valuable addition to modern educational settings. As technology continues to evolve, the integration of IoT devices in classrooms has the potential to further transform and improve the educational experience for students and educators alike(Rini et al., 2024).

Benefits of AI in Maintaining Classroom Order

Artificial Intelligence (AI) has rapidly evolved and begun to play a transformative role in various aspects of education, including maintaining classroom order. By leveraging AI technologies, educators can enhance classroom management, streamline administrative tasks, and create a more conducive learning environment. Here are some key benefits of AI in maintaining classroom order:

1. Enhanced Monitoring and Supervision

AI-driven tools can significantly improve monitoring and supervision in the classroom. Through the use of advanced sensors, cameras, and algorithms, AI systems can track student behavior and classroom dynamics in real-time. For instance, AI-powered video surveillance systems can analyze students' interactions, detect disruptions, and alert teachers to potential issues such as bullying or off-task behavior (Wang et al., 2019). This enhanced monitoring allows educators to address problems promptly and maintain a positive learning environment.

2. Automated Administrative Tasks

AI can automate various administrative tasks that contribute to maintaining classroom order. For example, AI systems can handle routine tasks such as taking attendance, grading assignments, and managing schedules. Automation of these tasks reduces the administrative burden on teachers, allowing them to focus more on instructional activities and student engagement (Jou, 2020). By streamlining administrative processes, AI helps maintain order and efficiency in the classroom.

3. Behavioral Analytics and Insights

AI technologies can analyze behavioral data to provide valuable insights into student behavior and classroom dynamics. Machine learning algorithms can identify patterns in students' actions, such as frequent disruptions or engagement levels. By analyzing this data, educators can gain a deeper understanding of individual and group behavior, identify underlying issues, and implement targeted interventions to address specific challenges (D'Mello et al., 2015). Behavioral analytics support proactive management strategies, helping to maintain classroom order effectively.

4. Personalized Learning and Engagement

AI can contribute to maintaining classroom order by facilitating personalized learning experiences. Adaptive learning systems powered by AI can tailor educational content to meet the needs and preferences of individual students. By providing personalized instruction, AI helps keep students engaged and focused, reducing the likelihood of disruptive behavior (Zhao et al., 2019). Personalized learning environments foster a sense of ownership and motivation, contributing to a more orderly and productive classroom atmosphere.

5. Predictive Behavior Management

AI systems can use predictive analytics to anticipate potential behavior issues and implement preventative measures. By analyzing historical data on student behavior, AI can identify students at risk of behavioral problems and suggest interventions before issues escalate. For example, predictive models can flag students who may need additional support or monitoring based on patterns of past behavior. Early intervention helps maintain classroom order and supports a positive learning environment (Miller et al., 2020).

6. Support for Classroom Interactions

AI-powered tools can assist in managing classroom interactions and facilitating smooth communication between teachers and students. For instance, AI-driven chatbots and virtual assistants can provide instant responses to common questions and administrative inquiries, reducing interruptions during class time. These tools can also help manage group activities and discussions by providing real-time feedback and moderation, ensuring that classroom interactions remain focused and orderly (Kukulska-Hulme et al., 2017).

7. Real-Time Feedback and Adjustments

AI systems can offer real-time feedback on classroom activities and behavior. For example, AI-powered platforms can provide teachers with immediate insights into student engagement levels and classroom dynamics. This real-time feedback allows educators to make quick adjustments to their teaching strategies, address disruptions as they occur, and maintain a more organized and effective learning environment (D'Mello et al., 2017).

8. Enhanced Security and Safety

AI technologies can enhance security and safety in the classroom by monitoring and managing access to the learning environment. AI-driven security systems can control entry and exit points, detect unauthorized access, and ensure that only authorized individuals are present in the classroom. Additionally, AI can monitor for safety hazards and provide alerts in case of emergencies. These security measures contribute to a safe and orderly classroom environment (Ribeiro et al., 2020).

9. Improved Resource Management

AI can assist in the efficient management of classroom resources, such as equipment, supplies, and digital tools. AI systems can track the usage and availability of resources, optimize their allocation, and ensure that they are used effectively. By managing resources efficiently, AI helps prevent disruptions related to shortages or misuse, contributing to a well-organized and orderly classroom (Jou, 2020).

AI offers numerous benefits for maintaining classroom order, including enhanced monitoring, automated administrative tasks, and personalized learning experiences. By leveraging AI technologies, educators can improve behavior management, streamline administrative processes, and create a more conducive learning environment. While there are challenges to consider, such as privacy and implementation costs, the potential benefits of AI in maintaining classroom order are significant. As technology continues to advance, AI will play an increasingly important role in supporting effective classroom management and promoting a positive educational experience for students and teachers alike.

Challenges of AI in Maintaining Classroom Order

While AI offers numerous advantages for maintaining classroom order, its implementation and use come with several challenges. These challenges can affect the effectiveness of AI systems and their overall impact on the educational environment. Understanding these challenges is crucial for educators, administrators, and policymakers to ensure that AI technologies are used responsibly and effectively. Here are some key challenges associated with using AI to maintain classroom order:

1. Privacy and Data Security

One of the primary concerns with AI in classrooms is the issue of privacy and data security. AI systems often rely on collecting and analyzing data from students, including behavioral patterns, speech, and biometric information. Ensuring that this data is securely stored and protected from unauthorized access is critical. Privacy breaches or misuse of data can have serious consequences, including legal and ethical implications. Educators and institutions must implement stringent data protection measures and comply with privacy regulations to safeguard student information (Liu et al., 2021).

2. Bias and Fairness

AI systems can unintentionally perpetuate or amplify biases present in the data they are trained on. For example, algorithms used in voice recognition or behavioral analysis may exhibit biases related to gender, race, or socioeconomic status. These biases can lead to unequal treatment of students and reinforce existing disparities. Addressing bias in AI systems requires careful design, diverse training data, and continuous monitoring to ensure fairness and equity in classroom management (Smith et al., 2020).

3. Accuracy and Reliability

AI systems are not infallible and may face challenges related to accuracy and reliability. For instance, speech recognition technology might struggle with accents, background noise, or overlapping conversations, leading to inaccuracies in tracking student participation. Similarly, behavioral analytics may misinterpret data or fail to capture the full context of student interactions. Ensuring the accuracy and reliability of AI systems is essential for effective classroom management. Regular updates, testing, and validation are necessary to address these issues (Miller et al., 2020).

4. Implementation Costs

Implementing AI technologies in the classroom can involve significant costs, including the purchase of hardware, software, and integration with existing systems. Additionally, there may be costs associated with training educators to use AI tools effectively and maintaining the technology over time. Budget constraints and financial considerations can limit the adoption of AI systems, particularly in under-resourced schools or districts. Careful planning and budgeting are required to manage these costs and ensure that the benefits of AI outweigh the expenses (Jou, 2020).

5. Ethical Considerations

The use of AI in classrooms raises ethical considerations related to surveillance and autonomy. Continuous monitoring of students' behavior, speech, and interactions can be perceived as intrusive, potentially impacting students' sense of privacy and autonomy. Educators and administrators must balance the benefits of AI with ethical considerations, ensuring that the technology is used in a way that respects students' rights and promotes a positive learning environment (Kukulska-Hulme et al., 2017).

6. Resistance to Change

The integration of AI into classroom management may face resistance from educators, students, and parents. Some educators may be hesitant to adopt new technologies due to concerns about their effectiveness, complexity, or potential impact on traditional teaching methods. Students and parents may also have concerns about how AI affects the learning experience. Overcoming resistance requires effective communication, professional development, and demonstrating the value of AI in enhancing classroom order and student outcomes (Zhao et al., 2019).

7. Integration with Existing Systems

Integrating AI technologies with existing classroom management systems and infrastructure can be complex. Compatibility issues may arise, and technical challenges may hinder seamless integration. For example, integrating AI tools with existing student information systems or learning management systems may require significant technical adjustments and coordination. Ensuring smooth integration involves careful planning, collaboration with technology providers, and addressing technical challenges (Liu et al., 2021).

8. Dependence on Technology

Heavy reliance on AI systems for maintaining classroom order can lead to potential issues if the technology fails or malfunctions. Technical glitches, system outages, or software errors can disrupt classroom management and hinder the learning process. It is important to have contingency plans and backup strategies to address potential technology failures and ensure that classroom management remains effective even when AI systems are not functioning optimally (Miller et al., 2020).

9. Lack of Personal Touch

AI systems may lack the human touch that is often crucial for effective class-room management. While AI can analyze data and provide insights, it cannot fully replace the interpersonal skills and empathy that educators bring to the classroom. Maintaining classroom order involves understanding students' emotions, building relationships, and providing personalized support. AI should complement, not replace, the role of educators in fostering a positive and supportive learning environment (Smith et al., 2020).

The integration of AI into classroom management offers numerous benefits, but it also presents several challenges that need to be addressed. Privacy and data security, bias and fairness, accuracy and reliability, implementation costs, ethical considerations, resistance to change, integration with existing systems, dependence on technology, and the lack of personal touch are all critical factors to consider. By acknowledging and addressing these challenges, educators and institutions can make informed decisions about the use of AI and ensure that the technology contributes positively to maintaining classroom order and enhancing the overall learning experience.

Ethical Issues Related to Surveillance and Privacy

The integration of surveillance and monitoring technologies in educational set-tings raises significant ethical issues related to privacy and the potential misuse of data. As educational institutions increasingly adopt technologies such as AI-driven surveillance systems, facial recognition, and behavioral analytics, it is crucial to address the ethical concerns that accompany these advancements. This discussion explores the key ethical issues associated with surveillance and privacy in education, providing a framework for understanding and addressing these challenges.

1. Invasion of Privacy

One of the primary ethical concerns with surveillance in educational settings is the invasion of students' privacy. Surveillance technologies, such as cameras and monitoring systems, often collect extensive data on students' behaviors, interactions, and activities. While these systems are designed to enhance safety and improve class-room management, they can also intrude on students' personal space and undermine their right to privacy. The constant monitoring of students can lead to feelings of discomfort and anxiety, affecting their overall learning experience (Liu et al., 2021).

2. Consent and Autonomy

The issue of consent is central to the ethical debate surrounding surveillance in education. Students, particularly minors, may not fully understand or be able to consent to the use of surveillance technologies. Educators and institutions must ensure that students and their guardians are informed about the nature, purpose, and scope of surveillance activities. Obtaining explicit consent and providing options for opting out are essential to respecting students' autonomy and ensuring that their participation is voluntary and informed (Kukulska-Hulme et al., 2017).

3. Data Security and Protection

The collection and storage of data from surveillance systems raise concerns about data security and protection. Sensitive information, such as behavioral patterns, ac-ademic performance, and biometric data, must be safeguarded against unauthorized access and potential misuse. Institutions are responsible for implementing robust data protection measures, including encryption, access controls, and regular audits, to ensure that students' data is kept secure. Failure to protect this data can lead to breaches, identity theft, and other negative consequences for students (Miller et al., 2020).

4. Potential for Misuse

Surveillance data can be misused or exploited if not properly managed. There is a risk that data collected for legitimate purposes, such as maintaining classroom order, could be used for unintended or unethical purposes. For example, data may be accessed by unauthorized individuals or used to unfairly target or discipline students. Ensuring that data is used solely for its intended purpose and establishing clear guidelines for its use and access are critical to preventing misuse (Smith et al., 2020).

5. Impact on Student Behavior

The presence of surveillance technology can influence student behavior, potentially leading to changes in how students interact and engage in the classroom. The awareness of being constantly monitored may lead students to modify their behavior, which can impact the authenticity of their interactions and participation. This phenomenon, known as the "Panopticon effect," can alter the natural learning environment and affect students' willingness to express themselves freely (Zhao et al., 2019).

6. Equity and Fairness

Ethical considerations also extend to issues of equity and fairness in the implementation of surveillance technologies. There is a risk that surveillance systems may disproportionately affect certain groups of students, particularly those from marginalized or disadvantaged backgrounds. Ensuring that surveillance practices are applied equitably and do not reinforce existing biases or inequalities is essential for maintaining fairness in the educational environment (Liu et al., 2021).

7. Transparency and Accountability

Transparency and accountability are crucial for addressing ethical issues related to surveillance. Educational institutions must be transparent about their use of surveillance technologies, including informing students, parents, and staff about the types of data collected, how it is used, and who has access to it. Establishing mechanisms for accountability, such as oversight committees and review processes, helps ensure that surveillance practices adhere to ethical standards and legal requirements (Kukulska-Hulme et al., 2017).

8. Long-Term Implications

The long-term implications of surveillance and data collection on students' futures are an important ethical consideration. Data collected during students' time in school may have implications beyond their educational years, potentially affecting their future opportunities and privacy. Institutions must consider the long-term impact of their data practices and take steps to ensure that students' data is handled responsibly and does not adversely affect their future prospects (Miller et al., 2020).

The integration of surveillance and monitoring technologies in education presents several ethical challenges related to privacy, consent, data security, and fairness. Addressing these challenges requires a careful balance between leveraging technology to enhance classroom management and safeguarding students' rights and well-being. By prioritizing transparency, consent, and robust data protection measures, educational institutions can navigate the ethical complexities of surveillance and ensure that technology is used in a manner that respects and protects students' privacy and autonomy.

CONCLUSION

The integration of advanced technologies in educational settings has the potential to significantly enhance teaching and learning experiences. From facial recognition systems for automating attendance to IoT devices for monitoring classroom environments and voice recognition technology for analyzing class participation, these innovations offer new ways to improve educational outcomes.

artificial intelligence (AI) has emerged as a transformative force in various fields, including education. AI-driven classroom management represents a significant shift in how educators approach teaching and learning, leveraging technology to enhance efficiency, engagement, and educational outcomes. However, this advancement comes with its own set of challenges and ethical considerations. Balancing the benefits of AI with its potential drawbacks is crucial for the effective and responsible implementation of these technologies in educational settings.

Enhancing Efficiency with AI

AI-driven tools can significantly improve classroom management by automating administrative tasks and streamlining processes. For instance, AI systems can handle routine activities such as grading assignments, tracking attendance, and managing schedules. This automation reduces the administrative burden on teachers, allowing them to focus more on instructional activities and individualized student support.

One prominent application of AI in enhancing efficiency is the use of intelligent tutoring systems (ITS). **Intelligent Tutoring Systems (ITS)** are computer systems designed to provide personalized instruction and feedback to learners, without the need for human intervention. These systems use artificial intelligence (AI) techniques to adapt educational content and interactions based on the needs and abilities of individual learners, helping them progress at their own pace.

Key features of ITS include:

1. **Personalization**: Tailors the learning experience to each student by analyzing their performance, learning style, and knowledge gaps.

2. **Feedback**: Offers real-time, context-specific feedback to help students understand concepts and correct errors.
3. **Adaptive Learning**: Adjusts difficulty levels, types of problems, or content sequencing based on the student's progress and abilities.
4. **Knowledge Representation**: Models the subject matter, student knowledge, and pedagogical strategies to guide the learning process effectively.
5. **Interactivity**: Engages learners through interactive problem-solving, dialogue, and exercises.

ITS are commonly used in various educational domains, from mathematics and science to language learning, with the goal of improving learning outcomes by delivering targeted, student-centered instruction.

ITS leverage machine learning algorithms to provide personalized instruction and feedback to students. These systems can assess individual student performance in real-time, identify areas of struggle, and offer tailored resources and interventions. As a result, educators can address learning gaps more effectively and allocate their time and resources where they are most needed (Kumar & Gupta, 2021).

AI can also assist in classroom management through behavior analysis and monitoring. Systems equipped with voice recognition and sentiment analysis can track student participation, engagement levels, and classroom dynamics. By analyzing patterns in student behavior and interactions, AI tools can help teachers manage classroom environments more proactively, address potential issues before they escalate, and create a more conducive learning atmosphere (Smith et al., 2018).

Enhancing Engagement with AI

AI technologies have the potential to increase student engagement by creating interactive and personalized learning experiences. Adaptive learning platforms, powered by AI, adjust content and instructional strategies based on individual student needs and progress. These platforms use data analytics to identify learning preferences, strengths, and areas for improvement, thereby offering a customized learning experience that can better engage students (Huang & Liu, 2019).

Adaptive learning platforms are educational systems that use technology, often powered by artificial intelligence (AI) and data analytics, to dynamically adjust the content, pace, and learning path according to the needs and progress of individual learners. These platforms aim to create a more personalized and efficient learning experience by continuously analyzing how a student interacts with learning materials and adjusts accordingly.

Key characteristics of adaptive learning platforms include:

1. **Personalized Learning Path**: The platform tailors content and learning activities based on the student's prior knowledge, learning style, and performance. It can modify the difficulty level or suggest different materials based on how well the student is progressing.
2. **Real-Time Feedback**: Adaptive systems provide instant feedback on performance, helping students identify and correct mistakes in real-time, while also offering hints or additional resources when needed.
3. **Data-Driven**: These platforms use data collected from student interactions, assessments, and progress reports to continuously refine the learning process, improving both the platform's recommendations and the student's outcomes.
4. **Flexibility**: The system adapts to students' learning speeds, providing more practice for difficult concepts or moving forward when mastery is demonstrated, ensuring that each learner works at their optimal pace.
5. **Assessment and Analytics**: Regular assessments are integrated into the learning process, often through formative quizzes or assessments, which inform the platform of the student's comprehension and readiness to proceed.

Examples of Adaptive Learning Platforms

- **Knewton**: A platform that customizes the sequence of instructional content based on the learner's individual needs.
- **DreamBox Learning**: An adaptive math platform for K-8 that changes lessons dynamically based on students' real-time performance.
- **Smart Sparrow**: Provides adaptive e-learning courses, allowing educators to tailor the learning experience while the platform adapts to individual learners.

Adaptive learning platforms are widely used in K-12 education, higher education, corporate training, and self-paced online courses to enhance learning outcomes by offering personalized instruction.

Gamification is another approach to enhancing engagement through AI. AI-driven educational games and simulations provide students with immersive and interactive experiences that make learning more enjoyable and motivating(Tuyen et al., 2023). By incorporating elements such as rewards, challenges, and real-time feedback, these technologies can increase student motivation and participation (Miller et al., 2020).

Furthermore, AI can support collaborative learning by facilitating group activities and discussions. AI tools can analyze group interactions, provide feedback on collaboration skills, and suggest ways to improve group dynamics. This helps create a more interactive and engaging classroom environment where students can learn from each other and work together more effectively (Zhou et al., 2020).

Addressing Ethical Considerations

While the benefits of AI in classroom management are substantial, it is essential to address the ethical implications of these technologies. Privacy concerns are a primary consideration, as AI systems often collect and analyze sensitive data about students, including their performance, behavior, and personal information. Ensuring data security and privacy is crucial to protect students' rights and maintain trust in educational institutions (Liu et al., 2021).

Bias and fairness are also critical ethical issues in AI-driven classroom management. AI algorithms are only as unbiased as the data they are trained on. If the training data reflects existing biases or inequalities, AI systems can perpetuate these biases, leading to unfair treatment of students. It is essential to design and implement AI systems with fairness and equity in mind, regularly auditing algorithms for bias and ensuring that all students are treated equitably (Choi et al., 2019).

Transparency and accountability are further ethical considerations. Educators and students should have a clear understanding of how AI systems operate, what data is collected, and how decisions are made. Providing transparency helps build trust and ensures that AI technologies are used responsibly and ethically in educational settings (Harris & Rea, 2018).

Balancing Efficiency, Engagement, and Ethics

To effectively balance efficiency, engagement, and ethics in AI-driven classroom management, several strategies can be employed:

1. **Integrative Design**: AI systems should be designed to complement, rather than replace, human educators. The goal is to enhance and support the teaching process, not to undermine the role of teachers. Integrating AI tools into existing teaching practices can help maintain the human element of education while leveraging technology to improve efficiency and engagement.
2. **Data Privacy and Security**: Implementing robust data protection measures is essential to safeguard student information. Educational institutions should establish clear policies and practices for data collection, storage, and use. Engaging with students and parents to obtain informed consent and explain data handling procedures can also help address privacy concerns.
3. **Bias Mitigation**: To address potential biases in AI systems, it is important to use diverse and representative data sets for training algorithms. Regularly reviewing and updating AI models to ensure fairness and equity is crucial. Involving educators, students, and other stakeholders in the development and evaluation of AI tools can help identify and address biases.

4. **Transparency and Communication**: Educators and students should be informed about how AI systems work and how they impact classroom management. Providing clear explanations and involving stakeholders in decision-making processes can foster trust and ensure that AI technologies are used ethically and effectively.
5. **Professional Development**: Training educators on the use of AI technologies and their ethical implications is important for successful implementation. Professional development programs can help teachers understand how to effectively integrate AI into their practices, use data responsibly, and address ethical challenges.

AI-driven classroom management offers the potential to enhance efficiency, engagement, and educational outcomes by automating administrative tasks, personalizing learning experiences, and improving classroom dynamics. However, the implementation of AI technologies must be approached with careful consideration of privacy, fairness, transparency, and accountability. By balancing these factors and employing thoughtful strategies, educational institutions can leverage AI to create more effective, engaging, and equitable learning environments for all students.

Facial recognition systems streamline the attendance process by providing real-time updates and reducing administrative burdens. These systems ensure accurate records and can facilitate more efficient classroom management. Similarly, IoT devices equipped with sensors for monitoring environmental factors such as noise levels, temperature, and air quality contribute to creating optimal learning conditions. By providing real-time data, these technologies help maintain a comfortable and healthy classroom environment, which can positively impact student well-being and academic performance.

Voice recognition technology further enhances classroom dynamics by tracking and analyzing student participation. This technology enables educators to monitor engagement levels, ensure equitable participation, and provide targeted feedback. By identifying students who may need additional support, voice recognition systems help create a more inclusive and responsive learning environment.

While the benefits of these technologies are substantial, their implementation also presents challenges. Privacy and security concerns, accuracy and reliability issues, and the costs of technology deployment must be carefully managed. Additionally, addressing potential biases and ensuring fair use of these systems are critical for their success.

Overall, the thoughtful application of these advanced technologies can lead to more effective teaching practices and improved student outcomes. As educational institutions continue to explore and integrate these innovations, they hold the promise of transforming classrooms into more engaging, responsive, and supportive learning environments.

REFERENCES

Aneesh, P. (2023). Developing an IoT-enabled smart classroom S3TH system. *Proceedings of ICIRCA 2023*. https://doi.org/DOI: 10.1109/icirca57980.2023.10220862

Baker, R. S., D'Mello, S. K., Rodrigo, M. M., & Graesser, A. C. (2010). Better to be frustrated than bored: The incidence, persistence, and impact of learners' emotions during interactions with three different computer-based learning environments. *International Journal of Human-Computer Studies*, 68(4), 223–241.

Baker, R. S., & Yacef, K. (2011). The state of educational data mining in 2009. *Proceedings of the 2nd International Conference on Educational Data Mining*, 3-16.

Choi, Y., Ko, J., & Lee, S. (2019). Analyzing student participation in class discussions using speech recognition technology. *Journal of Educational Technology*, 15(3), 45–60.

Conati, C., & Maclaren, H. (2009). Empathic and affective tutoring systems. *International Journal of Artificial Intelligence in Education*, 19(1), 1–24.

Cummings, J., & Schrum, L. (2018). *Designing for the future: The role of technology in educational reform*. Routledge.

D'Mello, S. K., Lehman, B., & Pekrun, R. (2011). Emotion and learning. In *The Cambridge Handbook of the Learning Sciences* (pp. 324–340). Cambridge University Press.

Dede, C. (2014). *The role of emerging technologies in transforming learning environments*. Harvard Education Press.

Devender, E.. (2023). IoT-enhanced learning environment optimization and student outcome. *International Journal on Recent and Innovation Trends in Computing and Communication*, 11(11). Advance online publication. DOI: 10.17762/ijritcc.v11i11.9954

Dora, C., Waddington, C., & Edwards, S. (2020). Indoor air quality and student performance: A review of the evidence. *Environmental Research Letters*, 15(5), 055002.

Ekman, P., & Friesen, W. V. (1971). *Constant variables in facial expressions of emotion*. Stanford University Press.

Harris, A., & Rea, T. (2018). Privacy and ethical concerns with emotion detection technologies. *Journal of Information Privacy and Security*, 14(2), 45–60.

Harrison, R., Bower, J., & Williams, K. (2017). The impact of classroom noise on student learning: A review of the literature. *Journal of Environmental Psychology*, 52, 1–10.

Hollis, V., Arnaud, M., & Jun, Y. (2020). Ethical considerations for emotion recognition technology in educational settings. *Educational Technology Research and Development*, 68(1), 123–139. PMID: 33199950

Huang, C., & Liu, R. (2019). IoT-based classroom environment monitoring and its impact on student performance. *International Journal of Computer Applications in Technology*, 60(3), 211–224.

Jung, J. Y., & Lee, K. S. (2020). Improving classroom acoustics: The impact of sound level meters on student concentration and behavior. *Journal of Educational Research and Practice*, 10(2), 121–135.

Koedinger, K. R., Corbett, A. T., & Perfetti, C. (2015). The knowledge component framework: A conceptual framework for describing students' knowledge. *International Journal of Artificial Intelligence in Education*, 25(3), 250–272.

Krupa, V., Khapper, I., Issa, W. A., AlHmoud, G., Balakrishna, G., Islam, A. K., & Graves, C. A. (2024). A low-power IoT-based smart desk integrated with a classroom response system. *Proceedings of SoutheastCon*, 2024, 1591–1598. DOI: 10.1109/southeastcon52093.2024.10500186

Kumar, R., & Gupta, S. (2021). Adaptive learning systems with real-time feedback: A review of voice recognition and emotion detection technologies. *Educational Technology Review*, 39(4), 145–162.

Liu, X., Zhao, Y., & Li, M. (2021). Privacy considerations in the use of voice recognition technology in education. *International Journal of Educational Technology*, 23(2), 89–102.

Mayer, J. D., Salovey, P., & Caruso, D. R. (2008). Emotional intelligence: New ability or eclectic traits? *The American Psychologist*, 63(6), 503–517. PMID: 18793038

Miller, R., Smith, A., & Johnson, P. (2020). Enhancing classroom dynamics with real-time speech analysis: A case study. *Educational Technology Research and Development*, 68(4), 1157–1176.

Mohammed, F. H., Sharif, H., Rahman, M. A., Khan, A. A., Islam, M. M., & Habib, M. T. (2023). Design and development of SEMS - An IoT-based smart environment monitoring system. *Proceedings of I-SMAC 2023*. https://doi.org/DOI: 10.1109/i-smac58438.2023.10290331

Mollahosseini, A., Chan, D., & Mahoor, M. H. (2017). AffectNet: A dataset for facial expression, valence, and arousal computing in the wild. *IEEE Transactions on Affective Computing*, 10(1), 18–31.

Picard, R. W., Vyzas, E., & Healey, J. (2001). Toward machine emotional intelligence: Analysis of affective states and affective computing. *IEEE Transactions on Pattern Analysis and Machine Intelligence*, 23(10), 1175–1191.

Rini, M., Lestari, A. D., & Muslim, M. A. (2024). IoT-integrated smart attendance and attention monitoring system for primary and secondary school classroom management. *Journal of Electronics Technology Exploration*, 2(1). Advance online publication. DOI: 10.52465/joetex.v2i1.381

Seneff, S., & Wang, C. (2019). The challenges of facial expression recognition in diverse settings. *Journal of Computer Vision*, 136(1), 85–97.

Smith, J., Green, H., & Roberts, K. (2018). Addressing challenges in voice recognition technology for educational settings. *Journal of Technology Education*, 32(1), 78–79.

Tuyen, P. T., Truong, A. T., Truong, D. P., Le, D. T., Pham, N. C., & Qui, N. C. (2023). Design and implementation of classroom environment monitoring system towards smart campus. *Proceedings of the 2023 International Conference on Smart Campus (ICSC)*. https://doi.org/DOI: 10.1145/3606150.3606177

Zhang, Y., & Li, X. (2022). Implementing smart classroom technologies: Benefits, challenges, and future directions. *Journal of Educational Technology Development and Exchange*, 15(1), 25–42.

Zhao, Y., Wang, Y., & Li, H. (2016). Temperature regulation and student comfort in classroom environments: An IoT approach. *Building and Environment*, 104, 221–229.

Zhou, L., Li, W., & Zhang, J. (2021). Ensuring equitable student engagement through voice recognition technology. *Journal of Educational Technology & Society*, 24(2), 123–136.

Zhou, L., Wang, Z., & Yang, F. (2020). Voice recognition for monitoring classroom participation: Benefits and limitations. *Journal of Classroom Interaction*, 55(1), 31–45.

Chapter 5
AI–Enhanced Peace Education:
AI's Impact on Student Learning Practices in Higher Education

Myla Arcinas
https://orcid.org/0000-0002-5795-031X
De La Salle University, Philippines

ABSTRACT

This chapter investigates the integration of artificial intelligence (AI) in higher education peace programs, examining its effects on student outcomes, engagement, and critical thinking. Employing a concurrent mixed-methods approach, the study collected data from 500 survey respondents and 50 interviewees across five institutions. Quantitative findings reveal significant improvements in learning outcomes, particularly in knowledge acquisition ($d = 0.82$) and critical thinking ($d = 0.70$), with increased student engagement ($d = 0.46–0.61$). AI integration emerged as the strongest predictor of learning outcomes ($\beta = 0.41$, $p < .001$). Qualitative analysis highlights AI's potential for enhancing engagement, personalization, and critical thinking, while also identifying implementation challenges and ethical concerns. The study concludes by recommending gradual AI integration, emphasizing personalized learning, and developing ethical guidelines, addressing issues such as technology overload and equitable access in AI-enhanced peace education.

DOI: 10.4018/979-8-3693-8191-5.ch005

INTRODUCTION

In an era marked by rapid technological advancements and persistent global conflicts, the intersection of artificial intelligence (AI) and peace education presents a unique opportunity to revolutionize learning practices in higher education. In navigating the complexities of the 21st century, the need for innovative approaches to fostering peace, understanding, and conflict resolution has never been more critical. This chapter explores the transformative potential of AI-enhanced peace education in shaping students' learning experiences and outcomes in higher education institutions.

Peace education, which promotes nonviolence, social justice, and human rights, has long been recognized as a crucial component of holistic education (Bajaj & Hantzopoulos, 2016). However, the traditional approaches to peace education often face challenges in engaging students effectively and addressing the rapidly evolving global landscape. Integrating AI technologies into peace education curricula offers a promising avenue to overcome these limitations and create more dynamic, personalized, and impactful learning experiences.

The significance of this study lies in its exploration of how AI can enhance the effectiveness of peace education in higher education settings. As AI continues to permeate various aspects of human lives, understanding its potential to shape educational practices becomes increasingly important. This research aims to bridge the gap between technological innovation and peace education, providing insights into how AI can be leveraged to cultivate a culture of peace among future generations of leaders, policymakers, and global citizens.

Research Objectives

The primary objectives of this study are:

1. To examine the current state of AI integration in peace education within higher education institutions.
2. To assess the impact of AI-enhanced peace education on student learning outcomes and engagement.
3. To identify the challenges and opportunities associated with implementing AI technologies in peace education curricula.
4. To develop a framework for effectively integrating AI in peace education programs at the higher education level.

Research Questions

To address these objectives, the following research questions guide this study:

1. How are AI technologies currently utilized in peace education programs within higher education institutions?
2. How does AI-enhanced peace education impact student learning outcomes, including knowledge acquisition, skill development, and attitudinal changes?
3. How does integrating AI in peace education affect student engagement and motivation?
4. What are the key challenges and opportunities associated with implementing AI-enhanced peace education in higher education settings?
5. How can a framework be developed to guide the effective integration of AI in peace education programs?

By addressing these questions, this chapter aims to contribute to the growing body of knowledge on educational technology and peace studies while providing practical insights for educators, administrators, and policymakers seeking to harness the power of AI in promoting peace education.

LITERATURE REVIEW

AI in Education

The application of AI in education has gained significant traction in recent years, with numerous studies highlighting its potential to transform teaching and learning practices. AI technologies have been shown to offer personalized learning experiences, adaptive assessments, and intelligent tutoring systems that can cater to individual student needs and learning styles (Roll & Wylie, 2016).

One of the key advantages of AI in education is its ability to process and analyze vast amounts of data to provide insights into student performance and learning patterns. AI-powered learning analytics can help educators identify at-risk students, tailor interventions, and optimize curriculum design (Siemens & Long, 2011). For instance, a study by Chatti et al. (2019) demonstrated how AI-driven learning analytics could predict student performance and provide timely support, leading to improved academic outcomes.

AI-powered chatbots and virtual assistants have also shown promise in providing 24/7 student support, answering queries, and facilitating self-directed learning. A study by Winkler and Söllner (2018) found that AI chatbots could effectively reduce instructors' workload while maintaining high student satisfaction and engagement levels.

Moreover, AI has been utilized to develop intelligent tutoring systems (ITS) that can adapt to individual student needs and provide personalized feedback. For example, VanLehn (2011) examined ITS effectiveness and found that these systems could be as effective as human tutors in certain contexts, particularly STEM subjects.

However, the integration of AI in education is not without challenges. Scholars such as Selwyn have raised ethical concerns regarding data privacy, algorithmic bias, and the potential dehumanization of the learning process (2019). Additionally, there is a need for ongoing professional development to ensure that educators are equipped to implement and leverage AI technologies in their teaching practices effectively (Zawacki-Richter et al., 2019).

Peace Education in Higher Education

Peace education in higher education has evolved significantly over the past few decades, moving beyond its initial focus on conflict resolution to encompass a broader range of issues related to social justice, human rights, and global citizenship (Bajaj & Hantzopoulos, 2016). Universities and colleges play a crucial role in shaping future leaders and decision-makers, making them ideal settings for cultivating a culture of peace and nonviolence.

Research has shown that peace education programs in higher education can have a significant impact on students' attitudes, knowledge, and skills related to peace and conflict resolution. For instance, a study by Kester and Cremin (2017) found that university students who participated in peace education courses demonstrated increased empathy, intercultural understanding, and conflict resolution skills.

Peace education in higher education often employs a variety of pedagogical approaches, including experiential learning, critical pedagogy, and transformative learning. These approaches engage students in critical reflection, dialogue, and action-oriented learning (Bajaj, 2015). For example, Brantmeier (2013) described intergroup dialogue as an effective method for promoting understanding and empathy among diverse student populations in higher education settings.

However, peace education in higher education also faces several challenges. These include the need for interdisciplinary approaches, the integration of peace education across various academic disciplines, and the development of assessment methods that can effectively measure the impact of peace education on students' attitudes and behaviors (Harris, 2004).

Integration of AI in Peace Education

The integration of AI in peace education represents a relatively new and unexplored area of research. However, preliminary studies suggest that AI technologies have the potential to enhance various aspects of peace education, including conflict simulation, cross-cultural communication, and perspective-taking exercises.

AI-powered virtual reality (VR) and augmented reality (AR) technologies offer immersive experiences that simulate real-world conflict scenarios, allowing students to practice conflict resolution skills in safe, controlled environments. For instance, Cuhadar and Kampf (2014) explored using AI-enhanced conflict simulations in peace education, finding that such tools could effectively improve students' conflict analysis and resolution skills.

Natural language processing (NLP) and machine translation technologies can facilitate cross-cultural communication and understanding, breaking down language barriers often contributing to conflicts. A study by Byram and Wagner (2018) highlighted the potential of AI-powered language tools in promoting intercultural competence among higher education students.

AI algorithms can also analyze large datasets related to conflicts and peace processes, providing students with insights into complex global issues. For example, Schrodt et al. (2014) demonstrated how machine learning techniques could be applied to analyze conflict data, offering new perspectives on conflict dynamics and resolution strategies.

Moreover, AI-enhanced learning management systems can provide personalized peace education curricula, adapting content and learning activities to individual student needs and interests. This personalization can potentially increase student engagement and the effectiveness of peace education programs (Luckin et al., 2016).

Gaps in Current Research

Despite the growing body of literature on AI in education and peace education in higher education, several gaps remain in our understanding of how these two fields can be effectively integrated:

1. Limited empirical studies: There is a scarcity of empirical research specifically examining the impact of AI-enhanced peace education on student learning outcomes in higher education settings.
2. Lack of comprehensive frameworks: Few studies have attempted to develop comprehensive frameworks for integrating AI technologies into peace education curricula in higher education.

3. Insufficient exploration of ethical considerations: The ethical implications of using AI in peace education, particularly concerning data privacy and algorithmic bias, have not been thoroughly explored in the context of higher education.
4. Limited focus on pedagogical approaches: There is a need for more research on how AI can support and enhance existing pedagogical approaches in peace education, such as experiential learning and critical pedagogy.
5. Absence of longitudinal studies: Long-term studies examining the sustained impact of AI-enhanced peace education on students' attitudes, behaviors, and career trajectories are currently lacking.

This study addresses these gaps by providing empirical evidence on the impact of AI-enhanced peace education in higher education settings, developing a framework for AI integration in peace education, and exploring the associated challenges and opportunities.

Conceptual Framework

The conceptual framework for this study is grounded in the intersection of three key domains: peace education, artificial intelligence in education, and higher education pedagogy. This interdisciplinary approach allows for a comprehensive examination of how AI can enhance peace education practices in the context of higher learning institutions.

Reardon (1988) defines peace education as a transformative process that equips individuals with the knowledge, skills, and attitudes necessary to build a culture of peace. It encompasses various dimensions, including conflict resolution, human rights education, and global citizenship (Harris & Morrison, 2013). The theoretical underpinnings of peace education draw from critical pedagogy (Freire, 1970), social learning theory (Bandura, 1977), and constructivism (Vygotsky, 1978), emphasizing the importance of experiential learning, dialogue, and critical reflection in fostering peace-oriented mindsets.

Artificial intelligence in education refers to applying AI technologies and techniques to enhance teaching and learning processes (Holmes et al., 2019). This includes using machine learning algorithms, natural language processing, and adaptive learning systems to personalize instruction, provide intelligent tutoring, and analyze educational data for improved decision-making (Luckin et al., 2016).

Higher education pedagogy focuses on the theories and practices of teaching and learning at the tertiary level. It encompasses various approaches, including active learning, problem-based learning, and technology-enhanced learning, all aimed at fostering critical thinking, deep understanding, and the development of transferable skills (Biggs & Tang, 2011).

Integrating these three domains forms the basis for exploring how AI can enhance peace education in higher education settings, potentially leading to more effective and engaging student learning experiences.

METHODOLOGY

This study employs a concurrent mixed methods design to comprehensively examine the impact of AI-enhanced peace education on student learning practices in higher education. This approach allows for the simultaneous collection and analysis of quantitative and qualitative data, providing a more nuanced understanding of the complex interplay between AI technologies and peace education (Creswell & Plano Clark, 2017).

Research Design

The concurrent mixed methods design was chosen for its ability to provide a comprehensive view of the research problem by combining the strengths of quantitative and qualitative approaches (Teddlie & Tashakkori, 2009). In this design, quantitative and qualitative data are collected concurrently, analyzed separately, and then merged for interpretation. This approach allows for triangulation of findings, enhancing the validity and reliability of the results (Johnson et al., 2007).

The quantitative component of the study focuses on measuring the impact of AI-enhanced peace education on student learning outcomes, engagement, and attitudes. The qualitative component explores the experiences, perceptions and challenges associated with implementing AI in peace education from the perspectives of both students and educators.

Participants and Sampling

Table 1 presents the participant profile for this mixed-methods study on AI-enhanced peace education. The study involved a quantitative phase with 500 undergraduate students and a qualitative phase with 50 key informants (25 students and 25 educators).

The quantitative sample was evenly distributed across five institutions (100 students each), with a slight majority of female participants (55%). The age range was typical for undergraduates, with 60% aged 18-21 and 40% aged 22-25.

In the qualitative phase, each institution contributed five students and five educators, ensuring balanced representation. The educator group was older (40% aged 26-35, 60% over 36) compared to the student group, allowing for exploration of generational perspectives.

Academic disciplines were consistently represented across phases, with Social Sciences dominating (40%), followed by Humanities, STEM, and other disciplines. This distribution reflects the interdisciplinary nature of peace education.

Participants' prior AI experience was predominantly moderate (45%) to low (40%), with only 15-16% reporting high experience levels. This suggests that AI-enhanced peace education is a novel approach for most participants.

This strategically structured sample provides a robust foundation for investigating AI-enhanced peace education across various contexts, disciplines, and levels of AI familiarity, enabling a comprehensive examination from multiple perspectives.

Table 1. Sampling distribution and participants' profile

Characteristic	Quantitative phase (n=500)	Qualitative phase (n=50)	
		Students (n=25)	Educators (n=25)
Role			
Students	500 (100%)	25 (100%)	-
Educators	-	-	25 (100%)
Institution			
Institution A	100 (20%)	5 (20%)	5 (20%)
Institution B	100 (20%)	5 (20%)	5 (20%)
Institution C	100 (20%)	5 (20%)	5 (20%)
Institution D	100 (20%)	5 (20%)	5 (20%)
Institution E	100 (20%)	5 (20%)	5 (20%)
Gender			
Female	275 (55%)	14 (56%)	13 (52%)
Male	220 (44%)	11 (44%)	12 (48%)
Non-binary	5 (1%)	-	-
Age Range			
18-21	300 (60%)	15 (60%)	-
22-25	200 (40%)	10 (40%)	-
26-35	-	-	10 (40%)
36+	-	-	15 (60%)
Academic Discipline			

continued on following page

Table 1. Continued

Characteristic	Quantitative phase (n=500)	Qualitative phase (n=50)	
		Students (n=25)	Educators (n=25)
Social Sciences	200 (40%)	10 (40%)	10 (40%)
Humanities	150 (30%)	8 (32%)	7 (28%)
STEM	100 (20%)	5 (20%)	5 (20%)
Others	50 (10%)	2 (8%)	3 (12%)
Previous AI Experience			
High	75 (15%)	4 (16%)	4 (16%)
Moderate	225 (45%)	11 (44%)	11 (44%)
Low	200 (40%)	10 (40%)	10 (40%)

Data Collection Instruments and Procedures

This study employed a mixed-methods parallel approach, utilizing quantitative and qualitative data collection instruments (Creswell & Plano Clark, 2018). For the quantitative phase, three primary instruments were developed and administered. The AI-Enhanced Peace Education Impact Survey (AIPEIS), a 40-item Likert-scale questionnaire, was designed specifically for this study to measure students' perceptions of AI's impact on their learning experiences in peace education, following guidelines for survey development in educational research (Artino et al., 2014). To assess learning outcomes, the Peace Education Outcome Assessment (PEOA), a standardized 30-item multiple-choice test, was used to evaluate students' knowledge and understanding of key peace education concepts, drawing on established principles of assessment in peace education (Kester, 2013). The AI in Education Readiness Scale (AIERS), a 20-item Likert-scale questionnaire, was employed to measure participants' readiness and attitudes toward AI integration in educational experiences, adapting concepts from technology acceptance models in education (Scherer et al., 2019).

For the qualitative phase, semi-structured interviews were conducted with all 50 key informants (25 students and 25 educators). These interviews were designed to explore participants' experiences, perceptions, and challenges related to AI-enhanced peace education in greater depth, providing rich, contextual data to complement the quantitative findings.

The data collection process spanned one academic semester (16 weeks) and was structured in three main phases. The first phase involved a pre-intervention assessment, where the AIPEIS, PEOA, and AIERS were administered to all 500 student participants, and initial interviews were conducted with the 50 key informants.

Following this, the implementation phase saw the integration of AI technologies into existing peace education curricula across the participating institutions. The final phase consisted of a post-intervention assessment, where the AIPEIS, PEOA, and AIERS were re-administered to all student participants and follow-up interviews were conducted with the key informants.

Data Analysis

Data analysis followed a concurrent mixed methods design, allowing for the integration of quantitative and qualitative findings. Quantitative data from the surveys and assessments were analyzed using descriptive and inferential statistical methods. Descriptive statistics provided an overview of the data, while inferential statistics, including paired t-tests and multiple regression analysis, were used to examine changes in learning outcomes and factors influencing these changes. Paired t-tests were particularly useful in comparing pre- and post-intervention scores on the PEOA, while multiple regression analysis helped identify predictors of learning outcomes.

Qualitative data from the semi-structured interviews were analyzed using thematic analysis, following the six-step approach outlined by Braun and Clarke (2006). This method involved familiarizing the data, generating initial codes, searching for themes, reviewing, defining, naming, and producing the report. This approach allowed for a systematic and rigorous analysis of the rich, textual data obtained from the interviews, identifying key themes and patterns in participants' experiences and perceptions.

Quantitative and qualitative data integration followed a concurrent design, where both data types were analyzed separately and then brought together for interpretation. This approach allowed for a comprehensive understanding of the impact of AI-enhanced peace education, with quantitative data providing measurable outcomes and qualitative data offering in-depth explanations and contextual insights. The convergence of these two data types enhanced the validity of the findings and provided a more nuanced understanding of the complex dynamics involved in integrating AI into peace education curricula. A joint display of findings represents the integration of quantitative and qualitative findings visually (Guetterman et al., 2015).

Ethical Considerations

This study strictly adhered to ethical guidelines to ensure the protection and respect of all participants. Before commencement, approval was obtained from all participating institutions, establishing a foundation of institutional oversight. Informed consent was secured from each participant following a comprehensive explanation of the study's purpose, procedures, and potential implications, emphasizing their right to withdraw without penalty. Participant identities were protected through pseudonyms and rigorous data anonymization techniques. Data security was ensured through robust measures, including encryption protocols and restricted access to research materials. The researcher communicated potential risks and benefits to participants, facilitating a clear understanding of their involvement. Although the study was deemed a minimal risk, participants were informed of potential discomforts, such as time commitments or engagement with sensitive topics. Upon completion of data collection, participants were offered referrals for debriefing sessions to address any concerns and provide further context about the study's objectives and implications. These comprehensive safeguards aligned the research process with established ethical standards in educational and social science research, ensuring the study's integrity and participants' well-being.

RESULTS

Results are presented in three sections. The quantitative findings present the -- 1. Prevalence of AI technologies in Peace Education Programs, 2. Impact of AI-enhanced Peace Education on Student Learning Outcomes, 3. Paired t-test results for PEOA, 4. Impact of AI-Enhanced Peace Education on Student Engagement and Motivation, and 5. Relationship between AI integration and Learning Outcomes. The qualitative findings generated these key themes – 1. Enhanced Engagement and Interactivity, 2. Personalized Learning Experiences, 3. Development of Critical Thinking and Analysis Skills, 4. Challenges in Implementation, and 5. Ethical Considerations. The last section presents the integration of quantitative and qualitative findings, showing the convergence or divergence of the results.

Quantitative Findings

Current Utilization of AI Technologies in Peace Education Programs. Table 2 presents the prevalence of various AI technologies implemented in peace education programs across the five participating institutions based on educator responses to the AI in Education Readiness Scale (AIERS). The data reveal notable variations in AI adoption across different technologies and institutions.

Chatbots for student support emerged as the most widely adopted AI technology, with an overall implementation rate of 92% across all institutions. Institutions A, C, and D reported 100% adoption of chatbots, while Institutions B and E showed 80% adoption. This high prevalence suggests that institutions prioritize AI technologies that offer immediate, scalable support to students.

Adaptive learning systems and AI-enhanced assessment tools showed the second-highest overall adoption rate at 76% each. Institution D demonstrated full implementation (100%) of these technologies, while other institutions varied between 60% and 80% adoption. This suggests a strong interest in personalized learning and data-driven assessment strategies across the participating institutions.

AI-powered simulations were less prevalent, with an overall adoption rate of 56%. Institution D led in this category with 80% implementation, while Institutions B and E reported the lowest adoption at 40%. This variability may reflect differences in resources, technical capabilities, or pedagogical priorities across institutions.

Virtual reality experiences showed the lowest overall adoption rate at 36%, indicating that this technology is still in the early stages of implementation in peace education programs. Institution D again led with 60% adoption, while Institutions B and E reported only 20% implementation.

Institution D consistently showed the highest adoption rates across all AI technologies, suggesting a more advanced integration of AI in their peace education curriculum. In contrast, Institutions B and E generally reported lower adoption rates, which may indicate challenges in implementing AI technologies or different strategic priorities.

These findings provide valuable insights into the current landscape of AI integration in peace education programs and highlight areas for potential growth and development in using AI technologies across higher education institutions.

Table 2. Prevalence of AI technologies in peace education programs

AI Technology	Institution A	Institution B	Institution C	Institution D	Institution E	Overall
Adaptive Learning Systems	80%	60%	80%	100%	60%	76%
AI-powered Simulations	60%	40%	60%	80%	40%	56%
Virtual Reality Experiences	40%	20%	40%	60%	20%	36%
Chatbots for Student Support	100%	80%	100%	100%	80%	92%
AI-enhanced Assessment Tools	80%	60%	80%	100%	60%	76%

Impact of AI-Enhanced Peace Education on Student Learning Outcomes. Table 3 presents the results of paired t-tests comparing pre- and post-intervention scores for student participants on the Peace Education Outcome Assessment (PEOA).

The results demonstrate statistically significant improvements across all dimensions of the PEOA ($p < .001$), with moderate to large effect sizes (Cohen's d ranging from 0.66 to 0.82). These findings suggest that the integration of AI technologies in peace education curricula has a substantial positive impact on student learning outcomes.

The largest improvement was observed in the Knowledge Acquisition dimension, with a mean difference of 13.6 points between pre-test ($M = 65.3$, $SD = 12.7$) and post-test ($M = 78.9$, $SD = 10.5$) scores. This improvement yielded the largest effect size ($d = 0.82$), indicating that AI-enhanced peace education was particularly effective in facilitating the retention and understanding of factual information related to peace studies.

Critical Thinking skills also showed significant enhancement, with a mean difference of 11.7 points between pre-test ($M = 61.8$, $SD = 14.2$) and post-test ($M = 73.5$, $SD = 12.8$) scores and a large effect size ($d = 0.70$). This suggests that AI technologies effectively supported the development of higher-order thinking skills crucial for peace education.

Intercultural competence demonstrated notable improvement, with a mean difference of 11.6 points and an effect size of 0.72, indicating that AI-enhanced learning experiences contributed to students' ability to understand and navigate cultural differences.

While showing significant improvement (mean difference = 11.3, $d = 0.66$), conflict resolution skills had the smallest effect size among the dimensions. Nevertheless, this still represents a substantial positive change in students' ability to address and resolve conflicts.

The Overall PEOA Score, reflecting a composite of all dimensions, showed a significant increase of 12.0 points from the pre-test ($M = 62.4$, $SD = 13.1$) to the post-test ($M = 74.4$, $SD = 11.2$), with a large effect size ($d = 0.78$). This overall improvement underscores the comprehensive positive impact of AI-enhanced peace education on student learning outcomes.

These results provide strong evidence for the effectiveness of AI-enhanced peace education in improving students' knowledge, skills, and competencies across multiple dimensions relevant to peace studies. The consistent pattern of significant improvements with moderate to large effect sizes suggests that integrating AI technologies in peace education curricula can substantially enhance learning outcomes in higher education settings.

Table 3. Paired t-test results for peace education outcome assessment (PEOA)

Dimension	Pre-test Mean (SD)	Post-test Mean (SD)	Mean Difference	t-value	p-value	Cohen's d
Knowledge Acquisition	65.3 (12.7)	78.9 (10.5)	13.6	8.42	<.001	0.82
Critical Thinking	61.8 (14.2)	73.5 (12.8)	11.7	7.63	<.001	0.70
Conflict Resolution Skills	58.9 (15.6)	70.2 (13.9)	11.3	6.87	<.001	0.66
Intercultural Competence	63.5 (13.8)	75.1 (11.7)	11.6	7.21	<.001	0.72
Overall PEOA Score	62.4 (13.1)	74.4 (11.2)	12.0	8.53	<.001	0.78

Impact of AI-Enhanced Peace Education on Student Engagement and Motivation. The Engagement and Motivation subscale of the AI-Enhanced Peace Education Impact Survey (AIPEIS) was used to examine the impact of AI-enhanced peace education on student engagement and motivation. Table 4 presents the pre-and post-intervention scores for this subscale.

Table 4. Pre- and Post-intervention scores for AIPEIS engagement and motivation subscale

Item	Pre-test Mean (SD)	Post-test Mean (SD)	Mean Difference	t-value	p-value	Cohen's d
Interest in course content	3.8 (0.9)	4.5 (0.7)	0.7	12.84	<.001	0.57
Motivation to learn	3.7 (1.0)	4.3 (0.8)	0.6	10.93	<.001	0.49
Active participation	3.5 (1.1)	4.2 (0.9)	0.7	11.76	<.001	0.53
Time spent on coursework	3.4 (1.0)	4.0 (0.9)	0.6	10.21	<.001	0.46
Perceived relevance	3.9 (0.8)	4.6 (0.6)	0.7	13.57	<.001	0.61
Overall subscale score	3.7 (0.8)	4.3 (0.6)	0.6	12.89	<.001	0.58

The results indicate statistically significant increases in all aspects of student engagement and motivation ($p < .001$), with moderate effect sizes (Cohen's d ranging from 0.46 to 0.61). The largest improvements were observed in the perceived relevance of the course content and interest in the course content.

Relationship Between AI Integration and Learning Outcomes. Multiple regression analysis was employed to examine the relationship between the level of AI integration and learning outcomes. The dependent variable was the overall PEOA score, while the independent variables included the AIERS score and control variables such as age, gender, and academic discipline. Table 5 presents the results of this analysis.

Table 5. Multiple regression analysis: Predictors of overall PEOA score

Predictor	B	SE B	β	t	p
(Constant)	23.15	4.87	-	4.75	<.001
AIERS Score	0.62	0.07	0.41	8.86	<.001
Age	0.84	0.23	0.15	3.65	<.001
Gender (Female)	1.76	0.89	0.08	1.98	.048
Academic discipline (ref: Social Sciences)					
- Humanities	-0.93	1.12	-0.04	-0.83	.407
- STEM	2.18	1.24	0.08	1.76	.079
- Other	-1.37	1.57	-0.04	-0.87	.384

$R^2 = .247$, Adjusted $R^2 = .237$, $F(6, 493) = 26.93$, $p < .001$

The regression model explained 24.7% of the variance in PEOA scores ($R^2 = .247$, $F(6, 493) = 26.93$, $p < .001$). The AIERS score was the strongest predictor of PEOA scores ($\beta = 0.41$, $p < .001$), indicating that higher levels of AI integration were associated with better learning outcomes. Age also emerged as a significant predictor ($\beta = 0.15$, $p < .001$), with older students tending to achieve higher PEOA scores. Gender had a small but significant effect, with female students scoring slightly higher than male students ($\beta = 0.08$, $p = .048$). Academic discipline did not have a significant impact on PEOA scores.

Qualitative Findings

Thematic analysis of the interview data revealed several key themes: Enhanced Engagement and Interactivity, Personalized Learning Experiences, Development of Critical Thinking and Analysis Skills, Challenges in Implementation and Ethical Considerations.

Table 6 presents a comprehensive overview of the qualitative findings, highlighting the perspectives of both students and teachers on various aspects of AI-enhanced peace education. It reveals areas of consensus, such as the positive impact on engagement and critical thinking, as well as shared concerns about ethical implications and implementation challenges. The table also illustrates some differences in perspective, with teachers often focusing more on pedagogical implications while students emphasize personal learning experiences.

Table 6. Qualitative results: Views of students and educators on AI-Enhanced peace education

Theme	Students' Views	Educators' Views
Engagement and Interactivity	• "AI simulations made conflict scenarios feel real. We were in them, making decisions and seeing the consequences." (Student 7, Institution C) • "The VR experiences were mind-blowing. I felt like I was actually in a conflict zone, which made me take the peace-building exercises much more seriously." (Student 15, Institution A) • "I found myself spending more time on coursework because the AI system kept challenging me with new scenarios based on my responses." (Student 22, Institution E)	• "AI tools have significantly increased student engagement. They are more eager to participate in discussions after interacting with simulations." (Educator 3, Institution B) • "The level of interaction in class has improved dramatically. Students come prepared with questions and insights from their AI-guided explorations." (Educator 8, Institution D) • "I have noticed students are more emotionally invested in the material. The AI simulations seem to create a personal connection to global issues." (Educator 17, Institution A)
Personalized Learning	• "The AI system understood my weaknesses and provided resources to help me improve in those areas." (Student 18, Institution E) • "It was like having a personal tutor. The AI adapted the content to my learning pace, which made difficult concepts much easier to grasp." (Student 5, Institution B) • "I appreciated how the system remembered my interests and brought up relevant case studies in future lessons." (Student 11, Institution D)	• "AI has allowed me to tailor content to individual student needs, something I could not do effectively before." (Educator 15, Institution C) • "The AI's ability to track student progress has transformed how I approach remedial support. I can now address issues before they become major obstacles." (Educator 6, Institution E) • "Personalization has led to more meaningful assignments. Students are working on peace projects that truly resonate with their concerns." (Educator 20, Institution A)
Critical Thinking and Analysis	• "Working with AI-powered data analysis tools helped me understand complex conflict dynamics in new ways." (Student 22, Institution D) • "The AI challenged my assumptions by presenting counter-arguments I had not considered. It pushed me to think critically." (Student 3, Institution A) • "Using AI to simulate different conflict resolution strategies made me realize how complex these situations are. There is rarely a simple solution." (Student 19, Institution B)	• "I have observed improved critical thinking skills as students engage with AI-generated scenarios and data sets." (Educator 9, Institution D) • "The AI tools have enhanced students' ability to see patterns in conflict data that they might have missed otherwise." (Educator 12, Institution C) • "Students are becoming more adept at questioning sources and considering multiple perspectives, thanks to the AI's prompts and challenges." (Educator 2, Institution E)

continued on following page

Table 6. Continued

Theme	Students' Views	Educators' Views
Challenges in Implementation	• "Sometimes the technology was overwhelming. There were so many features that it took time away from engaging with the content." (Student 3, Institution B) • "Not everyone in my class was comfortable with the AI tools. It sometimes created a divide between the tech-savvy students and others." (Student 14, Institution C) • "I worried that relying too much on AI might mean missing out on valuable human interactions and discussions." (Student 8, Institution E)	• "Ensuring equitable access to AI technologies was a significant challenge." (Educator 22, Institution E) • "Keeping up with the rapid advancements in AI technology is demanding. It requires constant professional development." (Educator 5, Institution A) • "Integrating AI tools seamlessly into the curriculum required a significant time investment and a complete overhaul of my teaching methods." (Educator 18, Institution D)
Ethical Considerations	• "I worry about how my data is being used by these AI systems. Who has access to this information?" (Student 12, Institution A) • "The AI sometimes seemed to have biases in how it presented historical conflicts. It made me question the objectivity of the system." (Student 25, Institution D) • "I am concerned that over-reliance on AI might lead to a loss of human empathy in peace studies." (Student 1, Institution C)	• "We need to be cautious about potential biases in AI algorithms. Peace education is about challenging biases, not reinforcing them." (Educator 11, Institution D) • "Ensuring the ethical use of student data while leveraging AI's benefits is a constant balancing act." (Educator 7, Institution B) • "There is a risk of students becoming too dependent on AI for moral reasoning. We need to ensure they develop their ethical frameworks." (Educator 14, Institution C)

Integration of Quantitative and Qualitative Findings

Integrating quantitative and qualitative findings reveals a comprehensive picture of AI-enhanced peace education's impact on student learning practices in higher education (see Table 7). The data demonstrate strong convergence across several key themes:

1. Learning Outcomes: Significant quantitative improvements in PEOA scores, particularly in Knowledge Acquisition ($d = 0.82$) and Critical Thinking ($d = 0.70$), align with qualitative reports from students and educators about enhanced understanding of complex concepts and improved analytical skills.
2. Engagement and Motivation: Quantitative increases in the AIPEIS Engagement and Motivation subscale correspond with qualitative accounts of increased student participation and time spent on coursework. The largest effect size in perceived relevance ($d = 0.61$) is reflected in students' comments about AI-generated content's challenging and relevant nature.

3. Personalized Learning: The strong correlation between AIERS scores and PEOA scores ($\beta = 0.41$, $p < .001$) is supported by qualitative data highlighting AI's ability to tailor content to individual student needs, demonstrating the effectiveness of personalized learning experiences.
4. Critical Thinking and Analysis: The significant improvement in the Critical Thinking dimension of PEOA ($d = 0.70$) is corroborated by qualitative accounts of AI challenging assumptions and promoting multiple perspectives, indicating AI's role in developing higher-order thinking skills.

A partial divergence is observed in Implementation Challenges. While quantitative data shows varying adoption rates of AI technologies across institutions, qualitative findings reveal specific challenges not captured by the quantitative measures, such as technology overwhelm and equity concerns. This provides a more nuanced understanding of the implementation process.

Ethical Considerations emerged as a prominent theme in the qualitative data but were not directly measured in the quantitative phase, suggesting an area for future quantitative assessment and research.

Table 7. Integration of quantitative and qualitative findings

Theme	Quantitative Findings	Qualitative Findings	Integration
Learning Outcomes	Significant improvements in PEOA scores: - Knowledge Acquisition (d = 0.82) - Critical Thinking (d = 0.70) - Conflict Resolution Skills (d = 0.66) - Intercultural Competence (d = 0.72)	Students: "Working with AI-powered data analysis tools helped me understand complex conflict dynamics in new ways." (Student 22, Institution D) Educators: "I have observed improved critical thinking skills as students engage with AI-generated scenarios and data sets." (Educator 9, Institution D)	Convergence: Quantitative data shows significant improvements across all PEOA dimensions, supported by qualitative reports of enhanced understanding and critical thinking skills. The large effect size in Knowledge Acquisition (d = 0.82) aligns with students' reports of a deeper understanding of complex concepts.
Engagement and Motivation	Significant increases in AIPEIS Engagement and Motivation subscale: - Interest in course content (d = 0.57) - Motivation to learn (d = 0.49) - Active participation (d = 0.53) - Time spent on coursework (d = 0.46) - Perceived relevance (d = 0.61)	Students: "I found myself spending more time on coursework because the AI system kept challenging me with new scenarios based on my responses." (Student 22, Institution E) Educators: "AI tools have significantly increased student engagement. They're more eager to participate in discussions after interacting with simulations." (Educator 3, Institution B)	Convergence: Quantitative improvements in engagement metrics align with qualitative themes of increased interactivity and time spent on coursework. The largest effect size in perceived relevance (d = 0.61) is reflected in students' comments about AI-generated content's challenging and relevant nature.

continued on following page

Table 7. Continued

Theme	Quantitative Findings	Qualitative Findings	Integration
Personalized Learning	Strong positive correlation between AIERS scores and PEOA scores (β = 0.41, p < .001)	Students: "The AI system understood my weaknesses and provided resources to help me improve in those areas." (Student 18, Institution E) Educators: "AI has allowed me to tailor content to individual student needs, something I could not do effectively before." (Educator 15, Institution C)	Convergence: The strong quantitative relationship between AI integration and learning outcomes is explained by qualitative reports of personalized learning experiences. Both data sets highlight the effectiveness of AI in tailoring educational content to individual needs.
Critical Thinking and Analysis	Significant improvement in Critical Thinking dimension of PEOA (d = 0.70)	Students: "The AI challenged my assumptions by presenting counter-arguments I had not considered. It pushed me to think critically." (Student 3, Institution A) Educators: "Students are becoming more adept at questioning sources and considering multiple perspectives, thanks to the AI's prompts and challenges." (Educator 2, Institution E)	Convergence: The large effect size in Critical Thinking is supported by qualitative accounts of AI challenging assumptions and promoting multiple perspectives. Quantitative and qualitative data suggest AI's effectiveness in developing higher-order thinking skills.
Implementation Challenges	Varied adoption rates of AI technologies across institutions (e.g., Chatbots: 92%, VR Experiences: 36%)	Students: "Sometimes the technology was overwhelming. There were so many features that it took time away from engaging with the content." (Student 3, Institution B) Educators: "Ensuring equitable access to AI technologies was a significant challenge." (Educator 22, Institution E)	Partial Divergence: While quantitative data shows varying adoption rates, qualitative data reveals specific challenges not captured in the quantitative measures. This provides a more nuanced understanding of implementation issues, such as technology overwhelm and equity concerns.
Ethical Considerations	Not directly measured in the quantitative phase		

This integration of findings underscores the value of a mixed-methods approach in capturing the multifaceted nature of AI-enhanced peace education, providing both measurable outcomes and rich contextual insights.

DISCUSSION

This study examined the impact of AI-enhanced peace education on student learning practices in higher education. The findings reveal a complex picture of both opportunities and challenges associated with integrating AI technologies in peace education curricula. This section interprets the key findings, compares them with existing literature, and discusses their implications for practice and future research.

Interpretation of Findings

Prevalence and Diversity of AI Technologies in Peace Education. The results indicate various AI integration across institutions, with chatbots for student support being the most widely adopted technology (92% overall), followed by adaptive learning systems (76%). This variability in adoption rates aligns with previous research on implementing educational technologies in higher education (Zawacki-Richter et al., 2019). The high prevalence of chatbots suggests that institutions are prioritizing technologies that can provide immediate, scalable support to students. However, the lower adoption rates of more complex technologies like virtual reality experiences (36%) indicate that there may be barriers to implementing more resource-intensive AI applications.

Impact on Learning Outcomes. The significant improvements observed across all dimensions of the Peace Education Outcome Assessment (PEOA) suggest that AI-enhanced peace education can positively impact student learning outcomes. The largest improvement in the Knowledge Acquisition dimension (mean difference = 13.6) indicates that AI technologies may be particularly effective in facilitating the retention and understanding of factual information related to peace studies. This finding is consistent with previous research on the effectiveness of adaptive learning systems in improving knowledge acquisition (VanLehn, 2011).

The moderate to large effect sizes observed (Cohen's d ranging from 0.66 to 0.82) are noteworthy, suggesting that the impact of AI-enhanced peace education is statistically significant and practically meaningful. These results support the potential of AI to transform educational practices in the field of peace studies.

Engagement and Motivation. The significant increases in student engagement and motivation, as measured by the AIPEIS subscale, corroborate the qualitative findings highlighting the immersive and interactive nature of AI-enhanced learning experiences. The largest improvements in perceived relevance and interest in course content suggest that AI technologies may be particularly effective in making peace education more engaging and applicable to students' lives and future careers. This aligns with previous research on the motivational benefits of technology-enhanced learning environments (Tsai et al., 2020).

Personalization of Learning. The strong predictive relationship between AI integration (as measured by AIERS scores) and learning outcomes (PEOA scores) underscores the potential of AI to provide personalized learning experiences in peace education. This finding is consistent with the qualitative theme of personalized learning experiences and supports previous research on the benefits of adaptive learning systems in higher education (Kulik & Fletcher, 2016). The ability of AI to tailor content, pace, and difficulty to individual student needs appears to be a key factor in its effectiveness in peace education contexts.

Development of Critical Thinking and Analysis Skills. The qualitative findings emphasize the development of critical thinking and analysis skills through AI-powered simulations and data analysis tools, which are particularly relevant to the goals of peace education. These findings suggest that AI technologies can go beyond mere knowledge transmission to facilitate higher-order thinking skills essential for conflict resolution and peace-building. This aligns with the objectives of critical peace education as outlined by Bajaj and Hantzopoulos (2016), which emphasize the importance of developing analytical and problem-solving skills in addressing complex global issues.

Challenges and Ethical Considerations. The challenges identified in the qualitative data, such as technology overwhelm and issues of equitable access, highlight important considerations for implementing AI in peace education. These findings echo concerns raised in the broader literature on educational technology adoption (Selwyn, 2019). The ethical considerations surrounding data privacy and potential algorithmic bias are particularly pertinent to peace education, which aims to promote equity and social justice. These concerns underscore the need for careful consideration of the ethical implications of AI integration in educational contexts.

Comparison with Existing Literature

The findings of this study both support and extend previous research on AI in education and peace education in higher education. The positive impact on learning outcomes aligns with meta-analyses of AI-enhanced learning in other disciplines (e.g., Kulik & Fletcher, 2016). However, this study provides novel insights into AI's specific applications and effects in peace education, which has received limited attention in previous research.

The emphasis on personalized learning experiences in our findings echoes the work of Holmes et al. (2019) on AI-enabled personalization in education. However, our study extends this work by demonstrating how personalization can be applied specifically to peace education contexts, where understanding diverse perspectives and adapting to complex scenarios is crucial.

Developing critical thinking and analysis skills through AI-enhanced simulations and data analysis tools aligns with the goals of peace education as outlined by Reardon (1988) and Harris and Morrison (2013). Findings suggest that AI technologies can serve as powerful tools in achieving these educational objectives, providing students with opportunities to engage with complex conflict scenarios in ways that were previously difficult to simulate in traditional classroom settings.

This study's challenges and ethical considerations reflect broader debates in AI ethics in education (Fenwick & Edwards, 2016). However, findings highlight the ethical concerns when applying AI to peace education, where bias, equity and social justice are central to the curriculum.

Implications for Practice

Based on the findings of this study, several implications for practice in AI-enhanced peace education can be identified:

1. Gradual and strategic implementation: Given the varying levels of AI adoption across institutions, a gradual and strategic approach to implementing AI technologies in peace education programs is recommended. Starting with widely adopted technologies like chatbots and adaptive learning systems may provide a foundation for more complex implementations in the future.
2. Focus on personalization: The strong relationship between AI integration and learning outcomes suggests that peace education programs should prioritize AI technologies that offer personalized learning experiences. This may include adaptive learning systems that tailor content and pacing to individual student needs.
3. Integration of simulations and data analysis tools: The qualitative findings on developing critical thinking skills suggest that peace education programs should incorporate AI-powered simulations and data analysis tools. These technologies allow students to apply theoretical knowledge to realistic scenarios and develop analytical skills crucial for peace-building.

4. Professional development for educators: To address the challenges identified in implementation, institutions should invest in professional development programs to enhance educators' technological literacy and ability to integrate AI tools into their teaching practices effectively.
5. Ethical guidelines and transparency: Given the ethical concerns of participants, institutions should develop clear guidelines for using AI in peace education, ensuring transparency in data collection and use, and implementing safeguards against potential biases in AI systems.
6. Promotion of digital equity: To address issues of equitable access, institutions should develop strategies to ensure that all students have access to the necessary technologies and support to engage with AI-enhanced peace education curricula fully.

SUMMARY, CONCLUSION AND RECOMMENDATIONS

This chapter has explored the impact of AI-enhanced peace education on student learning practices in higher education, comprehensively examining its potential, challenges, and implications. It is essential to synthesize the key findings, highlight the contributions to the field, and offer recommendations for future research and practice.

Summary of Key Findings

Integrating AI technologies in peace education programs has demonstrated significant potential to enhance student learning outcomes, engagement, and critical thinking skills. Key findings from this study include:

1. There are varied adoption of AI technologies across institutions, with chatbots and adaptive learning systems being the most widely implemented.
2. Significant improvements in student learning outcomes across all dimensions of peace education, particularly in knowledge acquisition and critical thinking skills.
3. Enhanced student engagement and motivation, with AI technologies making peace education more interactive and relevant to students' lives.
4. Strong evidence for the effectiveness of personalized learning experiences facilitated by AI leads to improved learning outcomes.
5. Developing critical thinking and analysis skills through AI-powered simulations and data analysis tools is crucial for addressing complex peace and conflict issues.

6. Identification of implementation challenges, including technology overwhelm and issues of equitable access.
7. Ethical considerations surrounding data privacy and potential algorithmic bias in AI systems used for peace education.

These findings collectively suggest that AI has the potential to transform peace education in higher education settings, offering new ways to engage students, personalize learning experiences, and develop essential skills for peace-building.

Contributions to the Fields of Peace Education and Educational Technology

This study makes several significant contributions to the fields of peace education and educational technology:

1. It provides empirical evidence on the effectiveness of AI-enhanced peace education, addressing a gap in the literature at the intersection of AI, education, and peace studies.
2. The study offers insights into how AI technologies can be specifically applied to peace education contexts, moving beyond general applications of AI in education.
3. It highlights the potential of AI to develop critical thinking and analysis skills crucial for peace-building, demonstrating how technology can support the core objectives of peace education.
4. The research identifies key challenges and ethical considerations for using AI in peace education, contributing to broader discussions on responsible AI implementation in educational settings.
5. The mixed-methods approach provides a comprehensive understanding of both the quantitative impacts and qualitative experiences of AI-enhanced peace education, offering a nuanced view of its effects.

CONCLUSION

The intersection of technological innovation and peace education and AI's potential to transform how the next generation is being prepared to be peacebuilders is both exciting and challenging. This study has demonstrated that AI-enhanced peace education can significantly improve learning outcomes, engagement, and critical thinking skills for addressing complex global conflicts.

However, the path forward requires careful navigation of ethical considerations, implementation challenges, and the need for equitable access. As educators, researchers, and practitioners in peace education, AI's integration must be seen cautiously to balance its potential and manifest critical awareness of its limitations and ethical implications.

The future of peace education in the AI era will depend on our ability to harness the power of technology while staying true to the core values of peace, justice, and human dignity. Integrating AI into our educational practices creates more dynamic, engaging, and effective learning experiences that prepare students to become skilled peacebuilders in an increasingly complex

In conclusion, this study demonstrates the significant potential of AI-enhanced peace education to improve learning outcomes, increase student engagement, and develop critical thinking skills essential for peace-building. However, it highlights important challenges and ethical considerations that must be addressed as AI technologies become more prevalent in higher education. By carefully navigating these opportunities and challenges, educators and institutions can harness the power of AI to create more effective, engaging, and impactful peace education programs for the next generation of peacebuilders.

Recommendations for Future Research and Practice

Based on the findings and limitations of this study, the following recommendations for future research and practice are being offered:

Research Recommendations:
1. Explore the effectiveness of specific AI technologies (e.g., virtual reality, machine learning algorithms) in peace education.
2. Investigate the ethical implications of AI use in peace education, including data privacy, algorithmic bias, and power dynamics.
3. Examine how cultural differences influence the effectiveness and reception of AI-enhanced peace education across diverse global contexts.
4. Study the integration of AI literacy into peace education curricula to prepare students for critical engagement with AI technologies in future peace-building work.

Practice Recommendations:
1. Prioritize AI technologies that offer personalized learning experiences, such as adaptive learning systems tailored to individual student needs.

2. Incorporate AI-powered simulations and data analysis tools to develop student's critical thinking and analytical skills in complex peace and conflict scenarios.
3. Invest in professional development programs to enhance educators' technological literacy and ability to integrate AI tools into peace education curricula effectively.
4. Develop clear ethical guidelines and transparency measures for using AI in peace education, addressing concerns about data privacy and algorithmic bias.
5. Implement strategies to ensure equitable access to AI-enhanced peace education, addressing potential disparities in technological access and literacy among students.

REFERENCES

American Educational Research Association. (2011). Code of ethics. *Educational Researcher*, 40(3), 145–156. DOI: 10.3102/0013189X11410403

Artino, A. R.Jr, La Rochelle, J. S., Dezee, K. J., & Gehlbach, H. (2014). Developing questionnaires for educational research: AMEE Guide No. 87. *Medical Teacher*, 36(6), 463–474. DOI: 10.3109/0142159X.2014.889814 PMID: 24661014

Bajaj, M. (2015). 'Pedagogies of resistance' and critical peace education praxis. *Journal of Peace Education*, 12(2), 154–166. DOI: 10.1080/17400201.2014.991914

Bajaj, M., & Hantzopoulos, M. (Eds.). (2016). *Peace education: International perspectives*. Bloomsbury Academic.

Bandura, A. (1977). *Social learning theory*. Prentice Hall.

Biggs, J., & Tang, C. (2011). *Teaching for quality learning at university* (4th ed.). Open University Press.

Brantmeier, E. J. (2013). Pedagogy of vulnerability: Definitions, assumptions, and applications. In Lin, J., Oxford, R. L., & Brantmeier, E. J. (Eds.), *Re-envisioning higher education: Embodied pathways to wisdom and social transformation* (pp. 95–106). Information Age Publishing.

Braun, V., & Clarke, V. (2006). Using thematic analysis in psychology. *Qualitative Research in Psychology*, 3(2), 77–101. DOI: 10.1191/1478088706qp063oa

Byram, M., & Wagner, M. (2018). Making a difference: Language teaching for intercultural and international dialogue. *Foreign Language Annals*, 51(1), 140–151. DOI: 10.1111/flan.12319

Chatti, M. A., Muslim, A., & Schroeder, U. (2019). Toward an open learning analytics ecosystem. In Ifenthaler, D., Mah, D. K., & Yau, J. Y. K. (Eds.), *Utilizing learning analytics to support study success* (pp. 195–212). Springer.

Creswell, J. W., & Plano Clark, V. L. (2017). *Designing and conducting mixed methods research* (3rd ed.). SAGE Publications.

Cuhadar, E., & Kampf, R. (2014). Learning about conflict and negotiations through computer simulations: The case of PeaceMaker. *International Studies Perspectives*, 15(4), 509–524. DOI: 10.1111/insp.12076

Fenwick, T., & Edwards, R. (2016). Exploring the impact of digital technologies on professional responsibilities and education. *European Educational Research Journal*, 15(1), 117–131. DOI: 10.1177/1474904115608387

Freire, P. (1970). Pedagogy of the oppressed. *Continuum : an Interdisciplinary Journal on Continuity of Care*.

Glaser, B. G., & Strauss, A. L. (1967). *The discovery of grounded theory: Strategies for qualitative research*. Aldine.

Guetterman, T. C., Fetters, M. D., & Creswell, J. W. (2015). Integrating quantitative and qualitative results in health science mixed methods research through joint displays. *Annals of Family Medicine*, 13(6), 554–561. DOI: 10.1370/afm.1865 PMID: 26553895

Harris, I. M. (2004). Peace education theory. *Journal of Peace Education*, 1(1), 5–20. DOI: 10.1080/1740020032000178276

Harris, I. M., & Morrison, M. L. (2013). *Peace education* (3rd ed.). McFarland & Company.

Holmes, W., Bialik, M., & Fadel, C. (2019). *Artificial intelligence in education: Promises and implications for teaching and learning*. Center for Curriculum Redesign.

Johnson, R. B., Onwuegbuzie, A. J., & Turner, L. A. (2007). Toward a definition of mixed methods research. *Journal of Mixed Methods Research*, 1(2), 112–133. DOI: 10.1177/1558689806298224

Kester, K., & Cremin, H. (2017). Peace education and peace education research: Toward a concept of poststructural violence and second-order reflexivity. *Educational Philosophy and Theory*, 49(14), 1415–1427. DOI: 10.1080/00131857.2017.1313715

Kulik, J. A., & Fletcher, J. D. (2016). Effectiveness of intelligent tutoring systems: A meta-analytic review. *Review of Educational Research*, 86(1), 42–78. DOI: 10.3102/0034654315581420

Luckin, R., Holmes, W., Griffiths, M., & Forcier, L. B. (2016). *Intelligence unleashed: An argument for AI in education*. Pearson.

Reardon, B. (1988). *Comprehensive peace education: Educating for global responsibility*. Teachers College Press.

Roll, I., & Wylie, R. (2016). Evolution and revolution in artificial intelligence in education. *International Journal of Artificial Intelligence in Education*, 26(2), 582–599. DOI: 10.1007/s40593-016-0110-3

Scherer, R., Siddiq, F., & Tondeur, J. (2019). The technology acceptance model (TAM): A meta-analytic structural equation modeling approach to explaining teachers' adoption of digital technology in education. *Computers & Education*, 128, 13–35. DOI: 10.1016/j.compedu.2018.09.009

Schrodt, P. A., Yilmaz, Ö., Gerner, D. J., & Hermrick, D. (2014). The CAMEO (Conflict and Mediation Event Observations) actor coding framework. *International Studies Perspectives*, 15(1), 145–161.

Selwyn, N. (2019). *Should robots replace teachers? AI and the future of education.* Polity Press.

Siemens, G., & Long, P. (2011). Penetrating the fog: Analytics in learning and education. *EDUCAUSE Review*, 46(5), 30–40.

Teddlie, C., & Tashakkori, A. (2009). *Foundations of mixed methods research: Integrating quantitative and qualitative approaches in the social and behavioral sciences.* SAGE Publications.

Tsai, Y. S., Poquet, O., Gašević, D., Dawson, S., & Pardo, A. (2020). Complexity leadership in learning analytics: Drivers, challenges and opportunities. *British Journal of Educational Technology*, 51(6), 2304–2320. DOI: 10.1111/bjet.12846

VanLehn, K. (2011). The relative effectiveness of human tutoring, intelligent tutoring systems, and other tutoring systems. *Educational Psychologist*, 46(4), 197–221. DOI: 10.1080/00461520.2011.611369

Vygotsky, L. S. (1978). *Mind in society: The development of higher psychological processes.* Harvard University Press.

Winkler, R., & Söllner, M. (2018). Unleashing the potential of chatbots in education: A state-of-the-art analysis. In *Academy of Management Annual Meeting Proceedings* (Vol. 2018, No. 1, p. 15903). https://doi.org/DOI: 10.5465/AMBPP.2018.15903abstract

Zawacki-Richter, O., Marín, V. I., Bond, M., & Gouverneur, F. (2019). Systematic review of research on artificial intelligence applications in higher education – where are the educators? *International Journal of Educational Technology in Higher Education*, 16(1), 39. DOI: 10.1186/s41239-019-0171-0

Chapter 6
Artificial Intelligence:
An Educational Advancement for Students With Visual Disabilities

Mansi Trivedi

https://orcid.org/0000-0001-5959-8324

Amity Law School, Amity University, Noida, India

Shantanu Bindewari

https://orcid.org/0000-0002-7048-5221

IILM University, India

ABSTRACT

A lot of industries, including education, are fast changing due to artificial intelligence (AI). Artificial Intelligence (AI) is evolving into a potent tool for meeting a variety of educational needs because to its ability to handle enormous volumes of data, recognize patterns, and carry out difficult tasks. One of its most exciting uses is the assistance it gives visually impaired pupils, giving them more chances to study, be involved, and be independent. Traditional teaching strategies and resources can provide serious difficulties for pupils who are visually impaired. A heavy emphasis on visual materials—like textbooks, whiteboards, and computer screens—can make it difficult for students to learn and participate.

DOI: 10.4018/979-8-3693-8191-5.ch006

1. INTRODUCTION

1.1. Understanding Visual Disabilities

1.1.1 Definition and Categories of Visual Impairments

Visual Impairment is a general term for all forms of vision issues (Wang, Wang, & Zhang, 2023; Luo & Pundlik, 2022) minor to severe, that impair a person's ability to see clearly. It can range from partial visual loss to total blindness. Blindness is the entire lack of vision (Luo & Pundlik, 2022) or very restricted vision, which is commonly characterized as the inability to perceive light or discern any visual features. A condition in which a person's eyesight is significantly reduced and cannot be rectified with ordinary glasses, contact lenses, or medical therapies (Wang, Wang, & Zhang, 2023).

1.1.2 Categories of Visual Impairments

1. **Blindness:** Total Blindness is complete lack of vision, often known as no light perception. Functional blindness occurs when a person's eyesight (Pundlik, Shivshanker, & Luo, 2023) is substantially damaged, limiting their ability to do daily chores.
2. **Low Vision:** Central vision (Luo & Pundlik, 2022; Nguyen, Weismann, & Trauzettel-Klosinski, 2009) loss causes difficulty seeing objects directly in front of you while peripheral vision stays intact. Common in situations such as macular degeneration. Peripheral Vision Loss is the difficulty seeing objects at the outside borders of your visual field, as in glaucoma or retinitis pigmentosa. Night Blindness (Nguyen, Weismann, & Trauzettel-Klosinski, 2009; Moshtael, Aslam, Underwood, & Dhillon, 2015; Deemer et al., 2018) is the difficulty seeing in low light or darkness, which can impair activities such as driving at night.
3. **Color Vision Deficiency (Color Blindness):** Red-Green Colour Blindness: The most prevalent type, in which discriminating between red and green hues is difficult. Blue-Yellow Colour Blindness is a less common condition characterised by difficulty differentiating blue and yellow hues. Total Colour Blindness is an extremely rare condition in which no colours are perceived at all (Luo & Pundlik, 2022; Moshtael, Aslam, Underwood, & Dhillon, 2015).
4. **Refractive Errors:** Myopia (nearsightedness) causes difficulty seeing distant objects hyperopia (farsightedness) causes difficulty seeing close objects. Astigmatism is a vision distortion caused by an irregularly shaped cornea or lens that affects both near and distance vision. Presbyopia is an age-related condition

where the eye's lens becomes less flexible, making it difficult to focus on close objects (Deemer et al., 2018)

5. **Other Visual Impairments:** Double vision (diplopia) is the perception of two images of the same object, which can be caused by problems with the eye muscles or nerves. Tunnel Vision: Severe loss of peripheral vision (Luo & Pundlik, 2022) results in a limited field of view. Visual Field Loss is the category includes disorders like hemianopia.

Figure 1. Categories of Visual Impairments

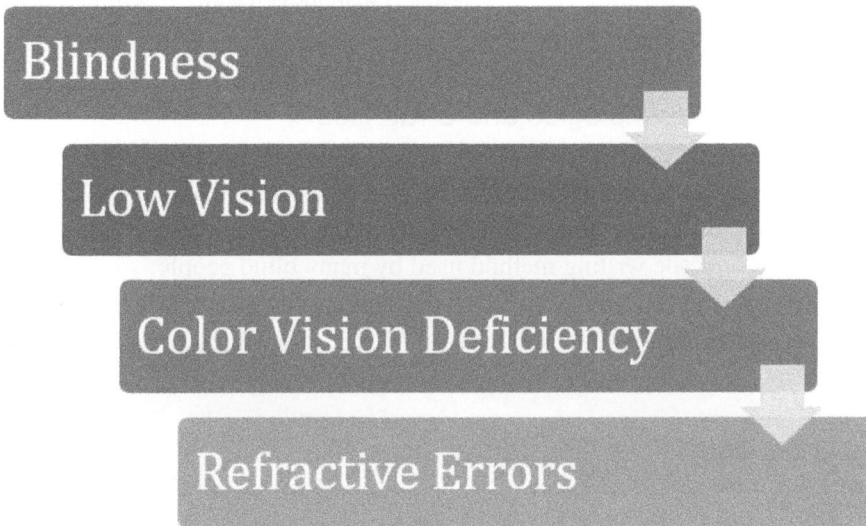

Severity and Impact: simple vision issues that can be resolved with corrective glasses or simple changes. Moderate visual impairment refers to significant vision problems that may necessitate the use of specialised instruments or strategies. Significant vision (Luo & Pundlik, 2022; Nguyen, Weismann, & Trauzettel-Klosinski, 2009) problems that interfere with daily functioning and may necessitate the use of adaptive devices or help.

1.1.3 Causes of Visual Disabilities

● Genetic conditions include retinitis pigmentosa and congenital cataracts.
● Diseases include diabetic retinopathy, glaucoma, and macular degeneration.

- Injuries: Trauma to the eye or head can cause vision (Luo & Pundlik, 2022) loss.
- Age-related changes include presbyopia (difficulty focusing on close things), which is common as we age.

1.1.4 Impact on Daily Life

- Difficulty moving around safely, necessitating the use of mobility aids such as white canes or guide dogs. Large print books, audiobooks, and screen readers can help to alleviate issues with traditional print sources. Visual impairments can disrupt social dynamics (Oyewumi, Isaiah, & Adigun, 2015) but adaptive communication tactics and technologies can help bridge the gap.

1.1.5 Assistive Technologies and Strategies

- Screen Readers: Software that reads text from a screen (Ahmadi, 2023).
- Magnification devices are tools or software that expand text and images.
- Braille is a tactile writing method used by many blind people.
- Voice-Controlled Technology: Devices and applications that can be operated via voice commands (Deemer et al., 2018; Pundlik, Shivshanker, & Luo, 2023).

1.1.6 Legal and Social Considerations

Various countries have laws in place to ensure accessibility in public venues, transportation, and digital material. Individuals with visual difficulties benefit greatly from inclusion in social and educational contexts (Zaraii Zavaraki, 2024; Oyewumi, Isaiah, & Adigun, 2015).

1.1.7 Promoting Inclusivity

Recognizing the needs and talents of people with visual difficulties promotes inclusivity and reduces stigma. Adaptive Design: Creating accessible environments, goods, and services benefits everyone, not just people with impairments (Ceoca & Dulf, 2024).

1.1.8 Global Statistics on Visual Disabilities Among Students

Global data on students (Zavaraki & Alimardani, 2023) with visual difficulties provide a sense of the group's prevalence and challenges. While precise estimates can vary by source and area, several significant data sources offer insight into the extent of visual problems.

Prevalence: The World Health Organisation (WHO) estimates that over 2.2 billion people worldwide suffer from vision impairment or blindness. While this figure covers people of all ages, children and adolescents are disproportionately affected. The World Health Organisation estimates that almost 19 million children under 15 have vision impairment (Luo & Pundlik, 2022; Nguyen, Weismann, & Trauzettel-Klosinski, 2009; Moshtael, Aslam, Underwood, & Dhillon, 2015). This image depicts disorders ranging from minor visual impairment to profound blindness.

1.1.9 Educational Impact

1. **Access to Education**: Children with visual difficulties frequently encounter barriers to receiving a quality education. According to UNESCO, almost 90% of children with impairments in underdeveloped countries do not attend school. In more developed locations, inclusive education policies and specialised programs are more frequent, although they are not without obstacles.
2. **Enrollment and Attendance:** According to data from the World Blind Union, pupils with visual impairments are significantly under-represented in education systems around the world.
3. **Educational Achievements:** Students with visual impairments frequently confront problems that have an influence on academic achievement, such as limited access to specialised educational (Zaraii Zavaraki, 2024) resources, technology, and qualified educators.

1.1.10 Regional Differences

1. Developed Countries: In countries with highly developed educational systems, students with visual impairments are more likely to be integrated into regular schools or special education programs. For example, in the United States, the National Centre for Education Statistics (NCES) says that approximately 1.2% of pupils get special education services for visual impairments.
2. Developing Countries: Many low- and middle-income countries have inadequate educational opportunities (Zaraii Zavaraki, 2024) for students (Zavaraki & Alimardani, 2023) with visual difficulties. The challenges include a lack of specialised schools, inadequate teacher training, and insufficient funding.

1.1.11 Initiatives and Support

○ **Inclusive Education:** There is a global movement towards inclusive education, which seeks to integrate children with visual difficulties into mainstream classes by providing necessary supports and accommodations.
○ **Assistive Technology:** Assistive technology advancements such as screen readers, braille e-books, and magnification equipment are contributing to better educational results for students with visual disabilities (Deemer et al., 2018).

Advocacy and Policy: Organisations such as the World Health Organisation, UNESCO, and numerous non-governmental organisations (NGOs) are striving to raise awareness, enhance access to education, and advocate for the rights of students with visual disabilities.

2. THE ROLE OF TECHNOLOGY IN EDUCATION FOR STUDENTS WITH DISABILITIES

Technology has a transformative impact on education for students (Zavaraki & Alimardani, 2023) with disabilities, giving tools and solutions that improve learning experiences (Zavaraki & Schneider, 2019), accessibility, and participation.

2.1 Assistive Technologies

a. **Screen Readers:** Software such as JAWS (Job Access With Speech) and NVDA (NonVisual Desktop Access) read text aloud from screens, allowing visually (Singh et al., 2023) challenged pupils to access digital content.
b. **Text-to-Speech (TTS):** Converts written text to spoken word. Students with reading challenges benefit from tools such as Google Text-to-Speech and Natural Reader, which provide aural input.
c. **Speech Recognition:** Dragon Naturally Speaking software enables students to manage their gadgets and enter text using voice commands, which is especially useful for people with motor disabilities or dyslexia.
d. **Magnification Software:** Programs like ZoomText magnify text and images on the screen, making it easier for students (Zavaraki & Alimardani, 2023) with impaired vision (NuEyes, n.d.) to view and interact with digital content.

e. **Braille Displays and Notetakers:** Braille embossers and electronic braille notetakers allow blind pupils to read and write in braille, increasing access to educational materials (Deemer et al., 2018; Pundlik, Shivshanker, & Luo, 2023).

Figure 2. Types of Assistive Technologies

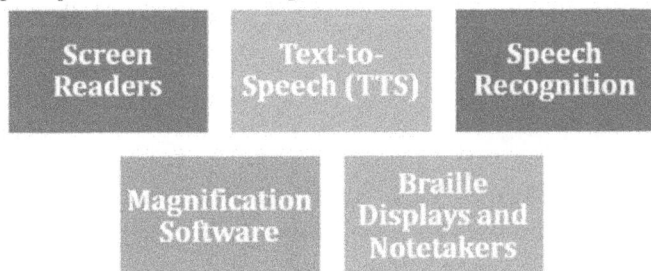

Screen Readers	Text-to-Speech (TTS)	Speech Recognition
Magnification Software	Braille Displays and Notetakers	

2. **Educational Apps and Software:** Apps such as Ghotit Real Writer for dyslexia and ModMath for children with dysgraphia give specialised support for individual learning requirements (Oyewumi, Isaiah, & Adigun, 2015). Tools such as SMART Boards can be tailored to accommodate different learning styles and disabilities, providing interactive and engaging ways to acquire knowledge. Apps and software that provide visual calendars and social stories assist kids with autism (Ahmadi, 2023) spectrum disorders in understanding routines and social interactions (Deemer et al., 2018).

2.2 Online Learning Platforms

a. **E-Learning Tools:** Platforms such as Khan Academy and Coursera provide a variety of accessible content, including subtitles and audio descriptions, which can be beneficial to students with varying learning requirements.
b. **Virtual Classrooms:** Remote learning tools such as Zoom and Microsoft Teams include screen sharing, live captioning, and breakout rooms, allowing for inclusive education regardless of physical location (Mina et al., 2023; Oyewumi, Isaiah, & Adigun, 2015).

2.3 Customizable Learning Environments

Systems that modify the level of difficulty and content kinds in response to individual student requirements and progress, allowing education to be tailored to each student's skills (Zavaraki & Schneider, 2019). Many educational technologies and platforms allow users to change text size, colour contrast, and layout, making content more accessible to students with visual or cognitive challenges.

2.4 Accessibility Features

a. **Built-In Device Features:** Many current gadgets include built-in accessibility capabilities like voice control, magnification, and closed captioning, which can be used to meet a variety of learning needs.
b. **Web Accessibility:** Adhering to web accessibility standards (e.g., WCAG) ensures that online educational content is accessible to students with impairments, including those who use assistive technologies (Deemer et al., 2018; Pundlik, Shivshanker, & Luo, 2023).

2.5 Current and Future Directions

Modern assistive technologies are increasingly focused on connecting with daily gadgets and tailoring solutions to match specific needs. Universal design concepts are becoming increasingly important, with the goal of creating goods and places that are accessible to all users, including those with impairments. The history of assistive devices reveals an ongoing process of innovation and adaptation. From early manual aids to sophisticated digital solutions, these technologies have had a significant impact on the lives of individuals with disabilities, encouraging independence, accessibility, and inclusion.

3. THE EMERGENCE OF ARTIFICIAL INTELLIGENCE IN EDUCATION

3.1 Overview of AI and its Applications in General Education

Artificial intelligence (AI) is the replication of human intelligence in robots that think and learn similarly to humans. It includes a variety of technologies such as machine learning, natural language processing, robotics, and computer vision (Ehrlich, Spaeth, Carlozzi, & Lee, 2017). AI systems can do activities that need human intelligence, such as language comprehension, pattern recognition, and decision making.

3.1.1 Applications of AI in General Education

- **Personalized Learning:** AI-powered platforms, such as DreamBox and Smart Sparrow, modify educational content and activities to individual students' requirements and learning paces, offering personalised feedback and adjusting difficulty levels in response to performance.
- **Intelligent Tutoring Systems:** Tools such as Carnegie Learning's MATHia and Khan Academy's AI-powered features provide personalised tuition in topics such as math and language arts, with rapid feedback and support available outside of typical classroom hours (Rani et al., 2024).
- **Administrative Efficiency:** AI systems can evaluate assignments and tests quickly and consistently, allowing teachers to focus on more interactive and creative parts of education.
- **Scheduling and Resource Management:** AI can optimise scheduling and resource allocation, resulting in more efficient use of educational resources and time.
- **Enhanced Engagement:** AI-powered educational games and simulations, such as those available in platforms like Classcraft, use gamification and immersive experiences to make learning more interesting and interactive.
- **Virtual Assistant:** AI chatbots and virtual assistants can offer students 24-hour support, answer queries, and direct them to learning materials (Mina et al., 2023; Walle, Serres, Gilles, & De Runz, 2022).
- **Language Processing and Translation:** Language Learning: Artificial intelligence applications such as Duolingo employ natural language processing to assist students in learning new languages through interactive activities and adaptive feedback. AI-powered translation services, such as Google Translate, aid in the removal of language barriers in multilingual classrooms, allowing for improved communication and resource access.
- **Special Education Support:** Assistive Technologies: AI tools help students with impairments by providing adaptive technologies such as speech-to-text software, text-to-speech programs, and personalised learning aids that are tailored to their specific needs.
- **Customised Learning Materials:** AI can provide tailored educational materials and tactics to solve specific learning obstacles encountered by students with varying needs.
- **Data-Driven Insights:** AI analyses data from many sources (e.g., student performance, attendance) to forecast future outcomes and identify potential

areas of concern, allowing for preemptive interventions. Artificial intelligence systems monitor and analyse student behaviour and participation, assisting educators in identifying patterns and adapting instructional tactics.

3.1.2 Professional Development for Educators

AI can suggest professional development materials and training programs depending on teachers' requirements and areas for improvement. AI systems help teachers control classroom dynamics by analysing student interactions and providing insights into effective management techniques.

3.1.3 Challenges and Considerations

1. **Data Privacy:** The application of AI in education necessitates the collection and analysis of student data, raising privacy and security concerns. It is critical to ensure data security and ethical use.
2. **Integration and Training:** To successfully apply AI in education, educators must be properly integrated with current systems and receive enough training in order to use and harness these technologies efficiently.
3. **Cost and Accessibility:** The development and deployment of AI technologies can be costly, and it is critical that these tools are available to all schools, including those with minimal resources.

4. LITERATURE REVIEW

In their paper The use of artificial intelligence in the education of people with visual impairments, Aikaterini Tsouktakou et al. provide a concise overview of current research on the use of AI in the education of individuals with visual impairments and whether it can help them have equal access to all educational levels and improve their quality of life. For a more thorough examination of the application of AI as an assistive technology, it also offers a case study, the "PeopleLens" system (Tsouktakou, Hamouroudis, & Horti, 2024).

In his paper Artificial Intelligence for Visually Impaired, Jiaji Wang discusses new studies on the creation of visual aids and artificial intelligence-based eye illness detection. According to the study's objectives, the research is separated into two categories: smart devices that assist visually impaired people in their daily lives and deep learning techniques used in the diagnosis of eye disorders. A synopsis of the potential future directions for artificial intelligence to help the blind and visually handicapped is provided at the end (Wang, Wang, & Zhang, 2023)

In their work, Shalini Garg and Shipra Sharma discuss how AI has affected special education. Focused interviews with instructors and kids with special needs were employed in qualitative research, which served as the foundation for the data gathering. The literature found in the academic databases EBSCO, which included Web of Science, Scopus, and Science Direct, as well as newspapers, magazines, and blogs, was another source of the data. Content analysis was used to examine the responses that were received. The study specifically examined whether the topic of examining how AI affects (a) special needs education and (b) how AI can assist educators in promoting special needs education was discussed in the literature. Based on targeted interviews, the study also attempted to suggest a framework for an inclusive future of special needs education (Garg & Sharma, 2020).

In their book AI-Assisted Special Education for Students With Exceptional Needs, Kumar, Ashish, Nayyar, Anand, et al. provide a summary of visually impaired youngsters and their unique requirements (Kumar, Nayyar, Sachan, & Jain, 2023).

Arshad Hashmi, Baig Muntajeeb Ali, M. Maheswari, P V V S D Nagendrudu, and D. Leela Rani wrote an article titled "Application of Artificial Intelligence Assisted Robots to Improve the Educational Outcome for Special Children in Disability Education (Kumari, 2024).

In the digital age, artificial intelligence (AI) is thriving, and its incorporation into the economy is an inevitable and natural trend for society's future. The advancement of science and technology is also essential to kids' academic growth. AI development has advanced to a point where it is expanding incredibly quickly and is changing every aspect of human life. There is no explanation of how to arrive at Artificial Intelligence + Curriculum, despite the state's requirement for a comprehensive curriculum. Computational tools for a range of jobs have been developed by artificial intelligence (AI) technology, simulating the astute problem-solving techniques used by people. By reducing their workload and improving special education pupils' access to pertinent knowledge, artificial intelligence is benefiting teachers. It goes without saying that very few educators do not believe AI will have some impact on their own professional development. Teachers are aware of the benefits of AI.

5. THE POTENTIAL OF AI IN SPECIAL EDUCATION, SPECIFICALLY FOR VISUALLY IMPAIRED STUDENTS

Artificial intelligence (AI) has significant potential for improving special education, particularly for visually impaired children. Here's a detailed look at how AI can improve their learning experience:

1. **Enhanced Accessibility:** JAWS and Voice-Over use OCR technology to turn printed or digital text into speech. This improves accessibility for visually impaired students to textbooks, articles, and educational materials. AI can increase the accuracy and timeliness of braille translations. Automated systems can transform a greater variety of digital content into braille more efficiently.
2. **Personalized Learning:** Artificial intelligence-powered adaptive learning platforms can customize instructional content to match the unique demands and learning styles of visually impaired pupils. For example, these systems may tailor font size, color contrast, and reading speed to individual preferences and needs.
3. **Navigation and Mobility:** AI-powered navigation apps and gadgets, such as those with GPS and computer vision (NuEyes, n.d.), can help visually impaired students navigate physical environments like school campuses or public areas. These gadgets can deliver real-time audio instructions as well as notifications about potential threats. Wearable (GiveVision, n.d.) technologies powered by artificial intelligence, such as smart glasses or haptic feedback systems, can provide spatial awareness and environmental information to visually impaired pupils, allowing them to move around more freely.
4. **Communication and Interaction:** AI-powered voice assistants and chatbots can help visually impaired students communicate by responding to queries in real time and assisting with tasks such as scheduling, homework support, and information access. This is particularly handy for class discussions, taking notes, and completing writing projects.
5. **Educational Content Enhancement:** Artificial intelligence can provide real-time audio descriptions of visual content including photos, charts, and films, making it more accessible to visually challenged pupils. This includes defining visual features, setting context, and communicating critical information. Artificial intelligence can help create tactile graphics and 3D-printed models that represent visual concepts, allowing visually impaired (Singh et al., 2023; Lin et al., 2023) students to interact with and comprehend complicated diagrams, maps, and other visual materials via touch.
6. **Data-Driven Insights:** AI can follow and analyze visually impaired students' academic achievement, finding trends and places where more assistance may be required. Artificial intelligence systems can track student engagement and behavior, offering feedback on how visually (Singh et al., 2023) impaired students interact with instructional content and recommending improvements or changes.

5.1 Challenges and Considerations

a. **Accessibility and Inclusion:** It is critical to ensure that AI technologies are accessible and usable by visually impaired pupils. This includes ensuring interoperability with existing assistive devices and meeting accessibility standards.
b. **Bias and Accuracy:** AI systems must be carefully constructed and trained to prevent biases while providing accurate representation and support for visually impaired (Lin et al., 2023) pupils. Continuous testing and refinement are required to ensure efficacy and fairness.
c. **Privacy and Security:** The application of AI requires the collection and analysis of personal data, which poses privacy and security problems. Ensuring that student data is protected and handled ethically is an important consideration..

5.2 AI-Powered Tools and Solutions for Visual Disabilities

5.2.1 Screen Readers and Voice Assistants

Description of Screen Readers and How They Utilize AI:

Screen readers are software applications that help people with visual impairments by translating text and other visual items on a screen into audible speech or braille.

5.2.2 Utilization of AI in Screen Readers

1. **Natural Language Processing (NLP):** AI-powered screen readers use natural language processing (NLP) to better grasp the context and meaning of text. AI can analyse the sentiment or tone of text, allowing screen readers to communicate emotions or emphasis in a more complex manner.
2. **Enhanced Text-to-Speech (TTS) Voices:** AI improves TTS engines by generating more natural-sounding voices that can be adjusted for pitch, speed, and accent. AI enables TTS engines to tailor voice output to the user's preferences and the context of the content, making the reading experience more personalised.
3. **Optical Character Recognition (OCR):** With AI-powered OCR technology, screen readers can extract text from photos, scanned documents, and other non-textual sources. This feature is particularly handy when reading text embedded in photos or PDFs. AI can also recognise and translate handwritten text into digital text, expanding the breadth of materials available to screen readers.

5.2.3 Examples of AI-Enhanced Screen Readers

- VoiceOver (Apple): Uses AI to deliver high-quality TTS and braille support, including context-sensitive feedback and voice customisation.
- JAWS (Job Access With Speech): Includes AI-driven TTS and advanced navigation functions, as well as integration with OCR for reading non-text content.
- NVDA (NonVisual Desktop Access) is an open-source screen reader that employs artificial intelligence to improve text-to-speech translation and navigation. It also supports braille displays (GiveVision, n.d.).

AI improves the operation of screen readers by enhancing text-to-speech quality, contextual comprehension, and accessibility to various content kinds. These improvements make it easier for visually impaired people to connect with digital material and navigate different contexts, promoting more independence and inclusivity (Singh et al., 2023; INDIAai, n.d.; Zaraii Zavaraki, 2024).

5.2.4 Popular AI-Driven Screen Readers (e.g., JAWS, NVDA)

Several popular AI-powered screen readers improve accessibility for visually challenged (INDIAai, n.d.) users by employing innovative technologies that improve text-to-speech conversion, navigation, and overall usability. Here's an overview of some popular screen readers and how they integrate AI.:

1. JAWS (Job Access With Speech)
   - Advanced Text-to-Speech (TTS): JAWS employs high-quality TTS (GiveVision, n.d.) engines to provide clear and natural-sounding speech. AI-enhanced TTS offers customisable speech settings, such as pitch, speed, and accent modifications.
   - Braille Support: Works with a variety of braille displays, converts text to braille, and provides real-time updates.

AI Integration: AI algorithms help to interpret the context of text and online items, increasing the accuracy and relevancy of spoken output. AI enhances features such as personalised (IrisVision, 2024) settings and user-specific modifications, resulting in a more tailored experience depending on user preferences (Isaksson-Daun, Jansson, & Nilsson, 2024).

2. NVDA (Non-Visual Desktop Access)

- NVDA is free and open-source, making it accessible to a wide spectrum of users. It is maintained by an active developer and user community.
- TTS and Braille: Uses high-quality TTS engines and supports braille displays, providing customizable speech and braille output.
- Web Accessibility: Provides tools for navigating and engaging with web content, including support for ARIA (Accessible Rich Internet Applications) landmarks and roles.

AI Integration: AI-driven TTS advances produce more natural and expressive voice output. Users can tailor speech qualities to their tastes.

3. Voice-Over:
- VoiceOver is incorporated into macOS and iOS devices, allowing for seamless integration with Apple hardware and applications.
- Advanced TTS uses AI-driven TTS technology to provide high-quality, customisable voice output. VoiceOver voices can be modified for pitch, speed, and modulation.
- Braille Support: Works with braille displays to generate braille output that changes in real time (IrisVision, 2024; GiveVision, n.d.).
    AI Integration:
- Contextual Feedback: AI improves VoiceOver's capacity to deliver detailed and context-sensitive feedback on user actions and information, resulting in better navigation and engagement.
- Dynamic Updates: AI assists in managing and interpreting dynamic content changes, ensuring that users are aware of updates and interactive features on their devices.

4. Narrator
- Built-In Screen Reader: Narrator is a built-in screen reader in Windows that requires no extra installation.
- TTS and Voice Customisation: Offers AI-enhanced TTS with customisable voices, pitch, and speed.
- Web and Document Reading: Provides tools for reading and navigating web pages, documents, and system interfaces.

AI Integration: AI-driven improvements improve the naturalness and clarity of Narrator's TTS voices. AI assists Narrator in understanding and interacting with complex site features and dynamic information, resulting in more accurate and useful feedback. AI-powered screen readers such as JAWS, NVDA, VoiceOver, and Narrator have greatly improved accessibility for visually impaired users by including powerful speech synthesis, dynamic content handling, and personalised user experiences.

5.2.5 Voice Assistants (e.g., Siri, Google Assistant) and Their Role in Aiding Visually Impaired Students.

Voice assistants such as Siri, Google Assistant, and others help visually impaired students by allowing them to access information and services hands-free and using their voices. Here's an in-depth look at how these voice assistants help visually impaired students and improve their learning experiences:

1. Accessibility and Navigation
   a. **Hands-Free Interaction**: Voice assistants allow visually impaired students to complete tasks and access information without having to interact with a screen. This hands-free feature is extremely useful for multitasking and exploring different locations.
   b. **Location-Based Assistance:** By connecting with GPS and mapping services, voice assistants may provide directions, assist with navigation on school campuses, and find specific rooms and amenities. For example, children can request directions to the nearest restroom or classroom.
2. **Educational Support:** Voice assistants can help students quickly find information on a number of topics, such as answering study questions or looking up definitions and explanations. This encourages independent investigation and learning. Voice assistants can help students organize homework assignments, create deadline reminders, and provide explanations or additional resources for academic subjects.
3. **Accessibility Features:** Voice assistants can control a wide range of smart devices and applications, including volume, lighting, and electronic gadgets in the classroom. This increases general accessibility and convenience. Many voice assistants feature settings for speaking speed, language, and accent, allowing students to personalize the assistant's responses to their own requirements.
   Challenges and Considerations

   a. **Privacy and Security:** Voice assistants gather and handle voice data, which raises privacy and security concerns. Ensuring that student data is managed appropriately and securely is critical.
   b. **Accuracy and Context:** While voice assistants are becoming more accurate, they may still fail to recognise context and provide precise responses in some instances. To meet these issues, natural language processing must be continuously improved.

c. **Requirement for Internet Connectivity:** Most voice assistants require an internet connection to function properly. Ensuring stable internet access is critical for smooth functioning.

Voice assistants such as Siri, Google Assistant, and Alexa greatly benefit visually impaired students by giving hands-free access to information, enabling conversation, and improving instructional support. Their ability to integrate with different technologies and conduct tasks using voice commands contributes to a more accessible and inclusive learning environment.

5.2.6 Optical Character Recognition (OCR) and Text-to-Speech (TTS)

How AI Enhances OCR for Visually Impaired Students:

Optical Character Recognition (OCR) technology is critical for visually impaired pupils because it allows them to access printed or handwritten information by transforming it into a digital version that can be read aloud or translated into braille. AI improves OCR in various areas, including accuracy, efficiency, and overall usability. Here is an in-depth look at how AI improves OCR for visually challenged pupils.:

1. Improved Text Recognition
   a. **Improved Accuracy:** AI algorithms, particularly those based on deep learning and neural networks, have considerably increased the accuracy of text recognition in OCR systems. These new algorithms can recognise complex fonts, different text sizes, and distorted or low-quality text images with more accuracy and dependability.
   b. **Contextual Understanding:** AI improves OCR by using natural language processing (NLP) to understand and interpret text in its context. This aids in correctly recognising and comprehending words that may be misunderstood owing to font variances or visual distortions.
2. Enhanced Handling of Diverse Text Formats
   a. **Complex Layouts:** AI-powered OCR systems can handle complex document layouts like multi-column text, tables, and mixed material (text and graphics). This gives visually challenged pupils access to a broader selection of educational resources, such as textbooks, articles, and scholarly papers.
   b. **Handwriting Recognition:** Advancements in artificial intelligence have increased OCR systems' capacity to recognise and interpret handwritten text. This is especially beneficial for retrieving handwritten notes, assignments, and documents that aren't available in digital form.

3. Real-Time Text Extraction
   a. **Live Text Extraction:** Artificial intelligence-powered OCR can extract text in real time from live video feeds or camera photos. For example, visually impaired students can utilise smartphone cameras to instantaneously capture and read text from books, whiteboards, or documents, allowing them to access material while on the road.
   b. **Image-to-Text Conversion:** Advanced artificial intelligence systems can instantly transform text images into digital formats, allowing students to engage with physical items and access educational content.
4. Integration with Assistive Technologies
   a. **Braille Translation:** AI-enhanced OCR systems can translate recognised text to braille formats for use in braille displays or embossers. This integration guarantees that visually impaired pupils who use braille have access to a greater selection of resources.
   b. **Educational Apps and Platforms:** AI-powered OCR is frequently integrated into educational apps and platforms, enabling easy access to learning resources. This comprises applications for reading textbooks, using web resources, and engaging with educational information.

   Examples of AI-Enhanced OCR Tools

1. **Google Lens:** Uses artificial intelligence to do real-time OCR on photos recorded by a smartphone camera, extracting and interpreting text from a variety of sources like books, signage, and papers.
2. **Microsoft Seeing AI:** Uses artificial intelligence to interpret text from photos, describe scenes, and recognise items. It is specifically designed for visually challenged people and provides real-time text recognition and voice feedback.

AI has significantly improved OCR technology, making it more accurate, adaptable, and usable for visually challenged pupils. AI-driven OCR systems improve text recognition, handle various formats, and integrate with other assistive technologies, promoting better accessibility and inclusion in education. These developments enable visually impaired students to access a broader selection of instructional resources and engage more completely in their learning environments.

5.2.7 Integration of TTS in Educational Materials

Text-to-speech (TTS) technology is essential for making educational materials accessible to visually impaired pupils. TTS improves the learning experience for students with visual impairments and other reading issues by translating written material into spoken words. Here's how TTS fits into educational resources to support varied learning demands.:

1. Reading and Accessibility
   a. **Textbooks and Reading Materials:** TTS can turn textbooks, articles, and other printed materials into audio files, allowing visually challenged students to listen to content. This conversion can be performed on digital files (such as PDFs and Word documents) or scanned photos using OCR technology. Users can change voice settings, such as speed, pitch, and loudness, to better fit their tastes and comprehension.
   b. **Web Content:** TTS can be added to web browsers as extensions or add-ons, allowing students to listen to online publications, educational resources, and interactive content.
   c. **Accessible Websites:** Educational websites and online platforms can immediately integrate TTS capability, making their information more accessible to visually impaired users.
2. Interactive Learning Tools
   a. **E-Learning Platforms:** E-learning platforms can use TTS to read aloud course materials such as lecture notes, quizzes, and instructional content. This enables visually challenged students to interact with the information in a way that meets their needs. TTS can be utilised in interactive features like virtual labs (Mina et al., 2023) or simulations to provide spoken instructions and feedback that improve the learning experience.
   b. **Educational Apps:** TTS is commonly used in educational apps such as language learning aids, reading apps, and study guides to assist students practice pronunciation, understand new terminology, and review content. Many apps allow users to tailor the TTS experience to their own learning needs, such as selecting multiple voices or modifying reading speed.
3. Assistive Technologies
   a. **Screen Readers:** Screen readers frequently integrate TTS functionality for reading aloud text from screens, such as educational materials, documents, and web pages. They collaborate with other assistive technologies to offer a full solution for visually impaired pupils.
   b. **Voice Assistants:** Voice assistants such as Siri, Google Assistant, and Alexa can read instructional materials aloud, answer questions, and provide explanations, thereby improving the learning experience via interactive voice commands.
4. Enhanced Engagement and Comprehension

a. **Audiobooks:** TTS may convert written texts into audiobooks, such as classic literature, textbooks, and additional reading resources. This offers an alternative format to pupils who benefit from aural learning. Audiobooks are particularly useful for disciplines that demand significant reading or for students who prefer to listen rather than read.

b. **Interactive Textbooks:** Interactive digital textbooks can use TTS to read chunks of text aloud, explain hard ideas or provide audio feedback on student involvement. Combining TTS with other multimedia elements like videos and interactive graphics promotes varied learning styles and improves comprehension.

5.2.8 Challenges and Considerations

a. Accuracy and Naturalness:
   - Voice Quality: While TTS technology has evolved, ensuring that synthesised speech is intelligible, natural-sounding, and easy to comprehend is critical for effective learning.
   - Pronunciation: Correct pronunciation of complex terms, names, or technical jargon is critical for comprehension, and TTS systems must be trained to handle these subtleties.

b. Integration and Compatibility:
   - System Compatibility: The TTS functionality must be interoperable with a variety of educational platforms, devices, and formats. Ensuring seamless connectivity across several systems is critical for providing a consistent user experience.
   - Customisation: Allowing users to alter TTS settings (e.g., voice selection, speed) helps adapt the experience to their specific preferences and needs.

6. AI IN BRAILLE TRANSLATION

6.1 Automated Braille Transcription Tools

Automated Braille transcription systems translate digital text into Braille, making written resources accessible to the blind and visually challenged. These tools ease the conversion process by utilising a variety of technologies such as Optical Character Recognition (OCR) and Text-to-Braille translation. Here's an overview of how these tools work, their benefits, and some popular examples:

6.1.1 How Automated Braille Transcription Tools Work

1. Text Extraction:
   - Digital Text: Tools for extracting text from digital files including Word documents, PDFs, and eBooks. They typically accept a variety of file types and employ algorithms to parse and process text.
   - OCR Integration: OCR technology is used to recognise and extract text from scanned pictures or photographs, as well as physical documents. The recognised text is then transformed to braille.
2. Braille Translation:
   - Text-to-Braille Conversion: The retrieved text is transformed to Braille using predetermined codes. Braille is made up of raised dots that correspond to letters, numerals, and punctuation marks. The translation procedure entails mapping these patterns onto the text.
3. Output Generation:
   - Braille Embossing: Some programs can generate files that are directly compatible with Braille embossers, which use embossing to create physical Braille documents on paper.
   - Digital Braille: The tools can also generate digital Braille files that can be viewed on Braille displays or converted to other formats.

6.1.2 Popular Automated Braille Transcription Tools

1. Duxbury Braille Translator (DBT):
   - Overview: DBT is one of the most used Braille translating software applications. It supports a wide range of Braille codes and can translate text from several formats to Braille.
   - Features: Advanced formatting choices, including support for complicated layouts and specialised Braille codes. It integrates with Braille embossers and displays.
2. Braille2000:
   - Overview: Braille2000 is another popular Braille translation software that includes capabilities for translating and formatting Braille texts.
   - Features include flexible formatting options, support for different Braille codes, and the ability to generate Braille files for embossers and digital displays.
   - Contracted Braille Translation Software (CBT):

Automated Braille transcription technologies improve the accessibility of educational and informational materials for visually impaired people by turning text into Braille swiftly and accurately.

6.1.3 AI's Role in Making Braille More Accessible and Accurate

AI plays a transformative role in making Braille more accessible and accurate by enhancing various aspects of Braille production and usage. Here's a detailed look at how AI contributes to these improvements:

1. Enhanced Braille Translation
   a. **Improved Accuracy:** Algorithms, particularly those utilizing natural language processing (NLP), can better understand the context and nuances of the text being translated into Braille. This leads to more accurate translations, particularly for complex or technical content. AI can identify and correct common translation errors that might occur during the conversion process, such as misinterpreting abbreviations or specialized terminology.
   b. **Dynamic Translation:** AI-powered translation tools can offer real-time Braille translation, allowing users to access content instantly in Braille as it becomes available. This is particularly useful for interactive and educational content.
2. Accessibility Enhancements
   a. **Adaptive Braille Formats:** AI can customize Braille output based on individual user needs and preferences. This includes adjusting formatting, spacing, and Braille codes to match specific requirements or preferences.
      - **Dynamic Layouts:** AI tools can handle various document layouts and formats, such as multi-column text or complex tables, ensuring that the Braille output is readable and well-organized.
3. **Optical Character Recognition (OCR) for Braille:** AI-driven OCR technology improves the accuracy of text extraction from printed or handwritten documents. This extracted text can then be converted into Braille with greater precision. AI helps in recognizing and processing complex document formats, such as textbooks with varied layouts, ensuring that the resulting Braille is accurate and readable.
4. **Braille Production and Embossing:** AI-powered systems can control Braille embossers with high precision, ensuring consistent and accurate Braille production. This includes managing complex layouts and formatting. AI can monitor and detect errors during the embossing process, allowing for adjustments and corrections to produce high-quality Braille documents.

5. **Educational and Interactive Content:** AI can create interactive educational materials that incorporate Braille, allowing visually impaired students to engage with dynamic content, such as interactive textbooks or educational games. AI tools can adapt educational content to meet individual learning needs, providing Braille materials that are tailored to specific subjects or learning styles. AI-powered apps can assist users in learning and practicing Braille by providing interactive exercises, feedback, and personalized learning paths.
6. **Braille Literacy and Training:** AI can support Braille literacy programs by offering interactive training tools that provide feedback, track progress, and adapt to individual learning needs. AI-driven resources, such as digital Braille books and educational materials, support Braille literacy development by providing diverse and engaging content

7. NAVIGATION AND MOBILITY ASSISTANCE

7.1 AI-Powered Apps for Indoor and Outdoor Navigation (e.g., Aira, Be My Eyes)

AI-powered navigation apps like Aira and Be My Eyes have significantly enhanced the mobility and independence of visually impaired individuals by providing real-time assistance for both indoor and outdoor navigation. Here's a detailed look at how these apps work and their features:

1. **Aira:** Aira is a navigation and assistance app designed specifically for visually impaired and blind users. It connects users with trained agents who provide real-time assistance via a smartphone or smart glasses.
   a. **Real-Time Assistance:** Aira connects users with live agents who can see through the user's device camera and provide assistance with navigation, reading signs, identifying obstacles, and more. Users communicate with agents via voice commands, allowing for hands-free assistance and guidance.
   b. **Indoor and Outdoor Navigation:** Agents help with route planning, identifying landmarks, and navigating streets. They can assist with crossing streets safely and finding specific locations. Aira can assist with navigating complex indoor environments such as malls, airports, and office buildings. Agents can provide guidance on finding stores, gates, or rooms.
   c. **Integration with Other Technologies:** Aira integrates with smart glasses like those from Aira's partner, allowing for a more immersive and hands-free experience. The app uses GPS and other location services to provide contextually relevant assistance.

d. **Customizable Assistance:** Users can set preferences for how they receive assistance, including the level of detail and type of guidance.

e. **Subscription-Based Service:** Aira offers various subscription plans, including options for frequent users and those who need occasional assistance.

2. **Be My Eyes:** Be My Eyes is a volunteer-based app that connects visually impaired individuals with sighted volunteers who provide assistance through live video calls.

a. **Volunteer Assistance:** Users make video calls to sighted volunteers who help with tasks such as reading labels, navigating environments, or identifying objects. The app has a large network of volunteers from around the world, offering diverse language support and availability.

b. **Indoor and Outdoor Help:** Volunteers can assist with identifying landmarks, finding public transportation, and navigating streets. Volunteers help with tasks such as organizing groceries, reading instructions, or navigating indoor spaces.

c. **AI Integration:** Be My Eyes has integrated AI technology to assist with certain tasks. For example, the app's "Visual Assistance" feature uses AI to recognize objects, text, and colors, providing automated assistance in addition to volunteer support.

d. **User-Friendly Interface:** The app is designed to be user-friendly, with a simple interface that allows users to quickly request assistance and connect with volunteers.

e. **Community and Support:** The app fosters a supportive community of volunteers who offer their time and expertise to assist those in need.

7.2 Smart Canes and AI-Driven Wearable Devices

Smart canes and AI-driven wearable devices represent a significant advancement in assistive technology for visually impaired individuals. These devices leverage artificial intelligence (AI) and other technologies to enhance navigation, safety, and overall mobility. Here's a comprehensive overview of smart canes and AI-driven wearable devices (GiveVision, n.d.):

1. **Smart Canes:** Smart canes are advanced versions of traditional white canes that incorporate technology to provide additional sensory feedback and navigation assistance. They integrate various sensors, including ultrasonic, radar, and GPS, to offer enhanced features for visually impaired users.

a. **Obstacle Detection:** Smart canes are equipped with sensors such as ultrasonic or radar sensors that detect obstacles in the cane's path. These sensors can identify objects at different heights and distances, alerting the user to potential obstacles.

b. Navigation Assistance:

    ●   **GPS Integration:** Some smart canes include GPS technology to provide location-based guidance and navigation. This helps users find specific locations or follow predefined routes.

    ●   **Geofencing:** Advanced models can create virtual (Mina et al., 2023; Walle et al., 2022) boundaries and alert users if they stray from a designated area or enter a restricted zone.

c. **Emergency Features:** Many smart canes are equipped with emergency alert SOS systems that can send distress signals or notifications to caregivers or emergency contacts if the user needs assistance.

d. **Smartphone Connectivity:** Smart canes often connect to smartphone apps, providing additional features such as route planning, real-time location sharing, and settings customization. Some apps can log travel data and provide insights into the user's navigation patterns or performance.

    Examples of Smart Canes:

a. **Sunu Band:** The Sunu Band is a wearable (GiveVision, n.d.) smart device that can be worn on the wrist or as a belt. It uses ultrasonic sensors to detect obstacles and provide haptic feedback. Includes adjustable vibration alerts, GPS navigation, and integration with a smartphone app for route planning and tracking.

b. **WeWALK Smart Cane:** WeWALK smart cane integrates with a smartphone app and includes features such as obstacle detection, GPS navigation, and voice assistance. Offers haptic feedback for obstacle detection, voice prompts for navigation, and integration with navigation apps like Google Maps.

2. **AI-Driven Wearable Devices:** AI-driven wearable devices for visually impaired users use artificial intelligence to enhance mobility, navigation, and interaction with the environment. These devices include smart glasses, wearable (GiveVision, n.d.) cameras, and other sensors that leverage AI to provide real-time assistance.

    Examples of AI-Driven Wearable Devices:

    a. **OrCam MyEye:** OrCam MyEye is a wearable (GiveVision, n.d.) camera that attaches to glasses and uses AI to provide real-time audio descriptions of text, faces, and objects. Includes text reading, facial recognition, object identification, and integration with smartphones for additional features.

b. **eSight Eyewear:** eSight glasses use high-definition cameras and AI to enhance vision for individuals with low vision (Ehrlich et al., 2017; Virgili et al., 2013). The glasses provide real-time image enhancement and magnification. Offers adjustable settings for contrast, brightness, and zoom, and provides real-time visual information through the wearable display (eSight Eyewear, 2023).

c. **Xenoma e-skin:** Xenoma e-skin is a smart wearable garment that uses embedded sensors to track movements and provide feedback for navigation and interaction. Includes haptic feedback for directional guidance and environmental awareness, and can be integrated with other assistive technologies.

Benefits:
- Enhanced Navigation: Both smart canes and AI-driven wearables provide users with better navigation and obstacle detection, improving safety and independence.
- Real-Time Assistance: AI technologies offer real-time feedback and assistance, making navigation and interaction with the environment more intuitive.
- Integration with Technology: Many devices integrate with smartphones and other technologies, providing additional features and customization options.

Smart canes and AI-driven wearable devices represent significant advancements in assistive technology for visually impaired individuals. They offer enhanced navigation, real-time assistance, and integration with modern technologies, improving mobility and independence.

7.3 AI in Content Accessibility

7.3.1 Enhancing Web Content Accessibility with AI

Enhancing web content accessibility with AI involves leveraging artificial intelligence technologies to make digital content more accessible to people with disabilities. AI can improve accessibility in various ways, from automatic content adjustments to real-time assistance. Here's a comprehensive look at how AI contributes to web accessibility:

1. Automated Content Adjustments
    a. **Text-to-Speech (TTS):** AI-driven TTS engines can convert written text into spoken words, making web content accessible to users with visual impairments or reading disabilities. Modern TTS systems use natural language processing (NLP) to produce more natural and expressive speech.
        - Examples: Tools like Google's Text-to-Speech, Amazon Polly, and Microsoft Azure Cognitive Services offer high-quality TTS capabilities.
    b. **Image and Video Descriptions:** Automatic Alt Text: AI can generate descriptive text (alt text) for images based on content recognition. This helps screen readers provide context for users who are visually impaired. AI-powered captioning tools can automatically generate subtitles for videos, making audiovisual content accessible to users with hearing impairments.
    c. **Content Summarization:** AI can summarize lengthy articles or web pages into shorter, more digestible content. This feature benefits users with cognitive disabilities or those who prefer concise information.
        - Examples: Tools like Sumnotes and Scholarcy use AI to provide summaries of text and research papers.
2. Improved Navigation and Interaction
    a. **Voice Navigation:** AI-powered voice recognition systems allow users to navigate websites and interact with content using voice commands. This is particularly useful for users with mobility impairments.
        - Examples: Voice assistants like Google Assistant and Amazon Alexa can be integrated with web content to provide voice-based navigation and interaction.
    b. Personalized Content:
        - Adaptive Interfaces: AI can adjust web interfaces based on user preferences and needs. For example, AI can customize font sizes, color contrasts, and layout based on user settings or accessibility requirements.
3. Real-Time Assistance
    a. **AI Chatbots:** AI chatbots can provide real-time assistance by answering questions, guiding users through processes, and offering help with accessibility features. This is valuable for users who need immediate support.
    b. **Automatic Accessibility Checking:** AI-powered tools can automatically scan web content for accessibility issues and suggest improvements to ensure compliance with standards such as WCAG (Web Content Accessibility Guidelines).
4. **Enhancing Cognitive Accessibility**
    a. Simplified Language:

AI Language Models: AI can simplify complex language and jargon on web pages, making content more accessible to users with cognitive disabilities or limited literacy.

b. Content Personalization:
- Tailored Experiences: AI can create personalized content experiences based on user preferences and needs, such as adjusting reading levels or providing additional context for complex topics.
- Examples: Adaptive learning platforms use AI to tailor content and learning materials to individual user needs.
    5. Enhancing Visual and Auditory Accessibility
    a. Color Contrast and Text Size Adjustments:

- AI-Based Enhancements: AI can automatically adjust color contrasts and text sizes to meet accessibility standards and user preferences, improving readability for users with visual impairments.
- Examples: Browser extensions and AI tools like High Contrast Mode and ZoomText offer customizable visual adjustments.
    b. Real-Time Audio Descriptions:
- Content Description: AI can provide real-time audio descriptions for multimedia content, describing visual elements of videos and images for users with visual impairments.
- Examples: AI tools integrated into video players can generate and deliver audio descriptions based on video content analysis.
    6. Detecting and Addressing Accessibility Issues
    a. AI-Powered Analysis:

- Issue Detection: AI can identify accessibility issues such as missing alt text, improper heading structures, and navigation problems. This helps web developers address these issues more efficiently.
- Examples: Accessibility audit tools powered by AI can generate detailed reports and recommendations for improving web accessibility.
    b. User Behavior Analysis:
- Usage Patterns: AI can analyze user behavior and interactions to identify accessibility barriers and optimize the user experience for individuals with disabilities.
- Examples: Analytics tools can track how users with disabilities interact with content and provide insights for improvements.
        Benefits:

- Increased Accessibility: AI technologies help make web content more accessible to a broader audience, including those with various disabilities.
- Efficiency: Automated tools and real-time assistance streamline the process of making content accessible, saving time and resources.
- Personalization: AI enables personalized user experiences, enhancing usability and accessibility based on individual needs.

AI is revolutionizing web content accessibility by providing automated adjustments, real-time assistance, and enhanced personalization. These advancements help create a more inclusive web environment for users with disabilities, making digital content more accessible and user-friendly. As AI technology continues to evolve, its role in improving web accessibility will likely become even more impactful, further supporting the needs of diverse user populations.

7.3.2 AI-Driven Image Recognition and Description Tools

AI-driven image recognition and description tools utilize advanced artificial intelligence technologies to analyze, interpret, and provide descriptive information about images. These tools are especially valuable for enhancing accessibility for visually impaired individuals and improving content management across various applications. Here's a detailed look at how these tools work, their features, and their applications:

8. HOW AI-DRIVEN IMAGE RECOGNITION AND DESCRIPTION TOOLS WORK

8.1 Image Recognition and Description Tools

a. Image Analysis:
   - Deep Learning Models: AI uses deep learning algorithms, particularly convolutional neural networks (CNNs), to analyze images. These models are trained on vast datasets to recognize patterns, objects, and scenes within images.
   - Feature Extraction: The AI extracts key features from images, such as shapes, colors, and textures, and identifies objects, people, and contexts.
b. Object and Scene Recognition:

- Object Detection: AI identifies and classifies objects within an image, such as cars, animals, or furniture. It can also detect the presence of multiple objects and their spatial relationships.
- Scene Understanding: AI analyzes the overall context of the image to describe the scene, such as identifying a beach, a cityscape, or a classroom.

c. Text Generation:
- Natural Language Processing (NLP): Once the image is analyzed, AI generates descriptive text using NLP techniques. This involves converting the recognized features and context into coherent, readable descriptions.
- Contextual Information: The generated text may include details about objects, their functions, interactions, and the overall setting of the image.

8.2 Key Features of AI-Driven Image Recognition and Description Tools

AI tools generate alternative text (alt text) for images, making web content accessible to users with visual impairments. This text describes the content and context of images. Tools like Google's Vision (Nguyen, Weismann, & Trauzettel-Klosinski, 2009) AI and Microsoft Azure Computer Vision provide automatic alt text generation. AI can provide real-time descriptions of images using smartphone cameras or wearable devices. This allows users to receive immediate information about their surroundings. Apps like Seeing AI by Microsoft and Aira offer real-time image recognition and description features.

9. CASE STUDIES AND REAL-WORLD APPLICATIONS

9.1 Successful Integration in Schools

9.1.1 Examples of Schools That Have Successfully Integrated AI Tools for Visually Impaired Students

Several schools and educational institutions worldwide have successfully integrated AI tools to support visually impaired students, enhancing their learning experiences and accessibility. Here are some notable examples:

1. **Perkins School for the Blind: Watertown, Massachusetts, USA:** Perkins School for the Blind incorporates AI technologies such as screen readers and AI-driven navigation tools into their curriculum. They use tools like the Aira app and OrCam MyEye to assist students in navigating the campus and accessing educational materials.
2. **Royal Blind School: Edinburgh, Scotland:** Royal Blind School utilizes a range of AI-driven assistive technologies, including text-to-speech software and AI-based image recognition tools. They employ tools like Google's Vision (Virgili et al., 2013, 2018; Envision, n.d.) AI and Microsoft's Seeing AI to support students with visual impairments in accessing and understanding educational content.
3. **Royal Institute for Deaf and Blind Children (RIDBC): Sydney, Australia:** RIDBC utilizes AI technologies to support visually impaired students through tools like AI-powered image recognition apps and adaptive learning platforms. They integrate these technologies into their educational programs to improve accessibility and learning outcomes (Gerich & Fellinger, 2012).

In India, several educational institutions have made significant strides in integrating AI tools to support visually impaired students. Here are some notable examples:

1. **The Blind Relief Association (BRA): New Delhi, India:** The Blind Relief Association integrates various AI-driven tools into their educational programs, such as screen readers and voice recognition software. They use these technologies to assist students in accessing digital content and enhancing their learning experience.
2. **Indian Institute of Technology (IIT) Delhi:** Delhi is involved in research and development projects focused on AI-driven assistive technologies for visually impaired students. This includes developing tools for real-time text-to-speech conversion, image recognition, and navigation assistance.
3. **National Institute for the Visually Handicapped (NIVH): Dehradun, India:** NIVH integrates AI tools like automated Braille transcription systems and AI-driven image recognition software into their curriculum. These tools help students access educational materials and improve their learning outcomes.

9.1.2 Companies Taking Initiatives for Visual Impaired

Organizations like Microsoft and Google have developed several initiatives to leverage AI for assisting visually impaired individuals. Here's an overview of some key initiatives:

Microsoft's Seeing AI

Overview: Microsoft's Seeing AI is a free mobile app designed to help visually impaired users understand their surroundings by providing audio descriptions of the environment. Launched in 2017, the app harnesses the power of AI and computer vision (Virgili et al., 2013, 2018; Envision, n.d.) to offer a range of functionalities. The app can identify and speak the denomination of various currency notes, making it easier for users to handle money independently.

10. CONCLUSION

10.1 Encouraging Continued Innovation and Inclusivity in AI

Encouraging continued innovation and inclusivity in AI for visually disabled individuals involves creating a supportive ecosystem that fosters research, collaboration, and practical application of technology. Here's a comprehensive approach to promoting ongoing progress in this field, Advocate for and secure funding for research initiatives focused on developing AI solutions tailored to visually disabled users. Support or organize competitions and hackathons to stimulate innovative solutions and attract talent to the field of assistive technologies. Encourage partnerships between academic institutions, technology companies, and non-profit organizations to pool resources and expertise. Develop shared research facilities and resources to accelerate the development of AI tools for visually disabled individuals. Implement pilot programs to test new AI technologies in real-world educational settings, gather feedback, and refine the tools based on practical experiences.

Ensure that pilot programs involve end-users—visually disabled students and educators—to validate the effectiveness and usability of AI solutions. Advocate for the adoption of universal design principles that make AI technologies accessible to all users, including those with varying levels of visual impairment. Support the development of AI tools with customizable features that allow users to adjust settings according to their specific needs and preferences. Promote adherence to accessibility standards, such as WCAG (Web Content Accessibility Guidelines) and ARIA (Accessible Rich Internet Applications), in the design of AI applications. Develop and disseminate best practices for creating inclusive AI technologies, ensuring that these practices are incorporated into development processes. Encouraging continued innovation and inclusivity in AI for visually disabled individuals requires a holistic approach that combines research and development, inclusive design, stakeholder engagement, education, policy support, and global collaboration. By fostering an environment that supports these efforts, we can drive advancements in AI that improve accessibility, enhance educational opportunities, and empower visually disabled individuals to achieve their full potential.

REFERENCES

Ahmadi, A. (2023). Designing an educational program based on social robot technology and its impact on social skills and academic achievement motivation of high-functioning autism spectrum disorder students [thesis]. Tehran, Iran: Allameh Tabataba'i University;

Ceoca, O., & Dulf, E.-H. "Assistive Helmet for Visually Impaired Human Beings", *2024 IEEE International Conference on Automation, Quality and Testing, Robotics (AQTR)*, pp.1-6, 2024.

Deemer, A. D., Bradley, C. K., Ross, N. C., Natale, D. M., Itthipanichpong, R., Werblin, F. S., & Massof, R. W. (2018). Low Vision Enhancement with Head-mounted Video Display Systems: Are We There Yet?. *Optometry and vision science: official publication of the American Academy of Optometry, 95*(9), 694–703. https://doi.org/ DOI: 10.1097/OPX.0000000000001278

Ehrlich, J. R., Spaeth, G. L., Carlozzi, N. E., & Lee, P. P. (2017). Patient-Centered Outcome Measures to Assess Functioning in Randomized Controlled Trials of Low-Vision Rehabilitation: A Review. *Patient, 10*(1), 39–49. DOI: 10.1007/s40271-016-0189-5 PMID: 27495171

Garg, S., & Sharma, S. (2020). Impact of artificial intelligence in special need education to promote inclusive pedagogy. *International Journal of Information and Education Technology (IJIET), 10*(7), 523–527.

Gerich, J., & Fellinger, J. (2012). Effects of social networks on the quality of life in an elder and middle-aged deaf community sample. *Journal of Deaf Studies and Deaf Education, 17*(1), 102–115. PMID: 21606089

GiveVision. (n.d.). https://www.givevision.net/en/sightplus

Goodrich, G. L., & Kirby, J. (2001). A comparison of patient reading performance and preference: Optical devices, handheld CCTV (Innoventions Magni-Cam), or stand-mounted CCTV (Optelec Clearview or TSI Genie). *Optometry (St. Louis, Mo.), 72*(8), 519–528. PMID: 11519714

Isaksson-Daun, J., Jansson, T., & Nilsson, J. (2024). Using Portable Virtual Reality to Assess Mobility of Blind and Low-Vision Individuals With the Audomni Sensory Supplementation Feedback. *IEEE Access : Practical Innovations, Open Solutions*, 12, 26222–26241.

Kumar, A., Nayyar, A., Sachan, R. K., & Jain, R. (Eds.). (2023). *AI-assisted special education for students with exceptional needs*. IGI Global.

Kumari, R. K. (2024). Artificial intelligence in special education. In Advances in educational technologies and instructional design book series (pp. 79–112). https://doi.org/DOI: 10.4018/979-8-3693-5538-1.ch003

Lin, N., Chen, B., Yang, M., Lu, F., & Deng, R. (2023). Low vision aids and age are associated with Müller-Lyer illusion in congenital visually impaired children. *Frontiers in Psychology*, 14. Advance online publication. DOI: 10.3389/fpsyg.2023.1278554 PMID: 38078226

Luo, G., & Pundlik, S. (2022). Usage patterns of Head-mounted vision assistance app as compared to handheld video Magnifier. In *Displays* (Vol. 75, p. 102303). Elsevier BV., DOI: 10.1016/j.displa.2022.102303

Mathews, K. M. (2016). Transformative models in K-12 education: The impact of a blended universal design for learning intervention. An experimental mixed methods study (Doctoral dissertation, University of San Diego).

Mina, P. N. R., Solon, I. M., Sanchez, F. R., Delante, T. K., Villegas, J. K., Basay, F. J., Andales, J.-r., Pasko, F., Estrera, M. F. R., Samson, R.Jr., & Mutya, R. (2023). Leveraging Education through Artificial Intelligence Virtual Assistance: A Case Study of Visually Impaired Learners. *International Journal of Educational Innovation and Research*, 2(1), 10–22. DOI: 10.31949/ijeir.v2i1.3001

Moshtael, H., Aslam, T., Underwood, I., & Dhillon, B. (2015). High Tech Aids Low Vision: A Review of Image Processing for the Visually Impaired. *Translational Vision Science & Technology*, 4(4), 6. DOI: 10.1167/tvst.4.4.6 PMID: 26290777

Nguyen, N. X., Weismann, M., & Trauzettel-Klosinski, S. (2009). Improvement of reading speed after providing of low vision aids in patients with age-related macular degeneration. In Acta Ophthalmologica (Vol. 87, Issue 8, pp. 849–853). Wiley. https://doi.org/DOI: 10.1111/j.1755-3768.2008.01423.x

Oyewumi, A., Isaiah, O., & Adigun, O. (2015). *Influence of social networking on the psychological adjustment of adolescents with hearing impairment in Ibadan.*

Pundlik, S., Shivshanker, P., & Luo, G. (2023). Impact of Apps as Assistive Devices for Visually Impaired Persons. In Annual Review of Vision Science (Vol. 9, Issue 1, pp. 111–130). Annual Reviews. https://doi.org/DOI: 10.1146/annurev-vision-111022-123837

Singh, S., Keller, P. R., Busija, L., McMillan, P., Makrai, E., Lawrenson, J. G., Hull, C. C., & Downie, L. E. (2023). Blue-light filtering spectacle lenses for visual performance, sleep, and macular health in adults. *Cochrane Library, 2023*(8). https://doi.org/DOI: 10.1002/14651858.cd013244.pub2

This AI-powered backpack helps the visually impaired navigate world. (n.d.). IN-DIAai. https://indiaai.gov.in/case-study/this-ai-powered-backpack-helps-the-visually-impaired-navigate-world

Tsouktakou, N. A., Hamouroudis, N. A., & Horti, N. A. (2024). The use of artificial intelligence in the education of people with visual impairment. *World Journal of Advanced Engineering Technology and Sciences*, 13(1), 734–744. DOI: 10.30574/wjaets.2024.13.1.0481

Rani, P. U., Angel, S., Janani, L., & Berista, S. (2024, March). Astute Assistance System for Blind and Visually Impaired People. In 2024 5th International Conference on Intelligent Communication Technologies and Virtual Mobile Networks (ICICV) (pp. 74-78). IEEE.

Virgili, G., Acosta, R., Bentley, S. A., Giacomelli, G., Allcock, C., & Evans, J. R. (2018). Reading aids for adults with low vision. *Cochrane Library, 2018*(4). https://doi.org/DOI: 10.1002/14651858.cd003303.pub4

Virgili, G., Acosta, R., Grover, L. L., Bentley, S. A., & Giacomelli, G. (2013). Reading aids for adults with low vision. *Cochrane Database of Systematic Reviews*, 10(10), CD003303. Advance online publication. DOI: 10.1002/14651858.CD003303.pub3 PMID: 24154864

Walle, H., Serres, B., Gilles, V., & De Runz, C. (2022). A Survey on Recent Advances in AI and Vision-Based Methods for Helping and Guiding Visually Impaired People. *Applied Sciences (Basel, Switzerland)*, 12(5), 2308. DOI: 10.3390/app12052308

Wang, J., Wang, S., & Zhang, Y. (2023). Artificial intelligence for visually impaired. *Displays*, 77(102391), 102391. DOI: 10.1016/j.displa.2023.102391

Wang, J., Wang, S., & Zhang, Y. (2023). Artificial intelligence for visually impaired. *Displays*, 77, 102391. DOI: 10.1016/j.displa.2023.102391

Wearable low vision glasses for visually impaired. IrisVision. (2024b, July 11). https://irisvision.com/esight-alternative/

Zaraii Zavaraki, E. (2024). *Artificial Intelligence for People with Special Educational Needs*. IntechOpen., DOI: 10.5772/intechopen.1004158

Zavaraki, E., & Schneider, D. (2019). Blended learning approach for students with special educational needs: A systematic review. *Journal of Education & Social Policy.*, 6(3), 1–2.

Zavaraki, E. Z., & Alimardani, F. (2023, July). The role of blended learning approach on interaction process of students with special educational needs. In EdMedia+ Innovate Learning (pp. 1243-1247). Association for the Advancement of Computing in Education (AACE).

Chapter 7
Artificial Intelligence in Education:
Insights From Gender and Locality–Based Perspectives

Jagneet Kour
https://orcid.org/0009-0003-0341-3636
Eternal University, India

Raino Bhatia
https://orcid.org/0000-0002-5379-3003
Eternal University, India

Richa Joshi
https://orcid.org/0009-0006-7286-6585
Eternal University, India

ABSTRACT

The incorporation of Artificial Intelligence in modern education has revolutionized the learning experience, but it also raises concerns about widening existing gaps in education, particularly in terms of gender and geographical location. This research delves into the effects of AI on students and educators, with a focus on the unequal access to digital technologies and its consequences for education. Our findings indicate notable differences in AI performance based on gender and location, with male students and urban areas performing better than their female and rural counterparts. We investigate how AI can both reduce and amplify existing disparities, and suggest approaches to ensure that the benefits of AI are shared fairly.

DOI: 10.4018/979-8-3693-8191-5.ch007

INTRODUCTION

Natural language processing, machine learning, and procedure development are all blended within the study of artificial intelligence. Several educational purposes of artificial intelligence can be utilized, such as personalized learning stages to encourage student learning, software for facial recognition to provide psychological insight, and mechanical assessment system for promoting student learning. The application of artificial intelligence in education has increased during the last several periods as a means of enhancing students' learning outcomes and experiences and improving our understanding of how youngsters learn. Artificial intelligence is beginning to have a big impact on education by changing educators' and parents views regarding what is required to learn and providing us opportunities for specified directions. The various applications of intelligent technology in education are addressed in this essay, with a focus on how such applications could help improve learning at all levels. In order to provide a more successful personalised learning environment, adaptive learning systems that are based on artificial intelligence have the ability to personalise the material of the course as well as the pace of the program to coincide with the particular requirements of each individual student. Through the utilisation of artificial intelligence, these algorithms are able to analyse enormous datasets in order to recognise patterns in student performance, identify areas of weakness, and put into action customised strategies in order combat particular learning issues. This procedure ultimately improves each students learning pathway. Furthermore, AI-powered educational solution allow immersive and engaging educational experiences using the integration of technologies like increased reality, virtual reality, and natural language processing. Firstly, AI was familiarized in USA in 1956 by McCarthy, and in India it started in the late 1960s by H.N. Mahabala. In Artificial intelligence, 'intelligence' use to the machines that have power to make purpose and actions depend on given information (Chen, 2020). In human being, we have different ability to learn, think and solve problems etc. In Artificial intelligence, intelligence is restoring by machines. They provided information and then programmed to disclose human intelligence. When a machine can take action by itself and use them, it will be considered as intelligent (Morley, 2020) . The growing presence of Artificial Intelligence (AI) in education has ignited a heated debate about its potential to transform the way we learn and teach. Advocates of AI argue that it can improve student outcomes, enhance teacher efficiency, and increase access to education, thereby bridging the gap between different socio-economic groups (Picciano, 2009). For instance, AI-powered adaptive learning systems can provide personalized instruction, helping to address individual learning needs and abilities. Additionally, AI-powered grading systems can help reduce teacher workload, freeing up time for more hands-on, human interaction with students.On the other hand, critics warn that AI may also exacerbate existing inequalities, particularly for students from disadvantaged backgrounds (Warschauer, 2003). For example, students who lack access to digital technologies, such as computers, smartphones, and internet connectivity, may be at a disadvantage compared to their peers who have access to these technologies. This digital divide can lead to a widening of the achievement gap, as students who are already disadvantaged may struggle to keep up with their peers. Furthermore, AI systems can perpetuate existing biases, particularly if they are trained on biased data sets (Hill, 2017). This can lead to unfair treatment of certain student groups, exacerbating existing inequalities. For instance, AI-powered systems may be more likely to provide biased feedback to students from certain racial or ethnic groups, perpetuating existing stereotypes and biases.

As AI becomes more integrated into education, it is essential to examine the implications of this technology on students and teachers, particularly in terms of the digital divide. This includes investigating how AI can both alleviate and worsen existing disparities, and suggesting strategies to ensure that the benefits of AI are shared fairly. By doing so, we can harness the potential of AI to improve education, while minimizing its negative consequences.

The integration of AI in education is a complex issue, with both positive and negative implications. While AI has the potential to enhance student outcomes and improve teacher efficiency, it also risks exacerbating existing inequalities. Therefore, it is essential to approach the integration of AI in education with caution, ensuring that its benefits are shared fairly and that its negative consequences are mitigated.

THE DIGITAL DIVIDE IN EDUCATION 5.0

The impact of AI on students and teachers in Education 5.0 is a multifaceted issue, with the digital divide being a critical concern. The digital divide refers to the unequal access to digital technologies, including computers, smartphones, and internet connectivity (Hargittai, 2002), which can exacerbate existing inequalities among students. In Education 5.0, AI-powered tools and platforms are increasingly used to deliver instruction and assess student learning, making it essential for students to have access to these technologies. Unfortunately, students who lack access to these technologies are at risk of being left behind, widening the existing achievement gaps (Wang et al., 2023).The digital divide is not a new issue, but it has become more critical in recent years due to the increasing reliance on digital technologies in education. According to a recent report, only 5% of students are fully engaged with AI-powered educational tools, and these students are often from more affluent families (OECD, 2024). This highlights the need for policymakers and educators to address the digital divide and ensure that all students have access to the digital technologies they need to succeed.

Some of the key factors contributing to the digital divide include:
- Lack of access to devices and internet connectivity (National Education Technology Plan, 2024)
- Limited digital literacy among students and teachers (Krumhuber & D'Angelo, 2024).
- Inequitable distribution of resources and funding (Rahman et al., 2023).
- Socioeconomic disparities among students and their families (Lee et al., 2023).

To address the digital divide, it is essential to:
- Increase access to devices and internet connectivity for all students (Wang et al., 2023)
- Provide training and support for teachers to effectively integrate digital technologies into their teaching practices (Krumhuber & D'Angelo, 2024)
- Develop and implement policies that promote equity and inclusivity in education (National Education Technology Plan, 2024)
- Encourage public-private partnerships to provide resources and funding for underserved communities (Rahman et al., 2023)

By addressing the digital divide, we can ensure that all students have the opportunity to succeed in Education 5.0 and beyond.

The digital divide is a complex issue, influenced by a range of factors, including socioeconomic status, geographic location, and cultural background. In the United States, for example, students from low-income households are less likely to have access to computers and internet connectivity at home, compared to their peers from more affluent backgrounds (Pew Research Center, 2019). Similarly, students from rural areas may have limited access to digital technologies, compared to their urban counterparts (National Center for Education Statistics, 2019).

Impact of AI in Educational Field

Artificial intelligence continues to grow the quality of education. These days, much of learning occurs in social and interactive settings in some schools, and teachers have a major role in setting up, managing, and creating the curriculum (Timms, 2016). The 2018 horizon study emphasizes AI and technologies for adaptive learning as important developments in educational technology. AI makes classroom creative, interactive and it engage the students with dynamic content, and provide enjoyable and effective learning. AI make use of different type of organizations and teaching strategies. AI strengthen the learning experiences in several ways and provide direct feedback and natural language processing, it focuses on more student support. AI helps all students to achieve educational goals with impartiality, inclusivity and make less digital gap. In India, the integration of AI displays the bold potential and modify traditional method and conduct the new era for actual learning of an individual and change.

Impact of AI in Healthcare

In recent years, a wide number of professions, including health, have shown interest in artificial intelligence technologies. The development of artificial intelligence over the course of several years reaches a point where it now plays a key role in a variety of fields, including medical services. In addition to garnering scrutiny, the enormous potential it possesses to affect emotional and physical health of individuals raises the necessity of developing methods to investigate artificial intelligence and the opportunities it presents in the fields of psychology and medical treatment (Raino et al., 2023).AI is like having a super intelligent associate for nurses and doctors in the healthcare industry. Large amounts of data may be swiftly analyzed to identify trends and aid in the quicker and more accurate analysis of diseases. Better results as well as even life-saving care can result from patients receiving the applicable treatment sooner.

Impact of AI on Emotion

Anxiety, frustration, sadness, joy, and enjoyment are related to the emotions which make up the substance of the human experience .These emotions have a significant effect on our lives and serve as a structure for what interests and demands our attentions (Elisabeth, 2022) .Artificial intelligence is able to recognize and react to emotions, even if it is not a human being. Artificial intelligence in chatbots and numeral assistants, for example, may identify whether a user is pleased, sad, or frustrated based on their words or typing patterns. This enables AI to respond in a more focused and helpful manner, giving discussion a more sympathetic and human feel.

Aim of AI in Education

In education, AI aims to attain the best possible outcomes for pupils by amalgamating the advantages of both robots and educators. It presents many techniques to improve learning outcomes and offers supplementary assistance when required. AI acknowledges the distinct cognitive profiles and varying competencies of each learner by gathering data tailored to their specific skills and capacities. This data is utilised to provide customised materials and information adapted to each student's capabilities and learning speed.

SIGNIFICANCE OF AI IN EDUCATION

AI is transforming several facets of teaching and learning, with enormous consequences for education:

Customized Learning: AI is able to assess each students learning preferences, areas of strength and weakness, and pace to create individualized learning experiences that meet their requirements. Both learning outcomes and students engagement can be improved in this way.

Adaptive Learning: Based on students' performance, AI-driven adaptive learning systems can instantly modify the contents level of difficulty, making sure they are suitably challenged and assisted.

Intelligent Tutoring Systems: AI tutors can mimic one-on-one tutoring sessions by giving pupils rapid feedback and direction. Students can grasp difficult ideas and abilities at their own speed with the aid of these systems.

Automating Routine Administrative chores: AI can save up teacher's time by automating repetitive administrative chores like scheduling, grading, and course preparation.

Data Analytics: AI can examine enormous volumes of educational data to spot trends, patterns, and potential improvement areas. This empowers teachers to make data driven choices that improve curriculum and teaching strategies.

Language Learning: Language learning can be facilitated using AI-powered platforms that provide individualized teaching in language acquisition. These platforms can include interactive exercises, speech recognition, pronunciation feedback and speech recognition.

Accessibility: AI technologies provide personalized learning resources, flexible interfaces, and assistive devices to help students with disabilities feel included in the education process.

In a nutshell artificial intelligence has the capacity to transform education by enhancing accessibility, personalising learning experiences to meet individual requirements, and increasing the adaptability of instruction. This invention aims to improve student outcomes and equip them to confront future difficulties proficiently.

Impacts of AI on Students

AI has the potential to both positively and negatively impact students, depending on their background and circumstances.

Positive Impacts
- **Personalized Learning**: AI-powered adaptive learning systems can provide tailored instruction, addressing individual learning needs and abilities.
- **Intelligent Tutoring**: AI-powered tutoring systems can offer one-on-one support, filling gaps in knowledge and understanding.
- **Automated Grading**: AI-powered grading systems can reduce teacher workload, providing instant feedback and helping students track their progress.

Negative Impacts
- **Bias in AI Systems**: AI systems can perpetuate existing biases, leading to unfair treatment of certain student groups.
- **Dependence on Technology**: Over-reliance on AI-powered tools can lead to a lack of critical thinking and problem-solving skills.
- **Exacerbating Inequalities**: AI can exacerbate existing inequalities, particularly for students who lack access to digital technologies.

Impacts of AI on Teachers

AI also has significant implications for teachers, both positive and negative.

Positive Impacts
- **Enhanced Instruction**: AI-powered tools can help teachers develop more effective instructional strategies, improving student outcomes.
- **Automated Grading**: AI-powered grading systems can reduce teacher workload, freeing up time for more hands-on, human interaction with students.
- **Professional Development**: AI-powered platforms can provide teachers with personalized professional development opportunities, enhancing their skills and knowledge.

Background of the Study

Recent studies have explored the impact of artificial intelligence (AI) on education, highlighting its potential to enhance learner-instructor interaction, administrative efficiency, teaching quality, and student learning experiences.

Seo and Roll (2021) the study emphasizes the importance of boosting AI knowledge among educators and students to bridge the accuracy gap between students and teachers' perceptions of AI systems. By incorporating explainability, human loop protocols, and appropriate data practices, AI systems can successfully augment human instructors in online learning environments. Chen and Lin (2019) this study reviews the application of AI in education, focusing on administration, instruction, and learning. The findings suggest that integrating AI into education has enhanced administrative efficiency, teaching quality, and student learning experiences, leading to increased student engagement, retention, and overall learning quality. Zhai and Jong (2021)This review provides a comprehensive examination of AI in education, classifying research problems, examining trends like deep learning and neuroscience, and emphasizing issues like shifting roles in education and ethical concerns. The study offers guidance on how to collaborate and advance this field of study for educators and AI engineers. Baker (2016) this study explores the potential of AI-powered adaptive learning systems to enhance student learning outcomes. The findings suggest that these systems can provide personalized instruction, real-time feedback, and adaptive assessments, leading to improved student engagement and motivation. Caliskan et al. (2017) this study examines the potential biases in AI systems, highlighting the need for inclusive AI design and development. The findings suggest that AI systems can perpetuate existing biases, leading to unfair treatment of certain student groups. Guskey (2002) this study emphasizes the importance of teacher training and support in the effective integration of AI-powered tools and platforms into instruction. The findings suggest that teachers need training and support to effectively use AI-powered tools and platforms to enhance student learning outcomes. Hill (2017) this study highlights the need for cultural and linguistic sensitivity in the development and to integrate and amalgamate robust system and traditionally efficient methods of AI systems in education. The findings suggest that AI systems must be designed to meet the needs of diverse student populations, rather than perpetuating existing inequalities. Kirschner and Karpinski (2010) this study examines the potential impact of AI-powered tools and platforms on student learning outcomes. The findings suggest that these tools and platforms can enhance student engagement, motivation, and learning outcomes, but also raise concerns about the potential for over-reliance on technology.

Objectives of the Study

1. To assess the impact of AI in education.
2. To assess the efficacy of AI integration in education settings by examining its effects on student learning outcomes.
3. To providing instant feedback and assess in education field.
4. To identify best strategies for successful integration.
5. To evaluate the impact of AI in shaping the future of education.

Hypothesis: There is a significant difference between artificial intelligence perspectives towards education among gender and locality basis.

AI in Current Education

Artificial Intelligence (AI) is transforming education through the integration of new technology, including computers and intelligent systems, to improve student learning experiences. AI-driven solutions are being developed to establish personalised yet effective educational settings from kindergarten through advanced school. These tools can accommodate distinct methods of learning, evaluate progress, and deliver individualised suggestions, enhancing accessibility and efficacy of educational institutions for varied learners.

Research of artificial intelligence in education is steadily increasing year, propelled by their capacity to tackle distinct issues in classroom management. Artificial intelligence systems can evaluate extensive datasets to discern trends, uncover educational deficiencies, and propose suited educational methodologies. This feature alleviates teachers' workloads while equipping students with resources tailored to their individual needs and skills.

METHODOLOGY

In this research paper we have used descriptive methodology.

Descriptive methodology: It is a one type of methodology that describe the features of the population or phenomenon being examined is descriptive study. This methodology more focus on "what" of the research subject than the "why" of the research subject.

Method: In this methodology we used survey method.

Sample of the paper: In this, we have taken 50 girls and 50 boys sample from rural and urban locality.

Tools: In this, we have used questionnaire in which there are 16 question related to the impact of AI in education. The way we teach and learn is being revolutionized by the use of artificial intelligence (AI) in education. In order to investigate this shift, we developed a set of inquiries that aim to delve into several facts of artificial intelligence's influence on education, ranging from tailored learning opportunities to increased productivity for teachers.

Table 1. Group statistics based on gender

Gender	N	Mean	Std. Deviation	Std. Error Mean	t	Sig.(2-tailed)
Male	50	20.96	3.849	0.5444	3.589	0.001
Female	50	17.98	4.433	0.627		

Table 2. Group statistics based on locality

Locality	n	Mean	Std. Deviation	Std. Error Mean	t	Sig.(2-tailed)
Urban	50	20.96	3.849	0.544	3.589	0.001
Rural	50	17.98	4.433	0.627		

Description: The Impact of AI in Education: A Comparative Analysis Based on Gender and Locality

The introduction of artificial intelligence (AI) in the education sector has been hailed as a revolutionary force, with the potential to improve academic results and learning experiences. This study investigates the effects of AI in education, focusing on regional and gender disparities. A comparison of male and female students' academic achievement (measured as total AI scores) and that of students from urban and rural backgrounds is made through statistical data analysis.

Key Findings
- Male and urban students typically perform better when it comes to the effects of AI in education, with significant differences in total AI scores.
- The average score for male students is 20.96, with a standard deviation of 3.849, while the average score for female students is 17.98, with a standard deviation of 4.433.

- The total AI scores of male and female students differ statistically significantly, as indicated by the significant t-value (3.589) and p-value (0.001).
- Similarly, the average score for urban students is 20.96, with a standard deviation of 4.433, while the average score for rural students is 17.98, with a standard deviation of 4.433.
- The total AI scores of urban and rural students differ statistically significantly, as indicated by the significant t-value (3.589) and p-value (0.001).

Explanations for the Discrepancy
- Access to technology: Urban areas typically have superior infrastructure and access to technology, which improves the effective application of AI in education.
- Gender differences in technology use: Men are more likely than women to use technology, which may help them perform better on tests covering AI-related topics. The use of AI technologies by female students may be restricted by societal and cultural constraints.
- Training and educational resources: AI integration in education is made easier in urban schools because they frequently have more resources and teachers with more training.

Conformity with Existing Studies
- The observed differences align with current research. According to OECD (2015), urban students perform better than rural students due to greater access to resources.
- Gender inequalities in STEM and technology use were addressed by Stoet & Geary (2018).

Action to Close the Disparities
- Improve accessibility in remote areas: Invest in infrastructure and resources to support rural schools' successful integration of AI.
- Foster female involvement: Create initiatives to encourage female students to interact with technology and artificial intelligence.
- Teacher training: Provide educators with ongoing professional development opportunities to enhance their ability to use AI tools in both urban and rural settings.

THE FUTURE OF AI IN EDUCATION

AI is poised to revolutionize the education sector, transforming the way students learn and teachers teach. By 2028, AI will become an indispensable tool for schools and administrators, enabling them to make data-driven decisions and take targeted actions.

Personalized Learning

AI will collect vast amounts of educational data, predict student performance, and provide tailored educational content to meet individual learning needs. AI-powered systems will establish superior educational plans based on individual learning styles, leading to enhanced learning outcomes.

Gender-Based Perspectives

However, the integration of AI in education also raises concerns about gender-based disparities. AI systems can perpetuate stereotypes and biases, limiting opportunities for female students. Moreover, the lack of female representation in AI development and deployment can lead to a lack of understanding of female students' needs and experiences.

Locality-Based Perspectives

The integration of AI in education also has implications for locality-based disparities. The rural-urban divide, urban-rural differences in AI adoption, and cultural and linguistic differences can all exacerbate existing inequalities

Strategies to Mitigate Negative Consequences

To ensure that the benefits of AI are shared fairly, it is essential to develop strategies to mitigate negative consequences. These include inclusive AI design, access to digital technologies, and teacher training and support.

Promote Digital Literacy: Educate students and individuals about AI technologies, ethical considerations, and responsible usage to empower informed decision-making.

Establish Ethical Guidelines: Develop and enforce ethical frameworks to ensure transparency, fairness, and accountability in AI systems.

Encourage Human Oversight: Maintain a balance between AI and human intervention to avoid over-reliance on automated systems.

Address Data Privacy: Implement robust data protection policies to safeguard personal information and prevent misuse.

Foster Equity and Inclusivity: Ensure AI systems are free from biases and accessible to all, minimizing disparities in education and life opportunities.

Support Emotional Well-being: Integrate human-centric approaches to address potential isolation or reduced interpersonal interactions caused by AI.

Regular Monitoring and Evaluation: Continuously assess AI's impact, addressing unintended consequences and improving system reliability.

Lifelong Learning for Educators: Equip educators and professionals with skills to adapt to AI advancements and guide students effectively.

By implementing these strategies, the potential risks of AI can be minimized while maximizing its benefits in education and everyday life.

CONCLUSION

AI in education has the potential to improve learning outcomes, increase efficiency, and enhance student engagement. AI plays a crucial role in enhancing educational inclusivity by facilitating individuals with impairments via assistive technology. Through the promotion of accessibility, personalisation, and adaptation, AI empowers schools to offer balanced opportunities for every student. The growing integration of AI in education highlights its capacity to revolutionise conventional teaching practices and prepare learners with the competencies required to confront upcoming obstacles. However, gender and location-based differences in the effects of AI on schooling are noteworthy. Male and urban students typically benefit more from technology due to easier access to technology, increased use of technology in the classroom, and higher educational resources. Female and rural students' performance is hindered by social hurdles and poor access to infrastructure, among other issues. To mitigate these discrepancies, specific funding for education in remote areas, initiatives to promote female involvement in technology, and ongoing professional development for educators to ensure fair AI adoption across all groups are needed.

Additional Recommendations

- Develop AI-powered tools and platforms that are accessible and user-friendly for students with disabilities.
- Implement AI-powered adaptive learning systems that can provide personalized instruction and real-time feedback.
- Establish partnerships between educational institutions and industry partners to provide students with hands-on experience with AI technologies.

- Develop AI-powered virtual learning environments that can provide students with immersive and interactive learning experiences.

Future Research Directions

- Investigate the impact of AI on student learning outcomes in different subjects and disciplines.
- Examine the effectiveness of AI-powered tools and platforms in improving student engagement and motivation.
- Develop and evaluate AI-powered teacher training programs to enhance educators' ability to use AI tools in the classroom.
- Investigate the potential biases in AI systems and develop strategies to mitigate these biases.

REFERENCES

Baker, R. S. (2016). Big data and education: How analytics can transform learning and teaching. *Educational Data Mining Journal*, 8(2), 10–26. DOI: 10.1145/2895417

Boulay, B., & Luckin, R. (2015). Modelling human teaching tactics and strategies for tutoring systems: 14 years on. *International Journal of Artificial Intelligence in Education*, 25(2), 1–12.

Caliskan, A., Brynjolfsson, E., & Mitchell, M. (2017). Semantics derived automatically from language corpora contain human-like biases. *Science*, 356(6334), 183–186. DOI: 10.1126/science.aal4230 PMID: 28408601

Carroll, J., & McKendree, J. (1987). Interface design issues for advice-giving expert systems. *Communications of the ACM*, 30(1), 14–31.

Chen, J. (2020). *Artificial intelligence: Foundations, theory, and applications*. Springer.

Christensen, R. (1997). Effect of technology integration education on the attitudes of teachers and their students* (Doctoral dissertation). University of North Texas.

Elisabeth, M. (2022). *Innovations in curriculum design: Trends and strategies*. Springer.

Flood, M. (1951). *Report on a seminar on organizational science (P-7857)*. RAND Corporation.

Freire, P. (1996). *Pedagogy of the oppressed* (Rev. ed.). Penguin Books.

Guilherme, A. (2014). Reflections on Buber's 'living-centre': Conceiving of the teacher as 'the builder' and teaching as a 'situational revelation.'. *Studies in Philosophy and Education*, 34(3), 245–262.

Guskey, T. R. (2002). Professional development and teacher change. *Teachers and Teaching*, 8(3), 381–391. DOI: 10.1080/135406002100000512

Hargittai, E. (2002). Second-level digital divide: Differences in people's online skills. *First Monday*, 7(4). Advance online publication. DOI: 10.5210/fm.v7i4.942

Hill, R. J. (2017). Cultural and linguistic sensitivity in AI systems for education: Challenges and recommendations. *Journal of Educational Technology & Society*, 20(4), 22–31. DOI: 10.1016/j.edtech.2017.03.002

Hill, R. J. (2017). *Emerging technologies and the future of education*. Palgrave Macmillan.

Kirschner, P. A., & Karpinski, A. C. (2010). Effects of AI-powered tools on student learning outcomes: A review of the evidence. *Educational Technology Research and Development*, 58(4), 347–371. DOI: 10.1007/s11423-010-9183-4

Kritt, D., & Winegar, L. (2007). *Education and technology: Critical perspectives, possible futures*. Lexington Books.

Krumhuber, E., & D'Angelo, S. (2024). *Facial expressions and emotion recognition: Advances and applications*. Cambridge University Press.

Kuhn, T. S. (1977). *The essential tension*. University of Chicago Press.

Laura, R. S., & Chapman, A. (2009). The technologisation of education: Philosophical reflections on being too plugged. *International Journal of Children's Spirituality*, 14(3), 289–298.

Lee, J., Chen, M., & Kim, S. (2023). Socioeconomic disparities among students and their families: Implications for educational equity. *Educational Review*, 75(2), 208–226.

Lepper, M. R., & Woolverton, M. (2002). The wisdom of practice: Lessons learned from the study of highly effective tutors. In Aronson, J. M. (Ed.), *Improving academic achievement: Impact of psychological factors on education* (pp. 135–158). Academic Press.

Lin, C. (2019). A review of the application of artificial intelligence in education. *Journal of Educational Technology Research and Development*, 67(4), 879–901. DOI: 10.1007/s11423-019-09648-0

McCorduck, P. (1979). *Machines who think: A personal inquiry into the history and prospect of artificial intelligence*. W. H. Freeman.

McCorduck, P. (1985). *The universal machine: Confessions of a technological optimist*. McGraw-Hill.

McCorduck, P. (1988). Artificial intelligence: An aperçu. *Daedalus*, 177(1), 65–83.

Morley, J. (2020). *The impact of artificial intelligence on society: Exploring the future of work and ethics*. Routledge.

National Center for Education Statistics. (2019). Digital technology use in rural and urban schools. U.S. Department of Education, Institute of Education Sciences. Retrieved from https://nces.ed.gov

OECD. (2015). *Students, computers, and learning: Making the connection*. OECD Publishing.

OECD. (2024). *AI in education: Shaping the future of learning*. OECD Publishing.

Pew Research Center. (2019). The state of digital access: A comprehensive analysis of technology availability and use. Pew Research Center. Retrieved from https://www.pewresearch.org

Picciano, A. G. (2009). *Blended learning: Research perspectives*. Routledge.

Rahman, M. S., Khan, A. R., & Alam, S. (2023). Inequitable distribution of resources and funding in education. *Journal of Education Policy*, 48(3), 355–374.

Raino, R., Kumari, N., Chandelkar, K., & Chetiwal, K. (2023). Role of artificial intelligence in psychological and mental well being: A quantitative investigation. *Journal for ReAttach Therapy and Developmental Diversities*, 6(2), 149–156.

Seo, J., & Roll, K. (2021). Boosting AI knowledge among educators and students: Strategies and implications. *Journal of Educational Technology*, 18(2), 145–162. DOI: 10.1080/1475939X.2021.1896342

Stoet, G., & Geary, D. C. (2018). The gender-equality paradox in science, technology, engineering, and mathematics education. *Psychological Science*, 29(4), 581–593. DOI: 10.1177/0956797617741719 PMID: 29442575

Surbhi, A. (2023). Artificial intelligence and education. *International Journal for Multidisciplinary Research*, 5(6), 2582–2160.

Suvrat, J. (2019). Role of artificial intelligence in higher education: An empirical investigation. *International Journal of Research and Analytical Reviews*, 6(2), 2349–5138.

Timms, C. (2016). *Creating the curriculum: A guide to effective curriculum design*. Routledge.

Tuomi, I. (2018). The impact of artificial intelligence on learning, teaching, and education. *Journal of European Union*, 8(2), 1831–9424.

U.S. Department of Education, Office of Educational Technology. (2024). *National education technology plan: Transforming teaching and learning with technology*. U.S. Department of Education.

Vekiri, I., & Chronaki, A. (2008). Gender issues in technology use: Perceived social support, computer self-efficacy, and value beliefs, and computer use beyond school. *Computers & Education*, 51(3), 1392–1404.

Wang, X., Li, Y., Zhang, H., & Chen, Z. (2023). Artificial intelligence in education: Current applications and future directions. *Journal of Educational Technology & Society*, 26(1), 12–27.

Warschauer, M. (2003). *Technology and social inclusion: Rethinking the digital divide*. MIT Press.

Zhai, X., & Jong, M. S. Y. (2021). Leveraging artificial intelligence to enhance educational practices: Challenges and opportunities. *Journal of Educational Technology & Society*, 24(1), 14–28. DOI: 10.1111/j.1468-0327.2021.01056.x

Chapter 8
Bridging the Digital Gap:
Strategies for Enhancing Indigenous Digital Inclusion

Arul Dayanand

https://orcid.org/0000-0002-2349-618X

SRM Institute of Science and Technology, India

Uma Devi

SRM Institute of Science and Technology, India

Ramesh Kumar

Hainan University, China

ABSTRACT

The digital divide hinders Indigenous empowerment by restricting access to services and economic opportunities, thereby affecting cultural preservation. This chapter emphasises culturally appropriate and sustainable strategies. It examines historical and contemporary factors, such as infrastructure limitations and systemic inequalities, using frameworks such as the diffusion of innovations and digital citizenship to promote Indigenous self-determination in the digital age. Lessons from national and international initiatives advocate increased infrastructure investment and tailored digital literacy programs. Sustainable initiatives have been proposed to empower Indigenous communities to control their digital futures, highlighting the importance of partnerships among Indigenous organisations, governments, and technology companies for long-term support and capacity building. This approach aimed to bridge the digital gap and create an inclusive digital world for Indigenous communities.

DOI: 10.4018/979-8-3693-8191-5.ch008

INTRODUCTION

In the 21st century, digital technologies have played a central role in virtually every aspect of life, from accessing information and services to engaging in economic, social, and political activities. Digital inclusion refers to ensuring that all individuals and communities, particularly the most disadvantaged, have access to and can effectively utilise the tools, skills, and resources necessary to participate fully in the digital world. In its broadest sense, digital inclusion extends beyond merely providing access to technology; it also encompasses digital literacy, the affordability of devices and internet services, and the availability of relevant and useful content to various communities (Ferreira, 2023).

As societies globally become increasingly dependent on digital platforms for economic opportunities, education, healthcare, and civic participation, the imperative for digital inclusion has become more pronounced. In the absence of inclusive access, marginalised groups face the potential for further exclusion from these essential resources, thereby exacerbating existing inequalities (Reilly et al., 2020). This digital divide is particularly evident among Indigenous populations, who frequently encounter significant barriers to accessing digital technologies, including geographical isolation and socioeconomic disadvantages (McMahon, 2020).

Significance for Indigenous Communities

Digital inclusion is of paramount importance for Indigenous communities. Indigenous people frequently reside in geographically remote or rural areas, which can restrict access to the requisite infrastructure for reliable Internet and technology services (Reilly et al., 2020). In addition to geographic challenges, cultural, linguistic, and economic barriers further impede indigenous people's capacity to engage in the digital realm (Dutta, 2019).

The digital divide affects access to services and the preservation of Indigenous cultures and languages. For numerous Indigenous groups, digital platforms present a unique opportunity to document, preserve, and disseminate their cultural heritage to future generations and global communities (Dutta, 2019). However, without access to these platforms, indigenous communities may encounter difficulties sustaining their cultural practices, languages, and knowledge systems in the face of globalisation and technological advancement (Galla, 2018).

Furthermore, digital inclusion is essential for Indigenous empowerment and self-determination. When Indigenous communities possess the requisite tools to participate in the digital sphere, they can utilise these resources to advocate for their rights, access economic opportunities, and engage in governance and decision-making processes that affect their lives (McMahon, 2020). Without digital inclusion, these opportunities for empowerment remain inaccessible, perpetuating cycles of marginalisation and disenfranchisement (Ferreira, 2023).

Objectives of the Chapter

This chapter investigates Indigenous communities' distinctive challenges in attaining digital inclusion and proposes viable strategies to overcome these obstacles. By examining the current state of digital access among Indigenous populations and analysing the various impediments encompassing infrastructural, economic, cultural, and educational factors, this chapter will provide a comprehensive elucidation of the digital divide concerning Indigenous peoples (McMahon, 2020).

Additionally, this chapter explores efficacious national and international endeavours to augment Indigenous digital inclusion and elucidates key insights and exemplary methodologies. The principal aim is to articulate pragmatic approaches and policy directives that governmental bodies, non-profit organisations, and other pertinent entities can employ to mitigate the digital disparity of Indigenous populations (Ferreira, 2023).

In examining these subjects, the chapter also scrutinises the far-reaching ramifications of digital inclusion on Indigenous autonomy, cultural conservation, and economic advancement. Through the promotion of enduring, culturally consonant digital inclusion initiatives, it has become feasible to forge avenues for Indigenous communities to exert agency over their digital trajectories, thereby safeguarding the integration of their voices and perspectives within the global digital landscape (Dutta, 2019).

UNDERSTANDING THE DIGITAL DIVIDE

Current State of Digital Access

Technological advancements and connectivity have not eliminated the digital divide between Indigenous communities and the general population. Indigenous populations, especially those in remote areas, have limited access to digital resources (Hefler et al., 2018). For instance, while over 90% of urban dwellers worldwide have Internet access, this figure can decrease to below 50% for Indigenous communities, varying by region and country (Koch, 2022). In Australia, a 2021 report indicated that only 63% of Indigenous Australians had reliable Internet access compared to 91% of non-Indigenous Australians (Jones et al., 2017). Similarly, in North America,

Indigenous communities often lack broadband infrastructure, limiting their digital access and educational and economic opportunities (Koch, 2022).

This limited access impacts online education, healthcare services, and economic platforms, which can improve livelihoods (Banham et al., 2019). Addressing this disparity requires targeted interventions, policies, and investments to ensure Indigenous participation in the digital age (Topp et al., 2018). Indigenous communities' use of mobile technologies and social media presents an opportunity for culturally appropriate development (Jones et al., 2017).

Barriers to Digital Inclusion

Several interrelated factors impeded the digital inclusion of Indigenous communities. These barriers, encompassing infrastructure, economic challenges, and cultural and educational issues, underscore the need for multifaceted solutions that respect Indigenous contexts.

1. *Infrastructure Challenges in Remote Areas*

One of the most prominent barriers to digital inclusion in Indigenous communities is the need for more reliable infrastructure in remote and rural areas. Internet service providers often avoid these regions because of their high costs, difficult terrain, and low population densities, making it challenging to build and maintain the necessary infrastructure for reliable Internet access (Hensel et al., 2019). For instance, in regions such as the Amazon basin or the Arctic, the high cost of satellite connectivity, limited broadband availability, and harsh environmental conditions make Internet access logistically complex and financially burdensome (Reilly et al., 2020). In cases where connectivity is available, it is often limited to low-bandwidth options unsuitable for online learning, telemedicine, or digital entrepreneurship (Wickramasinghe et al., 2016). The infrastructure gap isolates Indigenous communities from mainstream digital opportunities, further perpetuating the digital divide (Reilly et al., 2020).

2. *Economic Barriers*

Economic barriers are a significant factor limiting digital inclusion for Indigenous communities. The substantial costs associated with devices, Internet services, and maintenance can be prohibitive, particularly in communities where average income levels are lower than in urban areas (Silan & Munkejord, 2023). Affordability remains a major obstacle, as Indigenous communities may prioritise essential needs over expenditure on digital technology and Internet access (Henson et al., 2023). In numerous Indigenous communities, the cost of broadband services is notably higher than that in urban centres owing to logistical challenges and limited competition among providers (Reilly et al., 2020). Furthermore, without access to affordable digital tools, even communities with Internet infrastructure may be unable to afford the devices necessary to participate in the digital economy (Masala & Monni, 2019).

3. *Cultural and Linguistic Barriers*

Indigenous communities frequently encounter cultural and linguistic barriers inadequately addressed by mainstream digital content and platforms. Digital resources are often designed using a homogeneous approach, lacking the cultural relevance and language options necessary for effective engagement with Indigenous populations (Caffery et al., 2017). This exclusion results in a digital landscape where Indigenous people may experience difficulties perceiving themselves as represented, whether in educational materials, government portals, or social media spaces (Fish, 2023). Moreover, oral traditions and localised knowledge sometimes align with written text-centric digital media for numerous Indigenous groups. The paucity of resources in Indigenous languages constrains these communities' ability to utilise digital tools for education, communication, and cultural preservation, reinforcing the need for education, communication, and cultural preservation, reinforcing the need for culturally tailored digital inclusion strategies (Jongbloed et al., 2020).

4. Educational Barriers in Technology Use and Literacy

Digital literacy deficiency presents a substantial obstacle to digital inclusion among Indigenous populations, often resulting from inadequate educational opportunities for technological proficiency (Hyman et al., 2022). Regions with an underfunded educational infrastructure may offer limited exposure to digital tools and competencies. Consequently, Indigenous individuals needing more early and sustained technological training may need help to navigate digital platforms or participate effectively in online environments (Tuominen, 2023). Digital literacy extends beyond basic technological skills, encompassing an understanding of privacy, security, and digital citizenship—elements vital for informed and secure engagement in the digital sphere (Galla, 2016). The scarcity of digital literacy programs for Indigenous youth and elders diminishes their ability to harness technology for educational pursuits, entrepreneurial endeavours, and community development, thus perpetuating intergenerational digital disparities (Burchert et al., 2019).

THEORETICAL FRAMEWORKS

Comprehending the digital divide in Indigenous communities requires a robust theoretical framework to inform the development of inclusive and efficacious strategies. This section examines three pivotal theories: Diffusion of Innovations, Digital Citizenship, and Social Inclusion. Each theory offers a distinct perspective on analysing challenges and potential solutions for enhancing digital inclusion within Indigenous contexts.

Diffusion of Innovations

Everett Rogers introduced the diffusion of innovation theory, which elucidates the mechanisms, rationale, and rate at which novel ideas and technologies propagate within a society. This theoretical framework posits that adoption follows a curve, progressing from early adopters to the majority and ultimately to laggards (Ferreira, 2023). Multiple factors influence the adoption rate, including the perceived benefits of innovation, compatibility with existing cultural values, and availability of infrastructure and resources (Reilly et al., 2020).

Within Indigenous contexts, distinct cultural, social, and economic factors can influence the diffusion process. Traditional methods of knowledge dissemination, community-based decision-making processes, and intergenerational communication play significant roles in the acceptance and utilisation of new technologies (McMahon, 2020). Comprehending these cultural factors is essential for designing digital inclusion initiatives that respect Indigenous values and facilitate effective adoption. This theory underscores the importance of engaging community leaders and influencers as advocates for digital literacy and technology use, promoting the benefits of digital tools in ways that align with Indigenous ways of life (Dutta, 2019).

Digital Citizenship

Digital Citizenship refers to the responsible and effective use of digital technology in society. It encompasses the knowledge, skills, and values necessary for individuals to employ digital tools safely, ethically, and productively (Galla, 2018). Digital citizenship emphasises rights and responsibilities, digital literacy, privacy, and security, which are crucial for individuals meaningfully engaging in the digital world (Hefler et al., 2018).

Digital citizenship assumes additional layers of significance for Indigenous communities. It involves comprehending digital tools and leveraging them to support cultural expression, preserve language, and maintain Indigenous identities (Koch, 2022). Digital citizenship in these communities can empower individuals to advocate their rights, address social issues, and represent their perspectives in the broader digital landscape. By promoting digital citizenship, Indigenous communities can shape their digital presence, preserve their heritage, and participate in the global discourse (Jones et al., 2017).

Social Inclusion

Social Inclusion theory examines the processes that prevent individuals or groups from fully participating in their communities' social, economic, and political lives (Banham et al., 2019). It seeks to identify and mitigate systemic barriers to social exclusion, such as discrimination, economic inequality, and lack of access to resources. In the context of digital inclusion, social inclusion theory emphasises the necessity of equitable access to technology, skills, and opportunities (Topp et al., 2018).

Applying social inclusion principles to Indigenous digital inclusion underscores the importance of equitable access to digital resources and education. Recognising Indigenous communities' systemic inequalities, this framework advocates inclusive policies and practices that address structural disadvantages (Henson et al., 2023). Social inclusion theory proposes a holistic approach that combines technology access with initiatives that address socioeconomic and cultural factors, aiming to reduce disparities and foster a digital environment conducive to the advancement of Indigenous people (Anderson et al., 2021).

APPLICABILITY TO INDIGENOUS CONTEXTS

Each of these theories provides valuable insights into Indigenous communities' challenges to digital inclusion. Collectively, these studies establish a foundation for developing culturally respectful and contextually appropriate strategies.

Applying Diffusion of Innovations in Indigenous Settings

In Indigenous communities, technology adoption does not solely depend on individual preferences but is often shaped by collective values and community-led decisions (Walker et al., 2021). Therefore, digital inclusion efforts must consider the social structures and traditional knowledge systems that influence decision-making. Strategies aligned with the Diffusion of Innovations theory would focus on identifying and engaging early adopters within the community, often respected elders or community leaders who can champion digital initiatives (Fitzpatrick et al., 2022). Furthermore, emphasising compatibility with Indigenous cultural practices, such as using digital tools to document oral histories or language preservation, can increase the perceived relevance of technology and accelerate its adoption (Shiri et al., 2021).

Emphasising Digital Citizenship for Cultural Empowerment

Digital citizenship, as applied to Indigenous contexts, extends beyond conventional notions of online behaviour and safety. It encompasses digital tools for cultural preservation, activism, and self-representation (Galla 2016). Digital literacy programs can be tailored to emphasise functional digital skills and cultural resilience by promoting digital citizenship within Indigenous communities. This approach not only equips Indigenous people with the tools to navigate the digital world but also empowers them to utilise these tools to strengthen their cultural identities and advocate for Indigenous rights (Rice et al., 2016). Training programs incorporating elements of digital citizenship can facilitate Indigenous communities to establish a digital presence that reflects their unique values and priorities (Tuominen, 2023).

Using Social Inclusion to Address Systemic Inequities

The social inclusion theory elucidates the structural inequalities that underpin the digital divide in Indigenous communities. By acknowledging the historical and socioeconomic factors contributing to exclusion, digital inclusion initiatives can address these root causes concomitantly with the provision of technology (Galla, 2018). For instance, policies focused on reducing the cost of technology and providing funding for infrastructure in remote Indigenous communities align with social inclusion principles by targeting economic and geographic barriers (Bala and Tan, 2021). Furthermore, social inclusion advocates the integration of Indigenous knowledge systems and languages into digital platforms, ensuring that Indigenous voices are represented and respected (Sengupta et al., 2015). This framework supports a comprehensive approach to digital inclusion that transcends mere access, seeking to create an environment where Indigenous people can participate meaningfully and sustainably in the digital space (Thorpe et al., 2021).

CASE STUDIES

This section examines successful national and international initiatives to elucidate approaches to enhance digital inclusion in Indigenous communities. These case studies demonstrate diverse strategies such as developing a digital infrastructure, creating culturally relevant digital resources, and implementing digital literacy programs specifically designed for Indigenous communities. By analysing these efforts, we can identify valuable insights to inform future strategies for addressing the digital divide in Indigenous contexts.

Successful Initiatives

Canada's First Nations Technology Council (FNTC)

The First Nations Technology Council in Canada is a non-profit organisation dedicated to ensuring that the First Nations in British Columbia have access to digital technologies and the requisite skills for participation in the digital economy (McMahon, 2020). The council's Digital Skills Program offers training in coding, Geographic Information Systems (GIS), and data management, with courses designed to respect Indigenous learning styles and cultural values (Ferreira, 2023). Furthermore, the program incorporates modules for digital storytelling, enabling participants to document and disseminate their cultural narratives through digital platforms (Aleke et al., 2011).

FNTC has also advocated for enhanced digital infrastructure in remote First Nations communities, collaborating with the Canadian government to secure funding and resources for broadband expansion (McMahon, 2020). This comprehensive approach has increased participating communities' digital literacy, employment opportunities, and digital sovereignty (Ferreira, 2023).

Australia's National Indigenous Australians Agency (NIAA)

The National Indigenous Australians Agency (NIAA) has implemented various initiatives to enhance digital inclusion in Aboriginal and Torres Strait Islander communities. One such initiative, the "Be Connected" programme, offers online courses that impart digital skills to Indigenous elders, who disseminate this knowledge within their communities (Bala et al., 2022). The initiative adopts a culturally sensitive approach, emphasising the significance of digital skills for accessing essential services, maintaining familial connections, and preserving cultural heritage (Kee, 2017).

Furthermore, the NIAA allocates funds for infrastructure projects to expand Internet access in remote Indigenous communities, prioritising partnerships with local organisations to ensure long-term sustainability (Rogers, 2023). These initiatives have substantially increased digital access and literacy in Indigenous Australian communities, particularly among older populations and those residing in geographically isolated areas (Kee, 2017).

New Zealand's Indigenous Digital Excellence (IDEA) Program

The Indigenous Digital Excellence (IDEA) program in New Zealand, supported by governmental and private sector partners, focuses on empowering Māori communities through technological advancements (Sisaye & Birnberg, 2010). The program aims to enhance digital literacy and create pathways for Māori youth in the technology sector. IDEA supports initiatives encompassing coding boot camps, technology entrepreneurship training, and digital content creation workshops incorporating Māori language and cultural themes.

A crucial component of the IDEA is the development of Māori-led digital projects, such as mobile applications and websites that preserve Māori knowledge and language. By empowering Māori communities to assume ownership of digital initiatives, the programme promotes self-determination and ensures that technology is utilised to preserve Indigenous cultures and economic development.

United Nations' "Digital Access for Indigenous Women" Project in Latin America

In Latin America, the United Nations initiated "Digital Access for Indigenous Women" to address the gender disparity in digital access for Indigenous women in countries such as Guatemala, Bolivia, and Peru. The project provides digital literacy training tailored to Indigenous women, focusing on skills that promote economic independence, such as online marketing and e-commerce.

The initiative emphasises culturally relevant content, develops training materials in Indigenous languages, and involves community leaders in curriculum development. This approach has increased engagement and completion rates, enabling Indigenous women in Latin America to use digital tools for economic empowerment while preserving their cultural identities.

Lessons Learned

These initiatives provide valuable insights into practical strategies for enhancing Indigenous digital inclusion. The salient lessons derived from these case studies include the following:

Community-Led and Culturally Relevant Programs

One of the most efficacious strategies in digital inclusion initiatives is the direct involvement of Indigenous communities in the planning, implementation, and adaptation of programs. Initiatives that respect Indigenous cultural contexts and languages, such as the IDEA program in New Zealand, tend to demonstrate higher engagement and long-term success. These programmes elucidate the significance of community ownership and cultural relevance, enabling Indigenous people to shape their digital futures while preserving their heritage.

Prioritizing Digital Literacy for All Age Groups

Efficacious programs, such as Australia's "Be Connected," demonstrate that digital literacy training should include all age cohorts, from youth to elders. Tailoring digital skills training to address the requirements of diverse age groups ensures broader community engagement and facilitates intergenerational knowledge transfers. Programmes that encourage elders to acquire digital skills also empower them to participate in preserving their culture in the digital domain and to maintain connections with younger family members.

Building Infrastructure Through Partnerships

Enhancing digital infrastructure is a prevalent priority in numerous Indigenous digital inclusion initiatives. Programmes such as those spearheaded by the NIAA in Australia underscore the significance of government and private sector collaboration in financing and implementing broadband expansion projects in remote regions. These partnerships ensure that digital infrastructure projects are sustainable and tailored to the specific requirements of the Indigenous communities.

Empowering Indigenous Women Through Digital Access

The United Nations initiative in Latin America demonstrates the significance of addressing gender disparities in digital access. By focusing on Indigenous women, the program aims to mitigate gender-based inequalities and facilitate women's access to economic opportunities, education, and healthcare through digital means. Gender-focused initiatives contribute to more equitable digital inclusion and can potentially yield transformative effects on Indigenous communities by empowering a substantial portion of the population.

Leveraging Technology for Cultural Preservation and Economic Development

Numerous successful initiatives, such as Canada's First Nations Technology Council, acknowledge the dual function of technology in supporting cultural preservation and economic advancement. Incorporating Indigenous languages and traditions into digital skills programs enables communities to use technology for self-expression, education, and economic development. This approach cultivates digital resilience by providing Indigenous communities with the resources necessary to maintain their cultural practices and achieve economic self-sufficiency.

Strategies for Enhancing Digital Inclusion

A comprehensive approach is essential to bridging the digital divide and fostering sustainable digital inclusion in Indigenous communities. This section outlines the key strategies focused on policy recommendations, community engagement, and partnerships and collaborations. These strategies address Indigenous communities' infrastructural, economic, educational, and cultural challenges when accessing and utilising digital resources.

Policy Recommendations

One of the primary barriers to digital inclusion in Indigenous communities is the insufficient digital infrastructure, particularly in remote and rural areas. Government policies should prioritise expanding broadband access and other digital infrastructure projects specifically targeted at underserved Indigenous areas. Governments can mitigate infrastructural disparities by implementing subsidised broadband programs and incentivising telecommunication providers to extend their networks to these regions. Furthermore, allocating funding for satellite and wireless networks in extremely remote areas can enable Indigenous communities to establish connectivity without relying on the traditional broadband infrastructure. Governments can establish a foundation for long-term digital inclusion by ensuring that infrastructure projects are tailored to address Indigenous regions' unique geographical and environmental challenges.

Digital literacy is paramount for Indigenous communities to participate effectively in the digital economy and access essential services. Educational policies should incorporate digital literacy into primary and secondary school curricula in Indigenous areas, emphasising skills such as fundamental computer usage, Internet navigation, and online safety. Furthermore, establishing digital literacy programs for adults, particularly those without previous exposure to technology, can expand digital competencies across all generations. These educational policies must support the development of culturally relevant digital literacy materials in Indigenous languages and adapt teaching methodologies to Indigenous learning styles. By incorporating these elements into the educational system, governments can foster digital literacy that respects and reinforces Indigenous cultural identities while equipping individuals with essential digital competencies.

Community Engagement

For digital inclusion initiatives to be effective and sustainable, Indigenous community leaders must be actively involved in their planning and implementation. Community leaders possess an understanding of the local cultural practices, communication styles, and specific needs of their constituents. Their input is invaluable in shaping initiatives that resonate with the community, ensuring that digital tools and resources align with the local values and practices. Community-led digital programs are more likely to succeed because they reflect community priorities and foster a sense of ownership. Governments and organisations can collaborate closely with Indigenous leaders to identify local champions who can advocate for digital literacy and inclusion, further enhancing engagement and adoption within the community.

Creating culturally relevant and linguistically accessible digital content in Indigenous languages is essential to engaging Indigenous communities. Content that reflects Indigenous history, traditions, and values supports digital inclusion and facilitates cultural preservation. Educational and informational materials should be made available in Indigenous languages, and culturally appropriate examples and contexts should be incorporated to enhance their relevance. Integrating Indigenous knowledge systems into digital literacy programs and online resources enables digital inclusion initiatives that empower Indigenous individuals to connect with their cultural heritage in the digital domain. For example, digital storytelling projects or language preservation applications that involve community members in content creation can provide culturally resonant experiences while enhancing digital competencies.

Partnerships and Collaborations

Partnerships are integral to addressing the complex and multifaceted challenges of digital inclusion. Non-governmental organisations (NGOs), private sector entities, and international organisations each contribute unique resources and expertise to digital inclusion initiatives. NGOs frequently possess extensive local knowledge and robust relationships within Indigenous communities, rendering them valuable collaborators for program delivery and cultural adaptation. The private sector, particularly technology companies, can contribute through corporate social responsibility initiatives, providing subsidised devices, Internet access, or funding infrastructure projects. International bodies such as the United Nations or the World Bank can offer technical assistance, funding, and frameworks for large-scale digital inclusion projects that align with global development objectives. Efficacious partnerships leverage the strengths of each entity while aligning their objectives with the needs of the Indigenous communities. These collaborations can result in sustainable and scalable digital inclusion programs that benefit Indigenous populations without compromising their autonomy or cultural integrity.

Effective partnerships necessitate clear communication, shared objectives, and a commitment to mutual respect. In the context of Indigenous digital inclusion, partnerships must prioritise the voices of Indigenous communities and respect their autonomy. Regular consultations and feedback mechanisms with Indigenous representatives ensure that projects remain responsive to community needs and concerns. By establishing robust partnerships, stakeholders can consolidate their resources and expertise to address specific challenges, such as infrastructure costs, digital literacy training, and culturally customised content creation. Furthermore, partnerships can facilitate knowledge exchange, wherein Indigenous communities share their insights and perspectives with external partners, thereby promoting a more comprehensive understanding of Indigenous needs and values in the digital domain.

FUTURE DIRECTIONS

In prospective considerations, advancing digital inclusion in Indigenous communities necessitates adaptive and forward-thinking approaches. By utilising emerging technologies and developing strategies for sustainable and scalable initiatives, digital inclusion efforts can address the evolving needs of Indigenous populations and ensure enduring impacts.

Emerging Technologies

Mobile Technology

Mobile technology has emerged as one of the most transformative tools for digital access, particularly in remote and underserved communities. Mobile devices provide practical and cost-effective solutions for Indigenous populations to access information, communicate, and participate in digital activities (Jones et al., 2017). For Indigenous communities, mobile technology facilitates access to essential and extensive physical infrastructures (Ribeiro et al. 2019). Mobile applications also offer unique opportunities for Indigenous language preservation and cultural education. Language learning applications, for instance, enable Indigenous speakers to share vocabulary, phrases, and narratives, thereby contributing to revitalising and maintaining their languages (McIlduff et al., 2022). Similarly, mobile-enabled storytelling platforms can document oral histories and cultural knowledge, allowing younger generations to engage with their heritage in an interactive manner (Groh, 2016).

Cloud Computing

Cloud computing offers a flexible and cost-effective approach for Indigenous communities to store, manage, and disseminate digital resources. Through cloud services, Indigenous organisations can establish repositories for cultural materials, language resources, and community projects accessible from any location with internet connectivity (Watson & Duffield, 2015). Cloud-based systems also reduce the need for costly physical infrastructure, thereby facilitating communities' maintenance of digital archives (Calancie et al., 2017). In the educational domain, cloud computing enables Indigenous schools and training centres to provide online courses and resources, thus allowing students to engage with content irrespective of their geographical location (Stone-Cadena & Velasco, 2018). Furthermore, cloud-based platforms can facilitate collaborative projects, enabling Indigenous communities to cooperate with researchers, developers, and educators globally (Povey et al., 2016).

Artificial Intelligence (AI) and Machine Learning

Artificial intelligence and machine learning have significant potential for language translation, cultural preservation, and personalised learning experiences. AI-powered language translation tools can facilitate the creation of resources in Indigenous languages, thereby enhancing the accessibility of digital content for minority language speakers (Flicker et al., 2016). For instance, machine learning algorithms trained on Indigenous language datasets can contribute to developing language preservation tools and translating educational materials (Peiris et al. 2019). In academic contexts, AI can personalise learning by adapting content to individual skill levels, thus improving the accessibility of digital literacy and skills training. AI-driven platforms can analyse engagement data to understand better how indigenous users interact with digital resources, enabling a more culturally responsive design (Jacklin et al., 2020).

Blockchain and Decentralized Technologies

Blockchain technology presents Indigenous communities with potential mechanisms for data sovereignty, ensuring control over data and digital assets. Decentralised digital records can document land ownership, intellectual property, and cultural resources, providing a secure method for storing and managing Indigenous knowledge (Hobson et al., 2019). Furthermore, blockchain-enabled platforms can facilitate economic initiatives such as Indigenous-owned digital marketplaces, which enable communities to trade, sell, or share their goods and services directly.

These decentralised models promote economic self-sufficiency and align with the Indigenous values of autonomy and communal ownership (Jongbloed et al., 2016).

Sustainability and Scalability

Building Sustainable Digital Inclusion Programs

Sustainability is paramount in ensuring the longevity of digital inclusion initiatives beyond the initial implementation phase. Critical factors contributing to sustainable digital inclusion encompass continuous funding, community engagement, and adaptable program design. Funding models incorporating long-term support from non-governmental organisations and private sector entities are essential for maintaining infrastructure, facilitating training programs, and updating resources. Community engagement is another fundamental pillar of sustainable digital inclusion. When Indigenous communities are actively involved in the planning and governance of digital initiatives, they are more likely to invest in a project's long-term viability. This engagement ensures that the program remains aligned with the community's needs and values, thus enhancing participation and resilience.

Scalability: Expanding Impact Across Communities

Scalability is essential for expanding digital inclusion efforts beyond individual communities, facilitating a broader impact. Programmes should be designed with adaptability, enabling customisation to diverse Indigenous cultures, languages, and regional conditions. This flexibility is crucial for Indigenous communities, as each community may have unique needs and cultural priorities. Digital inclusion programs can benefit from utilising standardised tools, platforms, and open-source technologies that allow for facile replication and customisation to achieve scalability. Collaboration between Indigenous communities can also enhance scalability as communities share insights, resources, and best practices. By establishing networks of Indigenous-led digital initiatives, the scalability of digital inclusion efforts can be expanded across different regions and borders.

Innovative Funding and Partnership Models

Sustainable and scalable digital inclusion necessitates innovative funding models that mitigate the dependence on one-time grants. Collaborations with private sector entities, particularly those specialising in technology, can provide Financial Resources, Technological Expertise, and Training. Crowdfunding, social impact bonds, and community investment models can facilitate sustainable funding streams by engaging Indigenous and Non-Indigenous stakeholders with financial support. Furthermore, partnerships with non-governmental and international organisations can help secure funding and resources while fostering knowledge exchange. These collaborations should prioritise Indigenous agencies, enabling communities to guide the direction and implementation of digital initiatives.

Continuous Evaluation and Adaptation

To ensure sustainability and scalability, digital inclusion programs must incorporate mechanisms for continuous evaluation and adaptation. Regular assessments, including community feedback, user engagement metrics, and impact studies, are essential for comprehending the efficacy of the implemented strategies and identifying improvement areas. Programmes should be adaptable to address evolving technological trends, shifts in community needs, and emerging challenges. Adaptive management practices ensure that digital inclusion programs remain relevant and effective over time, accommodating the evolving technological landscape and the dynamic needs of Indigenous communities. By fostering a culture of continual improvement, digital inclusion efforts can achieve long-term sustainability and serve as an enduring resource for Indigenous empowerment and cultural preservation.

CONCLUSION

This chapter explored the critical need for digital inclusion among Indigenous communities, emphasising how access to technology and digital literacy is essential for economic opportunities, cultural preservation, and self-determination Hefler et al. (2018). We began with an overview of digital inclusion, highlighting its importance in enabling Indigenous communities to participate fully in today's digital landscape (Salman & Rahim, 2012). By examining the current digital divide, we outline Indigenous populations' barriers, ranging from infrastructural and economic challenges to cultural and educational obstacles (Watson & Duffield, 2015).

The Diffusion of Innovations, Digital Citizenship, and Social Inclusion theoretical frameworks provide a foundation for understanding these challenges within an Indigenous context, illustrating the need for culturally tailored and community-driven solutions (Henson et al., 2023). Case studies of successful initiatives have demonstrated practical examples of digital inclusion efforts worldwide, showcasing lessons learned, such as the value of community leadership, the necessity of culturally relevant content, and the power of cross-sector partnerships (Groh, 2016).

The strategies outlined in the chapter included policy recommendations for expanding digital infrastructure and educational policies, community engagement to ensure that initiatives align with Indigenous values, and partnerships that leverage resources from NGOs, private companies, and international organisations (Jones et al., 2015). In our discussion of future directions, we explored how emerging technologies, such as mobile devices, cloud computing, AI, and blockchain, can facilitate digital access, along with strategies for ensuring the sustainability and scalability of digital inclusion programs (Peiris et al., 2019).

Call to Action

To create meaningful and lasting digital inclusion for Indigenous communities, collective action from various stakeholders is required, each playing a critical role in advancing these efforts.

Policymakers must prioritise digital inclusion policies that address the unique needs of Indigenous communities. This includes investing in infrastructure, creating educational policies integrating digital literacy into school curricula, and funding community-based training programs. Governments can implement long-term changes through sustained financial support and policies that promote digital equity.

Community leaders within Indigenous populations are essential for guiding digital initiatives, ensuring they are culturally relevant and resonate with local values and practices. By involving community leaders in planning and implementation, digital programs can foster a stronger sense of ownership and engagement. Indigenous leaders can advocate for their communities' needs and represent their voices in partnerships and policymaking forums.

Non-governmental organisations (NGOs) and nonprofit organisations are uniquely positioned to bridge the gap between government initiatives and community needs. They can play a pivotal role in supporting digital literacy programs, delivering training in culturally relevant ways, and working closely with Indigenous communities to co-create digital content that preserves their cultural heritage. NGOs can also advocate for the rights of Indigenous communities, ensuring that their needs remain visible to policymakers and funders.

The private sector and technology companies possess the resources and expertise to realise digital inclusion. Technology companies can offer affordable devices, discounted Internet access, and technology training programs through partnerships with Indigenous communities. Corporate social responsibility initiatives can also drive innovative solutions tailored to Indigenous contexts, while long-term collaborations can promote sustainable digital infrastructure.

International bodies such as the United Nations and World Bank are important in promoting global initiatives and funding programs that support Indigenous digital inclusion. These organisations can provide technical assistance, set international standards for digital equity, and fund projects that significantly impact regions and borders.

The journey towards digital inclusion for Indigenous communities is both challenging and inspiring. By building partnerships, fostering culturally respectful practices, and committing to sustainable solutions, stakeholders can help close the digital divide and empower Indigenous communities to engage fully in the digital world. With collective efforts, digital inclusion can become a tool for Indigenous populations' self-determination, cultural preservation, and economic resilience, creating a more equitable and inclusive digital future.

REFERENCES

Aleke, B., Ojiako, U., & Wainwright, D. (2011). Social drivers for ICT diffusion among agrarian business enterprises in Nigeria. *International Journal of Technology Diffusion*, 2(2), 19–31. DOI: 10.4018/jtd.2011040102

Bala, P., Kulathuramaiyer, N., & Eng, T. (2022). *Digital socio-technical innovation and Indigenous knowledge.* IntechOpen., DOI: 10.5772/intechopen.101861

Bala, P., & Tan, C. (2021). Digital inclusion of the orang asli of peninsular Malaysia: Remote virtual mechanism for usability of telecentres amongst Indigenous peoples. *The Electronic Journal on Information Systems in Developing Countries*, 87(4). Advance online publication. DOI: 10.1002/isd2.12171

Banham, D., Roder, D., Eckert, M., Howard, N., Canuto, K., & Brown, A. (2019). Cancer treatment and the risk of cancer death among aboriginal and non-aboriginal South Australians: Analysis of a matched cohort study. *BMC Health Services Research*, 19(1). Advance online publication. DOI: 10.1186/s12913-019-4534-y PMID: 31665005

Burchert, S., Alkneme, M., Bird, M., Carswell, K., Cuijpers, P., Hansen, P., & Knaevelsrud, C. (2019). User-centred app adaptation of a low-intensity e-mental health intervention for Syrian refugees. *Frontiers in Psychiatry*, 9. Advance online publication. DOI: 10.3389/fpsyt.2018.00663 PMID: 30740065

Caffery, L., Bradford, N., Wickramasinghe, S., Hayman, N., & Smith, A. (2017). Outcomes of using telehealth for the provision of healthcare to Aboriginal and Torres Strait Islander people: A systematic review. *Australian and New Zealand Journal of Public Health*, 41(1), 48–53. DOI: 10.1111/1753-6405.12600 PMID: 27868300

Dutta, U. (2019). Digital preservation of Indigenous culture and narratives from the global south: In search of an approach. *Humanities (Washington)*, 8(2), 68. DOI: 10.3390/h8020068

Ferreira, G. (2023). Public policies for digital inclusion and indigenous peoples. *Revista Gênero E Interdisciplinaridade, 4(06)*, 500-520. https://doi.org/DOI: 10.51249/gei.v4i06.1766

Fish, J. (2023). "Inside of my home, I was getting a full dose of culture": Exploring the ecology of Indigenous peoples' development through stories. *The American Journal of Orthopsychiatry*, 93(6), 461–475. DOI: 10.1037/ort0000690 PMID: 37695347

Fitzpatrick, K., Ody, M., Goveas, D., Montesanti, S., Campbell, P., MacDonald, K., & Roach, P. (2022). Understanding virtual primary healthcare with Indigenous populations: A rapid evidence review. *Research Square*. https://doi.org/DOI: 10.21203/rs.3.rs-1953677/v1

Galla, C. (2018). Digital realities of indigenous language revitalization: A look at Hawaiian language technology in the modern world. *Language and Literature*, 20(3), 100–120. DOI: 10.20360/langandlit29412

Groh, A. (2016). The impact of mobile phones on indigenous social structures: A cross-cultural comparative study. *Journal of Communication*, 7(2), 344–356. DOI: 10.1080/0976691x.2016.11884917

Hefler, M., Kerrigan, V., Henryks, J., Freeman, B., & Thomas, D. (2018). Social media and health information sharing among Australian Indigenous people. *Health Promotion International*, 34(4), 706–715. DOI: 10.1093/heapro/day018 PMID: 29672684

Hensel, J., Ellard, K., Koltek, M., Wilson, G., & Sareen, J. (2019). Digital health solutions for Indigenous mental well-being. *Current Psychiatry Reports*, 21(8). Advance online publication. DOI: 10.1007/s11920-019-1056-6 PMID: 31263971

Henson, C., Chapman, F., Shepherd, G., Carlson, B., Rambaldini, B., & Gwynne, K. (2023). How older Indigenous women living in high-income countries use digital health technology: Systematic review. *Journal of Medical Internet Research*, 25, e41984. DOI: 10.2196/41984 PMID: 37071466

Hyman, A., Stacy, E., Mohsin, H., Atkinson, K., Stewart, K., Lauscher, H., & Ho, K. (2022). Barriers and facilitators to accessing digital health tools faced by South Asian Canadians in Surrey, British Columbia: Community-based participatory action exploration using photovoice. *Journal of Medical Internet Research*, 24(1), e25863. DOI: 10.2196/25863 PMID: 35023842

Jones, E., Peercy, M., Woods, J., Parker, S., Jackson, T., Mata, S., & Seely, E. (2015). Identifying postpartum intervention approaches to reduce cardiometabolic risk among American Indian women with prior gestational diabetes, Oklahoma, 2012–2013. *Preventing Chronic Disease*, 12. Advance online publication. DOI: 10.5888/pcd12.140566 PMID: 25837258

Jones, L., Jacklin, K., & O'Connell, M. (2017). Development and use of health-related technologies in indigenous communities: Critical review. *Journal of Medical Internet Research*, 19(7), e256. DOI: 10.2196/jmir.7520 PMID: 28729237

Jongbloed, K., Pearce, M., Thomas, V., Sharma, R., Pooyak, S., Demerais, L., & Spittal, P. (2020). The Cedar Project - mobile phone use and acceptability of mobile health among young Indigenous people who have used drugs in British Columbia, Canada: Mixed methods exploratory study. *JMIR mHealth and uHealth*, 8(7), e16783. DOI: 10.2196/16783 PMID: 32716311

Kee, K. (2017). Adoption and diffusion. *Encyclopedia of Communication*. https://doi.org/DOI: 10.1002/9781118955567.wbieoc058

Koch, K. (2022). The territorial and socio-economic characteristics of the digital divide in Canada. *The Canadian Journal of Regional Science*, 45(2), 89–98. DOI: 10.7202/1092248ar

Masala, R., & Monni, S. (2019). The social inclusion of indigenous peoples in Ecuador before and during the revolución ciudadana. *Development*, 62(1-4), 167–177. DOI: 10.1057/s41301-019-00219-y

McMahon, R. (2020). Co-developing digital inclusion policy and programming with indigenous partners: Interventions from Canada. *Internet Policy Review*, 9(2). Advance online publication. DOI: 10.14763/2020.2.1478

Peiris, D., Wright, L., News, M., Rogers, K., Redfern, J., Chow, C., & Thomas, D. (2019). A smartphone app to assist smoking cessation among Aboriginal Australians: Findings from a pilot randomized controlled trial. *JMIR mHealth and uHealth*, 7(4), e12745. DOI: 10.2196/12745 PMID: 30938691

Reilly, R., Stephens, J., Micklem, J., Tufănaru, C., Harfield, S., Fisher, I., & Ward, J. (2020). Use and uptake of web-based therapeutic interventions amongst Indigenous populations in Australia, New Zealand, the United States of America, and Canada: A scoping review. *Systematic Reviews*, 9(1). Advance online publication. DOI: 10.1186/s13643-020-01374-x PMID: 32475342

Rice, E., Haynes, E., Royce, P., & Thompson, S. (2016). Social media and digital technology use among Indigenous young people in Australia: A literature review. *International Journal for Equity in Health*, 15(1). Advance online publication. DOI: 10.1186/s12939-016-0366-0 PMID: 27225519

Rogers, J. (2023). Connecting in the gulf: Digital inclusion for aboriginal families on Mornington Island. *Visual Communication*, 23(2), 209–222. DOI: 10.1177/14703572231181598

Salman, A., & Rahim, S. (2012). From access to gratification: Towards an inclusive digital society. *Asian Social Science*, 8(5). Advance online publication. DOI: 10.5539/ass.v8n5p5

Sengupta, U., Vieta, M., & McMurtry, J. (2015). Indigenous communities and social enterprise in Canada: Incorporating culture as an essential ingredient of entrepreneurship. *Canadian Journal of Nonprofit and Social Economy Research*, 6(1). Advance online publication. DOI: 10.22230/cjnser.2015v6n1a196

Shiri, A., Howard, D., & Farnel, S. (2021). Indigenous digital storytelling: Digital interfaces supporting cultural heritage preservation and access. *The International Information & Library Review*, 54(2), 93–114. DOI: 10.1080/10572317.2021.1946748

Silan, W., & Munkejord, M. (2023). Pinhkngyan: Paths taken to recognizing, doing, and developing indigenous methodologies. *Alternative, an International Journal of Indigenous Peoples, 19(2)*, 407-416. https://doi.org/DOI: 10.1177/11771801231167727

Sisaye, S., & Birnberg, J. (2010). Organizational development and transformational learning approaches in process innovations. *Review of Accounting and Finance*, 9(4), 337–362. DOI: 10.1108/14757701011094562

Thorpe, K., Christen, K., Booker, L., & Galassi, M. (2021). Designing archival information systems through partnerships with indigenous communities. *AJIS. Australasian Journal of Information Systems*, 25. Advance online publication. DOI: 10.3127/ajis.v25i0.2917

Topp, S., Edelman, A., & Taylor, S. (2018). "We are everything to everyone": A systematic review of factors influencing the accountability relationships of Aboriginal and Torres Strait Islander health workers (AHWs) in the Australian health system. *International Journal for Equity in Health*, 17(1). Advance online publication. DOI: 10.1186/s12939-018-0779-z PMID: 29848331

Tuominen, I. (2023). Protecting and accessing Indigenous peoples' digital cultural heritage through sustainable governance and IPR structures - The case of Sámi culture. *Arctic Review on Law and Politics*, 14. Advance online publication. DOI: 10.23865/arctic.v14.5809

Walker, R., Usher, K., Jackson, D., Reid, C., Hopkins, K., Shepherd, C., & Marriott, R. (2021). Addressing digital inequities in supporting the well-being of young Indigenous Australians in the wake of COVID-19. *International Journal of Environmental Research and Public Health*, 18(4), 2141. DOI: 10.3390/ijerph18042141 PMID: 33671737

Watson, A., & Duffield, L. (2015). From garamut to mobile phone: Communication change in rural Papua New Guinea. *Mobile Media & Communication*, 4(2), 270–287. DOI: 10.1177/2050157915622658

Chapter 9
Era of Education 5.0:
Disruptive Technologies in a Learner–Cantered Educational Landscape

Yakkala B. V. L. Pratyusha
Infelearn, India

Bindi Varghese
Christ University, India

ABSTRACT

The chapter focuses on concepts of Education 5.0 and its competence in shaping future learning environments. It emphasises on learners social and personal growth by improving quality of life standards with the help of current technologies and digitalisation. (Shabir Ahmad, 2023) To deliver humanised approach by the application of new technologies is the primary use of Education 5.0. However, usage of new age technology in education doesn't mean giving laptop and tablet to each and every child and the usage of digital mediums for teaching and learning. After covid-19, digitisation becomes the integral part of our life, education is no exception for that. (Shabir Ahmad, 2023) Beyond digitalisation pandemic also remained us the importance of human hardships to social transformation with emotional intelligence driving technology as a tool. In short education 5.0. (SYDLE.com, 2023) referring to the significance of human, social and emotional abilities to enhance wellbeing of an individual by using technology advancement as a tool.

DOI: 10.4018/979-8-3693-8191-5.ch009

INTRODUCTION

Education 5.0 is not about advanced technology but more on human connectivity. Learning experience especially through human interaction is proposed explicitly is the primary advancement of Education 5.0. Improved infrastructure, wide range of connectivity, providing laptop and tablets to each and every learner and the usage of advanced digital tools and platforms in education sector is not its major focus. ((PwC), 2020) Besides these developments preparing future generations to be emotionally strong, Mindful of health and personal development to Intellectual, social and strong individual. (Dervojeda, 2021) It proposes appropriate strategic, pedagogical & methodological approaches will help in enhancing motivation, creativity and joy of learning. With infrastructure, digital equipment and technology platforms using as enablers which plays a prominent role in education instead purposes themselves. Moreover, education 5.0 focus on putting human qualities in the Centre of education, considering social (Shabir Ahmad, 2023) and learners needs alongside with market needs. Enabling learners as change agents to use these advancements Mindfully considering their safety and security at home, school and work.

Reflective Questions

· How educational setting or schools can drive value and address challenges using AI?
· Whether the educational landscape are teaching students the practical skills they need to engage with AI?
· Will AI replace the older systems and education 5.0 will make educators Future Ready & Future Fit for Teaching ?

The Future of Business is being rapidly reshaped by Artificial Intelligence (AI), Blockchain, Cyber Security, Data Science, Metaverse, Generative AI and Convergence of all. The Major Question arises, How can the educational landscape including the elementary schools prepare students for a world, where AI and Big Data are not just tools but the bedrock of strategy. Jobs are set to be transformed by AI – and the educational setting must adapt AI Integrated Teaching & Research practices quickly, so they can prepare students for the new world of work. The curriculums in schools need to Incorporating AI and Data Science into Curriculum Design & Development with a Multidimensional approach. The Current Status of Education in globally neds to be relevant, ill-resourced and battling old challenges of inadequate Technology Infrastructure. While AI may not completely replace; it will assist facilitators in efficiently and effectively managing multi-level/ multidimensional. In Future, many the educational settings will be shaped by the face of AI and Generative AI Trend.

The New Generations of learners need to be exposed to AI-Enabled Educational setting with 5.0 and will be likely to have a much greater comfort with and appetite for machine-moderated Education. The platform providers such as Coursera give learners the chance to upskill themselves.

Figure 1. Evolution of Education over the past years

Figure 1: Evolution of Education over the past years

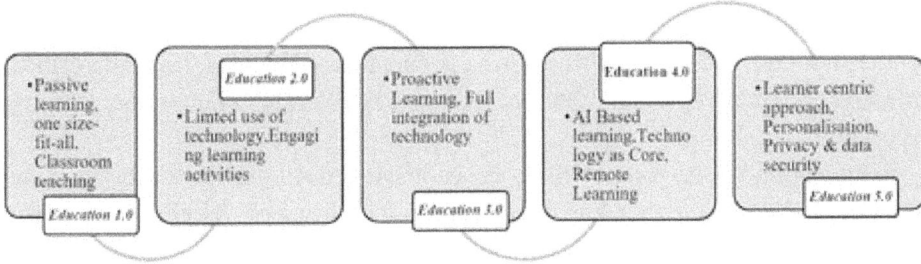

To meet the evolving needs of 21st century learners in education the imperative integration of cutting-edge technology has been emerged (Daron Cyr, 2022) The educational paradigm is undergoing major transformation which stands on the edge of fourth industrial revolution by amalgamating digital, biological and physical realms. (Hatice Leblebic, 2021) The evolvement of education can be observed multiple stages, conventional one -sized fit all approach is the beginning of the series and called as Education 1.0. (Trivedi, 2023) With infusion of technology into regular classrooms was shifted towards engaging and interactive learning experiences was initiated in Education 2.0. (Prakash Srinivasan, 2023) By laying foundation to current digital education era was initiated with web-based tools, collaboration with internet and incorporating student centric learning has been emphasised in education 3.0. (Rita Vieira, 2023) Modern age technologies like AI, Cloud computing, big data analytics, IOT were used as catalyst for the transformation of education in the landscape of Education 4.0. (Shabir Ahmad, 2023) Focusing on deepening commitment to individualised learning experiences the transition from education 4.0 to education 5.0 envisions a future where the symbiotic relationship between human intelligence and new age technologies (Elias Carayannis, 2023). Education 5.0 works towards rediscovering the importance of human element by focusing on overall individual growth but knowledge or qualifications, (SYDLE.com, 2023) as it tries to improves learners social and emotional learning, holistic development and lifelong learning.

Preparing learners for life lessons with relevant & personalised learning is the vision of Education 5.0. Certainly! Education 5.0 represents a paradigm shift in the way we approach teaching and learning by recognizing the importance of both human and digital technologies (H. Sandhya, 2022). At its core, Education 5.0 acknowledges that while new age technologies can excel at tasks like data analysis, personalized learning, and even grading, it cannot replace the nuanced understanding, empathy, and creativity that humans bring to education. One of the key principles of Education 5.0 (J, 2021) is augmented intelligence, where modern technologies serve as a supportive partner to humans, enhancing our capabilities rather than replacing them. This means that these technologies can assist teachers by automating routine tasks, providing insights into student learning patterns, and offering personalized recommendations for each student's unique needs. (Mollee Shultz, 2022) This frees up educators to focus on what they do best: mentoring students, fostering critical thinking, creativity, emotional intelligence, and facilitating collaborative learning experiences.

In Education 5.0, the role of educators becomes even more critical as they become facilitators of learning rather than just providers of information. (Nikum, 2022) They guide students in navigating the vast sea of information available, teaching them how to think critically, solve complex problems, and collaborate effectively with others. (Nitin Liladhar Rane, 2023) Mentorship takes centre stage, with educators providing guidance, support, and encouragement to help students reach their full potential. However, as we embrace the potential of technologies in education, it's crucial to address ethical considerations and ensure that digital tools are transparent, (Odier-Guedj, 2022) impartial, and adhere to ethical standards. This includes issues like bias in algorithms, data privacy, and security concerns. Building trust among stakeholders is essential for the successful implementation of Education 5.0.

AI INTEGRATION IN MANAGEMENT EDUCATION

Education 5.0 must strive for inclusivity by bridging the digital divide and ensuring that all students have equal access to the benefits of these modern age techniques in education. (Trivedi, 2023) This means addressing disparities in technology and internet access, particularly among marginalized communities. By making education more accessible and inclusive, we can unlock the full potential of Education 5.0 to empower learners and prepare them for the challenges of the future. (Tore Hoel, 2018) Education 5.0, the focus is on creating customized learning journeys that cater not only to academic excellence but also to the acquisition of crucial skills demanded by the contemporary job market. (Tiina Kivirand, 2021) This approach recognizes the lifelong nature of learning and emphasizes the importance of continuously developing skills beyond traditional educational milestones. By tailoring education to individual needs and incorporating essential (Alharbi, 2023) 21st-century workforce skills, learners are better equipped to thrive in a rapidly evolving professional landscape (Sandhya, H., & Varghese, B.,2023).

Education 5.0 encapsulate the fusion human intelligence with emerging technologies influencing considering various facets of educational landscape (Alharbi, 2023). The following are the key features of Education 5.0 realm.

Personalised Learning: Education 5.0 emphasises on catering personalised learning services according abilities and needs of students (SYDLE.com, 2023). Artificial intelligence can be used as tools to achieve personalised learning plan for each and every student (Tore Hoel, 2018). Education 5.0 aims to enhance learning trajectories by measuring students' engagement, motivation and (Pitshou Moleka, 2022)achievement along with understanding their abilities and needs which are fulfilled by personalised learning.

Adaptability: For the changing needs of society and workforce education 5.0 designed to be adaptable (Sebastian, 2023). Technologies like cloud computing and block chain technology could act as enabler for sharing resources and data among the stakeholders (Nitin Liladhar Rane, 2023). Flexibility and scalability are key metrics to evaluate assessing adaptability in Education 5.0. (Education Data Security: 5 Things to Implement Now, 2023) the ability to adjust to changing needs of students and workforce from time to tie can be referred as flexibility. (Pattanayak, 2023)

Accessibility: Education 5.0 wants to mitigate socio economic gaps in the society and made education more accessible to all (Dervojeda, 2021). These barriers can be removed with the help of technologies like 5G Network and cloud computing where data and information can be shared and transferred easily. (H. Sandhya, 2022) It is difficult to measure the success rate of accessibility in education 5.0. the rate of accessibility of educational resources and opportunities available regardless their location and socio-economic status (SYDLE.com, 2023) can its evaluate its success. Quality, quantity and relevancy to needs of students are considered to be factors of accessibility, (Trivedi, 2023) also educational resources like text books, online courses and availability of materials could also have impact on it.

Emotional well-being: Students physical, mental and emotional well-being will play a vital role in education 5.0. (Shabir Ahmad, 2023) overall performance of a student also depends on their well-being either it's their physical or mental health (Elias Carayannis, 2023). This can be measured by using technologies like internet of things, which can monitor student interests, engagement rates and motivation levels by conducting student satisfaction surveys, mental health assessments and physical health indicators. (Hatice Leblebic, 2021) On the basis feedback taken above mentioned forms we can rate student well being and help him/her to improve them. (Nikum, 2022)

Collaborative & Connectedness: Collaboration and connectedness among students, teachers and other stakeholders was emphasised by education 5.0. (Mollee Shultz, 2022) Communication skills, team work spirt, problem solving skills and conflict resolution could be considered as the factors for measuring the collaboration and connectedness (Education Data Security: 5 Things to Implement Now, 2023). Technologies like virtual reality, augmented reality can help in achieving collaboration and connectedness in education 5.0 (Tiina Kivirand, 2021). Working in group projects and assessment can assess the rate of collaboration in education 5.0. It improves engagement and effectiveness of students.

Rehumanising the Education

By creating a vision and strategizing directions for learning environment by using Education 5.0 (Shabir Ahmad, 2023) By aligning learning environments with current technological innovation by business & society alongside to foster direct engagement to rehumanise the learners in the age of machines and automation. Modern education reshaped itself with tec advancements like artificial intelligence, robotics, virtual reality and other digitalisation techniques. ((PwC), 2020) By plunging into these advancements all the stakeholders were forced to adapt the new normal overnight. Before covid-19 hit the world, the education sector is trying adopt itself for fourth industry revolution which revolves around the context of automation and cyber physical system and had a huge demand for soft skills and ability to understand the machines to gain 4x productivity (Shabir Ahmad, 2023). Currently we are running towards fifth industry revolution (industry 5.0) which works on the notion of humanising the processes by creating balance between humans and machines.

As making education 4.0 as foundation education 5.0 starts growing, but unlike education 4.0 its greater emphasis of human aspect of education. (Pattanayak, 2023) Focusing on holistic development of the student by enhancing creativity, emotional intelligent and critical thinking education 5.0 envisions for learning ecosystem which is far beyond possessing technical skills. (Education Data Security: 5 Things to Implement Now, 2023)Considering the socio-emotional wellbeing of the students, education 5.0 elevates on adaptive learning models and personalised learning styles as these models are in line with human centric approach by catering the diverse needs and aspiration of every learner. (Education Data Security: 5 Things to Implement Now, 2023) In contrast to the earlier educational paradigms these models emphasising on emotional wellbeing by nurturing essential life skill like self-awareness, resilience, empathy. Adaptive learning models in education 5.0 go beyond personalisation paths to encompass collaborative learning experience. (Nikum, 2022)By facilitating group activities, projects, discussions and promoting team work will improve social skills and communication skills. These models ensure the adaptability of the system aligns with collaborative activities to fulfil unique needs of learner journey (Nitin Liladhar Rane, 2023).

Understanding the significance of human qualities and placing them as centre of education by recognising skill and roles that humans are good at fulfilling them like (e.g.; critical thinking, compassion, analytical skills, creativity, Innovativeness, empathy etc;) (Alharbi, 2023). Besides the market needs(employability)we should consider about societal and learners needs which helps not only to grow professional but also to a responsible good individual (Dervojeda, 2021). Actively engaging learners in curriculum development and implementation by considering them as change agents. Preparing the young generations to be mindful while using digital innovations around them by teaching the learners about the safety and ergonomics at home, school and work (H. Sandhya, 2022). Making them to understand the significance of physical and mental health by explaining the consequences of misuse or excessive usage of technology along with what can be done about it ((PwC), 2020). Offering relevant personalisation and personal learning by ensuring freedom in choosing curriculum goal with possible outcomes from conventional educational frameworks.

By implying holistic educational transformation education 5.0 should also address all relevant elements besides technological innovation. (Prakash Srinivasan, 2023)

Strategy (Alharbi, 2023): In the context of education 5.0, recognise the purpose of education and redefine it with specific objectives

Collaboration (Elias Ratinho, 2023): creating effective learning ecosystems that will engage all the key stakeholders as communities by knowledge sharing with students from cultures and societies. By encouraging such practices not helps the students to grow but also the society.

Content (Alharbi, 2023): With corresponding to the strategy element choose the content which is in line to balance both technical and non-technical disciplines where learners can find the answers for ethical dilemmas, social inclusions, diversity and sustainability etc;

Learning Environment (Elias Carayannis, 2023): Creating an interactive learning environment which helps in objectifying the strategy element by stimulating multi-disciplinary orientation, risk taking behaviour, team spirit, collective problem-solving design thinking etc;

Delivery Mechanisms (Alharbi, 2023): To achieve the objective of strategy element, look for best possible tools and implement efficiently, (Pitshou Moleka, 2022)where the technology comes in to picture as enablers to survive the purpose.

Assessment & Recognition (Elias Ratinho, 2023): Developing and exploring different in formal and formal ways to assess education 5.0 criteria

Quality Assurance (Alharbi, 2023): keep a continuous track of progress of education 5.0 elements are serving the purpose or not.

Role of Technology in Education 5.0

The promotion of holistic development, the cultivation of creativity, fostering the skill that are necessary for future has to be changed is basic emphasis to be considered in moving towards education 5.0. (Nitin Liladhar Rane, 2023) This can be achieved by understanding the significance of new technology in facilitating and implementation of data informed educational experiences and providing customised and flexible environments. On the global scale, the methods of modern age technology like artificial intelligence, immersive technologies, IOT, Cloud computing, bigdata, block chain and 5G network has the potential to revolutionise the teaching methods, evaluation methods and educational administration. With the integration technology (Sebastian, 2023), the paradigm shift of education sector will be easier by surpassing the limitations of classroom based teaching and standardised curriculum. In the changing global society, educational ecosystem should be able to address current needs like acquisition of new skills for future, comprehensive growth and lifelong learning. (Tore Hoel, 2018) By incorporating technology this transformative journey will be seamless which serve to stimulate innovation, personalisation and generation of insights based on data. (Dervojeda, 2021)Enabling technology in education sector will help both learners and educators, can experience a novel journey of exploration and development through data analytics and adaptive learning within the education framework and intelligent automation. (Education Data Security: 5 Things to Implement Now, 2023) To provide a comprehensive understanding of complex relation between education and new age technologies, which seeks to explore numerous ways in influencing the future of education in line with global imperative of research and innovation through their applications.

The ever-changing expectations of society which are extremely independent and driven by knowledge are fundamental reason in the emergence of education 5.0. (Rodrigo Smiderle, 2020)We frequently encounter challenges in productively connecting academic concepts to practical implementation even though our conventional educational paradigms are fundamental imparting knowledge. (Trivedi, 2023)Emphasising on critical thinking skills, creative development and problem-solving abilities, nourishing multidisciplinary collaboration aims to eradicate existing limitation with the help of education 5.0. (H. Sandhya, 2022)This helps in processing new educational framework to ever changing needs of learners to navigate the intricacies of contemporary world by providing necessary skills. The primary aspect of education 5.0 is the concept tailored learning (Odier-Guedj, 2022). As each individual learner has a distinct combo of aptitude, areas of interest preferred mode of learning. (Nikum, 2022) The potential to customise educational experiences according to unique requirements of individual learners will be achieved by Ai since I possess the ability to handle quantify and evaluate extensive quantities of data efficiently within no time. (Alharbi, 2023)By responses and feedback given by the learners can generate individualised learning trajectories that can dynamically adjust in Realtime which are propelled by AI algorithms through adaptive learning platforms. Rather than a uniform progression through subject matters, it turns the education is a process of exploration. As we understand the prominence of new age technologies in previous stages of education series, ((PwC), 2020) currently we are focusing on using these advanced technologies like gamification, metaverse etc; in line with human interaction to create efficient and effective equitable education system. To achieve humanised approach by promoting personal learning, collaboration and wellbeing and develop skillset to 21st century skills (SYDLE.com, 2023) like critical thinking, creativity and problem-solving abilities.

Enabling Technologies of Education 5.0

In the new age technologies will act as building blocks of education 5.0. while the digital Equipment and infrastructure play a crucial role in attaining personalised and collaborative learning Spaces. (Pattanayak, 2023) AI based applications like smart teaching system can help in customisation and feedback in real time. (Prakash Srinivasan, 2023) Immersive technologies like augmented reality, virtual reality, extended reality will open gates to experiential learning and create interactive learning experience to students. (Nikum, 2022)Allowing for real time monitoring & analysis of student engagement by Internet of Things, which also helps in connecting multiple devices whereas accessing multiple digital resources was enabled by cloud computing. (J, 2021)For monitoring and tracking large amounts of data and analysing student progress, identifying gaps in learning trajectories and tailored instructions to each individual was made possible with the usage of easy by the usage of Big Data (Elias Carayannis, 2023). Moreover, data sharing by ensuring student privacy and security was intact because of Block Chain Technology. Finally, 5g Network take charge of above-mentioned technologies by proving (Trivedi, 2023) High Band width requirements and secure to attain seamless learning experience to the students.

Figure 2. Enablers of Education 5.0

Figure 2: Enablers of Education 5.0

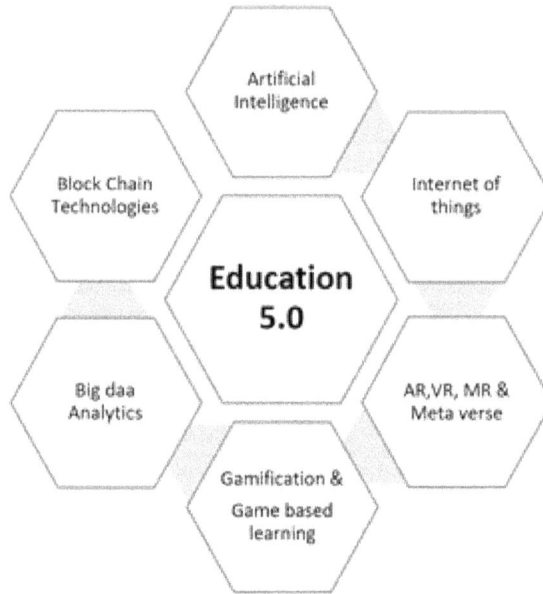

Artificial Intelligence: AI technologies has gone through continuous evolution and created a notable impact in various domains, like wise it has significant advancements in education as well. (Nitin Liladhar Rane, 2023)AI technologies can be used as enablers in achieving education 5.0 features like Personalisation and adaptive learning, Intelligent tutoring Assistants, Predictive analytics, collaboration etc;. (Odier-Guedj, 2022) Collaboration between human and powerful machines is the future of AI in education. With open AI coming into picture, it become an integral of our routine has an impact all aspects, including education. (Odier-Guedj, 2022) With the help of AI based applications like smart tutoring system we can reduce workload of a teacher as AI handling routine tasks and providing valuable insights whereas educators can focus on fostering creativity, interpersonal skills and creativity. (SYDLE.com, 2023)Applications like Collaborative automatic evaluation system, mobile game-based learning, interdisciplinary learning will benefit both student and teacher. In education 5.0 personalisation plays a crucial role which can be achieved by one AI technology called NLP. (H. Sandhya, 2022)Tools which work with the help of NLP have capabilities to examine students feedback and replies, measure their comprehension of their materials change the content and assignments accordingly. (H. Sandhya, 2022)By using these kind of tools learners can have a clear understanding about the concept and get real time feedback and progress at their own pace. Content, coherence, grammatical correctness, and pronunciations are being assessed even with open AI applications like Google Bard, Chat GPT & Microsoft Copilot as well. Besides NLP, Machine Learning plays vital role in AI applications and tools, its functionality helps in providing necessary feedback based on past trends and patterns. (Dervojeda, 2021)With the tools works with the principals of ML will help predict students' academic success based on their previous performance by considering various data points like their interests, learning goals and mode of study etc (Pratyusha, Y. B., & Varghese, B.,2024). Furthermore, it recommends some resources according to the individual choice and preferences like audio files, video lectures, books etc; (Pitshou Moleka, 2022)which helps them to overcome their weakness work towards the progress. ML based applications not helps the students but also the educators in fulfilling complex and tedious jobs like making institutional policies, setting curriculum, grading systems etc; (Rita Vieira, 2023)

Internet of Things: To achieve goal of lifelong learning education 5.0 is next evolution in education sector which is enabled by using modern technologies. (Pattanayak, 2023) Internet of things is one among them which plays pivotal role in education 5.0. Collecting data in real time on student learning and behaviour, providing a deeper understanding of individual student needs and abilities with the help of IOT enabled devices like wearables, sensors and sensors (Education Data Security: 5 Things to Implement Now, 2023). An approach to leverage technology for individualise instruction can facilitate personalised learning with the usage of IOT devices. (Mollee Shultz, 2022)With an adaptive learning system where pace and content of instruction can be changed according to performance of student and provided personalised feedback by tracking there with the help of IOT devices. (Nikum, 2022)This technology becomes an aid for the children with disabilities as they learn like other students using IOT devices as tools to create smart content which adapt to the individual needs and abilities of student. ((PwC), 2020) IOT devices helps in creating dynamic, interactive more engaging environments to the students to enhance their collaborative skills and improve their learning outcomes. (Tore Hoel, 2018)

AR, VR & Metaverse: Immersive learning can be created with the help of Augmented reality, virtual reality ad extended reality by incorporating these technologies in education 5.0. (Nitin Liladhar Rane, 2023)Unique features and capabilities possessed by immersive technologies make it promising tools as it was different from others. (Nitin Liladhar Rane, 2023)These technologies help to visualise complex concepts like human anatomy which are difficult to showcase in traditional classrooms. To produce immersive and engaging learning experience, students are given access to simulated settings where abstract ideas or real-life situations, where they can interact deeply and sense the material (SYDLE.com, 2023). Digitally stimulated environment called virtual environment is created and can be accessed with the help of VR tools or enhancements like headsets and vision goggles etc; when an individual wears a virtual reality headset he/she can completely lost into virtual world and imagine themselves being in that stimulated environment, as VR tools can sense the human moments with the help of sensors like hand movements, head movements etc; ((PwC), 2020) and reimagine themselves as they are interacting in virtual environment like watching, listening and experience things in virtual environment. Complex concepts like being in space, exploring historical monuments, analysing 3d models helps the learners to understand concepts in a better way. (Alharbi, 2023) These technologies have numerous advantages in the fields like aviation, architecture, medicine training or technical skills as it allow trainee to practice in risk free zone and improve their skill set. (Elias Ratinho, 2023) Emergencies or war like situation can be created in virtual environment and train them to handle the situations in a effective and efficient ways. (Rodrigo Smiderle, 2020)These immerse open gates to experiential learning where students can learn through experiencing real world situations instead of just listening or watching them on the screen. To meet the needs of a students, VR based education can be customised according to the learners' preferences. As per the competency of the student, content can be modified by making learning more efficient. (H. Sandhya, 2022)Learner Engagement, Social Learning Practices and mutual collaboration made accessible by connecting other learners through virtual world. (Elias Carayannis, 2023)

The technology to layer the virtual objects in physical environment enabled by the user can called as Augmented Reality (AR) (Prakash Srinivasan, 2023) allowing students to have more engaging and interactive sessions. Interactive learning materials like videos, 3d models, animations were being used in the classroom in education to have more engaging experience. Textbooks may come into life with the help of these technologies and students can perform better as they are learning in more efficient way. (Tore Hoel, 2018)

The technology which combines both real world and virtual world enables virtual objects to interact with physical environment called as Mixed Reality (MR) (Sebastian, 2023). with digital transformation and animation MR has capabilities to deliver blended learning experience to enhance students learning paths. Meanwhile, virtual shared space created by fusion of virtual and physical worlds is referred as Metaverse, (Tiina Kivirand, 2021) where users can interact with digital objects in seemingly real environment. Bridging gap between real and virtual these technologies like (Rita Vieira, 2023)AR, VR, XR, MR and Metaverse can provide immersive learning experience to deliver seamless, integrated learning experience through Education 5.0 (Prakash Srinivasan, 2023)

Gamification & Game based Learning: Game based learning plays key role in fulfilling the requirements of education 5.0 as it engage learners by using gaming elements in education like rewards, grades and badges and motivation to progress.

(Rodrigo Smiderle, 2020) (Rodrigo Smiderle, 2020)As it works as positive rein-forcement on students which we ca witness in conventional classroom setting. To enhance Engagement, motivation and knowledge retention in students use the power of gamification. (Sandhya H., 2023)To make learning enjoyable and effective explore innovative approaches like interactive quizzes to immersive simulations with the help of game-based learning. (Sebastian, 2023) Educators can elevate their methods and empower their students by incorporating gaming elements into instructional framework, fostering heightened engagement and motivation among students can be consider as revolution in education. ((PwC), 2020) To maximise retention and academic Success by taking advantage of gaming elements we can enrich learning journey more immersive and enjoyable for learners. (Hatice Leblebic, 2021) Apart from imparting knowledge games can also create an impact on improving problem solving skills, boosting team work, improving communication skills and encourage healthy competition with peers. (SYDLE.com, 2023) Moreover, games can also generate innovation, imagination and creativity in their participants. (Tore Hoel, 2018)By integrating games in education students would have following benefits like

- Higher motivation levels
- Increase knowledge retention
- Better student engagement
- Instant student feedback & reinforcement
- More enjoyable educational experience

As we discussed earlier creativity, analytical skills, critical thinking encompasses with education 5.0. by introducing gamification in education ecosystem will achieve it. (Pattanayak, 2023)

Block chain Technology: Block chain technology is considered as essential en-abler of education 5.0 because of its capability in managing the educational data. This technology is unique as it is decentralised and secure nature make way for secured and tamper proof storage of data (Trivedi, 2023). The ledger is maintained in series of transactions which are recorded in each block and validated by a com-puter network make up a block chain i.e.; made up of chain of blocks. Its highly challenging to alter the data once the block is entered into the chain as it cannot changed or removed without interrupting other blocks as each block has a copy of previous block. (Shabir Ahmad, 2023) Because of this nature the data entered is secured after the entry data once. Through the use of digital credentials which are immutable and easily verified because of Block chain technology as it can provide secured and reliable way of tracking and verifying educational achievements. (Tiina Kivirand, 2021)Moreover, it provides a streamlined way for individuals to showcase their skills and qualifications to potential employers or educational institutions alongside with security and authenticity of data. (Education Data Security: 5 Things to Implement Now, 2023)

Additionally, by enabling the creation of decentralised educational platforms to increase access of education to everyone. (Tiina Kivirand, 2021)Regardless of their location or financial background, these platforms can provide accessible, affordable and equitable education for all. (Tore Hoel, 2018)As it helps in addressing the long running issues of education for all and provide opportunity for every individual to learn and grow. Another significant aspect of block chain technology has a capability to increase transparency and accountability in education sector. (Rita Vieira, 2023) As it helps building trust among stakeholders which provides a clear understanding in educational landscape. Overall quality of education is increased because of improved transparency and trust which enables the stakeholders to make informed decisions based on up to date and accurate information. (Nitin Liladhar Rane, 2023)

Big data Analytics: Education 5.0 is about being learner centric and this can be achieved by customisation and personalisation and requires more and more data to work efferently. Exacting valuable and useful insights from large amounts data sets through analysis techniques and advanced data processing can referred as big data analytics (Pitshou Moleka, 2022). Decision making process will be easier if we have multiple data points and can analyse situations thoroughly top make informed decisions. Complex educational Processes are being transformed to big data analytics like organisational expansion, (Tore Hoel, 2018) faculty effectiveness, technical efficacy including academic success for seamless working. Time consuming things like maintaining students records, student enrolment scheduling and data management are streamlined by big data to improve the administrative process. (Elias Carayannis, 2023) To enhance students learning patterns by analysing multiple data points like previous test scores, demographic information, attendance records and interests, educators can gain multiple insights where they can identify weak areas of the students and guide them accordingly, (Prakash Srinivasan, 2023)could be possible by the usage of big data technology in education ecosystem. Big data allows the teachers to understand each student's strength, weakness and learning preference to provide individualised educational experience and improve student engagement to get better outcomes. (Alharbi, 2023) Not only students and administration it also helps teachers in evolving teaching methods and educational technologies. (Shabir Ahmad, 2023) Currently, AIED in conducting research in collaborative learning space to enhance social, cognitive and emotional view by using data mining and learning analytics. (Pattanayak, 2023)Big data analytics has greater potential in higher education as it can huge data sets and can solve complex problems within no time.

Privacy Protection and Ethical Stances for Students

The Concept of education 5.0 is beneficial, and it's in the welfare of society. With the help of education 5.0, the quality index of learner will increase exponentially, which will lead to the growth and development of the nation (SYDLE.com, 2023). To focus on safety and security is much required at the moment as automation is leading bigger concerns about privacy and protection. However, it's not about usage modern technology in education instead it's about making responsible choices and making the learners conscious about the aspects of privacy, safety, ethics and technological mindfulness. (Shabir Ahmad, 2023)It considers all its stakeholder groups will create a holistic approach towards transformation education by considering necessary elements for building a sustainable and bright future to our next generations. (Dervojeda, 2021)

As we are witnessing data is ruling the world, no longer student privacy is considered as legal requirement, it becomes a basic ethical imperative. To ensure the wellbeing of students, educational institutions should be more careful while handling student data as information is more valuable than ever. ((PwC), 2020) Besides the stakeholder's government should revise their policies according to the change of education ecosystem. (Nikum, 2022) While implementing certain changes in existing rules and policies one should consider the following suggestions (H. Sandhya, 2022)

Transparency and Consent: while the educators or the institutions are collecting data from their student its mandate to take their consent and should be transparent about its utilisation. Without the individual consent usage or sharing data to third parties should be considered as punishable offence.

Data Retention Policies: Every institution should revisit and revise their police especially considering digital transformation of education sector. Ensuring safety and security of the students 'data educators should come up with clear rules and polices regarding the retention of data.

Educating Stakeholders: Because of covid outbreak life becomes more digitalised, education has no exception. New trends like Hybrid learning, smart classrooms and intelligent learning system etc; becomes new normal. (Pattanayak, 2023) Not only the students but also the educators should adapt to these transformations. Besides adapting to the new normal all stakeholders should have awareness about ethical concerns while using these smart technologies, specially focusing on data privacy and security. (SYDLE.com, 2023) Responsible data handling is a primary topic to start with the training.

Data Encryption and security measures: In order to achieve personalisation, smart applications often collect numerous data points from each individual like their personal information, (Odier-Guedj, 2022)behaviour patterns including sleep cycles of an individual to give accurate results by using their applications. Even though there are numerous advantages by using these applications, there are some risks involved with privacy and security of an individual. To safeguard the privacy of the data, providers must be updated on cybersecurity technologies and practices. (Alharbi, 2023) To secure data from unauthorised access robust data encryption and straiten security measures were become essentials of Educational Providers.

Ethical Concerns in Edtech Landscape: In the ever-changing landscape of education eco system its much needed to address ethical issues including the confidentiality of information, algorithmic bias and full accountability. (Elias Ratinho, 2023)The development and deployment of new age technologies like Artificial intelligence, metaverse, AR, VR system must adhere to some standard principles in data collection, data sharing and its usage must be fair and transparent. Exchanging data with third parties should require prior authorisation from concerned personnel before sharing or selling it. (Education Data Security: 5 Things to Implement Now, 2023) To address the ethical challenges in digitalised education space, cross functional collaboration between educators, governments, technologists and ethical philosophers to set up standardised ethical norms, moral standards and legal framework must be established. (Nikum, 2022) The European commission report highlighted the significance availability of internet connectivity and basic resources to utilise technology advancement in education must be accessible to all.

The application of technologies in education background should poses multiple legal concerns, especially regarding privacy and data protection laws (Li et al., 2021). Federal student privacy laws mandate organizations to obtain consent before disclosing personally identifiable information and allow students to access and contest any inaccurate data (Limna et al., 2022). However, if institutions adhere to FERPA regulations, obtaining explicit approval may not be necessary for disclosing information to third parties (Lee et al., 2019). Accountability rests with both the developers and users of AI-enabled applications, as they risk causing harm or distress to students and educational institutions (de Saint Laurent, 2018). This potential harm can negatively impact students' cognitive growth, often leaving them to suffer alone without identifying the underlying cause (Lu, 2019). Efficient knowledge management facilitated by AI systems can enhance the learning experience for students (B Varghese, YBVL Pratyusha, 2022).

DISCUSSIONS AND IMPLICATIONS

The chapter focuses on the setting right direction for future generations with the help education 5.0. The way of education 5.0 exhibiting will pave path for future generation by gradual integration of ICT and automation in evolution of education sector ((PwC), 2020). To address the existing concerns about safety and privacy education 5.0 is the best possible direction and mitigate the aggressive automation in education sector by introducing humanising element and making learner is the primary benefactor (Alharbi, 2023). Furthermore education 5.0 has potential to revolutionise the sector but it requires a holistic approach with proper planning and implementation ongoing measures to ensure its success. To enhance learning experience with the help of new age technologies which focused on learner centric approach and personalisation future generations is theme of education 5.0. (Odier-Guedj, 2022) By addressing needs of the learner education 5.0 focused on being flexible, adaptable and transparent but it's not easy to implement education 5.0 in current scenario as they are major implication which we can ignore. Implementation cost is one among them, as we discussed earlier new age technologies were enablers of education 5.0 and these technologies comes with huge cost. (Pitshou Moleka, 2022) It would be difficult for schools and universities with limited budgets as maintaining and upgrading these technologies would be high.

Another implication of education 5.0 would lack of teacher training. Educators should be well trained to use newer technologies and teaching methods to effectively implement a personalised (Rita Vieira, 2023) and technology enabled education system. This could be major challenge especially in developing countries as most o the teachers are reluctant to adapt the transformation and may not be comfortable in using it in their classes. Digital divide could be the other implication which we can not ignore. (Nitin Liladhar Rane, 2023)As all the students shouldn't have same technologies and resources available to presume their education, creates a digital divide as accessibility of latest resources weren't available everyone. (Pattanayak, 2023) It would be difficult for the educators to reduce the gap between students from different socioeconomic backgrounds to provide personalised and technology enabled education for all, regardless of their background. (Rodrigo Smiderle, 2020) Moreover, without standardisation in platforms and technologies could make resource sharing exchange difficult among educational institutions. Security and privacy would be another major concern for education 5.0. (Trivedi, 2023)As sensitive and personal information are stored online, security of data becomes more important for the educators. Very often we hear about cyberattacks and data breaches, as stakeholders should ensure the protection of student data. (Tore Hoel, 2018)Some of the technologies like metaverse, VR /AR are complex in nature and needs more resources to develop education content. High speed internet, powerful servers, in-ternet access and hardware like AR/VR headsets should require to implement these technologies. (Elias Carayannis, 2023) Finally, educators should be able balance between offline and online learning as too much technology exposure may lead to lack of social interaction and Isolation.

CONCLUSION

Artificial Intelligence presents its potential to reshape Businesses, Industries and Societal Applications. This transformation is affecting the school curriculum, but more importantly, it is also calling into question the Employability of students and preparing them for life. The Digital age is far away from schools and it is happening so fast, and facilitators are slow in adapting & learning the Disruptive Technologies. It will take time, and it will be quite a challenge to speed up in the teaching and Education setting. Education 5.0 signifies the harmonious integration of human aspect and technology for adding value and effectiveness, where technology is used as enabler to achieve the goal of lifelong learning. (Alharbi, 2023) It represents latest evolution in learning by leveraging the potential of modern age technologies to create holistic and immersive experience as placing learner at centre of education ecosystem. (Education Data Security: 5 Things to Implement Now, 2023) Education 5.0 emphasises on the significance of privacy aspect, technology mindfulness, Ethics and safety towards educational transformation by considering all essential elements.

(Shabir Ahmad, 2023) It signifies the importance of real-world experience for engaging and enabling the students to deeply explore the topics through hands on experience in real world. (Tore Hoel, 2018)It advocates the importance of critical thinking, creativity, emotional intelligence and complex problem solving provided by improvement humanly skills. (Rodrigo Smiderle, 2020) While the technology handling the regular tasks and personalised learning experiences, educators can focus on nurturing the holistic development of student. moreover, addressing few implications like data security, digital divide, data privacy and ethical considerations are the critical that needs special attention. (Sebastian, 2023) All the stakeholders along with governments should come on board and address the concerns related to data security and availability of resources create some standardised polices to mitigate economical difference between the communities. Benefits of education 5.0 must accessible to all, irrespective of socio-economic backgrounds. The educational settings are creating the key to creating Multidisciplinary Talent and students who are not only Technologically astute but also aware of the scope and boundaries of current Technological progress and its applications in Society. The Curriculum needs to embed an Interdisciplinary Approach within Curriculum Design to ensure a solid understanding of AI Skills and Future Application. The biggest contribution that AI should make to the Educational landscape is to promote "Learner-Centred" learning, moving from the dominant "one-size-fits-all" approach.

REFERENCES

Alharbi, A. M. (2023). Implementation of Education 5.0 in Developed and Developing Countries: A Comparative Study. *Creative Education*, 14(5), 914–942. DOI: 10.4236/ce.2023.145059

Daniil Yaskevich, R.-o.-D. (2021). Digital Technologies, as a Factor in the Search for a New Quality of Inclusive Education. . 1-9.

Daron Cyr, J. W. (2022). Logics and the Orbit of Parent Engagement. *School Community Journal*, ●●●, 9–38.

Dervojeda, K. (2021, 7). Education 5.0: Rehumanising Education in the Age of Machines. 1-8.

Education Data Security: 5 Things to Implement Now. (2023, August 11). Retrieved from https://computersnationwide.com/education-data-security-5-things-implement-now/

Elias Carayannis, J. M. (2023). University and Education 5.0 for Emerging Trends, Policies and Practices in the Concept of Industry 5.0 and Society 5.0. 1-25.

Elias Ratinho, C. M. (2023). The role of gamified learning strategies in student's motivation in high school and higher education: A systematic review. *sciencedirect*.

Hatice Leblebic, A. T. (2021). Opinions of Teacher Candidates on Inclusive Education: A Parallel Mixed Method Study. *International Journal of Education and Literacy Studies*, 9(4), 32–44. DOI: 10.7575/aiac.ijels.v.9n.4p.32

Mollee Shultz, J. N. (2022). The role of epistemological beliefs in STEM pedagogy at Hispanic-Serving Institutions. *International Journal of STEM Education faculty's decisions to use culturally relevant*, 1-22.

Nikum, K. (2022). Answers to the Societal Demands with Education 5.0:Indian Higher Education System. *Journal of Engineering Education Transformations,*, 115-127.

Nitin Liladhar Rane, S. P. (2023). Education 4.0 and 5.0: integrating Artificial Intelligence (AI) for personalized and adaptive learning.

Odier-Guedj, C. C. (2022). Fostering Family–School–Community Partnership With Parents of Students With Developmental Disabilities: Participatory Action Research With the 3D Sunshine Model. *School Community Journal*, ●●●, 327–356.

Pattanayak, S. (2023, november 29). *HIGHER EDUCATION: Education 5.0 can address skill growth needed in evolving job market*. Retrieved from educationtimes. com: https://www.educationtimes.com/article/campus-beat-college-life/99734211/ higher-education-education-5-0-can-address-skill-growth-needed-in-evolving-job -market

Pitshou Moleka. (2022). *Dispelling the Limitations of Education 5.0 and Outlining the Vision of Education 6.0*. Managing Research African Network.

Prakash Srinivasan, S. N. (2023). Education 5.0 Revolutionizing Learning for the Future (Vol.1). *reasearch gate*.

Pratyusha, Y. B., & Varghese, B. (2024). Inclusive Educational Settings With Equity and Integration: Assessing Opportunities and Challenges. *Designing Equitable and Accessible Online Learning Environments*, 74-92.

Rita Vieira, J. O. (2023). Society 5.0 and Education 5.0: A Critical Reflection. *18th Iberian Conference on Information Systems and Technologies (CISTI)*. Aveiro, Portugal.

Rodrigo Smiderle, S. J. (2020). The impact of gamification on students' learning, engagement and behavior based on their personality traits. *springeropen*.

H. Sandhya, B. V. (2022). AI's Potential for Optimal Student Learning in Education: Ethical Implications.

Sandhya H., B. V. (2023). The Emerging Role of Innovative Teaching Practices in Tourism Education in the Post Covid Era. 1-15.

Sebastian, S. (2023). Education 5.0: A Paradigm Shift in Learning.

Shabir Ahmad, S. U. (2023). Education 5.0: Requirements, Enabling Technologies, and Future Directions. 1-24.

Tiina Kivirand, Ä. L. (2021). Designing and Implementing an In-Service Training Course for School Teams on Inclusive Education: Reflections from Participants. *Education Sciences*, 11(4), 1–19. DOI: 10.3390/educsci11040166

Tore Hoel, W. C. (2018). Privacy and data protection in learning analytics should be motivated by an educational maxim—Towards a proposal. *Research and Practice in Technology Enhanced Learning*. PMID: 30595748

Trivedi, D. R. (2023). *The Role of Industry 5.0 in Education 5.0 in Indian Perspective*. INTERNATIONAL JOURNAL OF INNOVATIVE RESEARCH IN TECHNOLOGY.

Chapter 10
Fostering Pro– Environmental Behaviors With AI–Driven Educational Psychology in Education 5.0

Minh Tung Tran
https://orcid.org/0000-0002-4238-882X
FPT School of Business and Technology, FPT University, Vietnam

ABSTRACT

This research proposes an innovative AI-driven educational psychology model, the AI-EcoCollaborative Educational Psychology Model, to foster pro-environmental behaviors in Education 5.0. By integrating AI technologies with educational psychology principles, the model aims to create personalized, engaging, and interactive learning experiences that promote environmental awareness and action. The model incorporates various components, including personalized interventions, virtual reality simulations, and ethical considerations, to ensure effective and responsible implementation. Through case studies and future directions, the research explores the potential of AI-driven educational psychology in shaping a sustainable future.

1. INTRODUCTION

Education 5.0 involves transforming schooling from the use of artificial intelligence (AI) to comfort and healing perspectives in the AI context with the hope of symbiosis. The aim is to deliberately engineer AI-driven materials and pedagogies

DOI: 10.4018/979-8-3693-8191-5.ch010

under the influence of energy conservation, carbon neutrality and sustainability, gender equality and women's empowerment, diversity and inclusion, equitable quality education. Alongside mathematics education, social, emotional and mental health (SEMH) education is among the priorities in Education 5.0 as a post COVID-19 pandemic education agenda. Fostering pro-environmental behaviors is needed for any educational efforts targeting climate change actions as climate change education concerns to potential climate change mitigation behaviors. Motivated by Education 5.0, a paradigm shift to non-invasive biophysiological AI-driven SEMH educational psychology is discussed with the intention of facilitating pre-service mathematics, computer science and special education teachers' educative pro-environmental behaviors (Ferreira Mello et al., 2023).

1.1. Background and Rationale

Education 5.0 strives to address the current issues that continue to evolve along the technological times in the Fourth Industrial Revolution (Industry 4.0) while predicting and preparing learners and the education system to prepare for the future of the world in the Fifth Industrial Revolution (Society 5.0). Society 5.0 is envisioned to ensure a balance between economic advancement and the resolution of the issues facing humanity. A key program in creating education systems, the personnel and areas that are deemed crucial for the Society 5.0 vision hinges upon the incorporation of advanced technologies that fill the gap between where the education and other education-related systems are at the moment, and to where they need to be, driving the transformation of Education 4.0 components such as learning contents and methods, learning environment, roles of stakeholders and the education ecosystem itself (Aliabadi et al., 2023). There is also the need to establish trustworthiness and openness, especially in the creation of artificial intelligence (AI) and education systems using AI. Education 5.0 strives to open the black box in and ensure outcome transparency, and addresses ethics and bias to serve societal needs as learning activities with AI in Education 4.0 may affect learners in the learning ecosystem and other stakeholders' decision-making at the individual, institution, society, and world levels (Porayska-Pomsta, 2024).

With the AI deep learning evolution, it became possible to modify and innovate educational psychology modelling by leveraging the large amount and diversified digital psychologists, learners and educators data in the open internet. A new educational psychology modelling paradigm is envisioned by employing unprecedented access to use the discovered knowledge in algorithmic educational models and systems. The objective of the new modelling paradigm is twofold. First, the modelling approach for the core stakeholders in the educational psychology modelling process are the learners and the educators interact with the AI systems, algorithms and contents used for learning and teaching, thereby fulfilling the diversity of learners and educators in various modalities, behaviours and education ecosystems. Second, the newly discovered knowledge and modelling frameworks are actively translated into AI based educational models and systems to be part of the AI learning and assessment ecosystem for Education 5.0. The vastly different core behaviours technologies are to be developed and deployed into educational models and systems.

1.2. Research Aim and Objectives

The research aims to develop an innovative educational psychology model called the AI-EcoCollaborative Educational Psychology Model focused on the promotion of pro-environmental behaviors in Education 5.0. The objectives include: designing the AI-EcoCollaborative Educational Psychology Model and its components to promote pro-environmental behaviors in the educational context, investigating the potential of the AI-EcoCollaborative Educational Psychology Model in promoting pro-environmental behaviors, and evaluating the feasibility of the AI-EcoCollaborative Educational Psychology Model as an interactive experiential educational tool.

Education 5.0 serves as the strategic framework for addressing the challenges stemmed from globalization and digital transformation. It acknowledges the pressing reality of climate change and the need for sustainability and resilience in educational systems. This concept emphasizes the holistic digital transformation of educational systems and aims to prepare individuals for the society of the future where advanced technologies are widely adopted. With the rise of Artificial Intelligence (AI) in education, there are many avenues for AI-supported educational systems. However, the opportunity of using educational systems to foster pro-environmental behaviors in the development of Education 5.0 has remained unrealized in existing empirical studies.

With the advancement of digital technologies including Augmented/Virtual Reality (AR/VR), and Natural Language Processing (NLP), there are many promising solutions for building interactive and experiential educational systems. As avenues for building empathetic and socially-aligned AI technologies, Psychological Models in Educational Systems on topics such as Trust, Emotions, and Empathy are of great interest. Nevertheless, the potential of AI-driven educational psychology models to foster pro-environmental behaviors have remained unexplored. AI is an enabling technology that raises new questions regarding initial conditions, strategies, and pathways of education. Addressing these gaps, this research will contribute to building resilient communities of educational systems for a sustainable future.

2. THEORETICAL FRAMEWORK

An understanding of the foundations of learning theories is essential for teachers to appreciate how people learn and how their own understanding of the learning process influences their effectiveness as educators (Sue Stover, 2018). Major learning theories and foundations are examined and discussed in this topic based upon a set of questions. The main focus is on learning theories and principles that effect pedagogical practices either directly or indirectly. There are six particular approaches to learning that stem from powerful schools of thought that have developed over the years; these are the Behavioral approach, the Cognitive approach, the Constructivist approach, the Humanistic approach, the Social Cognitive approach, and the Connectivism approach.

2.1. Educational Psychology Theories

Educational psychology is a field that focuses on understanding the psychological principles that govern educational practices. It provides a comprehensive framework for examining how people learn, how they are motivated to learn, and how cognitive processes evolve within educational settings. By exploring educational psychology theories, a broad understanding of complex psychological phenomena and their implications in educational contexts is gained. There are three primary categories of educational psychology theories: behavioral, cognitive, and constructivist (Tran et al., 2012). Both cognitive and behavioral theories investigate different aspects of learning and the underlying cognitive mechanisms, while constructivist theories emphasize the active role of learners in constructing knowledge and meaning.

Behavioral theories originated from the works of Pavlov and Skinner, focusing on the investigation of observable behaviors and external stimuli (Williamson, 2017). Prominent theories within the behavioral category include classical conditioning (Pavlov), operant conditioning (Skinner), and social learning theory (Bandura). Subsequent refinements of behavioral models led to the establishment of several theories of learning, such as Gagne's nine events of instruction, Keller's ARCS model, and Skinner's teaching machines. The cognitive category encompasses many theories derived from computer and brain metaphors, such as Piaget's cognitive development theory, Anderson's ACT model, learning-by-doing theory, and cognitive load theory. These theories share a common interest in understanding underlying cognitive processes of learning and knowledge representation. On the contrary, constructivism stems from the works of Dewey, Vygotsky, Bruner, and Papert, emphasizing learning as a constructive and contextual process wherein learners actively participate in interpreting and constructing knowledge and meaning.

2.2. AI in Education

Artificial Intelligence (AI) involves the integration of the necessary resources to solve a problem or perform a task as a human. Educational artificial intelligence (AIEd) is the involvement of AI methods in education, either impact on the education process and educational systems or aimed at improving how people learn, assisting in the dissemination of knowledge or teaching. Prior works have primarily focused on the technology and tools and highlighted both system and non-system issues that need to be considered in conjunction with educational AI use—professional training for teachers, educational policy, educating students about AI, public awareness, future skilling, and the social, economic, and ethical challenges (Mallik & Gangopadhyay, 2023).

Humanoid educational agents are allowing AI to enter classroom teaching roles. These need to address the general salient societal concerns about humanoid robots (for instance, labor replacing) but also discuss educational agent-specific concerns regarding the prerogative of algorithmic knowledge dissemination, control over curriculums, technology-induced constraints on socialization, and reduction of human-to-human interactivity (Schiff, 2021). The social relevance and need for intervention in education of AI in education could forestall technological determinism but may also benefit from attempts to devise intentional AIEd policies globally, rather than in piecemeal and incidental fashion.

3. PRO-ENVIRONMENTAL BEHAVIORS

The world is widely aware of the issues surrounding the environment and is siding with conservation efforts in order to work towards a sustainable future. In terms of education and educational psychology, pro-environmental behaviors could be included in the plans for instruction. Pro-environmental behaviors could be defined as voluntary behaviors taken by an individual or a group to lessen harm to the environment and help with the preservation of the natural resources of the planet (Zehui, 2023). These behaviors collectively address serious issues such as climate change, pollution, global warming, biodiversity loss, and many more that could greatly affect the existence of life on earth.

To achieve a common goal in pro-environmental behaviors, every single pro-social act counts regardless of the scale (Wang et al., 2022). Pro-environmental acts include but are not limited to: reducing the use of energy, water, and other consumables; recycling materials; minimizing waste; using eco-friendly products; substituting sustainable transportation; voting for a pro-environmental cause; supporting green initiatives; taking part in a clean-up campaign; planting trees and other efforts that contribute to saving the planet for future generations. Many countries have actively taken part in Earth Hour, car-free days, tree-planting, and coastal clean-up endeavors.

3.1. Definition and Importance

Pro-environmental behavior and actions are voluntary measures undertaken by individuals or groups to mitigate environmental damage and assist in its conservation. Such actions include, for instance, ecological lifestyles, recycling, using greener transport modes, conserving energy, and mobilizing against environmental decline. Pro-environmental behaviors have gained increasing interest in relation to a few of the most essential challenges faced by human societies namely climate change, biodiversity loss, and other forms of environmental degradation (Zehui, 2023). Comprehending the supporting factors and obstacles to pro-environmental behavior is necessary to formulate and enact effective policies, interventions, and communication strategies. In accordance with this growing interest, a wide body of research has been generated in sociology, political science, psychology, economics, and other fields that can inform debates on pro-environmental behavior. This manuscript endeavours to provide a comprehensive overview of the extant literature on pro-environmental behavior and actions, aiming to synthesize prevalent theoretical frameworks, empirical results, and practical implications.

The formative years of pro-environmental behavior and life-long habits are principally derived from childhood experiences and education. As a significant social context, schooling is the most important experience in children's lives, particularly with regard to their development of pro-environmental attitudes, awareness, and behaviors. Environmental Education (EE) in formal and non-formal settings has the potential to support positive environmental behavior, as well as to develop individuals' awareness about environmental issues. Numerous studies employing different data collection methods (surveys, interviews, observations) and research designs (prior/post-EE program comparisons; comparative studies) have been conducted to examine the long-term influences of both formal and non-formal EE on pro-environmental behaviors (Petsch, 2019).

3.2. Factors Influencing Pro-Environmental Behaviors

Various psychological, social, as well as environmental factors influencing pro-environmental behaviours at the individual level have been analysed systematically and discussed in this section. Pro-environmental behaviours are defined as deliberate individual actions which can positively affect the environment (Zehui, 2023). There exist a significant number of factors that can influence pro-environmental behaviours such as Knowledge/awareness, personal factors, values, norms, education, social encouragement or social interaction, littering context, independent assortment etc. Educational psychology can play a significant role in promoting pro-environmental behaviours. Education in conjunction with psychological factors might help to bring a more profound transformation in students. Significant attention to current techno-logical developments is also required and educational psychology ought to help us to adopt new digital tools including AI systems as new environments within class-rooms. With the development of effective deep-learning tools to address educational psychology including personality prediction, trait simulation, emotion detection, automatic labelling of educational contents etc., there is a high motivation to apply some of these tools in teaching and learning (Vinojini & Anton Arulrajah, 2018).

4. AI APPLICATIONS IN EDUCATION

4.1. Personalized Learning

As AI becomes more embedded in education, new opportunities arise for trans-forming learning into a more personalized and tailored experience. Simply stated, personalized learning means that the learning process becomes customized for each individual student according to their particular learning needs and preferences. Per-sonalization enables learning experiences in which students receive the right learning environment, individualized resources, and feedback at the appropriate time and complexity, hence leading to improved learning gains (E. August & Tsaima, 2021). An effective personalized learning approach in education considers the wide range of individual learner differences and involves responsive and adaptative feedback. While this opportunity is not new, as many attempts have been made in recent de-cades to personalize learning with technology, the renewed rise of AI techniques and tools provides increased capabilities to address complex and nuanced scenarios, such as individuality and diversity in education. (Tekin & van der Schaar, 2014)

Adaptive learning is one possible incarnation of pedagogical personalization, which refers to a subdomain of educational personalization in which automatic adjustment occurs in response to the changing needs of learners. In this approach, AI tools and algorithms can analyze massive amounts of data captured from ed-ucational environments and systems, and draw connections and inferences about learners, which allow metrics such as content difficulty and learning pathways to be adjusted in real-time. Moreover, allowing system predictions, current learner states, and content offload to be recombined in the leading of learning experiences means that adaptive is a more dynamic and fine-grained approach than non-adaptive personalization (Singh et al.2024), (Hutahaean et al.,2024).

4.2. Virtual Reality and Simulations

The use of Virtual Reality (VR) and Simulations in educational contexts have been explored with applications of Artificial Intelligence (AI). Even though VR and Simulations has seen a wide array of applications in the gaming and entertainment sector, their potential use in the educational world have not been fully realised. The characteristics of virtual reality and educational simulations allow for immersive and interactive experiences that enhance the learning outcomes (Mohamad Rasli et al., 2016) and also provides an overview of various AI applications in Virtual Reality and Educational Simulations. Put simply, Virtual Reality places the user inside an experience while the simulations model real world or fictional events for the user to control or observe from outside (Cheng Chye Tan et al., 2022). In the case of VR Educational simulations, the merging of these technologies within an environment of Pro-Environmental Behaviours promotes a combined effect. This combination allows an entrapped and interactive experience leading to an enhanced engagement learning experience. Virtual Reality and simulations are able to take the learner from a didactical learning context and provide a dynamic educational scenario to make Embedded pro-environmental behaviours.

5. INTEGRATION OF AI AND EDUCATIONAL PSYCHOLOGY

AI-driven educational systems (AIEd) are intelligent systems that make educational estimates, decisions, and interventions for learners and educators, responding proactively or reactively to perceived needs (Mallik & Gangopadhyay, 2023). This growing interest in the application of artificial intelligence in the educational sector, especially through the educational psychology domain, is evident from the increase in specific blends of AIEd systems and educational psychology-based educational interventions in recent years. Educational psychology is the discipline of psychology that specializes in education. Psychological principles are applied in the educational domain with the desire to enhance the teaching-learning experience and the overall student development process, both academically and behaviorally. AI technologies can be incorporated in educational settings to support and augment psychological strategies, extending their reach and increasing their effectiveness (Schiff, 2021). This section focuses mainly on the synergies between AI and educational psychology in Education 5.0, hoping to provide a brief overview of the potential that this integration holds.

Integration Benefits and Challenges The integration of AI and educational psychology has significant benefits, such as personalized assistance and scalability. However, there are also challenges, such as ethical and privacy concerns, technological complexities, and the need for collaboration and training. The challenge of inefficient interactions in mass education can be addressed by AI technologies and the well-established knowledge of educational psychology, which can create a more personal and effective educational environment. AIEd provides a much-needed pathway to make psychological coping strategies commonplace in education systems (Grassini, 2023).

5.1. Benefits and Challenges

Despite the challenges, the solution offers numerous potential benefits. First, engaging and interactive learning experiences can enhance pro-environmental behavior intention and disruption of inertia. Learning experiences that are immersive, engaging and interactive can foster pro-environmental behavior intention and help to break the inertia of it (Porayska-Pomsta, 2024). Additionally, with social interaction based on sentiment dynamic similarity, the learning experiences can provide group discussion opportunities for learners with similar feelings, thereby enhancing the learning experience. Second, rich behavioral and emotional data enable the provision of personalized interventions. By analyzing behavioral and emotional data related to the learning experience, dynamic models for behavioral and emotional engagement can be developed to provide personalized feedback and support for learners with different engagement levels (Luan et al., 2020). This is essential for educational endeavors in a pro-environmental context, as it helps to ensure that all learners achieve a desirable learning experience. Third, sufficient data privacy protection and transparency increase the acceptability of AI applications. By using federated learning with local personalization, only aggregated model parameters would be shared with the server, and learners' raw data remain on their devices. Additionally, learners would be informed about data use and given control of their own data. These measures can enhance learner protection of privacy and increase acceptability.

6. CASE STUDIES AND EXAMPLES

In presenting the case studies and examples, several real-world instances of successful implementations of AI-driven educational psychology are highlighted. The objective is to provide concrete illustrations of the application and impact of AI technologies in educational settings. Each case study showcases a different aspect of AI-driven educational psychology, whether it be the use of natural language processing for essay grading, AI chatbots for tutoring, personalized learning environments, or AI-powered recommendation systems for course selection (Mallik & Gangopadhyay,

2023). By analyzing these case studies, practical insights and lessons are offered that can inform the effective integration of AI and educational psychology.

In South Korea, the "AI Recommender" system was developed, which combined learning analytics, educational data mining, and natural language processing. The aim was to help students select online courses to improve e-learning personalization. The system was evaluated using survey results from students, who reported improved outcomes. In the American project "Firefly," a visual programming language was introduced to tutor early grade students in computer science. The use of intelligent agents monitored student learning and enhanced teacher capacity through data analysis. An experiment demonstrated that allowing more engaging agents led to higher engagement and performance, especially among at-risk students. In Saudi Arabia, the use of an AI chatbot for tutoring critical thinking skills was explored in a randomized controlled trial. The study showed that the chatbot service improved critical thinking performance among female freshmen students. In China, an AI recommendation system was implemented to increase the use of online learning platforms among K-12 students. The platform learned students' learning patterns and made personalized recommendations, resulting in higher content engagement. In Singapore, a multi-year pilot program using a series of AI-driven data tools was undertaken. The initiative aimed to foster teaching practices and professional accountability through data-driven transparency, enhancing student experiences and engagement with the curriculum (Schiff, 2021).

6.1. Successful Implementations

In a university in Indonesia, AI-driven educational psychology strategies were applied by developing an AI-enabled mobile app called SmartsWaste. This app allows students to input information about the waste produced using photos and descriptions of the waste. With the help of machine learning, students can identify in which waste container the waste should be thrown based on its group: organic, glass, plastic, or paper. With the help of chatbot technology, students can receive personalized information and advise about their waste treatment behavior, as well as information about recycling centers, waste treatment technology, and policies for waste treatment (Mallik & Gangopadhyay, 2023).

The SmartWaste application was implemented in 4 universities in Indonesia with a focus on an industrial engineering study program. The application was purchased by students in teams of 4 to 5 people, and each week they conducted literacy activities in the following areas: understanding the recyclable waste group, pro-environmental behavior, using the chatbot feature, and monitoring their behavior using the application. Data that can be collected from the application include chatbot conversation logs, monitoring of user behavior in using the application, and the number of questions received. The results of the implementation in 2021 showed that on average students had better knowledge about waste treatment after participating in the literacy activity (Schiff, 2021).

7. ETHICAL CONSIDERATIONS

The ethical considerations section scrutinizes the ethical implications and considerations associated with the integration of AI-driven educational psychology in fostering pro-environmental behaviors. By evaluating the potential ethical challenges and risks that may arise from leveraging AI technologies in educational settings, this section underscores the importance of privacy, data security, and ethical decision-making in the implementation of AI-driven educational strategies. The ethical challenges presented by AI in education, with a particular focus on pro-environmental behaviors, are examined and invites scholars and educators to contemplate the ethical nature in the design and implementation of AI systems to preeminently protect and improve the world in which pro-environmental behaviors are promoted (Nguyen et al., 2023).

The deployment of AI technologies in educational settings poses an array of challenges, including ethical considerations. While education is anticipated to be transformed by AI (Franco D'Souza et al., 2024), ethical dilemmas surrounding safety, accountability, and privacy across various domains (e.g., fairness, transparency, and reliability) have been raised. The expansion of AI in education hence demands careful scrutiny of its ethical implications since addressing ethical considerations in the development and adoption of AI technologies is of utmost importance in ensuring, sustaining, protecting, and improving people's freedoms.

7.1. Privacy and Data Security

Privacy is related to the protection of information considered sensitive. Such information can vary in nature and can include personal data (e.g., age, gender, and health), socio-demographic data (e.g., educational background and job position), and personal interests (e.g., hobbies and media consumption). The most valuable and protected sensitive information nowadays is private data about individuals, such as social security numbers, credit card numbers, and bank accounts. Another important category of private data is health-related information (Luan et al., 2020). The growing concern regarding privacy in the use of information systems or technologies has been using an essential driver for the emergence of laws and regulations in the area of privacy. This concern has also been an important topic of interest in artificial intelligence (AI) systems. Different models of AI, particularly machine learning (ML) algorithms, do not respect the confidentiality (i.e., privacy) of sensitive data upon which they are trained.

It covers previously discussed privacy concerns in the use of AI-driven educational psychology. Additionally, it extends the previous considerations in the area of types of sensitive data, data protection measures, and ethical responsibilities and legal aspects in the use of AI technologies in education (Schiff, 2021). Wherever such systems are used in education, likely, there will be AI-driven educational psychology regardless of any thought during their development. However, students and educators do not lose their rights outside the classroom regarding privacy and security of their socially, behaviorally, and emotionally sensitive AI-relevant data. Therefore, discussion of the rights of students or educators with respect to personally sensitive data is of utmost importance, as well as of ethical and security issues in operating AI-driven educational psychology systems.

8. FUTURE DIRECTIONS

The future directions section delineates the emerging technologies and potential advancements in AI-driven educational psychology. It highlights an ambitious vision of what AI-driven educational psychology may look like in the future. With the ever-growing influence of AI technologies, someone's perspective on the future landscape of educational practices and the burgeoning inclusion of AI technologies in education is envisaged. An effort will be taken to explore the trajectory of AI in education, focusing on educational psychology, and offering a forward-looking view of the possibilities and promises to exploit AI-driven educational psychology to foster pro-environmental behaviors (Mallik & Gangopadhyay, 2023).

Attention has to be paid to what AI-driven educational psychology looks like now, what it becomes at its most developed, imaginable stage in the future, and how it gets there step-by-step. It is important to note that there are various AI technologies to be taken into account, including intelligent tutoring systems and virtual agents. Each technology will have its own trajectory of advancement, leading educational practices to develop in different directions (Schiff, 2021).

8.1. Emerging Technologies

A plethora of emerging technologies hold the promise of shaping the future of AI-driven educational psychology includes but is not limited to: multi-sensory spaces, multi-modal interaction, extended reality, immersive learning spaces, learning environments as a service, learning-with-robots, learning-evolving and self-repairing systems, bringing-the-outside-in technologies, ambient learning, brain-computer interface and synthetic brains (Porayska-Pomsta, 2024). Several of them are innovative, some are more established but will have an influence nevertheless. Some of them are single technology but some rely on other technological developments and might be more like broader concepts or paradigms.

Competitive technologies, such as multi-sensory instructional aids, wearable multi-modal devices for learning, branched simulation interactions, adaptive avatars, learning based on brainwaves, learning based on stimuli effect on genes, stimuli for synthesizing and learning through biological neural networks and understanding learning though modeling with Artificial General Intelligence might offer unique opportunities for scaling up competitive testing environments in business education systems, public and private educational organisations by providing a wide range of transnational experimental conditions (Schiff, 2021). Educational Artificial Intelligence might contest because of its reliable, always-on capabilities, combining human like capabilities and learning mechanisms with unceasing number crunching and unlimited storage, with the opportunity of better understanding and simulating emotional development, learning behaviours, styles, patterns and mechanisms than present day knowledge of cognitive sciences.

9. CONCLUSION AND RECOMMENDATIONS

Education plays a crucial role in the sustainability transition towards sustainable lifestyles in everyday life. It is expected to provide awareness and promote pro-environmental behaviors starting from the early years, with developmentally suitable methods and techniques (Petsch, 2019). Young stakeholders should be motivated to participate in the environmental problems taking actions. Therefore, recent movements in education implement pro-environmental education as a cross-curricular competence, called sustainable education. In this context, artificial intelligence driven educational technologies, such as intelligent tutoring systems or educational agents, can support teachers and students by providing contextualized solutions and recommendations in order to facilitate and promote pro-environmental behaviors. Although there are great advances in the educational and social behavior modelling areas, strategies for using a context-aware educational psychology model in AI systems for pro-environmental education are still absent.

An AI-driven learning and discussion platform based on multi-agent social simulation framework and educational psychology model is proposed. Social reactions are computer simulated concerning students' and teachers' decisions in a pro-environmental education scenario. A pro-environmental educational agent considers these reactions in order to model the environmental impacts of students' and teachers' actions. Contextualized solutions based on the knowledge of the agent model and the context of each student, environment and society can promote the sustainable education and adoption of pro-environmental behaviors in AI-ed systems. The educational psychology framework is adapted to focus on the pro-environmental education domain, including approaches, indicators, strategies and actions. Pro-environmental educational agents can be characterized according to the educational psychology model and context. Educational technologies equipped with this model can have pro-environmental and psycho-pedagogical profiles to facilitate the implementation of the context-aware platform (Chen & Shi, 2024) (Guan et al.,2024).

REFERENCES

Aliabadi, R., Singh, A., & Wilson, E. (2023). Transdisciplinary AI Education: The Confluence of Curricular and Community Needs in the Instruction of Artificial Intelligence.

August, S. E., & Tsaima, A. (2021). Artificial intelligence and machine learning: an instructor's exoskeleton in the future of education. Innovative Learning Environments in STEM Higher Education: Opportunities, Challenges, and Looking Forward, 79-105.

Chen, L., & Shi, J. (2024). Communication Technology and Environmental Communication: Challenges, Opportunities, and Emerging Agendas. *Environmental Communication*.

Cheng Chye Tan, M., Yen Leng Chye, S., & Shu Min Teng, K. (2022). "In the shoes of another": immersive technology for social and emotional learning. Grassini, S. (2023). Shaping the future of education: exploring the potential and consequences of AI and ChatGPT in educational settings. *Education Sciences*.

Ferreira Mello, R., Freitas, E., Dwan Pereira, F., Cabral, L., Tedesco, P., & Ramalho, G. (2023). Education in the age of Generative AI: Context and Recent Developments.

Franco D'Souza, R., Mathew, M., Mishra, V., & Mohan Surapaneni, K. (2024). Twelve tips for addressing ethical concerns in the implementation of artificial intelligence in medical education.

Guan, B., Li, X., Luo, Z., & Liu, P. (2024). [Arouse You? The Impact of AI Services on Consumer Pro-Environmental Behavior. Journal of Hospitality & Tourism Research.]. *CANA*, •••, I.

Hutahaean, B., Telaumbanua, S., Tamba, L., Hutabarat, R. G. N., & Sumani, S. (2024). Analysis of Innovative and Adaptive Higher Education Curriculum Development to Education 5.0 Based Challenges in Indonesia. International Journal of Learning. *Teaching and Educational Research*, 23(4), 76–98.

Luan, H., Geczy, P., Lai, H., Gobert, J., J. H. Yang, S., Ogata, H., Baltes, J., Guerra, R., Li, P., & Tsai, C. C. (2020). Challenges and Future Directions of Big Data and Artificial Intelligence in Education.

Mallik, S. & Gangopadhyay, A. (2023). Proactive and Reactive Engagement of Artificial Intelligence Methods for Education: A Review. Schiff, D. (2021). Out of the laboratory and into the classroom: the future of artificial intelligence in education.

Mohamad Rasli, R., Md Norwawi, N., & Basir, N. (2016). Preliminary survey of educational simulations towards educational context.

Nguyen, A., Ngan Ngo, H., Hong, Y., Dang, B., & Thi Nguyen, B. P. (2023). Ethical principles for artificial intelligence in education.

Petsch, M. (2019). How Do Non-Formal Environmental Education Experiences Shape Pro-. *Environment and Behavior*.

Porayska-Pomsta, K. (2024). From Algorithm Worship to the Art of Human Learning: Insights from 50-year journey of AI in Education.

Singh, H., Chauhan, U., Chauhan, S. P. S., Saxena, A., & Kumari, P. (2024). Adaptive and Personalized Learning in Industry 5.0 Education. In Infrastructure Possibilities and Human-Centered Approaches With Industry 5.0 (pp. 1-19). IGI Global.

Sue Stover, T. (2018). A Case Study of Teachers Implementing The Framework for 21st-Century Learning.

Tekin, C., & van der Schaar, M. (2014). eTutor: Online Learning for Personalized Education.

Tran, C., Chen, J., Warschauer, M., Conley, A. M., & Dede, C. (2012). Applying Motivation Theories to the Design of Educational Technology.

Vinojini, M. & Anton Arulrajah, A. (2018). The Pro-Environmental Behaviour of Employee in an Apparel Manufacturing Organization in Nuwara-Eliya District of Sri Lanka.

Wang, Q., Kou, Z., Sun, X., Wang, S., Wang, X., Jing, H., & Lin, P. (2022). Predictive Analysis of the Pro-Environmental Behaviour of College Students Using a Decision-Tree Model.

Williamson, B. (2017). Moulding student emotions through computational psychology: affective learning technologies and algorithmic governance.

Zehui, Z. (2023). Pro-Environmental Behavior and Actions: Review of the literature and agenda for future research.

Chapter 11
Handling the AI Employment Landscape:
Gearing Up Students for Future Professions

Kalyani Nakul Satone
https://orcid.org/0009-0001-3927-352X
St. Vincent Pallotti College of Engineering and Technology, India

Pranjali B. Ulhe
https://orcid.org/0000-0002-6557-4334
School of Allied Sciences, Datta Meghe Institute of Higher Education and Research, India

Anushree Sandeep Deshmukh
Rajiv Gandhi Institute of Technology, India

Leena Mandurkar
St. Vincent Pallotti College of Engineering and Technology, India

ABSTRACT

Artificial intelligence (AI) is transforming education by being essential to the growth of students' digital literacy, critical thinking, and problem-solving abilities as well as their readiness for the quickly changing AI-driven labor markets. This abstract explores the multidimensional impact of AI on skill development in education. In order to prepare the complexity of the modern world, Students must be able to think critically and solve problems in order to be prepared for the complexity of the modern world. To develop skills, it gets achieved through adaptive assessments, real-world simulations, and tailored learning experiences. Through the use of AI, teachers may customize course materials to each student's unique learning style and speed,

DOI: 10.4018/979-8-3693-8191-5.ch011

improving comprehension and student engagement. The ability to effectively and ethically acquire, assess, and use information in digital environments is referred to as digital literacy.

I. INTRODUCTION

The objective of the U.S. Department of Education is to use technology to improve innovation, teaching, and learning in all educational institutions. This study emphasizes the growing significance of "Artificial Intelligence" (AI), a quickly developing technology that is becoming more widely available to the general public and incorporated into educational tools. AI, which is described as "automation based on associations," is a major development in educational technology. Establishing governance to direct the usage of AI systems in education is essential as these technologies become more commonplace. This chapter examines the possible advantages of artificial intelligence (AI) in education, points out potential drawbacks, and makes suggestions for future legislation.

Increasing Demand For AI Education

There are still many unreached priorities for enhancing teaching and learning. Thus, educators need to look for scalable, safe, and technology-enhanced alternatives. Teachers are investigating artificial intelligence (AI) technologies in light of the swift advancements in everyday technology. They see how these tools might help kids with disabilities, bilingual learners, and other learners who might gain from individualized digital learning experiences (Walton Family Foundation, 2023). They see ways AI can help with selecting materials, creating lessons, and modifying information for educational purposes.

Educators are aware of the threats that come with AI, about data privacy, the possibility of biased or unsuitable results, and the possibility that students may misidentify work produced by AI as their own. The Department of Education has seen an increase in both interest in and apprehension about artificial intelligence (AI), especially as more tech companies intend to use AI into educational programs. In 2022, hearings made clear how quickly action is needed to control artificial intelligence's growing influence in education. The necessity to weigh the advantages and disadvantages of artificial intelligence (AI) has been further highlighted by open dialogues and investigations of its potential, including generative chatbots.

Three Reasons to Address AI in Education Now

Firstly, AI has the ability to more affordably, scalable, and efficiently address educational concerns. By improving the adaptability of learning resources to students' needs and strengths, it could aid in addressing unfinished business from the pandemic. AI may also help educators by automating repetitive work, freeing them up to concentrate more on the unique needs of each student, and modifying course materials to better represent the communities and cultural backgrounds of their pupils.

Second, with the advent of AI, increasing student surveillance and worries about teachers being replaced. Algorithmic prejudice has drawn public attention in instances when specific student groups are unfairly targeted by exam monitoring systems or voice recognition algorithms that have trouble understanding regional languages. When AI functions covertly inside the framework of education, difficulties regarding transparency and trust arise. Additionally, there are questions regarding the veracity of material produced by AI and the possibility of algorithmic discrimination."

Third, the possibility of unanticipated consequences makes AI in education an urgent matter. For example, AI may unintentionally increase achievement gaps if it automates instructional decisions based on skewed or inadequate data. Similarly, if AI-driven hiring systems rely on erroneous historical data, they may inadvertently deprioritize diverse candidates. In order to take advantage of benefits, reduce risks, and control unforeseen effects, AI in education must be addressed today.

Approaching AI-Related Education Policies

The Stanford Institute for Human-Centered AI's 2023 AI Index Report notes a notable rise in AI funding and research, notably in the areas of ethics, justice, and transparency (Maslej et al., 2023). This increase is indicative of rising worries about AI's ethical implications, which are predicted to have an effect on education as well. The U.S. is concentrating on making sure AI is reliable and egalitarian, while the research highlights an increase in legislative initiatives addressing AI globally (Holmes & Porayska-Pomsta, 2022). A blueprint for an AI Bill of Rights was unveiled by the White House Office of Science and Technology Policy, providing guidelines for the application of AI in various industries (White House Office of Science and Technology Policy, 2022). The European Commission published ethical recommendations for AI and the use of data in education in Europe.

As AI develops quickly, society will need to adapt, necessitating a national policy response. However, in addition to broad policies, education-specific regulations are required to address the opportunities and challenges presented by AI, taking into account legal frameworks such as FERPA and IDEA. Educators must make sure that recommendations and actions derived from AI adhere to these legal frameworks, especially when it comes to protecting student privacy and providing support for students with disabilities (European Commission, Directorate-General for Education, Youth, Sport and Culture, 2022).

Figure 1. Number of publication using the concept of AI
Number of AI Publications by Field of Study (Excluding Other AI), 2010–21
Source: Center for Security and Emerging Technology, 2022 | Chart: 2023 AI Index Report

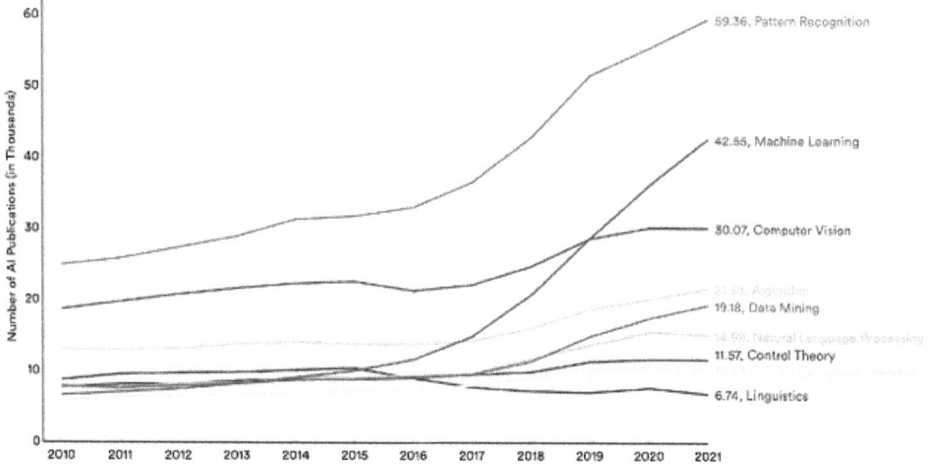

As per the figure 1, AI is progressing exponentially with powerful new AI features for generating images and text becoming available to the public.

Urgent Policies Are Needed To:

1. Utilize automation to enhance learning outcomes while preserving human decision-making and judgment.
2. Assess the quality of data used in AI models to ensure fair, unbiased pattern recognition and decision-making in educational applications, using accurate and context-appropriate information.
3. Evaluate how specific AI technologies within broader educational systems might impact or compromise student equity.
4. Protect and promote equity by implementing human oversight and restricting AI systems and tools that could undermine fairness.

II. WHAT IS AI?

Our initial definition, which is automation based on associations, needs to be expanded upon. Below, we examine three additional perspectives on what constitutes AI, which are important for educators to understand because they frequently come up in the marketing of AI features and are critical for assessing educational systems that use AI (Regona et al., 2022). AI is not a single thing; rather, it is an umbrella term that encompasses an expanding range of modeling capabilities.

Figure 2. AI based components (IEEE-USA Board of Directors, 2017)

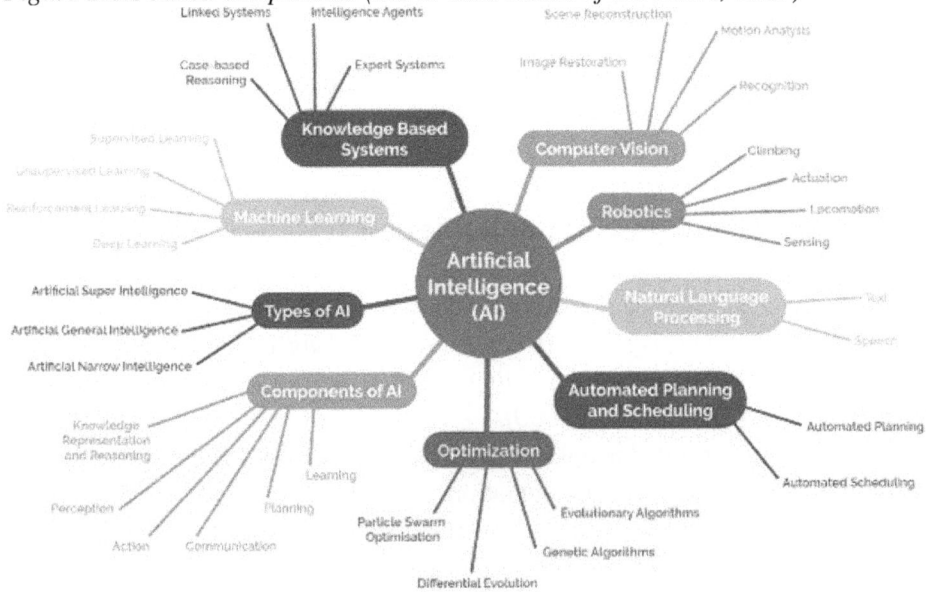

Perspective: Human-Like Reasoning

"The theory and development of computer systems able to perform tasks normally requiring human intelligence such as, visual perception, speech recognition, learning, decision-making, and natural language processing." (Russell, 2019)

As made prominent by the character HAL in 2001: A Space Odyssey, AI is frequently depicted as having reasoning similar to that of humans. The reasoning, speaking, and behaving human-like actions of HAL demonstrate the potential advantages and disadvantages of AI, particularly in the field of education. By interacting with teachers and students or co-directing classroom activities, AI can improve educational experiences and present new avenues for growth. But it's crucial to understand that AI analyzes information differently from humans, and oversimplifying this distinction could result in policies that are ineffectual.

Perspective: An Algorithm that Pursues a Goal

"Any computational method that is made to act independently towards a goal based on inferences from theory or patterns in data." (Russell, 2019).

AI systems see patterns and make decisions to accomplish particular objectives, including customizing educational sessions. By offering suggestions, such as when choosing teaching materials, these systems can improve the way that education is conducted. AI decision-making, however, needs to be carefully evaluated because it could not have the same sophisticated understanding of intricate educational situations that people do. For example, although AI may recommend educational materials, teachers need to evaluate if those recommendations are suitable, taking into account the possibility of errors (Gartner, n.d.).

Perspective: Intelligence Augmentation

"Augmented intelligence is a design pattern for a human-centered partnership model of people and artificial intelligence (AI) working together to enhance cognitive performance, including learning, decision making, and new experiences." (National Research Council, 2000).

By spotting patterns that people would miss, artificial intelligence (AI) supports human thinking in intelligent augmentation, placing the person at the center of the decision-making process. In contrast to AI, which focuses on what computers can accomplish, IA is intended to support human endeavors like education. Intelligent Advisory (IA) enables educators to make better judgments without being overburdened by offering tools that lessen instructors' workloads, such as reminding pupils of tasks.

III. PROCESS OF TEACHING AND LEARNING

A.   Learning

The Department sees its students as active learners who participate in class discussions, use simulations and visualizations, and gain from feedback and scaffolding. Technology must be in line with these empirically supported theories of learning. For information on efficient teaching methods, educators might consult the National Academies of Sciences, Engineering, and Medicine's *How People

Learn* and *How People Learn II* (Aleven et al., 2016). The development of AI-enhanced educational technology should prioritize helping people who have experienced learning difficulties, such as those brought on by wider injustices or the COVID-19 pandemic. Based on well-established learning theories, AI can improve learning by offering arithmetic instruction, accommodating unique needs, and promoting productive teamwork.

a. AI Enables Adaptivity in Learning

AI has the potential to greatly improve educational technology's adaptability, allowing it to better meet students where they are, make use of their talents, and foster their development (Forsyth et al., 2021). AI is an effective technique for increasing learning adaptivity because of its capacity to operate with natural inputs and the advantages of AI models. But the nature of the models AI utilizes limits its flexibility from the start. AI models may not fully represent the intricacy of human learning because they are approximations of reality, which could result in limited or fragile support. Therefore, it's critical to avoid limiting education to what AI can currently model and to create AI models that are in line with broader views of learning.

b. A Duality: Learning With and About AI

AI is an effective technique for increasing learning adaptivity because of its capacity to operate with natural inputs and the advantages of AI models; however, the nature of the models AI utilizes limits its flexibility from the outset. Given that AI models are approximations of reality, they may not fully represent the intricacy of human learning, which could result in limited or fragile support. As such, it's critical to avoid limiting education to what AI can currently model and to create AI models that are in line with broader views of learning.

Promising programs are being launched with the goal of teaching students about AI in addition to other crucial subjects like security and privacy (Hammerness, Darling-Hammond, & Bransford, 2005). Relevant learning objectives are also highlighted in the K–12 Computer Science Framework. From elementary school through high school, students can learn about artificial intelligence (AI) and use it to create products and simulations that they find engaging. Students also have strong opinions about the kinds of technologies they want to see in their schools and are keen to address the ethics of AI-driven items they use on a daily basis. Students must be involved in the design of future AI-enabled educational technologies, as mentioned in the Research section. In the end, it's critical to find a balance between teaching kids about AI and utilizing AI to enhance learning.

Challenge: Thinking About AI in Education

As AI enters the educational system, it's important to recognize that it will be applied in areas that may already be dysfunctional. AI isn't a solution for these broken systems and must be used cautiously in unstable contexts. Since AI tools don't fully align with learning goals, educational settings need to be designed to integrate AI appropriately, allowing educators to effectively use these tools. For example, AI can enhance math practice, but teachers should focus on roles like fostering mathematical practices and small-group work. Importantly, understanding culturally responsive learning remains a task for people, not AI, as AI isn't yet capable of connecting learning to a student's unique community and family strengths.

Questions to be Considered About AI for LEARNING

As we explore these opportunities, the open questions below deserve ongoing attention:

1. How much does AI help teachers adjust to their pupils' strengths rather than just their weaknesses?
2. Does AI make it possible for English language learners and learners with disabilities to receive better support?
3. How do young voices influence the selection and application of AI in education?
4. Are student data and privacy safeguarded when AI is used? Are parents and students informed about the use of their data?
5. How robust are the procedures or frameworks in place to keep an eye out for obstacles, prejudice, or other unfavorable effects when students utilize AI?
6. Are there any reputable studies or assessments of AI systems for education available?
7. Do we know who the system works for and under what circumstances, in addition to whether it works at all?

B. Teaching

Although educators have long anticipated the benefits that technology could have for their pupils and classrooms, nobody could have predicted the drastic changes brought about by the most recent pandemic. Nowadays, almost all teachers have unexpectedly come into contact with instructional technologies; some of these encounters have been pleasant, while others have not. As we continue to investigate the connection between teaching and technology, these experiences are essential.

In order to enable teachers to perform the amazing work they are dedicated to, it is imperative that the difficulties they encounter be addressed. It's also critical to keep in mind the motivations behind people's decisions to become teachers and to make sure they have the time to concentrate on the work that matters most. This section focuses on the ways in which artificial intelligence (AI) can assist educators, such as automating repetitive work, providing recommendations based on students' requirements, and assisting educators in planning, reflecting, and improving their instructional strategies.

Educators in Instructional Loops

Teachers must constantly be at the center of the process for AI to improve teaching and learning (ACE). Teaching with a human-centered perspective is a requirement of "ACE in AI" practice. The Department can state with confidence that AI will not replace teachers thanks to this premise. ACE aims to provide instructors more time to engage in activities they find most meaningful, such developing a deeper knowledge of their pupils and coming up with innovative ways to address instructional situations, rather than merely lightening their burden.

We examine the idea of human-in-the-loop AI to define how and where educators should be emphasized, and we ask: in which loops should teachers be central? Drawing inspiration from studies on adaptivity loops (Bryant et al., 2020).

1. The loop in which instructors decide in the moment while imparting knowledge.
2. The cycle in which educators plan, organize, and evaluate their instruction in addition to participating in professional development.
3. The loop in which educators participate in the development, application, and assessment of AI-enabled technology, impacting not just their own classrooms but also those of their peers.

Figure 3. Three approaches in adaptivity loop

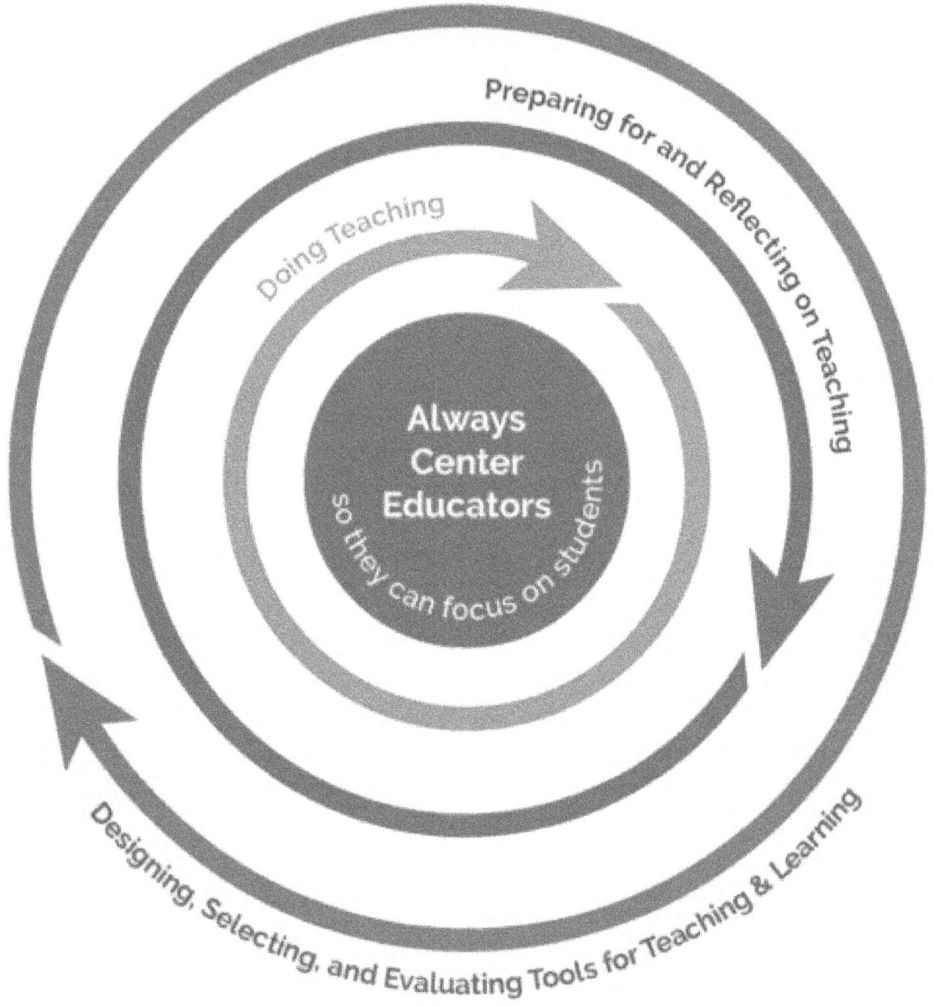

Note that we also address the crucial role teachers play in feedback loops that assist students and facilitate school improvement in the following section on formative assessment. The terms "bias" and "fairness," which are significant to educators, are also covered in that section.

IV. HOW TO IMPROVE TEACHING JOBS USING AI?

Teachers have a famously difficult profession because they have to make thousands of judgments every day. Teachers take part in procedures in the classroom, communicate with students outside of the classroom, collaborate with other educators, and perform administrative duties. Since they are expected to connect with families and caregivers, they are also expected to be members of their communities (Molenaar, 2022).

We consider how much simpler certain routine jobs have gotten over time. Notifications and alerts concerning events are available for request and receipt. Even with digital music, choosing the music we wanted to hear required multiple steps; however, these days, we can only say the name of the song we want to hear, and it will start to play. Similarly, planning a trip used to involve laboriously studying maps, but these days, cell phones allow us to select from a variety of ways to go where we're going. Why aren't educators able to recognize how students' needs are evolving and given the tools they need to implement a lesson plan that incorporates technology? Why is it so difficult for them to arrange their kids' educational paths? As things in a classroom always change, why don't the

Figure 4. Ratio of Teachers work in a week
Activity composition of teacher working hours, number of hours

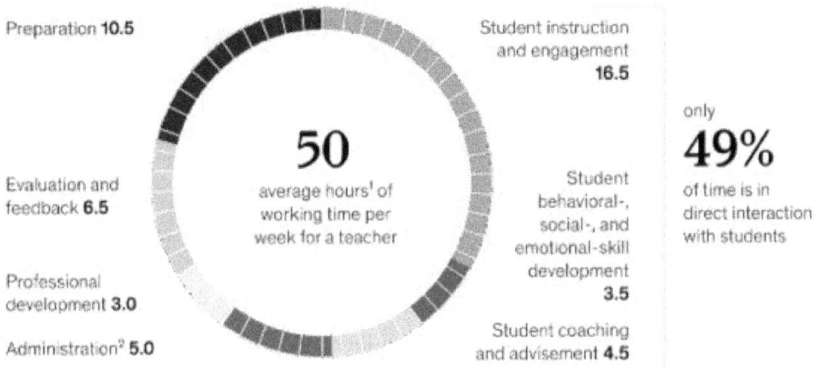

According to a McKinsey report (Wagner, Borenstein, & Howard, 2018), AI may initially help teaching positions by lessening low-level administrative or clerical labor pressures (Figure 4). Take note of the focus placed above on Sarah Hampton's remarks regarding the human touch at the listening session panel. When the necessary (but less meaningful) duties of teaching are lessened, teachers will feel that AI is supporting them in teaching with an emphasis on their human connection to their students.

Challenges

a. Balancing Human and Computer Decision-Making

The ability of AI to enable computer autonomy presents a significant new difficulty for teachers using these tools: when a teacher assigns work to an AI-enabled tool, it might continue that job in a semi-independent manner. Professor Inge Molenaar (2022) has pondered the difficulties with control in a situation including hybrid instruction: When is a teacher supposed to take charge? What tasks can be assigned to a computer system? How can an instructor keep an eye on the AI system, overturn its judgment, and regain control as needed?

Figure 5. The pressure between human and AI judgment making

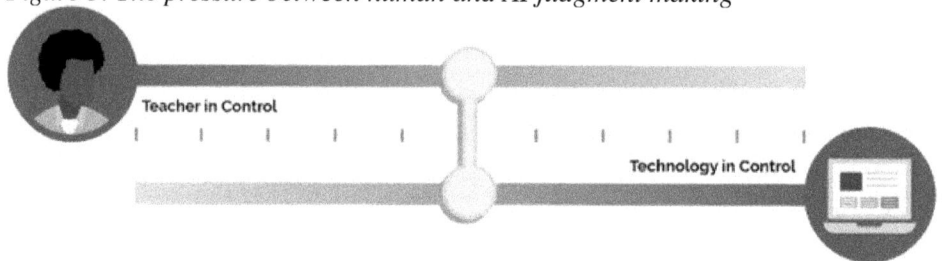

Figure 5 illustrates the conflict surrounding control. On the left, the instructor has complete control over the classroom and artificial intelligence is not used. On the right, the teacher is not there and the technology is in complete control—a situation that is rarely preferred. The middle ground involves multiple options and is not one-dimensional. After analyzing items, Molenaar makes the following recommendations:

The teacher assigns specific tasks to the technology, such as providing feedback on a particular math assignment or reminding students when an assignment is due.

● The teacher delegated more broadly to the technology, with clear protocols for alerts, for monitoring, and for when the teacher takes back control.
● The technology only provides information and recommendations to the teacher.

We must have an open discussion about these and other options. For instance, we should specify the various ways that a student may be affected by instructional decisions, and we should exercise extreme caution when giving up control over decisions that have significant ramifications (such placement in a subsequent course of study or disciplinary referrals). AI systems must enable teacher monitoring, have mechanisms to alert teachers when their judgment is required, and permit classroom, school, or district overrides when teachers disagree with an instructional decision for their pupils in order for the concept of "human in the loop" to become more completely realized. We must keep in mind that even if technology gives teachers more alternatives, as it should, it will take a considerable amount of time for them to consider and set up each one.

b. Making Teaching Jobs Easier While Avoiding Scrutiny

We acknowledge that tools intended to simplify tasks may also present hazards related to monitoring. A voice assistant in the kitchen, for example, may aid with tasks but could also listen in on private discussions. Analogously, AI programs that gather information to customize educational materials in classrooms might also be used to spy on teachers, which could have unfavorable effects. This is a problem: it will be challenging to develop reliable AI that actually enhances teachers' duties if it results in more surveillance.

Another issue is that putting instructors "in the loop" could unintentionally increase their workload, which would go against the intention of making their jobs simpler. Additionally, there's a fine line between over-trusting AI (risking monitoring or privacy invasion) and under-trusting it (losing out on its benefits). Studies indicate that individuals might obey a robot's commands even if they are aware of its flaws, emphasizing the necessity for educators to get guidance and assistance in determining when to rely on artificial intelligence and when to use their own discretion.

Figure 6. More teacher scrutiny versus highly tailored help

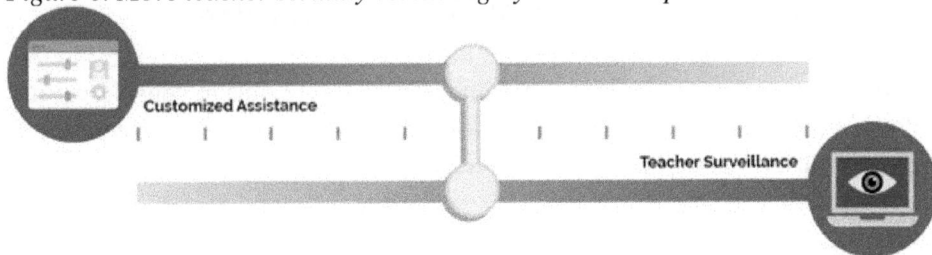

Customized Assistance

Teacher Surveillance

c. Responding to Students' Strengths While Protecting Their Privacy

By utilizing students' individual, community, and cultural strengths through culturally responsive techniques, educators work to solve learning disparities (Paris & Alim, 2017). AI could be of assistance by tailoring educational materials to students' needs and strengths, meeting them where they are. But doing so necessitates feeding intricate student data into AI algorithms, which raises data privacy concerns (Zacamy & Roschelle, 2022). Teachers need to make sure that student data exchanged with AI tools complies with privacy requirements at the federal or state level, such as FERPA, and that interactions with AI, such as using chatbots or automated tutors, are secure. This puts a conflict between protecting students' privacy and representing them effectively.

Figure 7. Replying to students' strengths while fully protecting student confidentiality

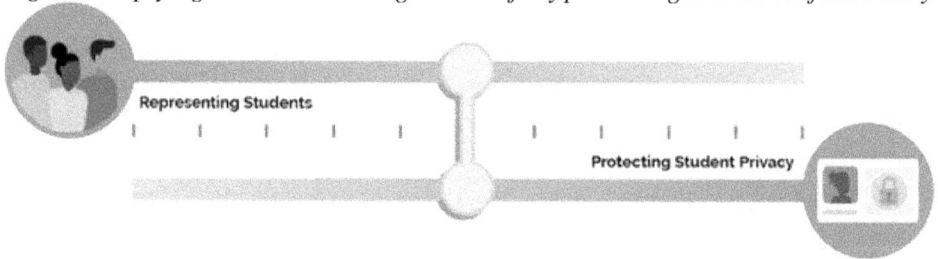

Moreover, representation would only be the beginning of the solution. As was previously mentioned in this report, bias in the data, code, or models used in AI-enhanced educational technology might lead to algorithmic discrimination (Shao et al., 2020). Engineers employ available data to build AI models that recognize patterns; however, the data they use might not be representative or might contain relationships that are inconsistent with policy objectives.

Questions to Be Considered About AI for Teaching

We implore everyone in the ecosystem to devote more time to considering the following concerns as leaders in pre-service and post-service teacher education, together with legislators, developers, and researchers, consider how AI may enhance teaching:

1. Does artificial intelligence raise the standard of a teacher's daily work?
2. Does AI lessen a particular kind of teaching burden?

3. Does using AI in the classroom give teachers greater in-depth understanding of their students' strengths while maintaining their privacy?
4. Are the AI systems that teachers utilize with their students under their supervision?
5. Are there sufficient safeguards against monitoring when AI systems are deployed to assist educators or improve learning?
6. How much can educators use their voice and decision-making skills to promote fairness and lessen bias?

V. FORMATIVE ASSESSMENT

Traditionally, formative assessment has been a major application of education since feedback loops are essential to enhancing instruction (Page, 1966). Keeping humans informed and in charge when employing AI is crucial, as we have underlined throughout this research. This includes paying close attention to the people involved in formative assessments, such as students, instructors, school administrators, families and caregivers, and other supporters of learners. Please take note of how the definitions of formative assessment and artificial intelligence (AI) overlap in the section below. Both terms deal with pattern recognition and decision-making (that adjusts to the requirements and strengths of learners).

1.Best Practices for evaluations

Formative evaluations could take on various forms in the future, and many of these could easily be extended to the realm of AI-enabled tools and systems. For instance, the 2017 NETP covered the following seven dimensions of how technology might improve formative assessments:

1.Enabling Enhanced Question Types:

to provide students with additional avenues to demonstrate their knowledge and abilities.

2. Complex Competency Assessment:

to more effectively elicit development in critical abilities that transcend conventional subject matter standards, such as in assessing practices, social skills like self-regulation and teamwork, and work-relevant abilities (e.g., leading teams or presenting).

3. Providing Real-Time Feedback:

to sustain and boost student interest and facilitate efficient learning, promptly and kindly respond to each learner's questions and offer suggestions.

4. Improving Availability:

to involve learners who are neuro-diverse and to maximize their communication skills as they impart their knowledge and abilities.

5. Adjusting for Knowledge and Skill of Learners:

help improve the accuracy and effectiveness of assessments.

6. Integrating Evaluation Into the Learning Process:

to highlight the function of assessments in enhancing instruction (this paper does not focus on assessment for accountability purposes).

5. Evaluation for Continued Education:

to demonstrate development throughout time rather to only reaching preset benchmarks.

Formative assessments could be improved by AI models and AI-enabled technologies. To help teachers better comprehend their students' understanding of concepts like "rate of change" in real-world contexts, AI can, for instance, assess student-drawn graphs or models and aggregate comparable replies for evaluation. In circumstances where rapid human evaluation is unavailable, AI can also offer feedback on complex abilities like speaking a foreign language or learning American Sign Language (Doewes & Pechenizkiy, 2021).

By managing the easier parts of students' responses, AI assistants might lighten the grading burden on teachers and free them up to concentrate on assessing more difficult material, such essays or projects. AI may also make feedback more accessible by speaking with students to help them with their arguments rather than having them type or read a screen. AI can also be integrated into the teaching and learning process, providing students with immediate feedback while they solve issues instead of having to wait until they get an incorrect response.

In spite of these advantages, teachers in our listening sessions voiced concerns about the state of formative assessments, emphasizing the time-consuming nature of exams and quizzes as well as the feedback loop's seeming lack of value for both teachers and students.

2. Feedback Loops

When "formative assessment" results in significant reflections and modifications to instruction or learning, it transcends tests and measurements. The idea of "feedback loops" draws attention to the fact that measurement is only one facet of the procedure. Students benefit most from effective feedback loops, or those that encourage educational improvements. Students gain from these feedback loops on several levels, whether they are used in small groups, individually, or during class discussions. They are beneficial "in the moment," when a learner is honing a talent, and in the long run, after a project is finished.

Feedback loops are essential for the continuous development of educational resources and initiatives since they assist educators in identifying trends in the way they respond to students. Formative evaluations are a good place to start investigating AI's possibilities in education because of their significance. AI can be used by educators to improve their current methods, and the assessment community offers resources to address concerns related to equity and prejudice. Though AI improves feedback loops, it's important to be aware of its limitations and the additional difficulties it poses.

3. Automated Essay Scoring

Intelligent Essay Scoring (AES) is a helpful illustration of AI in the classroom. For students to develop as proficient writers, teachers must provide them frequent, focused feedback, yet doing so takes time. AES technology has come a long way since Ellis Page first proposed computer-based essay scoring in 1966 (Doewes & Pechenizkiy, 2021), and programs like Grammarly and Turnitin are now well-known examples. While more recent AI tools seek to provide students with constructive comments to help them improve their writing skills—a critical life skill for success in college and the workplace—traditional AES (Reynolds & Suzuki, 2012) concentrates on scoring essays. AI-assisted human feedback could make writing assistance more widely available and equal.

The main suggestion is to use assessment expertise to lessen bias. Fairness and bias are important in traditional and AI-enabled evaluations. Bias in traditional evaluations might arise when test items favor some students over others based on unimportant details (Reynolds & Suzuki, 2012). AI measurement and feedback may be impacted by algorithmic discrimination resulting from datasets that do not fully reflect all student groups. Artificial intelligence (AI)-enabled evaluations must guarantee that the treatments and feedback given are just and equitable, preventing systemic disadvantages for any group. Although prejudice can be addressed by standard assessment methods, artificial intelligence presents new obstacles. Thus, when creating new formative assessments, it is crucial to pay close attention to bias and fairness.

VI. CONCLUSION

The advancements being made and the expanding conversations around AI's role in education are encouraging. In order to maximize benefits and minimize risks associated with artificial intelligence, the Department will work with various stakeholders to develop rules and regulations that are informed by the Blueprint for an AI Bill of Rights. In order to guarantee that AI in education is secure, fair, and efficient while adhering to our educational objectives, it is also possible to update the National Educational Policy (NEP). The goal of this chapter is to increase awareness, involve important parties, and promote appropriate usage of AI in education and various sectors of learning.

REFERENCES

Aleven, V., McLaughlin, E. A., Glenn, R. A., & Koedinger, K. R. (2016). Instruction based on adaptive learning technologies. In Mayer, R. E., & Alexander, P. A. (Eds.), *Handbook of research on learning and instruction* (pp. 522–560). Routledge.

Bryant, J., Heitz, C., Sanghvi, S., & Wagle, D. (2020, January 14). How artificial intelligence will impact K-12 teachers. McKinsey. https://www.mckinsey.com/industries/education/our-insights/how-artificial-intelligence-will-impact-k-12-teachers

Doewes, A., & Pechenizkiy, M. (2021). On the limitations of human-computer agreement in automated essay scoring. In Proceedings of the 14th International Conference on Educational Data Mining (EDM21). https://educationaldatamining.org/EDM2021/virtual/static/pdf/EDM21_paper_243.pdf

European Commission, Directorate-General for Education, Youth, Sport and Culture. (2022). Ethical guidelines on the use of artificial intelligence (AI) and data in teaching and learning for educators. Publications Office of the European Union. https://data.europa.eu/doi/10.2766/153756

Forsyth, S., Dalton, B., Foster, E. H., Walsh, B., Smilack, J., & Yeh, T. (2021, May). Imagine a more ethical AI: Using stories to develop teens' awareness and understanding of artificial intelligence and its societal impacts. In *2021 Conference on Research in Equitable and Sustained Participation in Engineering, Computing, and Technology (RESPECT)*. IEEE. DOI: 10.1109/RESPECT51740.2021.9620549

Friedman, L., Blair Black, N., Walker, E., & Roschelle, J. (2021, November 8). Safe AI in education needs you. Association for Computing Machinery Blog. https://cacm.acm.org/blogs/blog-cacm/256657-safe-ai-in-education-needs-you/fulltext

Gartner. (n.d.). Gartner glossary: Augmented intelligence. Gartner. https://www.gartner.com/en/information-technology/glossary/augmented-intelligence

Gay, G. (2018). *Culturally responsive teaching: Theory, research, and practice.* Teachers College Press.

Hammerness, K., Darling-Hammond, L., & Bransford, J. (2005). *Preparing teachers for a changing world: What teachers should learn and be able to do.* Jossey-Bass.

Holmes, W., & Porayska-Pomsta, K. (Eds.). (2022). *The ethics of artificial intelligence in education.* Routledge. DOI: 10.4324/9780429329067

IEEE-USA Board of Directors. (2017, February 10). Artificial intelligence research, development and regulation. IEEE. http://globalpolicy.ieee.org/wp-content/uploads/2017/10/IEEE17003.pdf

Maslej, N., Fattorini, L., Brynjolfsson, E., Etchemendy, J., Ligett, K., Lyons, T., Manyika, J., Ngo, H., Niebles, J. C., Parli, V., Shoham, Y., Wald, R., Clark, J., & Perrault, R. (2023). The AI index 2023 annual report. Stanford University: AI Index Steering Committee, Institute for Human-Centered AI.

Molenaar, I. (2022). Towards hybrid human-AI learning technologies. *European Journal of Education*, 00(4), 1–14. DOI: 10.1111/ejed.12527

National Research Council. (2000). *How people learn: Brain, mind, experience, and school*. The National Academies Press., DOI: 10.17226/9853National Academies of Sciences, Engineering, and Medicine. (2018). How people learn II: Learners, contexts, and cultures. The National Academies Press. DOI: 10.17226/24783

Page, E. B. (1966). The imminence of grading essays by computer. *Phi Delta Kappan*, 47(5), 238–243.

Paris, D., & Alim, H. S. (Eds.). (2017). *Culturally sustaining pedagogies: Teaching and learning for justice in a changing world*. Teachers College Press.

Regona, M., Yigitcanlar, T., Xia, B., & Li, R. Y. M. (2022). Opportunities and adoption challenges of AI in the construction industry: A PRISMA review. *Journal of Open Innovation*, 8(45), 45. Advance online publication. DOI: 10.3390/joitmc8010045

Reynolds, C. R., & Suzuki, L. A. (2012). *Bias in psychological assessment: An empirical review and recommendations* (2nd ed.). Handbook of Psychology, DOI: 10.1002/9781118133880.hop210004

Russell, S. (2019). *Human compatible: Artificial intelligence and the problem of control*. Viking.

Shao, Q., Sniffen, A., Blanchet, J., Hillis, M. E., Shi, X., Haris, T. K., & Balkcom, D. (2020). Teaching American sign language in mixed reality. *Proceedings of the ACM on Interactive, Mobile, Wearable and Ubiquitous Technologies*, 4(4), 1–27. DOI: 10.1145/3432211

Shute, V. J. (2008). Focus on formative feedback. *Review of Educational Research*, 78(1), 153–189. DOI: 10.3102/0034654307313795

Wagner, A. R., Borenstein, J., & Howard, A. (2018, September). Overtrust in the robotics age. *Communications of the ACM*, 61(9), 22–24. DOI: 10.1145/3241365

Walton Family Foundation. (2023, March 1). Teachers and students embrace ChatGPT for education. Walton Family Foundation. https://www.waltonfamilyfoundation.org/learning/teachers-and-students-embrace-chatgpt-for-education

White House Office of Science and Technology Policy. (2022, October). Blueprint for an AI bill of rights: Making automated systems work for the American people. The White House Office of Science and Technology Policy. https://www.whitehouse.gov/ostp/ai-bill-of-rights/

Zacamy, J., & Roschelle, J. (2022). Navigating the tensions: How could equity-relevant research also be agile, open, and scalable? Digital Promise. http://hdl.handle.net/20.500.12265/159

Baker, R. S., Esbenshade, L., Vitale, J., & Karumbaiah, S. (2022). Using demographic data as predictor variables: A questionable choice. DOI: 10.35542/osf.io/y4wvj

Zhang, H., Lee, I., Ali, S., DiPaola, D., Cheng, Y., & Breazeal, C. (2022). Integrating ethics and career futures with technical learning to promote AI literacy for middle school students: An exploratory study. *International Journal of Artificial Intelligence in Education*, ●●●, 1–35. DOI: 10.1007/s40593-022-00293-3 PMID: 35573722

Chapter 12
Impact of AI on Student Learning and Teacher Outcomes in Education 5.0

Dhruv Sabharwal
https://orcid.org/0000-0002-6973-7137
Sharda University, India

Archan Mitra
https://orcid.org/0000-0002-1419-3558
Presidency University, Bangalore, India

ABSTRACT

The role of Artificial Intelligence (AI) in Education 5. 0 is changing the paradigm of the student learning process and the teaching process as well. This chapter discusses the effects of AI on students and teachers for personalisation, student motivation and teacher practice. With the help of AI technologies, one gets better and more efficient educational process by providing better learning conditions and thus – making education more flexible. Teachers have less work load to handle or to be more precise the work load that teachers handle is now more intelligent, AI provides data, teachers use this data to imply a better teaching strategy. As Education 5. 0 narrative emerges, a conceptual balance of the role of AI can strengthen of learning spaces, enable innovation and preserve humanistic ideals. Thus, this chapter emphasis each of the four themes regarding the need for the responsible development and implementation of AI in order to create a future for education that will be inclusive, equitable and adaptable.

DOI: 10.4018/979-8-3693-8191-5.ch012

INTRODUCTION

Education 5.0 symbolizes a new culture where modern technologies especially AI brings a change into learning settings. It also differs from simple digitalisation in that the adaptive processes are powered by AI, which can then deliver individualised pathways of learning. When applied to education, AI, therefore, has a wide impact on how students and teachers learn and teach Introduction of AI in education brings change hence also some of the challenges.

In its essence it is an education system that is Education 5.0 is consistent with the requirement of Industry 4. 0, where AI, machine learning and automation are at the centre of changes. Moving away from AI as a tool to simply introduce technology into teachers' practices is not only a shift in methodology but in epistemology (Selwyn, 2019). AI's sophisticated data handling capability bendy Education systems that can monitor students' performance in the learning process and provides feedback to the learner indicating areas of relative weakness and offers recommendations on the relevant resources (Luckin et al., 2016).

To the students, it means that the application of artificial intelligence will be a perfect platform for individual learning. Particularly the one-way pedagogy models of instruction have been deemed irrelevant in an environment that is characterized by diverse learners. This is helped by AI to foster learning that is flexible with the pace, mode and mode of learning for each and every learner. For instance, Smart Sparrow and Dream Box make the use of algorithms to constantly evaluate the student performance, and in identifying areas of concern, the strategies applied in teaching will also be changed (Holmes et al., 2019). This not only increases the interest level but also guarantees that learning is done in a manner best suited to a learners capability.

Likewise, it has great importance to the teachers' profession and it changes them. Teachers in the present generation have a chance to use more advanced tools of artificial intelligence to analyse the results of their students in order to provide more effective remedial action. As noted by Luckin et al. (2016), these tools also help the teachers in time management in a way that reduces time spent on grading, attendance as well as course planning. This changes the teacher's role from dissemination of knowledge to the management of the learning process the process which has been revolutionized by AI at this stage. Furthermore, we continue to see these AI driven technologies are becoming apparent in immersive learning experiences. Two of the most effective pedagogy technologies are VR and AR which are supported by AI to allow for learning through experience that is not possible on a regular classroom setting (Cochrane et al., 2017). For instance, learners who are learning concepts such as history and scientific important events in the society can easily view and make real life experiences through these virtual worlds which makes understanding and even memorization much easier. Still, as seen from this discussion, the use of AI in education is thriving despite some of the difficulties that come with it such as ethical and privacy issues. Increased student data collection for AI algorithms also brings a number of concerns regarding data privacy, privacy and academic permission for data use, as well as AI's susceptibility to prejudice (West, 2019). They also face the danger of reliance on the AI to the extent that it distorts the important social emotional parts played by the teachers to students. Bearing in mind the integration of AI technologies in education requires a harmonisation process in order to ensure that learning is not fully mechanised and students are denied fluid social interaction, Education 5 mandates the following: Conversely, the least-used channel highlighted in Holmes et al., (2019).

Therefore, even though there is massive potential in applying AI to improve teaching-learning process, some of those issues have to be carefully tackled. As education 5.0 the technology of advances, so too will the role of AI, implying that everybody? Educators, policy makers and technologists, must develop systems that create the most benefit with the least amount of harm.

Figure 1. Multifaceted impact of AI in education (Kamalov, 2023)

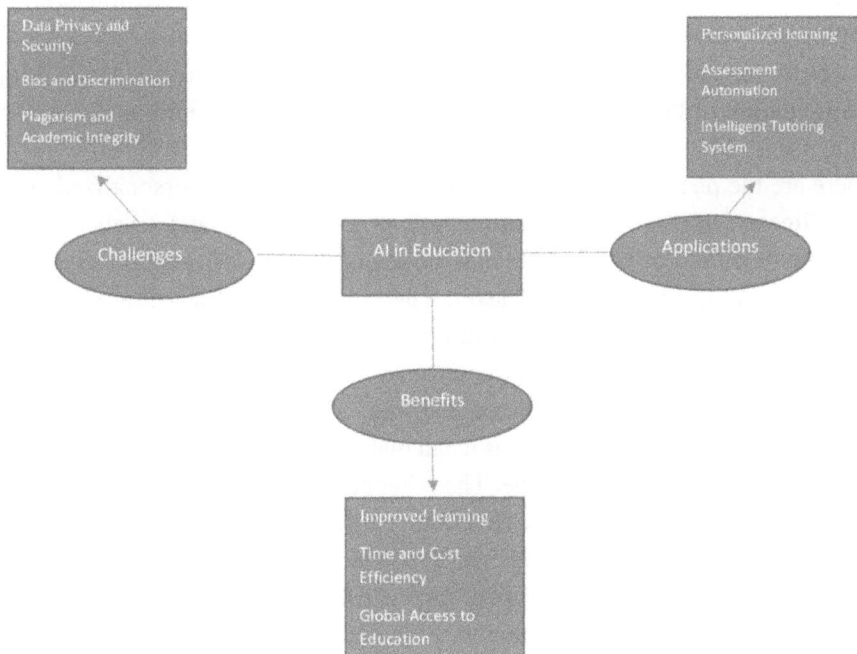

Applications: This section contains how artificial intelligence is used in education and they include the following: Personalized learning: AI can deliver knowledge and pace according to students' requirements. Assessment Automation: After class assessments, learners score low grades and AI technology is useful to assist teach in grading quickly and give feedback. Intelligent Tutoring System: Aids in the form of one on one quality tutoring are offered through AI controlled tutors.

Benefits: This section concerns with benefits of employing AI in education: Improved learning performance: AI is an essential tool in developing enhanced learning environment through provision of individualized learning. Time and Cost Efficiency: AI simplifies routine activities thus helping teaching institutions save time and costs which may be incurred in applying the traditional techniques of teaching. Global Access to Education: Education is made more democratic since there are learning resources that avail through the use of AI to students from all parts of the globe.

Challenges: In this section, future challenges or risks of AI implementation in education are provided: Data Privacy and Security: Since most AI applications are data-driven, the information input to the systems is of high sensitivity meaning that question arise on how the information is protected. Bias and Discrimination: Ml algorithms are known to reproduce or even enhance communicative prejudice; in other words, algorithms may perpetrate injustice. Plagiarism and Academic Integrity: Automation of tasks which might be seen as dishonesty could be done easily with the use of AI.

There are the possibilities of using AI in education such as personalized learning, intelligent tutoring system, automation of assessments and teacher student partnership. It should be pointed out that the use of AI allows for applying students learning at scale but in individual level. There are different learning techniques such as reinforcement learning that can be applied in order to gain more about a particular student and his/her requirements to optimize the learning process. In relation to the concept of personalized learning, one can designs intelligent tutor which can engage the students more as it can make interaction with the students and even provide the feedback if need be. The other equally strong area in AI relates to the automation of the assessments. Machine learning such as the computer vision and the natural language processing can as well be used to automate the process of grading homework, quizzes and exams. This is true in the sense that auto grading will offer significant relief to instructors who will have more time on their hands with the students. Beside, AI can also be of value in promoting the teacher-student cooperation by presenting several forms of feedback and analytics.

This shows the opportunities that exist with intelligent systems in terms of huge advantages in the area of application in education. The effects of AI can be observed in increased student achievement, cost reduction and time conservation, access to quality education for the people around the world and many others. For students, more effective ways of learning include personalized learning or the use of intelligent tutoring systems whose benefits are most felt amongst underprivileged students. Moreover the application of AI is not limited to a selected country but is implementable worldwide hence students; in the developed nations not to mention the developing nations, will have enhanced learning. There is no doubt that the use of automated grading will significantly reduce the costs and time used in learning. At present, about 40 percent of the time of the teachers is dedicated to grading and other related works. Saying goodbye to grading will enable teachers to have more time with the students and give more instruction.

1. AI AND STUDENTS: PERSONALIZED LEARNING

AI has improved the efficacy of a student's educational experience by making it possible to deliver content specific to the user. Unlike the conventional models of learning that give every learner similar content irrespective of the rate and way he or she grasps content, AI algorithms can, therefore, identify the learning patterns of students and present content, activities, and assessments that meet specific needs of the learners (Luckin et al., 2016). The overall transition to adaptive learning platforms has also provided the students with an opportunity to procure deeper study because they can make their own pace without the constriction of uniform study materials.

Contemporary examples of such transition are adaptive learning platforms such as DreamBox and Smart Sparrow. Such platforms are able to determine how much each student comprehends in real time and changes the difficulty of tasks accordingly. For example, if student is good in a certain area, it will pose more difficult questions, whereas if a student is having difficulty, the program will assist, or provide more basic material to review the basics. This level of personalization improves on the level of student commitment and skill acquisition as the students are constantly 'stretched' to their level of performance (Luckin et al., 2016). Many students could benefit from the use of AI systems especially in addressing a problem since the systems would present several ways of solving the problem – cater for the learners that learn by seeing, hearing and by feeling.

Moreover, with smart digital tutors like Carnegie Learning's wherein students can enhance their understanding of a certain subject as well as help them achieve mastery in a given course especially in Mathematics. These systems mimic the Tutoring Machines' natural language processing and incorporate new and sophisticated artificial intelligence. These standards in contrast to the traditional format of online resources are able to provide immediate and personalized feedback and justification based on the student's answers (Woolf et al., 2013). This enables students to have a more flexible approach to learning which is student cantered because they are able to ask questions, get feedback and engage in problem solving at their own convenience. In addition, AI-powered tutoring systems are especially useful for remote or distance learning environments, where students may not have direct access to a teacher. These platforms can serve as virtual tutors, offering explanations, guiding students through problem-solving, and adapting to each student's needs. For self-directed learners, who thrive on independent study, AI offers the autonomy to explore topics at their own pace while still receiving the support and structure traditionally provided by a teacher. As a result, AI fosters a more inclusive educational experience, ensuring that every learner—regardless of background or learning preference—can access a tailored education that meets their needs.

The impact of AI on personalized learning is substantial, not only improving academic outcomes but also promoting greater student autonomy and engagement. By aligning educational content with individual student profiles, AI makes learning more flexible and effective, offering an experience that is both student-cantered and adaptive to real-time performance.

2. AI AND STUDENT ENGAGEMENT

Several AI technologies increase students' learning experience by incorporating tablets and other modern learning gadgets that make learning more fun than ever before. These environments contributed with tools based on artificial intelligence such as virtual reality (VR) and augmented reality (AR) and that offer learning experiences that exceed traditional classroom lessons. It not only grabs the students' interest more effectively but also brings closer abstract ideas which makes them easier to understand.

One of the most trending platforms in the list is the class in which students can, for instance, experience with the simulator in virtual reality or augmented reality. In doing so they allow students to gain experiences while on the field that would otherwise be impossible or very hard to acquire within a normal classroom learning. For example, students studying science can virtually tour around a laboratory, perform lab experiments or tour inside a cell in gaining knowledge on biological process in an engaging manner. This kind of immersion helps students to understand various concepts since through the help of digital models of real-world objects, they are able to manipulate them (Cochrane et al., 2017).

These are especially beneficial in area of knowledge which includes spatial oriented skills or procedural knowledge in the learning process of the student. For instance, medical students can train themselves in the virtual environment on the complicated procedure of surgery and even engineering students build structures through VR. This kind of learning makes the theories taught learnable through making the knowledge accessible and tangible and hence easy to understand and retain.

In addition, AI based AR and VR platforms can also be dynamic and learn more about the student's interaction, thereby providing even more engagement in terms of the learning process. Thus, by observing the student's achievements and the given answers, the AI system may adapt the level of difficulty of the exercises or offer more tasks that will be relevant for the learner. This makes the learning environment to continue to be interesting and relevant to the students since the environment changes to correspond to the learning levels of the students (Holmes et al., 2019).

Aside from, VR and AR, AI chatbots and virtual assistants facilitate toward a higher engagement level of students by offering prompt support and feedback. For example, Cognii and Third Space Learning providers use natural language processing as a tool to communicate and discuss with students and offer an explanation or solve a problem in real time. Such an instant feedback maintains learner engagement in the learning process because instant feedback is given to the students as they do not have to wait for a human touch (Woolf et al., 2013).

In general, since AI makes learning more engaging and real-life like, it increases the interaction between the students and the learning process since the process is made more lively. AI also assist student to be more active in class for it brought simulation and learn abilities that help the students as well as the instructor in teaching as it helps in learning with understanding and memory.

3. IMPACT ON TEACHERS: NEW PEDAGOGICAL ROLES

There is no doubt that AI is changing the nature of the role of a teacher with moving from an information provider to a learning enabler. The use of AI is becoming integrated into the educational process, and today the teacher's tasks are to navigate, supervise and accompany the learning process, as well as individually approach the learner. That is due to the fact that teachers will be able to offer the required assistance based on analysis of voluminous data regarding the performance of the students. Applications like Chalk and Knewton provide teachers with analytics on learners' progress and those learners who need intervention in the form of suggestions on what they should do to improve (Holmes et al., 2019). They embrace the data-driven approach that helps the teachers paying more attention to the students who need intervention, improvement or special teaching at the right time and the right way.

In this new setting, all that has been depicted is how AI is promoting or aiding teachers to be more sensitive to the learners' situation. The advantages are AI applications can find some temporal and rather subtle tendencies in students' behavior and performance that even the attentive teacher can miss. For example, if the student demonstrates low performance in solving a certain type of problem, then AI can highlight this and recommend intervention methods, thus, enabling the teacher to offer interventions that are personalised to fit the student's needs (Luckin et al., 2016). This shift brings teaching closer to a 'guided experience' through which educators empower learners to find their way through education processes.

Additionally, AI is a promising way to bring innovations into the classroom, while easing the overload of paperwork, which is traditionally the main problem for teachers. Administrative tasks which previously require a considerable number of hours to complete including the grading system, attendance, and lesson plan preparations, among others are gradually being attained through AI learning platforms like Turnitin, Google classroom among others, and Gradescope. For instance, Turnitin has the feature that enables it to scan assignments for cases of plagiarism, whereas, Gradescope has features that aid in checking quizzes and Examination using machine learning. These automated tools do not only add efficiency into the equation but also decrease the likelihood of error in the repetitive tasks (Holmes et al., 2019).

Through the daily menial administrative operations, AI simplifies the work of teachers allowing them to engage more on the creative and evaluating type aspects in the teaching learning process. Students can get more time with teachers to implement interesting lesson plans, encourage professional growth and focus on problem-solving abilities. Automation in regard to administrative tasks therefore eases the interaction between teachers and learners from meaningless and mundane tasks meant for computers.

In addition teaching in an AI-supported learning environment can offer insights on the students' progress to the teacher in a way that allows the teacher to assess the learner's needs and plan for the future. This ability shows especially in teaching-learning on large-scale basis especially as the learners are diverse in terms of ability, modality or language. In such contexts, the AI tools provide instant feedback with the potential of helping teachers to customize their instructional practices according to the learners' differences (Woolf et al., 2013).

Altogether, as it was mentioned, AI creates much potential for intervention into the teaching profession, and yet, offers some difficulties (Sabharwal et al, 2022). One of the concerns related to increased use of technologies is that the role of a teacher may be reduced to that of providing instructions to the computer-based program; with little to no social or emotional support being provided to students. Teachers have to therefore find ways of fully harnessing the advantages offered by AI while at the same time being able to keep a human touch that is very important in the teaching learning process. However, if well incorporated into the learning process, it has the potential to aid teachers to become better educators to ensure they encourage the development of independent thinking, creativity and compassion in learners.

4.1 Teacher's Role: Facilitator, Curator, and Mentor

In the era of AI-powered education, the role of teachers has evolved significantly from traditional knowledge dispensers to becoming facilitators, curators, and mentors. As facilitators, teachers guide students through personalized AI-driven learning experiences, helping them navigate complex problems and engage with adaptive content. In the role of curators, teachers carefully select and organize resources from the vast array of digital tools and materials generated by AI systems, ensuring that students receive relevant, high-quality content. Meanwhile, as mentors, teachers focus on the holistic development of students, offering personalized support, fostering critical thinking, and encouraging creativity—qualities that AI cannot fully replicate. This shift allows teachers to concentrate on nurturing deeper intellectual and emotional connections with their students, while AI takes care of administrative tasks and personalized learning recommendations. However, it also requires educators to continuously adapt to new technologies and rethink traditional pedagogical approaches. This expanded role enhances the learning environment but also emphasizes the need for teachers to maintain a balance between AI-assisted strategies and human intuition.

4.1.1 The Evolving Role of Teachers in the AI-Infused Classroom

The integration of technology, particularly the use of artificial intelligence has altered the educational paradigm especially the changes in the role of teachers. With the advancements in AI technology and the increased implementation in teaching practices, improvement in the overall educational service, teachers are now expected to provide stewardship, selectivity and guidance for students in an ever-changing learning process. Many other tasks in a classroom like assignments compilation, students grading, and setting of numerous online quizzes are some ways through which the teachers will benefit most from AI in terms of getting administrative tasks done without being time consuming. The automation of some tasks like grading assignments, taking attendance and managing students records can be effectively performed by AI tools s so the teacher can spend time to learn better ways to communicate with the students and on instructional designing.

4.1.2 Administrative Efficiency and Time Savings

One of the most immediate benefits of AI for teachers is the automation of many time-consuming administrative tasks. AI-powered tools can handle tasks such as grading assignments, tracking attendance, and managing student records, freeing up teachers to focus on more meaningful interactions with their students and in-structional planning (Nguyen,2022)

- Automated Grading: The use of AI in grading learner work can also lead to more efficient evaluation of their performance and feedback can also be offered within a short span of time hence eliminating a lot of work which otherwise would have been done by hand. This enables teacher to spend ample of time with students giving them individual attention and guidance.
- Intelligent Attendance Tracking: Such systems are able to capture the attendance records of the students without any need for physical logging of this information and therefore are effective in capturing accurate information pertaining to the attendance of the students.
- Efficient Student Record Management: AI can help in minimizing the challenges associated with student records management thus enabling teachers to easily discover and use the records in the teaching process.

4.1.3 Data-Driven Insights for Personalized Instruction

AI can help teachers by giving them information about the performance and learning behaviour of students so that teacher can change their teaching methodology according to the students. When given data of the student's teachers are in a position to know which particular areas students may be having a challenge in.

- Predictive Analytics: With the help of predictive analytics, teachers can detect students that are not able to cope with the material on their own and give them additional help.
- Personalized Learning Paths: AI can help in designing or developing learning experiences that will fit the strengths, the weaknesses, and moreover the learning preferences of the students.
- Real-time Feedback: Integrated smart technologies should be able to offer the student feedback on assessments done, in real time and show them the areas that require changes on the learning modality being used.

4.1.4 Professional Development and Lifelong Learning

are critical aspects of ensuring that educators remain effective in an evolving digital landscape. AI is transforming the way teachers approach their own learning and growth, offering personalized, flexible, and up-to-date resources that enhance their skills and knowledge. Here's a deeper look into how AI supports teacher professional development:

1. Personalized Professional Development Plans: AI, with teacher performance data, their teaching style, and their development needs can create a specific training plan. Through these machine learning platforms, teachers can get suggestions on the specific courses, workshops or reading materials that are relevant to them and their career of interest. This focused approach does away with the generic model of professional development and enables the educators to concentrate on aspects that they consider they need more practice with, such as managing classroom, designing curriculums or implementing technology into lessons. Example: These platforms such as BloomBoard or Edthena support a teacher with feedbacks and resources depending in the interest and the performances recorded with the aim of creating a personalized learning pathway.

2. Access to Expert Knowledge: Based on what has been said, AI can further the collaboration between teachers and specialists of various fields and help get access to valuable knowledge. With the [L]AI [M]technology, the teachers are in a position to identify subject specialists and collaborate, consult and network with educators and subject specialists in real-time, from any part of the world. This not only enhances the teacher's know-how but also expose them to other ways of teaching they may have not been aware of. Example: Coursera or LinkedIn Learning for instance provide AI based education platforms where experts in various areas create their content and educators can directly engage with them and learn from them.

3. Continuous Learning: AI translates to more soak time for education as it offers educators the chance of being trained on a more progressive level, at their own free will. It allows intelligent platforms to filter and suggest continuous courses, workshops, webinars, and, in fact, peer-reviewed articles in precise subject areas of concern to a teacher or areas in which the teacher might require extra reinforcement. In this case, constant access to professional development materials enables a teacher to be updated with information regarding the trends, innovations and policies in their line of profession. Example: From FutureLearn and Udemy, teachers can also obtain an abundance of online courses and webinars that are related to educational technology as well as the teachers' subjects.

4. Interactive Learning Experiences: AI applications such as, training simulations and virtual learning environments are beneficial additions into teacher training as they provide practical, virtual practice-based experiences to teachers. The use of AI in simulation of classroom situations or distinct teaching-learning process can be experimented, and AI can provide feedback to the teachers on their performances without the actual danger of replicating the same in classroom teaching-learning situation.

5. Mentorship and Peer Collaboration: AI also enables the teacher to consult with other teachers either with professional who has been teaching for quite a number of years or with any other teacher who is facing similar issues (Zhang 2024). This encourages people to learn from one another and improve on their performances periodically. AI and software programmes also enables teachers to look for role models or get information from others about lesson plans, colleagues, or other disturbing information from forums, online groups, or professional learning community to seek guidance, advice, or learn more from other individuals on certain educational issues, concerns or problems Example: Applications of AI in education like the Teach Meets or Edmodo can foster the ideas of educational cooperation and support in which educators can share ideas, lessons and materials with their peers.

6. Real-Time Feedback and Reflective Practices: Using AI to augment these tools, decisions as to teaching approaches can be supported in real-time through data, including students' engagement levels, test performance, and even sentiment analysis about their instructors. Thus, they get to rethink the best strategies to adopt in teaching and change them within no time due to some students' poor performance. The use of AI in the collection of this data makes the process easier and more frequent hence promoting more self-evaluation and growth. Example: For example, there are Sibme or Swivl which provides teachers with means for recording lessons, getting AI analysis and metrics and involve in activities to reflect on their practice.

4.1.5 New Roles and Responsibilities

With the growth of AI in the educational setting, there might be a shift in the teacher's roles and responsibilities. Some may emerge as teachers, disseminators of knowledge and trainers that help the learners navigate the AI enriched learning process.

- Facilitator of Learning: It may mean that the teachers are required to forget about the conventional practice of delivering information right to the students.

- Curator of Educational Resources: Therefore, teachers may require filtering different educational resources such as digitized materials, technology tools as well as AI applications.
- Mentor and Coach: Teachers can have the dilemma of coaching and mentoring the students so that they are able to cope with the learning environment supported by artificial intelligence.

5. CHALLENGES AND ETHICAL CONSIDERATIONS

With such great benefits AI brings to education, however, its implementation is rife with challenges and ethical considerations. Data privacy is at the top of the list of problems. AI systems collect and process vast amounts of information that would otherwise not be accessible-including access to both academic performance data as well as behavioural data (Wang,2023). Not to forget even their own personal learning preferences in particular situations. The security of such data and its ethical use would be of great importance. What's instead emerging is a scenario where students' private information will be exposed through breaches in the AI systems and then likely misused or exploited. Secondly, the lack of transparency in AI algorithms may hinder fair decision-making since students are evaluated without a just foundation for judgment based on incomplete or skewed data (West, 2019). Protection of a student's data and a requisite that AI should function in a fair manner are the indispensable components for trust building in AI-driven education systems.

Another challenge posed by a paperless learning environment is the possible diminution of personal interaction among students and teachers. Of course, education essentially remains a human activity that not only pertains to the transfer of knowledge but also the acquisition of emotional as well as social skills. Teachers are actually some of the most indispensable catalysts in building these interpersonal skills through face-to-face interactions with students. However, in the instance of greater reliance on AI for a lot of the instruction to be done like grading, tutoring, even dispensing lesson plans, the crucial human touch that needs to flow within and out of the classroom can be sacrificed. The learning experience will become depersonalized as the student spends more time with machines than their instructors (Holmes et al., 2019). If AI replaces too much of the human element, emotional and social development in the students would be affected.

Finally, AI may exacerbate educational inequality unless placed within a thoughtfully structured framework for integration. Access to AI-based tools shares much in common with significant technological infrastructure and tips the balance against many schools-in particular, rural ones-in less well-endowed areas. This digital divide may then expand as the uncontained gains of AI will benefit those students who are likely to thrive in wealthier regions. That raises into question the feasible equity objectives coming out of these education systems; indeed, it is among the key issues that Selwyn (2019) advances. However, there exists the possibility that AI will also pass on existing biases within the education system. The AI algorithms are trained on past data, and such data may well be reflective of societal bias in areas such as gender, race, or socioeconomic status. If these biases are not addressed in the development of AI systems, they might influence the way a student gets assessed, graded, or recommended for interventions with the recourse of an unfair outcome. For example, predicting performance in students might become an area an AI system favors a student based on historical trends about a particular background; this may really entrench inequities rather than solve the fundamental cause.

Ultimately, then, automation of education processes by AI raises the question of what the future of the profession of teaching is. For one, even though AI may bear some of the burden of certain administrative burdens, there is a danger that teachers feel secondary to the enhancement of technological impact. Inspired mentoring and intimacy with the learner can't be duplicated by AI. Another major issue related to the development of Education 5.0 is that its utilization of AI should be managed in a way that it does not compromise the role of human teachers in generating creative thinking, critical thinking, and emotional intelligence.

In short, if AI promises to be an edifying forerunner in advancing education, there must be caution in its implementation. Thus, protecting the learner's data, fostering human links in learning situations, and ensuring that biases are unfurled may help in accomplishing an equitable and ethical AI-enhanced education system. Educators, policymakers, and technologists need to join forces in setting standards that allow AI support instead of undermining the core values of education.

Table 1. The Transformative Role of AI in Education: Impacts on Students, Teachers, and Ethical Considerations

	Description	Impact	Challenges	References
AI and Students: Personalized Learning	AI-driven systems tailor learning content to meet individual students' needs, preferences, and progress.	Enhances personalized learning by catering to diverse learning styles, improving academic outcomes.	Risk of over-reliance on technology, data privacy concerns, and algorithmic biases.	Holmes et al. (2019); Ross (2021)
AI and Student Engagement	AI tools, such as gamification and adaptive learning platforms, boost engagement by making learning interactive.	Increases student motivation and involvement through interactive lessons and instant feedback.	Dependence on technology may reduce real-world social interactions and critical thinking skills.	Tahiru (2021); Saura et al. (2022)
Impact on Teachers: New Pedagogical Roles	AI tools allow teachers to focus on creative and complex tasks by automating administrative functions.	Frees up time for teachers to engage in innovative pedagogical practices and focus on student development.	Teachers need to develop new skills to integrate AI effectively; resistance to change among educators.	Nawaz et al. (2020); Ahmed & Nashat (2020)
Teacher's Role: Facilitator, Curator, and Mentor	Teachers guide AI-driven learning by facilitating discussions, curating content, and mentoring students.	Strengthens teacher-student relationships by emphasizing the mentor role and personalized support.	Balancing human intuition with AI recommendations can be challenging; risk of reducing teacher autonomy.	Leeming (2021); Landwehr (2015)
Challenges and Ethical Considerations	Ethical issues include data privacy, security, bias in AI algorithms, and the replacement of human intuition.	Promotes innovation in education but raises significant ethical questions and the risk of dehumanizing learning.	Addressing data privacy, security, and the need for transparency in AI algorithms remains a critical issue.	Fjelland (2020); Stahl (2021); Köbis & Mehner (2021)

The table 1 presents a detailed overview of the transformative role of AI in education, focusing on personalized learning, student engagement, and the evolving pedagogical roles of teachers. AI's potential to enhance learning through tailored experiences and increased engagement is significant, but it also introduces new challenges, particularly in maintaining ethical standards and addressing the risk of over-reliance on technology. Teachers are increasingly becoming facilitators and mentors, focusing on critical thinking and emotional intelligence, while AI handles routine tasks. Balancing AI's benefits with ethical considerations is essential for fostering an inclusive and effective educational ecosystem.

6. BALANCED DISCUSSION OF BENEFITS AND CHALLENGES

Benefits
1. **Enhanced Learning Efficiency**: One of the primary advantages of AI in education is its ability to automate repetitive tasks, allowing teachers and students to focus on higher-order learning and engagement. AI-powered platforms can handle tasks such as grading, attendance tracking, and assignment feedback. This significantly reduces the workload for educators and creates more time for personalized instruction. AI also enables active learning by providing students with interactive tools like virtual labs, simulations, and intelligent tutoring systems. For example, platforms such as Carnegie Learning's MATHia have been shown to enhance learning efficiency by adapting to individual student needs, leading to better engagement and retention of information (Luckin, Holmes, Griffiths, & Forcier, 2016).
2. **Data-Driven Insights**: AI's data analytics capabilities are transforming how teachers assess student progress. AI systems can track and analyze vast amounts of student data, providing real-time insights into learning behaviors, strengths, and areas needing improvement. This data-driven approach allows educators to make informed decisions, tailor lesson plans, and offer personalized learning experiences. According to a study by Kose and Ocak (2020), data-driven insights from AI-based systems significantly improve educational outcomes by identifying learning gaps and predicting student success rates. This personalized instruction model helps in delivering targeted interventions, thereby improving overall student performance.

Challenges
1. **Ethical Issues**: The integration of AI in education raises important ethical concerns, particularly in relation to data privacy and surveillance. AI systems require access to personal student data to function effectively, and this creates the potential for data breaches or misuse. Additionally, the use of AI for performance assessments may lead to biased or inaccurate evaluations if not properly designed and implemented. Algorithms can unintentionally perpetuate biases based on race, gender, or socio-economic status, making it essential to prioritize ethical guidelines in AI system development. According to Williamson and Eynon (2020), there is a growing need for frameworks that ensure transparency, fairness, and accountability in the use of AI in educational settings. Furthermore, the ethical dilemma arises

when AI is used to monitor students, potentially infringing on their privacy and autonomy.

2. **Technical Barriers**: Integrating AI into schools requires substantial investment in technology infrastructure, professional development, and technical support, which can be a challenge, particularly for underfunded schools. Implementing AI-driven systems demands access to high-speed internet, compatible hardware, and trained personnel to operate and maintain the technology. Schools in rural or economically disadvantaged areas often lack the resources to adopt AI, thereby widening the digital divide. In their research, Miao, Holmes, and Huang (2021) highlight the technical and financial challenges schools face when implementing AI, stating that lack of infrastructure and ongoing technical support are significant barriers to widespread AI adoption in education. Additionally, continuous teacher training and support are necessary to ensure that AI is integrated effectively into curricula.

7. GLOBAL PERSPECTIVE AND DEEPENING THE ANALYSIS OF LONG-TERM IMPACTS

The global adoption of AI in education reflects varying levels of integration, depending on a country's economic development, technological infrastructure, and policy frameworks. By examining diverse regions, it becomes clear that the implementation of AI brings both opportunities and challenges, which differ significantly across geographies.

7.1 Global Adoption and Challenges

1. **High-Income Countries: Leading the AI Revolution in Education**: Countries such as the United States, the United Kingdom, and South Korea have made significant strides in incorporating AI into their educational systems. These nations have advanced technological infrastructures and access to substantial financial resources, enabling them to invest in AI-driven educational platforms. For example, the United States has seen rapid growth in AI-based educational tools like intelligent tutoring systems, which provide personalized learning experiences to students. According to Holmes et al. (2019), countries that invest in AI tend to experience a significant improvement in learning outcomes, especially in STEM (Science, Technology, Engineering, and Mathematics) fields. AI's adaptive learning algorithms help educators tailor instruction to meet individual needs, resulting in enhanced educational equity.

2. **Developing and Low-Income Countries: Bridging the Digital Divide**: However, the same level of AI adoption is not feasible in many developing or low-income countries due to resource constraints. For example, countries in sub-Saharan Africa and parts of Southeast Asia face challenges such as inadequate access to technology, insufficient infrastructure, and lack of teacher training, which limits their ability to integrate AI into education. The disparity between high- and low-income countries raises concerns about the widening global digital divide, where some students have access to cutting-edge AI-driven learning tools, while others struggle with basic resources like textbooks and classroom technology (Miao, Holmes, & Huang, 2021). In response to these disparities, international organizations like UNESCO and the World Bank have emphasized the need for equitable access to AI technology in education, advocating for targeted investments and policies that support underserved communities.

7.2 Long-Term Impacts on Education Systems

The long-term implications of AI adoption in education are complex and multi-faceted. As AI technologies continue to evolve, they will likely transform not only how students learn but also how teachers teach, and how education systems are managed on a macro level.

1. **Curriculum Design and Pedagogical Approaches**: One of the long-term impacts of AI in education will be the shift in curriculum design and teaching methods. AI will enable more personalized and adaptive curricula, which can evolve dynamically based on students' learning progress. As AI systems become more intelligent, they will offer more nuanced and customized learning experiences, making education more student-centered and less dependent on traditional one-size-fits-all approaches. Over time, this will lead to a reimagining of pedagogy, where teachers act more as facilitators of learning rather than dispensers of knowledge (Kose & Ocak, 2020). Furthermore, AI-driven learning platforms will empower students to learn at their own pace, leading to improved outcomes in terms of knowledge retention and application.
2. **Equity and Access to Education**: AI has the potential to democratize access to quality education by providing scalable solutions to under-resourced regions. Online learning platforms powered by AI, such as Coursera or Khan Academy, can offer courses to students across the globe, breaking down barriers related to geography and socio-economic status. However, the challenge remains in ensuring that all students have access to the technology and internet connectivity required to benefit from AI-powered learning. Long-term, the widespread adoption of AI in education will depend on governments' and institutions' ability to ensure

equitable access to these technologies, closing the digital divide and fostering inclusivity (Williamson & Eynon, 2020).

3. **Reshaping Teacher Roles and Professional Development**: In the long run, AI will also redefine the roles of teachers. As AI systems handle administrative tasks and provide real-time assessments of student progress, teachers will have more time to focus on higher-order skills, such as critical thinking, creativity, and problem-solving. This shift in focus requires significant investments in professional development for teachers. Educators will need ongoing training in digital literacy, AI tools, and new pedagogical approaches to leverage AI effectively in the classroom. According to Luckin et al. (2016), professional development programs that equip teachers with the skills to integrate AI into their teaching practices will be essential for the successful adoption of AI in education. Without adequate preparation, teachers may struggle to adapt to the evolving landscape, leading to a disconnect between AI tools and classroom practices.

8. FUTURE IMPLICATIONS FOR EDUCATION 5.0

Education 5.0, therefore, is a future where AI will be seen as the single enabler for teachers and students alike to produce more seamlessness, efficiency, personalization, and inclusivity in education. It will bridge education gaps by accessing quality education to very hidden populations, especially disadvantaged or underprivileged people living in outlying areas or impoverished regions. AI can automate part of teaching and provide students with a learning pathway, and this may not be possible because of resource constraints in most cases.

This role for AI in Education 5.0 in lifelong learning and reskilling activities is one of the most important implications; it will indicate which of these continuous learning requirements can be highly crucial for a future workforce significantly adapting to the rapid transformations due to the Fourth Industrial Revolution. AI can indeed bridge skills gaps and provide individualized, reskilling programs. Learners can freely learn new skills regarding emerging industries at their own speeds thanks to AI tools (Brynjolfsson & McAfee, 2014). Above all, the fluidity by this technology will be a necessity given that the rates of automation in most sectors are known to cause losses of jobs to be replaced with mechanized modes, and as such, they continue to build new skills just to win a competition.

Other than this, AI increases the accessibility of education. Artificial intelligence enables you to teach a wide range of students with different needs and backgrounds, such as making learning resources accessible for children with disabilities, language barriers, or even under-resourced schools. For example, a translation tool powered by AI can open up learning opportunities in any language for a non-native speaker, while an AI-based assistive technology allows students who are visually, audibly, or cognitively impaired to learn, as well. These applications of AI can democratize education to provide opportunities for the same set of students to be exposed to equal opportunities irrespective of any circumstances (Holmes et al., 2019).

CONCLUSION

AI in education 5.0 seems to bring transformative opportunities to the student as well as to the teacher. Some of the major benefits include allowing personalization, increasing engagement, and developing data-based pedagogical strategies. However, ethical considerations have topped the list of priorities, along with retaining human elements in education. A balanced and responsible integration of AI in education will bring forth an even more adaptive, more inclusive, and more effective learning environment. This has in turn opened the education sector to a new world of learning where the roles of students and teachers are being transformed. AI will become so much more powerful and prevalent, and its integration into education needs serious evaluation of implications and the potential challenges it poses in this new shift.

Although there are many benefits to AI, including personalized learning, increased engagement, and efficiency, it is very important to respond to concerns over data privacy, algorithmic bias, and job displacement. It is by considering these factors in conjunction with how ethical guidelines should be developed for using AI in education that we will enable such use to create a more just, effective, and engaging experience in learning for all.

It is also critical that in creating this future, educators, technologists, policymakers, and researchers would have enough interaction so that the implementation of AI reaches a point that would benefit and enhance learners and educators alike. However, realizing the complete potential of AI in Education 5.0 shall be rather through the collaborative approach among educators, technologists, and policymakers. AI tools are needed to be developed in accordance with educational goals and be designed in a manner that reassures the ethical concerns and will also be able to address equity concerns. Policymakers should ensure that data privacy, bias, and equitable access rules are strong and that AI systems are transparent and accountable. Simultaneously, educators must be involved in what the change in their classroom is going to look like so that AI technology supplements rather than supplants human interaction.

It will also require massive investment in infrastructure and staff training. On one hand, schools will need technological capacity that supports AI-driven platforms, as well as skilled teachers who can effectively use the tools pedagogically. For these purposes, professional development and training programs will continuously support teachers through the complexities in integrating AI.

In conclusion, flexibility, efficiency, and inclusivity in learning by AI power and future promises of Education 5.0 depend on a collective effort to position AI ways that ensure educational equity, protect student data, and maintain human connections that are key to learning. If these challenges are addressed, AI could be a powerful force in shaping a more adaptive, equitable educational landscape.

REFERENCES

Barnett, T. P., Adam, J. C., & Lettenmaier, D. P. (2005). Potential impacts of a warming climate on water availability in snow-dominated regions. *Nature*, 438(7066), 303–309. DOI: 10.1038/nature04141 PMID: 16292301

Bates, B. C., Kundzewicz, Z. W., Wu, S., & Palutikof, J. P. (2008). *Climate change and water*. IPCC Secretariat.

Becker, A., & Bugmann, H. (2001). Global change and mountain regions: The Mountain Research Initiative. *Bioscience*, 51(8), 641–647.

Beniston, M. (2003). Climatic change in mountain regions: A review of possible impacts. *Climatic Change*, 59(1-2), 5–31. DOI: 10.1023/A:1024458411589

Brynjolfsson, E., & McAfee, A. (2014). *The second machine age: Work, progress, and prosperity in a time of brilliant technologies*. W. W. Norton & Company.

Cochrane, T., Cook, S., Aiello, S., & Aguayo, C. (2017). Augmenting student engagement through AR/VR. *International Journal of Mobile and Blended Learning*, 9(1), 33–45. DOI: 10.4018/IJMBL.2017010103

Dirnböck, T., Essl, F., & Rabitsch, W. (2011). Disproportional risk for habitat loss of high-altitude endemic species under climate change. *Global Change Biology*, 17(2), 990–996. DOI: 10.1111/j.1365-2486.2010.02266.x

Gurung, G., & Banskota, K. (2009). *Mountain tourism in Nepal: Developing responsible mountain tourism for sustainable development*. ICIMOD.

Holmes, W., Bialik, M., & Fadel, C. (2019). *Artificial intelligence in education: Promises and implications for teaching and learning*. Center for Curriculum Redesign.

Holmes, W., Luckin, R., Griffiths, M., & Forcier, L. B. (2019). Intelligence Unleashed: An Argument for AI in Education. Pearson. https://www.pearson.com/

Immerzeel, W. W., Van Beek, L. P., & Bierkens, M. F. (2010). Climate change will affect the Asian water towers. *Science*, 328(5984), 1382–1385. DOI: 10.1126/science.1183188 PMID: 20538947

Kamalov, F., Santandreu Calonge, D., & Gurrib, I. (2023). New era of artificial intelligence in education: Towards a sustainable multifaceted revolution. *Sustainability*, 15(16), 12451. DOI: 10.3390/su151612451

Kohler, T., Wehrli, A., & Jurek, M. (2014). *Mountain ecosystems: Environmentally and socially sustainable development*. United Nations Environment Programme.

Kose, U., & Ocak, M. A. (2020). Artificial Intelligence-Based Personalized Learning in Education. *Education and Information Technologies*, 25(4), 3335–3355. DOI: 10.1007/s10639-019-10088-4

Luckin, R., Holmes, W., Griffiths, M., & Forcier, L. B. (2016). *Intelligence unleashed: An argument for AI in education*. Pearson.

Luckin, R., Holmes, W., Griffiths, M., & Forcier, L. B. (2016). *Intelligence Unleashed: An Argument for AI in Education*. Pearson.

Macchi, M. (2011). Framework for community-based climate vulnerability and capacity assessment in mountain areas. ICIMOD Working Paper 2011/13. International Centre for Integrated Mountain Development.

Miao, F., Holmes, W., & Huang, R. (2021). AI and Education: Guidance for Policy-Makers. *UNESCO*. https://unesdoc.unesco.org/ark:/48223/pf0000376709

Nguyen, A., Gardner, L., & Sheridan, D. (2022). Artificial intelligence in education: Applications, benefits, and challenges. *International Journal of Educational Technology in Higher Education*, 19(1), 1–21. DOI: 10.1186/s41239-021-00309-1 PMID: 35013716

Pauli, H., Gottfried, M., & Grabherr, G. (2012). Effects of climate change on the alpine and nival vegetation of the Alps. *Journal of Mountain Ecology*, 7, 9–12.

Sabharwal, D., Verma, M., & Sood, R. (2022). Studying the Relationship between Artificial Intelligence and Digital Advertising in Marketing Strategy. Journal of Content. *Community & Communication*, 16, 118–126. DOI: 10.31620/JCCC.12.22/10

Selwyn, N. (2019). *Should robots replace teachers? AI and the future of education*. Polity Press.

Struebig, M. J., Fischer, M., Gaveau, D. L., Meijaard, E., Wich, S. A., & Koh, L. P. (2015). The escalator to extinction: Emerging challenges for biodiversity conservation in tropical mountains. *Global Change Biology*, 21(8), 2829–2833. DOI: 10.1111/gcb.12843 PMID: 25846057

Viviroli, D., Weingartner, R., & Messerli, B. (2007). Assessing the hydrological significance of the world's mountains. *Mountain Research and Development*, 23(1), 32–40. DOI: 10.1659/0276-4741(2007)27[32:ATHSOT]2.0.CO;2

Wang, Z., Liu, X., & Jiang, C. (2023). AI in higher education: The influence on student performance and teacher engagement. *Educational Technology Research and Development*, 71(1), 123–140. DOI: 10.1007/s11423-022-10167-6

West, D. M. (2019). *The future of work: Robots, AI, and automation.* Brookings Institution Press.

Williamson, B., & Eynon, R. (2020). Datafied Education: Privacy and Online Learning. *Learning, Media and Technology, 45*(1), 3-https://doi.org/DOI: 10.1080/17439884.2020.1694943

Woolf, B. P., Lane, H. C., Chaudhri, V., & Kolodner, J. (2013). AI grand challenges for education. *AI Magazine*, 34(4), 66–84. DOI: 10.1609/aimag.v34i4.2499

Zhang, J., & Aslan, A. (2024). Teachers' perceptions of AI in education: Current use and future expectations. *British Journal of Educational Technology*, 55(3), 98–113. DOI: 10.1111/bjet.13242

Chapter 13
Integrating Effect of AR and VR in Sustained Learning Outcomes in Self–Directed Learning Environments

Debasis Pani
https://orcid.org/0009-0002-1706-5751
Gandhi Institute of Advanced Computer and Research, India

Narayana Maharana
https://orcid.org/0000-0003-2765-0866
Gayatri Vidya Parishad College of Engineering, India

Sunil Kumar Pradhan
https://orcid.org/0009-0006-1122-1468
Berhampur University, India

Saumendra Das
https://orcid.org/0000-0003-4956-4352
GIET University, Gunupur, India

ABSTRACT

Education 5.0 emphasises not only the integration of technology in education but also a humanitarian approach by incorporating artificial intelligence. This approach focuses on the emotional, social, and intellectual growth of students, aiming to enhance their overall learning experience and foster sustainable learning outcomes for holistic societal development. AR and VR play a crucial role in this transformation,

DOI: 10.4018/979-8-3693-8191-5.ch013

offering immersive and interactive learning environments. Despite their significant benefits, AR and VR technologies are still evolving, presenting new challenges for educators and students as they advance. This chapter explores the transformative potential of AR and VR in enhancing learning outcomes within self-directed learning programs. It examines how these immersive technologies can create interactive and engaging experiences that promote better retention and application of knowledge. This chapter bridges theory and practice, providing educators, designers, and policymakers with better insights on using AR and VR to enhance self-directed learning.

1. INTRODUCTION

Education 5.0 has brought a paradigm shift in the landscape of the teaching and learning profession by incorporating Augmented Reality (AR) and Virtual Reality (VR) technology in education. Such technology-enhanced learning practice is far beyond the conventional mode of teaching and results in better interactive learning experiences (Tan et al., 2022). Furthermore, such technology intervention in teaching and learning practices helps the students to understand and grasp complex topics in a simplified manner. The use of AR & VR technology in education provides a unique immersive experience by simplifying complex content into customised content as per the requirement and learning ability of the student (Childs et al., 2021). The website report of Maunder (2018) projects that by 2023, the VR and AR applications in the education industry will have grown to a value of 19.6 billion with an annual growth rate of 16.2%.

1.1 Evolution from Education 1.0 to Education 5.0

The evolution toward Education 5.0 reflects a transformative integration of technology and pedagogy, aligned with society's changing needs. This progression starts with Education 1.0, which is teacher-centred, focused on memorization, and dominated by lecture-based instruction, where the teacher holds full authority. Education 2.0 shifts to a more progressive, student-centred model that emphasizes critical thinking and problem-solving skills. Education 3.0 introduces digital tools, integrating computers and multimedia to enhance student engagement and active learning. Education 4.0 is characterized by customized, blended learning, incorporating AI and machine learning to tailor educational content, fostering critical thinking and creativity (Ahmad et al., 2023). Finally, Education 5.0 adopts a human-centred approach, utilizing augmented reality (AR) and virtual reality (VR) to provide interactive and experiential learning, enhancing learning outcomes.

1.2 AR and VR in Education 5.0

Augmented reality (AR) distinguishes itself from other interaction methods by allowing users to stay connected to their surroundings while keeping their focus on the real world. At the same time, AR enriches the experience by overlaying additional information onto the existing environment, enhancing the viewer's perception (Abad-Segura et al., 2020). According to Liberati (2016), "AR is the fusion of digital information with the physical environment, allowing users to interact with virtual elements effortlessly without concentrating on a device's screen". Virtual reality (VR) creates a simulated version of reality, offering a more immersive and interactive experience of real-world phenomena. It operates in a fully artificial environment, where users can choose to be either fully or partially immersed in the virtual world. (AlGerafi et al., 2023). Haptic interfaces allow users to completely participate in the virtual world while interacting with and manipulating computer-generated things in virtual reality. (Bermejo et al., 2023).

Both AR & VR technology help in amplifying the student's perspective of understanding the real-world situation and developing a coherent picture of it, which further leads to an impactful learning experience that is attributed to the student's attention, level of engagement and sustained learning. The use of AR & VR technology is extensively used in self-learning situations, such learning platforms have grown substantially during the period of the COVID-19 pandemic. Self-learning is another facet of the learning process, that navigates the students to observing, identifying, exploring, elaborating, developing, analysing, concluding and applying the educational activities. (Valladares Ríos et al., 2023). The technology-enabled self-learning practices allow the students to interact in peer-to-peer, which is mediated by technology in real-time virtual settings. Furthermore, such a self-directed learning platform helps to foster the cognitive ability, intellectual ability and vision for learning in a collaborative setup. Furthermore, AR & VR technology foster abilities like self-management, leadership qualities and innovative thinking by engaging students in the problem scenario in the real world through a virtual setup. Such practice further enhances their critical thinking and problem-solving attitude by analysing the environmental situation and applying the relevant knowledge and skills pertinent to the situation (Fainholc, 2016). Several studies have claimed the application of AR & VR technology in teaching and learning practices has provided substantial benefits to the students and teachers. However, the use of these technologies is nascent and undergoing rampant transformation. With every stage of change, this technology brought several implications before the students and teachers relating to its applicability, the feasibility of adaptation, and its contribution to sustained learning outcomes (Valladares Ríos et al., 2023).

2. THEORETICAL FRAMEWORK

The extent of immersion and interaction is the crucial factor differentiating AR and VR technology. VR completely replace the physical world and provides an immersive experience in a digital platform. AR is an extension of VR, where the user not only gets a similar immersive virtual experience but is also able to interact with gadgets like smartphones and AR glasses (Santana-Mancilla et al., 2012). Both the immersive experience through VR and the interactive experience through AR supplement the student's learning experience. Furthermore, there are several theories like Constructivist learning theories, Cognitive load theory, and Motivation and engagement theories underpinning the application of AR and VR technology in education. These learning theories play a crucial factor in developing VR-based learning experiences. The motivational components of these theories may be applied to VR and AR in developing interactive contents, that engage students and promote more effective and efficient learning practice. The upgradation of AR and VR technology will develop an implication for the teachers to understand how to apply learning theories in developing rich content that nurtures a unique learning experience.

2.1 Constructivist Learning Theories

Constructivist learning theory proposed by Dewey et al. (1997) focuses on the student's learning development by gaining several experiences form the environment. Another attribute of this theory is the learning is a continuous process and is beyond the classroom. It recognises that students have past knowledge and experiences that have been influenced by their social and cultural surroundings (Seifert & Sutton, 2019). In this way, the student develops knowledge about the environment and surroundings based on his or her experience in a cultural and social circumstance. Moreover, it places a strong emphasis on the value of social, contextual, and active learning. This theory holds that rather than passively acquiring information, learners develop knowledge either alone or in a group by relying on their past experiences and knowledge (Hein, 1991).

Constructivist learning theory provides a foundation for teachers to develop rich content using AR and VR, facilitating a deeper understanding of concepts. Moreover, it supports the integration of AR and VR in education, fostering interactive and immersive digital experiences that enhance student learning. VR technology offers engaging, interactive environments that promote experimentation, exploration, and critical thinking, encouraging students to ask thought-provoking questions and make real-world discoveries. By incorporating VR, educators enable students to actively participate in constructing their knowledge, leading to deeper and more lasting learning outcomes (Tene et al., 2024).

2.2 Cognitive Load Theory and its Implications for Immersive Learning

Figure 1.

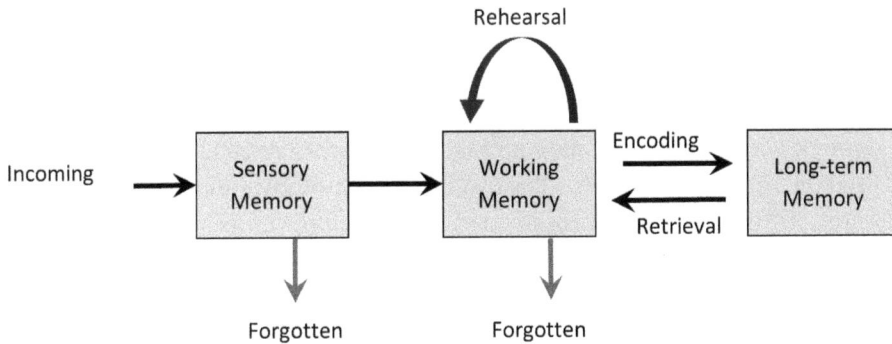

The cognitive load theory (CLT) was developed by John Sweller says that the human memory is classified into three parts sensory memory, working memory and long-term memory (Van Merriënboer & Sweller, 2005). Most of the information that is present in our environment is filtered out by sensory memory, which then transfers some of it to working memory for further processing. The purpose of the working memory is to either discard the information or to categorise it to store in long-term memory. The long-term memory keeps all the relevant information in the form of schemas. The quantity of information that our working memory can handle at any given time is referred to as cognitive load. All three forms of cognitive load must be taken into account by designers to maximize cognitive burden in VR learning environments.

2.2.1 Contribution of Cognitive Load Theory in Integrating AR and VR in Self-Directed Learning

Cognitive Load Theory (CLT) offers a foundational framework for using AR and VR technologies to create immersive and interactive learning experiences. Instructional content should be highly engaging and interactive to promote active learning and the construction of schemas. Additionally, the content should be realistic to motivate learners and support deeper understanding and retention. A broader application of CLT involves incorporating multimedia resources with advanced, customized content, which can enhance learning effectiveness and foster students' cognitive abilities. (Mayer, 2012).

2.3 Motivation Theories in the Context of AR and VR

One of the important motivation theories is the self-determination theory developed by Edward Deci and Richard Ryan provides a basic framework of how intrinsic and extrinsic motivation plays an important role in behaviour (Deci & Ryan, 2012). Although motivation is a broad term, in the perspective of education it can be associated with two primary subcategories: intrinsic and extrinsic motivation. Intrinsic motivation refers to the completion of a learning activity by own and feeling a sense of accomplishment, and internal pleasure for the completion of the course (Diseth et al., 2020). On the other hand, extrinsic motivation refers to conferring rewards, distinction in the form of good grades, appreciation and recognition from other students, such kind academic incentives motivate the overall progress of the student (Covington, 2000). Further, this theory proposes that a person's engagement and motivation level increase with the fulfilment of their psychological need for autonomy, competence, and relatedness. Motivation theory offers a foundational framework for integrating AR and VR into education, particularly in self-directed learning environments. By providing personalized content, both AR and VR address individual student needs and enable them to choose topics of interest, thereby fostering autonomy. To support competency, these technologies offer simulated environments that encourage skill and ability development, while incorporating levels and rewards to further enhance students' progress. Additionally, relatedness is nurtured through virtual classrooms, which create spaces for peer interaction, experience sharing, and instructor mentoring (Y. S. Chang, 2021)

2.4 Engagement Theories and Their Relevance With AR and VR

Engagement Theory developed by Kearsley & Shneiderman (1998) highlights the importance of engagement of students in a meaningful activity of creativity, collaboration and contribution to the outside world. The essence of this theory can be confined to an acronym of relate-create-donate. The related aspect of the engagement theory has a greater relevance to AR and VR, the technology-enabled learning platform should focus on collaborative learning regardless of their physical location, or virtual classroom and provide space for immersive interaction in a meaningful way that fosters sustained learning outcomes. The creativity aspect of the engagement theory should focus on fostering the creativity, problem-solving and critical thinking ability of the student. AR and VR in education should encourage students to work on projects with a broader societal impact, promoting sustainable development. Moreover, the combination of immersive and interactive experiences should facilitate collaborative problem-solving between students and instructors, creating a more meaningful and impactful learning environment (Vats & Joshi, 2023). These pedagogical theories offer a foundational understanding of different learning modes and provide a basis for integrating AR and VR to enhance teaching and learning. Incorporating these technologies allows instructors to create highly engaging environments that lead to impactful learning experiences.

3. AR AND VR TECHNOLOGIES: AN OVERVIEW

3.1 Description of AR and VR Technologies

Augmented Reality (AR): AR focuses on viewing the real-world scenario either directly or indirectly with the help of computer-generated programs, that further enrich the viewers viewing experience (Carmigniani et al., 2011). In another study, Azuma (1997) defines AR focus on supplementing more interactive digital elements in the virtual environment. Such addition of interactive digital experience in the form of 3d enriches the viewing experience and develops the interactive experience of the viewers. Further, Azuma (1997) "proposed that AR systems should exhibit three characteristics: (i) the ability to merge virtual and real objects in a real environment, (ii) support real-time interaction, and (iii) incorporate 3D virtual objects." In a similar study, Milgram & Kishino (1994) proposed another concept Mixed reality which incorporates both augmented reality (AR) and augmented virtuality (AV). To him, the MR stood in between AR and AV. AR portrays the real physical environment with the support of computer-generated graphics and interactive digital elements. Conversely, AV supplements actual aspects of the real environment into the virtual environment, bringing it closer to the real world (Milgram & Kishino, 1994). Another important feature of AR is that it eliminates the risk of social isolation. (Kiryakova et al., 2018). AR is considered a novice platform that has replaced the monotonous digital devices such as smartphones and computers with a more natural digital interactive device with real virtual world, enriches the viewing experience.

Virtual Reality (VR): Virtual reality is a new popular technology that allows users to interact with a virtual environment through a computer-generated simulation and this technology is widely used in the fields of engineering, STEM education and even medical education (Gao et al., 2022). One of the important features of the application of AR in teaching practices is it provides an immersive and interesting learning environment. VR can take students to such states that are difficult to reach, for instance, space, historical sites, and even the human body. Indeed, this is completely an alternative viewpoint of education practice, but this helps the students to get more involved connect with the course material and understand the subject matter (Marougkas et al., 2023). Providing students with immersive and fascinating experiences through the application of VR in education can improve their understanding of concepts and complex subjects in a better way. Furthermore, virtual reality in education holds the potential to completely transform the landscape of conventional methods of teaching. Offering students an immersive virtual reality experience may help them to correlate and connect between theory and real-world applications, boosting self-confidence so that they will be ready reckoner to face new challenges. With the rapid passage of technological development VR has a strong chance of becoming a fundamental part of the educational system and providing students with an impactful way to enhance their learning (Gonta, 2021)

3.2 Differences and Similarities Between AR and VR

3.2.1 Key Similarities Between AR and VR in the Context of Education

- Both technologies have their distinctive advantage and can be useful for educational purposes for better attainment of learning. The AR fosters the interactive experience, and the VR fosters the immersive experience, both are highly required in the context of teaching and learning for an impactful learning experience (Seo et al., 2024)
- Both technologies can integrate the gamified learning experience to make the student more competent and help to build their capacity. These interactive learning experiences can foster a sense of competitiveness among the students irrespective of their geographical location and instil confidence among them to accomplish a particular task (Chan et al., 2022).
- The interactive experience fostered by AR and the immersive experience fostered by VR creates a very plausible learning environment for the student, such experience together helps the students to develop intellectually, socially and emotionally (Zhang et al., 2022).
- A higher level of involvement and engagement of the student can be possible by using both technologies. Students got a platform for solving real-life problems in a virtual surroundings with a virtual collaboration. Furthermore, the immersive, interactive experience together fosters the attention and involvement level of the students and enriches their impactful learning experience (Verner et al., 2022).

3.2.2 Dissimilarities Between AR and VR in the Context of Education

- AR focuses on supplementing the interactive digital elements in the virtual surroundings focusing on making the real-world experience more interactive (Cook & Lischer-Katz, 2021)
- AR superimposes digital information by augmenting the digital interactive interface over the simulated virtual world. This mode of technology-enhanced learning practice improves the students' perception of the real world (Cook & Lischer-Katz, 2021).
- On the contrary, VR creates a unique experience by creating a perfect simulation of the physical world. A real-life situation through a virtual simulation can develop an immersive experience for the student and foster higher attention and involvement of the student (Zhang et al., 2022)).
- The immersive experience developed by the VR technology is a fictitious representation of the real physical world. Such virtual experience through a simulated computer programming environment deprives the student of getting connected with the real world (Chan et al., 2022).

3.3 Current Trends and Advancements in AR and VR for Education

By providing students with innovative and immersive ways to learn and interact with instructional content, augmented reality (AR) and virtual reality (VR) have the potential to completely change the educational landscape (Seyman Guray & Kismet, 2023).

- Both AR and VR can be used to facilitate virtual study tours for the student, which helps them to explore different distant places, which may not be practically possible form the student's point of view keeping their resource at stake (Solmaz et al., 2021). Furthermore, google provides services like google earth with satellite photos, 3D landscapes and buildings to visualise the real world virtually (McDaniel, 2022). Teachers and students can investigate both historical sites and monuments as well as a variety of natural features including mountains, rivers, and deserts on Earth (Hagge, 2021).
- Using AR and VR technology provides personalized and customised learning experiences that are required to fulfil the needs and abilities of the student, this is another significant development in education. In addition to meeting the needs of different student groups, this might help to boost student enthusiasm and engagement (Bucea-Manea- oniş et al., 2022). With the use

of AR and VR technologies, learning is expanded beyond memory and observation including the access of the students to a realistic physical world that facilitates understanding of difficult subjects (Su et al., 2023). With the application of VR technology, teachers can create more immersive learning environments that help the teachers to improve their curriculum and enrich content to ensure students learning enjoyment (Seyman Guray & Kismet, 2023).

- Academic contributions of AR and VR technology in education include studies on how effectively these technologies could be used to improve learning outcomes of students and to development of relevant and robust teaching methodology and learning resources with the help of these technologies (Solmaz et al., 2021). Moreover, there is more to be explored about the use of AR and VR technology in challenging areas including special education, STEM education, and language learning (Chan et al., 2022). Several studies indicate that experiential learning occurs either through virtual or real-world experience and has an equal impact on the learning ability of the student (Bansal et al., 2022). Several studies by Chinese researchers revealed that students form a positive sentiment, who are engaged in virtual classes compared with their boatmates who are not engaged in virtual set-ups (Zhang et al., 2022).

- Both the immersive and interactive experiences created by using AR and VR technology can create such a unique learning experience, which is impossible to create in a regular physical classroom. Several studies further suggested confirming performance improvement and students' results the technology should be sued very carefully under struct supervision in teaching-learning practices (Bucea-Manea- oniş et al., 2022).

- The immersive experience caused by VR with the help of 3D is completely different from the normal 2D and 3D imagery (Ouyang et al., 2020). The computer creates a realistic impression by displaying visuals that are frequently used in teaching instruction. Virtual reality (VR) may be utilized to teach students about subjects like engineering design and design thinking, as well as history and culture (Wang & Zhang, 2021). The idea of adopting AR and VR technology in education is in a nascent stage, it will transform the entire education practices in the days to come (Capone & Lepore, 2020).

- Another potential use of AR and VR is to introduce the gamified learning experience, which helps the student to increase their involvement, attention and pleasure of the learning experience by engaging them in a computer-generated graphical interface and by developing a competitive spirit among them. Virtual and augmented reality also uphold the promise of significantly enhancing the teaching and learning process and increasing the effectiveness in class through immersive and interactive learning experiences (Solmaz et al., 2021).

- VR technology is used in the teaching-learning profession to develop immersive learning environments, further, such experience can help to foster virtual field trips and gain knowledge about historical events through simulations (Hagge, 2021). Compared to a conventional standard textbook or traditional method of lecture, a virtual reality experience of a historical location can provide students with a more vivid and accurate picture of past events as if it was there.

4. IMPACT ON LEARNER ENGAGEMENT AND MOTIVATION

4.1 Immersive Learning Experiences Using AR and VR

The idea of immersive technology is very difficult to describe as it depends upon the different applications and perspectives of use. Tham et al. (2018) defined the immersive experience is "the vast domain of wearables and related embodied technologies that are not just about physical objects that extend human capacity but also software applications that create augmented simulations for more seamless, thus immersive, experiences in human-technology interactions". To Lee et al. (2021), other perspectives about immersive technologies advocate that their purpose is to enable users to minimise the barriers between the physical world and its simulation in a virtual format. However, in a broader term, this term can include software and hardware components used in VR and AR. VR and AR technology are being more widely used in education by replacing the conventional classroom, such platform helps the students to experience immersive interactive participation with their surroundings in a virtual setup and fosters engagement, involvement and helps them in a deeper understanding of the subject (Zhang et al., 2022). Moreover, research suggests that incorporating AR and VR technology into classroom activity positively impacts the engagement, involvement and learning experience of the student (Sun et al., 2023). A recent study revealed that students accustomed to AR and VR technology in teaching practices show higher levels of enthusiasm and engagement as well as improved academic performance (Alizadehsalehi et al., 2021).

4.2 Cases Demonstrating Increased Learner Engagement and Motivation

Application of AR in Biology Education: The study aimed to enhance high school students' biology learning experience in the Western Black Sea region of Turkey through a mobile AR application (Ciloglu & Ustun, 2023). It assessed the impact on self-efficacy, motivation, and attitude among 71 students, divided into a control group (26) and an experimental group (45). A quasi-experimental methodology with a pretest and post-test approach was employed. The AR content facilitated an interactive and immersive experience, enabling students to engage with complex subjects through 3D models.

Application of VR in Medical Training: The School of Medicine of Stanford University has introduced VR technology in complex surgery procedures (Silva et al., 2018). The intervention aimed to assess the impact of VR technology on the learning experience of medical students. By using VR technology, a real-life simulation was developed, that helped the student to practice surgery in a risk-free environment. Furthermore, the VR technology offers the student a real-life experience by providing real-time monitoring and haptic feedback. The study revealed that the students who underwent VR technology-based education and demonstrated simulation showed a higher level of confidence and engagement while conducting medical surgery practices in comparison with the students trained with the conventional method of training (Silva et al., 2018).

Application of AR in Language Learning: This study, conducted among Taiwan University students, investigated the impact of AR technology on enhancing English language learning outcomes (Y. S. Chang, 2021). The research examined how integrating AR technology could improve students' academic performance, engagement, and overall learning experience in English courses. AR-based content was designed to align with the curriculum, enabling students to practice language skills in a context-rich environment by responding to voice commands and interacting with virtual characters and objects. Course evaluation revealed a significant reduction in students' anxiety levels, boosting their confidence in presentations and improving language proficiency. The integration of AR in English education enhanced student engagement and motivation by offering a contextually immersive experience (Baxter & Hainey, 2024; Y. J. Chang et al., 2011; Gonta, 2021).

Application of VR in History Education: the University of Warwick has introduced the application of VR in history education intending to explore the understanding and engagement level of the student (Gibson et al., 2022). The instructors developed the VR-based content following the curriculum of the university. The developed VR-based simulation aimed to improve the historical understanding of the student relating to Rome and medieval Europe by providing an immersive learning experience with the help of historical figures and visiting historical sites virtually. It was found during the evaluation of the course outcome that the immersive experience has resulted in a deeper understanding of history by making it more relevant and tangible (Gibson et al., 2022). There was an improvement in the engagement and motivation level of the student compared with the conventional method of text-book learning.

Application of AR in STEM Education Forawi & Al Quraan (2022), evaluated the effectiveness of AR in improving the learning outcome and involvement of the students relating to the "Science, Technology, Engineering, and Mathematics" acronym as STEM subjects in United Arab Emeritus. Using AR tools, the interactive contents were developed covering the STEM syllabus. The interactive content with the help of simulation enhanced the real experience of the physical classroom and laboratory in a virtual setting. These interactive platforms helped the students to acquire a deeper understanding of the concepts of mathematics and science. At the evaluation of course outcomes, the students exhibited greater interest and involvement in STEM subjects. The students have shown a deeper understanding of STEM subjects in comparison with students educated through traditional methods. The study has exhibited application of AR in STEM education helped the student improve their learning experience by making concepts simple and interactive, which increased the motivation and involvement level of the students.

5. ENHANCING KNOWLEDGE RETENTION AND APPLICATION

5.1 Mechanisms Through Which AR and VR Aid in Knowledge Retention

The application of AR and VR technology in education has brought a paradigm shift in the teaching and learning profession by redefining the concept of immersive experience. This technology has enabled the students to participate in interactive learning scenarios, simulated scientific experiments, and visit historical locations inside the classroom. This evolution in teaching towards providing an immersive learning environment to students aims to improve knowledge retention and foster the development of practical skills with an increase in student engagement (Tewari et al., 2023). AR & VR uses several mechanisms to enhance the natural process of learning, memory and engagement of students. They are as follows.

1. **Immersive Learning Environments:** The integration of AR and VR will create a better interactive and immersive environment. In VR with the help of 3D objects an immersive environment is created and similarly with the help of AR digital content is supplemented over the real-world scenario. This sort of

experience simulates the various senses and brings the attention of the student, which plays a key role in controlling the amount of information and encoding these in the memory of the students (Capone & Lepore, 2020).

2. **Contextual Learning:** The instructors develop the content and the contextual aspect of the subject by applying AR and VR technology. Such contextual learning fosters their real-life experience about the subject, for instance visiting historical sites and various geographical locations of the earth (Hagge, 2021). Such experience helped the student to learn the content for a longer period.

3. **Emotional Engagement:** the interactive and immersive experience together triggers the emotional response of the student by involving them in a real-life situation through simulation (Lin et al., 2024). Such real-life experience develops the stress hormone and happy hormone in the brain and gets them emotionally connected with the subject (Marougkas et al., 2024). Further, emotional engagement supplements the coding and encoding of information in the memory of the student.

4. **Active Learning and Interactivity:** integration of AR and VR creates a unique, enjoyable learning environment, that helps the student to actively involve and engage with the subject and foster the knowledge retention process. Because the students involved in real-life situations can learn in a better way through active participation and manipulate the digital object as they do in real life (Solmaz et al., 2021).

5. **Repetition and Practice:** the application of AR and VR creates an interactive learning environment that provides a platform for the repetition of the concepts. Such repetition and practice of skill can be possible in the virtual environment without any interruption. The ability to practice and rehearse strengthens the memorising process of the students and helps them for better retention of these concepts (Zhang et al., 2022). For instance, the driving training conducted through simulation helps the trainee to acquire relevant skills over time.

6. **Personalization and Adaptive Learning:** content developed by applying AR and VR technology provides an opportunity for a personalised learning experience. The student can find a personalised experience by sharing their real-time feedback. Such personalise experience fosters the engagement and involvement level of the student and improves the retention of the concept by satisfying the unique requirement of the student (Su et al., 2023). For instance, students can learn language learning skills and vocabulary through interactive practice sessions.

7. **Reduction of Cognitive Load:** The application of AR and VR technology in education can help in segmenting the modules into simplified concepts, supplemented by visual aids and chunks of understandable information. These

simplified concepts reduce the stress level of the student and help them to improve their retention level effectively (Bucea-Manea- oniş et al., 2022).

8. **Spatial Memory Encoding:** An immersive experience caused by the application of AR and VR technology facilitates engaging the spatial memory of the student. Spatial memory is the ability of the brain to keep the information of the environment in the form of coding. The 3D content navigating experience of the environment helps the student to retain the difficult concept more enjoyably. For instance, students undergo scientific process in a virtual laboratory (Solmaz et al., 2021).

5.2 Examples of Successful Knowledge Transfer Through AR and VR Interventions

The integration of AR and VR in education has completely transformed the landscape of the teaching and learning profession. The new age of technology-enabled teaching practices has created a new horizon of teaching by providing an immersive and interactive experience to the student. (Tewari et al., 2023) Draw attention to how to use AR and VR technologies in transforming education in a self-directed learning environment and how this technology may be used to create a dynamic learning environment. VR enables students in self-directed learning environments to engage with the simulated environment by instantly emulating the attention of the student. The three primary characteristics of VR technology in educational settings are creating an immersive environment for the student, providing a platform to interact, and allowing the student to intervene in the virtual world. Immersion states a sense of being in the virtual world for the student while interaction reveals how well the student has modified the environment (Mccloy & Stone, 2001).

Virtual reality (VR) enables students to engage with their surroundings in a more meaningful way and the opportunity to interact with surroundings and explore by navigation creates an immersing learning experience in a virtual setup. Such practices effectively support experiential learning, it fosters the engagement level of the student with their surroundings and their memory of the material and development of practical skills. Chen et al. (2023) provide more evidence of the usefulness of virtual reality in enhancing the engagement and involvement level of the student. Cognitive engagement and procedural knowledge learning are more strongly impacted by immersive learning experiences caused due to VR encounters. Furthermore, the integration of VR and AR provides a unique way to improve traditional instructional materials. The effectiveness of AR in teaching complicated subjects like the solar system is investigated by de Moraes Rossetto et al. (2023). Their research revealed that AR has the potential to significantly improve the teaching process by improving the engagement level of the student and offering contextualized learning. Further, he draws attention to the difficulties and challenges in applying these technologies into practice, especially for the unprivileged section who faces the challenges of insufficient funds to invest and not having basic technological infrastructure.

5.3 Comparison with the Traditional Learning Methods

The integration of AR and VR in education offers an opportunity to transform teaching and learning through interactive and immersive experiences, potentially leading to improved learning outcomes compared to traditional methods. These technologies foster engagement, motivation, and understanding by allowing students to explore complex subjects tangibly, enhancing knowledge retention and self-directed learning (Al-Ansi et al., 2023; Oberdörfer et al., 2021). However, traditional methods remain prevalent due to their accessibility, adaptability, and lower resource requirements, although they often lack the same level of engagement and effectiveness in conveying complex concepts as AR and VR technologies. While AR and VR can enhance collaboration and social interaction in virtual environments, traditional classrooms naturally facilitate face-to-face interactions and group work. Despite their benefits, AR and VR require substantial investments in hardware, software, and training, which may limit their practicality. However, these technologies can also reduce costs associated with textbooks and travel, potentially increasing accessibility (Shibata, 2019). AR and VR are particularly effective in subjects requiring visualisation and experiential learning, such as medicine and STEM fields, providing realistic simulations that enhance skill development and practical knowledge (De Lorenzis et al., 2023; Mystakidis et al., 2021).

6. CHALLENGES IN INCORPORATING AR AND VR TECHNOLOGY IN EDUCATION

6.1 Technical Challenges: Cost, Accessibility, and Usability Issues

The integration of AR and VR technology in education offers a distinctive and immersive learning environment but faces significant challenges. Cost is a major barrier, as the necessary hardware and software require substantial investments and regular updates, increasing the financial burden on institutions (Al-Ansi et al., 2023). Accessibility is another concern, as not all students can access the required equipment. Institutions must ensure equal access to these technologies, considering students' varied experiences and maturity levels (Biswas et al., 2021). Moreover, exposure to AR/VR may overwhelm some students. Usability issues also arise; prolonged use of AR/VR headsets can cause discomfort, physical strain, and motion sickness. Students unfamiliar with immersive technology may find it distracting (Scavarelli et al., 2019). A socio-techno-economic study in Philippines by Ann Bautista et al. (2022) identified privacy and security concerns as key challenges, noting the risk of unauthorized data access. Additionally, the quality, equality, and accessibility of AR/VR education remain problematic in developing and underdeveloped countries (Hsiao et al., 2018). Addressing these challenges is crucial for the effective implementation of AR and VR in education.

6.2 Pedagogical Challenges

Integrating AR and VR into classroom environments presents various pedagogical challenges, particularly concerning student variability and curriculum alignment. These challenges are specific to handling student variability and curriculum alignment. According to Krauss et al. (2021), "developers of AR and VR applications have four distinct but interconnected roles: idea designers, interface designers, content writers, and technical developers." Throughout the process from conducting initial context studies to implementing the final product, a single designer may assume multiple responsibilities and face a diverse array of challenges.

a)   Curriculum Alignment

One of the major challenges in the design of a curriculum incorporating AR and VR is to align with established standards and learning objectives. The educational institution needs to ensure that technology-enabled teaching practice should not distract from its core learning goals. AR and VR are considered two of the most cutting-edge technological developments and have the potential to enhance and transform the educational system. Incorporating immersive technology in the teaching and learning profession is sometimes considered as sacred idea when it comes to instruction development, contextual learning, and even the training of teachers. Further, it is very important to know how the technology can be familiar among students and teachers who do not have prior knowledge to use it. How to apply this technology in developing course content and how the delivery of the course can be possible in hybrid mode (Baxter & Hainey, 2024).

b)   Learner Variability

Another important challenge in pedagogical development is to ensure the developed content caters to the requirements of the varied interests of the student. The students may vary in their learning style as visual, auditory, and kinaesthetic learners.

It is very complex for the developed content to be flexible enough to cater for the learning requirements of these learners. In a similar study by Alalwan et al. (2020), there he conducted interviews with 29 elementary-level teachers to learn more about their perspectives on the advantages and difficulties faced in integrating AR and VR into scientific instruction. An intriguing finding was that several teachers said AR is easier to use over VR as it requires less sophisticated hardware and software. Because AR is associated with mobile phones and use of mobile phones is also seen as a more convenient method of teaching and learning. Despite the acknowledged advantages of the application of AR and VR in higher education, Calvet et al. (2019) pointed out in their research that these technologies have not been widely accepted because of their perceived limitations relating to usability factors, display quality, lack of realism, and recognition inaccuracies.

c) Evaluation and Feedback

For an effective learning system, providing real-time feedback is very important. It is very difficult to provide real-time feedback to the student about their progress in a virtual setup. Hence the AR and VR-based content developer should focus on providing real-time feedback and providing space for the student for interaction and to allow them to clarify their doubts. Furthermore, monitoring students' academic performance and progress is very difficult in AR and VR settings. It becomes extremely difficult especially when connecting the progress data with current student information systems.

d) Scalability and Sustainability

Students belonging to different disciple have diverse demands of content and curriculum. It is very difficult for the AR and VR application to scale across different disciple, diverse curricula and different understanding levels of the student. Along with this adopting sustainable practices like maintaining technological instruments, updating study material regularly, and keeping up with changing educational requirements are all important aspects of successful adoption of AR and VR technology. The content developers must recognise and understand the importance of giving students additional opportunities to interact with the content by making it more interactive and immersive so that students can get a deeper comprehension of the subject matter being studied (Militello et al., 2021).

7. PROPOSED SOLUTIONS AND FUTURE RESEARCH DIRECTIONS

The emerging applications of AR and VR in education have the potential to transform the current educational landscape. These technology-enabled practices are expected to play a crucial role in shaping the future of education by addressing existing challenges with innovative solutions and opening new avenues for instructional development. Zhao et al. (2023) carried out a bibliometric and content analysis and revealed that future learning environments are more immersive and experienced, and may eventually replace conventional teaching practices by incorporating crucial elements of AR and VR like animation, 3D-visuals, and music. In a similar study, Kulikova & Poddubnaya (2021) focus on preparing aspiring teachers to effectively use mobile apps, AR, and VR in classroom instruction. Their work primarily addresses how educators can integrate technology into their teaching practices practically and efficiently. The delivery of education has been completely transformed by m-learning which is otherwise known as mobile learning (Bernacki et al., 2021)

Tewari et al. (2023) in his study highlight the transformative potential of AR and VR on education. To him, the application of AR and VR technology creates an opportunity to educate the special needs students and can address the customised requirement of the student. The research further indicates that personalisation with an opportunity to allow for customised learning experiences that satisfy the various demands of students would probably be the main emphasis of AR and VR in education in the future. However, advancements in AR and VR technology will also need to address challenges such as integrating these tools into current curricula and ensuring alignment with educational objectives.

8. PROPOSED FRAMEWORK FOR AR AND VR INTEGRATION

Figure 2.

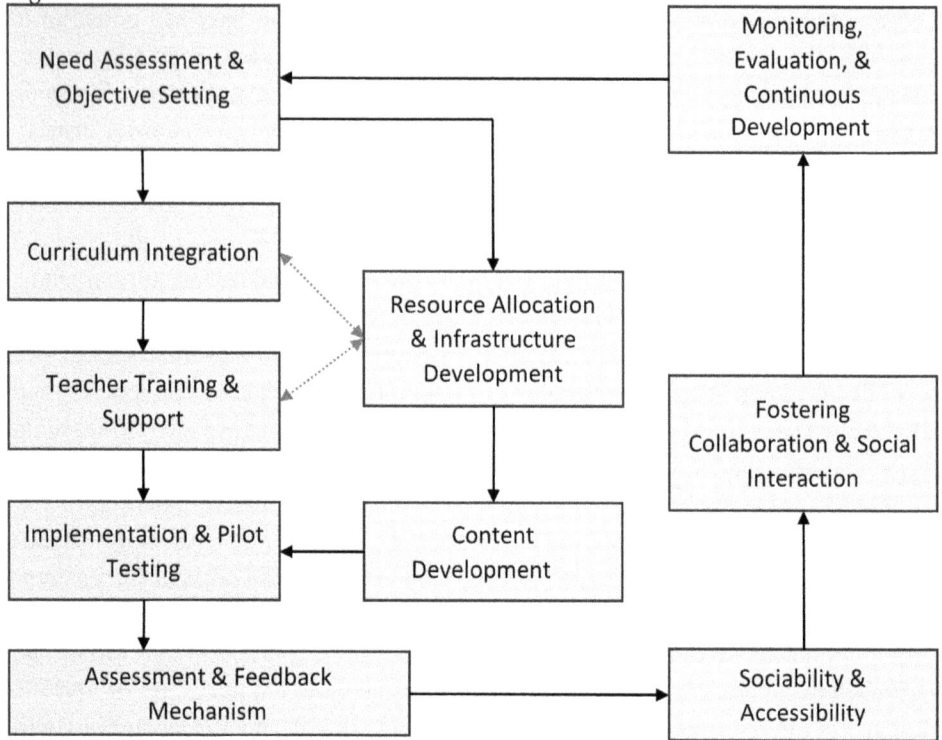

The proposed framework given in Figure 2, for integrating AR and VR in education begins with assessing needs and setting objectives to identify specific learning goals that these technologies can uniquely address. It then integrates AR and VR into the curriculum by aligning them with desired learning outcomes, especially in subjects like STEM and complex theoretical areas. Resources, including hardware, software, and infrastructure, must be allocated, and teachers need thorough training and ongoing support to effectively utilize these technologies. High-quality content is developed or curated in collaboration with educators and subject matter experts. Implementation starts with pilot testing in select classrooms, where feedback is gathered to refine the approach. Assessment tools measure the impact on learning outcomes, and data-driven insights inform adjustments. As AR and VR are scaled up, considerations for accessibility and cost-effectiveness are addressed.

The integration of AR and VR technology in education has the potential to transform the landscape of the teaching-learning environment. However, its successful implementation highly depends on the educators and instructional designers in reflecting their effort on effectively designing the course by aligning the curriculum with digital content. The instructional design usually depends on segmenting the learning activities that hover around the important theory, concepts and requisite skills to be included in the modules of the subject. A standardised instructional designing framework comprises of series of relevant learning activities, that are organised into four instructional stages Introduction, Presentation, Practice, and Application (Ipsita et al., 2024). The instructional development framework focuses on learning outcomes, prioritizing learner assessment and feedback aligning it with the background process. This integration ensures instructional activities should support student learning, measuring their progress through periodical assessments and taking real-time feedback from students.

9. CASES ILLUSTRATING THE INTEGRATION OF AR AND VR FRAMEWORK IN SELF-DIRECTED LEARNING

The evolution of immersive and interactive technology has given impetus to online distance education in the form of self-directed learning (SDL). Garrison (1997), "Self-directed learning is a popular theme since many adults desire to continue learning throughout their lives and enjoy choosing what to learn and how to learn it" Further this quick development in SDL through online distance education is amplified by the covid-19 pandemic. Distance education has its limitations as it relies on the imagination of the student, there are no physical instructors to supervise and finally, there is no scope for immediate feedback. This scenario highlights the importance of AR and VR technology in remote learning to overcome the challenges associated with it, especially one-to-one interactions and the problem of time constraints (Li et al., 2022).

Li et al. (2022) conducted a study in China with a sample size of 152 to evaluate the effectiveness of teaching calligraphy using AR and VR technology in a distance learning environment. The study employed a mixed-method research design, utilizing technological interventions such as Oculus Quest 2 VR equipment, a painting teaching application, and a virtual calligraphy painting application. The results indicated positive learning outcomes with high student engagement. However, the study acknowledged the ongoing challenge of developing comprehensive content for VR-based teaching and learning practices.

Çoban & Göksu (2022) conducted a study in Turkey aimed at enhancing motivation and socialization among undergraduate students through the use of AR and VR technology in a distance learning setting. The study involved 41 participants, with 21 in the experimental group and 20 in the control group, using a quasi-experimental design. The technologies utilized were "vAcademia" and "Adobe Connect."

Results showed a high level of motivation and engagement in socialization among the students. The study also highlighted that, beyond technological integration, the responsiveness of both instructors and students is a key factor in improving the effectiveness of learning.

Rawson et al. (2022) conducted an experimental study with 75 postgraduate students in the United Kingdom to assess the impact of VR technology on summative assessment outcomes for environmental management students. The study utilized low-immersive VR technology. The findings indicated promising learning outcomes, with a notably high level of student engagement. However, the study emphasized that improving VR-based content should take into account the varying levels of student understanding to further enhance learning effectiveness.

Lee et al. (2021) conducted a similar experimental study with 20 students in Korea to assess student responsiveness to real-time VR streaming for remote sensing, sharing, and interacting with the Solar Dynamics Observatory. The study used an "IVR-based distance education system." Results showed promising learning outcomes and high student engagement. However, students experienced discomfort and distraction from wearing the VR headset for extended periods during the study.

Gattullo et al. (2022) conducted an experimental study in Italy with 84 students to examine the impact of AR and VR-integrated content on STEM education, specifically in laboratory lectures. The study applied mixed reality technology and revealed promising learning outcomes, though student engagement was moderate during virtual classes. It was later determined that the lack of visually captivating design elements contributed to the lower levels of student involvement.

10. CONCLUSION

Augmented Reality (AR) and Virtual Reality (VR) hold immense potential to revolutionize education by creating immersive, interactive experiences that enhance teaching and learning. These technologies boost student engagement, enabling self-directed learning and fostering critical thinking, problem-solving, and creativity. AR and VR simplify complex concepts and facilitate collaborative learning environments, fostering deeper understanding and knowledge-building. Studies indicate that integrating AR and VR in higher education benefits various disciplines like STEM, History, Social Sciences, and Medical Education. However, challenges like cost, infrastructure, and pedagogy must be addressed to ensure seamless integration. Future trends should focus on enhancing learning experiences, equitable access, and effective implementation of AR and VR in education. Educational institutions must invest in the necessary infrastructure and train teachers to create high-quality content that maximizes these technologies' capabilities. This approach will enhance student learning outcomes, making AR and VR the new standard in education.

REFERENCES

Abad-Segura, E., Gonzalez-Zamar, M.-D., la Rosa, A. L., & Morales Cevallos, M. B. (2020). Sustainability of educational technologies: An approach to augmented reality research. *Sustainability*, 12(10), 4091.

Ahmad, S., Umirzakova, S., Mujtaba, G., Amin, M. S., & Whangbo, T. (2023). Education 5.0: requirements, enabling technologies, and future directions. *ArXiv Preprint ArXiv:2307.15846.*

Al-Ansi, A. M., Jaboob, M., Garad, A., & Al-Ansi, A. (2023). Analyzing augmented reality (AR) and virtual reality (VR) recent development in education. *Social Sciences & Humanities Open*, 8(1). Advance online publication. DOI: 10.1016/j. ssaho.2023.100532

Alalwan, N., Cheng, L., Al-Samarraie, H., Yousef, R., Ibrahim Alzahrani, A., & Sarsam, S. M. (2020). Challenges and Prospects of Virtual Reality and Augmented Reality Utilization among Primary School Teachers: A Developing Country Perspective. *Studies in Educational Evaluation*, 66. Advance online publication. DOI: 10.1016/j.stueduc.2020.100876

AlGerafi, M. A. M., Zhou, Y., Oubibi, M., & Wijaya, T. T. (2023). Unlocking the potential: A comprehensive evaluation of augmented reality and virtual reality in education. *Electronics (Basel)*, 12(18), 3953.

Alizadehsalehi, S., Hadavi, A., & Huang, J. C. (2021). Assessment of AEC students' performance using BIM-into-VR. *Applied Sciences (Basel, Switzerland)*, 11(7), 3225.

Ann Bautista, M. G., Roy Evangelista, I., Culaba, A., Concepcion, R., & Dadios, E. (2022). Technology Adoption of Augmented and Virtual Reality in a Progressive Philippines: A Socio-techno-economical Analysis. *2022 IEEE 14th International Conference on Humanoid, Nanotechnology, Information Technology, Communication and Control, Environment, and Management, HNICEM 2022*. https://doi.org/DOI: 10.1109/HNICEM57413.2022.10109429

Azuma, R. T. (1997). A Survey of Augmented Reality. *Presence: Teleoperators and Virtual Environments/MIT Press.*

Bansal, G., Rajgopal, K., Chamola, V., Xiong, Z., & Niyato, D. (2022). Healthcare in Metaverse: A Survey on Current Metaverse Applications in Healthcare. *IEEE Access: Practical Innovations, Open Solutions*, 10, 119914–119946. DOI: 10.1109/ ACCESS.2022.3219845

Baxter, G., & Hainey, T. (2024). Using immersive technologies to enhance the student learning experience. *Interactive Technology and Smart Education*, 21(3), 403–425. DOI: 10.1108/ITSE-05-2023-0078

Bermejo, B., Juiz, C., Cortes, D., Oskam, J., Moilanen, T., Loijas, J., Govender, P., Hussey, J., Schmidt, A. L., Burbach, R., King, D., O'Connor, C., & Dunlea, D. (2023). AR/VR Teaching-Learning Experiences in Higher Education Institutions (HEI): A Systematic Literature Review. *Informatics (MDPI)*, 10(2). Advance online publication. DOI: 10.3390/informatics10020045

Bernacki, M. L., Greene, M. J., & Lobczowski, N. G. (2021). A Systematic Review of Research on Personalized Learning: Personalized by Whom, to What, How, and for What Purpose(s)? *Educational Psychology Review*, 33(4), 1675–1715. DOI: 10.1007/S10648-021-09615-8

Biswas, P., Orero, P., Swaminathan, M., Krishnaswamy, K., & Robinson, P. (2021). Adaptive Accessible AR/VR Systems. *Conference on Human Factors in Computing Systems - Proceedings*. https://doi.org/DOI: 10.1145/3411763.3441324

Bucea-Manea- oniş, R., Kuleto, V., Gudei, S. C. D., Lianu, C., Lianu, C., Ilić, M. P., & Păun, D. (2022). Artificial Intelligence Potential in Higher Education Institutions Enhanced Learning Environment in Romania and Serbia. *Sustainability (Switzerland)*, 14(10). Advance online publication. DOI: 10.3390/su14105842

Calvet, L., Bourdin, P., & Prados, F. (2019). Immersive technologies in higher education: Applications, challenges, and good practices. *ACM International Conference Proceeding Series*, 95–99. https://doi.org/DOI: 10.1145/3371647.3371667

Capone, R., & Lepore, M. (2020). Augmented reality to increase interaction and participation: A case study of undergraduate students in mathematics class. *Augmented Reality, Virtual Reality, and Computer Graphics: 7th International Conference, AVR 2020, Lecce, Italy, September 7–10, 2020. Proceedings*, 7(Part II), 185–204.

Carmigniani, J., Furht, B., Anisetti, M., Ceravolo, P., Damiani, E., & Ivkovic, M. (2011). Augmented reality technologies, systems and applications. *Multimedia Tools and Applications*, 51, 341–377.

Chan, V. S., Haron, H. N. H., Isham, M. I. B. M., & Mohamed, F. Bin. (2022). VR and AR virtual welding for psychomotor skills: A systematic review. *Multimedia Tools and Applications*, 81(9), 12459–12493. DOI: 10.1007/s11042-022-12293-5 PMID: 35221778

Chang, Y. J., Chen, C. H., Huang, W. T., & Huang, W. S. (2011). Investigating students' perceived satisfaction, behavioral intention, and effectiveness of English learning using augmented reality. *Proceedings - IEEE International Conference on Multimedia and Expo.* https://doi.org/DOI: 10.1109/ICME.2011.6012177

Chang, Y. S. (2021). Applying the arcs motivation theory for the assessment of ar digital media design learning effectiveness. *Sustainability (Switzerland)*, 13(21), 12296. DOI: 10.3390/su132112296

Chen, Y., Li, M., Huang, C., Cukurova, M., & Ma, Q. (2023). A Systematic Review of Research on Immersive Technology-enhanced writing education: The current state and a Research Agenda. *IEEE Transactions on Learning Technologies.*

Childs, E., Mohammad, F., Stevens, L., Burbelo, H., Awoke, A., Rewkowski, N., & Manocha, D. (2021). An overview of enhancing distance learning through augmented and virtual reality technologies. *ArXiv Preprint ArXiv:2101.11000.*

Ciloglu, T., & Ustun, A. B. (2023). The Effects of Mobile AR-based Biology Learning Experience on Students' Motivation, Self-Efficacy, and Attitudes in Online Learning. *Journal of Science Education and Technology*, 32(3), 309–337. DOI: 10.1007/s10956-023-10030-7 PMID: 36844360

Çoban, M., & Göksu, İ. (2022). Using virtual reality learning environments to motivate and socialize undergraduates in distance learning. *Participatory Educational Research*, 9(2), 199–218. DOI: 10.17275/per.22.36.9.2

Cook, M., & Lischer-Katz, Z. (2021). Practical steps for an effective virtual reality course integration. *College & Undergraduate Libraries*, 27(2–4), 210–226.

Covington, M. V. (2000). Intrinsic versus extrinsic motivation in schools: A reconciliation. *Current Directions in Psychological Science*, 9(1), 22–25. DOI: 10.1111/1467-8721.00052

De Lorenzis, F., Pratticò, F. G., Repetto, M., Pons, E., & Lamberti, F. (2023). Immersive Virtual Reality for procedural training: Comparing traditional and learning by teaching approaches. *Computers in Industry*, 144. Advance online publication. DOI: 10.1016/j.compind.2022.103785

de Moraes Rossetto, A. G., Martins, T. C., Silva, L. A., Leithardt, D. R. F., Bermejo-Gil, B. M., & Leithardt, V. R. Q. (2023). An analysis of the use of augmented reality and virtual reality as educational resources. *Computer Applications in Engineering Education*, 31(6), 1761–1775.

Deci, E. L., & Ryan, R. M. (2012). Self-determination theory. *Handbook of Theories of Social Psychology, 1*(20), 416–436.

Dewey, J., Montessori, M., Strzemiński, W., Piaget, J., Vygotsky, L., von Foerster, H., Bruner, J., Simon, H., Watzlawick, P., & von Glasersfeld, E. (1997). Constructivism (learning theory). *Journal of Social Sciences, Literature and Languages*, 9–16.

Diseth, Å., Mathisen, F. K. S., & Samdal, O. (2020). A comparison of intrinsic and extrinsic motivation among lower and upper secondary school students. *Educational Psychology*, 40(8), 961–980. DOI: 10.1080/01443410.2020.1778640

Fainholc, B. (2016). Latin American present and future of teaching and learning in virtual environments related to university education. [RED]. *Journal of Distance Education*, 2(48).

Forawi, S. A., & Al Quraan, E. (2022). Status and Trends of STEM Education in the United Arab Emirates. *Status and Trends of STEM Education in Highly Competitive Countries: Country Reports and International Comparison.*

Gao, Y., Chang, C., Yu, X., Pang, P., Xiong, N., & Huang, C. (2022). A VR-based volumetric medical image segmentation and visualization system with natural human interaction. *Virtual Reality (Waltham Cross)*, 26(2), 415–424. DOI: 10.1007/s10055-021-00577-4

Garrison, D. R. (1997). Self-directed learning: Toward a comprehensive model. *Adult Education Quarterly*, 48(1), 18–33. DOI: 10.1177/074171369704800103

Gattullo, M., Laviola, E., Boccaccio, A., Evangelista, A., Fiorentino, M., Manghisi, V. M., & Uva, A. E. (2022). Design of a Mixed Reality Application for STEM Distance Education Laboratories. *Computers*, 11(4). Advance online publication. DOI: 10.3390/computers11040050

Gibson, L., Roberts-Smith, J., Llewellyn, K. R., & Llewellyn, J. (2022). A New Approach to Virtual Reality in History Education: The Digital Oral Histories for Reconciliation Project (DOHR). *History Education in the Digital Age*, 103–121. https://doi.org/DOI: 10.1007/978-3-031-10743-6_6

Gonta, I. (2021). Students' perspectives on online learning problems, opportunities and expectations. *ELearning and Software for Education Conference*, 157–161. https://doi.org/DOI: 10.12753/2066-026X-21-020

Hagge, P. (2021). Student perceptions of semester-long in-class virtual reality: Effectively using "Google Earth VR" in a higher education classroom. *Journal of Geography in Higher Education*, 45(3), 342–360.

Hein, G. E. (1991). Constructivist learning theory. *Institute for Inquiry. Available at:/*Http://Www. Exploratorium. Edu/Ifi/Resources/Constructivistlearning. *HtmlS.*

Hsiao, T. C., Tai, K. Y., Huang, Y. M., Chung, Y. F., Wu, Y. C., Kurniati, T., & Chen, T. S. (2018). An Implementation of Efficient Hierarchical Access Control Method for VR/AR Platform. *ICETA 2018 - 16th IEEE International Conference on Emerging ELearning Technologies and Applications, Proceedings*, 206–208. https://doi.org/DOI: 10.1109/ICETA.2018.8572099

Ipsita, A., Patel, M., Unmesh, A., & Ramani, K. (2024). Authoring instructional flow in iVR learning units to promote outcome-oriented learning. *Computers & Education: X Reality, 5*, 100074.

Kearsley, G., & Shneiderman, B. (1998). Engagement theory: A framework for technology-based teaching and learning. *Educational Technology*, 38(5), 20–23.

Kiryakova, G., Angelova, N., & Yordanova, L. (2018). The potential of augmented reality to transform education into smart education. *TEM Journal*, 7(3), 556.

Krauss, J. K., Lipsman, N., Aziz, T., Boutet, A., Brown, P., Chang, J. W., Davidson, B., Grill, W. M., Hariz, M. I., & Horn, A. (2021). Technology of deep brain stimulation: Current status and future directions. *Nature Reviews. Neurology*, 17(2), 75–87. PMID: 33244188

Kulikova, T. A., & Poddubnaya, N. A. (2021). Training of future educators for the introduction of mobile applications, AR and VR technologies into the educational process. *CEUR Workshop Proceedings*, 4, 231–240.

Lee, J., Surh, J., Choi, W., & You, B. (2021). Immersive virtual-reality-based streaming distance education system for solar dynamics observatory: A case study. *Applied Sciences (Switzerland)*, 11(19). Advance online publication. DOI: 10.3390/app11198932

Li, P., Fang, Z., & Jiang, T. (2022). Research Into improved Distance Learning Using VR Technology. *Frontiers in Education*, 7. Advance online publication. DOI: 10.3389/feduc.2022.757874

Liberati, N. (2016). Augmented reality and ubiquitous computing: The hidden potentialities of augmented reality. *AI & Society*, 31(1), 17–28. DOI: 10.1007/s00146-014-0543-x

Lin, X. P., & Li, B. Bin, Yao, Z. N., Yang, Z., & Zhang, M. (2024). The impact of virtual reality on student engagement in the classroom–a critical review of the literature. *Frontiers in Psychology*, 15. Advance online publication. DOI: 10.3389/fpsyg.2024.1360574 PMID: 38659670

Marougkas, A., Troussas, C., Krouska, A., & Sgouropoulou, C. (2023). Virtual Reality in Education: A Review of Learning Theories, Approaches and Methodologies for the Last Decade. *Electronics (Switzerland)*, 12(13). Advance online publication. DOI: 10.3390/electronics12132832

Marougkas, A., Troussas, C., Krouska, A., & Sgouropoulou, C. (2024). How personalized and effective is immersive virtual reality in education? A systematic literature review for the last decade. *Multimedia Tools and Applications*, 83(6), 18185–18233. DOI: 10.1007/s11042-023-15986-7

Mayer, R. E. (2012). Cognitive Theory of Multimedia Learning. *The Cambridge Handbook of Multimedia Learning*, 31–48. https://doi.org/DOI: 10.1017/cbo9780511816819.004

Mccloy, R., & Stone, R. (2001). Virtual reality in surgery. *BMJ (Clinical Research Ed.)*, 323(7318), 912–915. DOI: 10.1136/bmj.323.7318.912 PMID: 11668138

McDaniel, P. N. (2022). Teaching, Learning, and Exploring the Geography of North America with Virtual Globes and Geovisual Narratives. *The Journal of Geography*, 121(4), 125–140. DOI: 10.1080/00221341.2022.2119597

Milgram, P., & Kishino, F. (1994). A taxonomy of mixed reality visual displays. *IEICE Transactions on Information and Systems*, 77(12), 1321–1329.

Militello, C., Rundo, L., Vitabile, S., & Conti, V. (2021). Fingerprint classification based on deep learning approaches: Experimental findings and comparisons. *Symmetry*, 13(5). Advance online publication. DOI: 10.3390/sym13050750

Mystakidis, S., Fragkaki, M., & Filippousis, G. (2021). Ready teacher one: Virtual and augmented reality online professional development for k-12 school teachers. *Computers*, 10(10). Advance online publication. DOI: 10.3390/computers10100134

Oberdörfer, S., Birnstiel, S., Latoschik, M. E., & Grafe, S. (2021). Mutual Benefits: Interdisciplinary Education of Pre-Service Teachers and HCI Students in VR/AR Learning Environment Design. *Frontiers in Education*, 6. Advance online publication. DOI: 10.3389/feduc.2021.693012

Ouyang, Y., Wong, C. K., & Luo, X. (2020). Assessing students' hazard identification ability in virtual reality using eye tracking devices. *27th International Workshop on Intelligent Computing in Engineering of the European Group for Intelligent Computing in Engineering (EG-ICE 2020)*, 12–21.

Rawson, R., Okere, U., & Tooth, O. (2022). Using Low-immersive Virtual Reality in Online Learning: Field Notes from Environmental Management Education. *International Review of Research in Open and Distributed Learning*, 23(4), 211–221. DOI: 10.19173/irrodl.v23i4.6475

Santana-Mancilla, P. C., Garc'a-Ruiz, M. A., Acosta-Diaz, R., & Juárez, C. U. (2012). Service oriented architecture to support mexican secondary education through mobile augmented reality. *Procedia Computer Science*, 10, 721–727.

Scavarelli, A., Arya, A., & Teather, R. J. (2019). Circles: exploring multi-platform accessible, socially scalable VR in the classroom. *2019 IEEE Games, Entertainment, Media Conference, GEM 2019, 2019-Janua.* https://doi.org/DOI: 10.1109/GEM.2019.8897532

Seifert, K., & Sutton, R. (2019). The learning process. *Educational Psychology*.

Seo, S. H., Kim, M. Y., & Kim, Y. (2024). A Design and Implementation of an Online Video Lecture System based on Facial Expression Recognition. *International Journal on Advanced Science, Engineering and Information Technology*, 14(3).

Seyman Guray, T., & Kismet, B. (2023). Applicability of a digitalization model based on augmented reality for building construction education in architecture. *Construction Innovation*, 23(1), 193–212. DOI: 10.1108/CI-07-2021-0136

Shibata, T. (2019). Virtual reality in education: How schools use VR in classrooms. *Advances in Intelligent Systems and Computing*, 827, 423–425. DOI: 10.1007/978-3-319-96059-3_48

Silva, J. N. A., Southworth, M., Raptis, C., & Silva, J. (2018). Emerging applications of virtual reality in cardiovascular medicine. *JACC. Basic to Translational Science*, 3(3), 420–430. PMID: 30062228

Solmaz, S., Dominguez Alfaro, J. L., Santos, P., Van Puyvelde, P., & Van Gerven, T. (2021). A practical development of engineering simulation-assisted educational AR environments. *Education for Chemical Engineers*, 35, 81–93. DOI: 10.1016/j.ece.2021.01.007

Su, P.-Y., Hsiao, P.-W., & Fan, K.-K. (2023). Investigating the Relationship between Users' Behavioral Intentions and Learning Effects of VR System for Sustainable Tourism Development. *Sustainability*, 15(9), 7277.

Sun, J. C.-Y., Ye, S.-L., Yu, S.-J., & Chiu, T. K. F. (2023). Effects of wearable hybrid AR/VR learning material on high school students' situational interest, engagement, and learning performance: The case of a physics laboratory learning environment. *Journal of Science Education and Technology*, 32(1), 1–12.

Tan, Y., Xu, W., Li, S., & Chen, K. (2022). Augmented and virtual reality (AR/VR) for education and training in the AEC industry: A systematic review of research and applications. *Buildings*, 12(10), 1529.

Tene, T., Marcatoma Tixi, J. A., Palacios Robalino, M. D. L., Mendoza Salazar, M. J., Vacacela Gomez, C., & Bellucci, S. (2024, June). Integrating immersive technologies with STEM education: A systematic review. []. Frontiers Media SA.]. *Frontiers in Education*, 9, 1410163.

Tewari, V., Rahman, M., Mishra, A., Bajaj, K. K., & Shankar, A. U. (2023). Impact of Virtual Reality (Vr) and Augmented Reality (Ar) in Education. *Tuijin Jishu/Journal of Propulsion Technology, 44*(4), 1310–1318. https://doi.org/DOI: 10.52783/tjjpt.v44.i4.1014

Tham, J., McGrath, M., Duin, A. H., & Moses, J. (2018). Guest Editors' Introduction: Immersive Technologies and Writing Pedagogy. *Computers and Composition*, 50, 1–7. DOI: 10.1016/j.compcom.2018.08.001

Valladares Ríos, L., Acosta-Diaz, R., & Santana-Mancilla, P. C. (2023). Enhancing Self-Learning in Higher Education with Virtual and Augmented Reality Role Games: Students' Perceptions. *Virtual Worlds*, 2(4), 343–358. DOI: 10.3390/virtualworlds2040020

Van Merriënboer, J. J. G., & Sweller, J. (2005). Cognitive load theory and complex learning: Recent developments and future directions. *Educational Psychology Review*, 17(2), 147–177. DOI: 10.1007/s10648-005-3951-0

Vats, S., & Joshi, R. (2023). The Impact of Virtual Reality in Education: A Comprehensive Research Study. *International Working Conference on Transfer and Diffusion of IT*, 126–136.

Verner, I., Cuperman, D., Perez-Villalobos, H., Polishuk, A., & Gamer, S. (2022). Augmented and Virtual Reality Experiences for Learning Robotics and Training Integrative Thinking Skills. *Robotics (Basel, Switzerland)*, 11(5). Advance online publication. DOI: 10.3390/robotics11050090

Zhang, C., Wang, X., Fang, S., & Shi, X. (2022). Construction and Application of VR-AR Teaching System in Coal-Based Energy Education. *Sustainability (Switzerland)*, 14(23). Advance online publication. DOI: 10.3390/su142316033

Zhao, X., Ren, Y., & Cheah, K. S. L. (2023). Leading Virtual Reality (VR) and Augmented Reality (AR) in Education: Bibliometric and Content Analysis From the Web of Science (2018–2022). *SAGE Open*, 13(3). Advance online publication. DOI: 10.1177/21582440231190821

Chapter 14
Leveraging Data Analytics for Enhanced Academic Outcomes:
Strategies and Applications

Sakshi Saxena

Garden City University, Bangalore, India

Swetha Appaji Parivara

https://orcid.org/0009-0008-1215-154X

Presidency College, Bangalore, India

ABSTRACT

In the wake of the COVID-19 pandemic, educational institutions globally face unprecedented challenges, with data analytics emerging as a vital tool to bridge learning gaps across K-12 and higher education. This chapter explores how data analytics can transform education by personalizing learning, optimizing instructional strategies, and assessing academic progress. With access to vast amounts of data, institutions can make informed, data-driven decisions in curriculum design and resource allocation. By utilizing data sources such as demographics, engagement metrics, and performance data, educators gain insights into learning trends and outcomes. The chapter discusses practical applications, including adaptive learning tools and predictive analytics for early interventions to improve student retention. It also addresses challenges related to data privacy, equity, and ethical use. By embracing emerging technologies like AI, blockchain, and VR, educational institutions can foster a culture of continuous improvement, enhancing resilience and educational outcomes on a global scale.

DOI: 10.4018/979-8-3693-8191-5.ch014

INTRODUCTION

The educational landscape is transforming rapidly as institutions address diverse student needs and institutional goals. Educational institutions collect extensive data on learning styles, grades, attendance, and operational and financial factors, driving demand for robust data management and analytics in education (Greller & Drachsler, 2012). As educational platforms expand, the volume and complexity of data grow, enhancing the value of data evaluation. The COVID-19 pandemic, in particular, has prompted institutions to adopt data analytics to personalize learning, optimize strategies, and assess academic progress effectively. Demographic data, a critical component in this effort, informs educational practices by shedding light on student characteristics like age, gender, socio-economic status, and cultural background. Analyzing this data reveals performance patterns and disparities, enabling tailored instructional approaches that ensure equitable resource access.

Demographic data is collected through enrollment forms, surveys, and institutional records. When combined with engagement and performance metrics, demographic information provides insights that shape curriculum design and resource allocation. This enables institutions to foster inclusive learning environments that support success for all students. The pandemic has also highlighted existing educational challenges, including learning gaps and resource disparities. Data analytics offers educators strategic tools to analyze and respond effectively to diverse student needs.

The surge in interest in educational data analytics is fueled by advancements in big data and analytics technologies (Baker & Inventado, 2014). Tools for data aggregation and visualization tailored to education aid educators and teach students to communicate data effectively (Waskom, 2021). Data analytics plays a pivotal role in online learning, especially in higher education (Picciano, 2012), by revealing situational insights and addressing performance issues (Nistor & Hernández-Garcíac, 2018). For instance, Arnold et al. (2012) demonstrated the potential of data analytics to enhance student achievement, while Sibbetl (2009) underscored the collaborative opportunities enabled by new online learning technologies. Analytics in higher education allows institutions to explore and simulate instructional processes comprehensively (Nguyen, Gardner & Sheridan, 2020).

Many institutions now use Learning Management Systems (LMS) to monitor students, faculty, and administrative activities, collecting vast data volumes (Asif et al., 2017; Daniel, 2015). According to Bresciani et al. (2021), the ability to analyze and utilize extensive data is a key competitive differentiator. The development of data analytics also creates opportunities to address societal needs and global trends effectively (Nguyen, Gardner, & Sheridan, 2017). Murumba & Micheni (2017) highlighted that big data allows universities to strategically leverage IT resources to enhance educational quality and support students.

To fully harness analytics, colleges and universities should invest in data science programs and personnel. Data insights can illuminate student performance, highlight improvement areas, and enable targeted interventions, enhancing teaching strategies and ultimately improving educational outcomes. Adaptive learning systems offer another layer of customization, tailoring instructional approaches and support services to students' unique needs (Kerr, 2016).

Personalized resources and content derived from data insights boost student engagement, motivation, and retention, creating a more individualized learning environment. Active learning, tailored through analytics, makes lessons more engaging and relevant across various academic backgrounds (Donoghue et al., 2021; Romanow et al., 2020). Advanced data analysis tools also allow institutions to quantify and evaluate each aspect of a student's experience—from grades and attendance to test results and learning objectives. Through such analyses, institutions identify patterns and trends that provide valuable insights into student behavior and academic success.

Learning analytics also evaluates curricula effectiveness, instructional tactics, and teaching methods (Greller & Drachsler, 2012; Kerr, 2016). By examining data on student engagement, performance, and outcomes, educators can refine strategies to better meet student needs. Ethical and responsible data practices ensure that institutions safeguard student rights and privacy, enabling a balanced approach that enhances educational experiences without compromising trust. This proactive approach keeps institutions at the forefront of educational innovation and responsive to evolving societal and student needs.

In summary, data analytics presents significant opportunities for institutions to optimize educational practices. As data continues to grow in complexity and volume, educational institutions that embrace data-driven tools can better meet the diverse needs of students, educators, and society at large.

EMERGENCE OF DATA ANALYTICS IN EDUCATION

The rise of data analytics in education represents a shift from traditional assessments to data-driven approaches that enhance learning. Educational technologies like Edmodo and Schoology globally, and India's National Digital Education Architecture (NDEAR), use analytics to tailor learning experiences to individual student needs, adapting content based on strengths, weaknesses, and preferences. This personalized approach helps educators address learning gaps, improve teaching methods, and supports curriculum design. As data analytics becomes integral in education, it has the potential to elevate learning outcomes and foster growth within the ed-tech industry across both global and Indian contexts.

Global Perspective

The integration of data analytics in education gained traction in the early 2000s, especially in the U.S. and Europe. Educational institutions began using Learning Management Systems (LMS) like Blackboard and Moodle to collect data on student interactions, assignments, and grades, forming the basis for early analytics. A pioneering example is Purdue University's Course Signals system, launched in 2007, which used predictive analytics to identify students at risk of underperformance or dropout. By analyzing data on grades, attendance, and course engagement, the system issued real-time alerts, leading to significant improvements in student retention and performance.

As the advantages of data analytics became evident, institutions globally adopted more advanced tools. The Open University in the UK developed a comprehensive learning analytics platform that tracked over 250,000 students in its online courses. This system monitored metrics like login frequency, assignment time, and forum participation, providing personalized feedback and identifying students needing extra support. The initiative not only improved student satisfaction and retention but also informed course redesigns, underscoring the impact of data analytics in enhancing educational outcomes on a large scale.

Indian Perspective

In India, the rise of data analytics in education is closely tied to digital education platforms, spurred by initiatives like Digital India. Platforms such as Byju's, Unacademy, and the National Programme on Technology Enhanced Learning (NPTEL) utilize analytics to personalize learning and improve outcomes. Byju's, one of India's largest ed-tech companies, leverages data analytics to customize learning experiences. By tracking interactions with video lessons, quizzes, and assessments, Byju's can adapt its content to each student's learning pace and style. This adaptive approach, supported by data, has contributed to Byju's success with millions of users across India, exemplifying the impact of analytics on personalized education.

The Indian government also recognizes the value of data analytics for improving education. Initiatives like the National Digital Library of India (NDLI) and the Academic Bank of Credits (ABC) use data to make educational resources more accessible and to track academic progress effectively. NPTEL, a government-funded project, offers free courses primarily in engineering and technology. Through data analytics, NPTEL tracks student participation and performance, helping refine course content and better meet learner needs.

Indian institutions like the Indian Institute of Management (IIM) Bangalore have integrated data analytics into their practices. IIM Bangalore developed a learning analytics tool to monitor engagement and performance, aiding faculty in identifying students who may need additional support. The tool analyzes data from online discussions, assignments, and exams, providing timely insights that help improve student outcomes and instructional methods.

The emergence of data analytics in education, from early adopters like Purdue University to platforms like Byju's, marks a significant shift in educational practices. Globally and in India, analytics has become a powerful tool for enhancing student learning, personalizing instruction, and optimizing institutional processes. As technology advances, data analytics will continue to shape teaching and learning, transforming education across diverse contexts.

IMPORTANCE OF DATA ANALYTICS IN EDUCATION

Data analytics has become an essential tool in education, enhancing teaching quality, guiding informed decision-making, and promoting student success. With the growing use of digital technologies, educational institutions now generate vast amounts of data that, when analyzed effectively, can drive substantial improvements. Platforms like DreamBox and Khan Academy illustrate how adaptive learning, fueled by data analytics, customizes learning experiences, boosting engagement and comprehension by dynamically adjusting to each student's unique needs.

Figure 1. Data analytics in education

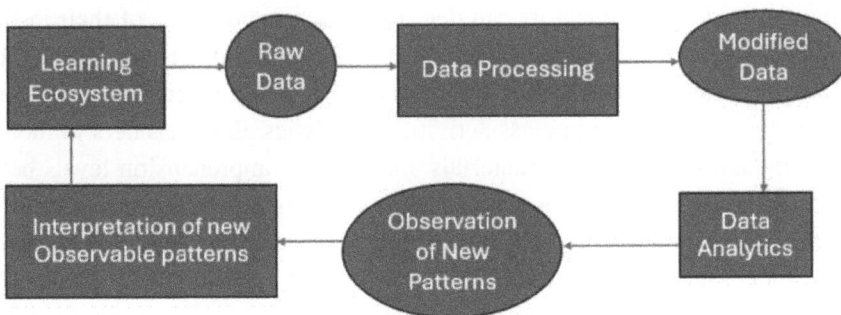

1. Enhancing Student Learning and Achievement

One of the most significant benefits of data analytics in education is its ability to improve student learning outcomes. By analyzing data from various sources, educators can identify patterns and trends in student performance, allowing for more targeted interventions and personalized learning experiences.

In many K-12 and higher education institutions, data analytics is used to create personalized learning pathways for students. For instance, platforms like Khan Academy utilize data analytics to track students' progress in real-time. By analyzing which concepts a student struggles with or excels at, the platform can adjust the content accordingly, providing additional resources or challenges as needed. This personalized approach ensures that students receive the right level of instruction, improving their overall learning outcomes.

Many schools and universities have implemented early warning systems (EWS) that leverage data analytics to identify students at risk of academic failure. For example, Georgia State University in the U.S. uses an EWS that tracks over 800 variables, including grades, attendance, and financial aid status. By analyzing this data, the system can predict which students are at risk of dropping out and trigger interventions such as academic advising or tutoring. As a result, Georgia State has significantly improved its retention and graduation rates, demonstrating the critical role of data analytics in supporting student success.

2. Improving Instructional Strategies

Data analytics empowers educators to refine teaching methods by providing insights into student engagement, comprehension, and assessment results. By examining these metrics, educators can determine the effectiveness of their instructional strategies and make data-driven adjustments. In a flipped classroom model, for example, students engage with pre-class materials like video lectures at home and apply their knowledge in class activities. Analytics allow teachers to monitor student interactions with these materials and assess comprehension levels before class, enabling them to tailor in-class sessions to focus on challenging topics.

Many institutions utilize learning analytics dashboards that offer real-time data on student performance. The University of Michigan's ECoach platform, for instance, provides instructors with analytics on student engagement, participation, and assessment results. This data enables instructors to personalize feedback, adapt teaching methods, and identify areas requiring additional support, enhancing student learning and engagement.

3. Data-Driven Decision Making in Curriculum Development

Data analytics is essential in curriculum development, providing actionable insights to improve educational quality and relevance. For instance, if standardized test data reveals consistent underperformance in math, schools might revise the curriculum to focus more on problem areas like algebra or geometry. Similarly, institutions like Arizona State University analyze online course data to identify when students struggle with specific modules, prompting curriculum adjustments to improve comprehension and engagement.

Data analytics also evaluates program effectiveness by examining graduation rates, job placements, and student satisfaction. For example, Georgia State University uses analytics to track students' progress through degree programs, identifying at-risk students early and offering tailored support, which has significantly improved graduation rates. In another case, a business school might analyze data showing that graduates face challenges in the job market, leading to curriculum updates that incorporate more practical skills or career readiness programs. This continuous, data-driven feedback loop keeps educational programs relevant, aligning them with student needs and job market demands.

4. Enhancing Institutional Efficiency and Accountability

Data analytics enhances efficiency and accountability in educational institutions by optimizing resource allocation and streamlining processes. For instance, the University of California, Irvine, used analytics to examine classroom utilization, identifying underused spaces and adjusting schedules accordingly to maximize occupancy. This proactive approach prevented resource wastage and ensured that space was effectively utilized across the campus.

Similarly, Georgia State University uses data analytics to manage faculty work-loads by tracking teaching hours, advising loads, and research output. This data-driven approach allows administrators to balance faculty responsibilities, preventing burnout and fostering a supportive environment for both educators and students.

Financial aid distribution also benefits significantly from data analytics. Arizona State University uses predictive models to identify students who are likely to succeed if provided with additional financial support. By analyzing academic performance and socioeconomic data, ASU directs financial aid to students with the highest potential impact, ensuring that scholarships and grants support those in genuine need.

Thus, data analytics enables educational institutions to not only optimize resources but also promote equitable access to education, ultimately enhancing institutional performance and accountability.

5. Promoting Equity and Inclusion

Data analytics plays a crucial role in advancing equity and inclusion within educational institutions (Clow, 2013; Nguyen, Gardner, and Sheridan, 2018). By examining data on student demographics, performance, and engagement, educators can identify achievement gaps among student groups based on factors like race, socioeconomic status, or gender. For instance, if data shows that students from low-income backgrounds are underperforming, educators can respond with targeted support, such as tutoring or mentoring, to bridge these gaps. This approach ensures equitable opportunities for success across diverse backgrounds.

Data analytics also guides the development of inclusive curricula by highlighting areas where certain groups are underrepresented. For example, by analyzing course enrollment patterns and student feedback, institutions can pinpoint programs lacking diversity and take steps to integrate broader perspectives. Such data-driven efforts support a more inclusive curriculum and help institutions respond to the unique needs of their student body.

Overall, data analytics enhances student learning, refines instructional strategies, and promotes equity, empowering educational institutions to make informed, impactful decisions. As the reliance on data-driven approaches grows, the role of analytics in shaping inclusive and effective education will continue to expand, fostering fairer learning environments for all students.

IMPROVING INSTRUCTIONAL STRATEGIES THROUGH DATA ANALYTICS

Data analytics has revolutionized teaching by providing valuable insights into student learning, engagement, and performance. Educators can now fine-tune their instructional strategies to improve learning outcomes and create more engaging classrooms. Through platforms like Google Classroom and Microsoft Teams, they can access real-time data that allows them to adapt their approaches, customizing instruction to better align with students' needs.

Figure 2. Improving instructional strategies through data analytics

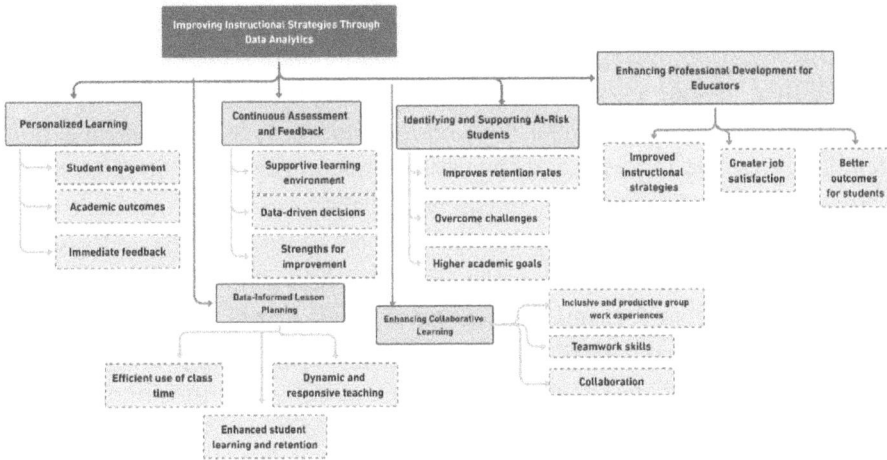

1. Personalized Learning

One of the most significant ways data analytics improves instructional strategies is by enabling personalized learning. Personalized learning tailors educational experiences to individual student needs, preferences, and learning styles. Data analytics allows educators to gather and analyze data on each student's progress, strengths, and areas of improvement, which can then be used to design customized learning pathways.

For example, Adaptive learning platforms like DreamBox and Knewton use data analytics to monitor student interactions with digital content. These platforms adjust the difficulty and pace of lessons based on real-time data about a student's performance. For instance, if a student struggles with a particular math concept, the platform might offer additional practice problems or present the concept in a different way. Conversely, if a student excels, the platform can introduce more advanced material. This adaptability ensures that each student is challenged appropriately and receives the support they need to succeed.

Impact: Personalized learning through adaptive technologies has been shown to improve student engagement and academic outcomes. Students are more likely to stay motivated when learning experiences are tailored to their needs, and they benefit from immediate feedback and targeted support.

2. Data-Informed Lesson Planning

Data analytics allows educators to refine their lesson plans by identifying which instructional methods are most effective for their students. By analyzing data on student performance, engagement, and feedback, teachers can determine which aspects of their lessons are working well and which need improvement.

In the flipped classroom model, students are introduced to new content at home (often through video lectures) and spend class time engaging in interactive activities that reinforce what they've learned. Data analytics plays a crucial role in this approach by tracking student engagement with pre-class materials and assessing their understanding before they come to class. Teachers can use this data to adjust their in-class activities, focusing on areas where students need the most help.

For example, if data reveals that many students struggled with a particular concept in the pre-class assignment, the teacher can dedicate more class time to collaborative exercises or discussions around that topic. Conversely, if students demonstrate strong understanding, the teacher can move on to more advanced material or application-based activities.

Impact: Data-informed lesson planning leads to more efficient use of class time, allowing educators to focus on areas where students need the most support. It also enables more dynamic and responsive teaching, which can enhance student learning and retention.

3. Continuous Assessment and Feedback

Data analytics facilitates continuous assessment and feedback, enabling educators to monitor student progress in real-time and provide timely interventions. Traditional assessment methods, such as end-of-term exams, often provide feedback too late to be actionable. In contrast, data analytics allows for ongoing assessment that informs instruction throughout the learning process.

In case of Formative assessments, such as quizzes, polls, and interactive exercises, digital learning platforms can be integrated to collect data on student understanding as they progress through a course. Learning analytics tools can then analyze this data to identify patterns, such as which students are consistently struggling with certain concepts or which topics require further clarification.

Educators can use these insights to adjust their teaching strategies, offer additional resources, or provide personalized feedback to students. For instance, if a formative assessment reveals that a large percentage of the class is struggling with a particular topic, the teacher might revisit the material, employ different teaching methods, or assign supplementary exercises.

Impact: Continuous assessment and feedback foster a more responsive and supportive learning environment. Students benefit from receiving timely feedback that helps them understand their strengths and areas for improvement, while educators can make data-driven decisions to enhance their instruction.

4. Enhancing Collaborative Learning

Collaborative learning, where students work together to solve problems or complete tasks, is a powerful instructional strategy that promotes deeper understanding and critical thinking. Data analytics can enhance collaborative learning by providing insights into group dynamics, participation levels, and the effectiveness of collaboration.

Educational platforms like Google Classroom and Microsoft Teams enable collaborative learning by allowing students to work together on assignments, participate in discussions, and share resources. Data analytics tools integrated into these platforms can track participation levels, identify which students are actively contributing, and measure the effectiveness of group work.

For instance, analytics might reveal that certain students are not participating as much as others, prompting the teacher to intervene and encourage more balanced participation. Additionally, data can be used to assess the outcomes of collaborative projects, helping educators understand which group configurations and activities are most effective.

Impact: By enhancing collaborative learning through data analytics, educators can create more inclusive and productive group work experiences. Students develop essential teamwork skills and benefit from diverse perspectives, while educators gain insights into how to structure and support collaboration effectively.

5. Identifying and Supporting At-Risk Students

Data analytics plays a critical role in identifying students who may be at risk of falling behind or dropping out. By analyzing data such as attendance, assignment completion, and assessment performance, educators can identify early warning signs and provide targeted interventions to support at-risk students.

Early Warning Systems (EWS) use predictive analytics to identify students who are at risk of academic failure or disengagement. These systems analyze a wide range of data points, including grades, attendance, and participation in extracurricular activities, to generate risk scores for each student.

Educators can use these risk scores to implement proactive measures, such as personalized academic counseling, tutoring, or mentoring. For example, if an EWS indicates that a student is at risk due to declining grades and poor attendance, the school might arrange a meeting with the student to discuss their challenges and offer support.

Impact: Identifying and supporting at-risk students through data analytics helps prevent academic failure and improves retention rates. By providing timely and targeted interventions, educators can help students overcome challenges and achieve their academic goals.

6. Enhancing Professional Development for Educators

Data analytics is not only valuable for improving student outcomes but also for enhancing educators' professional development. By analyzing data on teaching practices and student outcomes, institutions can identify areas where educators may benefit from additional training or support.

Some educational institutions use data analytics to assess the effectiveness of professional development programs for teachers. For instance, data might reveal that teachers who participated in a particular training session on classroom management techniques saw improvements in student behavior and engagement. This insight can guide future professional development efforts, ensuring that educators receive training that is most relevant and impactful.

Impact: By aligning professional development with data-driven insights, institutions can ensure that educators are equipped with the skills and knowledge they need to succeed. This leads to improved instructional strategies, greater job satisfaction for teachers, and better outcomes for students.

Data analytics is transforming instructional strategies by enabling personalized learning, data-driven lesson planning, and continuous assessment, creating more effective and responsive learning environments. As schools increasingly adopt data-driven methods, educators can better adapt teaching to meet diverse student needs, enhancing engagement and improving outcomes.

DATA ANALYTICS IN INSTITUTIONAL DECISION MAKING

Data analytics is essential for decision-making in education, helping institutions improve outcomes, allocate resources, and ensure accountability. By leveraging data, schools can make informed choices that enhance educational quality and student success. Tools like Civitas Learning analyze academic and behavioral data to identify at-risk students, supporting timely interventions that boost retention.

Figure 3.

Importance of Data Analytics in Institutional Decision Making

- **Strategic Planning and Resource Allocation**
  - Cost savings
  - Utilization of facilities
  - Alignment of
    - Institutional Resources
    - Student needs
    - Academci goals
- **Enhancing Student Retention and Success**
  - Enhanced student retention efforts
  - Higher graduation rates
  - Rreduced dropout rates
  - Academic achievement goals
- **Informing Curriculum Development and Program Evaluation**
  - Relevant
  - Competitive
  - Alignment of
    - Student Interest
    - Job market demand → Increased Emplaoyability & Instiution Reputation
- **Improving Financial Management and Accountability**
  - Efficient use of institutional resources
  - Better support for students
  - Enhanced financial sustainability
- **Supporting Accreditation and Compliance**
  - Regulatory requirements
  - Accreditation status
  - Enhanced quality
- **Enhancing Faculty Development and Performance Evaluation**
  - Eexcellence in teaching and research
  - Professional growth

Data Analytics in Institutional Decision Making

1. Strategic Planning and Resource Allocation

Data analytics is essential for institutional decision-making, particularly in strategic planning and resource allocation. For example, by analyzing student enrollment data, a university might discover that a specific classroom is consistently underutilized on certain days. This insight allows administrators to adjust class schedules or reallocate that space for other activities, ensuring more efficient use of facilities.

Additionally, institutions can examine data on student course preferences, as seen at Georgia State University, which has used analytics to identify popular courses and improve offerings accordingly. By aligning course offerings with student demand, schools can boost enrollment rates. This data-driven approach results in cost savings, improved facility utilization, and a better alignment of resources with student needs and academic goals.

2. Enhancing Student Retention and Success

Data analytics is vital for student retention and success initiatives. By analyzing performance, engagement, and behavior data, institutions can identify at-risk students and implement targeted interventions. For instance, Georgia State University utilizes a predictive analytics system that tracks over 800 variables related to student success, significantly increasing graduation rates through timely and personalized support. Similarly, universities can analyze data on grades, attendance, and financial aid status to develop predictive models for identifying students likely to face academic challenges. These data-driven approaches enable early interventions such as academic advising and tutoring, ultimately improving graduation rates and reducing dropout rates.

3. Informing Curriculum Development and Program Evaluation

Data analytics is essential for curriculum development and program evaluation, enabling institutions to make informed decisions based on student outcomes, enrollment trends, and job market demands. For example, by analyzing labor market data, universities can identify emerging skills in high demand. This insight may lead to the creation of new programs, such as data science or cybersecurity. The Indian Institute of Technology (IIT) Madras exemplifies this approach by using data analytics to align its curriculum with industry trends. By examining student placements and job market forecasts, IIT Madras has developed programs in artificial intelligence and machine learning, ensuring graduates are equipped for in-demand careers. This data-driven approach to curriculum development enhances employability, aligns educational offerings with market needs, and strengthens institutional reputation.

4. Improving Financial Management and Accountability

Data analytics offers critical insights for financial management and accountability in educational institutions, enabling informed decisions regarding budgeting, tuition pricing, and financial aid distribution. By analyzing financial data, institutions can enhance their financial operations and allocate resources effectively to support institutional priorities and student success.

For instance, data analytics can optimize financial aid distribution by identifying patterns in student demographics, academic performance, and retention rates. This allows institutions to predict which students would benefit most from additional support, ensuring that scholarships and grants are targeted to those in greatest need and likely to succeed. The University of Southern California (USC) exemplifies this approach by analyzing student demographics and financial need to tailor financial aid packages for its diverse student body. This data-driven strategy has improved access and retention rates among students.

By leveraging data analytics, institutions can achieve more efficient use of resources, provide better support for students, and enhance financial sustainability, ultimately fostering a more equitable educational environment.

5. Supporting Accreditation and Compliance

Accreditation and compliance are essential for educational institutions, ensuring programs meet established standards. Data analytics plays a vital role in this process by aggregating and analyzing data on student outcomes, faculty qualifications, and institutional performance, simplifying the generation of accurate accreditation reports. For example, universities often utilize analytics platforms to track key performance indicators (KPIs) like graduation rates and student satisfaction, which are critical for accreditation. This not only streamlines reporting but also provides insights for continuous improvement. By leveraging data analytics, institutions can maintain accreditation status and enhance the quality of their educational offerings.

6. Enhancing Faculty Development and Performance Evaluation

Data analytics is increasingly utilized in faculty development and performance evaluation, enabling institutions to enhance teaching effectiveness and research productivity. By analyzing data from teaching evaluations, research output, and student outcomes, institutions can offer targeted professional development and recognize faculty achievements. Many colleges use faculty performance dashboards to aggregate this data, providing a comprehensive view of faculty performance. For instance, a faculty member with low student evaluations may receive training on active learning techniques, while another with high evaluations and significant research output might be recognized through awards. This data-driven approach fosters a culture of excellence in teaching and research, ensuring continuous professional growth for faculty members.

The data analytics transforms institutional decision-making by offering insights for optimizing resource allocation, enhancing student success, informing curriculum development, and supporting accreditation. As the education sector evolves, the significance of data analytics in driving innovation and continuous improvement will only increase, enhancing the overall effectiveness of educational operations.

ROLE OF TEACHERS IN DATA-DRIVEN EDUCATION

Data analytics is transforming the role of teachers in education, shifting their traditional role as mere content deliverers to becoming facilitators of personalized, data-driven learning experiences. Educators now have access to vast amounts of data, enabling them to make informed decisions that enhance teaching methodologies and assess student progress more effectively.

1. Improving Teaching Methodologies

Data analytics empowers teachers to tailor their instructional strategies based on individual and group learning patterns. By analyzing data from various assessments, engagement metrics, and even behavioral data, teachers can identify the strengths and weaknesses of students, thereby adapting their teaching styles to address specific needs.

Example: A math teacher using a learning management system (LMS) can identify students who consistently struggle with fractions. With this data, the teacher can provide additional resources, such as video tutorials or interactive quizzes, to reinforce that concept. Additionally, real-time feedback on performance can help the teacher tweak lesson plans in response to what students are finding difficult.

2. Personalizing Learning

Data analytics significantly enhances personalized learning experiences by allowing educators to tailor instruction to individual student needs. Tools from platforms like LinkedIn, Coursera, Udemy, Khan Academy, and Duolingo evaluate student interaction data to create customized learning pathways. These adaptive learning systems adjust content difficulty and type based on each student's strengths and weaknesses. For example, students with exceptional needs benefit from individualized education plans (IEPs) that define their goals and accommodations.

In the Flipped Classroom model, students study new content online at their own pace, freeing up class time for personalized instruction and collaborative projects. Various instructional models, such as the Montessori Method, the Success Academy Model, the PACE (Program for Accelerated College Education) Model, the KIPP (Knowledge Is Power Program) Model, and RTI (Response to Intervention), ensure every student receives the support needed for academic success.

An example includes an English teacher using a digital platform to track a student's reading habits, identifying areas for improvement like comprehension or vocabulary. Based on this data, the teacher can recommend targeted reading materials and exercises. The Summit Learning Program, implemented in some U.S.

schools, employs data analytics to personalize education, resulting in increased student engagement and academic growth.

3. Assessing Student Progress

Continuous assessment is another key area where data analytics is helping educators. Instead of relying solely on periodic tests or exams, teachers can use real-time data to continuously monitor student progress. This allows for more timely interventions and better support for students who may be falling behind.

Example: A science teacher uses an LMS to track students' progress on lab assignments. Data on time spent on tasks, completion rates, and accuracy provides insights into which students need additional support and which ones are ready for more advanced material. In Singapore, many schools have adopted data analytics platforms that allow teachers to track student progress in real-time. Teachers can view visual dashboards that break down individual student performance in detail, enabling them to intervene early and provide personalized feedback. This system has helped improve overall student outcomes in key areas like mathematics and science.

4. Enabling Evidence-Based Decisions

Data-driven insights help teachers make evidence-based decisions about their instructional strategies. Rather than relying on intuition or past practices, educators can analyze data trends to determine the effectiveness of various teaching methods. This leads to more informed pedagogical choices that are aligned with student needs.

Example: A teacher might use data analytics to compare the effectiveness of traditional lectures with flipped classroom models. If data shows that students perform better with interactive activities, the teacher can adjust the classroom setup to include more hands-on exercises.

5. Supporting Professional Development

While data analytics offers immense potential, its effectiveness is tied to how well teachers understand and use these tools. Professional development is critical to ensuring that educators have the necessary skills to analyze data effectively and translate it into actionable teaching strategies. Teachers need ongoing training in how to interpret data, use data dashboards, and integrate insights into their instruction.

Example: School districts across the globe are now investing in teacher training programs focused on data literacy. Workshops on how to use analytics platforms, interpret performance data, and implement data-driven interventions are becoming common. In India, the Ministry of Education has launched several initiatives to train teachers in the use of technology and data analytics tools. These programs focus on building teachers' data literacy skills so they can better understand and act on student performance data.

6. Collaboration and Data Sharing

Data analytics enhances collaboration among educators by enabling them to share insights across classrooms and grade levels, providing a comprehensive view of student performance and facilitating coordinated support. For instance, teachers can analyze and discuss a student's performance data across different subjects to identify patterns that impact overall learning. If a student excels in math but struggles in language arts, teachers can collaborate to create interdisciplinary strategies that utilize the student's strengths in math while addressing the challenges in language arts. This collective approach ensures that students receive well-rounded support tailored to their unique needs.

In today's data-driven education landscape, teachers are crucial in interpreting and applying data to enhance student outcomes. By utilizing data analytics tools, educators can improve teaching methods, personalize learning experiences, and assess progress in real time. However, ongoing professional development is vital to equip teachers with the necessary skills to analyze data and integrate it into their instruction. This approach not only benefits students but also transforms teaching into a more strategic and evidence-based practice.

CHALLENGES AND ETHICAL CONSIDERATIONS

Integrating data analytics in education offers significant benefits but also raises challenges and ethical considerations that must be managed responsibly (Daniel, 2019; Klein et al., 2019). Ethical concerns are paramount, as exemplified by the Family Educational Rights and Privacy Act (FERPA) in the U.S., which mandates secure student data management. Similarly, India's National Education Policy (NEP) 2020 emphasizes ethical data practices, ensuring that student information is protected and used fairly.

1. Data Privacy and Security

Challenge: A major challenge in data analytics for education is safeguarding student privacy and data security. Institutions collect sensitive information, including personal details and academic records, which can be vulnerable to breaches if not properly managed. Due to the sensitive nature of this data, educational institutions are often targets of cyberattacks. Ensuring secure data transmission and storage can be difficult, especially with limited IT resources. Additionally, many stakeholders may not fully understand what data is collected, how it is used, or their rights regarding this data. Institutions may struggle with data reduction principles, leading to unnecessary data collection for analytics. Furthermore, inadequate training on ethical data practices among staff and educators can result in unintentional data misuse or policy violations. Many institutions also rely on third-party platforms for learning management and analytics, which raises further privacy concerns.

Ethical Consideration: To protect student information, institutions must adopt robust data protection measures, including encryption, access controls, and regular security audits. Compliance with regulations such as the General Data Protection Regulation (GDPR) in Europe and the Family Educational Rights and Privacy Act (FERPA) in the United States is essential for the proper handling of educational data. In India, technology plays a pivotal role in shaping policies, with the Digital Personal Data Protection (DPDP) Act, 2023, governing the processing of digital personal data collected both online and offline. Establishing strong privacy governance is vital for minimizing economic risks and safeguarding institutional reputations, contributing to the creation of a transparent and sustainable future. Implementing effective cybersecurity measures, such as encryption, multi-factor authentication, and frequent security audits, is crucial for protecting sensitive data from breaches and unauthorized access.

Example: The University of California experienced a significant data breach in 2021, affecting hundreds of thousands of individuals, highlighting the importance of stringent data security practices in educational institutions.

2. Bias and Fairness in Data Analytics

Challenge: Data analytics systems can unintentionally perpetuate or even exacerbate biases present in the data. If the data used for analysis reflects historical inequalities or is not representative of the diverse student population, the outcomes may unfairly disadvantage certain groups of students.

Ethical Consideration: Institutions must ensure that their data analytics practices are fair and unbiased. This involves using diverse data sources, regularly auditing algorithms for bias, and including a diverse range of stakeholders in the decision-making process to ensure that the tools developed are equitable.

Example: A predictive analytics tool used by some schools to identify at-risk students might disproportionately flag minority or low-income students as being at higher risk, not because of their abilities but due to biased data. Regular reviews and adjustments of these tools are essential to prevent such outcomes.

3. Transparency and Accountability

Challenge: The complexity of data analytics systems can lead to a lack of transparency in how decisions are made, which can cause distrust among students, parents, and educators. Without clear communication about how data is used and the criteria for decision-making, stakeholders may feel alienated or skeptical of the results.

Ethical Consideration: Institutions must strive for transparency in their data analytics processes by clearly communicating the purpose, methods, and implications of data-driven decisions. Additionally, there should be mechanisms for accountability, where students and educators can challenge or appeal decisions made by automated systems.

Example: In some cases, students have been automatically assigned to remedial courses based on analytics-driven assessments without understanding why. Clear explanations and the opportunity for students to discuss their placement with academic advisors can help mitigate this issue.

4. Ethical Use of Data

Challenge: The ethical use of data extends beyond privacy to include the responsible application of insights derived from analytics. For example, while predictive analytics can identify students who are likely to struggle, there is a risk of creating a self-fulfilling prophecy where students are treated differently based on predictions rather than their actual performance.

Ethical Consideration: Institutions must use data to empower and support students rather than to limit their opportunities. This involves setting clear ethical guidelines for how data can be used and ensuring that all analytics-driven interventions are designed to benefit students.

Example: Some schools have adopted "nudge" techniques, where analytics are used to encourage positive behaviors, like sending reminders to students about deadlines. While these can be effective, they must be carefully designed to avoid excessive surveillance or pressure on students.

The challenges and ethical considerations surrounding data analytics in education highlight the need for responsible and transparent practices. As institutions navigate issues of privacy, bias, and accountability, they must ensure that data-driven decisions are made with fairness and equity in mind.

INTERDISCIPLINARY USE OF DATA ANALYTICS IN EDUCATION

Data analytics has the transformative power to break down traditional academic silos and foster interdisciplinary research and collaboration within educational institutions. By integrating data from various fields—such as science, technology, social sciences, and the arts—educators and administrators can develop holistic insights into student learning, institutional practices, and academic success. This interdisciplinary approach can significantly enhance both teaching strategies and institutional outcomes.

Figure 4. Interdisciplinary use of data analytics in education

1. Enhancing Collaborative Learning and Research

Data analytics allows educators and researchers from different disciplines to come together and analyze diverse datasets, facilitating collaboration across departments. This enables a more comprehensive understanding of complex educational problems, as insights from multiple fields can be combined to create innovative solutions. Example: A collaboration between psychology and education departments can use data analytics to study the cognitive processes involved in learning. By combining data on student performance with cognitive metrics, researchers can gain insights into how different teaching methods affect memory retention, problem-solving, and creativity. At Stanford University, interdisciplinary teams use data analytics to study how students learn in online environments. By combining insights from computer science, education, and behavioral psychology, these teams have been able to optimize the design of digital learning platforms, leading to more engaging and effective learning experiences.

2. Integration of STEM and Humanities Data

One of the most beneficial aspects of interdisciplinary data analytics is its ability to bridge the gap between STEM (Science, Technology, Engineering, and Math) and the humanities. By analyzing data from both fields, institutions can develop a more rounded educational approach that values both quantitative and qualitative learning outcomes. Example: A university's engineering and history departments can work together to analyze data on how technological advancements have impacted societal structures. Using data analytics, students can explore trends and make predictions about the future based on historical patterns, thereby fostering a deeper understanding of both technology and human development. Harvard University's SEAS (School of Engineering and Applied Sciences) and its History Department collaborate on courses that combine data analytics and historical inquiry. By using computational tools to analyze historical data, students can visualize social changes over time, leading to a richer understanding of history and engineering's role in society.

3. Data-Driven Curriculum Design Across Disciplines

Data analytics can inform curriculum design by incorporating insights from different disciplines to address real-world challenges. By analyzing educational outcomes and student performance data across various departments, institutions can create interdisciplinary programs that foster critical thinking, creativity, and problem-solving. Example: A university might use data analytics to track the success of interdisciplinary courses that blend economics with environmental science.

If data shows that students in these courses perform better in critical thinking and problem-solving skills, the institution can invest in more interdisciplinary curricula to foster these skills across disciplines. The University of Michigan uses data analytics to design interdisciplinary programs that combine business, law, and public policy. Data collected from student performance in these programs is used to continuously refine curricula, ensuring that students are equipped with skills that are relevant in an increasingly interconnected world.

4. Improving Institutional Practices through Interdisciplinary Data

Data analytics allows educational institutions to make more informed decisions about institutional practices by analyzing data from various departments. This can lead to better resource allocation, optimized student support systems, and more effective teaching strategies that consider the broader context of student learning. Example: A university's health sciences, education, and counselling departments can collaborate to analyze data related to student well-being. By understanding the correlation between academic performance, physical health, and mental wellness, the institution can develop more targeted support services, such as wellness programs, tutoring, or counselling. Arizona State University integrates data from various departments—including student services, academic affairs, and campus health—to gain a complete picture of student success. By analyzing interdisciplinary data, they have improved student retention and graduation rates by addressing the full range of factors affecting student outcomes, from academic performance to social engagement.

5. Cross-Disciplinary Predictive Analytics

Predictive analytics, powered by interdisciplinary data, is a powerful tool for foreseeing educational outcomes and identifying students who may require additional support. By combining data from different fields, predictive models become more accurate and actionable, leading to better institutional practices and learning outcomes. Example: A predictive model that combines data from psychology, computer science, and education can identify students who are at risk of dropping out. The model might include academic data, attendance records, and even social engagement metrics to provide a full picture of student performance and identify early warning signs. Georgia State University has implemented an interdisciplinary predictive analytics system that uses data from multiple sources, including academic records, financial aid, and student engagement metrics, to improve retention rates. The system identifies students at risk of failing and provides timely interventions, leading to a significant increase in graduation rates.

6. Supporting Interdisciplinary Learning Experiences

Data analytics can also play a role in fostering interdisciplinary learning experiences for students. By analyzing data from various academic fields, institutions can create interdisciplinary projects and assignments that promote collaboration among students from different majors. Example: A data science project could involve students from computer science, sociology, and education, where the team works together to analyze data related to online learning behaviors. The project would benefit from different disciplinary perspectives, leading to richer insights and a deeper understanding of the topic. The Massachusetts Institute of Technology (MIT) runs interdisciplinary student programs where students from various fields, such as economics, biology, and political science, use data analytics to solve real-world challenges. These programs have resulted in several innovative projects, from sustainable energy solutions to public health initiatives.

7. Building Interdisciplinary Competencies Among Students

Using data analytics across disciplines helps students develop interdisciplinary competencies that are increasingly valued in the modern workforce. By analyzing data from multiple fields, students can enhance their problem-solving skills and become more adaptable to a variety of career paths. Example: A course that combines data analytics with environmental science might require students to analyze data on global climate patterns, economic impacts, and social behaviors. This helps students develop a multifaceted understanding of the issue, preparing them for careers that demand interdisciplinary knowledge. The University of Sydney offers a program where students from different disciplines collaborate on data-driven research projects. Through this interdisciplinary approach, students gain valuable experience in working across fields, a skill set that has become increasingly important in sectors like technology, healthcare, and policy-making.

The interdisciplinary use of data analytics in education not only enhances learning outcomes but also fosters a collaborative culture within educational institutions. By integrating data from various fields, educators and researchers can gain deeper insights into student success, improve curriculum design, and refine institutional practices. This interdisciplinary approach not only prepares students for the complexities of the real world but also helps institutions stay innovative and adaptable in an ever-evolving educational landscape.

EMERGING TRENDS AND TECHNOLOGIES IN EDUCATION

The education sector is evolving quickly due to advancements in technology and data analytics. These emerging trends have the potential to transform delivery, personalization, and assessment, resulting in more effective and equitable learning experiences. Technologies like AI, blockchain, and VR are reshaping education; for instance, Coursera uses AI to customize learning paths, blockchain enhances credential verification security, and VR platforms like zSpace provide immersive environments to help students grasp complex concepts.

1. Artificial Intelligence (AI) and Machine Learning

AI and machine learning are becoming increasingly integrated into educational platforms, enabling more personalized and adaptive learning experiences. These technologies can analyze vast amounts of data to understand each student's learning style, preferences, and challenges, tailoring instruction to meet individual needs. Example: Tools like IBM's Watson Education use AI to provide personalized learning paths for students, offering recommendations and resources based on their progress and learning behaviors. This can help students grasp complex concepts more effectively and at their own pace.

AI-powered adaptive learning systems are transforming traditional education models by making learning more student-centered and responsive to individual needs. As these systems become more sophisticated, they can offer even more granular insights, enabling educators to provide targeted support and resources.

2. Learning Analytics and Educational Data Mining

Learning analytics involves the collection and analysis of data related to student learning and behavior to improve educational outcomes. Educational data mining goes a step further by applying data mining techniques to educational data, uncovering patterns and relationships that can inform instructional strategies and curriculum design. For example, universities are increasingly using learning analytics platforms such as Moodle and Canvas to monitor student engagement in online courses. These systems provide dashboards that track student participation, assignment submissions, and quiz performance, alerting instructors to students who may need additional support, allowing for timely interventions.

Additionally, tools like Tableau and Google Data Studio help educators create visualizations and dashboards to uncover patterns and trends in educational data. Civitas Learning and Brightspace Insights utilize predictive analytics to identify at-risk students and suggest interventions. Learning analytics and educational data mining provide educators with actionable insights that can enhance teaching effectiveness, improve student engagement, and increase retention rates. As these tools evolve, they will offer even deeper insights, allowing for more predictive and preventative approaches to education.

3. Blockchain for Credentialing and Student Records

Blockchain technology is gaining attention in education for its potential to revolutionize the management of student records and credentials. Its decentralized and secure nature makes blockchain an ideal solution for storing and verifying educational credentials, transcripts, and achievements. For example, the Massachusetts Institute of Technology (MIT) has pioneered the use of blockchain for issuing digital diplomas, enabling graduates to securely share their credentials with employers and other institutions. This system ensures the authenticity of credentials and simplifies the verification process.

Various tools and platforms are emerging to facilitate blockchain integration in education. Learning Machine, for instance, allows institutions to issue secure digital diplomas on the blockchain, while Blockcerts provides an open standard for creating and sharing verifiable digital certificates. Additionally, Everledger focuses on maintaining transparent records of credentials, enhancing security and trust in the credentialing process.

Blockchain can streamline the management of student records, making it easier for students to control and share their academic achievements. This technology also offers the potential to create a more transparent and equitable system for credentialing, where all educational achievements are recorded and recognized.

4. Virtual and Augmented Reality (VR/AR) in Education

Virtual and augmented reality technologies are being used to create immersive learning experiences that go beyond traditional textbooks and lectures. These technologies can simulate real-world environments, allowing students to engage in hands-on learning in a controlled, virtual setting. For example, medical schools are increasingly using VR simulations, such as Osso VR and Immersive Touch, to train students in surgical procedures, providing them with a risk-free environment to practice and refine their skills. Similarly, AR applications like Merge Cube and Zspace are used in classrooms to bring abstract concepts to life, allowing students to visualize complex molecules in chemistry or explore historical events interactively.

VR and AR are transforming education by making learning more interactive, engaging, and experiential. These technologies have the potential to improve understanding and retention of complex concepts, particularly in fields that require practical, hands-on experience. With tools like Google Expeditions and Unity, educators can create customized immersive experiences that cater to diverse learning needs, further enhancing the educational landscape.

5. Gamification and Game-Based Learning

Gamification involves the use of game design elements in non-game contexts, while game-based learning utilizes actual games to teach specific skills or concepts. Both approaches are increasingly being used in education to enhance student motivation, engagement, and learning outcomes. For example, platforms like Kahoot! and Duolingo incorporate gamification elements, such as points, leaderboards, and challenges, to make learning more engaging. These tools have been particularly effective in language learning and basic skills development, where frequent practice and reinforcement are key to mastery.

Other notable tools include Quizizz, which allows teachers to create interactive quizzes that students can complete at their own pace, and Classcraft, which transforms classroom management into a role-playing game to encourage positive behavior and teamwork. Additionally, Minecraft: Education Edition provides a game-based learning environment where students can collaborate on projects and explore subjects like history and science in an interactive way.

Gamification and game-based learning have been shown to increase student motivation and engagement, leading to better retention and understanding of the material. As these approaches continue to evolve, they will likely become integral to the educational landscape, particularly in online and hybrid learning environments.

CONCLUSION

The integration of data analytics in education is transforming academic achievement and enhancing the learning experience. By systematically analyzing educational data, institutions can gain critical insights into teaching, learning, and administration, leading to improved academic outcomes and more effective instructional strategies. Data analytics allows for continuous assessment of educational initiatives, enabling real-time evaluations of teaching methods, curriculum changes, and interventions. For instance, institutions can analyze whether new teaching approaches help students understand complex concepts or if curricula need adjustments to better meet learner needs. This data-driven approach informs decisions on curriculum development, instructional strategies, and resource allocation, making educational practices more effective and personalized.

Emerging technologies like artificial intelligence (AI), blockchain, and virtual reality (VR) further enhance data analytics' role in education. AI can analyze student data to create personalized learning paths, while blockchain ensures secure and verifiable credentialing. VR offers immersive learning environments, allowing students to engage with concepts interactively, deepening understanding and fostering enthusiasm for learning. Together, these advancements make the educational process more adaptive, efficient, and responsive to the diverse needs of all learners.

The integration of data analytics and emerging technologies in education heralds a transformative era, enhancing academic achievement and the overall learning experience. By systematically analyzing a variety of educational data, institutions can derive valuable insights that improve teaching methodologies, personalize learning, and optimize administrative processes. This data-driven approach allows for continuous assessment of educational initiatives, enabling real-time evaluations of teaching methods, curriculum changes, and interventions. Consequently, institutions can make informed decisions that enhance academic performance and adapt educational practices to meet diverse learner needs.

Advanced technologies such as artificial intelligence (AI), blockchain, and virtual reality (VR) further amplify the impact of data analytics in education. AI can create personalized learning paths by analyzing student data, identifying strengths and weaknesses, and tailoring instruction accordingly. Blockchain technology ensures secure and verifiable credentialing, while VR offers immersive learning environments that engage students in hands-on experiences. Together, these advancements foster a more adaptive, efficient, and responsive educational landscape.

However, the integration of technology into education presents challenges. While technology democratizes access to resources, providing tools that extend beyond traditional textbooks, it also raises concerns about the digital divide. Not all students have equal access to technological resources, which can exacerbate educational disparities based on socioeconomic status and geographic location. Additionally, over-reliance on digital tools may detract from traditional teaching methods and critical thinking, leading to distractions and superficial engagement.

Privacy and cybersecurity concerns also emerge with the increased collection of student data through these technologies. Institutions must safeguard sensitive information while balancing the need to utilize data for educational improvement. Continuous professional development for educators is essential to ensure they remain adept at using these evolving tools effectively.

In the global context, data analytics has significant implications for both developed and developing nations. In India, with its vast and diverse student population, data analytics can help address educational disparities by identifying gaps in access and quality. Personalized learning initiatives can bridge the divide between urban and rural education, tailoring instruction to meet diverse needs.

Globally, data analytics is revolutionizing how academic institutions approach teaching, learning, and administration. It enhances student engagement, identifies strengths and weaknesses, and refines personalized learning experiences. This shift toward data-driven education fosters informed decision-making, greater efficiency, and improved academic outcomes. The interdisciplinary application of data analytics promotes collaboration among educators, administrators, and researchers, leading to innovative solutions and improved curriculum design.

The strategic application of data analytics provides a powerful framework for enhancing academic outcomes. It enables proactive student support, personalizes learning, refines educational interventions, and fosters evidence-based decision-making. As institutions adopt data-driven approaches, they will be better equipped to create responsive, inclusive, and innovative learning environments.

Ultimately, data analytics offers the potential to elevate academic performance, promote equity, and ensure education evolves to meet the challenges of the 21st century. By embracing these technological trends, educational institutions can foster a dynamic and individualized learning environment that adapts to each student's needs. AI and machine learning will increasingly provide tailored experiences while identifying structural inequalities in educational access, enabling targeted interventions for underrepresented groups. This approach not only enhances student success but also enriches the educational ecosystem, empowering educators and administrators to cultivate a culture of innovation and continuous improvement. The ongoing development of these technologies will further transform the teaching and learning process, creating a brighter future for students worldwide.

REFERENCES

Arnold, K., & Pistilli, M. D. (2012). Course Signals: Using Learning Analytics to Increase Student Success. *in Proceedings of the 2nd International Conference on Learning Analytics and Knowledge*, ACM, 267–270.

Asif, R., Merceron, A., Ali, S. A., & Haider, N. G. (2017). Analyzing undergraduate students' performance using educational data mining. *Computers & Education*, 113, 177–194. DOI: 10.1016/j.compedu.2017.05.007

Bresciani, S., Ciampi, F., Meli, F., & Ferraris, A. (2021). Using big data for co-innovation processes: Mapping the field of data-driven innovation, proposing theoretical developments and providing a research agenda. *International Journal of Information Management*, 60, 102347. DOI: 10.1016/j.ijinfomgt.2021.102347

Clow, D. (2013). An Overview of Learning Analytics. *Teaching in Higher Education*, 18(6), 683–695. DOI: 10.1080/13562517.2013.827653

Dahlstrom, E., Brooks, D. C., & Bichsel, J. (2014). The Current Ecosystem of Learning Management Systems in Higher Education: Student, Faculty, and IT Perspectives. *EDUCAUSE Review*. Retrieved https://www.educause.edu/ecar.2014

Daniel, B. (2015). Big Data and analytics in higher education: Opportunities and challenges. *British Journal of Educational Technology*, 46(5), 904–920. DOI: 10.1111/bjet.12230

Daniel, B. K. (2019). Big Data and data science: A critical review of issues for educational research. *British Journal of Educational Technology*, 50(1), 101–113. DOI: 10.1111/bjet.12595

Donoghue, T., Voytek, B., & Ellis, S. E. (2021). Teaching creative and practical data science at scale. *Journal of Statistics and Data Science Education : An Official Journal of the of the American Statistical Association*, 29(1), S27–S39. DOI: 10.1080/10691898.2020.1860725

Greller, W., & Drachsler, H. (2012). Translating Learning into Numbers: A Generic Framework for Learning Analytics. *Journal of Educational Technology & Society*, 15(3), 42–57.

Kerr, P. (2016). Adaptive Learning. *ELT Journal*, 70(1), 88–93. DOI: 10.1093/elt/ccv055

Klein, C., Lester, J., Rangwala, H., & Johri, A. (2019). Technological barriers and incentives to learning analytics adoption in higher education: Insights from users. *Journal of Computing in Higher Education*, 31(3), 604–625. DOI: 10.1007/s12528-019-09210-5

Murumba, J., & Micheni, E. (2017). Big Data Analytics in Higher Education: A Review [IJES]. *The International Journal of Engineering and Science*, 6(6), 14–21. DOI: 10.9790/1813-0606021421

Nguyen, A., Gardner, L., & Sheridan, D. (2017). A MultiLayered Taxonomy of Learning Analytics Applications. *In Proceedings of the Pacific Asia Conference on Information Systems*, Article 54.

Nguyen, A., Gardner, L. A., & Sheridan, D. (2018). A Framework for Applying Learning Analytics in Serious Games for People with Intellectual Disabilities. *British Journal of Educational Technology*, 49(4), 673–689. DOI: 10.1111/bjet.12625

Nistor, N., & Hernández-Garcíac, Á. (2018). What Types of Data are used in Learning Analytics? An Overview of Six Cases. *Computers in Human Behavior*, 89, 335–338. DOI: 10.1016/j.chb.2018.07.038

Picciano, A. G. (2012). The evolution of big data and learning analytics in American higher education. *Online Learning : the Official Journal of the Online Learning Consortium*, 16(3), 9–20. DOI: 10.24059/olj.v16i3.267

Romanow, D., Napier, N. P., & Cline, M. K. (2020). Using active learning, group formation, and discussion to increase stu- dent learning: A business intelligence skills analysis. *Journal of Information Systems Education*, 31, 218–231.

Waskom, M. L. (2021). Seaborn: Statistical data visualization. *Journal of Open Source Software*, 6(60), 3021. DOI: 10.21105/joss.03021

Chapter 15
Perception About Usage of GAI Tools in Teaching and Research by Teachers and Students in Higher Education Institutions

Chinna Suresh
https://orcid.org/0000-0002-3389-1116
SASTRA University, India

Sunkesula Mahammad Ali
https://orcid.org/0000-0002-5457-4689
AP Model School and Jr. College, Amarapuram, India

V. Devaki
https://orcid.org/0000-0002-7109-0205
SASTRA University, India

ABSTRACT

In recent days, due to the evolution of Artificial Intelligence, education and research are in the process of rapid development. The AI, particularly GAI tools such as individualized learning and intelligent tutoring systems, are recreating traditional pedagogies and research methodologies. Consequently, in this chapter, global practices of AI in higher education are explored together with their applications in Journal publications. Surveys on AI acceptance reveal mixed perceptions among

DOI: 10.4018/979-8-3693-8191-5.ch015

students and faculty. While students value AI's individualized learning experiences and self-paced study options, faculty acknowledge its ability to automate tasks but are worried about data privacy and students' ethical use of AI. Therefore, this chapter underlines a balanced method for AI integration, advocating for technical advancements that advocate educational values. To this end, recommendations and guidelines for adopting AI tools in higher education are provided with special emphasis on the role of educators to be aware and committed to conform with Institutional AI policies.

SECTION 1: INTRODUCTION

The rapid advancements in Generative Artificial Intelligence (GAI) have fundamentally reshaped various sectors in the short time, particularly the education sector. As GAI technologies become increasingly integrated into teaching and research processes, their impact on higher education institutions is profound and far-reaching (Akgun & Greenhow, 2021; Roll & Wylie, 2016). This chapter explores educators' and learners' attitudes and experiences toward adopting and using GAI tools in academic settings.

The GAI application in education, also known as Generative Artificial Intelligence in Education (GAIED), marks a shift from teacher-centric methods to student-centric methods(Akgun & Greenhow, 2021). These tools facilitate personalized instruction and improve the quality of education and learning outcomes by creating a more inclusive learning environment (Roll & Wylie, 2016). Additionally, GAI is being used to manage various administrative tasks, which permits educators to spend more time and energy in the teaching and learning process rather than being busy with administrative duties.

Understanding teachers' and students' GAI literacy levels is becoming more and more crucial as GAI is continuously incorporated into educational procedures. According to (Crompton & Burke, 2023) GAI literacy, in this sense, refers to the understanding of what GAI is, how to utilize it, and the ramifications of its integration into society and education. To teachers, especially in higher learning institutions and academics, GAI literacy is essential in the appropriate incorporation of the tools into practices and the ability to persist in working in an educational context (Zawacki-Richter et al., 2019). In this way, the educator who has mastered GAI can use it in various ways to advance the engagement of students, refine the delivery of instructions and self-advance the academic research as much as feasible (Tsai, 2019)

However, one cannot deny teaching-related benefits as well as a definite prospect of GAI in the future; nevertheless, numerous challenges and problems regarding the further application of GAI persist. One of the main challenges is associated with the level of awareness regarding the GAI among teachers and learners at different levels. While some people are acquainted well with the GAI tool technologies, they can easily incorporate these technologies, whereas others require more skills to incorporate GAI tools. Such a gap can lead to GAI literacy inaccessibility of GAI-driven educational resources and perpetuate the existing gaps in the educational system today, as seen by (Jiang et al., 2020). However, another problem is the rate of innovation of GAI technologies, which implies that one must switch to the technologies as they are developed.

In addition, giving GAI in education is still superlative for the ethical issue. One of the biggest problems of GAI is data privacy; then there are the questions of algorithmic bias and the problems that are associated with the use of GAI in replacing human educators in some tasks. Most importantly, as the type of tasks that can be automized and controlled by GAI tools steadily increases and expands into the teachers' sphere, there is a need to discuss the architecture of the tools in question. Hence, for the maintenance of academic integrity as well as quality in education, it is of paramount importance that GAI supplements human educators rather than replacing them. Besides, concerns about the accountability and transparency of GAI systems are still more relevant in terms of policy-making for the educational context as their functionality is wrapped around several ethical questions.

The role of GAI in research forms the final major topic of interest discussed in this chapter. GAI tools are gradually establishing themselves as primary tools used in the framework of academic research in activities like data analysis, data interpretation, and literature review, as well as for the extraction and formatting of the data. Of course, these tools can significantly enhance the quality and credibility of the research, but at the same, they pose a number of questions about academic integrity, academic dishonesty, originality of the work, research ethics and so on (Ifenthaler et al., 2024). Thus, there is a need to verify how these GAI tools in research affect knowledge generation and dissemination paradigms.

Comparing the attitudes of the teachers and students of the higher education institutions towards GAI tools is essential in identifying the effectiveness of the tools' implementation. Thus, with the help of data regarding educators' and learners' attitudes and experiences related to GAI, the study suggests revealing enablers and barriers to adopting these tools in educational contexts (Wirtz et al., 2023). In addition, it aims to identify potential trends regarding GAI utilisation for learning, teaching, and materials development, future research directions in higher education, and the ramifications foundational to educational practice and scholarly methods.

SECTION 2: OBJECTIVES OF THE RESEARCH STUDY

The study aims to achieve the following objectives.

1. Examine the guidelines established by various educational organizations worldwide regarding using Generative AI tools in research and teaching.
2. Explore students' perceptions about using Generative AI tools in their academic and research pursuits in the Indian context.
3. Assess faculty members' perceptions on employing Generative AI tools in their coursework and research activities in the Indian context.

This chapter examines the potential benefits and drawbacks of employing GAI technologies in research and educational contexts. As a result, relevant stakeholders can develop improved guidelines and policies to leverage the advantages of GAI tools while mitigating potential downsides by understanding the implications and possible challenges of integrating them into research and education.

The structure of this chapter is the following: The next section presents the overview of the literature concerning Generative AI, and the fourth section investigates international practices. The fifth section reveals additional information on the students' attitudes towards the application of GAI in their learning. Ongoing research with the target participants. The sixth section of interest, the last section, focuses on the PERC of the target faculty members on using GAI in the execution of their coursework and research agendas. The seventh section contains tips and suggestions for the application of GAI in teaching; the last section focuses on the questions of disclosure and attribution.

SECTION 3: REVIEW OF LITERATURE

Several studies have investigated how students in higher education perceive and use ChatGPT. For instance, (Romero-Rodríguez et al., 2023) examined the factors that influence Spanish university students' acceptance and use of ChatGPT, using the Unified Theory of Acceptance and Use of Technology Model-2. The results suggest that experience, performance expectancy, hedonic motivation, price value, and habit significantly impact students' intention to use ChatGPT. Additionally, the findings revealed that if it is easy to access and use, students are more likely to incorporate it into their regular study habits. However, this study was limited to the Spanish context and did not consider the perspectives of educators. (Strzelecki & ElArabawy, 2024) explores the impact of AI tools, specifically ChatGPT, on university students' acceptance and usage. It uses the Unified Theory of Acceptance and Use of Technology (UTAUT) framework and examines four constructs: performance expectancy, effort expectancy, social influence, and facilitating conditions. The findings suggest that these factors significantly influence behavioural intention and actual use behaviour, with gender and study level playing a moderating role. (Yijang Wang & Weining Zhang, 2017) Study explores factors driving Generation Z to embrace GenAI-assisted design using data from 326 participants on the mainland of China. Results show that effort expectancy, price value, and hedonic motivation positively influence intention to use GAI. At the same time, optimism and creativity significantly contribute to performance expectancy, effort expectancy, price value, and hedonic motivation. Trait curiosity positively impacts optimism and intention to use GAI.

Several studies have investigated teachers' perspectives on using ChatGPT in diverse educational settings. For instance, (Iqbal et al., 2022) Iqbal et al. conducted semi-structured interviews with 20 faculty members from a private university in Pakistan, providing qualitative insights into their perceptions and attitudes toward ChatGPT. The study findings indicate that teachers need more information and training on ChatGPT before they can use in their teaching learning process. This study emphasis the need for professional development to help educators effectively integrate new technologies into their practice.

Several research studies have engaged both students and teachers as participants to investigate the appropriate utilization of Generative AI in writing practices. A survey-based study by (Barrett & Pack, 2023) identified minor divergences between students and teachers regarding acceptable Gen AI usage for writing tasks, as well as a need for preparedness at the classroom and institutional levels. However, the study also showed that both students and teachers felt they needed more guidance and support to use these tools effectively. The study revealed the need for clearer rules and more training for teachers on how to effectively integrate AI into the classroom.

Research Gap

The present literature survey is also aware of various benefits and drawbacks of using ChatGPT but is scarce in terms of impressions that Indian college learners and teachers have about this technology. Therefore, this study seeks to fill this gap deliberately by enlisting participants from both groups and providing several theoretical contributions.

SECTION 4: GLOBAL PRACTICES ON GENERATIVE AI TOOLS

This section explores the diverse applications of generative AI tools, the need for Guidelines on GAI usage in HEIs, and examines the policies of the top 50 universities worldwide and the evolving policies shaping their future.

Need for Guidelines on GAI Usage in HEIs

The recent developments in Artificial Intelligence, remarkably Generative AI such as ChatGPT, Meta, Bard, and Gemini, have amplified calls for guidelines in its usage in higher education Institutions around the world. For example, (Gamage et al., 2023) suggest that HEIs, "develop policies and clear, easy-to-understand guidelines for the use of language models in learning and teaching - the guidelines should include information on the proper use of these tools and the consequence of cheating". This is because GAI can generate human-like content, videos, audio, images, simulations, etc, that are very difficult to identify even for the domain experts. Research studies worldwide uncovered that one out of five students are currently using GAI tools in their academics and these numbers may rise in future.

Early reports on the reactions of HEIs to GAI suggested various possibilities in response to the use of GAI tools in academics. Some universities prohibited the use of GAI tools in their academic programmes, by considering the usage of AI as cheating, while others have standard rules and regulations allowing their use, as long as that use is declared and acknowledged.

The primary concerns regarding the GAI tools in the HEI are that the students may use GAIs to cheat or plagiarise their written assignments and exams, which might dilute the academic integrity and encourage academic dishonesty (Chan, 2023). According to the Australian Government's Tertiary Education Quality and Standards (TEQSA), Academic Integrity is defined as "the expectation that teachers, students, researchers and all members of the academic community act with honesty, trust, fairness, respect and responsibility". Academic dishonesty, in contrast, refers to "a range of behaviours involving intentional violation of academic rules for personal gain, such as plagiarism, lying, and falsifications''. As per the TEQSA, examples of academic dishonesty include plagiarism, recycling, or resubmission of work, fabrication of information, collusion, exam cheating, contract cheating and impersonation as examples of academic dishonesty.

To promote Academic integrity and deter academic dishonesty, HEIs need to have Guidelines on using GAI in academics.

Guidelines of Top 50 Universities in the World on the Usage of GAI

Leading universities around the world have developed guidelines that address three key considerations:

1. Upholding academic integrity
2. Acknowledging the use of General Artificial Intelligence
3. Detecting the utilization of GAI.

Academic Integrity

The guidelines of the top 50 universities in the world on using GAI tools stress the importance of maintaining academic integrity. Three key areas were identified under this concept:

1. Forms of plagiarism involving GAI, such as directly copying AI-generated responses, running material through multiple generative AI tools to avoid detection, and failing to properly document the use of GAI in assessments.
2. Strategies for addressing plagiarism.
3. Instructors' responses to plagiarism.

The University College of London (UCL) and Duke University (DU) have suggested that students may use AI-generated content as a source of information or inspiration, but if they fail to cite or acknowledge the source correctly, this behaviour would be considered plagiarism (Holmes et al., 2022; Ka & Chan, 2023). Imperial College of London (ICL) stated that submitting AI-generated assessments as if they were the student's work constitutes plagiarism (Ka & Chan, 2023). The University of California, Los Angeles (UCLA) has noted that some students may attempt to bypass plagiarism detection tools by running their work through several GAI paraphrasing tools (Dalalah & Dalalah, 2023). To help students better understand academic integrity and the consequences of violating the university's plagiarism policy, UCLA and the University of Illinois at Urbana-Champaign (UIUC) have recommended that instructors incorporate relevant information into their course syllabi.

Acknowledgement of GAI

Most universities have properly acknowledged using Generative Artificial Intelligence in student assignments. The two primary commendations are acknowledging the use of GAI and limiting the inclusion of AI-generated content. The University of

Edinburgh has offered more detailed guidelines, suggesting that students specify the particular AI tool used, its version, and the access date. Additionally, the University of Toronto (UOFT) has stated that the appendix of each assessment should detail the tools employed, how they were used, and how the results from the GAI were incorporated into the submitted work. Similarly, UCL has emphasized that students must describe the prompts, the output received, and the modifications made to the GAI-generated output.

Detection of GAI Use

Most universities mentioned the availability of Generative Artificial Intelligence detection tools, but the acceptable percentage of AI-generated content remains unspecified. However, it is learned that in the Turnitin software, if the AI content is below 20 per cent it does not surface in the new reports but instead indicates this with an asterisk symbol in order to reduce the likelihood of misinterpretation. However, most guidelines discouraged instructors from relying on these tools to verify student adherence to academic integrity policies. Reasons for this recommendation included the tools' inaccuracy in identifying AI-generated content and concerns about privacy. For instance, Imperial College London and Duke University reminded their colleagues that GAI detection tools remain nascent, describing them as "unproven" and "by no means foolproof" in identifying AI-generated work. The University of Missouri (MU) also suggested that these detection tools cannot "keep pace with the latest developments." Some universities noted that having instructors input students' work into external sites could raise privacy and security issues, and the University of California, Berkeley (UCB) warned that this practice may lead to ethical, privacy, and copyright concerns. Accordingly, many universities advised that GAI detection tools should not be the sole factor in determining whether students have violated academic integrity.

A Survey of Journal Guidelines for Large Language Models and Generative AI

We reviewed the submission guidelines and ethics processes of the top 25 journals ranked by impact factor and categorized their approach to accepting generative AI and Large Language Models in the publishing process.

Non-Eligibility for Authorship: Most prominent journals, including those published by Nature, Science, Springer, Elsevier, the JAMA Network, and the British Medical Journal (BMJ), as well as specific journals like The Lancet and Cell, agree that generative AI tools and large language models do not meet the criteria for authorship. They explain that this is due to the inability of AI systems to be held accountable for the work, and they emphasize that accountability is a crucial aspect of authorship.

Mandatory Disclosure of GAI Use: Journals consistently require authors to disclose their use of AI and AI-assisted technologies, such as large language models and generative AI, during the writing process. This disclosure is typically expected to be included in the acknowledgements, methods section, or another appropriate part of the manuscript to provide transparency regarding the tools and techniques employed in the research and writing.

Limited Role of AI in Manuscript Preparation: Major academic publishers, such as Elsevier and the JAMA Network, as well as prestigious journals like The Lancet and Cell, state that AI should be used only to enhance readability and language and not for critical authoring responsibilities like generating scientific insights, concluding, or making recommendations. In this view, the role of AI is primarily as an assistive technology to support the writing process rather than to drive the research itself.

Transparency and Trust: Some academic journals, including those in the BMJ portfolio, promote transparency in using AI technology. This helps build trust among authors, readers, reviewers, and editors. The journals state that AI should be clearly described when it is used. Going forward, editors will assess the appropriateness of the AI usage outlined.

Bias and Accuracy: Multiple academic guidelines, including those from Sage, have identified concerns regarding the possibility of biases within content generated by generative AI systems, as well as the accuracy of such output. These guidelines recognize the limitations of GAI in comprehending contextual nuances and producing factually correct information.

Methods

The research participants were students and faculty members from Indian HEIs recruited via email invitations outlining the study's objectives. A pool of 127 individuals voluntarily shared perspectives on GAI usage in higher education through a Google Form survey administered in July 2024. Employing stratified sampling, 95 students and 32 teacher participants were selected to ensure diversity in experiences with GAI users. The participants had firsthand experience using GAI for academic tasks, ensuring their perspectives were well-informed and relevant to the study.

Table 1. Sample Distribution **127**

Students			Teachers		
UG	PG	PhD	Technical	Science	Arts, H & SS
34	41	20	13	10	9
95			32		

Table 1 shows the sample distribution of students and teachers who participated in the survey.

SECTION 5: STUDENT SURVEY SUMMARY

A survey was administered to 95 students' composition of undergraduate, postgraduate, and PhD students from various disciplines and HEIs to understand students' perceptions of GAI tools. The survey aimed to capture their experiences, attitudes, and concerns regarding using GAI in their education. The student survey questionnaire consists of 22 statements to express their viewpoints on using GAI tools in academics and research. The questionnaire was developed from an initial pool of 76 opinion statements gathered through a Google form questionnaire distributed to 283 students and 56 faculty members from HEIs.

Table 2. Familiar with Digital Technologies

Age group			
Up to 22 years (47)		23 years and above (58)	
High	Low	High	Low
74.47% (35)	25.53% (12)	55.17% (32)	44.83% (26)

From Table 2, it is observed that the survey showed that there was a generational gap in the acceptance of GAI tools. Younger students, who are more familiar with digital technologies, are likely to accept these tools easily when compared to their counterparts

Table 3. Acceptance Towards Digital Technologies and GAI

Field of Study			
Technology and Science (STEM) (64)		Arts, Humanities and Social Sciences (H&SS) (31)	
High	Low	High	Low
79.69% (51)	20.31% (13)	61.29% (19)	38.70% (12)

From Table 3, it is learned that additionally, there were variations in perceptions of students based on the field of study, where STEM students showed a much higher level of acceptance compared to students of humanities and social sciences.

The results reveal that students generally have a positive outlook on the potential of GAI tools to enhance their learning and academic performance (Zastudil et al., 2023).

Table 4. Which GAI Tool Did You Know and Use/Wish to Use in Your Coursework

Prefer to use GAI tool					
ChatGPT	**GitHub**	**Copilot**	**Meta Ai**	**Bard**	**Gemini**
75.79% (72)	4.21% (4)	5.26% (5)	3.16%(3)	8.42% (8)	3.16% (3)

From Table 4, it is learned that many of the students (76%) knew about and used ChatGPT as part of their coursework. In contrast, significantly fewer students had experience with GitHub Copilot and Meta Ai, possibly due to explicit restrictions imposed by their instructors. This may be due to its user-friendly user-interface, simple, availability multiple options in content development and first-ever AI in this 21st century.

Table 5. Especially For Which Purpose Did You Use GAI Tools

Purpose of use of GAI							
Technology and Science (STEM) (64)				**Arts, Humanities and Social Sciences (H&SS) (31)**			
Language related tasks	**Coding**	**Mathematical proofs**	**Problem-Solving**	**Language related tasks**	**Coding**	**Mathematical proofs**	**Problem-Solving**
50% (32)	25% (16)	15.62% (10)	9.38% (6)	87.10% (27)	NA	NA	12.90% (4)

Table 5 shows that sample from STEM half of the students were comfortable using AI tools for writing and language-related tasks, like finding different ways to say things or summarizing research papers. Around 24% had even used these tools for coding projects. However, using AI for things like mathematical proofs or problem-solving wasn't very common among the STEM students. Most students believed that coding and technical writing were areas where they could significantly benefit from AI tools. In contrast, they felt that mathematics and problem-solving were the domains where AI tools would be least useful.

Table 5 reveals that similarly sample from Arts, Humanities and Social Sciences (H&SS) (31) most students (87.10%) used AI tools to improve the quality of their written work. The majority were happy to use such tools, while the remaining sought to avoid dependence on them. Only about 10% of the students felt that AI tools were not very helpful for improving their writing.

Table 6. Rate/Evaluate the Efficiency of GAI Tools and State the Reason

Enhance Readability	Article Summarization	Code Debugging	Problem-Solving Abilities
5 (Very high)	2 (Low)	2 (Low)	1 (Very low)

From Table 6, it is learned that consistent with this pattern, when participants were asked to evaluate AI tools based on their capabilities, the highest score was given for enhancing readability, with successively lower ratings for article summarization and code debugging. The lowest score was assigned to the problem-solving abilities of AI tools, indicating the well-documented limitations of these tools in terms of their logical vulnerabilities.

Table 7. Do You Think Your Institute Should Provide Clear Guidelines for Using GAI Tools

Necessary	Undecided	Unnecessary
61.05% (58)	11.58% (11)	27.37% (26)

From Table 7, it is observed that the majority of students believed the Institute should provide clear guidelines for using GAI tools. However, a small but significant fraction felt such guidelines were unnecessary. The remaining students were undecided on the matter.

Table 8. Where Your Institute Should Provide Prescribed Guidelines for Using GAI Tools

Institute should provide clear guidelines for using GAI tools (95)	
Prescribe for individual courses/ Course Handbooks	On the Institution's website, as a general guideline
79.32% (75)	20.68% (20)

Table 8 shows that a significant portion of respondents who believed guidelines should be prescribed felt that the responsibility for specifying such guidelines should lie with individual courses or in the Student Handbook. Approximately 20% of student respondents suggested that this information could be provided on the Institution website, or during orientation.

Table 9: Restriction of use of GAI tools

Restriction of use of GAI tools (95)	
Unrestricted use of GAI tools	**Allowing GAI tools use only for specific tasks**
69.47% (66)	30.53% (29)

Table 9 shows for coursework, students were split nearly evenly between allowing unrestricted use of GAI tools versus allowing use only for specific tasks. Interestingly, a substantial portion of students sought to permit free usage but with the requirement of providing attribution.

*Table 10. The tasks the GAI tools are used in Research (*Exercised Multiple Options)*

Research & Idea Generation	Proposal Preparation	Literature Review	Statistical Analysis	Graphic Generation	Creating Tables from the Text	Extracting and reformatting the data
30.5% (29)	17.8% (17)	66.31% (63)	78.94% (75)	12.63% (12)	15.78% (15)	63.15% (60)

From Table 10, most of the students leverage the GAI tools in their research primarily for Data/Statistical Analysis (78.94%), and the literature review follows closely with 66.31%. Additionally 63.15% use GAI tools for formatting the data. However, it is observed that less portion of students rely on these tools for tasks like idea generation, proposal preparation and creating a table from the text. Interestingly the least common application is for graphic generation.

SECTION 6: FACULTY SURVEY SUMMARY

A similar survey was conducted among 32 Technical, Sciences, Arts and Humanities and Social Sciences faculty members to gauge their perceptions and experiences with GAI tools. The survey focused on how faculty members incorporate these GAI tools into their teaching and research and their concerns and recommendations for future use. The findings suggest that faculty members have mixed opinions on using GAI tools in higher education.

Table 11. Familiar With Digital Technologies

Field of Study			
Technology and Science (STEM) (23)		Arts, Humanities and Social Sciences (H&SS) (09)	
Yes	No	Yes	No
100% (23)	Nil	100% (9)	Nil

Table 11 shows the sample distribution of faculty from STEM and Arts, Humanities and Social Sciences.

Table 12. For Which Purpose Do You Use GAI Tools in General

To improve text readability	Simplify the complex passages or for writing	Debugging codes
46.88% (15)	28.12% (9)	25% (8)

From Table 12 it is learned that for the total sample in general, faculty members seem to be most knowledgeable about utilizing GAI tools to improve text readability (47%), to simplify the complex passages (29%), or for writing and 25% for debugging codes.

Table 13. For which Purpose Do you use GAI Tools in STEM and H&SS Disciplines

Technology and Science (STEM) (23)			Arts, Humanities and Social Sciences (H&SS) (09)		
To improve text readability	Simplify the complex passages or for writing	Debugging codes	To improve text readability	Simplify the complex passages or for writing	Debugging codes
43.47% (10)	21.74% (5)	34.78% (8)	55.55% (5)	44.45% (4)	NA

Table 13 compares the responses of the teachers from the STEM group and H&SS. In STEM, nearly 44% engage the GAI tools for improving the text readability, around 21% in simplifying complex passages or writing, and 34.78% in debugging codes. In contrast, around 55% of the faculty use GAI tools to improve text readability which is greater than the STEM faculty utilization, 44.45% on simplifying complex passages or writing while none report engaging in debugging codes. This reveals the differences in focus between the two groups, where STEM more engaged in technical tasks and H&SS more involved in textual clarity and writing.

Table 14. Weightage For Awarding the Grade to Un-Proctored Assignments

Weightage for awarding the grade when using GAI tools		
Less than 20%	**20% to 50%**	**50%**
40.625% (13)	21.875% (7)	37.50% (12)

Table 14 shows that Un-proctored work contributes a substantial portion to university course grades. Approximately 40% of faculty assign 20% to 50% of the grade weight to un-proctored work, while 12% allocate more than 50% to such work. In contrast, 38% of faculty give less than 20% weightage to un-proctored assignments.

The State Planning Commission of Tamilnadu, India, has recently initiated the use of AI technology to assess student's response sheets for end-semester examinations. Presently it is in the pilot phase, and the project is anticipated to be completed within the year. if the outcomes are satisfactory, there are plans to implement this methodology across all the universities in the state.

Table 15. Impact of GAI Tools on Student Learning

A mixed effect (both positive and negative)	To be solely detrimental	Negligible	Unsure
37.50% (12)	12.50% (4)	25.00% (8)	25.00% (8)

Table 15 shows that faculty are divided in their perceptions of the impact of GAI tools on student learning. While a significant portion (38%) believe that GAI tools have a mixed effect, both positive and negative, others feel that the impact is negligible (25%) or unsure (25%). Only a small fraction (12%) considers GAI tools to be solely detrimental to student learning.

Table 16. Opinion on GAI Tool Policies

Favour towards occasional use	Uncertainty	I have not yet thought about this
34.375% (11)	53.125% (17)	12.50% (4)

From Table 16, the findings suggest widespread uncertainty about GAI tool policies, with the largest group having "not yet thought about this" and only 35% favouring occasional student use. A minority of 12% strongly opposed allowing AI tool usage.

Table 17. Are You Comfortable to Use GAI Tools for Which of The Following Tasks

For more substantive academic tasks	To replace spelling and grammar checkers	For email composition	Not yet thought about this
15..625% (5)	43.375% (14)	21.875% (7)	18.75% (6)

Table 17 shows that the findings show a mix of perspectives among faculty. While 31% are comfortable using AI tools to replace spelling and grammar checkers, and 21% are fine with using it for email composition, only a small portion are willing to use it for more substantive academic tasks like presentations, research proposals, publications, or paper reviews.

Table 18. Higher Education Institutions Need to Maintain an Up-To-Date Resource Page for Faculty and Students Regarding Usage of GAI

Need	Uncertainty	No need
81.25% (26)	12.50% (4)	12.50% (4)

From Table 18, it is learned that the vast portion/majority of faculty (90%) recognize the need for higher education institutions to maintain an up-to-date resource page for faculty and students.

A very small portion (15%) are ready to contribute.

Table 19. Training/Orientation and Support to Effective Adoption of AI Tools In Their Teaching and Learning Practice

Need	Uncertainty	No need
62.50% (20)	25.00% (8)	12.50% (4)

Table 19 shows that 62% of faculties recognize the need for proper training and support to effective adoption of AI tools in their teaching and learning practice.

Table 20. Express Your Opinion on Incorporating GAI Tools In Teaching, Learning and Evolution

Incorporate up to a vast extent	Balancing GAI tools and preserving the human element of education	GAI tools can only be used as a complement to traditional teaching methods
31.25% (10)	43.75% (14)	25.00% (8)

From Table 20, it is learned that furthermore, faculty members emphasized the importance of balancing leveraging GAI tools and preserving the human element of education. They advocated for a blended approach, where GAI tools complement traditional teaching methods rather than replace them.

Table 21. The tasks the GAI tools are used in Research (*Exercised Multiple Options)

Research & Idea Generation	Proposal Preparation	Literature Review	Data/ Statistical Analysis	Graphic Generation	Creating Tables from the Text	Extracting and reformatting the data
6 (18.75%)	9 (28.12%)	25 (78.12%)	17 (53.12%)	11 (34.37%)	7 (21.8%)	19 (59.3%)

Table 21 shows that most of the faculty members use GAI tools for the purpose of Literature Review (78.12%). A considerable portion (59.3%) uses GAI tools for Extracting and Reformatting Data and 53.12% apply them for Data/Statistical Analysis. Proposal Preparation (28.12%) and Graphic Generation (34.37%) are moderately used. However less portion of faculty members use GAI tools for Creating Tables from Text (21.8%) and Research & Idea Generation (18.75%), marking these the least common applications.

SECTION 7: GUIDELINES AND RECOMMENDATIONS FOR TEACHING

The use of AI tools in education is rapidly changing the learning landscape. While educational advancements are usually slow and calculated, the arrival of AI tools presents a sudden shift (Becker et al., n.d.). This brings exciting possibilities and unknown challenges, placing students and educators at a crossroads. Although the best way forward is still being determined, there's a collective awareness that AI can reshape the classroom. Surveys show various opinions on AI tools in higher education, from hindering learning to acting as personal tutors (Bala et al., 2023; Cardona et al., 2023). This contrast in viewpoints between faculty and students emphasizes the need for careful consideration and a balanced approach as we explore the potential of AI in education.

7.1 Managing Nerves and Excitement

The rapid emergence of AI tools in education casts a critical turning point for pedagogical practices. This technological invasion contrasts sharply with the historically measured pace of educational evolution, introducing promising possibilities and unique challenges for all involved. While the standard approach to integrating AI tools remains a subject of ongoing exploration, there is a shared understanding that these technologies hold the power to deeply reshape the educational experience (Copur-Gencturk et al., 2024). Significantly, surveys examining faculty and student perspectives on AI in education reveal diverse viewpoints, from concerns about potential negative impacts on learning to enthusiastic support for AI's potential as a personalized learning aid. This difference in stakeholder perspectives underscores the need for careful consideration and context-specific methods to AI integration to ensure fairness and pedagogical effectiveness. As educational institutions navigate this transformative period, they must carefully consider the trade-offs and potential unintended consequences of AI integration while binding the technology's capabilities to enhance student learning, engagement, and outcomes (Demmer et al., 2023). Integrating AI tools in education needs a refined, evidence-based approach that prioritizes pedagogical goals, addresses stakeholder concerns, and maintains the integrity of the educational process.

The passion for incorporating AI tools into teaching stems from the disconnection between the reality of education and our understanding of learning. Students significantly benefit from personalized course content, instructor attention, and interactive classroom discussions. AI tools may offer capable and scalable solutions to achieve these anticipated educational outcomes. For instance, AI-powered adaptive learning platforms can design lesson plans and content to individual student needs, while AI-driven virtual aides can provide personalized guidance and feedback. Additionally, AI-based collaboration tools can assist in more engaging and interactive classroom discussions. Integrating AI technologies can boost the overall quality and effectiveness of teaching and learning in higher education.

7.2 Acceptable Instructional Use Cases for AI Tools

Solving Complex Problems Using AI Tools

For certain types of problems, the ability of students to "get the answer" using AI tools may not necessarily reflect their true understanding of the relevant concepts(Martin et al., 2024). While recognizing that students can leverage such tools to assist with their coursework, faculty must reconsider whether these problems remain an effective means of promoting deeper student learning(Marx et al., 2023).

In some domains, faculty may find opportunities to present more complex, open-ended questions, where students must learn to break down an unstructured problem into a sequence of simpler, targeted questions (Alnasyan et al., 2024; Gao et al., 2024; Weng & Chiu, 2023).

Developing the critical skill to ask the right questions in a manner that facilitates effective problem-solving is a valuable asset that students will gain (Ismail & Yusof, 2023). Furthermore, as AI tools become increasingly integrated into professional workflows across various industries, students will benefit significantly from firsthand experience before graduation (Song et al., 2024). With companies rapidly adopting AI technologies, which may herald the next phase of an industrial revolution, students are eager to be an integral part of this transformative process. Consequently, the Institute and its faculty must carefully contemplate how exposing students to solving complex problems using AI tools may help better prepare them for the AI-driven world of the future (Su et al., 2022).

Customized and Comprehensive Educational Programs

Higher education institutions should offer courses catering to students with varying learning speeds, providing ample time to grasp and apply new concepts (Moorhouse et al., 2023). Students come from diverse backgrounds and would greatly benefit from such adaptability in the curriculum. However, those who need more support often end up in the lower tiers of grading curves, struggling to keep pace with pre-planned course trajectories (Kizilcec et al., 2024).

AI-powered tools present the possibility of delivering personalized assistance to students. These tools can serve as virtual tutors, answering questions that students may hesitate to ask in a classroom setting or as a source of practice problems before exams (Renkema & Tursunbayeva, 2024). Spending an hour interacting with ChatGPT or similar AI assistants, prompting dozens of questions without the fear of judgment, can ensure active engagement - a difficult feat to achieve in larger classes.

A prime example of the transformative potential of such learning tools comes from programming education. Coding skills vary widely among university students, and nothing short of personalized guidance can effectively help students with limited prior experience become proficient. AI-powered tools offer exciting possibilities in this regard, such as integrating tutor bots in introductory computer science courses or developing mobile applications for personalized learning experiences.

Beyond programming, AI tools enable the creation of immersive and interactive learning environments across various disciplines. The virtual AI/VR museum project, for instance, can provide hands-on experiments like earthquake simulators, while Google Expeditions can take students on virtual field trips to ancient historical sites or underwater ecosystems. Interactive 3D simulators from ZSpace offer engaging learning opportunities in pure and natural sciences, and platforms like Labster deliver virtual science labs for education (Rapaka et al., 2025a) . Personalized math instruction is made possible through platforms like Dreambox Learning, which caters to students from kindergarten to eighth grade, while AI-powered learning management systems, such as Canvas LMS with AI Analytics and Coursera's Learning Platform, integrate intelligent features to enhance the overall educational experience (Caccavale et al., 2024).

These AI-powered tools and platforms have the potential to revolutionize the way higher education institutions deliver content and support student learning. By creating personalized, adaptive, and immersive learning experiences, these technologies can cater to students with diverse backgrounds and learning styles, ultimately improving educational outcomes and fostering a more inclusive and engaging academic environment (Bressane et al., 2024).

The exemplified use cases, although not necessarily directly replicable, may serve as a source of inspiration. The integration of artificial intelligence within the educational domain remains an emerging field, yet anticipated advancements in AI technology could facilitate the development of increasingly personalized and immersive learning environments (Ayanwale et al., 2024). Furthermore, AI possesses the potential to support students from underrepresented communities by providing them access to high-quality educational resources. This could contribute to bridging the divide between diverse educational backgrounds and ensuring equitable opportunities for student success.(Renkema & Tursunbayeva, 2024)

Language Assistance

Many students at higher education institutions struggle with developing proficiency in the English language. Insufficient mastery of the language can significantly impede their ability to effectively communicate their ideas and research findings through oral presentations, academic manuscripts, and theses (Bedington et al., 2024). To address these language-related challenges, tools like Grammarly, which are widely used on university campuses, provide real-time feedback and suggestions for improving grammar, spelling, and sentence structure(Pahi et al., 2024; Wang et al., 2024). This can help students enhance the clarity and coherence of their written work. Additionally, incorporating AI-powered language assistance tools into the curriculum, such as through a semester-long course, could further strengthen students' academic writing skills (von Garrel & Mayer, 2023). The short-term course on leveraging AI tools for scientific writing offered by ETH Zurich provides a valuable example in this context, offering students hands-on experience in utilizing these technologies to refine the quality of their research papers and publications (Gayed et al., 2022; Rahimi & Sevilla-Pavón, 2024).

Course Administration

According to (Moundridou et al., 2024), GAI tools have the potential to greatly simplify a variety of teaching activities, freeing up faculty members to spend more time and energy with their student's insightful, tailored feedback on their work. For example, AI-powered grading and automated lecture transcription can free up class time for interactive discussions and hands-on learning rather than note-taking. Furthermore, these AI-enabled features can greatly benefit students who miss a lecture, enabling them to catch up more easily by reviewing the automatically transcribed content and focusing their energy on comprehending the material rather than frantically trying to record everything.

7.3 Recommendations for Teaching

Technology is a Supplement to the Faculty but not a Replacement

While it is clear that faculty members will retain a central role in the classroom, AI technologies cannot fully replicate the capacities of human instructors in generating meaningful course content (Maqbool et al., 2024a; Robinson et al., 2021). As the recent COVID-19 pandemic has demonstrated, students require the guidance and expertise of instructors to learn effectively, as well as the collaborative learning opportunities provided by interactions with their peers. Concurrently, the pandemic has underscored the need to evolve teaching methods and make them more impactful. In this context, AI tools can drive this evolution by augmenting and enhancing the teaching and learning process rather than entirely substituting it(Shwartz-Asher et al., 2022). Faculty must be equipped to leverage these tools to improve student engagement, facilitate personalized learning, and foster deeper understanding of the subject matter. By utilizing AI-powered tools, instructors can allocate more time to high-value activities, such as one-on-one mentoring, facilitating group discussions, and providing personalized feedback (Gupta et al., 2023). Additionally, AI-driven adaptive learning platforms can tailor the learning experience to individual students' needs, enabling them to progress at their own pace and address specific knowledge gaps. When employed effectively, these technologies can enhance the role of faculty, enabling them to create more dynamic and interactive learning environments that better meet the diverse needs of today's students (Maqbool et al., 2024b; Saini & Salim Al-Mamri, 2019).

AI Tools will not be Virtual Teaching Assistants

Teaching assistants are vital in our academic framework, serving as indispensable facilitators of student learning and development. They provide personalized guidance, mentorship, and support that AI tools cannot readily replicate. While AI tools may offer supplementary capabilities in specific tasks, they fundamentally lack the sophisticated understanding, empathy, and multifaceted responsibilities that make teaching assistants indispensable to our educational system (Jackson & Panteli, 2023). The diverse functions of teaching assistants, from leading discussions and providing feedback to serving as academic and career mentors, are essential to cultivating transformative learning experiences that empower students to reach their full potential.

Regularly Evaluate and Update Course Goals, Teaching Methods, and Assessments

The institutional policy should actively encourage the thoughtful integration of AI tools into courses as instructors deem appropriate. This allows students to engage with the technology constructively and meaningfully. Many courses have traditionally focused on a key learning objective centred around students' ability to create complex artefacts such as code, proofs, and designs - skills often considered cognitively demanding for students.

However, as AI tools increasingly demonstrate the capability to generate such artefacts, faculty must diligently monitor their evolving capabilities and limitations within their respective academic domains (Xiaolei & Teng, 2024). Based on this subtle understanding, faculty should carefully consider revising course learning objectives to better prepare students for the significant impact of these rapidly advancing technologies on their future professional endeavours. Teachers who rely heavily on plagiarism checks are at a great disadvantage because GAI tools can easily bypass such measures. Instead of that, they can focus on the percentage of AI-generated content in the submitted work.

For instance, instead of primarily emphasizing students' ability to independently create complex artefacts, faculty could focus on developing students' capacity to critically evaluate and assess the quality, accuracy, and reliability of artefacts generated by AI tools. This revised approach would require modest modifications to pedagogical and assessment strategies, such as incorporating examples of plausible yet flawed AI-generated artefacts into lectures and designing quiz and exam questions that challenge students to identify errors, biases, or limitations in the AI-produced content (Rapaka et al., 2025b). These strategic adjustments would better align course objectives and assessments with the evolving landscape of technological capabilities, thereby better equipping students for the realities of their future professional workspaces.

Transparent and Simple Course Policies

Institutions should adopt a clear, comprehensive policy that allows the strategic use of AI tools in teaching and research, while emphasizing the importance of proper attribution and academic integrity (Lee et al., 2024). This policy should provide detailed guidelines on the appropriate integration of AI-powered technologies, such as requirements for citation, disclosure of AI-generated content, and ethical considerations. Faculty must clearly and consistently communicate the applicable policy to students at the start of each course, emphasizing that students are fully accountable for the work they submit and must adhere to rigorous academic integrity standards (Chauncey & McKenna, 2023). Given the rapid evolution of AI and its growing impact on higher education, it is critical that institutions periodically re-evaluate these policies in a measured, thoughtful manner rather than taking reactive or impulsive stances. This periodic review process should involve substantive input from faculty, students, and other relevant stakeholders to ensure the policies remain relevant, effective, and adaptable in the face of technological advancements (Steele, 2023).

Infrastructure and Administrative Support

The rapid advancements in AI technology necessitate a proactive response from the Institute to adequately support students and faculty in staying current with these developments for this, the institutions can have specificized offices to train the faculty and students. Comprehensive training workshops can significantly enhance AI-related knowledge and skills across the diverse campus community (Kajiwara & Kawabata, 2024). Demonstrations of cutting-edge AI tools by specialized centres like IKEN can improve technology adoption and encourage responsible and ethical utilization of these powerful capabilities. Furthermore, lectures delivered by subject matter experts on the ethical implications and appropriate use of AI will remind users to leverage the technology judiciously, with a keen awareness of the potential risks and societal impacts. Additionally, the Institute can conduct periodic surveys to thoroughly assess how the campus community engages with AI tools in teaching and research activities (Steele, 2023). This data-driven approach will enable the development of relevant and well-informed policies that promote innovation and ensure the responsible use of AI technologies.

SECTION 8: GUIDELINES AND RECOMMENDATIONS FOR RESEARCH

Generative AI is a powerful research tool that is expected to become increasingly capable over time. Researchers in science, engineering, and mathematics aim to utilize the best available tools to produce high-quality work. However, generative AI must be employed responsibly. It is crucial to recognize that while AI tools can serve as a valuable resource, they should complement, not replace, traditional academic mentorship and guidance. Students should critically evaluate the information and recommendations provided by AI tools and seek expert advice from their professors, advisors, and peers within their specific areas of study.

Disclosure and Attribution

Generative artificial intelligence tools require explicit disclosure, providing clear attribution and detailed information. Researchers must adhere to the guidelines the relevant journal, conference, or publisher established when incorporating GAI in published academic works. Similarly, for theses and other institutional documents, authors should follow the publication guidelines provided by the institution. Importantly, it is advisable for all academic publications, regardless of the publisher, to align with the institution's guidelines for using GAI and other technologies.

- When employing generative AI software tools to produce new content such as text, images, tables, code, and the like, the use of these tools must be disclosed either in the Methods section or the Acknowledgements section of the work. Furthermore, the extent to which these tools were utilized must be detailed.
- If a significant portion of a work, such as sections containing tables, graphs, images, and other content, was generated using AI tools, the specific sections and the particular AI tools and versions must be disclosed. Additionally, the text of the prompts provided as input to the AI systems and any subsequent editing done on the AI-generated content should be detailed. These AI tools should only be employed to produce portions of a Related Work or similar section and not to generate novel findings or interpretations.
- ·If the amount of AI-generated text is limited, including a footnote referencing the utilization of such a system in the relevant section of the work and a general disclaimer in the Acknowledgements section would be acceptable.
- Suppose one utilizes generative artificial intelligence software tools to edit and enhance the quality of pre-existing text in a manner analogous to employing a writing assistance application such as Grammarly to improve spelling,

grammar, punctuation, clarity, and engagement, or a basic word processing system to correct orthographic and grammatical errors. In that case, there is no requirement to disclose the use of these tools within the academic work.

CONCLUSION

The study explores a range of perspectives on integrating GAI tools within Indian higher education institutions, from enthusiastic adoption to cautious implementation and ethical examination. This underscores the complex considerations involved in utilizing AI tools in the educational setting. The findings highlight the need to recognize and address the distinct concerns of both students and faculty through constructive dialogue and collaboration.

Higher education institutions are encouraged to develop comprehensive ethical guidelines and balanced policies that address concerns about academic integrity, privacy, and potential misuse, while also enhancing creativity, productivity, and personalized learning experiences. Ensuring equitable access to digital resources and addressing infrastructural challenges are crucial steps for maximizing the potential of ChatGPT in higher education.

Instead of banning GAI tools, the study recommends a balanced approach that encourages responsible usage, critical thinking, and ethical considerations. This includes exploring alternative assessment methods that accommodate AI tools, cultivating critical thinking and creativity skills, and preparing students for an AI-shaped future. Creating an inclusive future where learners are knowledgeable and adaptable technology users is essential, ensuring their responsible stewardship of emerging technologies.

REFERENCES

Akgun, S., & Greenhow, C. (2021). Artificial intelligence in education: Addressing ethical challenges in K-12 settings. *AI and Ethics 2021 2:3, 2*(3), 431–440. DOI: 10.1007/s43681-021-00096-7

Alnasyan, B., Basheri, M., & Alassafi, M. (2024). The power of Deep Learning techniques for predicting student performance in Virtual Learning Environments: A systematic literature review. In *Computers and Education: Artificial Intelligence* (Vol. 6). Elsevier B.V. DOI: 10.1016/j.caeai.2024.100231

Ayanwale, M. A., Adelana, O. P., Molefi, R. R., Adeeko, O., & Ishola, A. M. (2024). Examining artificial intelligence literacy among pre-service teachers for future classrooms. *Computers and Education Open*, 6, 100179. DOI: 10.1016/j.caeo.2024.100179

Bala, K., Colvin, A., Christiansen, M. H., Heinemann, A. W., Kreps, S., Levine, L., Liang, C., Mimno, D., Rush, S., Snyder, D., Tarlow, W. E., Thoemmes, F., Vanderlan, R., Stevenson Won, A., Zehnder, A., & Ziewitz, M. (2023). *Generative Artificial Intelligence for Education and Pedagogy*.

Barrett, A., & Pack, A. (2023). Not quite eye to A.I.: Student and teacher perspectives on the use of generative artificial intelligence in the writing process. *International Journal of Educational Technology in Higher Education*, 20(1), 1–24. DOI: 10.1186/s41239-023-00427-0

Becker, B. A., Denny, P., Finnie-Ansley, J., Luxton-Reilly, A., Prather, J., & Santos, E. A. (n.d.). *Programming Is Hard – Or at Least It Used to Be: Educational Opportunities And Challenges of AI Code Generation*.

Bedington, A., Halcomb, E. F., McKee, H. A., Sargent, T., & Smith, A. (2024). Writing with generative AI and human-machine teaming: Insights and recommendations from faculty and students. *Computers and Composition*, 71, 102833. Advance online publication. DOI: 10.1016/j.compcom.2024.102833

Bressane, A., Zwirn, D., Essiptchouk, A., Saraiva, A. C. V., Carvalho, F. L. de C., Formiga, J. K. S., Medeiros, L. C. de C., & Negri, R. G. (2024). Understanding the role of study strategies and learning disabilities on student academic performance to enhance educational approaches: A proposal using artificial intelligence. *Computers and Education: Artificial Intelligence*, 6, 100196. Advance online publication. DOI: 10.1016/j.caeai.2023.100196

Caccavale, F., Gargalo, C. L., Gernaey, K. V., & Krühne, U. (2024). Towards Education 4.0: The role of Large Language Models as virtual tutors in chemical engineering. *Education for Chemical Engineers*, 49, 1–11. DOI: 10.1016/j.ece.2024.07.002

Cardona, M. A., Rodríguez, R. J., & Ishmael, K. (2023). *Artificial Intelligence and the Future of Teaching and Learning Insights and Recommendations Artificial Intelligence and the Future of Teaching and Learning.* https://tech.ed.gov

Chan, C. K. Y. (2023). A comprehensive AI policy education framework for university teaching and learning. *International Journal of Educational Technology in Higher Education*, 20(1), 38. Advance online publication. DOI: 10.1186/s41239-023-00408-3

Chauncey, S. A., & McKenna, H. P. (2023). A framework and exemplars for ethical and responsible use of AI Chatbot technology to support teaching and learning. *Computers and Education: Artificial Intelligence*, 5, 100182. Advance online publication. DOI: 10.1016/j.caeai.2023.100182

Copur-Gencturk, Y., Li, J., Cohen, A. S., & Orrill, C. H. (2024). The impact of an interactive, personalized computer-based teacher professional development program on student performance: A randomized controlled trial. *Computers & Education*, 210, 104963. Advance online publication. DOI: 10.1016/j.compedu.2023.104963

Crompton, H., & Burke, D. (2023). Artificial intelligence in higher education: The state of the field. *International Journal of Educational Technology in Higher Education*, 20(1), 22. Advance online publication. DOI: 10.1186/s41239-023-00392-8

Dalalah, D., & Dalalah, O. M. A. (2023). The false positives and false negatives of generative AI detection tools in education and academic research: The case of ChatGPT. *International Journal of Management Education*, 21(2), 100822. DOI: 10.1016/j.ijme.2023.100822

Demmer, T. R., Kühnapfel, C., Fingerhut, J., & Pelowski, M. (2023). Does an emotional connection to art really require a human artist? Emotion and intentionality responses to AI- versus human-created art and impact on aesthetic experience. *Computers in Human Behavior*, 148, 107875. Advance online publication. DOI: 10.1016/j.chb.2023.107875

Gamage, K. A. A., Dehideniya, S. C. P., Xu, Z., & Tang, X. (2023). ChatGPT and higher education assessments: More opportunities than concerns? *Journal of Applied Learning and Teaching*, 6(2), 358–369. DOI: 10.37074/jalt.2023.6.2.32

Gao, R., Merzdorf, H. E., Anwar, S., Hipwell, M. C., & Srinivasa, A. R. (2024). Automatic assessment of text-based responses in post-secondary education: A systematic review. In *Computers and Education: Artificial Intelligence* (Vol. 6). Elsevier B.V. DOI: 10.1016/j.caeai.2024.100206

Gayed, J. M., Carlon, M. K. J., Oriola, A. M., & Cross, J. S. (2022). Exploring an AI-based writing Assistant's impact on English language learners. *Computers and Education: Artificial Intelligence*, 3, 100055. Advance online publication. DOI: 10.1016/j.caeai.2022.100055

Gupta, T., Shree, A., Chanda, P., & Banerjee, A. (2023). Online assessment techniques adopted by the university teachers amidst COVID-19 pandemic: A case study. *Social Sciences & Humanities Open*, 8(1), 100579. Advance online publication. DOI: 10.1016/j.ssaho.2023.100579 PMID: 37287633

Holmes, W., Porayska-Pomsta, K., Holstein, K., Sutherland, E., Baker, T., Shum, S. B., Santos, O. C., Rodrigo, M. T., Cukurova, M., Bittencourt, I. I., & Koedinger, K. R. (2022, September). Ig, &, Bittencourt, I., & Koedinger, K. R. (2022). Ethics of AI in Education: Towards a Community-Wide Framework. *International Journal of Artificial Intelligence in Education*, 32(3), 504–526. Advance online publication. DOI: 10.1007/s40593-021-00239-1

Iqbal, N., Ahmed, H., & Azhar, K. A. (2022). EXPLORING TEACHERS' ATTITUDES TOWARDS USING CHATGPT. *Global Journal for Management and Administrative Sciences*, 3(4), 97–111. DOI: 10.46568/gjmas.v3i4.163

Ismail, N., & Yusof, U. K. (2023). A systematic literature review: Recent techniques of predicting STEM stream students. In *Computers and Education: Artificial Intelligence* (Vol. 5). Elsevier B.V. DOI: 10.1016/j.caeai.2023.100141

Jackson, S., & Panteli, N. (2023). Trust or mistrust in algorithmic grading? An embedded agency perspective. *International Journal of Information Management*, 69, 102555. Advance online publication. DOI: 10.1016/j.ijinfomgt.2022.102555

Jiang, L., Yu, S., & Wang, C. (2020). Second language writing instructors' feedback practice in response to automated writing evaluation: A sociocultural perspective. *System*, 93, 102302. DOI: 10.1016/j.system.2020.102302

Ka, C., & Chan, Y. (2023). Open Access International Journal of Educational Technology in Higher Education A comprehensive AI policy education framework for university teaching and learning. *International Journal of Educational Technology in Higher Education*, 20(1), 38. Advance online publication. DOI: 10.1186/s41239-023-00408-3

Kajiwara, Y., & Kawabata, K. (2024). AI literacy for ethical use of chatbot: Will students accept AI ethics? *Computers and Education: Artificial Intelligence*, 6, 100251. Advance online publication. DOI: 10.1016/j.caeai.2024.100251

Kizilcec, R. F., Huber, E., Papanastasiou, E. C., Cram, A., Makridis, C. A., Smolansky, A., Zeivots, S., & Raduescu, C. (2024). Perceived impact of generative AI on assessments: Comparing educator and student perspectives in Australia, Cyprus, and the United States. *Computers and Education: Artificial Intelligence*, 7, 100269. DOI: 10.1016/j.caeai.2024.100269

Lee, D., Arnold, M., Srivastava, A., Plastow, K., Strelan, P., Ploeckl, F., Lekkas, D., & Palmer, E. (2024). The impact of generative AI on higher education learning and teaching: A study of educators' perspectives. *Computers and Education: Artificial Intelligence*, 6, 100221. Advance online publication. DOI: 10.1016/j.caeai.2024.100221

Maqbool, M. A., Asif, M., Imran, M., Bibi, S., & Almusharraf, N. (2024a). Emerging E-learning trends: A study of faculty perceptions and impact of collaborative techniques using fuzzy interface system. *Social Sciences & Humanities Open*, 10, 101035. Advance online publication. DOI: 10.1016/j.ssaho.2024.101035

Maqbool, M. A., Asif, M., Imran, M., Bibi, S., & Almusharraf, N. (2024b). Emerging E-learning trends: A study of faculty perceptions and impact of collaborative techniques using fuzzy interface system. *Social Sciences & Humanities Open*, 10, 101035. Advance online publication. DOI: 10.1016/j.ssaho.2024.101035

Martin, F., Zhuang, M., & Schaefer, D. (2024). Systematic review of research on artificial intelligence in K-12 education (2017–2022). In *Computers and Education: Artificial Intelligence* (Vol. 6). Elsevier B.V. DOI: 10.1016/j.caeai.2023.100195

Marx, E., Leonhardt, T., & Bergner, N. (2023). Secondary school students' mental models and attitudes regarding artificial intelligence - A scoping review. In *Computers and Education: Artificial Intelligence* (Vol. 5). Elsevier B.V. DOI: 10.1016/j.caeai.2023.100169

Moorhouse, B. L., Yeo, M. A., & Wan, Y. (2023). Generative AI tools and assessment: Guidelines of the world's top-ranking universities. *Computers and Education Open*, 5, 100151. DOI: 10.1016/j.caeo.2023.100151

Moundridou, M., Matzakos, N., & Doukakis, S. (2024). Generative AI tools as educators' assistants: Designing and implementing Inquiry-based lesson plans. *Computers and Education: Artificial Intelligence*, 100277, 100277. Advance online publication. DOI: 10.1016/j.caeai.2024.100277

Pahi, K., Hawlader, S., Hicks, E., Zaman, A., & Phan, V. (2024). Enhancing active learning through collaboration between human teachers and generative AI. *Computers and Education Open*, 6, 100183. DOI: 10.1016/j.caeo.2024.100183

Rahimi, A. R., & Sevilla-Pavón, A. (2024). The role of ChatGPT readiness in shaping language teachers' language teaching innovation and meeting accountability: A bisymmetric approach. *Computers and Education: Artificial Intelligence*, 7, 100258. Advance online publication. DOI: 10.1016/j.caeai.2024.100258

Rapaka, A., Dharmadhikari, S. C., Kasat, K., Mohan, C. R., Chouhan, K., & Gupta, M. (2025a). Revolutionizing learning − A journey into educational games with immersive and AI technologies. *Entertainment Computing*, 52, 100809. Advance online publication. DOI: 10.1016/j.entcom.2024.100809

Rapaka, A., Dharmadhikari, S. C., Kasat, K., Mohan, C. R., Chouhan, K., & Gupta, M. (2025b). Revolutionizing learning − A journey into educational games with immersive and AI technologies. *Entertainment Computing*, 52, 100809. Advance online publication. DOI: 10.1016/j.entcom.2024.100809

Renkema, M., & Tursunbayeva, A. (2024). The future of work of academics in the age of Artificial Intelligence: State-of-the-art and a research roadmap. *Futures*, 163, 103453. DOI: 10.1016/j.futures.2024.103453

Robinson, G. M., Hardman, M., & Matley, R. J. (2021). Using games in geographical and planning-related teaching: Serious games, edutainment, board games and role-play. *Social Sciences & Humanities Open*, 4(1), 100208. Advance online publication. DOI: 10.1016/j.ssaho.2021.100208

Roll, I., & Wylie, R. (2016). Evolution and Revolution in Artificial Intelligence in Education. *International Journal of Artificial Intelligence in Education*, 26(2), 582–599. DOI: 10.1007/s40593-016-0110-3

Romero-Rodríguez, J. M., Ramírez-Montoya, M. S., Buenestado-Fernández, M., & Lara-Lara, F. (2023). Use of ChatGPT at University as a Tool for Complex Thinking: Students' Perceived Usefulness. *Journal of New Approaches in Educational Research*, 12(2), 323–339. DOI: 10.7821/naer.2023.7.1458

Saini, D. K., & Salim Al-Mamri, M. R. (2019). Investigation of Technological Tools used in Education System in Oman. *Social Sciences & Humanities Open*, 1(1), 100003. Advance online publication. DOI: 10.1016/j.ssaho.2019.100003

Shwartz-Asher, D., Raviv, A., & Herscu-Kluska, R. (2022). Teaching and assessing active learning in online academic courses. *Social Sciences & Humanities Open*, 6(1), 100341. Advance online publication. DOI: 10.1016/j.ssaho.2022.100341

Song, Y., Weisberg, L. R., Zhang, S., Tian, X., Boyer, K. E., & Israel, M. (2024). A framework for inclusive AI learning design for diverse learners. In *Computers and Education: Artificial Intelligence* (Vol. 6). Elsevier B.V. DOI: 10.1016/j.caeai.2024.100212

Steele, J. L. (2023). To GPT or not GPT? Empowering our students to learn with AI. *Computers and Education: Artificial Intelligence*, 5, 100160. Advance online publication. DOI: 10.1016/j.caeai.2023.100160

Strzelecki, A., & ElArabawy, S. (2024). Investigation of the moderation effect of gender and study level on the acceptance and use of generative AI by higher education students: Comparative evidence from Poland and Egypt. *British Journal of Educational Technology*, 55(3), 1209–1230. DOI: 10.1111/bjet.13425

Su, J., Zhong, Y., & Ng, D. T. K. (2022). A meta-review of literature on educational approaches for teaching AI at the K-12 levels in the Asia-Pacific region. In *Computers and Education: Artificial Intelligence* (Vol. 3). Elsevier B.V. DOI: 10.1016/j.caeai.2022.100065

Tsai, S.-C. (2019). Computer Assisted Language Learning Using google translate in EFL drafts: A preliminary investigation. *Computer Assisted Language Learning*, 32(5-6), 510–526. Advance online publication. DOI: 10.1080/09588221.2018.1527361

von Garrel, J., & Mayer, J. (2023). Artificial Intelligence in studies—Use of ChatGPT and AI-based tools among students in Germany. *Humanities & Social Sciences Communications*, 10(1), 799. Advance online publication. DOI: 10.1057/s41599-023-02304-7

Wang, C., Li, Z., & Bonk, C. (2024). Understanding self-directed learning in AI-Assisted writing: A mixed methods study of postsecondary learners. *Computers and Education: Artificial Intelligence*, 6, 100247. Advance online publication. DOI: 10.1016/j.caeai.2024.100247

Wang, Y., & Zhang, W. (2017). Factors Influencing the Adoption of Generative AI for Art Designing among Chinese Generation Z: A Structural equation modeling approach. *IEEE Access*. https://www.mendeley.com/reference-manager/reader-v2/91a8830d-70ac-34d3-a5c7-0743720fa9c1/6fc85f02-f390-2d55-11b9-4ff6473ab798

Weng, X., & Chiu, T. K. F. (2023). Instructional design and learning outcomes of intelligent computer assisted language learning: Systematic review in the field. In *Computers and Education: Artificial Intelligence* (Vol. 4). Elsevier B.V. DOI: 10.1016/j.caeai.2022.100117

Xiaolei, S., & Teng, M. F. (2024). Three-wave cross-lagged model on the correlations between critical thinking skills, self-directed learning competency and AI-assisted writing. *Thinking Skills and Creativity*, 52, 101524. Advance online publication. DOI: 10.1016/j.tsc.2024.101524

Zastudil, C., Rogalska, M., Kapp, C., Vaughn, J., & MacNeil, S. (2023). Generative AI in Computing Education: Perspectives of Students and Instructors. *Human - Computer Interaction*. http://arxiv.org/abs/2308.04309

Zawacki-Richter, O., Marín, V. I., Bond, M., & Gouverneur, F. (2019). Systematic review of research on artificial intelligence applications in higher education-where are the educators? *International Journal of Educational Technology in Higher Education*, 16(1), 39. Advance online publication. DOI: 10.1186/s41239-019-0171-0

Chapter 16
Predictive Model for Enhancing Learning Skill Through Biometric Integration:
A Review

Surekha Yashodharan
https://orcid.org/0009-0006-9688-7524

Government Engineering College, A.P.J. Abdul Kalam Technological University, India

K. S. Vijayanand
https://orcid.org/0000-0001-5002-5554

A.P.J. Abdul Kalam Technological University, India

ABSTRACT

In the field of education, early identification of students who require additional support due to learning difficulties is paramount importance. This paper offers a pioneering approach to revolutionize education by harnessing biometric data for personalized and effective learning experiences. This research provides a foundation for further exploration in the field of adaptive learning technologies and their potential to transform the way we educate and acquire knowledge. This study proposes the development of a predictive model that leverages biometric information, such as physiological and behavioural data, to provide real-time insights into the learning process. The predictive model is designed to adapt and personalize learning experiences based on the individual's biometric responses. By continuously monitoring and analyzing biometric data, the system can dynamically adjust the difficulty level of educational content, provide timely interventions, and optimize learning strategies.

DOI: 10.4018/979-8-3693-8191-5.ch016

INTRODUCTION

There are various types of learners like Fast learners, Bright learners, Average learners and slow learners in education field. Fast Learners have very good cordial relationships and good leadership qualities. They are almost well in all subjects. Bright learners are the ones who succeed better in a typical school setting. These learners always learn with ease, good memoriser and complete assignment. Average learners manifest average ability. Majority of learners can be classified into his group. Average learners are also known as Normal Learners. They need a teacher to bring out their skills and up bring them. A teacher must be there for providing learning style to each average learner. Slow learner is a child who qualifies for special education services. They exhibit numerous learning difficulties that seem to defy all learning methodologies and procedures. They have no interest in learning and their memory capacity is very low. They have poor communication skills, oral and writing skills are not also good. They are not able to mingle with their peers. Their scores in all tests are very low. They need repeatedly remedial classes. They are having poor eye-hand coordination. Several factors can influence the learning activity and overall academic performance of a student. These factors can be broadly categorized into personal, environmental, psychological, and social influences. Here are some key factors:

a) Personal Factors:
- Cognitive Abilities: Intelligence, memory, and critical thinking skills play a significant role in a student's ability to learn and process information.
- Motivation: A student's intrinsic and extrinsic motivation affects their engagement and willingness to participate in learning activities.
- Physical Health: General health, including nutrition, sleep quality, and physical fitness, can impact energy levels, concentration, and cognitive functioning.
- Learning Styles: Different students have varied learning preferences, such as visual, auditory, kinesthetic, or reading/writing styles, which can affect how they absorb and retain information.
- Self-Discipline: A student's ability to manage time, maintain focus, and follow through on tasks is crucial for successful learning.
- Prior Knowledge: The background knowledge and skills a student brings to a learning activity influence how well they can grasp new concepts.

b) Environmental Factors:

- Learning Environment: The physical and digital learning environments, including classroom setup, availability of resources, and online platforms, can either enhance or hinder learning.
- Teacher Quality: The effectiveness of the instructor, including their teaching style, expertise, and ability to engage students, is a critical factor.
- Class Size: Smaller class sizes generally allow for more personalized attention, which can benefit student learning.
- Access to Resources: Availability of learning materials, technology, and extracurricular support (e.g., tutoring, libraries) can significantly affect learning outcomes.

c) Psychological Factors:
- Stress and Anxiety: High levels of stress or anxiety can impair concentration, memory, and problem-solving abilities, affecting learning.
- Self-Efficacy: A student's belief in their ability to succeed in a specific task influences their approach to learning and perseverance in the face of challenges.
- Emotional Well-being: A student's emotional state, including happiness, depression, or fear, can greatly impact their ability to focus and learn.
- Attention Span: The ability to maintain attention during learning activities is crucial for effective learning and information retention.

d) Social Factors:
- Peer Influence: Interaction with classmates and friends can either positively or negatively influence a student's attitudes towards learning and academic performance.
- Parental Support: Parental involvement, encouragement, and support in educational activities are significant contributors to a student's academic success.
- Cultural Background: Cultural values and norms can shape attitudes towards education and influence a student's approach to learning.
- Socioeconomic Status: Economic factors can affect access to educational resources, extracurricular activities, and even basic needs, which in turn can impact learning.

e) Technological Factors:
- Access to Technology: The availability and use of digital tools and internet access can facilitate or hinder learning, especially in modern education systems.
- Digital Literacy: A student's ability to effectively use technology for learning is increasingly important in today's educational landscape.

f) Institutional Factors:
- Curriculum Design: The structure and content of the curriculum, including how well it aligns with students' needs and learning styles, can influence learning activity.
- Assessment Methods: The type and frequency of assessments (e.g., exams, projects, quizzes) can affect how students engage with the material.
- Support Services: Availability of counseling, academic advising, and special education services can support students with diverse needs.

g) Societal and Policy Factors:
- Educational Policies: Government policies on education funding, curriculum standards, and access to education can have broad impacts on student learning.
- Economic Conditions: The overall economic environment, including job prospects and the perceived value of education, can influence a student's motivation and engagement.

Understanding these factors is crucial for educators, parents, and policymakers to create supportive learning environments and address the diverse needs of students. As traditional educational paradigms face the challenge of catering to diverse learning styles and individual needs, the amalgamation of biometric data and predictive modelling stands as a promising frontier for revolutionizing the learning process. The convergence of biometrics and education represents a paradigm shift, leveraging real-time physiological and behavioural data to gain profound insights into the cognitive and emotional states of learners. Biometric indicators such as heart rate variability, eye tracking, and electroencephalography (EEG) provide a nuanced understanding of how students engage with learning materials. By harnessing this wealth of information, predictive model is constructed which is capable of dynamically adapting educational content to suit the unique requirements of each learner.

The objective of this paper is to critically review and analyze the development of predictive models aimed at enhancing learning skills through the integration of biometric data. This review seeks to understand how biometric indicators, such as eye-tracking, heart rate, and facial expressions, can provide insights into learning behaviors and cognitive states. The paper aims to evaluate existing models and techniques, identify key challenges and limitations, and propose directions for future research. The ultimate goal is to offer a comprehensive overview of how biometric integration can improve personalized learning experiences and contribute to more effective educational outcomes.

Related Works

Vasudevan (2017) developed a work which indicates details about slow learners. It also dictates situations which makes a child a slow learner. This paper also deals with the remedial measures that should be taken by a teacher or a parent to up bring a slow learner child. It discusses the challenges faced by slow learners in the classroom and provides potential remedies to help them succeed, including providing additional support and time in the regular classroom environment, identifying the causes of slow learning, and implementing effective educational programs tailored to their needs.

Sassirekha and Vijayalakshmi (2022) proposed an algorithm known as SLASAFP (Supervised Learning Approach For Student's Academic Future Progression) which is a best fit machine learning algorithm for predicting success in higher education. The real data set was subjected to six various techniques namely Support Vector Machine, Linear Discriminant Analysis, Principal Component Analysis, Naïve Baye's Classification, K-Nearest Neighbour and Random Forest. It focuses on the importance of predicting academic progression for educational institutions and students alike, as it can help identify at-risk students, provide early interventions, and improve overall educational outcomes The study aims to identify key factors influencing academic success and develop predictive models that can help educators and institutions support students more effectively. Academic progression refers to the continuous advancement of students through their educational journey, marked by successful completion of courses, improvement in grades, and overall academic performance. Predicting academic progression is important for identifying students at risk of underperformance or dropout. Predicting academic outcomes can be challenging due to the complex interplay of various factors, including students' personal, social, and academic characteristics. Traditional methods of monitoring student progress may not capture these complexities effectively. Machine learning offers a powerful approach to analyzing large and complex datasets, allowing for the development of predictive models that can uncover patterns and trends not easily visible through traditional analysis. In education, machine learning can be used to predict academic outcomes, identify at-risk students, and provide personalized interventions.

Alqahtani et al. (2020) proposed a system in which physiological signals are used for affect detection in a computerised English Language Test. In this work, wearable physiological sensors are used to record EEG,ECG and EMG signals of 27 individuals who are participants of the test. Feature extraction is done on these acquired recordings and which are used by machine learning models to determine the difficulty level of each individual for attending particular question and it also helps in finding out the number of questions answered correctly by the participant. Mainly four algorithms are used for classification namely Linear SVM,SVM-RBF,

Decision Tree and Linear Discriminant Analysis. This study showed classification F1-score of 74.21% for prediction of self-reported difficulty level of questions and F1-score of 59.14% for predicting correctly answered questions. These systems aim to enhance the educational experience by adapting to the emotional and cognitive states of students in real-time. ITS are computer-based systems designed to provide personalized instruction to students, mimicking the guidance of a human tutor.

Alban et al. (2023) developed a system in which wearable sensors are used to detect the challenging behaviour of children showing ASD. Heart Rate Variability (HRV) is used as the major factor for detecting challenging behaviour in this study. The four main machine learning techniques used in this work are-SVM, DT, MLP and XGBoost. Among these, XGBoost showed the best prediction performance. The study investigates how physiological signals, specifically heart rate, collected through wearable sensors, can provide insights into the emotional and behavioral responses of children with ASD in these interactions. Children with ASD often experience difficulties with social interactions and communication, which can lead to challenging behaviors, particularly in unfamiliar or stressful situations

Masri and Member (n.d.) introduced a paper which deals with the review of mental stress assessment methods and strategies in workplace. Electroencephalography (EEG), Electrocardiography (ECG), Galvanic Skin Response (GSR) and Functional near infrared spectroscopy (fNIRS) are found to be the most useful modalities to assess mental stress. Furthermore, the integration of these multimodalities with AI technology in stress assessment tools opens up new possibilities for real-time monitoring and intervention. Wearable devices, mobile applications, and data analytics can provide valuable insights into the dynamic nature of stress in the workplace, facilitating proactive measures to mitigate its impact. The review examines various tools, techniques, and approaches for monitoring and evaluating stress levels among employees, highlighting their advantages, limitations, and applications.

Lim et al. (2022) developed a paper which focuses on the exploration of the application of eye-tracking technology in the context of biometric machine learning. Biometrics involves the measurement and statistical analysis of people's unique physical and behavioural characteristics, and eye-tracking is a technology that monitors and records eye movement. This review paper helps in identifying meaningful features from eye-tracking data for the development of biometric machine learning models. The study focuses on extracting and analyzing eye movement features to develop machine learning models for accurate and reliable biometric authentication. Biometric identification involves using unique physiological or behavioral characteristics, such as fingerprints, facial recognition, or iris patterns, to verify an individual's identity. These systems are widely used for security and authentication purposes. Eye-tracking technology captures the movement and behavior of the eyes, providing a rich set of data that can be used for various applications, including biometrics. Eye movements are unique to individuals, making them a potential biometric identifier. Extracting relevant features from biometric data is crucial for developing accurate machine learning models. The challenge lies in identifying the most distinctive features that can reliably differentiate between individuals.

Odule et al. (2020) introduced a paper which proposed multimode framework for two dimensional space using affiliation rule mining and article based data. Favourite and non-favourite items of items of a specific customer can be predicted. The paper proposes a two-dimensional (User × Item)-space multimode referral scheme that uses a combination of affiliation rules mining and content-based methods to provide recommendations to users with a large user base but relatively few items. Referral systems are commonly used in various domains, such as e-commerce and social networks, to suggest relevant products, services, or connections based on user behavior and preferences.

Hung et al. (2012) introduced a generic model for educational data mining. This study focussed on case study approach for demonstrating how online teaching and learning can be made efficient. This paper proposes a generic model for Educational Data Mining (EDM) studies and demonstrates the procedures of this EDM model through a case study approach, which revealed patterns and relationships that could be used to improve online teaching and learning and predict student academic performance. The rise of online teaching and learning has created a wealth of data related to students' interactions, performance, and engagement. This data has the potential to provide insights into educational processes and outcomes. EDM involves applying data mining techniques to educational data to uncover patterns, trends, and relationships. The goal is to use these insights to inform and improve teaching practices, student support, and educational strategies. The study collects data from online learning platforms, which may include student interaction logs, course participation records, assessment results, discussion forum posts, and feedback surveys.

Tharay et al. (2020) proposed Dermatoglyphics as a novel method for finding IQ of Children of age group five to eleven years. In this method, fingertip patterns of left and right hands are analysed to find the intelligence of children. The paper aims to measure the IQ and record dermatoglyphic patterns of children aged 5-11 years, including those with intellectual disabilities, and to correlate them, finding that dermatoglyphic patterns can be used to estimate IQ range and are easier to record than traditional IQ testing methods. Dermatoglyphics refers to the scientific study of the patterns of ridges on the fingers, palms, toes, and soles. These patterns are unique to each individual and are formed during fetal development. The study posits that since dermatoglyphic patterns are influenced by genetic factors, they may be correlated with cognitive abilities and intelligence.

Raja and Raja (2020) proposed a study based on the brain lobes and fingerprint patterns. There exists 10 lobes in human brain and each lobe is related to the finger. Therefore, this study helps in identifying the inborn talent of a child and hence improvising his behavioural qualities. Cognitive science helps in studying human behaviour, emotions etc. The study aims to develop and evaluate techniques for understanding and measuring cognitive functions and intelligence potential by analyzing patterns in brain activity and other relevant data. Understanding cognitive abilities and inborn intelligence potential is important for various applications, including educational planning, career guidance, and psychological assessment.

Ahsan et al. (2021) introduced an intelligent computational approach for authenticating finger prints for identifying and verifying a person. This method showed performance with accuracy of 99.87%. Fingerprint identification is one of the most widely used biometric techniques for personal identification due to its uniqueness and permanence. However, improving the accuracy and reliability of fingerprint identification systems remains a challenge, particularly in scenarios involving noisy, low-quality, or partial fingerprints. The paper aims to develop an intelligent fingerprint identification system that combines the strengths of Gabor filters, a traditional image processing method, with deep learning techniques. The goal is to improve the accuracy, robustness, and efficiency of automatic fingerprint identification systems. Gabor filters are widely used in image processing due to their ability to capture both spatial frequency and orientation information, which are critical for identifying unique patterns in fingerprints. The features extracted using Gabor filters are fused to create a comprehensive representation of the fingerprint. Feature fusion enhances the discriminative power of the features, improving the system's ability to distinguish between different fingerprints.

Lynn and Emanuel (2020) introduced data mining techniques for predicting student's performance. Decision tree was found to be the best classification method for predicting performance of a student. This study helped in improving results of students. It explores the commonly used data mining techniques to predict students' performance, and finds that the decision trees algorithm is the best classification technique for this purpose. The study evaluates various methods, models, and approaches used to analyze educational data and make predictions about student outcomes. In the context of education, data mining techniques are used to analyze large volumes of data collected from students' interactions, assessments, and behaviors

Li et al. (2022) proposed a model which is based on Deep Neural Network is used for predicting student's academic behaviour. In this study, data set on student's heterogeneous behaviour from multiple sources is made which is used for feature extraction .This work helped a lot in improving student's academic performance. It proposes an end-to-end deep learning model that automatically extracts features from students' multi-source heterogeneous behavior data to predict academic performance, which outperforms several machine learning algorithms. The study utilizes diverse datasets collected from campus environments, including academic records, demographic information, behavioral data (such as library usage and class attendance), and social interactions. This comprehensive data provides a holistic view of a student's academic environment and behavior.

Shinghal and Saxena (2020) proposed a dermatoglyphics Multiple Intelligence test cum Psychometric test based on questionnaire for finding the entrepreneurship mind set in engineering students. It analyzes the entrepreneurial mindset of engineering students using a Dermatoglyphics Multiple Intelligence Test (DMIT) and a psychometric test, and then evaluates the impact of an entrepreneurship training program on the students' mindset. The study emphasizes the importance of fostering entrepreneurial thinking within engineering education to prepare students for innovation, problem-solving, and leadership roles in their future careers. In today's rapidly evolving technological landscape, there is a growing recognition of the need for engineers to possess not only technical skills but also an entrepreneurial mindset.

Nguyen and Nguyen (2019) proposed method for fingerprint classification using random Forest and SVM method with more than 96% accuracy. Computer vision algorithms were used in the image pre-processing stage. This method introduced an effective feature extraction with speedy and accurate classification. The paper proposes a fingerprint classification system that combines computer vision techniques for image pre-processing and machine learning algorithms, specifically Random Forest and Support Vector Machine, to achieve high accuracy in classifying fingerprints into three types: arch, loop, and whorl.

Qiao et al. (2024) introduced a paper in which an EEG emotion recognition model based on attention and generative adversarial networks achieves high accuracy on the SEED dataset. This model is used to effectively solve the problem of emotion classification using EEG signals, which had previously suffered from weak features and disturbances, and their proposed model achieved a detection accuracy of 94.87% on the SEED dataset. Emotion recognition is a crucial component in various applications, including human-computer interaction, mental health monitoring, and personalized user experiences. Accurately identifying emotions from data such as facial expressions, voice, or physiological signals is a challenging task due to the complexity and variability of human emotions.

Persson et al. (2021) developed a paper focuses on the growing concern of driver fatigue, which is a leading cause of road accidents. The researchers aim to determine whether HRV, which reflects autonomic nervous system activity, can be used as a reliable indicator to classify drivers as alert or sleep-deprived. By analyzing HRV data from drivers in real-world driving conditions, the study seeks to develop a non-invasive method to monitor driver fatigue and potentially prevent accidents. The study aims to develop a classification model that can effectively identify driver alertness levels based on HRV measurements, with the goal of improving road safety by detecting drowsy driving. Random forest provided best accuracy with 85%.

Santosh et al. (2023) introduced a paper which investigates the use of combined eye-tracking and physiological sensing technologies to assess readers' interest levels during reading activities. The study employs methodologies such as tracking pupil dilation, fixation duration, and saccades through eye-tracking, along with monitoring heart rate variability (HRV), galvanic skin response (GSR), and electromyography (EMG) for physiological responses. It explores the combination of these modalities to develop a more comprehensive understanding of a reader's engagement and interest in the material. Interest and engagement are crucial factors in the learning process, affecting comprehension, retention, and overall academic performance.

Masri et al. (2023) proposed a paper which provides an overview of various methods and technologies used to assess mental stress in work environments. The review covers both traditional and modern approaches, examining their effectiveness, advantages, and limitations in monitoring and managing stress among employees. It states that there are many effective methods for assessing mental stress in the workplace, each has its strengths and limitations. A multimodal approach, combining different assessment techniques, offers the most promise for accurately monitoring and managing stress. It examines both subjective and objective approaches to stress assessment, including self-report questionnaires, physiological measurements, and behavioral monitoring techniques. The paper also discusses modern approaches like wearable devices, mobile applications, and artificial intelligence (AI)-based methods that can continuously monitor stress levels with minimal intrusion. These technologies are becoming increasingly popular due to their ability to provide real-time feedback.

Choi et al. (2023) introduced a paper which uses machine learning approach can forecast personal learning performance in VR-based construction safety training using real-time biometric responses such as eye-tracking and EEG data, and demonstrates that a simplified forecast model using only principal features as independent variables can achieve better prediction performance compared to a full forecast model. It investigates the use of biometric data to predict individual learning outcomes in a virtual reality (VR) environment designed for construction safety training. The study focuses on how physiological signals can be used to assess and forecast the effectiveness of training programs. Biometric data were analyzed to extract relevant features that correlate with learning performance. These features included physiological indicators of stress, engagement, and cognitive load during the training.

Changa et al. (2020) introduced a paper which presents a novel approach for identifying and classifying familiar and unfamiliar individuals using electroencephalography (EEG) data. SVM and KNN are main two machine learning techniques used for classification purpose. SVM performed well with accuracy of 90.58%. The proposed system demonstrates a high level of accuracy in distinguishing between familiar and unfamiliar individuals. The use of both feature extraction and directed functional brain networks enhances the system's ability to capture the complex dynamics of brain activity associated with facial recognition. The study leverages feature extraction techniques and directed functional brain networks to achieve accurate person identification and classification, focusing on the brain's response to familiar and unfamiliar stimuli.

Hernández-Mustieles et al. (2024) proposed a paper which includes details about 140 wearable sensor technology studies in educational environment. WBT uses data collection, analysis, biofeedback techniques, and qualitative questionnaires to investigate the efficacy of teaching and learning. According to this review, the most common NPM utilized in studies on schooling is EEG. Some research use EEG alone or in combination with other biometrics including blood pressure, eye tracking, ECG, EMG, and EDA. The review systematically examines how these technologies are being utilized to enhance learning, monitor student engagement, and improve educational outcomes.

Khosravi et al. (2022) introduced a paper which provides a systematic review of the use of wearable devices in higher education, particularly for engineering education, discusses the advantages and disadvantages of different types of wearable devices based on their placement on the body, and recommends a three-step acceptability route for implementing wearable devices in higher education. It explores the application of wearable sensor technology to improve learning experiences and outcomes in higher education settings. The study investigates how these sensors can be used to monitor and enhance various aspects of student learning, providing insights into the physiological and psychological factors that influence academic performance

Ferrier et al. (2022) developed a paper which describes the development and evaluation of a wearable sensor-based educational program called "STEMfit" that aims to engage students in learning biomechanical concepts through the use of wearable technology. It reviews various types of wearable sensors, such as fitness trackers, smart watches, and EEG headsets that can monitor physiological and behavioural data like heart rate, movement, stress levels, and brain activity. Wearable sensors, such as smart watches, EEG headsets, and fitness trackers, have become increasingly popular in various fields, including healthcare, sports, and wellness

Hammoud et al. (2019) proposed a paper which Stress and Heart Rate Variability during University Final Examination among Lebanese Students. This study aims to explore how the stress experienced by university students during final exams affects their heart rate variability (HRV), a physiological marker that reflects autonomic nervous system activity and stress levels. University final exams are known to be a significant source of stress for students, often leading to heightened anxiety and potential negative impacts on both mental and physical health.

Hunasgi et al. (2018) introduced a paper focuses on identifying and assessing stress levels among dental students using smart phone sensors and specialized software. The study leverages the widespread availability of smart phones to collect data, making it a convenient and non-invasive method for monitoring stress. The study aims to evaluate the feasibility of using smart phone sensors combined with specific software to monitor stress levels in dental students, who are known to experience significant stress due to the demands of their education and clinical responsibilities

Bustos-Lopez et al. (2022) dictated paper which explores the use of wearable technology to monitor and assess student engagement in educational settings. Engagement is a critical factor in effective learning, and wearable offer a novel approach to detecting and analyzing engagement in real-time. The review aims to consolidate and analyze existing research on the use of wearable devices to detect and measure engagement in learning environments. It seeks to understand the potential of wearable in providing continuous, non-invasive monitoring of students' engagement levels. The paper discusses various types of wearable devices, such as smart watches, fitness trackers, and EEG headsets, which are equipped with sensors that can capture physiological and behavioral data.

Wu et al. (2018) introduced a paper presents a biometric authentication system based on EEG signals, which are electrical activities of the brain, with a particular emphasis on eye blinking signals. The proposed system is designed to function in an open-set environment, meaning it can differentiate between enrolled (known) users and those who are not part of the system (unknown users). The inclusion of eye blinking signals in the analysis is key, as these signals are distinct and unique to individuals, adding an extra layer of security to the authentication process. The system is evaluated on its ability to correctly authenticate users, reject impostors, and handle situations where an individual is not part of the registered user set, demonstrating high accuracy and robustness in various scenarios.

Apicella et al. (2022) introduced a paper which presents a novel approach to assessing student engagement in educational settings using EEG (electroencephalogram) signals. The paper aligns with the principles of Learning 4.0, which emphasize personalized, technology-enhanced learning experiences. The concept of Learning 4.0 involves integrating advanced technologies, such as artificial intelligence, big data, and IoT, into educational practices to create more personalized and adaptive learning environments. In this context, monitoring student engagement becomes crucial, as engagement is strongly correlated with learning outcomes. Student engagement is a critical factor in effective learning. Engaged students are more likely to retain information, participate actively, and achieve better academic results.

Zheng and Lu (2017) presents a study on developing a system to estimate human vigilance levels by analyzing brain activity (EEG) and eye movements (EOG). The research aimed to create an accurate and reliable method to estimate a person's vigilance level—a measure of their alertness or attentiveness—by combining data from electroencephalography (EEG) and electrooculography (EOG) signals. The study collected EEG and EOG data from participants engaged in tasks that required sustained attention. EEG signals provide information on brain activity, while EOG signals capture eye movements, including blinks and saccades. Features were extracted from both EEG and EOG signals, focusing on time-domain, frequency-domain, and nonlinear aspects to capture relevant information about vigilance states

Gui et al. (2019) introduced a paper which provides a comprehensive review of the field of brain biometrics, which involves using brain signals, particularly electroencephalography (EEG), for biometric identification and authentication. Brain biometrics involves using EEG signals, which are unique to each individual, as a biometric identifier. Unlike traditional biometrics (fingerprints, iris, etc.), brain biometrics are based on internal physiological characteristics. The paper discusses various methods of acquiring EEG data, including different types of EEG devices (e.g., wet vs. dry electrodes) and the conditions under which the data is collected (e.g., at rest, during tasks, etc.).

Materials and Methods

Physiological Signals affecting Learning Activity. Physiological signals are intimately connected to the learning process, providing valuable insights into a learner's cognitive and emotional states. Understanding these relationships enables the development of more responsive, adaptive, and effective educational environments. Physiological signals, such as EEG, heart rate, skin conductance, brain activity, and eye movement, are closely related to cognitive and emotional processes involved in learning. By monitoring these signals, researchers can gain insights into a learner's state of engagement, attention, stress, and cognitive load, which are all critical factors in the learning process. Some of the physiological signals are listed below:-

a) **Heart Rate (HR) and Heart Rate Variability (HRV):**
  o **Engagement and Attention**: Heart rate and HRV can indicate levels of engagement and attention. A moderate increase in heart rate might correlate with heightened attention and cognitive effort, while HRV is often associated with emotional regulation and stress levels. Low HRV can indicate stress or anxiety, which might negatively impact learning, while higher HRV is linked to a relaxed and focused state conducive to learning.
  o **Stress and Anxiety**: Elevated heart rates can also signal stress or anxiety, which can interfere with learning by reducing the ability to focus and retain information.

b) **Skin Conductance (Galvanic Skin Response, GSR):**
- o **Emotional Arousal**: GSR measures changes in skin conductivity due to sweat gland activity, which is controlled by the sympathetic nervous system. High skin conductance levels typically indicate emotional arousal, which can be related to either positive excitement or negative stress. Both types of arousal can influence learning, with moderate levels potentially enhancing focus and high levels potentially causing distraction or cognitive overload.

c) **Electroencephalography (EEG) – Brain Activity:**
- o **Cognitive Load**: EEG measures electrical activity in the brain and can provide insights into the cognitive load, which refers to the amount of mental effort being used in the working memory. Different EEG patterns are associated with different cognitive states, such as focus, relaxation, or mental fatigue. For example, an increase in theta waves might indicate cognitive effort or problem-solving, while alpha waves are often associated with a relaxed but alert state.
- o **Attention and Focus**: Specific EEG signals, like those found in the beta frequency band, are linked to focused attention and active thinking, which are essential for effective learning.

d) **Eye Movements and Pupil Dilation:**
- o **Attention and Information Processing**: Eye-tracking data, including fixation duration and pupil dilation, can reflect a learner's attention and cognitive processing. Longer fixation on a particular element of a learning material might indicate deeper cognitive processing. Pupil dilation can indicate cognitive load; larger pupils suggest higher mental effort.
- o **Reading Patterns**: Eye movement patterns can reveal how a learner interacts with text, such as how often they backtrack or reread sections, which can indicate comprehension difficulties or areas of confusion.

e) **Facial Expressions and Posture:**
- o **Emotional States**: Facial expressions and body posture, often analyzed through computer vision, can provide cues about a learner's emotional state, such as confusion, frustration, or satisfaction. These emotional responses are crucial for understanding how learners are interacting with the material and whether they are struggling or progressing smoothly.

Some of the main applications of physiological signals in learning environment are the following:-

- **Real-Time Feedback**: Monitoring physiological signals allows educators to provide real-time feedback and adapt instructional methods to better suit the learner's current state. For instance, if sensors detect high cognitive load or stress, the learning pace can be adjusted, or additional support can be provided.

- **Personalized Learning**: Physiological data can be used to personalize learning experiences by tailoring content and challenges to match the learner's cognitive and emotional state, optimizing both engagement and retention.
- **Early Intervention**: By continuously monitoring physiological signals, it's possible to identify when a learner is disengaged, stressed, or overwhelmed, allowing for timely interventions that can help mitigate these issues and keep the learner on track.

Techniques used for analyzing physiological signals in context of learning. Machine learning (ML) and deep learning (DL) techniques are widely used to analyze physiological signals in the context of learning. These techniques help to process and interpret complex physiological data, enabling the detection of engagement, cognitive load, stress, and other learning-related states. These techniques are highly relevant in analyzing physiological signals due to their ability to handle complex, high-dimensional data and extract meaningful patterns that are often difficult to identify with traditional methods. Below is a list of common ML and DL techniques associated with physiological signals and learning, along with a block diagram.

MACHINE LEARNING TECHNIQUES

ML algorithms can be used to preprocess physiological signals, such as filtering noise, normalizing data, and extracting relevant features (e.g., heart rate variability from ECG signals). Techniques like Principal Component Analysis (PCA) and Independent Component Analysis (ICA) help in reducing the dimensionality of data, making it easier to analyze.

1. Support Vector Machines (SVM)
    o Application: SVM is used for classification tasks, such as distinguishing between different levels of engagement or stress based on physiological data (e.g., heart rate, GSR).
    o Advantages: Effective in high-dimensional spaces, works well with clear margins of separation.
2. Random Forest (RF)
    o Application: RF is an ensemble method used for both classification and regression tasks. It is commonly used to predict learning outcomes or detect emotional states from a combination of physiological signals.

- o   Advantages: Handles large datasets with higher dimensionality, reduces overfitting through averaging multiple decision trees.
3. k-Nearest Neighbors (k-NN)
    - o   Application: k-NN is a simple, instance-based learning algorithm used for classifying physiological states (e.g., relaxed vs. stressed) based on nearest data points in feature space.
    - o   Advantages: Intuitive and easy to implement, especially effective with small datasets.
4. Naive Bayes
    - o   Application: Naive Bayes is used for probabilistic classification tasks, such as predicting a learner's engagement level based on physiological data.
    - o   Advantages: Works well with small datasets, particularly for tasks with categorical inputs.
5. Logistic Regression
    - o   Application: Used for binary or multi-class classification, such as determining whether a learner is engaged or disengaged based on physiological signals.
    - o   Advantages: Interpretable model, especially useful for binary outcomes.

DEEP LEARNING TECHNIQUES

Deep Learning models can automatically learn to extract features directly from raw physiological data without the need for manual feature engineering. This is particularly useful in complex signals like EEG or PPG, where patterns may be subtle or hidden.

1. Convolutional Neural Networks (CNN)
    - o   Application: CNNs are used for extracting spatial features from physiological data, such as EEG signals or images of facial expressions. They can classify different cognitive states or emotional responses.
    - o   Advantages: Excellent at capturing local features and patterns, particularly in image or spatial data.
2. Recurrent Neural Networks (RNN) and Long Short-Term Memory Networks (LSTM)
    - o   Application: RNNs and LSTMs are ideal for sequential data like time-series physiological signals (e.g., heart rate variability, EEG). They are used to predict engagement levels or cognitive load over time.

o   Advantages: Handles time dependencies well, effective for modeling sequential data and long-term dependencies.
3. Autoencoders
   o   Application: Autoencoders are used for unsupervised learning tasks like anomaly detection in physiological data, dimensionality reduction, or generating low-dimensional embeddings of complex signals.
   o   Advantages: Useful for feature learning and data compression, can model complex non-linear relationships.
4. Deep Belief Networks (DBN)
   o   Application: DBNs are used for unsupervised learning and feature extraction from physiological signals. They can be applied to tasks like detecting subtle changes in cognitive load or engagement.
   o   Advantages: Effective for learning hierarchical representations of data.
5. Generative Adversarial Networks (GANs)
   o   Application: GANs can be used for data augmentation, generating synthetic physiological data that mimic real signals, useful for training models when data is scarce.
   o   Advantages: Powerful generative model that can improve model robustness.

Block Diagram. The block diagram below in figure 1 represents how machine learning and deep learning techniques can be applied to physiological signals in learning environment.

Figure 1. Working of ML/DL Techniques in analyzing physiological signals

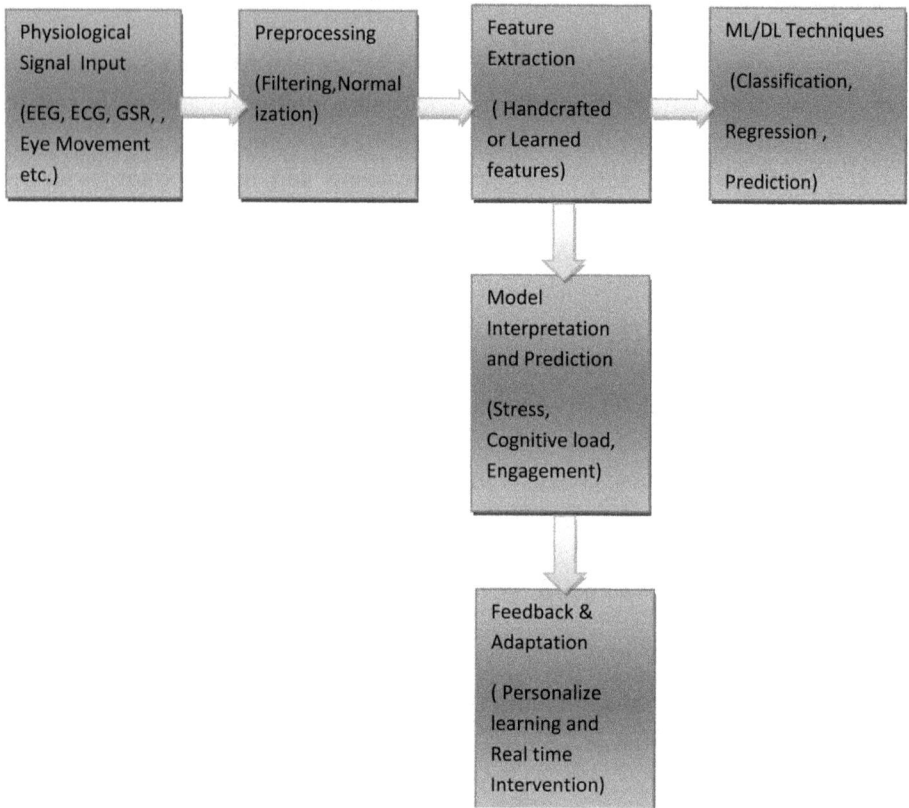

Architecture

A predictive model architecture that enhances learning skills through biometric integration typically includes the following components:

1. Data Collection Layer
   - Biometric Sensors: Collect data through various biometric devices such as eye-trackers, EEG headsets, heart rate monitors, facial recognition cameras, and skin conductance sensors.

- Learning Environment Sensors: Capture non-biometric data like mouse clicks, keystrokes, and screen interactions within digital learning platforms.
- Wearable Devices: Devices like smartwatches gather continuous physiological data, especially useful for non-intrusive, real-time monitoring.

2. Data Preprocessing Layer
   - Signal Processing: Raw biometric data, often noisy or inconsistent, undergoes filtering and normalization. This includes processes such as artifact removal in EEG signals or noise reduction in heart rate data.
   - Data Synchronization: Synchronizes data from various sources (e.g., eye movements with heart rate changes) for cohesive, time-aligned analysis.

3. Feature Extraction Layer
   - Feature Extraction: Relevant features are extracted from processed signals, such as pupil dilation from eye-tracking data, emotional indicators from facial recognition, or stress markers from heart rate variability.

4. Machine Learning and Deep Learning Techniques
   - Machine Learning Models: Uses algorithms such as neural networks, decision trees, or support vector machines (SVMs) to analyze biometric data patterns and predict cognitive and emotional states like attention, stress, or engagement levels.
   - Deep Learning Techniques: Employs deep learning models, like convolutional neural networks (CNNs) for image-based data or recurrent neural networks (RNNs) for time-series data, to capture complex, non-linear patterns within biometric data.
   - Training and Validation: Model training is conducted on labeled datasets that match biometric responses to learning outcomes. Models are iteratively validated to ensure accurate and meaningful predictions.

5. Model Interpretation and Prediction Layer
   - Edge Computing: Processes data on the local device (edge) to reduce latency, making it possible to adapt learning materials in real-time based on detected states like cognitive load or emotional state.
   - Adaptation Engine: Dynamically adjusts learning content, pace, and delivery methods. For instance, if the model detects stress, the system might slow down or offer additional explanations, providing a responsive learning experience.

6. Feedback and Intervention Layer
   - Feedback Mechanism: Provides feedback to both learners and educators. This could be visual cues for the learner or alerts for the educator if a student is disengaged or stressed.

- Personalized Recommendations: Suggests personalized learning materials, techniques, or break times based on real-time data and predictive insights.
- Data Dashboard: Displays relevant insights for educators, allowing them to monitor student progress, engagement levels, and emotional states, facilitating informed, timely interventions.

This architecture enables the predictive model to analyze a diverse range of biometric signals, derive meaningful insights into cognitive and emotional states, and adapt learning environments accordingly. Such a structure ensures adaptability, privacy, and personalization, supporting an enhanced learning experience powered by biometric integration.

Table 1. Summary is given below

Sl.No. of References.	Methodology	Advantages	Limitations/Future Enhancements
(Vasudevan, 2017)	• Causes of Slow learners • Problems and remedial measures	• Early identification and diagnosis • Giving proper guidance and motivation	Beneficial for adolescent group only
(Sassirekha & Vijayalakshmi, 2022)	• This paper focuses on best machine learning algorithm for predicting success in higher education. • KNN, SVM,NaïveBayes, PCA, Linear Descriminant Analysis and RF were used.	Provided an accuracy of 90% in predicting student's academic behaviour	Limitations in analysing students' online learning assessment.
(Alqahtani et al., 2020)	• LSVM,SVM-RBF,DT,LDA	• Predicting self –reporting difficulty level of question • Predicting correct answers	• Integrating this system into real time ITS • User friendliness should be improved
(Alban et al., 2023)	SVM MLP, DT, XGBoost	• To detect challenging behaviour among children with Autism	• Enhanced to predict performance in learning
(Masri & Member, n.d.)	ECG,EEG, GSR and Functional near infrared spectroscopy (fNIRS), Regression, Clustering	• Identifying stress level of employee	• Needed more accurate assessment • Limitations of workplace environment • Using XAI to build trust in prediction models

continued on following page

Table 1. Continued

Sl.No. of References.	Methodology	Advantages	Limitations/Future Enhancements
(Lim et al., 2022)	ML algorithms like SVM, KNN and RF	• Used for classification	• Enhanced to computational ntelligence domain
(Odule et al., 2020)	Two dimensional Space multimodal referral scheme is used	• Improved versatility • Better forecast exactness	Can be enhanced for finding the areas of interest of students
(Hung et al., 2012)	EDM model was proposed based on Knowledge Data Discovery	Improves online teaching and learning method	Limited to student's learning management system
(Tharay et al., 2020)	• Raven's colored progressive matrices • Finger tip pattern analysis	Determination of IQ with finger tip pattern	• Limited to age group 9-11 • Gender based differences not evaluated
(Raja & Raja, 2020)	Cognitive Science, Cognitive Informatics and Pattern Recognition	Early detection of inborn talents	Can be enhanced to find out birth defects
(Ahsan et al., 2021)	• Gabor filters and CNN were used • PCA algorithm applied for feature map	Provided accuracy of 99.87%	Study can be extended using other biometric measures
(Lynn & Emanuel, 2020)	Decision Tree, Naïve Bayes, KNN and SVM	Easiest method for predicting student's academic behaviour	Can be used for predicting performance of staff in any organisation
(Li et al., 2022)	Deep Neural Networks, LSTM	Academic performance can be predicted dynamically over time	More data is needed to enhance the interpretability of the model
(Shinghal & Saxena, 2020)	DMIT Test,Psychometric test	Helps in improving students	Can be enhanced to many higher education systems
(Nguyen & Nguyen, 2019)	CNN, Random forest and SVM	Classification with accuracy >=96%	Deep learning methods can be used for optimization.
(Qiao et al., 2024)	Generative Adversarial Network, CNN	• Improved Accuracy of emotion recognition • Expansion of brain map data	Graphical features can be made unlimited
(Persson et al., 2021)	KNN, Ada Boost, SVM, RF	• Early detection of driver fatigue • Non-invasive monitoring	• Environmental Factors • Individual Variability • Limited dataset

continued on following page

Table 1. Continued

Sl.No. of References.	Methodology	Advantages	Limitations/Future Enhancements
(Santosh et al., 2023)	CNN-LSTM	• Enhanced Accuracy • Real time monitoring • Personalized learning experience	• Data integration complexity • High costs • Privacy Concerns
(Masri et al., 2023)	EEG,GSR,fNIRS	• Improved Accuracy • Comprehensive Assessment	• Integration of multisensory stimulation and multimodalities for stress mitigation
(Choi et al., 2023)	Ridge, SVR, MLP	• Enhance the safety of workers • Robust system	• Improved to handle multiple accidents • Need to integrate VR simulations with biometric responses.
(Changa et al., 2020)	SVM,KNN	• Helpful in BCI studies • Helps in detection of brain diseases • Helps in deception detection	• Complexity of signal processing • Extension of datasets • Low Spatial Resolution
(Hernández-Mustieles et al., 2024)	Physiological signals	• Helps in improving academic performance • Helps in improving mental health	Generation of better predictive algorithms for forecasting academic performance
(Khosravi et al., 2022)	Wearable devices, Physiological signals	• Enhance student's learning	• Inclusion of real world cases
(Ferrier et al., 2022)	Wearable devices	• Cost effective wearable • User friendly	• Scalability • Enhanced to other student cohorts
(Hammoud et al., 2019)	ECG	• Real time monitoring systems.	• Limited sampling rate of ECG • Number of participants can be increased
(Hunasgi et al., 2018)	Android,HRV, Oxygen Saturation	Detection of stress	Large dataset needed

continued on following page

Table 1. Continued

Sl.No. of References.	Methodology	Advantages	Limitations/Future Enhancements
(Bustos-Lopez et al., 2022)	Physiological signals	Early engagement detection	• Need of comparative analysis of wearable devices • Analysis of actual contribution of wearable devices needed • Examining of mobile applications for physical sign monitoring • Analysis of user acceptance needed
(Wu et al., 2018)	CNN, BPNN	• High Accuracy • Real-time capability	Improve practicability of system
(Apicella et al., 2022)	SVM, TCA	• Assessment of cognitive engagement • Assessment of emotional engagement	Implementation in real educational situation
(Zheng & Lu, 2017)	EEG,EOG,ML	• Improved accuracy • Real time montitoring	• Complexity of data processing • Intrusiveness for sensors
(Gui et al., 2019)	SVM, NN, Ensemble learning, LDA, PCA	Improved Accuracy	• Lack of real world applications • Scalibility Issues

Issues and Challenges

- Data Privacy and Ethical Concerns: Collecting and processing biometric data raise significant privacy issues. Ensuring the confidentiality and ethical use of sensitive biometric information, especially in educational settings, poses a challenge. Policies and protocols must be established to protect students' rights and data.
- Data Quality and Variability: Biometric data is often prone to noise, variability, and inconsistency, which can lead to inaccuracies in the predictive models. Variability in data collection methods and equipment, along with the influence of external factors (e.g., environment, stress levels), can complicate data standardization and model reliability.
- Integration of Diverse Biometric Indicators: Combining multiple biometric inputs—such as eye movement, heart rate, and facial expressions—requires complex, multivariate data processing and fusion techniques. Ensuring that

these diverse inputs are accurately interpreted and integrated into a unified predictive model is a major technical hurdle.

- Model Accuracy and Interpretability: While predictive models may show promising accuracy in controlled studies, translating them to real-world educational environments can be challenging. Furthermore, the complexity of these models often reduces interpretability, making it difficult for educators and students to understand the model's outputs and take actionable steps.

- Real-time Processing and Scalability: The practical application of these models in educational settings requires real-time data processing capabilities. Achieving this in a scalable manner, especially in large institutions, is challenging due to computational demands and the need for infrastructure that supports continuous biometric data monitoring.

- Individual Differences and Adaptive Learning: Biometric responses to learning stimuli vary widely between individuals due to differences in cognitive processing, cultural background, and learning styles. Developing models that can adapt to such individual differences, rather than applying a one-size-fits-all approach, is essential for achieving meaningful improvements in learning outcomes.

- High Cost of Biometric Equipment: Implementing biometric sensors and tools for educational purposes can be costly, which may limit the accessibility and widespread adoption of these models, especially in resource-constrained environments.

- Lack of Longitudinal Studies: The lack of long-term studies assessing the impact of biometric integration on learning outcomes limits the evidence supporting the effectiveness of these predictive models. More longitudinal research is needed to validate these models over time and across different learning contexts.

Addressing these challenges is essential for the successful implementation of biometric-based predictive models that can reliably enhance learning skills and provide valuable insights in educational settings.

Current Trends

- Personalized Learning through Real-Time Feedback: Predictive models are increasingly focused on providing real-time feedback by analyzing biometric data, enabling adaptive learning pathways. These models use data such as eye-tracking, heart rate variability, and facial expressions to gauge student engagement, stress, and focus, tailoring educational content based on individual cognitive states.

- Integration of Multi-Modal Biometrics: There is a shift towards using multiple biometric indicators to create more comprehensive models of student engagement and learning states. By integrating diverse data sources—such as EEG, eye movements, and facial expressions—researchers are improving the accuracy of these predictive models and gaining richer insights into complex cognitive and emotional responses during learning.
- Machine Learning and Deep Learning for Enhanced Prediction Accuracy: Advanced machine learning algorithms, including deep learning and neural networks, are being employed to handle the complex, non-linear nature of biometric data. These models can detect subtle patterns in biometric signals, leading to better predictions of cognitive load, motivation, and readiness to learn.
- Emotion-Aware Learning Models: Emotion recognition, derived from facial expressions, voice tone, and physiological data, is being incorporated to predict learning outcomes and adjust learning strategies. These models aim to detect emotional states that can impact learning, such as frustration or boredom, allowing the system to prompt educators or modify the learning content.
- Edge Computing for Real-Time Biometric Processing: To manage the challenges of real-time processing, edge computing is being explored, allowing biometric data to be processed locally on devices. This reduces latency, enhances data privacy, and enables more responsive adaptive learning interventions in real-time.
- Wearable Technology for Continuous Monitoring: Wearable devices like smartwatches and headbands are gaining popularity for continuous biometric monitoring in learning contexts. These wearables can track physiological signals—such as heart rate and galvanic skin response—in real-time, contributing to non-intrusive, continuous data collection.
- Focus on Privacy-Preserving Techniques: With increasing concerns over data privacy, predictive models now often incorporate privacy-preserving methods such as data anonymization and federated learning, allowing the analysis of biometric data without compromising personal information. This trend is crucial for the ethical implementation of biometric-based learning models in educational environments.
- Longitudinal Studies for Predictive Model Validation: Researchers are placing more emphasis on longitudinal studies to evaluate how biometric-driven predictive models impact learning outcomes over time. This trend is aimed at validating the long-term effectiveness of such models and identifying patterns that only emerge in extended study periods.

- Cross-Cultural and Inclusivity Research: Recognizing that biometric responses may vary across cultural and demographic lines, there is a growing trend towards studying how predictive models perform across diverse populations. This inclusivity focus aims to refine models to ensure they're effective and fair across different cultural and socio-economic backgrounds.

These trends reflect a growing interest in using biometric data to enable more adaptive, personalized, and effective learning experiences while addressing key issues related to data privacy, inclusivity, and model reliability.

Application Areas

- **K-12 and Higher Education**: Predictive models using biometric data are being used in schools and universities to personalize learning experiences. By monitoring engagement and cognitive load, these models help educators identify students who may need additional support or customized content, enhancing learning outcomes across diverse age groups.
- **Corporate Training and Professional Development**: In corporate settings, biometric-integrated predictive models are applied to evaluate employee engagement and retention during training sessions. This approach helps identify effective training modules and allows real-time adjustments to maintain engagement, ensuring that employees acquire essential skills more effectively.
- **Special Education**: For students with learning disabilities, such as ADHD or autism, biometric data can be invaluable for understanding attention patterns, emotional responses, and engagement levels. Predictive models help educators adjust teaching approaches based on real-time feedback, creating more inclusive and supportive learning environments.
- **Remote and E-Learning Platforms**: In online education, predictive models with biometric integration provide insights into student engagement levels, even in virtual environments. Biometric data such as facial recognition and eye-tracking allow platforms to detect signs of distraction or fatigue, enabling real-time adjustments to content pacing and interaction styles.
- **Language Learning**: Language learning applications benefit from biometric models by monitoring learners' stress levels, engagement, and focus during speaking exercises. This allows platforms to provide customized feedback and adaptively present challenges that match the learner's cognitive state, enhancing retention and skill acquisition.
- **Gaming-Based Learning (Edutainment)**: In educational gaming, biometrics help track player engagement and emotional responses to game content. Predictive models can adapt the game's difficulty and offer tailored feedback

based on biometric cues, making learning both enjoyable and effective, particularly for young learners.

- **Medical and Healthcare Education**: In medical training, predictive models use biometrics to assess students' emotional and cognitive responses during simulations. Monitoring parameters like heart rate and gaze patterns helps evaluate readiness to perform under stress, giving trainers feedback on areas where learners may need additional support or practice.
- **Workplace Safety and Skills Assessment**: In high-stress or safety-critical industries (e.g., aviation, manufacturing), predictive models help in training simulations by tracking biometric indicators that signify stress, attention, and reaction times. This allows employers to assess employee readiness and address potential safety concerns through targeted training interventions.
- **Test Preparation and Assessment**: Biometric data can be used in test prep and assessment tools to monitor focus, anxiety, and cognitive load during practice exams. Predictive models can then provide personalized feedback and suggest techniques to improve focus and reduce test anxiety, ultimately enhancing performance on assessments.
- **Sports Education and Coaching**: In athletic training and sports education, predictive models use biometric data to monitor mental engagement, focus, and stress levels. By adapting training techniques based on cognitive and emotional states, coaches can optimize performance and skill development in sports settings.

These application areas highlight how predictive models with biometric integration are transforming the learning process across a broad range of educational and training contexts, making learning more responsive, personalized, and adaptive.

Pros

- Personalized Learning Experiences: By analyzing biometric data, predictive models can deliver highly tailored educational experiences that adapt to a student's cognitive and emotional states, leading to better engagement and comprehension.
- Enhanced Engagement and Motivation: Real-time feedback based on biometric indicators can help educators and learners address disengagement, stress, and fatigue, making learning experiences more interactive and enjoyable.
- Insightful Feedback for Educators: Predictive models provide educators with actionable insights about student learning patterns, allowing them to identify students who may need additional support and adapt their teaching strategies accordingly.

- Support for Special Education Needs: These models can provide individualized support for learners with special needs by tracking attention levels and cognitive load, which helps educators implement effective and supportive teaching methods.
- Reduced Test Anxiety: By monitoring stress and emotional responses during assessments, predictive models can help students practice stress management, which could lead to improved test performance and overall confidence.
- Lifelong Learning Applications: Predictive models have potential applications beyond traditional education, supporting skills training, professional development, and lifelong learning by providing insights into learners' engagement and readiness.
- Encouragement of Social-Emotional Learning (SEL): By tracking emotional responses, predictive models can support SEL by helping students become aware of and manage their emotions, ultimately fostering empathy, resilience, and interpersonal skills.

Cons

- Privacy and Ethical Concerns: The collection and analysis of sensitive biometric data raise privacy and ethical concerns. Protecting data confidentiality, ensuring informed consent, and adhering to ethical guidelines are challenging but crucial.
- Data Sensitivity and Noise: Biometric data can be inconsistent due to environmental factors, individual differences, and sensor variability, which can affect the reliability and accuracy of predictions and lead to potential misinterpretations.
- High Implementation Costs: Biometric sensors and the computational infrastructure needed to support real-time processing can be costly, potentially limiting access to these technologies for under-resourced institutions and students.
- Risk of Over-Reliance on Technology: Heavy reliance on predictive models may reduce educators' focus on traditional teaching methods and intuitive observations, which are also essential for effective teaching and engagement.
- Complexity of Model Interpretation: Advanced predictive models, especially those involving machine learning, can be difficult for educators and students to interpret. This lack of transparency could limit the model's usability and trustworthiness in educational settings.
- Dependence on Infrastructure and Connectivity: Real-time biometric monitoring requires robust infrastructure and internet connectivity, which may be

challenging to implement in remote or rural areas and other under-resourced settings.
- Ethical Use in Testing and Assessment: The use of biometric data for assessments raises ethical questions about fairness and transparency. Misinterpretation of biometric cues may impact a student's evaluation unfairly.

CONCLUSION AND FUTURE WORK

This paper has delved into the evolving landscape of educational technology, specifically focusing on the integration of biometrics to develop predictive models for enhancing learning skills. In this review, several biometric modalities have been explored ranging from fingerprint analysis to physiological measurements such as heart rate variability. These modalities, when harnessed effectively, offer unique insights into the cognitive and emotional states of learners, enabling the development of predictive models that can anticipate individual learning needs and tailor educational interventions accordingly. The real-time feedback provided by biometric data can inform educators about the engagement levels, cognitive load, and emotional states of learners. In future, the challenges and ethical considerations associated with biometric data usage in education must be carefully addressed. Striking a balance between the benefits of enhanced learning experiences and the protection of privacy and data security is paramount.

Future Scope is as follows:

- Advanced Personalization of Learning: As predictive models evolve, they will enable even finer-grained personalization by adjusting content, pacing, and teaching methods according to real-time cognitive and emotional states. This hyper-personalized learning will cater to diverse individual needs, making education more inclusive and effective.
- Enhanced Real-Time Adaptability: Future models will likely achieve true real-time adaptability, where biometric data instantly adjusts learning environments to suit the learner's current state. This will empower systems to reduce frustration, improve engagement, and provide immediate support based on detected stress, fatigue, or disengagement.
- Integration with Virtual and Augmented Reality (VR/AR): The integration of predictive models with VR and AR environments could offer immersive, interactive, and adaptive learning experiences. Biometrics could track learners' physiological responses within VR/AR, adjusting scenarios and feedback to maintain engagement and maximize cognitive benefits in real-time.

- Emotionally Intelligent Learning Systems: As emotion recognition technology becomes more sophisticated, future predictive models could interpret nuanced emotional cues such as confusion, satisfaction, or boredom. Emotionally intelligent systems would then provide empathetic responses or interventions, creating a supportive learning experience that enhances emotional well-being.
- Cross-Domain and Multi-Context Applications: Predictive models could be deployed across diverse learning contexts, from academic and corporate settings to personal development and mental health training. By incorporating multi-context learning, models could adapt skills learned in one environment to another, fostering continuous, lifelong learning.
- Artificial Intelligence-Driven Tutors: Future predictive models will likely drive AI tutors capable of interacting naturally with learners while sensing their emotional and cognitive states. These AI-driven tutors could dynamically adjust teaching strategies, employ more engaging narratives, and maintain learner interest by "reading" the learner's responses.
- Integration with Brain-Computer Interfaces (BCIs): Advances in BCIs could integrate directly with predictive learning models, providing unprecedented insights into cognitive load and focus levels. BCIs, in tandem with traditional biometrics, could facilitate even deeper, more accurate monitoring and support of cognitive and emotional states, helping to optimize learning in real time.
- Scalable Implementation in Large-Scale Educational Settings: With advances in cloud computing and edge computing, biometric-based predictive models will become more scalable, allowing widespread use in classrooms, universities, and online learning platforms. Scalability will enable broader adoption, making adaptive learning technologies accessible to more students and institutions.
- Data-Driven Policy and Curriculum Development: Aggregated insights from predictive models could guide educational policy and curriculum design, identifying effective learning methods, challenging subjects, and key focus areas for various demographics. This data-driven approach will support curriculum improvements that reflect how students learn best.
- Incorporation of Soft Skills and Social-Emotional Learning (SEL): Future models could expand their focus beyond academic skills, using biometrics to enhance soft skills, such as empathy, resilience, and teamwork, by analyzing physiological responses to social and collaborative learning experiences.

REFERENCES

Ahsan, M., Based, M. A., Haider, J., & Kowalski, M. (2021). An intelligent system for automatic fingerprint identification using feature fusion by Gabor filter and deep learning. *Computers & Electrical Engineering*, 95, 107387.

Alban, A. Q., Alhaddad, A. Y., Al-Ali, A., So, W. C., Connor, O., Ayesh, M., & Cabibihan, J. J. (2023). Heart rate as a predictor of challenging behaviours among children with autism from wearable sensors in social robot interactions. *Robotics (Basel, Switzerland)*, 12(2), 55.

Alqahtani, F., Katsigiannis, S., & Ramzan, N. (2020). Using wearable physiological sensors for affect-aware intelligent tutoring systems. *IEEE Sensors Journal*, 21(3), 3366–3378.

Apicella, A., Arpaia, P., Frosolone, M., Improta, G., Moccaldi, N., & Pollastro, A. (2022). EEG-based measurement system for monitoring student engagement in learning 4.0. *Scientific Reports*, 12(1), 5857.

Bustos-Lopez, M., Cruz-Ramirez, N., Guerra-Hernandez, A., Sánchez-Morales, L. N., Cruz-Ramos, N. A., & Alor-Hernandez, G. (2022). Wearables for engagement detection in learning environments: A review. *Biosensors (Basel)*, 12(7), 509.

Changa, W., Wang, H., Yan, G., & Liu, C. (2020). An EEG based familiar and unfamiliar person identification and classification system using feature extraction and directed functional brain network. *Expert Systems with Applications*, 158, 113448.

Choi, D., Seo, S., Park, H., Hong, T., & Koo, C. (2023). Forecasting personal learning performance in virtual reality-based construction safety training using biometric responses. *Automation in Construction*, 156, 105115.

Ferrier, B., Lee, J., Mbuli, A., & James, D. A. (2022). Translational Applications of Wearable Sensors in Education: Implementation and Efficacy. *Sensors (Basel)*, 22, 1675. DOI: 10.3390/s22041675 PMID: 35214578

Gui, Q., Ruiz-Blondet, M., Laszlo, S., & Jin, Z. (2019). A survey on brain biometrics. *ACM Computing Surveys*, 51(6), 1–38.

Hammoud, S., Karam, R., Mourad, R., Saad, I., & Kurdi, M. (2019). Stress and Heart Rate Variability during University Final Examination among Lebanese Students. *Behavioral Sciences (Basel, Switzerland)*, 9(3). Advance online publication. DOI: 10.3390/bs9010003 PMID: 30591634

Hernández-Mustieles, M. A., Lima-Carmona, Y. E., Pacheco-Ramírez, M. A., Mendoza-Armenta, A. A., Romero-Gómez, J. E., Cruz-Gómez, C. F., & Lozoya-Santos, J. D. J. (2024). Wearable Biosensor Technology in Education: A Systematic Review. *Sensors (Basel)*, 24(8), 2437.

Hunasgi, S., Koneru, A., Rudraraju, A., Manvikar, V., & Vanishree, M. (2018). Stress recognition in dental students using smartphone sensor and a software: A pilot study. *Journal of Oral and Maxillofacial Pathology : JOMFP*. PMID: 30651673

Hung, J.-L., Rice, K., & Saba, A. (2012). An Educational Data Mining Model for Online Teaching and Learning. *Journal of Educational Technology Development and Exchange*, 5(2).

Khosravi, S., Bailey, S. G., Parvizi, H., & Ghannam, R. (2022). Wearable Sensors for Learning Enhancement in Higher Education. *Sensors (Basel)*, 22, 7633. DOI: 10.3390/s22197633 PMID: 36236732

Li, X., Zhang, Y., Cheng, H., Li, M., & Yin, B. (2022). Student achievement prediction using deep neural network from multi-source campus data. *Complex & Intelligent Systems*, 8(6), 5143–5156.

Lim, J. Z., Mountstephens, J., & Teo, J. (2022). Eye-tracking Feature Extraction for Biometric Machine Learning. *Frontiers in Neurorobotics, 15*.

Lynn, N. D., & Emanuel, A. W. R. (2020). Using Data Mining Techniques to Predict Students' Performance. a Review. ICIMECE 2020 IOP Conf. Series: Materials Science and Engineering, 1096. DOI: 10.1088/1757-899X/1096/1/012083

Masri, G., Al-Shargie, F., Tariq, U., Almughairbi, F., Babiloni, F., & Al-Nashash, H. (2023). Mental stress assessment in the workplace: A review. *IEEE Transactions on Affective Computing*.

Masri, G., & Member, G. S. (n.d.). Mental Stress Assessment in the Workplace. *RE:view*. Advance online publication. DOI: 10.1109/TAFFC.2023.3312762

Nguyen, H. T., & Nguyen, L. T. (2019). Fingerprints classification through image analysis and machine learning method. *Algorithms*, 12(11), 241.

Odule, T. J., Adesina, A. O., Abdullah, A. K. K., & Ogunyinka, P. I. (2020). Using Affiliation Rules-based Data Mining Technique in Referral System. *Iraqi Journal of Science*, 3095–3103.

Persson, A., Jonasson, H., Fredriksson, I., Wiklund, U., & Ahlström, C. (2021). Heart Rate Variability for Classification of Alert Versus Sleep Deprived Drivers in Real Road Driving Conditions. *IEEE Transactions on Intelligent Transportation Systems*, 22(6).

Qiao, W., Sun, L., Wu, J., Wang, P., Li, J., & Zhao, M. (2024). EEG emotion recognition model based on attention and GAN. *IEEE Access : Practical Innovations, Open Solutions*.

Raja, R., & Raja, H. (2020). Assessment Methods of Cognitive Ability of Human Brains for Inborn Intelligence Potential Using Pattern Recognitions. DOI: 10.5772/intechopen.93268

Santosh, J., Dzsotjan, D., & Ishimaru, S. (2023). Multimodal Assessment of Interest Levels in Reading: Integrating Eye-Tracking and Physiological Sensing. *IEEE Access : Practical Innovations, Open Solutions*, 11.

Sassirekha, M. S., & Vijayalakshmi, S. (2022). Predicting the academic progression in student's standpoint using machine learning. *Automatika Journal for Control, Measurement, Electronics,Computer Communications*, 63(4), 605–617.

Shinghal, K., & Saxena, A. (2020). Analysis of Entrepreneurial Mindset in Engineering Students. *International Journal of Advances in Engineering and Technology*, 13–23.

Tharay, N., Nirmala, S. V. S. G., Bavikati, V. N., & Nuvvula, S. (2020). Dermatoglyphics as a Novel Method for Assessing Intelligence Quotient in Children Aged 5–11 Years: A Cross-sectional Study. *International Journal of Clinical Pediatric Dentistry*, 13(4), 355.

Vasudevan, A. (2017). Slow learners – Causes, problems and educational programmes. *International Journal of Applied Research*, 3(12), 308–313.

Wu, Q., Zeng, Y., Zhang, C., Tong, L., & Yan, B. (2018). An EEG-Based Person Authentication System with Open-Set Capability Combining Eye Blinking Signals. *Sensors (Basel)*, 18(335). Advance online publication. DOI: 10.3390/s18020335 PMID: 29364848

Zheng, W. L., & Lu, B. L. (2017). A multimodal approach to estimating vigilance using EEG and forehead EOG. *Journal of Neural Engineering*, 14, 026017. DOI: 10.1088/1741-2552/aa5a98 PMID: 28102833

Chapter 17
Promoting Inclusive and Equitable Quality Education for Indigenous Peoples Through E-Learning and Digital Resources

Myla Arcinas
https://orcid.org/0000-0002-5795-031X
De La Salle University, Philippines

ABSTRACT

This study explores the transformative potential of e-learning technologies in indigenous education, addressing persistent educational disparities. Through comprehensive literature analysis and international case studies, it investigates how digital resources and innovative educational strategies can overcome geographical barriers, preserve indigenous languages and foster culturally responsive education. The paper critically analyzes successful digital learning initiatives and identifies best practices in implementation. It concludes with actionable recommendations for researchers, educators, and policymakers, advocating for indigenous leadership, investment in digital infrastructure, and the respectful integration of indigenous and Western knowledge systems. By navigating these complexities, the study posits that e-learning is a powerful tool for creating global equitable, culturally affirming and effective educational experiences for indigenous learners.

DOI: 10.4018/979-8-3693-8191-5.ch017

INTRODUCTION

Indigenous peoples, comprising approximately 476 million individuals world-wide, represent a rich tapestry of cultures, languages, and traditional knowledge systems (United Nations, 2020). Despite their significant contributions to global cultural diversity and sustainable practices, indigenous communities often need help accessing quality education. The United Nations Declaration on the Rights of Indigenous Peoples (UNDRIP) emphasizes the right of indigenous peoples to establish and control their educational systems in a manner appropriate to their cultural methods of teaching and learning (United Nations, 2007).

The reality of indigenous education globally presents a complex picture. While some countries have made strides in incorporating indigenous perspectives into their national curricula, others need help providing even primary educational access to indigenous communities. A study by Naylor et al. (2020) across various countries revealed that indigenous students consistently underperform compared to their non-indigenous counterparts in standardized educational assessments, highlighting a persistent achievement gap.

The challenges in providing quality education to indigenous communities are multifaceted and deeply rooted in historical, socioeconomic, and geographical factors. The remoteness of many indigenous settlements often results in limited access to educational infrastructure and qualified teachers (Wilks et al., 2020). This geographical isolation is compounded by socioeconomic disparities, with many in-digenous communities experiencing higher rates of poverty, which further impedes educational access and resources (Biddle & Markham, 2018).

Language barriers present another significant challenge. Many indigenous languages are endangered, and education systems often prioritize dominant na-tional languages, leading to a disconnect between home and school environments for indigenous learners (Hornberger, 2019). This linguistic mismatch can result in cognitive dissonance and reduced learning outcomes. Furthermore, the lack of culturally relevant curricula and pedagogies that respect and incorporate indigenous knowledge systems has been identified as a significant barrier to effective learning among Indigenous students (Nakata et al., 2020). Traditional educational models often need to recognize the unique ways of knowing and learning intrinsic to indig-enous cultures, leading to disengagement and high dropout rates.

In the face of these challenges, e-learning and digital resources present promising opportunities for enhancing educational access and quality for indigenous learners. The flexibility and scalability of digital technologies offer potential solutions to overcome geographical barriers and resource limitations (Rennie et al., 2019). E-learning platforms can be tailored to incorporate indigenous languages and cultural content, promoting linguistic diversity and cultural preservation. Lockard and De

Maio (2021) demonstrated how digital inclusion initiatives in Australian Aboriginal communities have improved educational outcomes and strengthened connections to cultural heritage.

Moreover, digital resources' interactive and multimedia capabilities align well with indigenous pedagogical approaches emphasizing experiential and narrative-based learning. For instance, virtual and augmented reality technologies can create immersive learning experiences that bridge traditional knowledge with modern educational content (Pulla, 2017).

This chapter aims to provide a comprehensive overview of the intersection between indigenous education and e-learning technologies. This chapter aims to:

1. To analyze the current global landscape of indigenous education, highlighting both progress and persistent challenges.
2. To critically examine the potential of e-learning and digital resources in addressing the unique educational needs of indigenous communities.
3. To explore case studies and best practices in implementing digital learning solutions for indigenous education.
4. To discuss the ethical considerations and potential pitfalls of applying e-learning technologies in indigenous contexts.
5. To outline a framework for developing culturally responsive and technologically innovative educational strategies for Indigenous learners.

This chapter addresses these objectives to contribute to the growing knowledge of inclusive and equitable education for indigenous peoples. It intends to provide educators, policymakers, and technology developers with insights and strategies for leveraging e-learning to enhance educational outcomes while respecting and promoting indigenous cultural identities.

GLOBAL LANDSCAPE OF INDIGENOUS EDUCATION: PROGRESS AND PERSISTENT CHALLENGES

The state of indigenous education worldwide presents a complex tapestry of advancements and ongoing obstacles. This section analyzes the current global landscape, shedding light on both the progress made and the challenges that continue to impede equitable educational access and outcomes for indigenous populations.

Progress in Indigenous Education

In recent years, notable improvements in indigenous education have been witnessed across various regions. Many countries have acknowledged the importance of indigenous education and developed specific policies to address it. For instance, New Zealand's Te Whāriki curriculum framework integrates Māori perspectives, promoting cultural responsiveness in early childhood education (McLachlan et al., 2018). Similarly, Canada's Truth and Reconciliation Commission has increased its national policy focus on indigenous education (Archibald & Hare, 2017).

The implementation of Mother Tongue-Based Multilingual Education (MTB-MLE) programs has gained traction globally. In the Philippines, the introduction of MTB-MLE has positively impacted indigenous students' academic performance and cultural preservation (Metila et al., 2016). A study by Walter and Dekker (2011) found that MTB-MLE programs in Papua New Guinea significantly improved literacy outcomes for indigenous children.

There has also been a rise in educational programs developed and managed by indigenous communities. The First Nations School of Toronto in Canada exemplifies this trend, offering a curriculum that integrates traditional knowledge with provincial standards (Toulouse, 2016). In Australia, the Stronger Smarter Institute, founded by indigenous educator Chris Sarra, has been instrumental in transforming expectations of indigenous student achievement (Sarra et al., 2018).

Many educational systems now incorporate indigenous knowledge and practices. Australia's incorporation of Aboriginal and Torres Strait Islander histories and cultures as a cross-curriculum priority in its national curriculum represents a significant step forward (Lowe & Yunkaporta, 2013). In Latin America, countries like Bolivia and Ecuador have constitutionally recognized the importance of indigenous knowledge in education (Osuna, 2013).

Several countries have implemented affirmative action policies and scholarship programs to boost indigenous participation in higher education. Brazil's quota system for public universities has significantly increased indigenous student enrollment (Schwartzman & Knobel, 2016). In New Zealand, the University of Auckland's Vision 2020 and Strategic Plan 2013-2020 prioritized Māori and Pacific student success, increasing enrollment and completion rates (Theodore et al., 2016).

Persistent Challenges

Despite these advancements, significant challenges remain. Indigenous students continue to face substantial gaps in educational attainment compared to non-indigenous populations. A study by the OECD (2017) found that Indigenous students were likelier to leave school early and less likely to attain tertiary education across member countries' movements; despite some improvements, the gap in Year 12 attainment between Indigenous and non-indigenous students remains significant (Biddle & Edwards, 2017).

Indigenous students still need help with education systems primarily using dominant languages and cultural frameworks. This linguistic mismatch can decrease engagement and academic performance (Skutnabb-Kangas & Dunbar, 2010). A study in Peru by Hynsjö and Damon (2016) found that Indigenous students performed significantly better when taught in their native language.

Remote indigenous communities often need more access to quality educational resources and infrastructure. A World Bank report (2015) highlighted how geographical isolation compounds economic disadvantages, creating significant educational barriers for Latin American indigenous populations. In Canada, Ottmann (2017) noted that many First Nations schools on reserves receive less funding per student than provincial schools, exacerbating educational inequities.

More teachers from Indigenous communities must be adequately trained in culturally responsive pedagogies. This gap affects the quality and relevance of education provided to Indigenous students (Santoro et al., 2011). In Norway, Keskitalo and Olsen (2019) found that many teachers in Sámi schools felt unprepared to effectively teach Sámi culture and language.

Despite progress, many curricula must adequately reflect indigenous histories, knowledge systems, and perspectives. This lack of representation can alienate indigenous students and perpetuate historical inaccuracies (Battiste, 2013). A study in Chile by Webb and Radcliffe (2016) revealed that despite policy changes, textbooks continue to marginalize indigenous knowledge and experiences.

The legacy of colonialism and forced assimilation policies continues to impact Indigenous communities' relationship with formal education systems. Historical trauma and systemic discrimination create ongoing challenges for educational engagement and success (Bombay et al., 2014). In the United States, Brayboy and Maaka (2015) argue that addressing historical trauma is crucial for improving educational outcomes for Native American students.

There is a global need for comprehensive, disaggregated data on indigenous education. This lack of information hinders evidence-based policy-making and targeted interventions (UNESCO, 2019). Guimond et al. (2014) highlight the challenges in collecting and interpreting data on indigenous populations in Canada, emphasizing the need for improved data collection methods.

Overall, the global landscape of indigenous education is characterized by a tension between promising advancements and persistent, deeply rooted challenges. While there has been notable progress in policy recognition, cultural integration, and community-led initiatives, significant disparities and structural barriers impede equitable educational outcomes for indigenous populations worldwide.

Addressing these challenges requires sustained commitment, increased resources, and a fundamental shift towards inclusive and culturally responsive educational systems. Future efforts must focus on bridging the implementation gap between policy and practice, amplifying indigenous voices in educational decision-making, and fostering genuine partnerships between indigenous communities, governments, and educational institutions.

As Tuck and McKenzie (2015) argue, decolonizing educational approaches are essential for meaningful change. This involves incorporating indigenous knowledge into curricula and transforming educational systems' structures and power dynamics. Only through such concerted and culturally grounded approaches can we create an educational landscape that honors indigenous rights, knowledge, and aspirations while providing equitable opportunities for all.

THE POTENTIAL OF E-LEARNING AND DIGITAL RESOURCES IN INDIGENOUS EDUCATION

Integrating e-learning and digital resources into indigenous education presents promising opportunities and significant challenges. This section critically examines the potential of these technologies in addressing the unique educational needs of indigenous communities, considering both the benefits they may offer and the barriers to their effective implementation.

Increased Access to Education

One of the primary advantages of e-learning is its potential to overcome geographical barriers that often limit educational access for indigenous communities in remote areas. Rennie et al. (2019) highlight how online courses and digital resources can bring educational content to students who might otherwise be unable to attend traditional schools due to distance or other logistical challenges. Lockard and Huss (2016) found that mobile learning technologies in Native American schools in the United States improved student engagement and academic performance.

However, the digital divide remains a significant challenge. Gonzales (2018) found that many indigenous communities, particularly in remote areas, lack the necessary technological infrastructure and internet connectivity to fully engage with e-learning resources. This disparity in access could potentially exacerbate existing educational inequalities if not addressed systematically.

Preservation and Transmission of Indigenous Knowledge

Digital technologies offer innovative ways to document, preserve, and transmit indigenous knowledge and languages. Galla (2016) discusses how digital archives and language learning apps have supported indigenous language revitalization efforts. For example, the First Voices initiative in Canada has developed online platforms for preserving and teaching indigenous languages (Carpenter et al., 2018). These digital preservation efforts are crucial, given the endangered status of many indigenous languages.

However, Suri et al. (2019) caution that the design of educational technologies often reflects Western paradigms, which may not align with indigenous ways of knowing and learning. They emphasize the importance of involving indigenous communities in designing and developing digital learning resources to ensure cultural appropriateness and relevance. This collaborative approach is essential to avoid the risk of digital colonialism and to ensure that technology serves as a tool for cultural preservation rather than assimilation.

Culturally Responsive and Flexible Learning

E-learning platforms can be designed to incorporate culturally responsive pedagogies and content. Keskitalo et al. (2019) describe how digital learning environments can be adapted to reflect Sámi cultural values and ways of knowing in Nordic countries. This flexibility allows for greater customization to meet the diverse needs of indigenous learners, potentially increasing engagement and learning outcomes.

However, implementing culturally responsive e-learning requires careful consideration of indigenous pedagogies. Battiste (2013) argues that the uncritical application of Western educational technologies can lead to "cognitive imperialism," marginalizing indigenous knowledge systems and ways of learning. She emphasizes the need for "two-eyed seeing" – an approach that respectfully brings together indigenous and Western knowledge systems. This balanced approach ensures that e-learning enhances rather than supplants traditional knowledge transmission methods.

Enhancing Digital Literacy

Incorporating e-learning and digital resources into indigenous education can help bridge the digital divide. Resta and Laferrière (2015) argue that developing digital literacy skills is crucial for indigenous students' future academic and professional success in an increasingly technology-driven world. Educators can prepare indigenous learners to navigate their traditional cultures and the global digital landscape by integrating digital skills into culturally relevant curricula.

However, Salazar et al. (2020) note that many indigenous communities face challenges related to low levels of digital literacy, which can hinder the adoption and effective use of e-learning tools. They argue for the need to couple the introduction of digital technologies with comprehensive digital literacy programs. This holistic approach ensures that technology adoption is accompanied by the skills necessary to use these tools effectively and critically.

While e-learning and digital resources offer significant potential for enhancing indigenous education, their successful implementation requires a nuanced, culturally grounded approach. Key considerations include:

1. Ensuring equitable access to technology and internet connectivity,
2. Involving indigenous communities in the design and development of digital learning resources,
3. Balancing the preservation of traditional knowledge with the development of contemporary digital skills and
4. Addressing challenges related to digital literacy and technological adoption.

By carefully navigating these considerations, e-learning can be a powerful tool for creating equitable, culturally affirming educational experiences for indigenous learners. The path forward requires ongoing collaboration between indigenous communities, educators, technologists, and policymakers to ensure that digital solutions are technologically advanced, culturally appropriate, and pedagogically sound.

CASE STUDIES AND BEST PRACTICES IN IMPLEMENTING DIGITAL LEARNING SOLUTIONS FOR INDIGENOUS EDUCATION

Implementing digital learning solutions in indigenous education has yielded valuable insights and best practices. This section explores several case studies worldwide, highlighting successful approaches and critical lessons learned.

First Voices Initiative (Canada)

The First Voices initiative in British Columbia, Canada, exemplifies the effective use of digital technologies for language revitalization and cultural preservation (Carpenter et al., 2016). This online platform for archiving and teaching indigenous languages features a user-friendly interface for creating custom language lessons and mobile apps for language learning.

Carpenter et al. (2016) report that the initiative has archived over 60 indigenous languages and dialects. A follow-up Galla (2018) study found that participating communities reported increased youth engagement with traditional languages and improved intergenerational knowledge transfer. Essential best practices identified include:

1. Community-driven content creation,
2. Integration of multimedia resources (audio, video, text), and
3. Accessibility across multiple devices.

Ara Irititja Project (Australia)

The Ara Irititja Project in Central Australia demonstrates the potential of digital archives in preserving and sharing indigenous cultural heritage (Hughes & Dallwitz, 2007). This project features a digital archive of historical and cultural materials, custom-designed software for culturally appropriate access and use, and community-controlled data management.

Hughes and Dallwitz (2007) report that the project has digitized over 150,000 historical items. Kral (2010) found that the digital archive has become a valuable educational resource, supporting intergenerational learning and cultural continuity. Best practices identified include:

1. Customized technological solutions respecting cultural protocols,
2. Emphasis on community ownership and control, and
3. Integration with existing educational programs.

Te Reo Māori Project (New Zealand)

The Te Reo Māori Project in New Zealand showcases the potential of social media and digital platforms to support indigenous language learning (Keegan et al., 2015). This initiative uses Twitter for language practice and engagement, develops Māori language keyboards and predictive text, and creates online Māori language communities.

Keegan et al. (2015) found that the project increased participants' daily use of te reo Māori. A subsequent study by Olsen-Reeder et al. (2017) reported improved language proficiency and cultural connection among young Māori learners engaged with digital platforms. Best practices identified include:

1. Leveraging popular social media platforms
2. Developing language-specific digital tools
3. Fostering online learning communities

Sámi Pedagogy and Digital Learning (Nordic Countries)

Integrating Sámi pedagogy with digital learning environments in Nordic countries offers insights into culturally responsive e-learning design (Keskitalo et al., 2019). This approach features digital learning environments reflecting Sámi cultural values, integrating traditional knowledge with digital literacy skills, and involving Sámi educators and technologists in collaborative design.

Keskitalo et al. (2019) report improved engagement and academic performance among Sámi students using these culturally tailored digital learning environments. Rahko-Ravantti (2020) found that this approach strengthened cultural identity while developing crucial digital skills. Best practices identified include:

1. Incorporation of indigenous pedagogical principles in digital design
2. Collaborative development with indigenous educators
3. Balancing cultural content with contemporary skill development

Mobile Learning in Aboriginal Communities (Australia)

The use of mobile technologies in remote Aboriginal communities in Australia demonstrates the potential of m-learning in overcoming geographical and infrastructure barriers (Auld et al., 2012). This initiative uses mobile devices for literacy and numeracy development, creates locally relevant digital content, and provides offline functionality to address connectivity issues.

Auld et al. (2012) report increased student engagement and improved literacy outcomes. A follow-up study by Featherstone (2017) found that the initiative also enhanced community involvement in education and improved digital literacy among adults. Best practices identified include:

1. Utilization of mobile technologies to overcome infrastructure limitations,
2. Development of culturally relevant, localized content, and
3. Design for offline use in areas with limited connectivity.

The comparison of the five case studies presented in the paper is presented in Table 1. The table includes the following columns: Case Study: The name of the initiative, Location: The country or region where the study took place, Key Features:

Main characteristics of the project, Outcomes: Reported results of the initiative, and Best Practices: Key lessons learned or successful strategies identified.

Table 1. Comparison of the five case studies based on their key features, outcomes and best practices

Case Study	Location	Key Features	Outcomes	Best Practices
First Voices Initiative	Canada	- Online platform for archiving and teaching indigenous languages - User-friendly interface for creating custom language lessons - Mobile apps for language learning	- Archived over 60 indigenous languages and dialects - Increased youth engagement with traditional languages - Improved intergenerational knowledge transfer	1. Community-driven content creation 2. Integration of multimedia resources 3. Accessibility across multiple devices
Ara Irititja Project	Australia	- Digital archive of historical and cultural materials - Custom-designed software for culturally appropriate access and use - Community-controlled data management	- Successfully digitized over 150,000 historical items - Became a valuable educational resource - Supported intergenerational learning and cultural continuity	1. Customized technological solutions respecting cultural protocols 2. Emphasis on community ownership and control 3. Integration with existing educational programs
Te Reo Māori Project	New Zealand	- Use of Twitter for language practice and engagement - Development of Māori language keyboard and predictive text - Creation of online Māori language communities	- Increased daily use of te reo Māori among participants - Improved language proficiency and cultural connection among young Māori learners	1. Leveraging popular social media platforms 2. Developing language-specific digital tools 3. Fostering online learning communities

continued on following page

Table 1. Continued

Case Study	Location	Key Features	Outcomes	Best Practices
Sámi Pedagogy and Digital Learning	Nordic Countries	- Digital learning environments reflecting Sámi cultural values - Integration of traditional knowledge with digital literacy skills - Collaborative design involving Sámi educators and technologists	- Improved engagement and academic performance among Sámi students - Strengthened cultural identity while developing crucial digital skills	1. Incorporation of indigenous pedagogical principles in digital design 2. Collaborative development with indigenous educators 3. Balancing cultural content with contemporary skill development
Mobile Learning in Aboriginal Communities	Australia	- Use of mobile devices for literacy and numeracy development - Creation of locally relevant digital content - Offline functionality to address connectivity issues	- Increased student engagement and improved literacy outcomes - Enhanced community involvement in education - Improved digital literacy among adults	1. Utilization of mobile technologies to overcome infrastructure limitations< 2. Development of culturally relevant, localized content 3. Design for offline use in areas with limited connectivity

Synthesis of Best Practices

Drawing from these case studies, several overarching best practices for implementing digital learning solutions in indigenous education emerge:

1. Community Involvement and Ownership: Successful initiatives prioritize indigenous community involvement in all stages of development and implementation (Sinti et al., 2021). This ensures cultural relevance and promotes long-term sustainability.
2. Cultural Responsiveness: Digital learning solutions should be designed to reflect and respect indigenous cultural values, knowledge systems, and learning styles (Keskitalo et al., 2019).
3. Language Support: Given language's critical role in cultural identity, effective digital solutions often incorporate features for indigenous language learning and preservation (Galla, 2016).

4. Flexible and Accessible Design: Considering the diverse contexts of indigenous learners, successful digital solutions are often designed for use across multiple devices and in areas with limited connectivity (Rennie et al., 2019).
5. Integration with Traditional Practices: The most effective approaches balance digital learning with traditional, land-based, and experiential learning practices (Schwartz et al., 2016).
6. Capacity Building: Successful implementation often includes programs to develop digital literacy skills within the community, ensuring that users can fully engage with and maintain the digital learning solutions (Salazar et al., 2020).
7. Ongoing Evaluation and Adaptation: Given the rapidly evolving nature of technology and educational needs, successful initiatives incorporate mechanisms for ongoing evaluation and adaptation (Sinti et al., 2021).

The case studies and best practices presented here demonstrate the potential of digital learning solutions to address the unique educational needs of indigenous communities. However, they also underscore the importance of thoughtful, culturally grounded implementation. Successful digital learning initiatives in indigenous education contexts are characterized by deep community involvement, cultural responsiveness, and a balanced approach that leverages technology while respecting traditional knowledge and practices.

As technology evolves, ongoing research and collaboration with indigenous communities will be crucial to refine these best practices and develop innovative approaches that support indigenous learners' educational success while strengthening cultural identities and knowledge systems.

ETHICAL CONSIDERATIONS AND POTENTIAL PITFALLS OF APPLYING E-LEARNING TECHNOLOGIES IN INDIGENOUS CONTEXTS

Implementing e-learning technologies in indigenous educational contexts presents a complex landscape of ethical considerations and potential pitfalls. While these technologies offer significant opportunities for enhancing educational access and outcomes, their application must be approached with careful consideration of the unique cultural, social, and historical contexts of indigenous communities. This section explores key ethical issues and potential risks associated with e-learning in indigenous education.

Cultural Appropriateness and Representation

One of the primary ethical concerns in implementing e-learning technologies in indigenous contexts is ensuring cultural appropriateness and accurate representation. Ethical considerations include respect for indigenous knowledge systems and ways of learning, accurate and respectful representation of indigenous cultures in digital content, and avoidance of cultural appropriation or misrepresentation.

Potential pitfalls include imposing Western educational paradigms through technology (Suri et al., 2019), misrepresenting or oversimplifying complex cultural concepts (Fairlie et al., 2014), and perpetuating stereotypes or outdated information about indigenous cultures.

Suri et al. (2019) emphasize the importance of co-designing e-learning technologies with indigenous communities to ensure cultural appropriateness. Their study of digital learning initiatives in Malaysia found that projects developed without significant indigenous input often failed to resonate with learners and, in some cases, presented inaccurate or stereotypical cultural information.

Data Sovereignty and Intellectual Property Rights

Data collection, storage, and use in e-learning platforms raise significant ethical questions regarding data sovereignty and intellectual property rights. Ethical considerations include respect for indigenous data sovereignty, traditional knowledge and cultural intellectual property protection, and ensuring community control over data and its uses.

Potential pitfalls include unauthorized collection or use of indigenous cultural knowledge (Kukutai & Taylor, 2016), exploitation of indigenous intellectual property for commercial gain, and loss of community control over culturally sensitive information.

Kukutai and Taylor (2016) argue that Indigenous data sovereignty is crucial in the digital age. They highlight cases where Indigenous communities have lost control over their cultural and intellectual property due to digitization projects failing to consider data ownership and control issues adequately.

Digital Divide and Equitable Access

The implementation of e-learning technologies can exacerbate existing inequalities if not carefully managed. Ethical considerations include ensuring equitable access to technology and internet connectivity, addressing disparities in digital literacy, and avoiding creating new forms of educational disadvantage.

Potential pitfalls include widening the educational gap between connected and unconnected communities (Rennie et al., 2019), excluding learners needing necessary technology or skills, and creating a two-tiered educational system within indigenous communities.

Rennie et al. (2019) found that introducing digital learning platforms in some Australian indigenous communities inadvertently widened educational disparities. Students in areas with better internet connectivity and access to devices benefited, while those in more remote or under-resourced areas fell further behind.

Language Preservation vs. Digital Inclusion

The choice of language in e-learning platforms presents a complex ethical dilemma. Ethical considerations include supporting indigenous language preservation and revitalization, ensuring learners can access various educational resources, and balancing local language needs with broader educational goals.

Potential pitfalls include reinforcing the dominance of colonial languages in education (Hornberger, 2019), limiting access to global knowledge if only indigenous languages are used, and creating linguistic barriers within heterogeneous indigenous communities.

Hornberger (2019) discusses the tension between using indigenous languages in education to support cultural preservation and the pressure to use dominant languages to access wider educational and economic opportunities. E-learning platforms must navigate this complex linguistic landscape carefully.

TRADITIONAL KNOWLEDGE SYSTEMS AND WESTERN EDUCATION MODELS

Integrating e-learning technologies often bring Western educational models into Indigenous contexts, raising questions about preserving traditional knowledge systems. Ethical considerations include respecting and incorporating indigenous pedagogies and knowledge systems, avoiding the marginalization of traditional learning methods, and balancing traditional and contemporary knowledge in curricula.

Potential pitfalls include undermining traditional knowledge transmission methods (Battiste, 2013), privileging Western scientific knowledge over indigenous ways of knowing, and creating conflict between traditional and technology-based learning approaches.

Battiste (2013) argues that the uncritical application of Western educational technologies can lead to "cognitive imperialism," marginalizing indigenous knowledge systems and ways of learning. She emphasizes the need for "two-eyed seeing" – an approach that respectfully brings together indigenous and Western knowledge systems.

Community Autonomy and External Dependencies

Introducing e-learning technologies can create new dependencies on external expertise and resources. Ethical considerations include maintaining community autonomy in educational decision-making, building local technology management and content creation capacity, and ensuring the long-term sustainability of e-learning initiatives.

Potential pitfalls include creating dependency on external technical expertise (Resta & Laferrière, 2015), diminishing community control over educational content and delivery, and implementing unsustainable projects that fail when external support ends.

Resta and Laferrière (2015) highlight the importance of capacity building within indigenous communities to manage and sustain e-learning initiatives. They argue that without local expertise, e-learning projects risk creating new forms of educational colonialism.

Privacy and Safe Learning Environments

E-learning platforms raise essential privacy considerations, particularly in small, close-knit indigenous communities. Ethical considerations include protecting learner privacy and data security, creating safe online learning environments, and respecting cultural information-sharing norms.

Potential pitfalls include exposing sensitive personal or cultural information (Galla, 2016), creating opportunities for cyberbullying or online harassment, and violating cultural protocols around knowledge sharing and dissemination.

Galla (2016) discusses how some indigenous language learning apps have faced challenges in balancing the need for user engagement with cultural protocols around who can share certain types of knowledge. This highlights the complex intersection of digital privacy and cultural norms in e-learning contexts.

Applying e-learning technologies in indigenous contexts offers significant potential benefits but presents various ethical challenges and pitfalls. To navigate these complex issues, it is crucial to:

1. Indigenous leadership and participation should be prioritized in all stages of e-learning development and implementation (Suri et al., 2019).
2. Develop clear protocols for data sovereignty and intellectual property protection (Kukutai & Taylor, 2016).
3. Address infrastructure and digital literacy gaps to ensure equitable access (Rennie et al., 2019).
4. Adopt flexible, multilingual approaches that support language preservation and broader educational goals (Hornberger, 2019).
5. Integrate indigenous and Western knowledge systems respectfully, avoiding cognitive imperialism (Battiste, 2013).
6. Build local capacity to ensure community autonomy and project sustainability (Resta & Laferrière, 2015).
7. Implement robust privacy protections that respect cultural norms (Galla, 2016).

By carefully considering these ethical dimensions and potential pitfalls, educators and technologists can work towards e-learning solutions that respect indigenous rights, preserve cultural integrity, and provide meaningful educational opportunities for indigenous learners. The path forward requires ongoing dialogue, collaboration, and a commitment to ethical, culturally responsive practices in developing and implementing e-learning technologies for indigenous education.

A FRAMEWORK FOR DEVELOPING CULTURALLY RESPONSIVE AND TECHNOLOGICALLY INNOVATIVE EDUCATIONAL STRATEGIES FOR INDIGENOUS LEARNERS

Developing educational strategies that are both culturally responsive and technologically innovative for Indigenous learners requires a thoughtful, multifaceted approach. This section outlines a comprehensive framework based on current research and best practices in Indigenous education and educational technology.

1. Cultural Grounding and Indigenous Knowledge Systems

The foundation of any effective educational strategy for Indigenous learners must be deeply rooted in the relevant Indigenous culture and knowledge systems. Battiste (2013) emphasizes the importance of "two-eyed seeing," which involves bringing together Indigenous and Western ways of knowing. This approach ensures that technological innovations are grounded in cultural relevance.

Fundamental Components: a) Integration of Indigenous epistemologies and ontologies (Battiste, 2013), b) Incorporation of local Indigenous languages (McCarty & Nicholas, 2014), and c) Recognition of traditional teaching and learning methods (Barnhardt & Kawagley, 2005)

Implementation Strategies:

- Collaborate with Indigenous elders and knowledge keepers in curriculum development.
- Develop digital resources that showcase Indigenous stories, art, and cultural practices.
- Create language learning apps and digital dictionaries for Indigenous languages.

2. Community-Driven Design and Ownership

Successful educational strategies must be developed in partnership with Indigenous communities, ensuring local ownership and relevance. Galla (2016) demonstrates how participatory design in digital language resources leads to more effective and sustainable educational tools.

Fundamental Components: a) Participatory design methodologies (Galla, 2016), b) Community control over educational content and delivery (Castell et al., 2015), and c) Capacity building within the community (Resta & Laferrière, 2015)

Implementation Strategies:

- Establish community advisory boards for educational technology projects
- Train local community members in content creation and technology management
- Implement feedback mechanisms for continuous community input and improvement

3. Culturally Responsive Pedagogy

Educational strategies must reflect Indigenous ways of teaching and learning, adapted for the digital age. Cajete (1994) describes Indigenous education as inherently holistic, integrating spiritual, environmental, and communal aspects of learning.

Fundamental Components: a) Holistic and relational approaches to learning (Cajete, 1994), b) Place-based education (Greenwood, 2013), and c) Storytelling and oral traditions in digital formats (Iseke & Moore, 2011)

Implementation Strategies:

- Develop virtual reality experiences that connect learners to significant cultural sites.
- Create digital storytelling platforms that allow elders to share traditional knowledge.
- Design collaborative online projects that reflect communal learning practices.

4. Technological Innovation and Digital Literacy

While grounding strategies in cultural responsiveness, leveraging cutting-edge technology to prepare learners for the digital age is crucial. Mills et al. (2019) highlight the importance of critical digital literacy in empowering Indigenous youth to navigate and shape the digital world.

Fundamental Components: a) Access to up-to-date hardware and software (Rennie et al., 2019), b) Development of critical digital literacy skills (Mills et al., 2019), and c) Exposure to a range of digital tools and platforms (Sánchez et al., 2015)

Implementation Strategies:

- Provide training in coding and app development tailored to Indigenous contexts
- Implement maker spaces that blend traditional crafts with digital fabrication
- Develop e-portfolios that showcase both cultural knowledge and digital skills

5. Flexible and Adaptive Learning Environments

Educational strategies should accommodate diverse learning needs and contexts within Indigenous communities. Lockard and Huss (2016) demonstrate how blended learning can effectively combine face-to-face cultural instruction with online resources in Indigenous education.

Fundamental Components: a) Blended learning approaches (Lockard & Huss, 2016), b) Mobile learning solutions for remote areas (Auld et al., 2012), and c) Asynchronous learning options (Dipartimento et al., 2018)

Implementation Strategies:

- Develop offline-capable mobile apps for areas with limited internet connectivity.
- Create modular, self-paced online courses that allow for flexible learning schedules.

- Implement virtual tutoring programs that connect learners with Indigenous mentors.

6. Culturally Appropriate Assessment and Evaluation

Assessment strategies must reflect Indigenous values and ways of demonstrating knowledge. Castagno and Brayboy (2008) argue for assessment methods that value Indigenous ways of knowing and expressing knowledge.

Fundamental Components: a) Performance-based assessments (Castagno & Brayboy, 2008), b) Incorporation of Indigenous metrics of success (Cajete, 2015), and c) Formative assessment techniques that support holistic development (Kaka'e et al., 2019)

Implementation Strategies:

- Develop digital portfolios that showcase cultural competencies alongside academic achievements.
- Create assessment rubrics that incorporate Indigenous values and knowledge systems.
- Implement peer and community assessment features in online learning platforms.

7. Sustainable and Scalable Implementation

To ensure long-term success, educational strategies must be sustainable within individual communities and scalable across diverse Indigenous contexts. Kral (2010) emphasizes the importance of sustained investment in digital infrastructure and skills development in Indigenous communities.

Fundamental Components: a) Long-term funding and resource allocation (Kral, 2010) b) Ongoing professional development for educators (Singleton et al., 2015) c) Adaptable frameworks that can be customized for different Indigenous groups (Deepa et al., 2019)

Implementation Strategies:

- Establish partnerships with tech companies for long-term support and upgrades
- Create online professional learning communities for Indigenous educators
- Develop open-source platforms that can be easily adapted to different cultural contexts

Below is the summary of the key components, key features, and implementation strategies for the Framework for Developing Culturally Responsive and Technologically Innovative Educational Strategies for Indigenous Learners (see Table 2). The table includes the following columns: Framework Component: The seven main components of the framework. Key Features: The primary characteristics of each component, and Implementation Strategies: Practical approaches to implement each component.

Table 2. Summary of the key components, key features and implementation strategies to developing framework that is culturally responsive and technologically innovative educational strategies for indigenous learners

Framework Component	Key Features	Implementation Strategies
1. Cultural Grounding and Indigenous Knowledge Systems	- Integration of Indigenous epistemologies and ontologies - Incorporation of local Indigenous languages - Recognition of traditional teaching and learning methods	- Collaborate with Indigenous elders and knowledge keepers in curriculum development - Develop digital resources showcasing Indigenous stories, art, and cultural practices - Create language learning apps and digital dictionaries for Indigenous languages
2. Community-Driven Design and Ownership	- Participatory design methodologies - Community control over educational content and delivery - Capacity building within the community	- Establish community advisory boards for educational technology projects - Train local community members in content creation and technology management - Implement feedback mechanisms for continuous community input and improvement
3. Culturally Responsive Pedagogy	- Holistic and relational approaches to learning - Place-based education - Storytelling and oral traditions in digital formats	- Develop virtual reality experiences connecting learners to significant cultural sites - Create digital storytelling platforms allowing elders to share traditional knowledge - Design collaborative online projects reflecting communal learning practices

continued on following page

Table 2. Continued

Framework Component	Key Features	Implementation Strategies
4. Technological Innovation and Digital Literacy	- Access to up-to-date hardware and software - Development of critical digital literacy skill - Exposure to a range of digital tools and platforms	- Provide training in coding and app development tailored to Indigenous contexts - Implement maker spaces blending traditional crafts with digital fabrication - Develop e-portfolios showcasing both cultural knowledge and digital skills
5. Flexible and Adaptive Learning Environments	- Blended learning approaches - Mobile learning solutions for remote areas - Asynchronous learning options	- Develop offline-capable mobile apps for areas with limited internet connectivity - Create modular, self-paced online courses allowing for flexible learning schedules - Implement virtual tutoring programs connecting learners with Indigenous mentors
6. Culturally Appropriate Assessment and Evaluation	- Performance-based assessments - Incorporation of Indigenous metrics of success - Formative assessment techniques supporting holistic development	- Develop digital portfolios showcasing cultural competencies alongside academic achievements - Create assessment rubrics incorporating Indigenous values and knowledge systems - Implement peer and community assessment features in online learning platforms
7. Sustainable and Scalable Implementation	- Long-term funding and resource allocation - Ongoing professional development for educators - Adaptable frameworks customizable for different Indigenous groups	- Establish partnerships with tech companies for long-term support and upgrades - Create online professional learning communities for Indigenous educators - Develop open-source platforms easily adaptable to different cultural contexts

The framework for developing culturally responsive and technologically innovative educational strategies for Indigenous learners emphasizes the importance of grounding all initiatives in Indigenous knowledge systems and community ownership.

By integrating cultural responsiveness with technological innovation, this approach aims to create educational experiences that are relevant, empowering, and effective for Indigenous learners.

Successful implementation of this framework requires ongoing collaboration between Indigenous communities, educators, technologists, and policymakers. It also demands a commitment to continuous evaluation and adaptation to ensure educational strategies remain relevant and practical in rapidly changing technological landscapes and evolving community needs.

By following this framework, educators and communities can develop educational strategies that honor Indigenous knowledge and learning methods while equipping learners with the skills and knowledge needed to thrive in the digital age. The path forward is one of respectful collaboration, innovative thinking, and unwavering commitment to the educational empowerment of Indigenous learners.

CONCLUSION

This comprehensive review of e-learning and digital resources in indigenous education reveals a complex interplay of opportunities and challenges in promoting inclusive and equitable quality education for indigenous peoples. The global landscape of indigenous education shows significant progress in policy recognition and community-led initiatives, yet persistent disparities underscore the need for continued efforts and innovative approaches. E-learning technologies offer promising solutions for enhancing educational access, preserving indigenous languages, and promoting culturally responsive education. Successful initiatives such as Canada's First Voices, Australia's Ara Irititja Project, and New Zealand's Te Reo Māori Project demonstrate the potential of digital technologies to bridge geographical barriers, support language revitalization, and preserve cultural knowledge. However, implementing these technologies must carefully navigate ethical considerations, including cultural appropriateness, data sovereignty, and the digital divide. The proposed framework for developing culturally responsive and technologically innovative educational strategies emphasizes the importance of grounding initiatives in indigenous knowledge systems while leveraging the benefits of digital technologies. This approach aligns with calls for decolonizing education and respecting indigenous ways of knowing, learning, and teaching.

To ensure the successful integration of e-learning and digital resources in indigenous education, the following is being recommended:

1. Prioritize indigenous leadership and participation in all stages of e-learning development and implementation.

469

2. Invest in digital infrastructure and literacy programs to ensure equitable access across indigenous communities.
3. Develop clear protocols for data sovereignty and protection of indigenous intellectual property.
4. Adopt multilingual approaches that support both language preservation and broader educational goals.
5. Integrate indigenous and Western knowledge systems respectfully, avoiding cognitive imperialism.
6. Build local capacity to ensure community autonomy and long-term sustainability of digital learning initiatives.
7. Implement culturally sensitive privacy protections that respect indigenous norms and values.

By adhering to these recommendations and the best practices identified in successful case studies, it is possible to harness the power of digital technologies to create educational experiences that are not only accessible and effective but also deeply respectful of indigenous cultures and ways of knowing. The path forward requires ongoing collaboration between indigenous communities, educators, technologists, and policymakers and a commitment to continuously evaluating and adapting digital learning strategies.

To promote a more inclusive and equitable educational landscape for indigenous learners, it is crucial to recognize that technology is not a panacea but a tool that can significantly enhance educational opportunities and outcomes when wielded thoughtfully and aligned with indigenous values and aspirations. The ultimate goal remains to empower indigenous communities through education that honors their cultural heritage while equipping learners with the skills needed to thrive in the contemporary world.

REFERENCES

Archibald, J., & Hare, J. (2017). *Learning, knowing, sharing: Celebrating successes in K-12 Aboriginal education in British Columbia*. Office of Indigenous Education/Indigenous Education Institute of Canada, University of British Columbia.

Archibald, J., & Hare, J. (2017). *Learning, knowing, sharing: Celebrating successes in K-12 Aboriginal education in British Columbia*. Office of Indigenous Education/Indigenous Education Institute of Canada, University of British Columbia.

Auld, G., Snyder, I., & Henderson, M. (2012). Mobile phones are used as resources for literacy learning in a remote Indigenous community in Australia. *Language and Education*, 26(4), 279–296. DOI: 10.1080/09500782.2012.691512

Barnhardt, R., & Kawagley, A. O. (2005). Indigenous knowledge systems and Alaska Native ways of knowing. *Anthropology & Education Quarterly*, 36(1), 8–23. DOI: 10.1525/aeq.2005.36.1.008

Battiste, M. (2013). *Decolonizing education: Nourishing the learning spirit*. Purich Publishing Limited.

Biddle, N., & Edwards, B. (2017). The characteristics and potential effects of the schools that Indigenous Australians attend. CAEPR Working Paper No. 119/2017. Centre for Aboriginal Economic Policy Research, Australian National University. https://doi.org/DOI: 10.25911/5c21c77718a8c

Biddle, N., & Markham, F. (2018). Indigenous population change in the 2016 Census. CAEPR 2016 Census Paper No. 1. Centre for Aboriginal Economic Policy Research, Australian National University. https://doi.org/DOI: 10.25911/5b4efd3bc2959

Bombay, A., Matheson, K., & Anisman, H. (2014). The intergenerational effects of Indian Residential Schools: Implications for the concept of historical trauma. *Transcultural Psychiatry*, 51(3), 320–338. DOI: 10.1177/1363461513503380 PMID: 24065606

Brayboy, B. M. J., & Maaka, M. J. (2015). K–12 Achievement for Indigenous Students. *Journal of American Indian Education*, 54(1), 63–98.

Cajete, G. (1994). *Look to the mountain: An ecology of indigenous education*. Kivaki Press.

Cajete, G. (2015). *Indigenous community: Rekindling the teachings of the seventh fire*. Living Justice Press.

Carpenter, J., Guerin, A., Kaczmarek, M., Lawson, G., Lawson, K., Nathan, L. P., & Turin, M. (2018). Digital language resource and database development in support of indigenous language revitalization in northeastern British Columbia. *Journal of Northern Studies*, 12(1), 37–56.

Castagno, A. E., & Brayboy, B. M. J. (2008). Culturally responsive schooling for Indigenous youth: A review of the literature. *Review of Educational Research*, 78(4), 941–993. DOI: 10.3102/0034654308323036

Featherstone, D. (2017). The Aboriginal invention of broadband: How Yarnangu is using ICTs in the Ngaanyatjarra Lands of Western Australia. In Crouch, A., Rozentals, L., & Simovic, V. (Eds.), *Digital Participation through Social Living Labs* (pp. 299–316). Chandos Publishing., DOI: 10.1016/B978-0-08-102059-3.00016-6

Galla, C. K. (2016). Indigenous language revitalization, promotion, and education: Function of digital technology. *Computer Assisted Language Learning*, 29(7), 1137–1151. DOI: 10.1080/09588221.2016.1166137

Galla, C. K. (2018). Digital realities of indigenous language revitalization: A look at Hawaiian language technology in the modern world. *Language and Education*, 32(3), 212–226. DOI: 10.1080/09500782.2018.1434097

Gonzales, A. L. (2018). Technology maintenance: A new frame for studying poverty and marginalization. *Communication Theory*, 28(2), 129–148. DOI: 10.1093/ct/qtx009

Greenwood, D. A. (2013). A critical theory of place-conscious education. In Stevenson, R. B., Brody, M., Dillon, J., & Wals, A. E. J. (Eds.), *International handbook of research on environmental education* (pp. 93–100). Routledge.

Guimond, E., Kerr, D., & Beaujot, R. (2014). Charting the growth of Canada's Aboriginal populations: Problems, options and implications. *Canadian Studies in Population*, 31(1), 55–82. DOI: 10.25336/P6HW3B

Hornberger, N. H. (2019). Ethnography in language planning and policy research. In King, K. A., Lai, Y. J., & May, S. (Eds.), *Research Methods in Language and Education* (pp. 193–204). Springer., DOI: 10.1007/978-3-319-02249-9_15

Hughes, M., & Dallwitz, J. (2007). Ara Irititja: Towards culturally appropriate IT best practice in remote Indigenous Australia. In Dyson, L. E., Hendriks, M., & Grant, S. (Eds.), *Information Technology and Indigenous People* (pp. 146–158). Information Science Publishing.

Hynsjö, D., & Damon, A. (2016). Bilingual education in Peru: Evidence on how Quechua-medium education affects indigenous children's academic achievement. *Economics of Education Review*, 53, 116–132. DOI: 10.1016/j.econedurev.2016.05.006

Iseke, J., & Moore, S. (2011). Community-based indigenous digital storytelling with elders and youth. *American Indian Culture and Research Journal*, 35(4), 19–38. DOI: 10.17953/aicr.35.4.4588445552858866

Kaka'e, K., Taum, R. P., & Magee, L. (2019). Indigenous ways of assessing student learning: A Polynesian perspective. AlterNative. *An International Journal of Indigenous Peoples*, 15(1), 77–84. DOI: 10.1177/1177180119828769

Keegan, T. T., Mato, P., & Ruru, S. (2015). Using Twitter in an Indigenous language: An analysis of te reo Māori tweets. AlterNative. *An International Journal of Indigenous Peoples*, 11(1), 59–75. DOI: 10.1177/117718011501100105

Keskitalo, P., Frangou, S. M., & Chohan, I. (2019). Educational design research in collaboration with students: Using digital tools to learn about reindeer herding within a vocational Sámi pedagogical context. *Education in the North*, 26(2), 62–85. DOI: 10.26203/3jca-m555

Keskitalo, P., & Olsen, T. (2019). Historical and political perspectives on Sámi and inclusive school systems in Norway. In Petrovic, J., & Mitchell, R. (Eds.), *Indigenous Philosophies of Education Around the World* (pp. 177–198). Routledgc., DOI: 10.4324/9781351069410-11

Kral, I. (2010). Plugged in: Remote Australian Indigenous youth and digital culture. Centre for Aboriginal Economic Policy Research, Working Paper No. 69/2010. https://doi.org/DOI: 10.25911/5d7bdbde8a9c5

Kukutai, T., & Taylor, J. (2016). *Indigenous data sovereignty: Toward an agenda.* ANU Press., DOI: 10.22459/CAEPR38.11.2016

Lockard, W., & De Maio, F. (2021). Digital inclusion initiatives in Aboriginal communities in Australia: A systematic review. *International Journal of Environmental Research and Public Health*, 18(6), 3080. DOI: 10.3390/ijerph18063080 PMID: 33802715

Lockard, W., & Huss, J. (2016). Learning to be Webbed: A Case Study of a Native American High School's Integration of Technology. *Journal of American Indian Education*, 55(2), 4–27.

Lowe, K., & Yunkaporta, T. (2013). The inclusion of Aboriginal and Torres Strait Islander content in the Australian National Curriculum: A cultural, cognitive and socio-political evaluation. *Curriculum Perspectives*, 33(1), 1–14.

McCarty, T. L., & Nicholas, S. E. (2014). Reclaiming Indigenous languages: A reconsideration of the roles and responsibilities of schools. *Review of Research in Education*, 38(1), 106–136. DOI: 10.3102/0091732X13507894

McLachlan, C., Fleer, M., & Edwards, S. (2018). *Early childhood curriculum: Planning, assessment and implementation*. Cambridge University Press.

Metila, R. A., Pradilla, L. A. S., & Williams, A. B. (2016). The challenge of implementing mother tongue education in linguistically diverse contexts: The case of the Philippines. *The Asia-Pacific Education Researcher*, 25(5-6), 781–789. DOI: 10.1007/s40299-016-0310-5

Mills, K. A., Davis-Warra, J., Sewell, M., & Anderson, M. (2019). Indigenous ways with literacies: Transgenerational, multimodal, placed, and collective. *Language and Education*, 33(5), 400–420. DOI: 10.1080/09500782.2019.1629942

Nakata, M., Nakata, V., & Day, A. (2020). Dreaming, knowing and knowledge sharing: Indigenous knowledges and higher education. In Frawley, J., Larkin, S., & Smith, J. A. (Eds.), *Indigenous Pathways, Transitions and Participation in Higher Education* (pp. 3–16). Springer., DOI: 10.1007/978-981-10-4062-7_1

Naylor, R., Baik, C., Arkoudis, S., & Dabrowski, A. (2020). Exploring the experiences of Aboriginal and Torres Strait Islander students in higher education. In Frawley, J., Russell, G., & Sherwood, J. (Eds.), *Cultural Competence and the Higher Education Sector* (pp. 63–80). Springer., DOI: 10.1007/978-981-15-5362-2_4

OECD. (2017). *Promising Practices in Supporting Success for Indigenous Students*. OECD Publishing., DOI: 10.1787/9789264279421-

Olsen-Reeder, V., Higgins, R., & Ratima, M. (2017). *Te Ahu o te Reo Māori: Reflecting on Research to Understand the Well-Being of Te Reo Māori*. Victoria University Press.

Osuna, C. (2013). Educación intercultural y revolución educativa en Bolivia. Un análisis de procesos de (re) esencialización cultural. *Revista Española de Antropología Americana*, 43(2), 451–470. DOI: 10.5209/rev_REAA.2013.v43.n2.44020

Ottmann, J. (2017). Canada's Indigenous peoples' access to post-secondary education: The spirit of the 'New Buffalo. In Frawley, J., Larkin, S., & Smith, J. A. (Eds.), *Indigenous Pathways, Transitions and Participation in Higher Education* (pp. 95–117). Springer., DOI: 10.1007/978-981-10-4062-7_7

Pulla, S. (2017). Mobile learning and indigenous education in Canada: A synthesis of new ways of learning. *International Journal of Mobile and Blended Learning*, 9(2), 39–60. DOI: 10.4018/IJMBL.2017040103

Rahko-Ravantti, R. (2020). Sámi education in Finland: A multilayered context. In *Educational Equity* (pp. 109–124). Springer., DOI: 10.1007/978-981-15-4526-9_7

Rennie, E., Thomas, J., & Wilson, C. (2019). Aboriginal and Torres Strait Islander people and digital inclusion: What is the evidence and where is it? *Communication Research and Practice*, 5(2), 105–120. DOI: 10.1080/22041451.2019.1601148

Resta, P., & Laferrière, T. (2015). Digital equity and intercultural education. *Education and Information Technologies*, 20(4), 743–756. DOI: 10.1007/s10639-015-9419-z

Salazar, J. F., Radoll, P., Cardoso-Castro, P., Rodrigues, R., & Dezuanni, M. (2020). Digital inclusion, indigenous peoples, and the Global South: A critical perspective from the margins. In Servaes, J. (Ed.), *Handbook of Communication for Development and Social Change* (pp. 1–19). Springer., DOI: 10.1007/978-981-15-2014-3_128

Sánchez, J., Salinas, A., Sáenz, M., & de Benito, B. (2015). Computer-supported collaborative learning in a 1:1 laptop initiative in Chilean classrooms. In Spada, H., Rummel, N., & McLaren, B. M. (Eds.), *CSCL 2015 Proceedings* (pp. 409–416). International Society of the Learning Sciences.

Santoro, N., Reid, J. A., Crawford, L., & Simpson, L. (2011). Teaching Indigenous children: Listening to and learning from Indigenous teachers. *The Australian Journal of Teacher Education*, 36(10), 65–80. DOI: 10.14221/ajte.2011v36n10.2

Sarra, C., Spillman, D., Jackson, C., Davis, J., & Bray, J. (2018). High-expectations relationships: A foundation for enacting high expectations in all Australian schools. *Australian Journal of Indigenous Education*, 47(1), 32–45. DOI: 10.1017/jie.2018.10

Schwartz, D. L., Lin, X., Brophy, S., & Bransford, J. D. (2016). Toward the development of flexibly adaptive instructional designs. In Reigeluth, C. M. (Ed.), *Instructional-design theories and models: A new paradigm of instructional theory* (Vol. 2, pp. 183–213). Routledge.

Schwartzman, L. F., & Knobel, M. (2016). The Transformative Potential of Affirmative Action in Brazilian Higher Education. In Stevens, P. A. J., & Dworkin, A. G. (Eds.), *The Palgrave Handbook of Race and Ethnic Inequalities in Education* (pp. 247–290). Palgrave Macmillan., DOI: 10.1057/978-1-137-51944-1_8

Singleton, J., Straits, K. J. L., & Straits, K. (2015). Professional development for educators teaching in Indigenous contexts. In Reyhner, J., Martin, J., Lockard, L., & Gilbert, W. S. (Eds.), *Honoring our elders: Culturally appropriate approaches for teaching Indigenous students* (pp. 165–184). Northern Arizona University.

Sinti, M. E., Sánchez, F. M., & Vargas, R. C. (2021). Digital technologies for revitalizing indigenous languages: The case of the Kukama-Kukamiria people in the Peruvian Amazon. *International Journal of Educational Technology in Higher Education*, 18(1), 1–18. DOI: 10.1186/s41239-021-00244-3

Skutnabb-Kangas, T., & Dunbar, R. (2010). Indigenous children's education as linguistic genocide and a crime against humanity? A global view. Gáldu Čála – Journal of Indigenous Peoples Rights, 1, 1-128.

Suri, V. R., Ling, R., & Teo, C. L. (2019). Leveraging indigenous knowledge for sustainable development: A case study of the Bidayuh community in Sarawak, Malaysia. *Information Development*, 35(3), 447–466. DOI: 10.1177/0266666918754829

Theodore, R., Tustin, K., Kiro, C., Gollop, M., Taumoepeau, M., Taylor, N., Chee, K.-S., Hunter, J., & Poulton, R. (2016). Māori university graduates: Indigenous participation in higher education. *Higher Education Research & Development*, 35(3), 604–618. DOI: 10.1080/07294360.2015.1107883

Toulouse, P. R. (2016). What matters in Indigenous education: Implementing a vision committed to holism, diversity and engagement. In Measuring What Matters, People for Education. Toronto: March, 2016.

Tuck, E., & McKenzie, M. (2015). *Place in research: Theory, methodology, and methods*. Routledge., DOI: 10.4324/9781315764849

UNESCO. (2019). *Indigenous Peoples' Right to Education*. UNESCO.

United Nations. (2007). United Nations Declaration on the Rights of Indigenous Peoples. https://www.un.org/development/desa/indigenouspeoples/declaration-on-the-rights-of-indigenous-peoples.html

United Nations. (2020). Indigenous Peoples at the United Nations. https://www.un.org/development/desa/indigenouspeoples/about-us.html

Walter, S. L., & Dekker, D. E. (2011). Mother tongue instruction in Lubuagan: A case study from the Philippines. *International Review of Education*, 57(5-6), 667–683. DOI: 10.1007/s11159-011-9246-4

Webb, A., & Radcliffe, S. (2016). Whitened geographies and education inequalities in southern Chile. *Journal of Intercultural Studies (Melbourne, Vic.)*, 37(3), 267–285. DOI: 10.1080/07256868.2016.1141757

Wilks, J., Wilson, K., & Kinnane, S. (2020). Promoting engagement and success at university through strengthening the online learning experiences of Indigenous students living and studying in remote communities. In Frawley, J., Russell, G., & Sherwood, J. (Eds.), *Cultural Competence and the Higher Education Sector* (pp. 231–252). Springer., DOI: 10.1007/978-981-15-5362-2_13

World Bank. (2015). *Indigenous Latin America in the Twenty-First Century: The First Decade*. World Bank., DOI: 10.1596/978-1-4648-0325-9

Chapter 18
Quantum Pedagogy:
A 21st Century Framework for Education 5.0

Robertas Damaševičius
https://orcid.org/0000-0001-9990-1084
Vytautas Magnus University, Lithuania

ABSTRACT

This chapter introduces a pioneering educational paradigm that integrates the principles of quantum computing to redefine teaching and learning. Quantum Pedagogy leverages quantum mechanics concepts such as superposition, entanglement, and quantum tunneling to create highly personalized, adaptive, and immersive learning environments. By harnessing the unprecedented computational power of quantum computing, this framework offers innovative solutions for real-time curriculum adjustment, individualized tutoring, and predictive analytics for student success. The chapter explores the transformative potential of Quantum Pedagogy through key themes including quantum-adaptive learning systems, quantum-enhanced collaborative platforms, and quantum data analytics. Case studies demonstrate the practical applications and benefits of this framework, while addressing the challenges and ethical considerations inherent in its implementation.

1. INTRODUCTION

The rapid advancements in technology over the past few decades have fundamentally transformed various sectors, including education (Westfall and Leider, 2018). Traditional educational models, which have remained relatively unchanged for centuries, are now being challenged by innovative approaches that leverage cutting-edge technologies (Seegerer et al., 2021). In this context, quantum computing

DOI: 10.4018/979-8-3693-8191-5.ch018

emerges as a groundbreaking force with the potential to revolutionize how education is delivered and experienced (Kushimo and Thacker, 2022). Quantum Pedagogy, a novel educational framework, integrates the principles of quantum computing to create learning environments that are highly personalized, adaptive, and immersive (Pagano et al., 2023). This chapter explores the concept of Quantum Pedagogy within the broader framework of Education 5.0, examining its potential to redefine teaching and learning in the 21st century (Uhlig et al., 2019).

1.1 The Evolution of Educational Paradigms

Educational paradigms have evolved significantly over time, reflecting changes in societal needs, technological advancements, and pedagogical theories (Mermin, 2002). The earliest educational systems were largely teacher-centered, focusing on rote memorization and the transmission of knowledge from teacher to student (Pagano et al., 2023). The Industrial Revolution brought about a shift towards standardized education, emphasizing efficiency and uniformity to prepare students for factory work (Ozlem Salehi et al., 2020). The late 20th century saw the rise of more student-centered approaches, influenced by constructivist theories that advocate for active learning, critical thinking, and collaboration (Angara et al., 2022).

In recent years, the integration of digital technologies has given rise to Education 4.0, characterized by the use of online learning platforms, artificial intelligence, and data analytics to enhance educational outcomes (Pagano et al., 2023). Despite these advancements, many challenges remain, including the need for more personalized learning experiences, better support for diverse learning needs, and improved global collaboration (Seegerer et al., 2021). As we look to the future, it is clear that a new paradigm is needed—one that leverages the unique capabilities of emerging technologies to address these challenges and create a more holistic and equitable education system (Westfall and Leider, 2018).

Education 5.0 represents the next evolutionary step in educational paradigms, integrating advanced technologies to create personalized, efficient, and equitable learning experiences (George and Wooden, 2023). This paradigm shift is characterized by a human-centered approach that emphasizes the development of both cognitive and affective skills (Chang et al., 2022). At the core of Education 5.0 is the integration of artificial intelligence, big data, and quantum computing, which together enable the creation of highly adaptive learning environments (Pagano et al., 2023).

Quantum Pedagogy, as a key component of Education 5.0, utilizes the principles of quantum computing—such as superposition, entanglement, and quantum tunneling—to enhance educational practices (Zable et al., 2020). These principles allow for the development of quantum-adaptive learning systems that can process vast amounts of data to create personalized learning paths, provide real-time feedback, and simulate complex scenarios for deeper understanding (Liu et al., 2020). Quantum-enhanced collaborative platforms facilitate global communication and teamwork, breaking down traditional barriers and fostering a more interconnected and inclusive educational environment (Lampou, 2023).

By harnessing the power of quantum computing, Education 5.0 aims to transcend the limitations of current educational models, offering a vision for the future where learning is tailored to individual needs, continuously adaptive, and globally connected (Duran et al., 2020). This chapter focuses on the foundational principles of Quantum Pedagogy, explores its practical applications, and discusses the potential benefits and challenges associated with its implementation (Liu et al., 2020). Through this exploration, we seek to provide a comprehensive understanding of how Quantum Pedagogy can transform education in the 21st century, preparing students and educators for the challenges and opportunities of the future (Chang et al., 2022).

The rapid pace of technological advancement and the increasing complexity of societal challenges have underscored the inadequacies of traditional pedagogical models (da Silva Frasseto et al., 2022). These models, rooted in the industrial era, emphasize standardized testing, uniform curricula, and one-size-fits-all teaching approaches, which often fail to address the diverse learning needs of students in a globalized world (Volkova et al., 2021). The contemporary educational landscape demands a shift towards more flexible, adaptive, and personalized learning environments that can cater to individual student needs and prepare them for the future workforce (Rodrigues, 2020). The proliferation of digital technologies has created new opportunities for learning, but has also highlighted the need for pedagogical frameworks that can effectively integrate these technologies to enhance educational outcomes (Makarova and Makarova, 2018).

The introduction of Quantum Pedagogy represents a significant innovation in the field of education, offering a novel approach that addresses the limitations of traditional pedagogical models. Its reliance on quantum computing principles allows for the creation of educational environments that are not only highly personalized and adaptive but also capable of fostering deep, experiential learning. This pedagogical framework contributes to the advancement of Education 5.0 by integrating cutting-edge technology with a human-centered approach, emphasizing the development of both cognitive and affective skills. The novelty of Quantum Pedagogy lies in its ability to harness the unique capabilities of quantum computing to provide tailored educational experiences, facilitate global collaboration, and enhance the overall learning process. As such, Quantum Pedagogy prepares students for the complexities of the 21st-century workforce, equipping them with the skills and knowledge necessary to thrive in an increasingly interconnected and technologically advanced world.

2. RELATED WORKS

The concept of Quantum Pedagogy is gaining significant attention as researchers explore its potential to revolutionize educational practices. Biersteker (Biersteker, 2022) focuses on the integration of quantum principles within educational frameworks, particularly focusing on their application in the broader context of international relations. Biersteker argues that Quantum Pedagogy can provide a new lens through which to understand and teach complex global interactions, highlighting how the probabilistic nature of quantum mechanics mirrors the uncertainties and dynamics in world politics. This work sets the foundation for understanding Quantum Pedagogy not just as a technological innovation, but as a transformative educational approach that challenges traditional deterministic paradigms.

Building on these foundational ideas, (Lehka et al., 2023) extend the discussion into the realm of school informatics with their study, Exploring the Quantum Frontier in School Informatics: A Pedagogical Journey. This research highlights the practical application of Quantum Pedagogy in the classroom, particularly in the teaching of informatics and computer science at the school level. The authors argue that introducing quantum concepts early in the educational journey can demystify the complexities of quantum computing and prepare students for future technological advancements. Their work emphasizes the importance of curriculum development that integrates quantum principles, suggesting that such an approach can foster a deeper understanding of both classical and quantum computing among students. The study underscores the potential of Quantum Pedagogy to reshape the educational landscape by making cutting-edge scientific concepts accessible and engaging for younger learners.

Furthering the exploration of Quantum Pedagogy, Dobson and Scaff (Dobson and Scaff, 2024) introduce an innovative framework that combines quantum learning with AI-driven tutoring systems. The Qurio platform exemplifies how Quantum Pedagogy can be operationalized through technology, leveraging quantum bits (QBits) to create adaptive learning environments that respond to student needs in real-time. Dobson and Scaff's research demonstrates the practical application of Quantum Pedagogy in personalized education, where AI tutors can provide tailored feedback and learning pathways based on quantum algorithms. This study not only reinforces the feasibility of Quantum Pedagogy in modern educational settings but also highlights its potential to enhance student engagement and learning outcomes through the integration of AI and quantum technologies.

Together, these studies provide a comprehensive overview of the emerging field of Quantum Pedagogy, illustrating its theoretical foundations, practical applications, and technological implementations.

In response to these evolving needs, Quantum Pedagogy emerges as a revolutionary framework that leverages the principles of quantum computing to transform educational practices (Westfall and Leider, 2018). Quantum Pedagogy is predicated on the unique characteristics of quantum mechanics, such as superposition, entanglement, and quantum tunneling, to develop educational systems that are more adaptive, personalized, and immersive (Nita et al., 2020). By utilizing quantum algorithms and computational power, this pedagogical approach enables the creation of learning environments that can dynamically adjust to the cognitive and emotional states of students, providing real-time feedback and support tailored to their individual learning trajectories (Mykhailova, 2020). Quantum Pedagogy also facilitates the development of advanced simulation and modeling tools, allowing students to engage with complex, real-world problems in a deeply interactive and experiential manner (Alvarez-Rodriguez et al., 2016).

Quantum computing may play a key role in the realization of Education 5.0, a holistic and human-centered educational paradigm that integrates advanced technologies to enhance learning experiences (Lampou, 2023). Unlike classical computing, which relies on binary processing, quantum computing exploits the probabilistic nature of quantum bits (qubits) to perform complex calculations at unprecedented speeds (Biamonte et al., 2016). This capability is particularly valuable in education, where the processing and analysis of large datasets are crucial for personalized learning, predictive analytics, and adaptive systems (Wootton et al., 2020). Quantum computing enables the development of sophisticated educational tools that can analyze vast amounts of data in real-time, providing insights into student performance, learning patterns, and potential areas for intervention (Mykhailova, 2021). The ability of quantum computers to simulate complex systems and phenomena opens up new avenues for experiential learning, allowing students to explore and understand complex scientific and mathematical concepts in a more intuitive and engaging manner (Zable et al., 2020).

3. MAIN PRINCIPLES OF QUANTUM PEDAGOGY

Quantum Pedagogy, as an innovative educational framework, draws upon the fundamental principles of quantum mechanics to create a transformative learning environment. The core principles of Quantum Pedagogy—superposition, entanglement, and quantum tunneling—offer unique advantages that traditional pedagogical models cannot achieve. These principles (Table 1) facilitate highly personalized, adaptive, and immersive educational experiences that cater to the diverse and evolving needs of students. By integrating these quantum principles into educational practices,

Quantum Pedagogy seeks to enhance both the cognitive and affective dimensions of learning, preparing students for the complexities of the future.

3.1 Quantum Superposition in Learning

Superposition, a foundational concept in quantum mechanics, refers to the ability of quantum systems to exist in multiple states simultaneously (Dong et al., 2005). In the context of Quantum Pedagogy, superposition can be harnessed to create multiple, parallel learning pathways that adapt to the individual needs and preferences of students (Silva et al., 2010). Traditional educational models often rely on linear and uniform approaches to teaching, which may not accommodate the diverse learning styles and paces of all students (Altman and Zapatrin, 2009). Superposition in learning, however, allows for the simultaneous exploration of different instructional strategies, content delivery methods, and assessment techniques (Araujo and Silva, 2020). By leveraging superposition, educators can design adaptive learning environments where students can engage with various forms of content—such as videos, interactive simulations, and textual materials—concurrently (Dong et al., 2005). This multiplicity of learning experiences ensures that students can find the mode of instruction that best suits their learning preferences, thereby enhancing their engagement and comprehension (Altman and Zapatrin, 2009). Superposition enables real-time adjustments to the learning process, allowing educators to provide immediate feedback and alternative explanations when students encounter difficulties (Silva et al., 2010). This dynamic and responsive approach to teaching fosters a more personalized and effective learning experience, promoting deeper understanding and retention of knowledge (Araujo and Silva, 2020).

Table 1. Summary of Main Principles of Quantum Pedagogy

Principle	Technology Aspects	Educational Characteristics
Superposition in Learning	Utilizes quantum algorithms to create multiple, parallel learning pathways.	Provides highly personalized learning experiences, allowing students to explore various instructional methods.
Entanglement in Collaboration	Leverages quantum entanglement for real-time, secure communication networks.	Facilitates seamless global collaboration, enabling students and educators to interact synchronously regardless of physical location.
Quantum Tunneling In Problem Solving	Employs quantum computing to explore multiple solutions to complex problems.	Encourages innovative and non-linear problem-solving approaches, fostering creativity and resilience in students.
Adaptive Learning Algorithms	Uses quantum-powered adaptive algorithms to analyze student performance data in real-time.	Continuously adjusts learning content and strategies to individual student needs, promoting effective and personalized education.

continued on following page

Table 1. Continued

Principle	Technology Aspects	Educational Characteristics
Real-Time Data Analysis	Processes vast amounts of educational data instantaneously using quantum processors.	Provides immediate feedback and insights, enabling timely interventions and support for students.
Immersive Simulations	Integrates quantum-enhanced simulations and virtual reality environments.	Offers interactive and experiential learning experiences, helping students understand complex concepts through hands-on activities.
Scalability	Quantum computing enables scalable solutions that can support large numbers of students simultaneously.	Ensures equitable access to high-quality education for all students, regardless of geographic and resource limitations.
Resource Integration	Seamlessly integrates diverse digital resources, leveraging multimedia and interactive tools.	Enhances the learning experience by providing rich, varied, and up-to-date educational materials.
Security	Implements quantum-resistant cryptography for data protection and secure communications.	Maintains the integrity and privacy of student data, ensuring a safe learning environment.

3.2 Entanglement in Collaboration

Entanglement, another key principle of quantum mechanics, describes the phenomenon where quantum particles become interconnected in such a way that the state of one particle instantly influences the state of another, regardless of the distance between them (Choi et al., 2010). This concept of entanglement can be applied to educational settings to enhance collaboration and communication among students and educators (Kimble, 2008). In Quantum Pedagogy, entanglement in collaboration involves creating interconnected learning networks that facilitate real-time, synchronous interactions and knowledge sharing across different geographical locations (Wei et al., 2022). Entangled collaboration platforms can leverage advanced technologies such as quantum-enhanced communication tools and virtual reality (VR)/Metaverse environments (Pant et al., 2017) to enable seamless and immersive collaborative experiences. These platforms allow students to work together on complex projects, participate in global classroom discussions, and engage in cross-cultural exchanges without the constraints of physical proximity (Humphreys et al., 2017). The instantaneous nature of entangled communication ensures that collaborative efforts are fluid and cohesive, promoting a deeper sense of community and shared purpose among learners (Choi et al., 2007). Entanglement in collaboration extends to the relationship between students and educators. Quantum Pedagogy encourages the development of mentorship networks where teachers can provide personalized guidance and support to students, regardless of their location (Kimble, 2008). This interconnected approach to education fosters a more inclusive and supportive learning environment, enabling students to benefit from diverse perspectives and expertise (Wei et al., 2022). By cultivating a sense of interconnectedness and mutual support, entangled collaboration enhances the overall learning experience and prepares students for the collaborative nature of the modern workforce (Pant et al., 2017).

3.3 Quantum Tunneling in Problem Solving

Quantum tunneling, a phenomenon where particles can pass through energy barriers that would be insurmountable in classical mechanics, offers a powerful metaphor for problem-solving in Quantum Pedagogy (Razavy, 2003). Traditional problem-solving approaches often involve linear and incremental strategies that may not be effective for tackling complex and multifaceted challenges (Domert et al., 2005). Quantum tunneling in problem-solving, however, encourages students to explore multiple potential solutions simultaneously and to approach problems from unconventional angles (Mu~niz and Oliver-Hoyo, 2014). By incorporating the principle of quantum tunneling, educators can design problem-solving activities that encourage creative and non-linear thinking (Morgan et al., 2004). Students can be presented with open-ended problems that require them to consider a wide range of possibilities and to experiment with different approaches (Lamichhane, 2012). This exploratory and iterative process allows students to develop resilience and adaptability, as they learn to navigate obstacles and to find innovative solutions to challenging problems (Siahaan et al., 2022). Quantum tunneling also emphasizes the importance of persistence and perseverance in the face of difficult tasks (Morgan and Wittmann, 2006). By fostering a mindset that views challenges as opportunities for growth and discovery, Quantum Pedagogy helps students to develop critical thinking and problem-solving skills that are essential for success in the 21st century (Domert et al., 2005). The application of quantum tunneling in educational contexts encourages interdisciplinary learning, as students draw upon knowledge and techniques from various fields to solve complex problems (Domert et al., 2005).

3.4 Distinguishing Quantum Pedagogy from Classical Pedagogy

Quantum Pedagogy represents a fundamental departure from classical pedagogical models, leveraging the principles of quantum mechanics to create learning experiences that are deeply personalized, adaptive, and immersive (Freericks, 2023). Classical pedagogy, rooted in the industrial era, emphasizes standardized curricula, uniform teaching methods, and a linear progression of knowledge acquisition. This approach often relies on fixed schedules, traditional classroom settings, and a one-size-fits-all methodology, which can fail to accommodate the diverse learning needs and styles of individual students (Silva et al., 2010).

In contrast, Quantum Pedagogy embraces the inherent complexity and variability of the learning process by utilizing the principles of superposition, entanglement, and quantum tunneling (Grant and Humble, 2019). These principles enable the creation of educational environments that are dynamic and responsive, continuously adapting to the individual needs and preferences of students. For instance, superposition allows for the simultaneous exploration of multiple learning pathways, providing students with a variety of instructional materials and methods to choose from (Freericks, 2023). This contrasts sharply with the linear and uniform approach of classical pedagogy, where all students are expected to follow the same path regardless of their unique abilities and interests (Silva et al., 2010).

Entanglement, another key principle of quantum mechanics, facilitates a level of collaboration and interconnectedness that classical pedagogy cannot achieve. In traditional educational settings, collaboration is often limited by physical proximity and time constraints, with group work and discussions confined to scheduled class periods. Quantum Pedagogy, however, leverages advanced communication technologies to create real-time, synchronous learning networks that transcend geographical boundaries (Pant et al., 2017). This enables students to engage in collaborative projects and discussions with peers from around the world, fostering a global perspective and a deeper sense of community (Grant and Humble, 2019).

Quantum tunneling, which allows particles to pass through barriers that would be insurmountable in classical mechanics, inspires a more innovative and creative approach to problem-solving in education. Classical pedagogy often emphasizes rote memorization and the application of predefined algorithms to solve problems, which can stifle creativity and critical thinking (Silva et al., 2010). Quantum Pedagogy, on the other hand, encourages students to explore multiple potential solutions simultaneously and to approach problems from unconventional angles (Lamichhane, 2012). This fosters a mindset that values experimentation and resilience, preparing students to tackle the complex, real-world challenges they will encounter in the future.

Table 2 provides a detailed comparison of the characteristics of Quantum Pedagogy versus Traditional Pedagogy.

3.5 Impact of Quantum Pedagogy on Education 5.0

Table 2. Comparison of Quantum Pedagogy with Traditional Pedagogy

Aspect	Quantum Pedagogy	Traditional Pedagogy
Learning Approach	Utilizes principles of quantum mechanics to create dynamic, adaptive, and personalized learning environments.	Relies on fixed curricula, standardized tests, and uniform teaching methods.
Personalization	Highly personalized, providing individualized learning paths and real-time adjustments based on student data.	Limited personalization, often follows a one-size-fits-all approach with minimal adaptation to individual needs.
Data Utilization	Leverages quantum computing to analyze vast amounts of data for real-time insights and personalized learning experiences.	Uses periodic assessments and standardized tests to gather data, which is less frequently analyzed.
Interactivity	Enhances learning with interactive simulations, virtual environments, and quantum-enhanced tools.	Primarily uses lectures, textbooks, and traditional classroom activities with limited interactivity.
Scalability	Scalable to support numerous students simultaneously, with individualized learning experiences for each.	Scalability is limited by physical classroom size and teacher-student ratios.
Feedback	Provides instantaneous, data-driven feedback and continuous assessment to guide student learning.	Feedback is often delayed, based on periodic testing and teacher evaluations.
Adaptability	Continuously adapts to the learner's progress, adjusting content and pace in real-time.	Adaptations are infrequent and often require significant manual intervention by the teacher.
Resource Integration	Seamlessly integrates diverse digital resources, including multimedia, simulations, and real-time data.	Relies heavily on physical textbooks and static digital content, with limited integration of interactive resources.
Engagement	High levels of student engagement through personalized, interactive, and adaptive learning experiences.	Varies widely, often dependent on the teacher's ability to engage students within a fixed curriculum framework.
Cost Efficiency	Potential for lower long-term costs due to automation and scalability, though initial setup may be expensive.	Ongoing costs include physical materials, periodic curriculum updates, and larger staff requirements.
Technology Integration	Integrates advanced technologies such as quantum computing, AI, and virtual reality.	Utilizes basic digital tools, with limited integration of advanced technologies.
Support for Diverse Learning Styles	Highly adaptable to different learning styles and needs, providing customized support for each student.	Limited adaptation to different learning styles, often adhering to a standard teaching approach.

to enhance both cognitive and affective development (Marsico et al., 2013). Quantum Pedagogy aligns perfectly with these goals, offering innovative solutions that address many of the limitations of current educational models (Nazaretsky et al., 2021).

One of the most significant impacts of Quantum Pedagogy on Education 5.0 is its ability to provide highly personalized learning experiences (Guo et al., 2020). By utilizing quantum algorithms and computational power, educational systems can process vast amounts of data to tailor learning paths to the individual needs and preferences of each student (Fern´andez-Morante et al., 2021). This ensures that students receive instruction that is not only aligned with their academic abilities but also attuned to their personal interests and learning styles (Blumenstein, 2020). The result is a more engaging and effective educational experience that promotes deeper understanding and retention of knowledge (Marsico et al., 2013).

The principle of entanglement enhances collaborative learning, a core component of Education 5.0 (Rodr´ıguez-Triana et al., 2011). Quantum Pedagogy facilitates the creation of interconnected learning networks that enable students to collaborate seamlessly with peers and educators, regardless of their physical location (Mart´ınez-Cerd´a et al., 2018). This global interconnectedness enriches the learning experience by exposing students to diverse perspectives and ideas, fostering a more inclusive and empathetic worldview (Jagust and Boticki, 2019). The ability to engage in real-time, synchronous collaboration helps to build strong communication and teamwork skills, which are essential for success in the modern workforce (Marsico et al., 2013).

Quantum tunneling, as applied to problem-solving, encourages a more innovative and interdisciplinary approach to learning (Charlton and Avramides, 2016). By promoting creative and non-linear thinking, Quantum Pedagogy helps students to develop the critical thinking and problem-solving skills that are crucial for addressing the complex challenges of the 21st century (Guo et al., 2020). This approach also supports the development of resilience and adaptability, as students learn to navigate obstacles and to view failures as opportunities for growth and discovery (Marsico et al., 2013).

The impact of Quantum Pedagogy extends beyond the classroom, influencing the broader educational ecosystem (McLoughlin and Lee, 2010). For instance, the use of quantum-enhanced data analytics allows educators and administrators to gain deeper insights into student performance and learning patterns (Nazaretsky et al., 2021). This data-driven approach supports more informed decision-making and helps to identify areas where interventions are needed, ensuring that all students receive the support they need to succeed (Blumenstein, 2020). The integration of quantum computing into educational research accelerates the pace of discovery and innovation, leading to the development of more effective teaching methods and technologies (Fern´andez-Morante et al., 2021).

4. ELEMENTS OF QUANTUM-ADAPTIVE LEARNING SYSTEMS

The advent of quantum computing introduces a new frontier in education, where the capabilities of quantum-adaptive learning systems hold the potential to revolutionize how students learn and interact with educational content (Biamonte et al., 2016). These systems are designed to leverage the principles of quantum mechanics to provide personalized, responsive, and immersive learning experiences (Kaul et al., 2021). The core elements of these systems include quantum algorithms for personalization, quantum tutors, and dynamic quantum curricula (Naqa and Ten, 2016). Each of these elements plays a crucial role in enhancing the adaptability and efficacy of educational processes, ensuring that learning is tailored to the unique needs of each student (Heese et al., 2023).

4.1 Quantum Algorithms for Personalization

Quantum algorithms represent the backbone of personalization in quantum-adaptive learning systems (Kaul et al., 2021). Unlike classical algorithms that rely on binary processing, quantum algorithms utilize qubits and the principles of superposition and entanglement to process information in fundamentally new ways (Schuld et al., 2014). This allows for the simultaneous exploration of multiple data points, enabling the rapid analysis and synthesis of vast amounts of educational data (Montanaro, 2015). In the context of education, quantum algorithms can analyze student performance data, learning styles, and preferences in real-time, creating highly individualized learning paths (Heese et al., 2023). For instance, a quantum algorithm might evaluate a student's responses to various types of content, such as textual, visual, or interactive materials, to determine which mode of instruction is most effective for that particular learner (Biamonte et al., 2016). This continuous, real-time analysis ensures that the educational content adapts to the student's evolving needs, providing a more engaging and effective learning experience (Kaul et al., 2021).

Quantum algorithms can identify patterns and correlations that are too complex for classical systems to detect (Naqa and Ten, 2016). This capability is particularly valuable in understanding the multifaceted nature of learning, where cognitive, emotional, and environmental factors all play a role (Schuld et al., 2014). By integrating data from these diverse sources, quantum algorithms can offer holistic insights into a student's learning process, helping educators to design more effective interventions and support mechanisms (Montanaro, 2015).

4.2 Quantum Tutors

Quantum tutors represent an innovative application of quantum computing in education, providing personalized guidance and support to students (Mykhailova, 2021). These AI-driven entities leverage the computational power of quantum systems to offer real-time, adaptive feedback that is tailored to the individual learner's needs (Hentschel and Sanders, 2010). Quantum tutors can simulate complex scenarios and problem-solving tasks, providing students with a rich, interactive learning environment (Zable et al., 2020).

The primary advantage of quantum tutors lies in their ability to respond dynamically to student inputs. Unlike traditional tutoring systems, which may rely on predefined scripts or limited datasets, quantum tutors can analyze and adapt to a wide range of variables simultaneously (DeVore and Singh, 2016). This enables them to provide nuanced feedback that is specific to the student's current understanding and progress. For example, a quantum tutor might detect that a student is struggling with a particular concept and immediately adjust its teaching strategy, offering alternative explanations, additional practice problems, or even suggesting relevant real-world applications to enhance comprehension.

Quantum tutors can facilitate a more engaging and interactive learning experience. By incorporating elements of gamification, virtual reality, and simulation, these tutors can make learning more enjoyable and immersive (Zable et al., 2020). This not only helps to maintain student motivation but also allows for deeper and more experiential learning, where students can explore concepts in a hands-on, interactive manner (Hentschel and Sanders, 2010).

Table 3 provides a comparison of the capabilities and limitations of both Quantum Tutors and Traditional Tutors.

4.3 Dynamic Quantum Curricula

Dynamic quantum curricula are the third pillar of quantum-adaptive learning systems, designed to offer flexible and continuously evolving educational content (Wootton et al., 2020). Traditional curricula are often static and rigid, failing to accommodate the diverse and changing needs of students. In contrast, dynamic quantum curricula leverage the principles of quantum computing to adapt in real-time, ensuring that educational content remains relevant, engaging, and effective (C´orcoles et al., 2021).

A dynamic quantum curriculum is characterized by its ability to adjust to the individual learning trajectories of students (Hughes et al., 2020). Using quantum algorithms, the curriculum can analyze student performance data and continuously update its content and structure to align with each learner's needs (Mykhailova,

2020). For example, if a student demonstrates a strong understanding of a particular topic, the curriculum can advance to more challenging material, providing opportunities for deeper exploration and mastery (Fingerhuth et al., 2018). Conversely, if a student encounters difficulties, the curriculum can offer additional resources, such as remedial content or alternative instructional methods, to support their learning (Polizzi and Beratan, 2015).

Dynamic quantum curricula can incorporate real-time data from various sources, including educational research, student feedback, and technological advancements (Sim et al., 2018). This ensures that the curriculum remains cutting-edge and evidence-based, reflecting the latest insights and innovations in education (Genç et al., 2021). By continuously integrating new information and adapting to the changing educational landscape, dynamic quantum curricula help to create a more responsive and effective learning environment (Havlícek et al., 2018a).

Table 3. Comparison between Quantum Tutors and Traditional Tutors

Aspect	Quantum Tutors	Traditional Tutors
Personalization	Utilize quantum algorithms to provide highly personalized learning paths based on real-time data analysis.	Tailor instruction based on observed student needs and interactions, which may not be as immediate or precise.
Adaptability	Continuously adapt to the learner's progress and interactions in real-time, providing dynamic support.	Adapt teaching strategies based on periodic assessments and feedback, often with a delay.
Feedback	Provide instant, detailed, and data-driven feedback using quantum computing capabilities.	Offer feedback based on personal observation and periodic evaluations, which may be less frequent.
Data Processing	Can analyze vast amounts of data simultaneously to identify patterns and insights for personalized learning.	Limited to analyzing smaller sets of data, often manually, which can be less efficient and comprehensive.
Interactivity	Support immersive and interactive learning experiences through quantum-enhanced simulations and virtual environments.	Relies on direct interaction and traditional methods, such as verbal explanations and written exercises.
Scalability	Capable of scaling to support numerous students simultaneously, leveraging the power of quantum computing.	Limited scalability, as one tutor can only handle a finite number of students effectively.
Availability	Available 24/7, providing continuous support and learning opportunities without the constraints of time zones.	Availability is restricted to scheduled sessions and the tutor's personal time constraints.
Resource Integration	Seamlessly integrate a wide range of digital learning resources and real-time updates.	Integration of resources depends on the tutor's access to and familiarity with available materials.

continued on following page

Table 3. Continued

Aspect	Quantum Tutors	Traditional Tutors
Cost	Potential for lower costs in the long run due to scalability and automation, though initial setup may be expensive.	Often more costly due to the need for individual or small-group sessions, with ongoing hourly fees.
Emotional and Social Support	Limited in providing emotional and social support, relying on algorithms and simulations.	Capable of offering nuanced emotional and social support through human interaction and empathy.

Table 4 provides a detailed comparison of the capabilities and limitations of Dynamic Quantum Curricula versus Traditional Curricula.

5. QUANTUM-ENHANCED COLLABORATIVE LEARNING

Quantum-enhanced collaborative learning represents a transformative approach in education, leveraging the unique capabilities of quantum computing to foster

Table 4. Comparison between Dynamic Quantum Curricula and Traditional Curriculam

Aspect	Dynamic Quantum Curricula	Traditional Curricula
Adaptability	Continuously adapts to individual student progress and learning styles using real-time data analysis.	Fixed structure with periodic updates, often requiring manual intervention to adapt to student needs.
Personalization	Highly personalized, offering customized learning paths and resources based on real-time feedback.	Limited personalization, typically offering the same content and pace to all students in a class.
Content Update	Real-time updates integrating the latest research, resources, and educational advancements.	Updated infrequently, usually on an annual or semi-annual basis, often lagging behind current research and trends.
Interactivity	Provides interactive and immersive learning experiences through quantum-enhanced simulations and digital tools.	Primarily relies on textbooks, lectures, and traditional classroom activities with limited interactivity.
Scalability	Scalable to accommodate numerous students simultaneously, leveraging quantum computing power.	Scalability limited by classroom size and teacher-student ratio.
Data Integration	Seamlessly integrates a wide range of data sources, including real-time student performance and feedback.	Limited integration of data, often relying on standardized tests and periodic assessments.

continued on following page

Table 4. Continued

Aspect	Dynamic Quantum Curricula	Traditional Curricula
Flexibility	Highly flexible, allowing for adjustments in pacing, content, and learning methods tailored to each student.	Rigid structure with predetermined pacing and content, offering little flexibility for individual adjustments.
Resource Utilization	Efficiently utilizes diverse digital resources, incorporating multimedia, simulations, and interactive modules.	Heavily reliant on physical textbooks and static digital content, with limited use of interactive resources.
Feedback Mechanisms	Instantaneous, data-driven feedback mechanisms that continuously inform and improve the learning process.	Feedback is often delayed, based on periodic tests and teacher evaluations.
Cost	Potential for lower costs in the long run due to automation and scalability, though initial setup may be expensive.	Ongoing costs associated with physical materials, periodic curriculum updates, and larger staff requirements.
Student Engagement	High student engagement through personalized, interactive, and adaptive learning experiences.	Varies widely, often dependent on the teacher's ability to engage students within a fixed curriculum framework.

deeper and more effective collaboration among students and educators (Ngoen-riang et al., 2022). This paradigm shift in educational methodology addresses the limitations of traditional collaborative learning by creating dynamic, real-time, and interconnected learning environments (Pagano et al., 2023). The core components of this approach include quantum collaboration platforms, simulated quantum environments, and global quantum classrooms, each of which plays a crucial role in enhancing the collaborative learning experience (Melnikov et al., 2023).

5.1 Quantum Collaboration Platforms

Quantum collaboration platforms are designed to utilize the principles of quantum mechanics to facilitate seamless and efficient collaboration among students and educators (Leymann et al., 2020). Traditional collaboration tools often struggle with latency, limited interactivity, and scalability issues, which can hinder effective teamwork and communication. Quantum collaboration platforms, on the other hand, harness the power of quantum entanglement and superposition to create highly interconnected and responsive networks (Havl´ıcek et al., 2018a).

These platforms enable real-time synchronization of information, allowing students to work together on projects, share resources, and exchange ideas instantaneously, regardless of their geographical location (Gen¸c et al., 2021). The use of quantum communication technologies ensures that data transmission is not only fast but also secure, protecting the privacy and integrity of collaborative efforts (Melnikov et al., 2023). This level of connectivity fosters a sense of community and shared purpose among learners, encouraging more meaningful and productive interactions (Ngoenriang et al., 2022).

Quantum collaboration platforms can integrate advanced analytical tools powered by quantum computing to provide insights into group dynamics and individual contributions (Pagano et al., 2023). By analyzing patterns of interaction and feedback, these platforms can help educators identify areas where additional support or intervention may be needed, ensuring that all students are engaged and contributing effectively (Gen‚c et al., 2021). This data-driven approach to collaboration enhances the overall learning experience, making it more inclusive and equitable (Havl´ıcek et al., 2018a).

The Quantum Collaboration Platform architecture, as depicted in Figure 1, presents a sophisticated and integrated system designed to leverage the unique capabilities of quantum computing to enhance collaborative learning. This platform is built upon several key components, each playing a crucial role in creating a seamless, efficient, and secure educational environment. At the forefront of the platform are the users—students, teachers, and administrators—who access the system through a variety of devices, including mobile phones, desktops, and tablets. This multi-device accessibility ensures that users can engage with the platform from anywhere, facilitating continuous learning and interaction. The diagram illustrates how these different devices connect users to the Quantum Communication Network, which serves as the backbone of the platform. Central to the platform is the Quantum Communication Network, represented by the Quantum Entanglement Network and a Quantum Router. This network employs the principles of quantum entanglement and superposition to enable secure, real-time communication. The Quantum Router manages the flow of information, ensuring that data is transmitted instantaneously and securely between users. This network forms the foundation for all collaborative tools and interactions within the platform, providing the necessary infrastructure for high-speed and secure data exchange.

The Quantum Collaboration Tools package includes essential components such as chat, video conferencing, document sharing, and collaborative whiteboards.

These tools are designed to facilitate various forms of interaction and teamwork among users. The chat interface (IChat) allows for real-time text communication, while the video conferencing interface (IVideo) supports high-fidelity video streams. Document sharing (IDocument) ensures secure exchange and collaborative editing of files, and the collaborative whiteboard (IWhiteboard) enables interactive brainstorming and problem-solving sessions. These tools are integrated with the Quantum Router to ensure that all communications are processed efficiently and securely. Behind these collaborative tools lies the Quantum Computing Backend, featuring a Quantum Processor that handles complex computations and data analysis. This backend is equipped with adaptive learning algorithms and real-time data analysis capabilities, allowing the platform to process large volumes of educational data swiftly and accurately. The Quantum Processor ensures that the platform can adapt to the individual needs of users, providing personalized learning paths and insights based on real-time performance data.

Given the sensitive nature of educational data, the platform incorporates a robust Security and Encryption Layer. This layer includes components for quantum-resistant cryptography, user authentication, and data encryption. Quantum-resistant cryptography ensures that the platform's security measures are future-proof against potential quantum attacks. User authentication verifies the identities of all users accessing the platform, while data encryption safeguards the integrity and privacy of all stored and transmitted data. The Data Storage and Management package comprises databases for user data, learning materials, and collaboration artifacts. These databases are crucial for organizing and managing the vast amounts of information generated and used within the platform. User data includes personal information and performance metrics, learning materials encompass educational content and resources, and collaboration artifacts involve documents and records of collaborative activities. This organized data storage facilitates efficient access and retrieval, supporting the platform's adaptive learning capabilities.

To enhance the learning experience further, the platform integrates AI and Machine Learning Modules. These modules provide personalized recommendations, performance tracking, and real-time analytics. The personalized recommendations component analyzes individual learning patterns and preferences to suggest tailored educational content and activities. Performance tracking monitors student progress, offering insights and feedback to help students and educators identify strengths and areas for improvement. Real-time analytics use the data collected to generate actionable insights, guiding instructional strategies and decision-making processes. Finally, the Integration APIs connect the Quantum Collaboration Platform with external educational tools and resource libraries. These APIs expand the platform's functionality by allowing seamless integration with other digital learning resources and technologies. This connectivity ensures that users have access to a wide range of educational materials and can benefit from the latest advancements in educational technology.

Figure 1. Quantum collaboration platform architecture

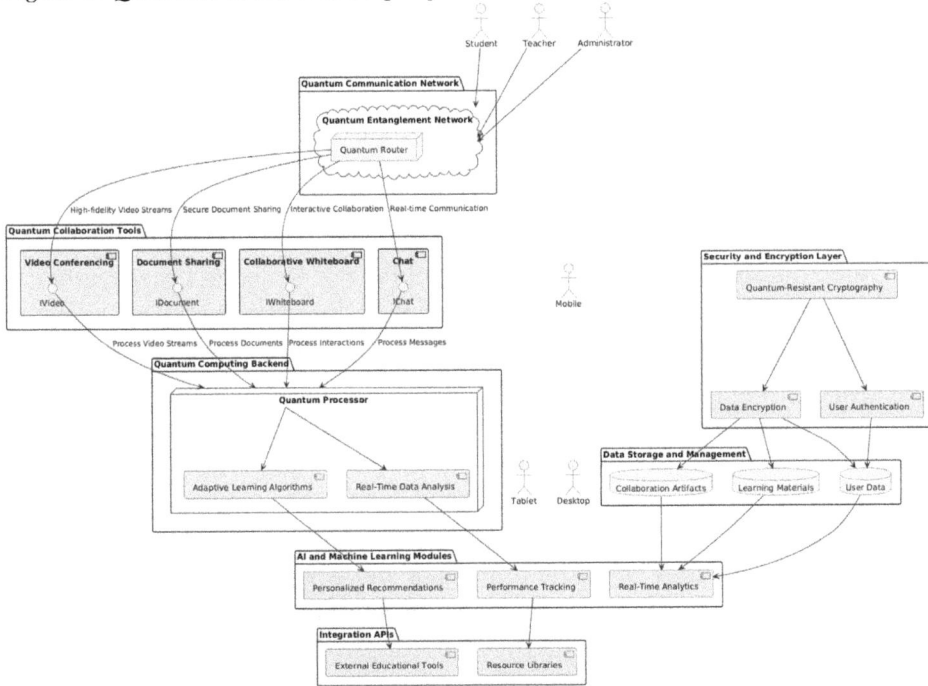

5.2 Simulated Quantum Environments

Simulated quantum environments represent another innovative application of quantum computing in education, offering immersive and interactive learning experiences that go beyond traditional classroom settings (Zable et al., 2020). These environments utilize the computational power of quantum systems to create realistic simulations of complex phenomena, allowing students to explore and experiment in ways that were previously impossible (Li, 2023).

In a simulated quantum environment, students can engage with detailed models of scientific processes, historical events, or engineering challenges, gaining a deeper understanding through hands-on experience (Santos et al., 2013). For example, a simulation of a quantum particle's behavior could help students grasp abstract concepts in quantum mechanics by visualizing and manipulating the particle's state in real-time (Li, 2023). Similarly, a simulation of a historical battle could provide a rich, contextual understanding of the event, highlighting the interplay of various factors and decisions (Squire and Klopfer, 2007).

These immersive experiences are further enhanced by the use of virtual and augmented reality technologies, which can make the simulations more engaging and realistic (Avila Herrera and Guevara, 2021). By placing students in a lifelike setting, these technologies facilitate deeper cognitive and emotional connections to the material, promoting retention and comprehension (Beck, 2019). The ability to experiment and explore within a simulated environment encourages a more active and inquiry-based approach to learning, fostering critical thinking and problem-solving skills (Gen¸c et al., 2021).

Figure 2 illustrates the comprehensive workflow of Quantum Pedagogy-based educational processes within Simulated Quantum Environments. This complex system leverages the unique capabilities of quantum computing to create an immersive, adaptive, and personalized learning experience for students, while providing teachers with the tools to monitor and guide these interactions effectively. At the forefront of the system are the students and teachers, who interact with the platform through various user devices. Students engage in the simulations using VR/AR headsets, which provide an immersive learning environment. Teachers, on the other hand, use desktops or tablets to monitor and guide the students. This dual interaction setup ensures that both students and teachers are seamlessly integrated into the learning process.

The backbone of this platform is the Quantum Communication Network, consisting of a Quantum Network and a Quantum Router. The Quantum Network facilitates real-time data transmission using quantum communication principles, ensuring secure and instantaneous communication. The Quantum Router manages the flow of data between the user devices and the simulated environment, directing interaction data from the students and monitoring inputs from the teachers to the appropriate components within the system.

Within the Simulated Quantum Environment, several critical components work together to create and manage the learning experiences. The Simulation Engine processes the simulation based on real-time interaction data received from the Quantum Router. The Scenario Manager handles the different simulation scenarios, loading and saving them as needed to provide varied and dynamic learning experiences. The Interaction Tracker continuously monitors user actions and interactions within the simulation, providing valuable data for real-time analysis and adaptation.

The Quantum Computing Backend is the core computational engine of the platform. The Quantum Processor, a key component of this backend, handles the complex computations required for running adaptive learning algorithms and real-time data analysis. These algorithms are designed to personalize the learning experience based on the unique interactions and progress of each student. Real-time data analysis further enhances this personalization by continuously processing interaction data to generate insights and feedback.

Effective data management is crucial for the functionality of this system. The Data Storage and Management component includes databases for Student Profiles, Simulation Data, and Learning Resources. Student Profiles store historical data and profiles of each student, providing a rich source of information for personalized learning. Simulation Data stores information related to the various simulation scenarios, ensuring that the simulations can be easily accessed and managed. Learning Resources include educational materials and resources that are integrated into the simulations to provide comprehensive learning content.

To further enhance the learning experience, the platform incorporates AI and Machine Learning Modules. These modules provide Personalized Feedback, Progress Analytics, and Content Recommendations. Personalized Feedback is generated based on the adaptive learning algorithms and real-time data analysis, offering tailored guidance to students to improve their learning outcomes. Progress Analytics track and analyze student progress, providing teachers with detailed insights into each student's performance and areas that may require additional support. Content Recommendations suggest next activities and learning materials based on the student's progress and interactions, ensuring that the learning experience remains engaging and relevant.

The workflow begins with the student engaging in the simulation through VR/AR headsets, while the teacher monitors and guides using a desktop or tablet. Interaction data from both the student and teacher is transmitted in real-time through the Quantum Network and managed by the Quantum Router. This data is then processed by the Simulation Engine, with the Scenario Manager handling different simulation scenarios. The Interaction Tracker sends user interaction data to the Quantum Processor for analysis.

The Quantum Processor, utilizing adaptive learning algorithms, generates personalized feedback and content recommendations, which are transmitted back to the student and teacher. The student receives this feedback through the VR/AR headset, while the teacher receives progress analytics on their desktop. Historical data from student profiles, simulation data, and learning resources are integrated into this process to enhance the personalization and relevance of the learning experience.

Figure 2. Simulated quantum environment

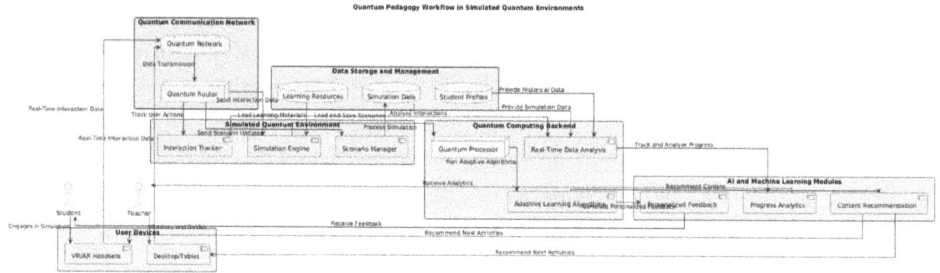

5.3 Global Quantum Classrooms

Global quantum classrooms extend the principles of quantum-enhanced collaborative learning to a global scale, breaking down geographical and cultural barriers to create a truly interconnected educational experience (Arias-Masa et al., 2014). These classrooms leverage quantum communication and networking technologies to facilitate real-time, synchronous interactions among students and educators from different parts of the world (Simon, 2017).

In a global quantum classroom, students can participate in joint lessons, collaborative projects, and cross-cultural exchanges, gaining exposure to diverse perspectives and ideas (Lock and Duggleby, 2018). This global interaction not only enriches the learning experience but also fosters a sense of global citizenship and mutual understanding (Hastie et al., 2010). By working together on common goals and challenges, students develop the skills and attitudes necessary for effective collaboration in an increasingly interconnected world (Sun et al., 2017).

The use of quantum-enhanced natural language processing and translation tools further supports communication and collaboration in global quantum classrooms (Michailidou and Economides, 2003). These tools can provide real-time translation and interpretation, ensuring that language differences do not pose a barrier to interaction (Villanueva et al., 2020). This capability allows students to engage in meaningful discussions and collaborations, regardless of their native language, promoting inclusivity and equity (Arias-Masa et al., 2014).

Global quantum classrooms can be integrated with quantum collaboration platforms and simulated quantum environments, creating a comprehensive and cohesive learning ecosystem (Lonchamp, 2006). This integration enables students to collaborate on complex projects, engage with immersive simulations, and access a wide range of educational resources, all within a unified framework (Jara et al., 2012). The combination of these technologies provides a rich, interactive, and holistic learning experience that prepares students for the challenges and opportunities of the 21st century (Simon, 2017).

The Global Quantum Classrooms (Figure 2) presents a sophisticated and detailed framework for leveraging quantum computing and advanced technologies to create a highly secure, adaptive, and interconnected educational environment. This complex system integrates various components to facilitate seamless and effective collaborative learning across multiple classrooms worldwide. At the heart of the system is the Global Quantum Network, which comprises the Quantum Entanglement Server and the Quantum Communication Link. The Quantum Entanglement Server plays a crucial role in facilitating quantum entanglement communication between different classrooms, ensuring real-time, secure data transmission. The Quantum Communication Link acts as the backbone of the network, enabling instantaneous communication and interaction among users. The deployment includes multiple Classrooms, each equipped with VR/AR Headsets and Desktop/Tablet devices. Students use VR/AR headsets to engage with the quantum classroom environment, experiencing immersive and interactive simulations. Teachers and students also utilize desktops or tablets to monitor activities and interact with the system. Each classroom is equipped with a Local Cache to store frequently accessed data, reducing latency and improving performance by caching data locally.

The Central Data Center is a pivotal component of this architecture, housing essential databases and the quantum computing infrastructure. The data center contains the User Profiles Database (UserDB), which stores user information and profiles, the Learning Resources Database (LearningDB) for educational materials, and the Collaboration Artifacts Database (CollabDB) for data related to collaborative projects. The Quantum Computing Cluster within the data center consists of the Quantum Processor (QProcessor), which performs complex computations, Real-Time Analytics (RTAnalytics) for analyzing data and providing insights, and Adaptive Learning Algorithms (AdaptiveAlgo) that adapt learning experiences based on real-time data.

The AI and Machine Learning Services module provides critical functionalities for personalized education. The Personalized Feedback Service (FeedbackService) generates tailored feedback for students based on their performance and interactions. The Progress Tracking Service (ProgressService) monitors and analyzes student progress, providing valuable insights to both students and teachers. The Content Recommendation Service (ContentService) suggests relevant learning materials and activities tailored to each student's needs, ensuring an engaging and effective learning experience.

Security is a paramount concern in this system, addressed by the Security and Authentication components. Quantum-Resistant Cryptography (QCrypto) ensures that all data is protected against potential quantum computing threats, while User

Authentication (Auth) verifies the identities of users accessing the system, maintaining a secure environment. Data Encryption (Encryption) further protects data during transmission and storage, ensuring confidentiality and integrity.

Students and teachers interact with the quantum classroom environment using VR/AR headsets and desktop/tablet devices. These devices connect to the Quantum Communication Link, which ensures real-time, secure communication facilitated by the Quantum Entanglement Server. In each classroom, a local cache stores frequently accessed data to reduce latency and improve performance. The Quantum Communication Network transmits interaction data to the Central Data Center, where the Quantum Computing Cluster processes the data using quantum processors, real-time analytics, and adaptive learning algorithms. The Central Data Center houses databases for user profiles, learning resources, and collaboration artifacts. These databases support the AI and Machine Learning Services, which provide personalized feedback, progress tracking, and content recommendations. These services communicate back to the user devices in the classrooms, delivering personalized educational experiences and insights. Security and authentication components ensure that all communications and data storage are protected using quantum-resistant cryptography, user authentication, and data encryption techniques. This comprehensive system creates a highly secure, adaptive, and interconnected global quantum classroom environment, facilitating advanced collaborative learning and personalized education.

6. LEARNING SCENARIOS BASED ON QUANTUM PEDAGOGY

6.1 Collaborative Problem-Solving in Quantum Simulated Labs

Quantum Simulated Labs provide an innovative platform for collaborative problem-solving, leveraging the principles of Quantum Pedagogy to create immersive and interactive learning environments (Arango et al., 2007). In these simulated labs, students

Figure 3. Components of global quantum classrooms

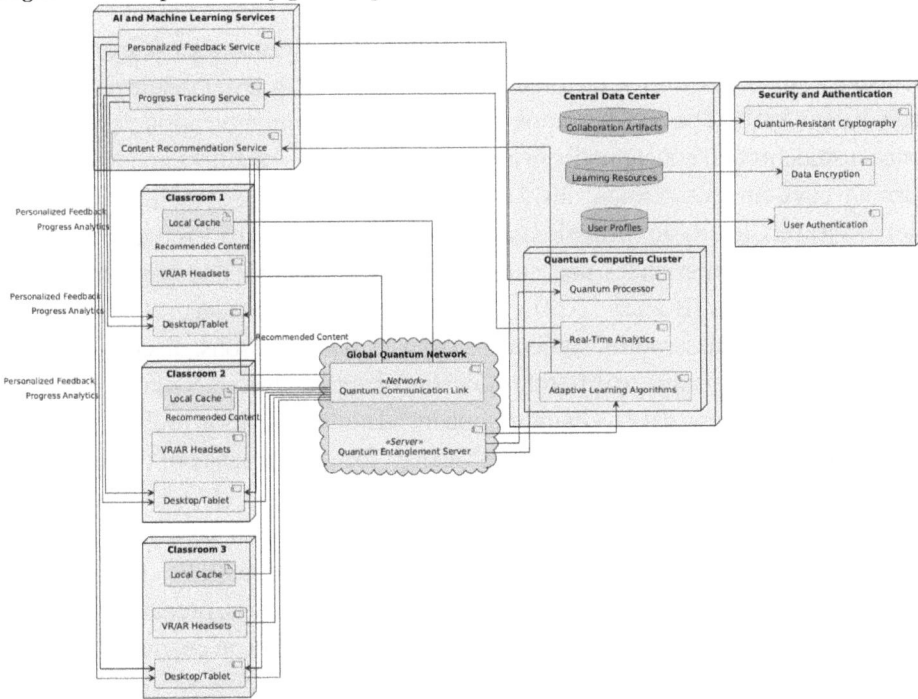

from diverse geographical locations can work together in real-time to tackle complex scientific and engineering challenges (Ghazinejad et al., 2021). The use of quantum computing allows these labs to simulate complex systems and phenomena that are beyond the capabilities of classical computing (Tomandl et al., 2015). For instance, students can explore quantum chemical reactions, model complex biological systems, or simulate advanced materials with unprecedented precision (Jankiewicz et al., 2022).

These labs foster a collaborative spirit by enabling students to share data, insights, and strategies instantaneously, thanks to the secure and instantaneous communication facilitated by quantum entanglement (Seskir et al., 2022). This interconnectedness ensures that all participants can contribute equally, regardless of their physical location (Torre et al., 2013). Additionally, the labs can adapt to the individual learning paces and styles of each student, providing personalized guidance and resources (Okamoto, 2004). This adaptability is powered by quantum algorithms that continuously analyze student interactions and progress, offering real-time feedback and support (Pedersen et al., 2015). As a result, students develop critical thinking, teamwork, and problem-solving skills in a dynamic and supportive environment (Valdez et al., 2014).

6.2 Global Virtual Classrooms and Cross-Cultural Learning

Global Virtual Classrooms represent a significant advancement in educational inclusivity and accessibility, facilitated by Quantum Pedagogy (Prasolova-Førland and Chang, 2007). These classrooms utilize quantum communication networks to connect students and educators from around the world in a seamless and interactive learning environment (Simon, 2017). By breaking down geographical barriers, Global Virtual Classrooms provide students with the opportunity to engage in cross-cultural learning experiences that enrich their understanding and appreciation of diverse perspectives (Borger, 2022).

In these virtual classrooms, students participate in joint lessons, discussions, and projects, gaining exposure to different educational approaches and cultural contexts (Ove and Christensen, 2013). Quantum-enhanced communication tools ensure that these interactions are real-time and high-fidelity, fostering a sense of presence and community among participants (Kostic et al., 2011).

The cross-cultural experiences facilitated by Global Virtual Classrooms promote empathy, global awareness, and intercultural communication skills (Canto et al., 2014). Students learn to navigate and appreciate cultural nuances, preparing them for a globalized workforce and society. Educators can collaborate on curriculum development and pedagogical strategies, sharing best practices and innovative approaches to teaching and learning (Harper et al., 2004). This global exchange of knowledge and ideas enriches the educational experience for all participants, fostering a more inclusive and connected educational landscape (Coppola et al., 2002).

6.3 Quantum-Enhanced STEM Education

Quantum-Enhanced STEM Education leverages the computational power and unique capabilities of quantum computing to transform the teaching and learning of science, technology, engineering, and mathematics (STEM) subjects. Traditional STEM education often struggles to convey the complexity and intricacies of advanced scientific concepts and phenomena (Gong et al., 2015; Damasevicius and Zailskaite-Jakste, 2024b). Quantum computing addresses this challenge by enabling the simulation and visualization of complex systems and processes that are otherwise difficult to model with classical computers (Zulehner and Wille, 2017).

In Quantum-Enhanced STEM Education, students can engage with interactive simulations that bring abstract concepts to life. For example, quantum simulations can demonstrate the behavior of subatomic particles, the dynamics of chemical reactions, or the properties of new materials (Hughes et al., 2020). These visualizations provide students with a deeper and more intuitive understanding of the underlying principles, enhancing their comprehension and retention of complex topics (Ahmed et al., 2021). Quantum algorithms can analyze vast amounts of scientific data, identifying patterns and correlations that might not be evident through classical analysis. This capability supports inquiry-based learning, where students formulate hypotheses, conduct experiments, and analyze results using quantum-powered tools (Havl´ıcek et al., 2018b). The immediate feedback and adaptive learning pathways enabled by quantum computing ensure that students receive personalized support tailored to their learning needs and progress (Melnikov et al., 2023).

Quantum-Enhanced STEM Education also prepares students for the emerging fields and industries driven by quantum technologies. By equipping students with the knowledge and skills to work with quantum systems, this approach ensures that they are well-prepared for future careers in quantum computing, quantum chemistry, quantum engineering, and other related fields (Carrascal et al., 2020). The interdisciplinary nature of quantum-enhanced learning fosters a holistic understanding of STEM subjects, promoting creativity, innovation, and problem-solving skills that are essential for success in the 21st century (Ozlem Salehi et al., 2020).

6.4 Assessment and Evaluation in Quantum Learning Scenarios

Assessment and evaluation in Quantum Learning Scenarios are fundamentally transformed by the capabilities of quantum computing. Traditional assessment methods, such as standardized tests and periodic evaluations, often fail to capture the dynamic and multifaceted nature of student learning (Carrascal et al., 2020).

Quantum Pedagogy, however, enables continuous and adaptive assessment, providing a more comprehensive and nuanced understanding of student performance (Melnikov et al., 2023). Quantum algorithms can process vast amounts of data generated from student interactions within simulated environments, collaborative projects, and individual learning activities (Zulehner and Wille, 2017). This data is analyzed in real-time to assess not only the correctness of student responses but also the process and strategies used to arrive at those responses (Havl´ıcek et al., 2018b). By evaluating factors such as problem-solving approaches, time taken to complete tasks, and the frequency of revisions, quantum-powered assessments offer a deeper insight into a student's cognitive and metacognitive skills (Gong et al., 2015).

The adaptability of quantum systems allows for the creation of dynamic assessment environments. Instead of static test questions, students can be presented with adaptive challenges that evolve based on their performance (Ozlem Salehi et al., 2020). For example, a student demonstrating proficiency in a particular area might be given increasingly complex problems, while another student struggling with a concept might receive additional support and simpler tasks (Hughes et al., 2020). This continuous and adaptive assessment ensures that evaluations are tailored to individual learning paths, providing more accurate and personalized feedback (Melnikov et al., 2023).

Quantum-enhanced assessments can incorporate a broader range of competencies, including collaborative and interpersonal skills, creativity, and critical thinking (Ahmed et al., 2021). By analyzing data from group projects, discussions, and interactive simulations, these assessments can provide a holistic view of student abilities, going beyond traditional academic metrics (Gong et al., 2015). This comprehensive evaluation framework supports a more balanced and inclusive approach to measuring student success, recognizing diverse talents and learning styles (Angara et al., 2020).

6.5 Feedback and Improvement Mechanisms in Quantum Pedagogy

Effective feedback is crucial for learning and development, and Quantum Pedagogy enhances this process by leveraging real-time data analysis and adaptive learning algorithms (Akavova et al., 2023). In quantum-enhanced educational environments, feedback mechanisms are designed to be immediate, personalized, and actionable, providing students with continuous guidance and support throughout their learning journey (Liu et al., 2017).

The integration of quantum computing enables the system to analyze student performance data instantaneously and generate tailored feedback based on individual needs and progress (Fernandes et al., 2023). This feedback is not limited to correcting mistakes but also includes suggestions for improvement, alternative strategies, and resources for further learning (Siadaty and Taghiyareh, 2007). For instance, if a student struggles with a particular concept, the system might recommend targeted exercises, visualizations, or peer tutoring sessions to address the gap (Akavova et al., 2023).

The dynamic nature of quantum-enhanced feedback ensures that it evolves with the student's learning trajectory (Peng et al., 2019). As students progress and their understanding deepens, the feedback adapts accordingly, offering more advanced insights and challenges (Clark et al., 2018). This continuous loop of feedback and improvement fosters a growth mindset, encouraging students to view learning as an ongoing process rather than a series of discrete events (Biamonte et al., 2016).

Teachers also benefit from these advanced feedback mechanisms (Hentschel and Sanders, 2010). Quantum Pedagogy provides educators with detailed analytics and visualizations of student performance, highlighting trends, strengths, and areas for improvement (Pagano et al., 2023). These insights enable teachers to tailor their instruction to better meet the needs of their students, implement targeted interventions, and monitor the effectiveness of their teaching strategies (Fernandes et al., 2023). By integrating real-time data into their instructional practices, teachers can create a more responsive and supportive learning environment (Siadaty and Taghiyareh, 2007).

The collaborative nature of Quantum Pedagogy enhances peer feedback and group learning (Biamonte et al., 2016). Students can engage in reflective discussions and collaborative assessments, supported by quantum-powered tools that facilitate secure and efficient communication (Clark et al., 2018). This peer-to-peer feedback not only reinforces individual learning but also builds interpersonal skills and fosters a sense of community and shared responsibility (Liu et al., 2017).

Figure 4 represents the comprehensive workflow of feedback and improvement mechanisms in Quantum Pedagogy, illustrating how quantum computing and advanced AI technologies facilitate real-time, personalized feedback and continuous learning improvement. At the heart of the system are the students and teachers, who interact with the platform through various devices. Students use VR/AR headsets to engage with immersive simulations, while teachers monitor and guide students using desktops or tablets. These interactions generate a wealth of data, which is sent through the Quantum Communication Link, a secure network facilitated by the Quantum Entanglement Server. This server ensures real-time, instantaneous data transmission using quantum entanglement principles. In each classroom, local caches store frequently accessed data to reduce latency and ensure seamless interaction. The interaction data from the students' VR/AR headsets and the teachers' devices is transmitted to the Quantum Entanglement Server, which processes the data using the Quantum Processor within the Central Data Center. This processor performs complex computations required for real-time analysis and adaptive learning. The Real-Time Data Analysis component processes the interaction data, integrating information from the Student Profiles Database, Learning Resources Database, and Performance Data Database. This comprehensive analysis allows the Adaptive Learning Algorithms to tailor the learning experience to each student's needs. The algorithms adapt based on the real-time data, providing a personalized learning pathway that evolves with the student's progress. The Personalized Feedback Generator then creates tailored feedback for each student, which is delivered through the VR/AR Feedback Interface for students and the Desktop Feedback Interface for teachers. This feedback is immediate and actionable, helping students understand their mistakes and providing guidance on how to improve. Teachers receive detailed analytics and visualizations of student performance, enabling them to tailor their instruction and provide targeted support. The Progress Tracker continuously monitors and analyzes each student's progress, sending detailed reports to the teacher. This ensures that educators have a clear understanding of each student's development and can intervene when necessary. Simultaneously, the Content Recommender suggests relevant learning materials and activities to the student based on their current progress and performance. This ensures that the learning experience remains engaging and appropriate for each student's level of understanding.

7. DISCUSSION

7.1 Application Considerations

The application of Quantum Pedagogy is challenging, making it more practical for technologically advanced institutions with substantial financial resources and skilled personnel. Due to the significant computational requirements, infrastructure demands, and expertise needed, institutions with limited resources may find it difficult to adopt this model without substantial adjustments or external support. Quantum Pedagogy is applicable in specific fields and learning levels that benefit most from high computational power and data-driven insights. For example, it is well-suited to STEM-focused higher education programs, particularly in advanced areas like physics, computer science, and engineering, where students and faculty can engage with quantum concepts and applications directly. Graduate and postgraduate education levels are also ideal, as students at this stage often

Figure 4. Feedback and improvement mechanisms in quantum pedagogy

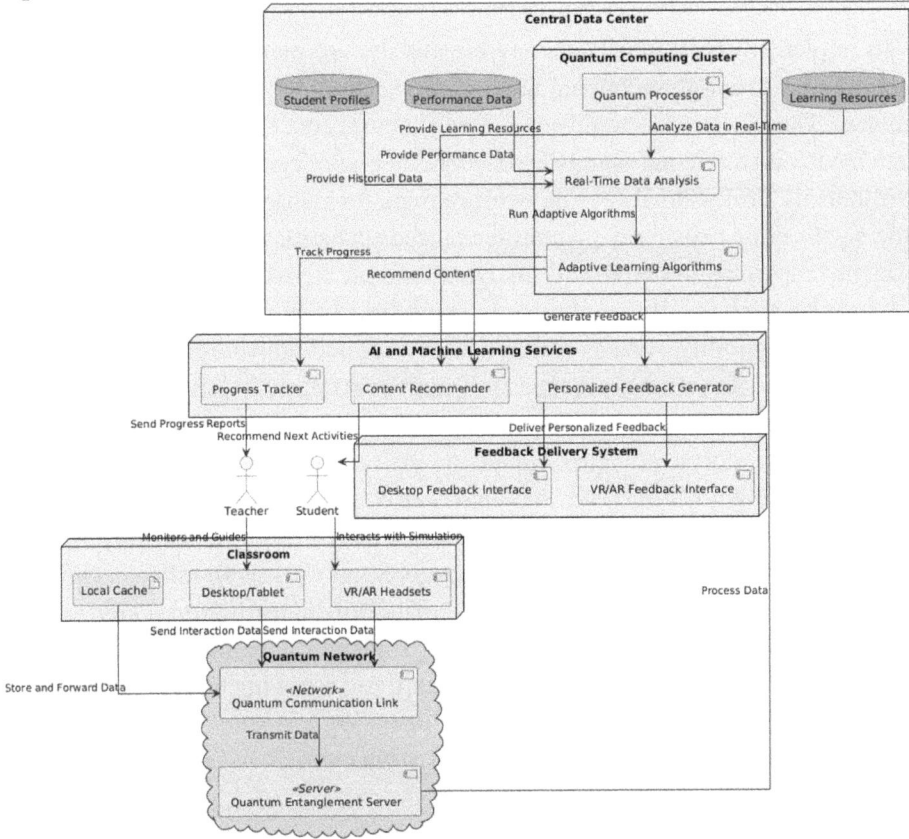

possess the foundational knowledge needed to interact effectively with quantum-enhanced learning environments.

In professional and continuing education, Quantum Pedagogy could provide flexible, advanced learning paths for professionals in fields like data science, AI, and quantum computing, supporting reskilling and upskilling initiatives. Research-intensive learning environments, such as those focused on scientific research, can leverage Quantum Pedagogy to enhance complex problem-solving and data analysis, particularly in fields like molecular biology, environmental science, and cognitive neuroscience. These areas are well-suited to the unique capabilities of Quantum Pedagogy, making it a valuable tool for institutions dedicated to cutting-edge research and advanced technological education.

7.2 Managerial Implications

To implement Quantum Pedagogy effectively, top management should begin by building a strong foundational understanding through targeted workshops and seminars. These sessions should cover core quantum concepts—superposition, entanglement, and tunneling—and demonstrate their application to adaptive learning environments. Professional development programs for management can further equip leaders with skills to oversee quantum-enhanced educational frameworks, focusing on adaptive learning systems, data analytics, and predictive modeling.

Assessing current infrastructure is essential to identify any upgrades needed for quantum compatibility, such as secure data storage and scalable cloud solutions to handle the high data volumes produced by quantum systems. Investment in quantum-enabled learning platforms will allow management to provide personalized, real-time feedback and support to students, enhancing their learning experiences.

Understanding quantum data analytics is also crucial, as it enables institutions to make data-driven decisions based on real-time insights into student performance and engagement. Additionally, fostering a global network with other institutions implementing Quantum Pedagogy will help management learn from shared experiences and support global classrooms, enriching student collaboration across regions.

Finally, continuous feedback mechanisms are key, allowing for real-time adjustments based on input from educators and students. By focusing on these elements, top management can lead a smooth transition to Quantum Pedagogy, advancing the institution's position in innovative education.

8. CONCLUSION

Quantum Pedagogy represents a transformative approach to education that leverages the principles of quantum mechanics—such as superposition, entanglement, and quantum tunneling—to create a more personalized, adaptive, and immersive learning environment. This innovative educational framework addresses the limitations of traditional pedagogical models, which often fail to accommodate the diverse learning needs of students and the dynamic nature of modern education. By utilizing the computational power of quantum systems, Quantum Pedagogy enables the development of quantum-adaptive learning systems that can process vast amounts of educational data in real-time, providing tailored learning experiences that adjust to the individual needs of each student. Key elements of Quantum Pedagogy include quantum algorithms for personalization, quantum tutors, and dynamic quantum curricula. Quantum algorithms analyze student performance data to create individualized learning paths, ensuring that each student receives the most effective instructional strategies. Quantum tutors provide real-time, adaptive feedback and guidance, enhancing student engagement and understanding. Dynamic quantum curricula continuously adapt to student progress, integrating the latest educational research and technological advancements to maintain relevance and efficacy. Quantum Pedagogy enhances collaborative learning through quantum collaboration platforms, simulated quantum environments, and global quantum classrooms. These components facilitate seamless and secure communication, immersive and interactive learning experiences, and real-time global collaboration. By fostering a sense of interconnectedness and shared purpose, Quantum Pedagogy prepares students for the collaborative and interdisciplinary nature of the modern workforce.

The vision for 21st-century education, as embodied by Quantum Pedagogy, is one of a highly personalized, adaptive, and interconnected learning environment that leverages advanced technologies to enhance both cognitive and affective development. Education in the 21st century will be characterized by its ability to provide individualized learning experiences that cater to the unique needs and preferences of each student. The use of quantum computing will enable the continuous analysis and adaptation of educational content, ensuring that learning remains engaging, relevant, and effective. In this vision, the boundaries of traditional classrooms will be transcended, creating a global learning ecosystem where students can collaborate with peers and educators from around the world.

Quantum-enhanced communication and collaboration tools will facilitate real-time interactions and knowledge sharing, fostering a sense of global citizenship and mutual understanding. This interconnectedness will not only enrich the learning experience but also prepare students to navigate and contribute to an increasingly globalized and interconnected world. The integration of quantum computing with other emerging technologies, such as artificial intelligence (Damasevicius and Sidekerskiene, 2024), virtual and augmented reality, digital twins (Damasevicius and Zailskaite-Jakste, 2024a) and blockchain, will further enhance the educational landscape. These technologies will provide new opportunities for experiential and inquiry-based learning, allowing students to explore complex concepts and engage with real-world challenges in innovative ways. The combination of these advanced tools will create a comprehensive and cohesive educational ecosystem that supports lifelong learning and continuous personal and professional development.

REFERENCES

Ahmed, S. Z., Weidner, C., Jensen, J. H. M., Sherson, J., & Lewandowski, H. (2021). Student use of a quantum simulation and visualization tool. *European Journal of Physics*, ●●●, 43.

Akavova, A., Temirkhanova, Z., & Lorsanova, Z. Adaptive learning and artificial intelligence in the educational space. In: E3S Web of Conferences (2023)

Altman, C., & Zapatrin, R. (2009). Backpropagation training in adaptive quantum networks. *International Journal of Theoretical Physics*, 49, 2991–2997.

Alvarez-Rodriguez, U., Lamata, L., Escandell-Montero, P., Martín-Guerrero, J. D., & Solano, E. (2016). Quantum machine learning without measurements. arXiv preprint arXiv:1612.05535.

Angara, P., Stege, U., & MacLean, A. Quantum computing for high-school students an experience report. *2020 IEEE International Conference on Quantum Computing and Engineering (QCE)* pp. 323–329 (2020)

Angara, P., Stege, U., MacLean, A., Müller, H. A., & Markham, T. (2022). Teaching quantum computing to high-school-aged youth: A hands-on approach. *IEEE Transactions on Quantum Engineering*, 3, 1–15.

Arango, F., Chang, C., Esche, S. K., & Chassapis, C. (2007, October). A scenario for collaborative learning in virtual engineering laboratories. In 2007 37th annual frontiers in education conference-global engineering: knowledge without borders, opportunities without passports (pp. F3G-7). IEEE.

Araujo, I. C., & Da Silva, A. J. (2020, July). Quantum ensemble of trained classifiers. In *2020 International Joint Conference on Neural Networks (IJCNN)* (pp. 1-8). IEEE.

Arias-Masa, J., Alonso-D'ıaz, L., Cubo-Delgado, S., Guti'errez-Esteban, P., & Yuste-Tosina, R. (2014). Assessment of the use of synchronous virtual classrooms in higher education. *The New Educational Review*.

Ávila-Herrera, S., & Guevara, C. (2021). Development of a Methodology for the Learning-Teaching Process Through Virtual and Augmented Reality. In Intelligent Human Systems Integration 2021: Proceedings of the 4th International Conference on Intelligent Human Systems Integration (IHSI 2021): Integrating People and Intelligent Systems, February 22-24, 2021, Palermo, Italy (pp. 651-656). Springer International Publishing.

Beck, D. (2019). Special issue: Augmented and virtual reality in education: Immersive learning research. *Journal of Educational Computing Research*, 57, 1619–1625.

Biamonte, J., Wittek, P., Pancotti, N., Rebentrost, P., Wiebe, N., & Lloyd, S. (2016). Quantum machine learning. *Nature*, 549, 195–202. PMID: 28905917

Biersteker, T. (2022). Quantum Pedagogy. Quantum International Relations: A Human Science for World Politics, 197.

Blumenstein, M. (2020). Synergies of learning analytics and learning design: A systematic review of student outcomes. *Journal of Learning Analytics*.

Borger, J. G. (2022, October). Getting to the CoRe of Collaborative Online International Learning (COIL). []. Frontiers Media SA.]. *Frontiers in Education*, 7, 987289.

Canto, S., de Graaff, R., & Jauregi, K. (2014). Collaborative tasks for negotiation of intercultural meaning in virtual worlds and video-web communication. In *Technology-mediated TBLT* (pp. 183–212). John Benjamins.

Carrascal, G., Barrio, A. D. D., & Botella, G. (2020). First experiences of teaching quantum computing. *The Journal of Supercomputing*, ●●●, 1–30.

Chang, Q., Pan, X., Manikandan, N., & Ramesh, S. (2022). Artificial intelligence technologies for teaching and learning in higher education. *International Journal of Reliability Quality and Safety Engineering*.

Charlton, P., & Avramides, K. (2016). Knowledge construction in computer science and engineering when learning through making. *IEEE Transactions on Learning Technologies*, 9, 379–390.

Choi, K. S., Deng, H., Laurat, J., & Kimble, H. (2007). Mapping photonic entanglement into and out of a quantum memory. *Nature*, 452, 67–71. PMID: 18322529

Choi, K. S., Goban, A., Papp, S., Enk, S. J., & Kimble, H. (2010). Entanglement of spin waves among four quantum memories. *Nature*, 468, 412–416. PMID: 21085175

Clark, R. M., Kaw, A., & Delgado, E. (2018). Do Adaptive Lessons for Pre-class Experience Improve Flipped Learning? Proceedings of the ASEE Annual Conference & Exposition..

Coppola, N., Hiltz, S. R., & Rotter, N. (2002). Becoming a virtual professor: Pedagogical roles and asynchronous learning networks. *Journal of Management Information Systems*, 18, 169–189.

Córcoles, A. D., Takita, M., Inoue, K., Lekuch, S., Minev, Z. K., Chow, J. M., & Gambetta, J. M. (2021). Exploiting dynamic quantum circuits in a quantum algorithm with superconducting qubits. *Physical Review Letters*, 127(10), 100501.

Damasevicius, R., & Sidekerskiene, T. (2024). Ai as a teacher: A new educational dynamic for modern classrooms for personalized learning support. AI-Enhanced Teaching Methods. IGI Global Scientific Publishing.

Damaševičius, R., & Zailskaitė-Jakštė, L. (2023, November). From STEAM to STREAM: Integrating Research as a Part of STEAM Education. In International Conference on New Media Pedagogy (pp. 318-335). Cham: Springer Nature Switzerland.

Damasevicius, R., & Zailskaite-Jakste, L. (2024a). *Digital twin technology: Necessity of the future in education and beyond.* Automated Secure Computing for Next-Generation Systems. Wiley.

De Marsico, M., Sterbini, A., & Temperini, M. (2013). A framework to support social-collaborative personalized e-learning. In Human-Computer Interaction. Applications and Services: 15th International Conference, HCI International 2013, Las Vegas, NV, USA, July 21-26, 2013 [Springer Berlin Heidelberg.]. *Proceedings*, 15(Part II), 351–360.

DeVore, S., & Singh, C. (2016). Interactive learning tutorial on quantum key distribution. *Physical Review. Physics Education Research.*

Dobson, S., & Scaff, J. (2024). Qurio: QBit Learning, Quantum Pedagogy, and Agentive AI Tutors. Joint Mathematics Meetings, San Francisco, USA, January 3-6, 2024.

Domert, D., & Linder, C. (2005). Ingerman: Probability as a conceptual hurdle to understanding one-dimensional quantum scattering and tunnelling. *European Journal of Physics*, 26, 47–59.

Dong, D., Chen, C., Li, H. X., & Tarn, T. (2005). Quantum reinforcement learning. *IEEE Transactions on Systems, Man, and Cybernetics. Part B, Cybernetics*, 38, 1207–1220. PMID: 18784007

Duran, M., Simon, S., & Blasco, F. (2020, June). Science Education and Artificial Intelligence–A Chatbot on Magic and Quantum Computing as an Educational Tool. In EDEN Conference Proceedings (No. 1, pp. 137-142).

El Naqa, I., & Ten, R. (2016). SU-D-BRB-05: Quantum Learning for Knowledge-Based Response-Adaptive Radiotherapy. *Medical Physics*, 43(6Part4), 3338–3338.

Fern'andez-Morante, C., Cebreiro-L'opez, B., Rodr'ıguez-Malmierca, M. J., & Casal-Otero, L. (2021). Adaptive learning supported by learning analytics for student teachers' personalized training during in-school practices. *Sustainability*.

Fernandes, C. W., Rafatirad, S., & Sayadi, H. (2023, June). Advancing personalized and adaptive learning experience in education with artificial intelligence. In 2023 32nd Annual Conference of the European Association for Education in Electrical and Information Engineering (EAEEIE) (pp. 1-6). IEEE.

Fingerhuth, M., Babej, T., & Wittek, P. (2018). Open source software in quantum computing. *PLoS One*, ●●●, 13. PMID: 30571700

Freericks, J. (2023). Focus on conceptual ideas in quantum mechanics for teacher training. *Journal of Physics: Conference Series*, ●●●, 2490.

Gen c, H., Aydin, S., & Erdal, H. (2021). Designing a virtual reality programming environment for quantum computers. *Computer Applications in Engineering Education*, 30, 690–707.

George, B., & Wooden, O. (2023). Managing the strategic transformation of higher education through artificial intelligence. *Administrative Sciences*.

Ghazinejad, M., Khoshnoud, F., & Porter, S. (2021). *Enhancing interactive learning in engineering classes by implementing virtual laboratories. In: 2021 IEEE Frontiers in Education Conference*. FIE.

Gong, M. Y., Yuksel, T., Magana, A., & Bryan, L. (2015, June). Engineering and Physics Students' Perceptions about Learning Quantum Me-chanics via Computer Simulations. In *2015 ASEE Annual Conference and Exposition Proceedings* (Vol. 26, No. 1, p. 23952).

Grant, E. K., & Humble, T. S. (2020). Adiabatic quantum computing and quantum annealing. In Oxford Research Encyclopedia of Physics.

Guo, S., Zeng, D., & Dong, S. (2020). Pedagogical data analysis via federated learning toward education 4.0. *American Journal of Education and Information Technology*, 4(2), 56–65.

Harper, K. C., Chen, K., & Yen, D. (2004). Distance learning, virtual classrooms, and teaching pedagogy in the internet environment. *Technology in Society*, 26, 585–598.

Hastie, M., Hung, I. C., & Chen, N. (2010). Kinshuk: A blended synchronous learning model for educational international collaboration. *Innovations in Education and Teaching International*, 47, 24–29.

Havl'ıcek, V., C'orcoles, A., Temme, K., Harrow, A., Kandala, A., Chow, J., & Gambetta, J. (2018a). Supervised learning with quantum-enhanced feature spaces. *Nature*, 567, 209–212. PMID: 30867609

Heese, R., Gerlach, T., M¨ucke, S., M¨uller, S., Jakobs, M., & Piatkowski, N. (2023). *Explainable quantum machine learning*. ArXiv.

Hentschel, A., & Sanders, B. C. (2010, April). Machine learning for adaptive quantum measurement. In *2010 Seventh International Conference on Information Technology: New Generations* (pp. 506-511). IEEE.

Higher, T. B. (2014). [ITHET]. *Education + Training*, •••, 1–5.

Hughes, C., Isaacson, J., Perry, A., Sun, R. F., & Turner, J. (2020). Teaching quantum computing to high school students. *The Physics Teacher*.

Humphreys, P., Kalb, N., Morits, J. P. J., Schouten, R., Vermeulen, R., Twitchen, D., Markham, M., & Hanson, R. (2017). Deterministic delivery of remote entanglement on a quantum network. *Nature*, 558, 268–273. PMID: 29899475

Jagušt, T., & Botički, I. (2019). Mobile learning system for enabling collaborative and adaptive pedagogies with modular digital learning contents. *Journal of Computers in Education*, 6(3), 335–362.

Jara, C., Her'ıas, F. A. C., Medina, F., Dormido, S., & Esquembre, F. (2012). Synchronous collaboration of virtual and remote laboratories. *Computer Applications in Engineering Education*, •••, 20.

Kaul, D., Raju, H., & Tripathy, B. K. (2021). Quantum-Computing-Inspired Algorithms in Machine Learning. In Research Anthology on Artificial Intelligence Applications in Security (pp. 429-448). IGI Global.

Kimble, H. (2008). The quantum internet. *Nature*, 453, 1023–1030. PMID: 18563153

Kostic, Z. O., Jevremovic, A. D., Markovic, D. S., & Popovic, R. M. (2011, October). Virtual educational system and communication. In 2011 10th International Conference on Telecommunication in Modern Satellite Cable and Broadcasting Services (TELSIKS) (Vol. 1, pp. 373-376). IEEE.

Kushimo, T., & Thacker, B. (2022). Investigating students' strengths and difficulties in quantum computing. arXiv preprint arXiv:2212.03726.

Lamichhane, S. K. (2012). Instructional design for student learning on quantum tunneling. *The Himalayan Physics*, 3, 27–34.

Lampou, R. (2023). The integration of artificial intelligence in education: Opportunities and challenges. *Review of Artificial Intelligence in Education*, 4, e15–e15.

Lehka, L. V., Shokaliuk, S. V., & Semerikov, S. O. (2023). Exploring the quantum frontier in school informatics: A pedagogical journey. *Educational Dimension*, 8, 112–142.

Leymann, F., Barzen, J., Falkenthal, M., Vietz, D., Weder, B., & Wild, K. (2020). Quantum in the cloud: application potentials and research opportunities. arXiv preprint arXiv:2003.06256.

Li, W. (2023, April). Simulating Quantum Turing Machine in Augmented Reality. In *Proceedings of the 2023 8th International Conference on Multimedia and Image Processing* (pp. 107-112).

Liu, D. Y. T., Bartimote-Aufflick, K., Pardo, A., & Bridgeman, A. (2017). Data-driven personalization of student learning support in higher education. In *Higher Education Learning Analytics: Navigating between Learning and the Digital Realm* (pp. 143–169). Springer.

Liu, S., Wang, Y., & Zheng, Y. (2020, June). Computational Intelligence in Science Education. In *Proceedings of the 6th International Conference on Frontiers of Educational Technologies* (pp. 34-38).

Lock, J., & Duggleby, S. (2018). Exploring quality of life through an online international collaboration. *Technology, Pedagogy and Education*, 27, 533–548.

Lonchamp, J. (2006). Supporting synchronous collaborative learning: A generic, multi-dimensional model. *International Journal of Computer-Supported Collaborative Learning*, 1, 247–276.

Machado, L. S. R., Frasseto, L. D. S., Bilessimo, S. M. S., Silva, J. B. D., & Silva, I. N. D. (2022, August). Pedagogical models focused on the integration of ICT in basic education: A systematic review. *International Journal of Advanced Engineering Research and Science. Jaipur.*, 9(8), 129–134.

Makarova, E. A., & Makarova, E. L. (2018). Blending pedagogy and digital technology to transform educational environment. International Journal of Cognitive Research in Science, Engineering and Education:(IJCRSEE), 6(2), 57-66.

Mart'ınez-Cerd'a, J. F., Torrent-Sellens, J., & Gonz'alez-Gonz'alez, I. (2018). Promoting collaborative skills in online university: Comparing effects of games, mixed reality, social media, and other tools for ict-supported pedagogical practices. *Behaviour & Information Technology*.

McLoughlin, C., & Lee, M. J. W. (2010). Personalised and self regulated learning in the web 2.0 era: International exemplars of innovative pedagogy using social software. *Australasian Journal of Educational Technology.*

Mermin, N. (2002). From cbits to qbits: Teaching computer scientists quantum mechanics. *American Journal of Physics*, 71, 23–30.

Michailidou, A., & Economides, A. (2003). Elearn: Towards a collaborative educational virtual environment. *Journal of Information Technology Education*, 2, 131–152.

Montanaro, A. (2016). Quantum algorithms: an overview. npj Quantum Information, 2(1), 1-8.

Morgan, J., Wittmann, M. C., & Thompson, J. R. (2004). Student understanding of tunneling in quantum mechanics: Examining interview and survey results for clues to student reasoning. *University of Maine Physics Education Research Laboratory*, 720, 97–100.

Morgan, J. T., & Wittmann, M. C. (2006, February). Examining the evolution of student ideas about quantum tunneling. In *2005 Physics Education Research Conference* (Vol. 818, pp. 73-76).

Mu˜niz, M. N., & Oliver-Hoyo, M. (2014). Investigating quantum mechanical tunneling at the nanoscale via analogy: Development and assessment of a teaching tool for upper-division chemistry. *Journal of Chemical Education*, 91, 1546–1556.

Mykhailova, M. (2020, February). The Quantum Katas: Learning Quantum Computing Using Programming Exercises. In *Proceedings of the 51st ACM Technical Symposium on Computer Science Education* (pp. 1417-1417).

Mykhailova, M. (2021, March). Developing Programming Exercises for Teaching Quantum Computing. In *Proceedings of the 52nd ACM Technical Symposium on Computer Science Education* (pp. 1376-1376).

Nazaretsky, T., Bar, C., Walter, M., & Alexandron, G. (2022, March). Empowering teachers with AI: Co-designing a learning analytics tool for personalized instruction in the science classroom. In *LAK22: 12th International Learning Analytics and Knowledge Conference* (pp. 1-12).

Ngoenriang, N., Xu, M., Kang, J., Niyato, D., Yu, H., & Shen, X. (2023). Dqc ^2 o: Distributed quantum computing for collaborative optimization in future networks. *IEEE Communications Magazine*, 61(5), 188–194.

Nita, L., Smith, L. M., Chancellor, N., & Cramman, H. (2020). The challenge and opportunities of quantum literacy for future education and transdisciplinary problem-solving. *Research in Science & Technological Education,* ●●●, 1–17.

Okamoto, T. (2004). Collaborative technology and new e-pedagogy. In E-Learn: World Conference on E-Learning in Corporate, Government, Healthcare, and Higher Education (pp. 3064-3077). Association for the Advancement of Computing in Education (AACE).

Ove, C. (2013). Virtual classroom in the cloud—Transnational scandinavian teaching with digital technology. *Journal of Literature and Art Studies,* 3, 669–676.

Pagano, A., Angelelli, M., Calvano, M., Curci, A., & Piccinno, A. (2023, December). Quantum computing for learning analytics: an overview of challenges and integration strategies. In *Proceedings of the 2nd International Workshop on Quantum Programming for Software Engineering* (pp. 13-16).

Pant, M., Krovi, H., Towsley, D., Tassiulas, L., Jiang, L., Basu, P., ... & Guha, S. (2019). Routing entanglement in the quantum internet. npj Quantum Information, 5(1), 25.

Pedersen, M. K., Skyum, B., Heck, R., Müller, R., Bason, M., Lieberoth, A., & Sherson, J. F. StudentResearcher-A virtual learning environment for interactive engagement with advanced quantum mechanics.

Peng, H., Ma, S., & Spector, J. (2019). Personalized adaptive learning: An emerging pedagogical approach enabled by a smart learning environment. *Smart Learning Environments,* 6, 1–14.

Polizzi, N., & Beratan, D. (2015). Open-access, interactive explorations for teaching and learning quantum dynamics. *Journal of Chemical Education,* 92, 2161–2164.

Prasolova-Førland, E., & Chang, T. W. (2007, July). Building a Babel Tower in 21st Century: Supporting Cross-Cultural Collaboration and Learning in a 3D CVE Spanning Three Continents. In *Seventh IEEE International Conference on Advanced Learning Technologies (ICALT 2007)* (pp. 295-299). IEEE.

Razavy, M. (2013). *Quantum theory of tunneling.* World Scientific.

Rodr'ıguez-Triana, M., Mart'ınez-Mon'es, A., & Asensio-P'erez, J. I. (2011). Monitoring collaboration in flexible and personal learning environments. [s]. *Interaction Design and Architecture,* 11-12, 51–63.

Rodrigues, A. L. (2020). Digital technologies integration in teacher education: the active teacher training model. Journal of e-learning and knowledge society, 16(3), 24-33.

Salehi, O. (2020). Seskir, Z.C., Tepe, I.: A computer science-oriented approach to introduce quantum computing to a new audience. *IEEE Transactions on Education*, 65, 1–8.

Santos, L., Escudeiro, P., & de Carvalho, C. V. (2013, September). Evaluating virtual experiential learning in engineering. In *2013 International Conference on Interactive Collaborative Learning (ICL)* (pp. 42-48). IEEE.

Schuld, M., Sinayskiy, I., & Petruccione, F. (2014). An introduction to quantum machine learning. *Contemporary Physics*, 56, 172–185.

Seegerer, S., Michaeli, T., & Romeike, R. (2021, October). Quantum computing as a topic in computer science education. In *Proceedings of the 16th Workshop in Primary and Secondary Computing Education* (pp. 1-6).

Seskir, Z. C., Migdał, P., Weidner, C., Anupam, A., Case, N., Davis, N., & Chiofalo, M. (2022). Quantum games and interactive tools for quantum technologies outreach and education. *Optical Engineering (Redondo Beach, Calif.)*, 61(8), 081809–081809.

Seskir, Z. C., Migdał, P., Weidner, C., Anupam, A., Case, N., Davis, N., & Chiofalo, M. (2022). Quantum games and interactive tools for quantum technologies outreach and education. *Optical Engineering (Redondo Beach, Calif.)*, 61(8), 081809–081809.

Siadaty, M., & Taghiyareh, F. (2007, July). PALS2: Pedagogically adaptive learning system based on learning styles. In *Seventh IEEE International Conference on Advanced Learning Technologies (ICALT 2007)* (pp. 616-618). IEEE.

Siahaan, J. H., Marson, F., & Forsyth, O. (2022). Transforming Primary School Science Education: The Quantum Teaching Revolution. Jurnal Ilmu Pendidikan dan Humaniora, 11(1), 35-51.

Silva, A. J., Ludermir, T. B., & de Oliveira, W. R.Jr. (2010, October). Superposition based learning algorithm. In *2010 Eleventh Brazilian Symposium on Neural Networks* (pp. 1-6). IEEE.

Sim, S., Cao, Y., Romero, J., Johnson, P. D., & Aspuru-Guzik, A. A framework for algorithm deployment on cloud-based quantum computers. arXiv: Quantum Physics (2018)

Simon, C. (2017). Towards a global quantum network. *Nature Photonics*, 11, 678–680.

Squire, K., & Klopfer, E. (2007). Augmented reality simulations on handheld computers. *Journal of the Learning Sciences*, 16, 371–413.

Sun, Z., Liu, R., Luo, L., Wu, M., & Shi, C. (2017). Exploring collaborative learning effect in blended learning environments. *Journal of Computer Assisted Learning*, 33, 575–587.

Tomandl, M., Mieling, T. B., Kroon, C. M. L. V., Hopf, M., & Arndt, M. (2015). Simulated interactive research experiments as educational tools for advanced science. *Scientific Reports*, ●●●, 5. PMID: 26370627

Torre, L. D. L., Heradio, R., Jara, C., S'anchez, J., Dormido, S., Medina, F., & Her'ıas, F. A. C. (2013). Providing collaborative support to virtual and remote laboratories. *IEEE Transactions on Learning Technologies*, 6, 312–323.

Uhlig, R. P., Dey, P., Jawad, S., Sinha, B., & Amin, M. (2019). *Generating student interest in quantum computing. In: 2019 IEEE Frontiers in Education Conference.* FIE.

Villanueva, A., Zhu, Z., Liu, Z., Peppler, K., Redick, T., & Ramani, K. (2020, April). Meta-AR-app: an authoring platform for collaborative augmented reality in STEM classrooms. In *Proceedings of the 2020 CHI conference on human factors in computing systems* (pp. 1-14).

Volkova, L.V., Lizunova, L.R., Komarova, I.A.: (2021). Digital pedagogy. Revista on line de Pol'ıtica e Gest˜ao Educacional

Wei, S., Jing, B., Zhang, X., Liao, J., Yuan, C., Fan, B. Y., Lyu, C., Zhou, D., Wang, Y., Deng, G., Song, H., Oblak, D., Guo, G., & Zhou, Q. (2022). Towards real-world quantum networks: A review. *Laser & Photonics Reviews*, ●●●, 16.

Westfall, L., & Leider, A. (2019). Teaching quantum computing. In Proceedings of the Future Technologies Conference (FTC) 2018: Volume 2 (pp. 63-80). Springer International Publishing.

Wootton, J. R., Harkins, F., Bronn, N. T., Vazquez, A. C., Phan, A., & Asfaw, A. T. (2021, October). Teaching quantum computing with an interactive textbook. In *2021 IEEE International Conference on Quantum Computing and Engineering (QCE)* (pp. 385-391). IEEE.

Zable, A., Hollenberg, L., Velloso, E., & Goncalves, J. (2020, November). Investigating immersive virtual reality as an educational tool for quantum computing. In *Proceedings of the 26th ACM Symposium on Virtual Reality Software and Technology* (pp. 1-11).

Zulehner, A., & Wille, R. (2017). Advanced simulation of quantum computations. *IEEE Transactions on Computer-Aided Design of Integrated Circuits and Systems*, 38, 848–859.

Chapter 19
The State of Artificial Intelligence (AI) Use in Higher Education Institutions (HEIs) in the Philippines

John Mark R. Asio
https://orcid.org/0000-0002-6096-4595
Gordon College, Philippines

Imelda D. P. Soriano
Gordon College, Philippines

ABSTRACT

Artificial Intelligence (AI) is a technology slowly gaining traction in the Philippine educational landscape. This chapter intends to investigate and share the different perspectives and insights of higher education institutions in the country regarding the use of AI in faculty and students' teaching and learning experiences. Given that the Philippines is a developing country with numerous educational issues and problems, the impact of the previous COVID-19 pandemic has led to the emergence of additional challenges. The abrupt transition from face-to-face to online learning paved the way for students and faculty to use AI as a helpful tool to adapt to the changes in the education spectrum. The authors argued that there were essential mechanisms that higher education institutions must look over before embracing AI in the curriculum. The institutions must first weigh the benefits and risks to arrive at a sound policy regulating AI within the educational system.

DOI: 10.4018/979-8-3693-8191-5.ch019

INTRODUCTION

Artificial Intelligence (AI) has seen unprecedented development and innovation in recent years, transforming numerous industries across the globe. As the Asian region embraces AI innovations, upholding equity, inclusivity, and ethical principles is crucial to forge a more resilient and equitable educational landscape (Hara, 2024). With AI's growing technological impact in the global arena, it is inevitable that AI will be part of everyone's everyday lives for the next century. The landscape of artificial intelligence in the Philippines is rapidly evolving, with increasing adoption across various sectors such as healthcare, finance, and agriculture. Some Filipino professionals, at the same time, generally view AI as an opportunity rather than a threat. They also imply their willingness to train and incorporate AI into their workflows (de Leon et al., 2024). The Fourth Industrial Revolution, characterized by technological diversity and the Internet of Things, has ushered in this trend, enabling us to adapt firmly to the rapid evolution of humanity. The Internet of Things (IoT) is one of the disruptive technologies (aside from AI) that is also a part of the Fourth Industrial Revolution. This emerging technology also offers extraordinary opportunities to develop new models. It can provide automation and monitoring in everything we do, especially in the education system (Illahi et al., 2019). Both AI and IoT benefit different stakeholders, especially society.

The Philippines, a developing country in Southeast Asia, also has a fair share of technological innovations as it tries to embrace the growing demands of technology in its countryside slowly. AI has already significantly impacted the financial sector (Samonte & Ong, 2023), human resource management (Kshetri, 2021), public administration (Moreno, 2023), public health (Corpuz, 2023), small and medium enterprises (Hernandez et al., 2023), even the hospitality industry (Pinpin-Lucero, 2022), and the quality management systems (QMS) of higher education institutions (HEIs) in the country (Tobias et al., 2023). Accordingly, the QMS leans towards sustainability, big data, and applied technological innovation based on the analysis of Minglana et al. (2021). Even in disaster management, the AI application has its own practical use (Escolano et al., 2023).

The government is taking steps to promote AI development through initiatives such as funding for research and development. However, there is a need for robust policies to address ethical considerations and ensure that AI technologies benefit society as a whole. The development of AI has paved the way for many innovative procedures and systems. Some of the nation's higher education institutions (HEIs) have already adopted AI to enhance the educational experience and address new challenges. Some of the leading universities in the country (e.g., University of the Philippines, Far Eastern University, Mindanao State University) have already imposed some measures for the appropriate use of AI in their educational system.

However, the application of AI in higher education requires significant processing power and technological infrastructure (Estrellado & Miranda, 2023). Funding and human resources also play an important role in the integration of AI into the system. The operation guidelines and maintenance are also equally crucial in monitoring the pace and utilization of AI within the institution. The use of AI in education has also become a disruptive force, reshaping the educational system and industry expectations (Barajas et al., 2024). Artificial Intelligence (AI) is already at the frontiers of the current generation. Crafting an appropriate means of utilizing such technology is imperative to regulate its unforeseen effects later. That is the reason why some institutions are still adamant about integrating AI into their learning process, as it has unseen and long-term impacts. In a conference paper by Chua and Valencia (2020), they imparted the idea that AI will play a substantial role in the education landscape, particularly in digital technology, in order to pursue learning among students and faculty. Collaboration between the government, industry stakeholders, and academia is crucial to harnessing the full potential of AI while mitigating risks and ensuring inclusivity in its deployment across the Philippines.

This chapter provides a comprehensive overview of the use of AI in Philippine higher education institutions, focusing on the significant issues, emerging trends, and challenges administrators and teachers face. The upcoming discussions will be crucial in policy-making and implementing safeguards and pertinent mechanisms to regulate AI use in higher education. Additionally, this chapter will provide essential points to enhance the invigorating and motivating nature of the learning experience for students while fostering a more digitalized and technology-driven learning environment and experience for students and youth.

BACKGROUND

AI in Philippine education could transform learning experiences and outcomes. Recently, the country has steadily integrated AI technologies into numerous schooling systems. It promoted innovation and changed instruction from traditional to technologically advanced. Philippines universities can benefit from artificial intelligence, which can improve student outcomes, streamline administrative processes, and inspire creativity. Early COVID-19 pandemic effects enhanced higher education technology utilization. Pahuriray et al. (2022) said the COVID-19 pandemic introduced AI, which improved academia and higher education. The immediate deployment of blended learning hurt Philippine education, according to Vidal (2022). Chua and Valencia (2020) believed AI will improve schooling. For instance, AI-powered learning management systems (LMS) are being used to give students individualized learning experiences at home. AI technologies are being tested in schools to improve teaching and learning. Students acknowledge AI's educational benefits in Valerio's recent piece (2024). In contrast, Baron's 2024 study stated that understanding AI's function in education did not just affect psychological maturity. We offer AI technologies for student behavior and response assessment and performance analysis. This context helps instructors identify student needs and facilitate focused interventions to improve learning outcomes. Some US institutions and colleges use AI for personalized learning, evaluation, and predictive analytics to evaluate student performance.

AI simplifies administrative work at educational institutions and gives dependable answers. Amado et al. (2024) have provided a solid foundation for AI solutions that improve administrative efficiency. AI can integrate with enrollment, admissions, and record-keeping. Organizational efficiency can be improved by automating system-powered processes and operations. This efficiency lets educators focus on teaching, research, and community service.

AI adoption in Philippine higher education is slow, although most universities and colleges face some challenges. Higher education institutions should consider technological proficiency, AI tool comprehension, and perceived AI use (Labrague et al., 2023). To maximize AI's potential, talent, data privacy and security, and infrastructure are needed. However, they stress the need for transparency and ethical guidelines. The sector is gradually adopting AI, but maximizing its benefits and ensuring its appropriate and fair integration into higher education will involve tackling digital gap, ethical challenges, and professional development. According to Barajas and colleagues' 2024 study, numerous universities have implemented fundamental AI concepts, but complete integration requires a more comprehensive plan. Dela Rosa et al. (2024) advocate harsher AI checkers and educating college students AI responsibility to reduce academic dishonesty. Diano and colleagues (2023) also stressed the importance of technology in global education and the need to close the digital divide to give Filipino students equal access to digital resources.

Local viewpoints on AI's influence support fair access to digital learning tools for diverse groups (Espartinez, 2024). Panoy et al. (2022) also found that pupils can master technology, especially online. Abrenilla et al. (2023) noted that educators, researchers, and policymakers must promote inclusive, student-centered, and ethical AI-driven education. Thus, technology proficiency affects student learning outcomes and expectations. HEIs can educate students for a future where AI will shape education and develop many professions and activities by embracing AI technologies and promoting innovation.

AI PERSPECTIVES AMONG HIGHER EDUCATION INSTITUTIONS

The Philippines' AI landscape is changing due to the increased interest in using AI to improve operational efficiency and decision-making. AI has helped Philippine universities improve instruction, student experiences, and efficiency. AI boosts productivity and service delivery, according to Moreno (2023). AI can tailor educational content to students' requirements and learning styles in adaptive learning platforms. Private schools (Umali, 2024) and one Catholic institution have examined AI-enhanced IT programs (Ang & Aragon, 2020). This tailored strategy can boost student engagement and learning. Teachers use AI-powered tools like virtual assistants, adaptive learning platforms, and intelligent tutoring systems to give pupils tailored education. Thus, the complicated dynamics of AI in education, which balances the benefits and drawbacks of over-reliance, must be examined (Fontanilla et al., 2023). Institutions can optimize expenses and resource distribution via AI. Faculty activities like grading and monitoring student records can be automated with AI. Alda and colleagues (2020) found that capacity-building programs equipped administrators and faculty to select and integrate digital resources for teaching and learning. AI application in education is hindered by infrastructure issues, digital access inequities, and the need for educational institutions to adapt their courses to the changing technology world.

Faculty agree that AI in teaching and evaluation is widely accepted and strongly linked to technological acceptability (Clifford, 2024). Santiago et al.'s (2023) article emphasizes the importance of culture and language concerns because AI fails to match Filipino academic writing's distinctive linguistic and cultural nuances. Cadiz et al. (2024) examined how HEIs use technology innovation to promote academic performance and resilience in the changing educational landscape. AI is changing higher education by boosting teaching and learning, administrative efficiency, research, and workforce readiness.

HEIs use AI-driven data analytics to analyze enormous educational data and make evidence-based decisions and predictive models for student success. AI adoption and management in education require collaboration between academics, industry, and government. This cooperation promotes information sharing, skills development, resource sharing, and co-creation of 21st-century education innovations. One's idea of how AI's application can interact with local or global organizations is limited by its possibilities. Students must anticipate AI and technology advancements to prepare for the digital economy. To prepare children for life in this fast-paced world, education should emphasize 21st-century abilities like critical thinking, cooperation, adaptability, and digital literacy.

AI Application in Education

AI Applications in Teaching and Learning

Individualized learning, adaptable assessments, and efficient administrative procedures are possible with AI. These technologies can enhance education and address accessibility and inclusivity. Philippine universities are exploring artificial intelligence applications to improve teaching and learning. According to Cortez and colleagues (2024), students utilize communication AI to boost productivity and enjoy using it. Junio and Bandala (2023) found that students are knowledgeable about using AI-powered tools in academic writing. Intelligent tutoring systems can use AI algorithms to customize instruction and feedback for students. To navigate the digital realm and employ artificial intelligence ethically, students need digital literacy abilities. Several educators have benefited from using artificial intelligence (AI) tools to give students immediate feedback on their work and performance (Ambit, 2024). Our educators should also emphasize cybersecurity to teach pupils about data protection and internet security, especially in an AI-driven environment.

Educational programs use AR and VR to create dynamic and immersive learning environments. Alda et al.'s 2020 study found that administrators and academics need augmented reality, robot, and digital enablement abilities. Interactive multimedia content, virtual field trips, and hands-on simulations are possible with these technologies. Additionally, generative artificial intelligence techniques improve student and teacher learning. Balahadia et al. (2023) note teachers' expertise in ChatGPT and other generative AI technologies. This allows such technology to be integrated into educational courses, improving teaching and student engagement. Goli-Cruz (2024), "the efficacy of artificial intelligence and its incorporation in the realm of education were contingent upon the conscientiousness of faculty and administrators in the facilitation of students' analytical and evaluative proficiencies." Gelacio and company (2024) revealed a strong correlation between students' technical preparedness and AI adoption. This is crucial for integrating AI into graduates' academic and professional careers. Teachers are the key to raising generations who can confidently and compassionately navigate the complex global world powered by artificial intelligence (Eslit, 2023). Despite data privacy, algorithm bias, and ethical problems, institutions can adopt artificial intelligence technology. Responsible and inclusive use of AI in the classroom is needed.

AI-Driven Student Support and Engagement

Researchers are now investigating the use of AI-powered solutions, such as personalized learning platforms, intelligent tutoring systems, and data analytics, to adapt to a wide range of learning requirements and enhance educational outcomes. Mupaikwa's (2024) research links students' academic achievement to their level of engagement and their use of artificial intelligence (AI) in the classroom. Researchers are now investigating applications of artificial intelligence to personalize learning experiences, optimize administrative tasks, and provide real-time feedback to both students and teachers. For example, artificial intelligence can supply designers and developers of mobile applications with valuable insights that can help them create more engaging and user-friendly platforms specifically to assist students (Chavez & Palaoag, 2024). Balaquiao (2024) highlighted in his most recent paper the enhancement in student performance resulting from the integration of AI technology. This revelation underscores the positive impact that enhancing instructional efficacy can have. On the other hand, this concept seeks to advocate for the significantly more extensive implementation and investigation of artificial intelligence in educational contexts. According to Cortez et al. (2024), students' behavioral intentions and their actual academic use of artificial intelligence as an educational tool significantly impact individuals. The integration of artificial intelligence, according to Millora et al. (2024), results in more profound knowledge and understanding for pupils, taking into account their individual learning methods. In addition, Obenza et al. (2024) revealed that the students who participated in their research projects had excellent comprehension, knowledge, perception, attitude, and a solid intention to use artificial intelligence technology. Additional applications of artificial intelligence include analyzing student data and identifying trends. This process enables early detection and the implementation of tailored interventions that enhance student performance and engagement.

Students with a variety of learning challenges can also benefit from AI technology because it can provide individualized learning experiences and interventions. Labrague et al. (2023) found in a previous article that students' perceived utilization of artificial intelligence (AI) positively influenced their attitude towards AI and their intention to maximize its potential. From this study, we can only conclude that students exhibit a positive attitude towards the future application of artificial intelligence (AI) in their professional activities, and they have strong intentions to implement AI technology moving forward. In addition, Amado and colleagues (2024) suggested that artificial intelligence tools gave significant benefits in the field of educational administration and supervision. Data-driven decision-making and increased operational efficiency were among these benefits. As a means of catering to pupils' educational requirements, the adaptive mechanism of artificial intelligence can be applied to learning materials and assistive technology. In the paper that Mindajao created in 2023, the proponent investigated the efficacy of chatbots as a novel approach to reporting student performance. The study proved successful, presenting novel concepts and potential for improving the feedback students receive on their performance evaluations. Implementing this concept will create an inclusive learning environment in which students with special needs will still be able to navigate the learning process. Artificial intelligence-powered solutions have the potential to enhance accessibility and inclusivity in education. This approach will guarantee that all students succeed by providing them with the necessary assistance and attention.

Data-Driven Decision Making

Higher learning institutions in the Philippines use data analytics powered by artificial intelligence to mine huge volumes of educational data and gain insights. Amado et al. (2024) state that AI tools offer several benefits, particularly administration and supervision. Institutions in this department saw improvements in their operational efficiency and ability to make data-based decisions. Educational institutions can get insights into various data sources, including student performance records, feedback surveys, and learning management systems, through data mining and analysis. Artificial intelligence is able to perform an analysis by assessing a variety of data, including academic performance, attendance, and other learning performance results. Based on this analysis, the institution is able to intervene and provide help to students who are considering dropping out. Ligot and colleagues (2022) emphasized the importance of trends in fostering the development of analytics in the labor sector, such as women's participation, work from arrangements, online learning, and the significance of data and AI ethicality. The paper they wrote highlighted these trends. Predictive modeling and machine learning algorithms can identify at-risk students, adjust course offerings, and improve resource allocation. In addition, Osorio (2023) found that putting in place data-driven regulation, using artificial intelligence analytics, promoting a principle-based regulatory process, improving incentives, and teaching consumers more can give the country enough power to change. Higher education institutions can identify students at risk of dropping out or performing poorly by using artificial intelligence-powered predictive analysis. Zabala (2023) asserted that implementing AI successfully requires overcoming significant obstacles such as limited technical skills, poor infrastructure, and limited financial resources. Taer and Taer (2024) suggest that modernization policies and locally tailored capacity-building initiatives, aided by partnerships between the academic community and the business sector, should provide significant institutional support to overcome gaps. Another paper said that using data-driven methods to improve state universities and colleges (SUCs) could help policymakers and administrators make the schools better prepared to support procedures that are effective, clear, and accountable (Sulasual, 2023).

Research and Innovation

Universities and other research institutions in the Philippines regularly participate in a wide variety of research initiatives that are both innovative and groundbreaking. Artificial intelligence (AI) is growing in research and innovation at higher education institutions. Artificial intelligence is gradually transforming the research capabilities of the university. Ilham et al. (2023) assert that artificial intelligence, which processes data more efficiently and accurately, empowers us to make more informed and intelligent decisions. Artificial intelligence facilitates the development of creative ways to facilitate more effective data analysis, pattern identification, and even model simulations. This notion is because artificial intelligence generates technical innovation, which can boost productivity (Bonsay et al., 2021). These efforts, which investigate the cutting-edge application of artificial intelligence (AI) in pedagogy, curriculum development, and even educational technology, drive the advancement and digitization of students' learning experiences. In their study, Ilham and colleagues (2023) found that artificial intelligence (AI) in education was a popular research area for AI. Specifically, they focused on general learning, medical education, and higher education. Aquino and Sancon (2022) assert that the Philippines must prioritize addressing the rapidly increasing institutionalization. Researchers are investigating the application of artificial intelligence techniques in a variety of domains such as data analysis, computer vision, and natural language processing. In their discussion, Santiago et al. (2023) pointed out that artificial intelligence presents prospects for global learning, tailored training, and efficient resource management. In addition, Kabalisa and Altmann (2021) stated that there is compelling evidence that adopting artificial intelligence affects a country's economy. They published their analysis of artificial intelligence technologies and the reasons countries embrace AI. Consequently, they recommended that the formulation of policies is essential for the nation to flourish appropriately. Artificial intelligence-driven research programs are addressing a wide range of issues, spanning from the fields of medicine and agriculture to the social sciences and engineering. Additionally, higher education institutions collaborate with government organizations and commercial partners to advance artificial intelligence research and development. According to Kim and Castillejos-Petalcorin's 2020 research, innovation is an essential factor behind the expansion of a nation's economy and improving its social well-being. According to a previous paper by Marcial (2020), the expansion of technological advancements in domains such as robotics, artificial intelligence, the Internet of Things, and 5G, among others, disrupted the teaching and learning processes of all education institutions. These creative approaches and strategies are introducing the concept of education in the classroom. Among the topics under the introduction are organization, management, assessment, pedagogy and ethics, and professional development.

Skills Development and Workforce Readiness

The country's educational environment is already making efforts to integrate artificial intelligence into the curriculum. In order to better prepare students for their future employment in a technology-driven environment, commonly referred to as the Fourth Industrial Revolution, the primary objective is to provide them with the necessary information and abilities related to artificial intelligence (AI). According to Bernardo et al. (2022), a few characteristics are essential predictors when it comes to global competency indices. The accompanying research identified these variables. This category includes indicators such as the readiness to participate in classroom disputes, worry about pollution, connectedness to people from other nations, and opinions about the significance of learning. We can also draw a comparison between this concept and the Sustainable Development Goals established by the United Nations. SDG 4 (Quality Education) and SDG 8 (Decent Work and Economic Growth) align with this philosophy. The purpose of training programs for educators is to assist them in developing their foundations and essentials to facilitate their professional development and enable them to use artificial intelligence technologies in the process of teaching and learning within the institution.

Because of artificial intelligence, the landscape of skills in higher education is shifting. As a result, artificial intelligence can also be useful in professional development to a certain degree. Institutions can offer training programs and seminars that focus on integrating various artificial intelligence tools and technologies into diverse professional applications. Rosales et al. (2020) assert that properly trained artificial intelligence can enhance employment opportunities across all economic sectors. Higher education institutions in the Philippines are realizing that it is of the utmost importance to equip students with skills linked to artificial intelligence to enhance their employability in the digital age. Verdate (2019) asserts that the rapid adoption of new technological trends has significant implications for the workforce and the essential skills expected of workers. We are expanding currently available curricula to incorporate new classes and modules covering topics like artificial intelligence (AI), machine learning, data analytics, and other pertinent subjects. According to Eslit (2023), the instructors are the ones who hold the key to developing the next generation that is capable of accepting the complicated parts of a global landscape driven by artificial intelligence. In addition, higher education institutions offer training classes, hackathons, and seminars to assist students in gaining practical experience with artificial intelligence and working on projects. The purpose of placing such an emphasis on the development of AI skills is to ensure that graduates are prepared to meet the ever-evolving demands of the labor market.

Accessible AI Education

In addition, higher education institutions in the Philippines are working to broaden the availability of artificial intelligence (AI) courses to a greater number of students. According to Julien (2024), artificial intelligence is primarily a tool for knowledge imparting, comprehension stimulation, intelligence elevation, and a treasure to promote learning. In the same vein, Labrague et al. (2023) said that technological skill is one criterion that should be considered when determining whether or not pupils are ready for artificial intelligence. The development of online platforms, Massive Open Online Courses (MOOCs), and other e-learning efforts is currently underway with the goal of making AI-related courses accessible to a more extensive student audience. Additionally, with the help of artificial intelligence virtual assistance, students were able to unlock their potential and receive assistance in completing challenging academic assignments (Mina et al., 2023). According to Agbong-Coates (2024), the incorporation of artificial intelligence into individualized learning among students explained a major portion of the variability. By participating in these programs, students from all across the country, especially those who live in remote areas, have the opportunity to have access to artificial intelligence education and further their careers in this rapidly emerging field. In accordance with this, Rogers and colleagues (2025) emphasized the importance of optimizing the learning management system (LMS) in schools to cultivate a digital learning environment that supports students, staff, and administration. Moron and Diokno (2023) found that their participants were somewhat prepared and accustomed to the artificial intelligence software application they utilized in their line of work. Both the teaching staff and the students viewed a particular learning management system (LMS) that facilitates the acquisition of information and skills favorably (Mendoza et al., 2023). The positive feedback from both groups indicated this. In addition, Oluyinka and Cusipag (2021) discussed the trialability and purposefulness of a specific learning management system (Google Classroom) among educational institutions of higher learning during the COVID-19 epidemic. In their research, they discovered that the trialability and purposefulness of the learning management system (LMS) were two elements that contributed to its acceptance and implementation in educational institutions of higher learning. On the other hand, there are still considerable obstacles to overcome, such as the digital divide, concerns around data privacy, and the requirement for teacher training in the integration of AI.

Ethical Considerations and Responsible AI Use

When it comes to the topic of artificial intelligence deployment, higher education institutions in the Philippines emphasize the importance of ethical issues and responsible AI activities. When implementing AI in educational settings, addressing ethical concerns is of the utmost importance. Students of Generation Z stated that proper education and technological capacity development can accelerate people's comprehension of these artificial intelligence technologies (Jabar et al., 2024). Within academia, discussions and research on artificial intelligence ethics, justice, accountability, and transparency are gaining increasingly significant attention. For instance, a student at a state university in the Philippines attempted to analyze the use of ChatGPT and its potential threat to the integrity of academic studies in a paper. When it comes to the employment of artificial intelligence technologies in education, Robledo and colleagues (2023) observed that instructors have expressed worries regarding ethical issues, academic dishonesty, and technology dependence among pupils. Ventayen (2023) illustrated another work, demonstrating that an online artificial intelligence tool (ChatGPT) computed a similarity index that exceeded the university's threshold. According to the findings of another study, the use of artificial intelligence tools by educators can result in a lack of academic integrity when it comes to citation and attribution (Ambit, 2024). According to Goli-Cruz (2024), ChatGPT is a valuable tool for both students and teachers in the field of education because it makes the duties that teachers have to perform easier to complete. To ensure the ethical and responsible development and deployment of AI systems, HEIs incorporate ethical frameworks and principles into their processes. In addition, Millora et al. (2024) suggested that to guarantee the successful incorporation of artificial intelligence, educators should address the ethical concerns of data privacy and security. This idea would guarantee the protection of both educators and students. In their previous article, Abrenilla and colleagues (2023) revealed that ethical considerations in integrating artificial intelligence necessitate fair access to AI technology and extensive training programs. This concept was a key finding of their research. Legaspi et al. (2024) demonstrated that a comprehensive validation process and a cross-referencing mechanism must support using artificial intelligence (AI) as a detection tool to verify the results. In the Philippines, the application of artificial intelligence (AI) in education is continuously developing, with the primary focus being on utilizing AI to address particular difficulties that are already present within the educational system.

POTENTIAL ISSUES AND CHALLENGES OF AI IN HIGHER EDUCATION

Despite the fact that artificial intelligence has a promising future in higher education, there are still a number of challenges and impediments to overcome. Some higher education institutions do not have equal access to artificial intelligence technology and resources because of infrastructure, finance, and technological know-how differences. According to Labrague et al. (2023) and Mina et al. (2024), one obstacle that makes access to artificial intelligence technology is the need for more computer skills to limited awareness of AI among students and professors. The digital gap is one of the most compelling reasons for concern in the world today. In order to discourage marginalization and encourage inclusion among students and institutions, it is necessary to ensure that everyone has equitable access to artificial intelligence technologies and training. Joe and his colleagues (2022) proposed three different strategies for preparing the nation for artificial intelligence's impact on our educational system and economy. In their study, Batucan et al. (2022) imply that students' intention toward online learning technology still complies with the rising trends despite the difficulties associated with internet access in the country. Internet access is crucial, especially for the institution's library services (Dagdag & Galiza, 2020), as it facilitates quick and complete information searches and enhances the user's experience in the library. Vidal (2022) also brought to light the experiences of educators overwhelmed by a plethora of new information, leading to a range of worries about their educational abilities and competency. Despite the potential advantages, there are still obstacles to overcome. These obstacles include the digital divide, which restricts access to technology for certain pupils; concerns regarding the privacy and security of data in educational settings; and the requirement that teachers obtain training on how to use AI technologies successfully.

Concerns regarding algorithmic bias, data privacy, and the moral application of AI on the classroom surface are also a source of difficulty. Another challenge is the ethical issues that accompany the employment of artificial intelligence (AI) as AI systems become more self-sufficient. The widespread use of artificial intelligence technologies to assist students in completing their homework and other activities has given rise to numerous issues in the field of education, including the problem of academic dishonesty. Booc et al. (2023) conducted a study and found that a significant number of students were using artificial intelligence-powered tools for their summative evaluations. Consequently, to govern this incorrect scenario, there needs to be a certain degree of control and a regulatory framework in place. Junio and Bandala's (2023) work aligns with this concern. In that paper, the authors highlight a few potential negative repercussions, including biases or inaccuracies, dangers of plagiarism, and an excessive reliance on technology. Academic dishonesty among students is another scenario that students may abuse (Ventayen, 2023). Booc et al.'s (2023) research confirmed that students attending a Catholic tertiary institution experienced such a scenario. In this context, students can exploit their academic performance. Additionally, Legaspi and his colleagues were of the opinion that the widespread use of artificial intelligence tools was becoming increasingly prominent among students, posing a threat to the academic integrity of the learning process. Higher education institutions must manage these complex challenges, develop stringent laws, and foster accountability and openness within AI-driven decision-making processes. In order to establish trust and defend the rights of learners, it is vital to establish standards and regulations that are clear, precise, and flexible. These guidelines and regulations should preserve data, provide transparency, and minimize bias.

Additionally, with the rapid advancement of technology, administrators and educators must participate in continual professional development to maintain current knowledge of the most effective practices and capabilities of artificial intelligence. The nation must strengthen its cyber security to protect the data and information stored on the World Wide Web. According to Aquino and Norona (2021), the most effective use of artificial intelligence in cyber security is to put out the fire before it gets out of hand and completely out of control. Taking this action will prevent data breaches, which are known to inflict harm to both individuals' lives and assets. According to Verdote (2019), the perspective of Industry Revolution 4.0, which will revolve around the era of artificial intelligence, has impacted how universities and colleges approach and offer education. Notwithstanding this, Eslit (2023) suggested that educators show resiliency and adaptability by utilizing technology (i.e., instruments driven by artificial intelligence) to impose pupils who are prepared for the future. Prioritizing upskilling and reskilling programs will enable academics and staff members to successfully integrate artificial intelligence tools into their teaching, research, and administrative responsibilities. Furthermore, Alda et al. (2020) emphasized the importance of administrators and faculty members at teacher education institutions rethinking infrastructure layout, redesigning research projects, and strengthening faculty training capacities. As stated in the previous paper by De La Cruz (2022), "Industry 4.0" brought about rapid change, presenting challenges to the country's implementers to adapt to the emergence of technologies like artificial intelligence and robots. For the nation to successfully adjust to its expanding significance and embrace artificial intelligence for future generations, proper coordination and decision-making based on research are vital factors.

SOLUTIONS AND RECOMMENDATIONS

Philippine Higher Education Institutions (HEIs) can benefit much from AI implementation because it can improve many education and administrative processes. We advocate extensive investigation and analysis before applying AI for students, professors, and the institution. To maximize AI's educational potential, educators, policymakers, and technology providers must collaborate. This idea will ensure ethical deployment, effective use, and advantages for all Filipino students in varied educational settings. The following are suggestions for using artificial intelligence in higher education:

1) Conduct an assessment of the student's competencies and the Cross-Cultural Exchange program.

AI serves not only as a tool but also as a source of motivation for students. The advent of this phenomenon paves the way for students to explore and improve their learning experiences by providing them with new avenues and chances. Participating in virtual exchange programs powered by artificial intelligence better prepares students for an increasingly interconnected and varied world.

2) Strengthening and expanding the institution's technological infrastructure.

Implementing artificial intelligence in educational settings may be difficult due to financial restrictions. On the other hand, beginning with the fundamentals and progressively expanding can be a plan that successfully works. Additionally, organizations can seek additional funding by soliciting sponsorships or donations from businesses and private entities dedicated to fulfilling their corporate social responsibility obligations.

3) Making judgments and formulating policies for the institution based on current research.

Educational institutions can foster innovation and develop vigilant policies to ensure the maintenance of proper measures and standards while incorporating artificial intelligence (AI) into the curriculum. All of the procedures and processes that make use of artificial intelligence ought to have relevant and suitable safeguards in place to prevent misbehavior and misuse.

4) The institution should provide substantial education, training, and skill development opportunities for the teaching staff and faculty.

In order to provide students with a learning experience that will be memorable, the institution must prepare and upgrade all of its personnel, regardless of whether they are teaching staff or individuals who are not teaching. By keeping them up to date with the most recent technical advances and processes, it is possible to facilitate their adaptation more seamlessly and with less resistance. The provision of adaptable and self-directed learning opportunities for people of all ages is one of how AI-based personalized learning platforms contribute to the advancement of lifelong learning efforts.

5) The integration of AI into the curricula among universities that are prepared for AI.

A concerted effort from policymakers, educators, technology developers, and communities is required to ensure that the incorporation of artificial intelligence (AI) in education is not only successful but also inclusive and ethical. This mechanism is necessary to overcome these obstacles and maximize the benefits of AI for all Filipino learners. As a means of adapting to the ever-changing demands of the market and the improvements in technology, the creation of platforms can make it possible for students and professionals to acquire new skills, acquire new skills, and seek continuous learning.

6) Collaboration and benchmarking with established organizations that have capabilities driven by artificial intelligence.

In order to effectively harness the potential of artificial intelligence in education, stakeholders need to work together to develop comprehensive strategies that address these challenges while emphasizing ethical considerations, equity in access, and the cultivation of a supportive ecosystem that empowers educators and learners to thrive in the digital age. Artificial intelligence-powered collaboration platforms facilitate global learning experiences, cultural exchanges, and collaborative projects between students and instructors from various countries.

7) Continuous monitoring and evaluation of the impact of artificial intelligence on education.

Artificial intelligence technologies can significantly enhance students' learning experiences, necessitating a deeper investigation of contextual elements to achieve more acceptable educational outcomes for both the institution and the student. In order to protect data, reduce the likelihood of bias in artificial intelligence algorithms, and guarantee that AI systems operate ethically and transparently, stakeholders need to set explicit principles.

In order to develop innovation, boost efficiency, and deliver value to customers, higher education institutions can fully embrace artificial intelligence technology. Putting these solutions into practice and maintaining compliance with the rules can accomplish this. There are several applications of artificial intelligence (AI) in the real world, operating in a wide variety of industries, and its potential is continually expanding. By implementing AI in education while considering these solutions and recommendations, educational institutions can improve educational results through tailored and data-driven interventions, increase student learning, and assist teachers in their instructional approaches.

FUTURE RESEARCH DIRECTIONS

The Philippines is making efforts to harness artificial intelligence to enhance teaching methodologies, student engagement, and administrative operations. In the Philippines, the incorporation of AI in education is steadily gaining traction. Artificial intelligence (AI) in education has a wide range of potential study topics that are constantly growing. A few potential areas of concentration for future studies in artificial intelligence and education are as follows:

1) The societal implications of artificial intelligence for both pupils and teachers are worth considering.

This study aims to conduct a comprehensive inquiry into the ways in which artificial intelligence (AI) interacts with society and the potential effects it may have on the day-to-day lives of students, as well as on their families and the community at large. Both quantitative and qualitative research can facilitate this kind of endeavor.

2) Improvements to the assessment methods and feedback mechanisms employed in intelligence

Future researchers can investigate the various methods and procedures that artificial intelligence will use to offer students a reliable evaluation, as well as its ability to determine the most favorable outcome for student performance. In this particular area, the sorts of studies that are in demand include assessment, instrument creation, and validation.

3) Studies focus on developing emotional and social intelligence among students who use AI.

This idea is an excellent area for research to establish artificial intelligence's impact on students in terms of their emotional and social intelligence. Phenomenological research has the potential to be the driving force behind this topic, and more exploratory studies can capitalize on its promise.

4) The use of augmented and virtual reality in education.

Future researchers can analyze students' underlying performance in their learning experience using augmented or virtual reality education. This area is yet another field of innovative learning. We can use experimental research to conduct an in-depth investigation of the benefits and drawbacks associated with these themes.

5) The Ethical Application of AI in Education.

Ethical concerns may arise because artificial intelligence is not typically a common technology for casual use. Future researchers may also choose to do a qualitative inquiry in addition to conducting an exploratory style of research in order to accomplish the objective at hand.

6) The influence of artificial intelligence on educational policy.

In light of the enormous potential that artificial intelligence possesses, as well as its innovative data analytics and functionalities, data-driven decision-making is an approach that is unavoidable and should be the subject of further exploration. The subjects above are amenable to the application of more advanced quantitative research methods, such as structural equation modeling (SEM).

CONCLUSION

Higher education institutions in the Philippines have a chance to benefit tremendously from artificial intelligence, which offers a huge deal of promise and potential. It provides opportunities to improve the teaching and learning experiences of both instructors and students, as well as to optimize administrative procedures among personnel and stimulate creativity. When it comes to higher education teaching and learning experiences, the application of artificial intelligence (AI) in education in the Philippines has enormous potential to assist both students and staff. Before implementing artificial intelligence (AI) in the educational system, the government and institutions must address several concerns and difficulties. Artificial intelligence in higher education requires institutions to conduct in-depth examinations, investigations, and capacity analyses to exploit and fully optimize this technology's possibilities. To maximize the benefits of artificial intelligence and ensure its responsible and equitable integration into the landscape of higher education, it will be critical to address challenges such as the digital divide, ethical considerations, and professional development. While AI adoption in other sectors is rising, these challenges must be addressed.

REFERENCES

Abrenilla, E. M., Redido, C., Abendan, C. F., & Kilag, O. K. (2023). The Next Chapter of ELT: Embracing AI-Infused Pedagogies and Evolving Educational Strategies in the Post-Pandemic Landscape. *Excellencia: International Multidisciplinary Journal of Education (2994-9521), 1*(5), 124-135. https://multijournals.org/index .php/excellencia-imje/article/view/106

Agbong-Coates, I. J. G. (2024). ChatGPT integration significantly boosts personalized learning outcomes: A Philippine study. *International Journal of Educational Management and Development Studies*, 5(2), 165–186. DOI: 10.53378/353067

Alda, R., Boholano, H., & Dayagbil, F. (2020). Teacher education institutions in the Philippines towards education 4.0. *International Journal of Learning. Teaching and Educational Research*, 19(8), 137–154. DOI: 10.26803/ijlter.19.8.8

Amado, J. A., Dayson, C. J. P., Gipaya, P. N., Hipos, A. M. G., Ortile, F. F., & Digo, G. S. (2024). Assessing the Impact of AI Generative Tools on Administrative and Supervisory Practices in Education. *Asia Pacific Journal of Management*, ●●●, 32–40.

Ambit, M. (2024). Artificial Intelligence Tools: Teachers' Pedagogical Adaptation in English Curriculum. *Nexus International Journal of Science and Education, 1*(2), 1–30. https://nijse.org/index.php/home/article/view/92

Ang, S. M. O., & Aragon, M. J. D. (2020). *Development of AI-Enhanced Information Technology Program: Preparing Today's Students in AI Era* (No. 4049). EasyChair. https://easychair.org/publications/preprint/dQmN

Aquino, J. M. D., & Sancon, R. J. S. The Philippine Legal Framework on the utilization of Artificial Intelligence (AI) in strengthening initiatives in combating climate change: an analysis on AI roles, opportunities and legal issues. UP Los Baños Journal, 20(2), 6.

Aquino, M. F. M., & Noroña, M. I. (2021, March). Enhancing cyber security in the Philippine academe: A risk-based IT project assessment approach. In *Proceedings of the international conference on industrial engineering and operations management* (pp. 5166-5179). http://dx.doi.org/DOI: 10.46254/AN11.20210878

Balahadia, F. F., Miranda, J. P. P., & Hernandez, H. E. (2023, November). Teachers' and Students' Awareness on the Uses of ChatGPT: A Cross-Sectional Case Study. In *2023 IEEE 15th International Conference on Humanoid, Nanotechnology, Information Technology, Communication and Control, Environment, and Management (HNICEM)* (pp. 1-5). IEEE. https://doi.org/DOI: 10.1109/HNICEM60674.2023.10589186

Balaquiao, E. C. (2024). Optimizing Students' Performance through Artificial Intelligence (AI) Technology: A Gamified Approach to Smart Learning Environment. *Journal of Pedagogy and Education Science*, 3(02), 104–114. DOI: 10.56741/jpes. v3i02.515

Barajas, J. R., Sangil, M. J., Aspra, N., Gealone, P. J., Lucero, A., Ramos, M., Padua, O., & Oropesa, R. (2024, May). Exploratory Data Analysis of Artificial Intelligence Integration in Philippine Engineering Programs Offered by State Universities and Colleges: A Preliminary Assessment. In *2024 Systems and Information Engineering Design Symposium (SIEDS)* (pp. 360-365). IEEE. https://doi.org/DOI: 10.1109/ SIEDS61124.2024.10534634

Baron, J. V. (2024). A Double-Edged Sword: Examining the Link between Students' Dependence on Artificial Intelligence (AI) and their Psychosocial Maturity. *TWIST*, 19(3), 339–344. DOI: 10.5281/zenodo.10049652#236

Batucan, G. B., Gonzales, G. G., Balbuena, M. G., Pasaol, K. R. B., Seno, D. N., & Gonzales, R. R. (2022). An extended UTAUT model to explain factors affecting online learning system amidst COVID-19 pandemic: The case of a developing economy. *Frontiers in Artificial Intelligence*, 5, 768831. DOI: 10.3389/frai.2022.768831 PMID: 35573898

Bernardo, A. B., Cordel, M. O., Ricardo, J. G. E., Galanza, M. A. M. C., & Almonte-Acosta, S. (2022). Global citizenship competencies of Filipino students: Using machine learning to explore the structure of cognitive, affective, and behavioral competencies in the 2019 Southeast Asia Primary Learning Metrics. *Education Sciences*, 12(8), 547. DOI: 10.3390/educsci12080547

Bonsay, J. O., Cruz, A. P., Firozi, H. C., & Camaro, P. J. C. (2021). Artificial Intelligence and Labor Productivity Paradox: The Economic Impact of AI in China, India, Japan, and Singapore. *Journal of Economics. Finance and Accounting Studies*, 3(2), 120–139. DOI: 10.32996/jefas.2021.3.2.13

Booc, N. B., Sobremisana, K. H. R. I. S. N. A., Ybañez, A. N. G. I. E., Tolosa, R. O. W. E. N. A., Ladroma, S. M., & Caparoso, K. M. (2023). Artificial intelligence-powered calculator application usage in mathematics summative assessments. *Iconic Research and Engineering Journal*, 6(10), 446-474. https://www.irejournals.com/ paper-details/1704266

Cadiz, M. C. D., Manuel, L. A. F., Reyes, M. M., & Natividad, L. R. (2024). Technology Integration in Philippine Higher Education: A Content-Based Bibliometric Analysis. *Jurnal Ilmiah Ilmu Terapan Universitas Jambi*, 8(1), 35–47. DOI: 10.22437/ jiituj.v8i1.31807

Chavez, O. J., & Palaoag, T. (2024). AI-driven mobile application: unraveling students' motivational feature preferences for reading comprehension. *Journal of Research in Innovative Teaching & Learning*. Vol. ahead-of-print No. ahead-of-print. https://doi.org/DOI: 10.1108/JRIT-02-2024-0045

Chua, C. P., & Valencia, L. D. (2020). The Role of Artificial Intelligence in Education Amidst of the COVID-19 Pandemic. https://www.researchgate.net/publication/343691393_The_Role_of_Artificial_Intelligence_in_Education_Amidst_of_the_COVID-19_Pandemic

Clifford, P. L. R. (2024). AI in Higher Education: Faculty Perspective Towards Artificial Intelligence through UTAUT Approach. *Ho Chi Minh City Open University Journal of Science-Social Sciences*, 14(4), 3–21. DOI: 10.46223/HCMCOUJS.soci.en.14.4.2851.2024

Corpuz, J. C. G. (2023). Artificial intelligence (AI) and public health. *Journal of Public Health*, 45(4), e783–e784. DOI: 10.1093/pubmed/fdad074 PMID: 37309563

Cortez, P. M., Ong, A. K. S., Diaz, J. F. T., German, J. D., & Jagdeep, S. J. S. S. (2024). Analyzing Preceding factors affecting behavioral intention on communicational artificial intelligence as an educational tool. *Heliyon*, 10(3), E25896. Advance online publication. DOI: 10.1016/j.heliyon.2024.e25896 PMID: 38356557

De La Cruz, R. J. D. (2022). Science education in the Philippines. In *Science Education in Countries Along the Belt & Road: Future Insights and New Requirements* (pp. 331-345). Singapore: Springer Nature Singapore. https://doi.org/DOI: 10.1007/978-981-16-6955-2_20

de Leon, L. C. R., Flores, L. V., & Alomo, A. R. L. (2024). Artificial intelligence and Filipino academic librarians: Perceptions, challenges and opportunities. *Journal of the Australian library and information association, 73*(1), 66-83. https://doi.org/DOI: 10.1080/24750158.2024.2305993

Dela Rosa, A. C. C., Dacuma, A. K. B., Ang, C. A. R., Nudalo, C. J. J., Cruz, L., & Vallespin, M. R. (2024). Assessing AI Adoption: Investigating Variances in AI Utilization Across Student Year Levels in Far Eastern University-Manila, Philippines. *International Journal of Current Science Research and Review*, 6, 1–8. DOI: 10.47191/ijcsrr/6-i00-00

Diano, F., Jr., Kilag, O. K., Malbas, M., Catacutan, A., Tiongzon, B., & Abendan, C. F. (2023). Towards Global Competence: Innovations in the Philippine Curriculum for Addressing International Challenges. *Excellencia: International Multidisciplinary Journal of Education, 1*(4), 295-307. https://multijournals.org/index.php/excellencia-imje/article/view/66/71

Escolano, V. J. C., Caballero, A. R., Albina, E. M., Hernandez, A. A., & Juanatas, R. A. (2023, May). Acceptance of Mobile Application on Disaster Preparedness: Towards Decision Intelligence in Disaster Management. In *2023 8th International Conference on Business and Industrial Research (ICBIR)* (pp. 381-386). IEEE. https://doi.org/DOI: 10.1109/ICBIR57571.2023.10147638

Eslit, E. (2023). Thriving beyond the crisis: Teachers' reflections on literature and language education in the era of artificial intelligence (AI) and globalization. *Preprints*, 2023072151. https://doi.org/DOI: 10.20944/preprints202307.2151.v1

Eslit, E. R. (2023). Thriving Beyond the Crisis: Teachers' Reflections on Literature and Language Education in the Era of Artificial Intelligence (AI) and Globalization. *International Journal of Education and Teaching*, 3(1), 46–57. DOI: 10.51483/IJEDT.3.1.2023.46-57

Estrellado, C. J., & Miranda, J. C. (2023). Artificial intelligence in the Philippine educational context: Circumspection and future inquiries. *International Journal of Scientific and Research Publications*, 13(5), 16–22. DOI: 10.29322/IJSRP.13.04.2023. p13704

Fontanilla, J. B., Bautista, K. H., Lactao, M.Jr, Villacorte, M. A., & Santos, R. (2023). Educators' Perspectives on the Impact of Artificial Intelligence on Writing Competence. *International Journal of Multidisciplinary Research and Publications*, 6(6), 29–34. https://www.researchgate.net/publication/375769974

Gelacio, B. A., Amodia, L., Cabaya, I. M., Toylo, K. J., & Dacula, J. (2024). Steering the Artificial Intelligence Landscape: Technological Readiness and Acceptance of Accountancy Students. *Psychology and Education: A Multidisciplinary Journal*, 21(1), 95-102. https://doi.org/DOI: 10.5281/zenodo.12191798

Goli-Cruz, M. J. (2023). Perceptions of Higher Education Faculty Regarding the Use of Chat Generative Pre-Trained Transformer (ChatGPT) in Education. *International Journal on Open and Distance e-Learning, 9*(2). https://doi.org/DOI: 10.58887/ijodel.v9i2.249

Hara, M. (2024). Roles of artificial intelligence in education for sustainable development in Asia-Pacific contexts. *Global Journal of Business and Integral Security*, 1(2), 1–17. https://www.gbis.ch/index.php/gbis/article/view/350

Hernandez, A. A., Caballero, A. R., Albina, E. M., Balmes, I. L., & Niguidula, J. D. (2023, May). Artificial Intelligence for Sustainability: Evidence from select Small and Medium Enterprises in the Philippines. In *2023 8th International Conference on Business and Industrial Research (ICBIR)* (pp. 818-823). IEEE. https://doi.org/DOI: 10.1109/ICBIR57571.2023.10147579

Ilham, R., Muhammad, I., Aji, L. J., Rizal, S. U., & Özbilen, F. M. (2023). Artificial intelligence research in education: A bibliometric analysis. *Journal of Education Global*, 1(1), 45–55. https://penaeducentre.com/index.php/JEdG/article/view/25

Illahi, A. A. C., Culaba, A., & Dadios, E. P. (2019, November). Internet of Things in the Philippines: a review. In *2019 IEEE 11th International Conference on Humanoid, Nanotechnology, Information Technology, Communication and Control, Environment, and Management (HNICEM)* (pp. 1-6). IEEE. https://doi.org/DOI: 10.1109/HNICEM48295.2019.9072882

Jabar, M., Chiong-Javier, E., & Pradubmook Sherer, P. (2024). Qualitative ethical technology assessment of artificial intelligence (AI) and the internet of things (IoT) among Filipino Gen Z members: Implications for ethics education in higher learning institutions. *Asia Pacific Journal of Education*, ●●●, 1–15. DOI: 10.1080/02188791.2024.2303048

Jose, J. A. C., Bandala, A. A., Culaba, A. B., Chu, T. S., & Dadios, E. P. (2022, December). Artificial Intelligence for Developing Countries: Philippine Context. In *2022 IEEE 14th International Conference on Humanoid, Nanotechnology, Information Technology, Communication and Control, Environment, and Management (HNICEM)* (pp. 1-5). IEEE. https://doi.org/DOI: 10.1109/HNICEM57413.2022.10109550

Julien, G. (2024). How Artificial Intelligence (AI) impacts inclusive education. *Educational Research Review*, 19(6), 95–103. DOI: 10.5897/ERR2024.4404

Kabalisa, R., & Altmann, J. (2021). AI technologies and motives for AI adoption by countries and firms: a systematic literature review. In *Economics of Grids, Clouds, Systems, and Services: 18th International Conference, GECON 2021, Virtual Event,September 21–23, 2021,Proceedings 18* (pp. 39-51). Springer International Publishing. https://doi.org/DOI: 10.1007/978-3-030-92916-9_4

Kim, J., & Castillejos-Petalcorin, C. (2020). The role of government research & development in fostering innovation in Asia. *Asian Development Bank*. https://www.adb.org/documents/asian-development-outlook-2020-background-papers

Kshetri, N. (2021). Evolving uses of artificial intelligence in human resource management in emerging economies in the global South: Some preliminary evidence. *Management Research Review*, 44(7), 970–990. DOI: 10.1108/MRR-03-2020-0168

Labrague, L. J., Aguilar-Rosales, R., Yboa, B. C., & Sabio, J. B. (2023). Factors influencing student nurses' readiness to adopt artificial intelligence (AI) in their studies and their perceived barriers to accessing AI technology: A cross-sectional study. *Nurse Education Today*, 130, 105945. DOI: 10.1016/j.nedt.2023.105945 PMID: 37625351

Labrague, L. J., Aguilar-Rosales, R., Yboa, B. C., Sabio, J. B., & de Los Santos, J. A. (2023). Student nurses' attitudes, perceived utilization, and intention to adopt artificial intelligence (AI) technology in nursing practice: A cross-sectional study. *Nurse Education in Practice*, 73, 103815. DOI: 10.1016/j.nepr.2023.103815 PMID: 37922736

Legaspi, J. B., Licuben, R. J. O., Legaspi, E. A., & Aguinaldo, J. (2024). Comparing AI detectors: Evaluating performance and efficiency. *International Journal of Science and Research Archive*, 12(2), 833–838. DOI: 10.30574/ijsra.2024.12.2.1276

Ligot, D. V., Melendres, R. L., Tayco, F. C., Vizmonte, E. J., Toledo, M., Gerlock-Barretto, A., Martinez, J. E., Benardo, G., Sindol-Ritualo, M., Neri, C., Nungcaras, J., & Pelayo, S. (2022). Philippines Data Analytics Sector Labor Market Intelligence Report. https://dx.doi.org/DOI: 10.2139/ssrn.4027384

Marcial, D. E. (2020). Education 4.0: Disrupting education towards creativity, innovation, and commercialization. *International Journal of Scientific Engineering and Science*, 4(12), 25–33. https://ijses.com/volume-4-issue-12

Mendoza, J. R., Catapang, R. G., & Aquino, J. M. (2023). The Impact of Moodle-Cloud on Faculty and Graduate Students' User-Independence Engagement in a State University in the Philippines. *International Journal of Learning. Teaching and Educational Research*, 22(12), 299–325. DOI: 10.26803/ijlter.22.12.15

Milloria, B. R. B., Marzon, A. M. D., & Derasin, L. M. C. (2024). Investigating AI-Integrated Instruction in Improving Academic Performance of Senior High School Students in the Philippines. *Journal of Harbin Engineering University*, 45(6), 61–66. https://www.researchgate.net/publication/382299009

Mina, A., Tumanglao, M., & Bugarin, M. (2023). Enhancing clinical instructors' preparedness: A holistic approach to integrating artificial intelligence in nursing education. *Filipino Multidisciplinary Research Journal in Education*, 3(1), 1021. DOI: 10.5281/zenodo. 10777491

Mina, P. N. R., Solon, I. M., Sanchez, F. R., Delante, T. K., Villegas, J. K., Basay, F. J., Andales, J.-r., Pasko, F., Estrera, M. F. R., Samson, R.Jr, & Mutya, R. (2023). Leveraging Education through Artificial Intelligence Virtual Assistance: A Case Study of Visually Impaired Learners. *International Journal of Educational Innovation and Research*, 2(1), 10–22. DOI: 10.31949/ijeir.v2i1.300

Mindajao, B. Y. (2023). Effectiveness of Chatbot as an innovative modality in grade reporting in the new normal. *European Journal of Education Studies*, 10(2), 244–252. DOI: 10.46827/ejes.v10i2.4686

Minglana, J., Tobias, R. R., & Roxas, R. E. (2021, December). Artificial intelligence applications in quality management system: a bibliometric study. In *TENCON 2021-2021 IEEE Region 10 Conference (TENCON)* (pp. 947-952). IEEE. https://doi.org/ DOI: 10.1109/TENCON54134.2021.9707340

Moreno, F. G. (2023, July 13). AI readiness of Philippine Public Administration: A review of literature. https://doi.org/DOI: 10.31219/osf.io/kpzt6

Moron, C. E., & Diokno, C. O. B. (2023). Level of readiness and adoption on the use of artificial intelligence technologies in the accounting profession. *Open Journal of Accounting*, 12(3), 37–54. DOI: 10.4236/ojacct.2023.123004

Mupaikwa, E. (2024). Artificial Intelligence-Driven Instruction and Its Impact on Heutagogy and Student Engagement. In *AI Algorithms and ChatGPT for Student Engagement in Online Learning* (pp. 101–123). IGI Global., DOI: 10.4018/979-8-3693-4268-8.ch007

Obenza, B., Salvahan, A., Rios, A. N., Solo, A., Alburo, R. A., & Gabila, R. J. (2024). University Students' Perception and Use of ChatGPT: Generative Artificial Intelligence (AI) in Higher Education. *International Journal of Human-Computer Studies*, 5(12), 5–18. https://papers.ssrn.com/sol3/papers.cfm?abstract_id=4724968

Oluyinka, S., & Cusipag, M. (2021). Trialability and purposefulness: Their role towards Google classroom acceptance following educational policy. *Acta Informatica Pragensia*, 10(2), 172–191. https://www.ceeol.com/search/article-detail?id=1020610

Osorio, C. P. (2023). Regulating the Regulators: Economic Assessment of Philippine Electricity Regulation. *International Journal of Energy Economics and Policy*, 13(3), 191–196. DOI: 10.32479/ijeep.14213

Pahuriray, A. V., Basanta, J. D., Arroyo, J. C. T., & Delima, A. J. P. (2022). Flexible Learning Experience Analyzer (FLExA): Sentiment Analysis of College Students through Machine Learning Algorithms with Comparative Analysis using WEKA. *International Journal of Emerging Technology and Advanced Engineering*, 12, 1–15. DOI: 10.46338/ijetae1222_01

Panoy, J. F., Andrade, R., Febrer, L., & Ching, D. (2022). Perceived proficiency with technology and online learning expectations of students in the graduate program of one state university in the Philippines. *International Journal of Information and Education Technology (IJIET)*, 12(7), 615–624. DOI: 10.18178/ijiet.2022.12.7.1661

Robledo, D. A. R., Zara, C. G., Montalbo, S. M., Gayeta, N. E., Gonzales, A. L., Escarez, M. G. A., & Maalihan, E. D. (2023). Development and Validation of a Survey Instrument on Knowledge, Attitude, and Practices (KAP) Regarding the Educational Use of ChatGPT among Preservice Teachers in the Philippines. *International Journal of Information and Education Technology (IJIET)*, 13(10), 1582–1590. DOI: 10.18178/ijiet.2023.13.10.1965

Rogers, J. K. B., Mercado, T. C. R., & Decano, R. S. (2025). Moodle interactions and academic performance: Educational data mining in a Philippine university. [EduLearn]. *Journal of Education and Learning*, 19(1), 542–550. DOI: 10.11591/edulearn.v19i1.21549

Rosales, M. A., Jo-ann, V. M., Palconit, M. G. B., Culaba, A. B., & Dadios, E. P. (2020, December). Artificial intelligence: the technology adoption and impact in the Philippines. In *2020 IEEE 12th International Conference on humanoid, nanotechnology, information technology, communication and control, environment, and management (HNICEM)* (pp. 1-6). IEEE. https://doi.org/DOI: 10.1109/HNICEM51456.2020.9400025

Samonte, M. J. C., & Ong, A. P. L. (2023, November). Analyzing the Impact of Artificial Intelligence in the Financial Industry. In *2023 IEEE 15th International Conference on Humanoid, Nanotechnology, Information Technology, Communication and Control, Environment, and Management (HNICEM)* (pp. 1–6). IEEE. https://doi.org/DOI: 10.1109/HNICEM60674.2023.10589026

Santiago, C. S.Jr, Embang, S. I., Conlu, M. T. N., Acanto, R. B., Lausa, S. M., Ambojia, K. W. P., Laput, E. y., Aperocho, M. D. B., Malabag, B. A., Balilo, B. B.Jr, Paderes, J. J., Cahapin, E. L., & Romasanta, J. K. N. (2023). Utilization of writing assistance tools in research in selected higher learning institutions in the Philippines: A text mining analysis. *International Journal of Learning. Teaching and Educational Research*, 22(11), 259–284. DOI: 10.26803/ijlter.22.11.14

Sulasula, J. (2023). Towards Algorithmic University: Assessing the readiness of State Universities and Colleges (sucs) in Zamboanga Peninsula, the Philippines. https://dx.doi.org/DOI: 10.2139/ssrn.4505296

Taer, A. N., & Taer, E. C. (2024). Transforming Philippine Agriculture Through Data-driven Innovation: A Quantitative Landscape Assessment to Prioritize Technological Solutions. https://doi.org/DOI: 10.21203/rs.3.rs-3943832/v1

Tobias, R. R., Minglana, J., Hernandez, D. K., Mital, M. E., & Roxas, R. E. (2023). Artificial intelligence applications in quality management systems of Philippine higher education institutions. In *Intelligent Sustainable Systems: Selected Papers of WorldS4 2022, Volume 2* (pp. 159-172). Singapore: Springer Nature Singapore. https://doi.org/DOI: 10.1007/978-981-19-7663-6_16

Umali, J. N. D. (2024). Artificial Intelligence Technology Management of Teachers, Learners Motivation and Challenges Encountered. *Educational Research*, 6(3), 821–880. https://www.ijmcer.com/volume-6-issue-3/

Valerio, A. (2024). Anticipating the Impact of Artificial Intelligence in Higher Education: Student Awareness and Ethical Concerns in Zamboanga City, Philippines. *Cognizance Journal of Multidisciplinary Studies*, 4(6), 10–47760. DOI: 10.47760/cognizance.2024.v04i06.024

Verdote, R. J. M. (2019). The Philippines, Part 1: The University of Cordilleras and Its Place in Philippines Higher Education. In *The Global Phenomenon of Family-Owned or Managed Universities*. Brill., DOI: 10.1163/9789004423435_014

Vidal, J. (2022). Digital education: The approach of a modern teacher. *Jozac Academic Voice*, 71-76. https://doi.org/DOI: 10.57040/av.vi.246

Zabala, C. (2023). Exploring the applicability of Artificial Intelligence in Local Government Units (LGUs) in Zamboanga Peninsula (Region IX), Philippines. https://dx.doi.org/DOI: 10.2139/ssrn.4506110

ADDITIONAL READING

Alibudbud, R. (2024). Artificial intelligence and inequality: Insights from the Philippines. *Journal of Public Health*, ●●●, fdae109. Advance online publication. DOI: 10.1093/pubmed/fdae109 PMID: 38879184

Arcilla, A. O., Espallardo, A. K. V., Gomez, C. A. J., Viado, E. M. P., Ladion, V. J. T., Naanep, R. A. T., Artificio, E. B., & Tubola, O. D. (2023, September). Ethics in AI Governance: Comparative Analysis, Implication, and Policy Recommendations for the Philippines. In *2023 27th International Computer Science and Engineering Conference (ICSEC)* (pp. 319-326). IEEE. https://doi.org/DOI: 10.1109/ICSEC59635.2023.10329756

Concepcion, R. S., Bedruz, R. A. R., Culaba, A. B., Dadios, E. P., & Pascua, A. R. A. R. (2019, November). The technology adoption and governance of artificial intelligence in the Philippines. In *2019 IEEE 11th International Conference on humanoid, nanotechnology, information technology, communication and control, environment, and management (HNICEM)* (pp. 1-10). IEEE. https://doi.org/DOI: 10.1109/HNICEM48295.2019.9072725

Dagdag, J. D., & Galiza, C. C. (2020). Perceived use, satisfaction level and benefits among student library users of a higher education institution in Isabela Province, Philippines. *International Journal of Psychosocial Rehabilitation*, 24(05), 5630–5637. https://www.researchgate.net/publication/341051267

De Jesus, F. S., Ibarra, L. M., Pasion, B. J., Villanueva, W., & Leyesa, M. (2024). ChatGPT as an Artificial Intelligence Learning Tool for Business Administration Students in Nueva Ecija, Philippines. *International Journal of Learning. Teaching and Educational Research*, 23(6), 348–372. DOI: 10.26803/ijlter.23.6.16

Diloy, M. A., Comparativo, C. P. E., Reyes, J. C. T., Eusebio, B. J. M., & Morona, L. I. C. (2023, December). Exploring the Landscape of AI Tools in Student Learning: An analysis of commonly utilized AI Tools at a university in the Philippines. In *Proceedings of the 2023 6th Artificial Intelligence and Cloud Computing Conference* (pp. 266-271). https://doi.org/DOI: 10.1145/3639592.3639629

Espartinez, A. S. (2024). Exploring student and teacher perceptions of ChatGPT use in higher education: A Q-Methodology study. *Computers and Education: Artificial Intelligence*, 7, 100264. DOI: 10.1016/j.caeai.2024.100264

Gutierrez, K. L. T., & Viacrusis, P. M. L. (2023). Bridging the Gap or Widening the Divide: A Call for Capacity-Building in Artificial Intelligence for Healthcare in the Philippines. *Journal of Medicine. University of Santo Tomas*, 7(2), 1325–1334. DOI: 10.35460/2546-1621.2023-0081

Junio, D. A., & Bandala, A. A. (2023, November). Utilization of Artificial Intelligence in Academic Writing Class: L2 Learners Perspective. In *2023 IEEE 15th International Conference on Humanoid, Nanotechnology, Information Technology, Communication and Control, Environment, and Management (HNICEM)* (pp. 1-6). IEEE. https://doi.org/DOI: 10.1109/HNICEM60674.2023.10589003

Prestoza, M. J. R., & Banatao, J. C. M. (2024). Exploring the Efficacy of AI Passion-Driven Pedagogy in Enhancing Student Engagement and Learning Outcomes: A Case Study in Philippines. *Asian Journal of Assessment in Teaching and Learning*, 14(1), 45–54. DOI: 10.37134/ajatel.vol14.1.5.2024

Rivera, M. K. (2022). The appropriate legal framework for text and data mining exception to build an AI-driven economy in the Philippines. https://ruj.uj.edu.pl/xmlui/handle/item/288749

Ventayen, R. J. M. (2023, April). OpenAI ChatGPT-Generated Results: Similarity Index of Artificial Intelligence-Based Contents. In *International Conference on Soft Computing for Security Applications* (pp. 215-226). Singapore: Springer Nature Singapore. https://doi.org/DOI: 10.1007/978-981-99-3608-3_15

KEY TERMS AND DEFINITIONS

Accessible AI Education: The use of AI technology to improve the accessibility of individuals with education regardless of status and geographical locality.

Artificial Intelligence: The ability of a digital computer or computer-controlled robot to perform tasks commonly associated with intelligent beings.

Ethical Artificial Intelligence: A system of moral principles and mechanisms intended to inform AI technology's development and responsible use.

Higher Education Institutions (HEIs): Universities or colleges that offer courses in different disciplines, such as law, medicine, business, theology, music, arts, and humanities.

Data-Driven Decision-Making: The use of facts, metrics, and data to guide strategic business or organizational decisions that align with the institution's goals, objectives, and initiatives.

Research and Innovation: They are the processes of creating new ideas, processes, technologies, services, or techniques introduced to an organization but not necessarily new to the outside world.

Student Support and Engagement: This term provides comprehensive support to help students become more connected to and engaged in school.

Teaching and Learning: This process includes different variables that interact as learners work toward their goals and incorporate new knowledge, behaviours, and skills into their wide range of learning experiences.

Chapter 20
Transforming Higher Education Through Technology:
The Impact of Artificial Intelligence in Education 5.0

Elisha Mupaikwa
https://orcid.org/0000-0002-0313-7139
National University of Science and Technology, Zimbabwe

ABSTRACT

This chapter analyses recommended journal articles to explore the impact of AI in Education 5.0. These reviews indicated that the establishment of intelligent tutoring systems, personalized learning, curriculum development and evaluation, research support, learning analytics, and gamification of learning were the main uses of artificial intelligence in Education 5.0. The key findings from the chapter are the transformative role that artificial intelligence has played in education by creating a more independent, student-centred and student-directed learning environment that enables learners to demonstrate their innovative skills. The main obstacles to the adoption of Education 5.0 were concerns about ethics, security, and finances as well as legislation. The chapter went on to suggest investments in infrastructure development, user training, and policy initiatives.

DOI: 10.4018/979-8-3693-8191-5.ch020

INTRODUCTION

The exponential expansion in computer power has facilitated the rapid development of information processing technologies and processes, which has resulted in multiple artificial intelligence advancements that have spread to various sectors of the global economy. The education industry has not been immune to the swift advancements in artificial intelligence (AI)-driven breakthroughs, as evidenced by the growing adoption of AI advances dubbed Artificial Intelligence in Education (AIEd). Globally, educational systems have also changed to meet the needs of the populations they serve and from literature; it is society's duty to keep education relevant. Due to these advancements in both education and the digital world, there is no room for education to change. As a result, many new educational paradigms, including Education 1.0, Education 2.0, Education 3.0, Education 4.0, and Education 5.0, have emerged. When it comes to the use of AIEd and the endorsement of Industry 4.0, Industry 5.0, Society 4.0, and Society 5.0, the latter two paradigms have triumphed. Conversely, three AIEd paradigms—AI-directed, learner-as-recipient; AI-supported, learner-as-collaborator; and AI-empowered, learner-as-leader—have arisen from the advancements of AI-mediated learning (Ouyang and Jiao, 2021). Intelligent tutoring systems, recommender systems, learning analytics, teaching robots and chatbots, language translators, essay writing and scoring systems, and more are examples of AIEd developments that have surfaced. Artificial neural networks, machine learning, and natural language processing are a few examples of AI technology techniques that have been employed. Several categorization and prediction models that have been utilized by teachers and students to make judgments about teaching and learning have been developed as a result of these being used to create intelligent learning environments for behavioural detection. The advancements in AI and education, as well as the advancements in education and the internet, have significant roles in all these processes. Studies have also revealed a substantial correlation between the aspiration of nations to have education-driven breakthroughs in businesses and to align education with the industrial demands of their economy and education reforms. The developmental goals of communities must therefore be addressed in educational programs, and for several years, state ideology has been driving these changes based on the necessity of addressing socio-political concerns, some of which may be historical. But in other countries, the necessity to meet industry's demands for human capital—which includes producing a trained labour force and conducting evidence-based research that frequently spurs inventions and industrialization—may be the driving factor behind improvements in education. However, the literature identifies a variety of strategies that different countries have used to embrace different educational systems. Since the focus of this chapter is AI's role in Education 5.0, the authors acknowledge that there is no agreement among researchers regarding the principles of Education 5.0, and as a result, the paradigm's characteristics have not been universal, depending on national ideology and industry desires. While a lot of research has been done on AI in education, and there has also been a lot of interest in Education 5.0, especially in light of the fourth industrial revolution (4IR), little research has been done on how AI has changed education through Education 5.0. Education 5.0 is a paradigm shift in learning that incorporates disruptive technology to facilitate student-directed learning in a setting where learners are expected to engage in creative learning. Innovations that drastically change how customers, industries, or businesses function are known as disruptive technologies. Consequently, these technologies have permeated every field, including education. As such, these technologies have spread across all disciplines, including education. Therefore, the goal of this study is to show how AI has been incorporated into Education 5.0 and changed the larger educational landscape. Thus, the development of education from Education 1.0 to Education 5.0 is covered in this chapter. It then goes over the ideas behind AIEd and how AI has made Education 5.0 possible. The chapter also covers the difficulties educational institutions have had implementing Education 5.0, which is technology-driven. Finally, it offers implementation solutions for AI-assisted Education 5.0. Through a synthesis of journal articles, the chapter further analyses the effectiveness of AI in education.

BACKGROUND

Providing widespread access to education is just one of the ways that the current educational systems have succeeded. This is demonstrated by the fact that literacy rates have risen globally, especially in rural places. Sadly, despite the sophisticated pedagogical approaches and tactics used in the current educational system, students' curiosity is not encouraged, which could further encourage them to follow their interests (Rahate et al., 2023). When it comes to concerns regarding the current teaching-learning methodologies and associated procedures, students frequently hesitate to speak up (Xia, Li, and Cao, 2023). This is because the current system has mostly been limited to the realm of classroom instruction. The chalkboard system, for example, restricts student interaction within the walls of the classroom, where students' understanding is assessed using conventional methods that do not fully reveal their potential in related fields of study (Li and Rutab, 2023). Even with technology-enabled learning, the potential is not completely realized by utilizing the most cutting-edge academic experiences available today. These restrictions came to light during the pandemic, when most kids and young adults had trouble adjusting to the internet and hybrid forms of instruction. As a result, face-to-face communication has decreased, and the technology supporting instructors has constraints that influence their choices. To promote successful communication between humans and technologies, it is necessary to incorporate Industry 5.0 and associated technologies into education (Patil et al., 2022). Therefore, integrating technology into Industry 5.0 and Education 5.0 helps society produce intelligent, emotionally stable, and socially adept persons. This can be accomplished by utilizing its distinctive teaching and learning strategies, which prioritize and highlight the human traits at the centre of the educational process by helping each student find the roles and talents that best fit them. It can encourage creativity, help people showcase their special talents, and sharpen their critical thinking skills. Additionally, it can foster the growth of their problem-solving and design abilities (Carayannis and Morawska, 2023). The demands of society as a whole are also emphasized, in addition to employability. Furthermore, in accepting these educational reforms, innovation is now recognized as a critical element for maintaining educational institutions' competitiveness as well as for making additional contributions to the knowledge economies. AI and other more recent digital technologies have been major drivers of this advancement.

The implementation of Education 5.0 is one of several changes that have been made in the worldwide education sector. Nonetheless, historically, while examining changes in education, countries have looked to determine how well these programs fit the demands of their societies and their attempts at industrialization. Therefore, Kuru-Çetin, Nayir, and Taşkın (2020) used graphics to explain the relationship between education and national economies in their discussion, as seen in Figure 1 below:

Figure 1. Education-Industrial Revolution relationship (Kuru-Çetin, Nayir and Taşkın, 2020)

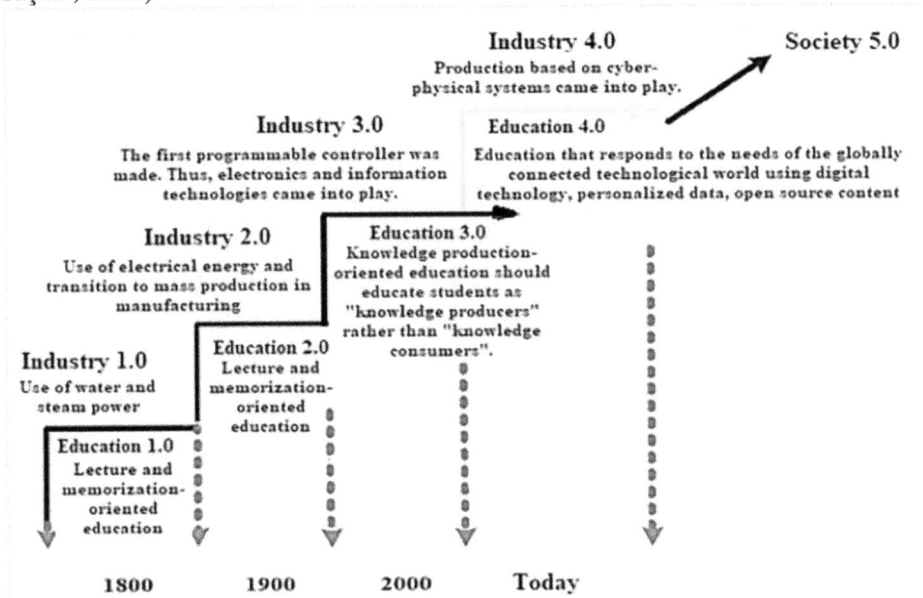

Industry 4.0
Production based on cyber-physical systems came into play.

Society 5.0

Industry 3.0
The first programmable controller was made. Thus, electronics and information technologies came into play.

Education 4.0
Education that responds to the needs of the globally connected technological world using digital technology, personalized data, open source content

Industry 2.0
Use of electrical energy and transition to mass production in manufacturing

Education 3.0
Knowledge production-oriented education should educate students as "knowledge producers" rather than "knowledge consumers".

Industry 1.0
Use of water and steam power

Education 2.0
Lecture and memorization-oriented education

Education 1.0
Lecture and memorization-oriented education

1800   1900   2000   Today

The figure shows how the futuristic breakthroughs of Education 3.0, Education 4.0, and Education 5.0 have been impacted by the latest advancements in the digital environment. Researchers have realized the great potential of these technologies in aiding in instructional delivery, improving educational services, and supporting the Fourth Industrial Revolution (4IR). As a result, they have advocated for the integration of AI in education, even though these phased processes to the evolution of educational paradigms have varied according to the level of countries' digitization. Wang et al. (2021) list several AIEd innovations, including the AI tutor, which uses GPT-U's ability to deliver personalised learning, Khanmingo, which provides intelligent feedback at Khan Academy, Duolingo for language learning, iFlytek for intelligent assessment, and learning management systems Absorb and Docebo. Softbank Robotics, Nao, and Pepper are a few more robot-based systems that have been created as social robots for language instruction (Wang et al., 2021).

Even though the concept of Education 5.0 is relatively new, especially when considering the developing world, care must be taken to take into account the various ways that different countries and institutions understand Education 5.0 when researching the role of AI in Education 5.0. For instance, in developing countries like Zimbabwe, the goal of utilizing heritage-based resources to make education relevant for innovation and industrialization was the driving force for the implementation of

Education 5.0. In addition, this was intended to tackle the nation's socioeconomic problems; according to Alhrabi (2023), the main goal of the new model was to close the knowledge gap between the nation's industrial market demands and university curricula. As a result, Education 5.0 evolved into a research-focused paradigm that combined industrialization and innovation, even though it appears that emerging technologies like AI, the Internet of Things (IoT), blockchain technology, cloud computing, data mining, and big data analytics are not given as much attention. In the Zimbabwean setting, teaching, research, community services, innovation, and industrialization were the main components of Education 5.0 (Alharbi, 2023). Additionally, Alharbi (2023) mentions a few instances of Education 5.0 implementation from Sri Lanka and Malaysia. According to Alharbi's (2023) report, developing nations like Malaysia regularly invest in educational technologies, and their citizens frequently seek out opportunities and services for higher education in an environment that is characterized by the use of contemporary technologies that would help them meet the developmental needs of their industries and societies. According to Alharbi (2023), Saudi Arabia's educational change appears to have been driven by the needs of the market and the country's Vision 2030. There, learners were expected to acquire new personalities, talents, and a creative spirit in an atmosphere that was exciting and provided with integrated, supportive services. Strong industry partnership was expected to enable learners to meet the country's growing expectations for economic and social development.

METHODOLOGY

The following search phrases were used to download 130 journal articles in total: "Education 5.0," "Education 5.0 AND AI," and "Impact of AI on Education." 77 articles were chosen from this total depending on the author's assessment of their applicability. Therefore, these 77 journal papers are the source of the main conclusions in this chapter.

The Education 5.0 History

In the countries where this educational paradigm has gained traction, the concept of education has been used in diverse ways. Alharbi (2023) defined Education 5.0 as a learning environment where students participate in the learning process and have a role in education, despite these variations. In this setting, learning is guided, controlled, and centred on the learners themselves. Alharbi (2023) and Gerstein (2014) offer a historical account of Education 1.0 to Education 5.0, which is necessary to comprehend the essence of Education 5.0. Technology is not allowed in Education

1.0, a behaviourist educational program built on the three Rs: receiving, reacting, and regurgitating. Under this authoritarian, teacher-centred method, students are treated as passive recipients of knowledge, and their responses are repeated notes, text study, and repetitive exams. Education 1.0 was mostly a one-way process in which teachers provided students with information through class notes in a teaching and learning environment. This is similar to the first generation of the web (Alharbi, 2023). Among its many drawbacks include rote learning, a dearth of technology, passive learning, and the presumption of a one-size-fits-all strategy that ignores the unique requirements and characteristics of each student.

Education 2.0, according to Gerstein (2014), is a paradigm for learning that allows for interaction between users and the content as well as amongst users. With the help of technology, this method replaced rote learning with more active, collaborative learning in the classroom (Ahmad et al., 2023). With the help of blended learning and remote learning, students were able to study whenever and wherever they wanted. Among the technologies utilized were social bookmarking, podcasts, and blogs. This learning style is characterized by knowledge memorization but also includes communication and teamwork, as well as some degrees of student-centred learning (Makrides, 2020). With its emphasis on constructivism and andragogy, Education 2.0 integrates active, interactive, authentic, relevant, and socially networked learning events into the course structure and classroom. This method did, however, continue to view the instructor as the main knowledge source.

Education 3.0 places a significant emphasis on collaborative learning and completely incorporates technology into teaching and learning. The two main features of Education 3.0 are personalized and interactive material. The flipped classroom is another aspect of this strategy, in which students hear live or recorded lectures, complete their homework using AI-powered tools at home, and then participate in interactive discussions during class. According to this self-determined, interest-based learning paradigm, education is driven by creativity, invention, and problem-solving skills (Gerstein, 2014). This paradigm places a great emphasis on social networking as a learning tool and gives students a significant role as providers of knowledge or artefacts. Thus, the 3Cs (Connectivity, Creativity, and Constructivism) are the focus of this learning paradigm (Gerstein, 2014), and among learners who also engage in research, the instructor takes on the roles of coordinator, advisor, facilitator, learner, and practice guide.

Education 4.0 is a 4IR-related educational paradigm that aims to apply smart technologies to change earlier paradigms in education. Thus, this approach necessitates cutting-edge technology-based teaching and learning strategies. The goals of Education 4.0 are to increase students' capacity for critical thought, teamwork, communication, and digital literacy (Ahmad et al., 2023). To facilitate learning through simulations backed by AI, it has also integrated the concepts of augmented reality and virtual reality. Co-creation and innovation are hallmarks of this type of learning environment, where students learn outside of the classroom in a setting of individualized instruction (Makrides, 2020). However, under this strategy, the teacher's background and attitude toward technology have an impact on how well students learn and teach. Similar to Education 4.0, the core of Education 5.0 is defined by all stakeholders involved in education. According to this concept, learning is centred around, motivated by, and linked to the learner (Alharbi, 2023). Technology is all around the students, giving them choices about what to study when to study, where to study, why to study, and who to study with (Melluso et al, 2020; Alharbi, 2023). The following are the main areas where Education 5.0 should be implemented to reap the greatest benefits, according to Universiti Teknologi Mara (2019): applying creative thinking to problem-solving, creating a value-based learning culture, and improving and blending the concept of personalized learning. To foster progressive thinking learners who are agents of their learning, Education 5.0 at the University Teknologi Mara should focus on five key areas: learning that goes beyond achieving good grades on campus; personalization and personalised learning experiences; space design for learning and creation; provision of challenging tasks and content; and instillation of a values-based learning culture. A coherent and relevant curriculum, innovative delivery and assessment, meaningful learning experiences, transformative learning, and inspiring educators are all important elements of Education 5.0, according to Universiti Teknologi Mara's implementation of the program in 2019.

According to Judijanto, Ili, and Wardhana (2024), the idea of Education 5.0 has arisen as a novel strategy that emphasizes the development of students' technologically integrated adaptable, collaborative, and creative skills. Over time, Education 5.0 has placed a strong emphasis on a comprehensive approach to education that develops students' social and emotional intelligence as well as their ability to positively impact society and their surroundings (Chen, 2022). The emphasis on sustainability is growing, with an emphasis on how education can promote sustainable development and train students to be global problem solvers. The emphasis in this educational progression is on the interaction of general knowledge, real-world applications, and technology to foster creativity and innovation in the classroom as well as the application of moral and business principles. The goal of Education 5.0 is to create people who, in addition to possessing the skill sets required for the future, also have the understanding and social responsibility to promote a better world (Dec et al., 2022). Education 5.0 introduces five fundamental principles—collaboration, creativity, critical thinking, communication, and connectivity—that serve as the cornerstones for enhancing the calibre of education and forming students' character to meet future problems (Duan and Zhao, 2023). These guidelines are intended to incorporate life skills that are pertinent to the demands of the modern world, enabling pupils to flourish in a high-tech, constantly evolving setting (Dupri et al., 2021). Students who get instruction that promotes teamwork learn how to function in groups, utilizing the skills and abilities of each individual to accomplish a shared objective. This teaches them the importance of empathy and teamwork in reaching sustainable solutions, in addition to preparing them for future work contexts (Garcia, 2020). It has lately been recognized that academic institutions can increase research productivity and quality through collaborative research. This has been made possible by combining several research data management techniques that have improved study findings and data sharing through the use of web-based digital repositories. It is also anticipated that AI technology will increase the reproducibility of science. In the past, scientists studying AI have tried to create systems that can mimic the methods used in scientific discovery (Langley, 2000). However, as AI systems can readily record and perform experiments, methods, and results, researchers anticipate an improvement in data sharing and replicability of experimental results with the advancement of AI applications (King et al. 2009, Bianchini et al, 2020). Amigoni and Schiaffonati (2007) suggest a method of using AI systems that could be able to explain scientific findings as well as promote scientific endeavours, thus leading to the development of more explainable AI. While the complexity of the phenomena scientists are trying to understand and the ever-increasing data availability frequently overwhelm scientists, there is hope that AI methods will help scientists overcome analytical limitations and explore new scientific avenues (Gil et al., 2014, Kitano, 2016, Mannocci et al., 2017). Through improved data access and an increased ability to predict valuable combinations of existing knowledge, advanced AI technologies like deep learning could facilitate the search over large and complex sets of unstructured data, leading to the discovery of new knowledge (Gil and Hirsh, 2012, Agrawal et al., 2018). It is anticipated that data-driven science would be especially helpful in scientific fields with large amounts of data but few hypotheses (Kell and Oliver, 2004).

The capacity to think creatively and devise original solutions to issues is highly regarded. With learning exercises meant to promote creativity and inquiry, Education 5.0 helps students to grow in their ability to think creatively. The curriculum is adaptable to complement this approach, giving pupils unrestricted opportunities to investigate and express their ideas (Gonçalves and Rua, 2022). It is anticipated that the cultivation of creativity will equip students to become future leaders who can invent fresh approaches to the world's most difficult problems (González et al., 2022). It has been established that virtual assistants foster creativity in students. AI-powered virtual assistants can assist students with time management, reminders, and scheduling, among other administrative duties. With the aid of these resources, students can better manage their time and finish their assignments on time by remaining focused and organized.

Critical thinking abilities are vital in the fast-paced, international world of today. The intersection of AI and critical thinking is a fascinating field of study in the ever-changing realm of education, particularly in the context of teaching literature. As the cornerstone of effective learning, critical thinking is essential to helping students develop their analytical abilities, critical interpretation skills, and intellectual autonomy. Simultaneously, the swift progression of AI technologies presents innovative opportunities for improving and innovating education. In both academic and practical contexts, critical thinking is essential for assessing data, resolving issues, and coming to well-informed conclusions (Quinn et al., 2020; Shanta and Wells, 2022). Students who engage in critical thinking learn how to evaluate arguments and information in a reasoned and systematic manner. This idea is crucial in the digital age because students are exposed to a variety of information sources and need to be able to discern between logical ideas and those that are not, as well as between facts and opinions. Students who get instruction that has a strong focus on critical thinking are better equipped to make responsible judgments and find practical answers to problems they confront in the real world (Gupta et al., 2024). A growing body of research has demonstrated how AI technologies are essential for improving language learning and critical thinking abilities (Rusdin et al., 2023). According to studies by Muthmainnah et al. (2022) and Hapsari and Wu (2022), AI tools like chatbots function as self-regulated learning platforms to enhance speaking skills and reduce emotional barriers like anxiety. The research conducted by Xiao and Zhi (2023) highlights the dual role of AI in skill and emotional development. It also highlights the unique possibilities of ChatGPT as a personalized learning assistant. Furthermore, several studies have underscored the importance of AI in fostering critical thinking abilities, hence validating its function as an enabler of higher-order cognitive abilities in 21st-century education. The results showed a nuanced understanding of critical thinking that entails challenging conventions, assessing the evidence, and examining the context. Students praised the value of AI in enhancing academic research and theoretical inspection, among other aspects of critical thinking. Academic research has also profited from AI's encouragement of critical thinking, as AI tools such as Natural Language Processing (NLP) are essential. By examining enormous volumes of text data, NLP, which uses algorithms to comprehend and manipulate human language, can conduct thorough literature assessments. It can help with the development and improvement of research questions by pointing out important themes, trends, and gaps in the body of current literature. NLP is a useful tool in academic contexts because of its capacity to process and interpret complicated linguistic patterns, which speeds up research and improves the accuracy and depth of literature study. Raharjana et al.'s (2021) demonstration of NLP's ability to effectively sort through massive academic literature serves to emphasize this utility. This is further supported by Duman and Akdemir (2021), who contend that AI can significantly increase research capacities by automating repetitive and time-consuming processes like issue identification and literature reviews. These efficiencies allow researchers to focus more of their cognitive resources on difficult activities that are essential to developing higher-order cognitive skills, such as forming hypotheses and interpreting data.

The efficacy of the other three principles is reinforced by the essential principle of communication. In any collaborative or negotiation setting, the capacity for effective and clear communication is essential to understanding and being respected (Huang, 2021). Education 5.0 helps students become more proficient communicators by teaching them how to express complicated ideas in a variety of ways in addition to words. These abilities are essential not just in daily life but also in work settings where cross-disciplinary and cross-cultural collaboration are required (Husaeni et al., 2024). Effective communication has also been accomplished in Education 5.0 thanks to features like selective information transmission, which has aided in the development of recommender systems. Recommendation systems are among the functions that are supported by AI and machine learning technologies, which are becoming more and more popular in aiding research in academic libraries. Systems that provide recommendations make an effort to find content that a particular user is likely to find interesting. This information is individualized since it is based on the user's past reading, listening, and accessing habits. Currently, a variety of methods and resources are employed to evaluate, categorize, or filter the vast quantity of data accessible on the Internet to examine user behaviour or preferences. These tools include recommender systems, natural language processing (NLP), big data, and machine learning. These methods frequently enable us to analyze user behaviour to forecast future actions or ascertain preferences. The automatic and focused release of personal information about people according to their unique interests and preferences is known as "selective dissemination of information" (SDI) (Saeidnia, 2023). It is an idea with scientific and IT roots that seeks to efficiently filter and present people with pertinent content. To handle the growing amount of information available, SDI systems were created to provide individualized information distribution and retrieval (Rzheuskyi et al., 2019). A person is always kept up to date on new advancements and developments that are pertinent to their field through selective dissemination of information, or SDI. Lastly, Connectivity acknowledges the value of networking in the globalization period. The development of students' physical and digital capacity to connect and engage in global networks is emphasized by this idea. To provide students with a broader perspective on the world and equip them to be engaged, informed global citizens, Education 5.0 investigates the use of technology to connect students with ideas, sources, and communities outside of the traditional classroom (Hwang and Tu, 2021). Students get an appreciation for diversity and the significance of cross-cultural cooperation in addressing global difficulties through an awareness of global connectedness (Ismaya et al., 2021).

APPLICATION AI IN EDUCATION 5.0

Numerous AI technologies, including machine learning, natural language processing (NLP), robots, expert systems, and image identification, are becoming more and more common in educational settings. Curriculum development and evaluation, instructional delivery and assessment, personalized learning, intelligent tutoring, virtual learning environments, automated grading, learning analytics, gamification of the learning process, and research support have all been applied to the Education 5.0 environment.

AI and Curriculum Development and Evaluation in Education 5.0

Students in Education 5.0 are given access to a real-world setting where they can acquire and use flexible skills and competencies in an actual business or industry. The curriculum must be logical and pertinent to address issues and requirements that are pertinent to the community and industry. Based on research, several authors have acknowledged the use of AI technologies, such as machine learning and the associated classification and clustering algorithms, in determining the needs of communities to include in the curriculum and to make use of when assessing the curriculum. The majority of recent research on AI and the curriculum, according to a review by Chiu and Chai (2020), has concentrated on what information and abilities should be taught in the classroom and what resources work best for teaching students. These studies have looked into the questions of what the intended curriculum results are. These issues can be answered by utilizing AI and ML technologies. For instance, the predictive powers of machine learning algorithms can ascertain the relationship between the intended results and the instructional content. Chiu and Chai (2020) support four curriculum approaches for the creation of a cogent and pertinent curriculum. These approaches are curriculum as a content, product, process, and praxis, and they are all influenced by educational, philosophical, psychological, and sociological perspectives. While each of these approaches has a distinct and independent understanding, they are all essential to the building of any comprehensive, relevant, and coherent curriculum. When curriculum is viewed as content, learners experience education as a transforming process where new skills and information are imparted through meticulous design and creation of a cogent curriculum. All of this is supported by literature, which demonstrates how AI and related technologies—such as robotics, machine learning, natural language processing, expert systems, and robotics—all help curriculum planners by identifying societal needs that can be incorporated into and assessed through the curriculum. As a result, AI is becoming more heavily incorporated into studies on curriculum quality. For instance, according to Liu et al. (2023), the use of AI to evaluate how well learning materials align with the curriculum has embraced machine learning algorithms like clustering and classification algorithms, as well as K-nearest neighbours, support vector machines, regression algorithms, and artificial neural networks to identify and predict curriculum demands as well as evaluate the connections between curriculum content and the intended curriculum outcomes. Furthermore, curriculum authors and teachers received trustworthy input from the pattern analysis of learners. By enabling personalized learning experiences and automating the use of external datasets to assess student performance, AI technologies like machine learning and natural language processing also significantly improved educational practices, according to Oluyemisi's (2023) study on the impact of AI on curriculum development in Nigeria. This implies that AI is crucial in the development of adaptive learning systems that meet the needs of both individual students and society as a whole, in the effort to create a cohesive and pertinent curriculum. Ayadole et al. (2023) are other authors who have looked into the use of AI in curriculum building and management. They also made the case that AI may enhance educational procedures and results.

AI and Instructional Delivery and Assessment in Education 5.0

The use of technology in Education 5.0 has changed the classroom setting and allowed students to take an active role in their education. An environment focused on the learner has been established through the integration of AI, the Internet of Things, and big data analytics (Huang, 2018). Instructional delivery and evaluation are the two main areas of education that have benefited from these disruptive and emergent technologies. Tests, assessments, and evaluations related to education measurement are among the various tasks that have received support in these domains. These resources can give teachers insightful knowledge of student performance, learning objectives, and the efficacy of their instruction. To assist students in identifying their areas of strength and weakness, AI-powered assessment systems, for instance, can evaluate assignment replies from students and offer tailored feedback (Nazaretsky et al., 2022). These resources can also give educators feedback on how well their lessons are working and point out areas in which they might need to modify their pedagogical approaches. Furthermore, a lot of the evaluation process can be automated with the use of AI-powered tools, which will free up instructors' time and ease their workload. Teachers' time spent evaluating essays can be reduced by using AI-powered grading tools, which can evaluate student essays and offer feedback on grammar, structure, and topic (Huang et al., 2023). According to Delgado et al. (2020), AI-powered solutions can also assist in identifying students who may be in danger of falling behind or who might benefit from extra support or remediation. These technologies can examine student data, including attendance logs and test results, and spot trends that might point to the need for intervention. This can assist educators in giving pupils who most need focused support. As a result, the creation of AI-powered tools and applications has completely changed the educational landscape by giving teachers insightful data on student performance, learning objectives, and the efficacy of their teaching. As technology develops further, it has the potential to completely change education by giving students individualized, data-driven learning and empowering educators to maximize their use of instructional methodologies to raise student achievement. As a result, these tools have produced creative ways to conduct training and evaluations.

Personalized Learning in Education 5.0

A range of educational initiatives that allow for the customization of instruction and learning pace to meet the individual needs of each student are referred to as personalized learning programs. The experience is customized to each learner's unique interests and learning preferences. This AI-powered learning application can adjust to each person's unique learning style and keep giving them increasingly challenging assignments to quicken their learning. AI-based tools and systems can personalize lessons, increase instructor productivity, and increase student engagement (Mena-Guacas et al., 2023). Using information about each student's learning trajectory, talents, and shortcomings, AI can assist in developing individualized learning programs for them. By evaluating data from several sources, including quizzes, homework, and assessments, AI can determine students' learning needs and offer tailored feedback. AI tools can be utilized for customized instruction in addition to creating lesson plans and learning activities (Adiguzel et al., 2023). This allows students to focus on the areas where they need extra guidance and learn at their own speed. Personalized learning plans for students are generated using AI-powered adaptive learning tools, such as DreamBox and Knewton, through data analysis and assessment of their strengths and shortcomings. Students can, for instance, finish a pre-assessment test to create a personalized learning plan with recommendations and targeted targets. As a result, learners of all speeds can keep going at their rate. For instance, Holotescu and Grosseck (2018) created Buddy, a teaching robot for a MOOC (Massive Open Online Course) that offers students individualized, focused learning materials.

Personalized learning systems, a crucial element of Education 5.0, are among the innovations that have arisen as AI has continued to change educational institutions. For instance, Prahani et al. (2022) state that personalized learning platforms in Education 5.0 facilitate student-directed and student-centred learning. Chen et al. (2022) have built an AI-driven model for personalised learning. This gave rise to chances in Education 5.0 for learners to generate self-directed innovations. Smart education may offer individualized learning experiences that cater to each learner's requirements, preferences, and abilities by utilizing AI and ML (Palanivel, 2020). This makes it possible for students to acquire knowledge and skills more effectively since they can concentrate on their weak points or take their time learning new subjects.

Intelligent Tutoring Systems In Education 5.0

AI-driven tutoring programs can offer kids individualized help and feedback. By providing education and support that is specifically suited to each student's learning style, these systems can help students achieve better learning results. By giving quick feedback, these systems can support students in maintaining their motivation and interest in what they are learning. Intelligent tutoring solutions powered by AI offer pupils individualized help in real time. According to Rane et al. (2024), these systems provide direction, evaluation, and extra resources based on each student's unique performance. Intelligent tutoring systems make learning more efficient and interesting by continuously evaluating knowledge and adjusting to learning speeds.

Automated Grading in Education 5.0

It has long been anticipated that AI will assist teachers in increasing productivity and saving time when grading assignments, tests, and other work that is time-consuming and costly. AI auto-graders have been implemented to evaluate student-written assignments. Modern auto graders may also determine the nature of the problem and suggest to the student how to solve it, while some can evaluate student responses with a reliability of about 90%, depending on the subject (Ahmad et al., 2023). AI can assist in automating the grading process, saving professors time and giving students instant feedback on their papers. Teachers can save a lot of time by focusing on important duties like lesson planning and student support when they use automated grading systems (Adiguzel et al., 2023). Both pupils' writing abilities and teachers' workloads may benefit from this. Furthermore, given how much time teachers spend grading assignments and examinations, AI can be used as an evaluation tool to learn how teachers grade, remove biases resulting from human brains and emotions, and free up teacher time. Essays are also evaluated by AI, in addition to multiple-choice exams. NLP algorithms are used by automated essay scoring (AES) software to assess and mark essays and other written tasks. Teachers may ensure consistent and impartial evaluation, save time on grading, and provide students instant feedback on their writing by utilizing AES software. When scoring essays automatically, a model is trained using texts that have already been manually evaluated. Subsequently, machine learning techniques are employed to ascertain the degree to which fresh texts align with, or incorporate components from, the texts utilized in the model's creation.

Predictive Analytics and Learning Analytics Tools

Learning analytics tools evaluate student learning data and offer insights into student performance, engagement, and learning outcomes using data mining and AI algorithms. AI is progressively employed in adaptive learning to gather and evaluate student learning data, identify each student's unique learning preferences and features, and then automatically modify the pace, content, and manner of instruction to best meet their needs (Wu, 2019). As more data is gathered over time, AI will become increasingly "smart" and accurate in adjusting to students' learning. This will create a positive feedback loop where students' learning efficiency will increase, the results will get better and better, and their confidence will rise as well (Yufei et al, 2020). To improve student learning outcomes, educators can use learning analytics tools to track student progress, identify kids who are at risk, and make data-driven decisions. Open Learning Analytics (OLA) and Learning Analytics and Knowledge (LAK) are two examples. The goal of educational data mining is to provide learners with automated and methodical responses. The goal of AI-based educational data mining is to create natural association rules and provide students with knowledge objects tailored to their individual needs. For instance, from a limited number of written tasks, data on students' demographic characteristics and grades can be evaluated. A machine learning regression technique that also forecasts a student's performance in the future can be utilized to do it. Additionally, data mining is becoming a potent tool for enhancing knowledge acquisition and the learning process, which will enhance our comprehension of both learners and educational environments. Put another way, teachers can use data mining to improve curriculum development in the educational system by applying predictive modelling and pattern discovery to retrieve hidden information. Personalized learning from knowledge field data, where students complete their education at their speed and choose their AI-assisted learning approach, is one of the significant uses of data mining-based AI. In a perfect world, students would select their interests through individualized learning, and teachers would modify their lesson plans and delivery strategies accordingly (Kim et al., 2018). AI can develop its intelligence more precisely and produce more dependable results by using data mining. Data from student characteristics and knowledge objects from the learner model and knowledge field model are the main focus of learning analytics. The goal is to adapt teaching strategies to the requirements and aptitude of each student, such as assisting at-risk pupils or offering feedback and course materials. It makes use of methods from the learning sciences, data visualization, machine learning, and semantics. Institutions can take proactive measures by using AI-based competency learning, for example, which produces vital data from the students and can efficiently get insights into the students and forecast the essential competencies they can pursue. Apart from competency-based learning, learning analytics leverage AI's varied learning capabilities. When it comes to drop-out problems, AI can take into account many factors to categorize prospective students according to their propensity to leave school, producing early warning systems and useful information for the universities.

Gamification Tools in Education 5.0

Gamification is the process of "engaging people, motivating action, promoting learning, and solving problems through the use of game-based mechanics, aesthetics, and game thinking." Teachers can encourage learning, raise student engagement, and give students quick feedback on their performance by utilizing gamification technologies. Students highly regard gamification as an effective educational approach that can increase their learning outcomes, engagement, productivity, and motivation and trigger both their intrinsic and extrinsic motivation, which are crucial components of Education 5.0, according to Lampropoulos and Sidiropoulos (2024), among others who have studied the effect of gamification on learning. Students' essential needs in terms of autonomy, competence and sufficiency, relatedness and sense of belonging were addressed, and the learning process became more pleasurable. In comparison to online and traditional learning, gamification is an effective learning strategy that improves academic performance, learning outcomes, motivation, engagement, and retention rates in both theoretical and applied course contexts. In their study on the effects of the gaming tool Kahoot on students' learning, Altawalbeh and Irwanto (2022) found that game-based learning promoted enjoyment, engagement, motivation, and usefulness for learning. AI and gamification work together to change traditional education into a dynamic, participatory process that offers a personalized, pleasurable learning environment (Rane et al., 2024).

VIRTUAL REALITY AND AUGMENTED REALITY TOOLS

As AI technology advances, additional technologies will be incorporated into modern education, including blockchain, augmented and virtual reality, image identification, voice semantic recognition, and machine learning. The world is now the classroom where augmented reality (AR) and virtual reality (VR) are used in education instead of only small spaces, whiteboards, and PowerPoints. Immersion technologies are used by VR and AR applications to give students dynamic, hands-on learning opportunities. Teachers can improve student learning outcomes, give students real-world experiences, and include students in hands-on learning activities by utilizing VR and AR tools. These technologies can be combined with AI in an AI-powered university to improve their capabilities and provide individualized learning experiences (Luck and Aylett, 2000).

Inspiring Educators through AI in Education 5.0

The institution wants its teachers to be outstanding educators who are proactive in their own study and skill development. Universiti Teknologi Mara (2019) defines inspiring instructors as kind, empathetic, demanding, uplifting, knowledgeable, and optimistic. Teachers can benefit from individualized learning experiences, adaptive content creation, and real-time student support by utilizing AI. By guaranteeing alignment with learning objectives and improving the efficacy of teaching tactics, the use of an instructional design matrix gives the educational process structure and coherence. By combining these two strategies, teachers may build more engaging and motivating virtual classrooms that are inclusive of all students (Ruiz-Rojas, 2023). Providing insightful and focused feedback to students is one of the most significant duties of a lecturer or class teacher. As a result, interactive learning environments (ILE) are being used by several colleges to raise the standard of mentorship and feedback.

AI in Research in Education 5.0

In addition to supporting educational AI research and innovation, fostering innovations and fostering the local development of AI technologies and tools would proactively address inequality, prejudice, and opportunity adoption. According to Salam et al. (2023), AI models like ChatGPT can help make research articles easier to read and write, but they can't take the position of writers' primary responsibilities, such as analyzing data and coming to valid findings. AI can support academic research in several ways, as studies by Wade and Wang (2016), DesRoches (2022), and de Jong and Bus (2023) show. These consist of reviewing the literature, analyzing data, forecasting and prediction, designing experiments, and working together. By automating time-consuming processes, offering fresh perspectives, and facilitating research collaboration, AI has the potential to greatly increase the efficacy and efficiency of academic research.

CHALLENGES

Even though AI has a lot of potential for use in education, there are still obstacles and limitations. Because of several new issues, the poor world continues to have relatively limited acceptance and utilization of this cutting-edge technology. According to Patel and Ragolane (2024), these difficulties include learning the requisite skills, the lack of a structured data environment, moral dilemmas, governmental regulations, poor infrastructure, and poor network connectivity. Therefore, if these issues are not resolved, they may have a major negative influence on the economic development of Africa (Wang'ang'a, 2024). Concerns about the ethical implications of AI algorithms in educational settings have been brought up in recent literature. For example, studies have shown that AI-based assessment tools may contain algorithmic bias, which unintentionally maintains current educational disparities. Furthermore, concerns about data security and privacy have become important factors to take into account when implementing AI in educational settings (Rane et al., 2024). Since ChatGPT and other AI systems analyze large volumes of data, particularly sensitive data, data security is crucial. It is crucial to set up strong cyber security procedures to protect sensitive data against breaches and illegal access. Furthermore, the generated content's accuracy and dependability are of the utmost importance. Inaccuracies or false information can result in expensive mistakes in both industrial and educational contexts. Therefore, improving the accuracy and relevance of generative AI by fine-tuning its underlying algorithms is still a challenge. AI is used in education to provide pupils with personalized learning experiences. The difficulty, therefore, is in creating a curriculum that respects moral principles and advances constructive educational ideals while simultaneously catering to the unique requirements and learning preferences of each student. Additionally, a lot of universities—especially those in developing nations—have had to deal with social and economic issues that have made it more difficult for them to successfully implement Education 5.0. While universities in poor nations are gradually moving toward including their goals for development in their curricula, organized efforts to incorporate the community are still absent. Universities continue to function as separate entities, mostly focused on internal matters (Togo and Gandidzanwa, 2020).

CONCLUSIONS

The need to meet social demands and adopt new digital technologies, such as AI, the Internet of Things, and big data analytics, has caused the field of education to alter over time. Education 5.0 has emerged as a result of these developments. Although this paradigm has been interpreted differently around the world, research indicates that its essential component is the emerging and disruptive technologies that have improved learning overall by offering research support, intelligent tutoring systems, automated grading systems, curriculum development and review, personalized learning, and assessment. Despite these advantages, educational institutions have encountered many obstacles in their attempts to implement AI in Education 5.0.

Recommendations

To address these issues, academics and decision-makers support a sophisticated approach to AI integration in education that puts an emphasis on ethical issues and provides protection against unfavourable outcomes. New developments in AI research, such as differential privacy and federated learning, offer viable solutions for resolving privacy issues and maintaining the benefits of personalized learning. Educators may leverage AI's potential to enhance learning outcomes while protecting sensitive student data by implementing privacy-preserving strategies and decentralizing AI model training. To guarantee the ethical and fair application of AI in educational settings, significant obstacles such as data privacy issues, ethical concerns, and the possibility of biases in AI algorithms must be overcome. The success and long-term viability of AI-driven education depend critically on finding a balance between technological innovation and moral considerations (Rane et al., 2024).AI innovations like ChatGPT and generative AI can continue to spur innovation, increase productivity, and positively impact society through responsible development, considerate regulations, and ongoing research. This will help to shape a future in which technology and people coexist peacefully (Rane, 2024). The requirement for thorough strategic planning and institutional frameworks to direct the application of AI in higher education institutions is another significant obstacle. As of right now, a small number of emerging nations have embraced AI on an as-needed basis, which has resulted in disjointed and uneven applications. Consequently, customized strategic frameworks that may harmonize technology breakthroughs with the distinct requirements of higher education administration in these emerging nations are desperately needed. Therefore, institutions in the developing world can more effectively utilize AI's promise to improve educational outcomes and operational efficiency when higher education institutions create strong policies and invest in infrastructure and training.

REFERENCES

Adiguzel, T., Kaya, M. H., & Cansu, F. K. (2023). Revolutionizing education with AI: Exploring the transformative potential of ChatGPT. *Contemporary Educational Technology*, 15(3), ep429.

Agrawal, A., McHale, J., & Oettl, A. (2018). Finding needles in haystacks: artificial Intelligence and recombinant growth. National Bureau of Economic Research, Working paper.

Ahmad, S., Umirzakova, S., Mujtaba, G., Amin, M. S., & Whangbo, T. (2023). *Education 5.0: Requirements*. Enabling Technologies, and Future Directions.

Al Husaeni, D. F., Al Husaeni, D. N., Nandiyanto, A. B. D., Rokhman, M., Chalim, S., Chano, J., & Roestamy, M. (2024). How technology can change educational research? definition, factors for improving quality of education and computational bibliometric analysis. *ASEAN Journal of Science and Engineering*, 4(2), 127–166.

Alharbi, A. M. (2023). Implementation of Education 5.0 in Developed and Developing Countries: A Comparative Study. *Creative Education*, 14, 914–942.

Altawalbeh, K., & Irwanto, I. (2023). Game-Based Learning: The Impact of Kahoot On a Higher Education Online Classroom. *Journal of Educational Technology and Instruction*, 2(1), 30–49.

Amigoni, F., & Schiaffonati, V. (2007). The multi-agent technology and paradigm Within the Scientific discovery. *International Journal of Artificial Intelligence Tools*, 16(2), 219–242.

Association of African Universities. (2023). Artificial Intelligence in African Higher

Bassey, B. A., Ubi, I. O., Anagbogu, G. E., & Owan, V. J. (2020). Permutation of UTME multiple-choice test items on performance in the use of English and mathematics among prospective higher education students. *The Journal of Social Sciences Research*, 6(4), 483–493.

Bianchini, S., Muller, M., and Pelletier, P. (2020). Deep Learning in Science, Papers 2009.01575, *arXiv.org, revised Sep 2020.*

Carayannis, E. G., & Morawska, J. (2023). University and Education 5.0 for emerging trends, policies and practices in the concept of Industry 5.0 and Society 5.0,' in *Industry 5.0: Creative and Innovative Organizations*. Springer, (2023):1–25.

Chen, W. (2022). Research on the design of intelligent music teaching systems based on virtual reality technology. *Computational Intelligence and Neuroscience*.

Chen, X., Zou, D., Xie, H., Cheng, G., & Liu, C. (2022). Two Decades of Artificial Intelligence in Education: Contributors, Collaborations, Research Topics, Challenges, and Future Directions. *Journal of Educational Technology & Society*, 25(1), 28–47.

Chiu, T. K. F., & Chai, C. (2020). *Sustainable Curriculum Planning for Artificial Intelligence Education: A Self-determination Theory Perspective*. Sustainability. MDPI.

Cipolla, R., Gal, Y., & Kendall, A. (2018). Multi-task Learning Using Uncertainty to Weigh Losses for Scene Geometry and Semantics. *2018 IEEE/CVF Conference on Computer Vision and Pattern Recognition*.

de Jong, R. M., & Bus, D. (2023). Searching Scholarly Literature with Artificial Intelligence: An Introduction. *Research Software Community Leiden*, 12, 8–21.

Dec, G., Stadnicka, D., Paśko, Ł., Mądziel, M., & Figliè, R. (2022). Role of academics in Transferring knowledge and skills on artificial intelligence, the internet of things and edge computing. *Sensors (Basel)*. PMID: 35408110

Delgado, H. O. K., de Azevedo Fay, A., Sebastiany, M. J., & Silva, A. D. C. (2020). Artificial intelligence adaptive learning tools. *BELT-Brazilian English Language Teaching Journal*, 11(2), e38749–e38749.

DesRoches, A. (2022). Harnessing the Power of Artificial Intelligence in Scholarly Publishing. *Editorial Office News*, 15, 9–11.

Duan, S., & Zhao, Y. (2023). Knowledge graph analysis of artificial intelligence Application research in the nursing field based on visualization technology. *Alexandria Engineering Journal*.

Duman, M. Ç., & Akdemir, B. (2021). A study to determine the effects of industry 4.0 technology components on organizational performance. *Technological Forecasting and Social Change*, 167(6), 1–14.

Dupri, D., Candra, O., & Nazirun, N. (2021). The Implementation of Mini Volleyball in Physical Education to Increase Students' Creative Thinking Ability. *International Journal of Human Movement and Sports Sciences*, 9(4A), 89–93.

Garcia, L. (2020). Strategic intelligence teaching to leverage professional success.

Gerstein, J. (2014). *Moving from Education 1.0 Through Education 2.0 Towards Education 3.0*. Educational Technology Faculty Publications and Presentations. Boise State University Scholar Works.

Gil, Y., Greaves, M., Hendler, J., & Hirsh, H. (2014). Amplify scientific discovery with Artificial intelligence. *Science*, 346(6206), 171–172. PMID: 25301606

Gil, Y., & Hirsh, H. (2012). Discovery Informatics: AI opportunities in scientific Discovery. *AAAI Fall Symposium.*

Gonçalves, C., & Rua, O. (2022). *Learning Creativity and Students' Performance: The Academia Contributions. Developing Entrepreneurial Ecosystems.* IGI Global.

González, L., Neyem, A., Contreras, I. and Molina, D. (2022). Improving learning Experiences in software Engineering capstone courses using artificial intelligence virtual assistants. *Computers in Engineering education. 30(2).*

Gupta, A. K., Aggarwal, V., Sharma, V., & Naved, M. (2024). *Education 4.0 and Web 3.0 Technologies Application for Enhancement of Distance Learning Management Systems in the COVID–19 Era.* Education Improvement.

Hapsari, I. P., & Wu, T. (2022). AI chatbot learning model in English-speaking Skill: Alleviating speaking anxiety, boosting enjoyment, and fostering critical thinking. In Lecture Notes in Computer Science: 444–453.

Holotescu, C., & Grosseck, G. (2018). Towards a MOOC-related Strategy in Romania. *BRAIN.Broad Research in Artificial Intelligence and Neuroscience*, 9, 99–109.

Huang, S. (2021). Design and development of educational robot teaching resources using artificial intelligence technology. *Journal of Emerging Technologies in Learning,* Huang, X., Zou, D., Cheng, G., Chen, X., and Xie, H. (2023). Trends, research Issues and applications of artificial intelligence in language education. *Journal of Educational Technology & Society*, 26(1), 112–131.

Huang, S. P. (2018). Effects of using artificial intelligence teaching system for environmental education on environmental knowledge and attitude. *Eurasia Journal of Mathematics, Science and Technology Education*, 14(7), 3277–3284.

Hwang, G., & Tu, Y. (2021). Roles and Research Trends of Artificial Intelligence In Mathematics Education: A Bibliometric Mapping Analysis and Systematic Review. *Mathematics*, 2021, 9.

Ismaya, B., Perdana, I., Arifin, A., Fadjarajani, S., Anantadjaya, S. P.D., and Muhammadiah, M. (2021). Merdeka Belajar in the Point of View of Learning Technology in the Era of 4.0 and Society 5.0. *A l- Ishlah: Ju rnal Pendidikan.. 13 (3): 1777-1785.*

Judijanto, L., Ili, L., & Wardhana, M. G. (2024). Education 5.0: Collaboration and Creativity in improving students' digital intelligence. [INJOSEDU]. *The International Journal of Social Education*, 1(3), 682–693.

Kell, D. B., & Oliver, S. G. (2004). Here is the evidence, now what is the Hypothesis? The complementary roles of inductive and hypothesis-driven science in the post-genomic era. *BioEssays*, 26, 99–105. PMID: 14696046

Kim, Y., Soyata, T., and Behnagh, R.F. (2018). Towards emotionally aware AI Smart classroom: Current issues and directions for engineering and education, *IEEE Access*, (6) 5308_5331.

King, R. D.. (2009). The Automation of Science. *Science*, 324(5923), 85–89. PMID: 19342587

Kitano, H. (2016). Artificial Intelligence to Win the Nobel Prize and Beyond: Creating The Engine for Scientific Discovery. *AI Magazine*, 37(1), 39–49.

Kotecha, K. (2023). Employing multimodal co-learning to evaluate the robustness of sensor fusion for Industry 5.0 tasks. *Soft Computing*, 27(7), 4139–4155.

Kuru-Çetin, S., Nayir, F., & Taşkın, P. (2020). Okul yöneticilerin eğitimde değişime ilişkin görüşleri. [MSKU Journal of Education]. *Muğla Sıtkı Koçman Üniversitesi Eğitim Fakültesi Dergisi*, 7(1), 12–23.

Lampropoulos, G., & Sidiropoulos, A. (2024). Impact of Gamification on Students' Learning Outcomes and Academic Performance: A Longitudinal Study Comparing Online, Traditional, and Gamified Learning. *Education in Science*, 14(367). Advance online publication. DOI: 10.3390/educsci14040367

Langley, P. (2000). The computational support of scientific discovery. *International Journal of Human-Computer Studies*, 53, 393–410.

Li, S., & Rutab, N. M. P. (2023). An analysis of education problems in the post-pandemic era of COVID-19. *Adult Higher Educ.*, 5(1), 60–64.

Liu, J., Li, H., Zhu,H. Li, H, Zhang, X., Zhou, G., Lou, D, and Chen, Y. (2023).

Machine Learning Based Analysis of the Curriculum Standards and Textbooks of Middle School Biology Teaching. (2023). Case of "Curriculum Ideological and Political". *ICEKIM 2023. AHCS*, 13, 292–303.

Makrides, G. (2020). The evolution of Education 1.0 to Education 4.0: Is it an Evolution or a revolution? Anniversary Scientific Conference "Synergetics and Reflection in Mathematics Education", 16-18 October 2020, Pamporovo, Bulgaria.

Mannocci, A., Salatino, A. A., Osborne, F., & Motta, E. (2017). 2100 AI: Reflections on the mechanisation of scientific discovery. In: Recoding Black Mirror @ ISWC '17, 21-25 Oct 2017, Wien, Austria.

Melluso, N., Fareri, S., Fantoni, G., Bonaccorsi, A., Chiarello, F., Coli, E., Giordano, V., Manfredi, P., & Manafi, S. (2020). *Lights and shadows of COVID-19, Technology and Industry 4.0*. https://doi.org/DOI: 10.48550/ARXIV.2004.13457

Mena-Guacas, A. F., Urueña Rodríguez, J. A., Santana Trujillo, D. M., Gómez-Galán, J., & López-Meneses, E. (2023). Collaborative learning and skill development for the educational growth of artificial intelligence: A systematic review. *Contemporary Educational Technology*, 15(3), ep428.

Muthmainnah, S., Ibna Seraj, P. M., Oteir, I., & Balakrishnan, B. (2022). Playing

Nazaretsky, T., Ariely, M., Cukurova, M., & Alexandron, G. (2022). Teachers' trust in AI-powered educational technology and a professional development program to improve it. *British Journal of Educational Technology*, 53(4), 914–931.

Oluyemisi, O. M. (2023). Impact of Artificial Intelligence in Curriculum Development in Nigerian Tertiary Education. *International Journal of Educational Research*, 12(2), 2023.

Ouyang, F and Jiao, P. (2021). Artificial intelligence in education: The three

Palanivel, K. (2020). Emerging Technologies to Smart Education. *International Journal of Computer Trends and Technology*, (68), 5–16.

(2021). Paradigms. Computers and Education. *Artificial Intelligence*, 2, 100020.

Patel, S., & Ragolane, M. (2024). The Implementation of Artificial Intelligence in South African Higher Education Institutions: Opportunities and Challenges. *Technium Education and Humanities*, (9), 51–65.

Patil, A., Thakur, K., Gandhi, K., Savale, V., & Sayyed, N. (2022). A review on Industry 5.0: The techno-social revolution. *Int. J. Mech. Eng.*, 7(5), 1–5.

Prahani, B. K., Rizki, I. A., Jatmiko, B., Suprapto, N. and Amelia, T.(2022). Artificial Intelligence in Education Research During the Last Ten Years: A Review and Bibliometric Study. *iJET 17(08)*.

Quinn, S., Hogan, M., Dwyer, C., Finn, P., & Fogarty, E. (2020). Development and Validation of the student-educator negotiated critical thinking dispositions scale (SENCTDS). *Thinking Skills and Creativity*, 38(4), 100710–100717.

Raharjana, I. K., Siahaan, D., & Fatichah, C. (2021). User stories and natural Language processing: A systematic literature review. *Institute of Electrical and Electronics Engineers Access*, 9(1), 53811–53826.

Rane, N. L., Choudhary, S. P., & Rane, J. (2024). Education 4.0 and 5.0: Integrating Artificial Intelligence (AI) for personalized and adaptive learning. *Journal Of Artificial Intelligence And Robotics*, 1(1), 29–43.

Rane, N. T. (2024). ChatGPT and similar generative artificial intelligence (AI) for smart industry: Role, challenges, and opportunities for Industry 4.0, Industry 5.0, and Society 5.0. *Innovations In Business And Strategic Management*, 2(1), 10–17.

Ruiz-Rojas, L.I., Acosta-Vargas, P., De-Moreta-Llovet, J., and Gonzalez-Rodriguez, M. (2023). Empowering Education with Generative Artificial Intelligence

Rzheuskyi, A., Matsuik, H., Veretennikova, N., & Vaskiv, R. (Eds.). (2019).

Saeidnia, H. (2023). Using ChatGPT as a digital/smart reference robot: how may ChatGPT impact digital reference services? *Information Matters, 2(5).*

Salam, M. Y., Taman, M. M. and Mudinillah, A. (2023). Using Artificial Intelligence for Education in the Education 5.0 Era to Improve Reading Skills. *Arabiyat: Jurnal Pendidikan Bahasa Arab dan Kebahasaaraban. 10(2): 149-162.*

Shanta, S., & Wells, J. G. (2022). T/E design-based learning: Assessing student Critical thinking and problem-solving abilities. *International Journal of Technology and Design Education*, 32(1), 267–285.

Togo, M and Gandidzanwa, C. P. (2021). The role of Education 5.0 in accelerating

Wade, A. D., & Wang, K. (2016). The Rise of Machines: Artificial Intelligence Meets scholarly content. *Learned Publishing*, 29, 201–205.

Wang, Y., Liu, C., & Tu, Y.-F. (2021). Factors affecting the adoption of AI-based Applications in higher education: An analysis of teachers perspectives using structural equation modelling. *Journal of Educational Technology & Society*, 24(3), 116–129.

Wang'ang'a, A. W. (2024). Consequences of Artificial Intelligence on Teaching and Learning in Higher Education in Kenya: Literature Review East African. *Journal of Education Studies*, 7(1), 202–215.

Wu, B. (2019). Personalized Education for Graduate Students Driven by Artificial Intelligence and Big Data. *Teaching of Forestry Region*, (7).

Xia, C., Li, X., & Cao, S. (2023). Challenges for the government-controlled higher Education system in China. *International Journal of Educational Development*, (97), 102721.

Xiao, Y., & Zhi, Y. (2023). An exploratory study of EFL learners' use of ChatGPT For language Learning tasks: Experience and perceptions. *Languages (Basel, Switzerland)*, 8(3), 1–12.

Yufei, L., Saleh, S. Jiahui, H, Mohamad, S., and Abdullah,S. (2020). Review of The Application of Artificial Intelligence in Education. *International Journal of Innovation, Creativity and Change. 12(8).*

KEY TERMS AND DEFINITIONS

Artificial Intelligence: The ability of machines to reason and perform actions associated with humans.

Chatbot: An online conversational agent.

Education 5.0: A paradigm of education that integrates technology in solving real-world problems.

Personalised Learning: Learning that is individualised.

Intelligent Tutoring Systems: Online AI-driven learning platforms.

Learning Analytics: AI technologies that harness computing power to analyse the learning patterns of learners

Selective Dissemination of Information: Targeted communication as per users' needs.

Virtual Reality: Immersive technologies for supporting virtual learning of real-world experiences.

Compilation of References

Abad-Segura, E., Gonzalez-Zamar, M.-D., la Rosa, A. L., & Morales Cevallos, M. B. (2020). Sustainability of educational technologies: An approach to augmented reality research. *Sustainability*, 12(10), 4091.

Abrenilla, E. M., Redido, C., Abendan, C. F., & Kilag, O. K. (2023). The Next Chapter of ELT: Embracing AI-Infused Pedagogies and Evolving Educational Strategies in the Post-Pandemic Landscape. *Excellencia: International Multidisciplinary Journal of Education (2994-9521)*, *1*(5), 124-135. https://multijournals.org/index.php/excellencia-imje/article/view/106

Adiguzel, T., Kaya, M. H., & Cansu, F. K. (2023). Revolutionizing education with AI: Exploring the transformative potential of ChatGPT. *Contemporary Educational Technology*, 15(3), ep429.

Agbong-Coates, I. J. G. (2024). ChatGPT integration significantly boosts personalized learning outcomes: A Philippine study. *International Journal of Educational Management and Development Studies*, 5(2), 165–186. DOI: 10.53378/353067

Agrawal, A., McHale, J., & Oettl, A. (2018). Finding needles in haystacks: artificial Intelligence and recombinant growth. National Bureau of Economic Research, Working paper.

Ahmad, S., Umirzakova, S., Mujtaba, G., Amin, M. S., & Whangbo, T. (2023). Education 5.0: requirements, enabling technologies, and future directions. *ArXiv Preprint ArXiv:2307.15846*.

Ahmadi, A. (2023). Designing an educational program based on social robot technology and its impact on social skills and academic achievement motivation of high-functioning autism spectrum disorder students [thesis]. Tehran, Iran: Allameh Tabataba'i University;

Ahmad, S., Umirzakova, S., Mujtaba, G., Amin, M. S., & Whangbo, T. (2023). *Education 5.0: Requirements*. Enabling Technologies, and Future Directions.

Ahmed, S. Z., Weidner, C., Jensen, J. H. M., Sherson, J., & Lewandowski, H. (2021). Student use of a quantum simulation and visualization tool. *European Journal of Physics*, ●●●, 43.

Ahsan, M., Based, M. A., Haider, J., & Kowalski, M. (2021). An intelligent system for automatic fingerprint identification using feature fusion by Gabor filter and deep learning. *Computers & Electrical Engineering*, 95, 107387.

Akavova, A., Temirkhanova, Z., & Lorsanova, Z. Adaptive learning and artificial intelligence in the educational space. In: E3S Web of Conferences (2023)

Akgun, S., & Greenhow, C. (2021). Artificial intelligence in education: Addressing ethical challenges in K-12 settings. *AI and Ethics 2021 2:3*, 2(3), 431–440. DOI: 10.1007/s43681-021-00096-7

Aktaş, H., & Çağman, N. (2007). Hacı Akta¸ s and Naim C¸a˘gman. Soft sets and soft groups. *Information Sciences*, 177(13), 2726–2735. DOI: 10.1016/j.ins.2006.12.008

Al Husaeni, D. F., Al Husaeni, D. N., Nandiyanto, A. B. D., Rokhman, M., Chalim, S., Chano, J., & Roestamy, M. (2024). How technology can change educational research? definition, factors for improving quality of education and computational bibliometric analysis. *ASEAN Journal of Science and Engineering*, 4(2), 127–166.

Alalwan, N., Cheng, L., Al-Samarraie, H., Yousef, R., Ibrahim Alzahrani, A., & Sarsam, S. M. (2020). Challenges and Prospects of Virtual Reality and Augmented Reality Utilization among Primary School Teachers: A Developing Country Perspective. *Studies in Educational Evaluation*, 66. Advance online publication. DOI: 10.1016/j.stueduc.2020.100876

Al-Ansi, A. M., Jaboob, M., Garad, A., & Al-Ansi, A. (2023). Analyzing augmented reality (AR) and virtual reality (VR) recent development in education. *Social Sciences & Humanities Open*, 8(1). Advance online publication. DOI: 10.1016/j.ssaho.2023.100532

Alban, A. Q., Alhaddad, A. Y., Al-Ali, A., So, W. C., Connor, O., Ayesh, M., & Cabibihan, J. J. (2023). Heart rate as a predictor of challenging behaviours among children with autism from wearable sensors in social robot interactions. *Robotics (Basel, Switzerland)*, 12(2), 55.

Alda, R., Boholano, H., & Dayagbil, F. (2020). Teacher education institutions in the Philippines towards education 4.0. *International Journal of Learning. Teaching and Educational Research*, 19(8), 137–154. DOI: 10.26803/ijlter.19.8.8

Aleandri, G. (2021). lifelong, lifewide y lifedeeP learning. análisis y PersPectivas Pedagógicas. EXPERIENCIAS Y APRENDIzAJES A LO LARGO DE LA VIDA, 19.

Aleke, B., Ojiako, U., & Wainwright, D. (2011). Social drivers for ICT diffusion among agrarian business enterprises in Nigeria. *International Journal of Technology Diffusion*, 2(2), 19–31. DOI: 10.4018/jtd.2011040102

Aleven, V., McLaughlin, E. A., Glenn, R. A., & Koedinger, K. R. (2016). Instruction based on adaptive learning technologies. In Mayer, R. E., & Alexander, P. A. (Eds.), *Handbook of research on learning and instruction* (pp. 522–560). Routledge.

AlGerafi, M. A. M., Zhou, Y., Oubibi, M., & Wijaya, T. T. (2023). Unlocking the potential: A comprehensive evaluation of augmented reality and virtual reality in education. *Electronics (Basel)*, 12(18), 3953.

Alharbi, A. M. (2023). Implementation of Education 5.0 in Developed and Developing Countries: A Comparative Study. *Creative Education*, 14(5), 914–942. DOI: 10.4236/ce.2023.145059

Aliabadi, R., Singh, A., & Wilson, E. (2023). Transdisciplinary AI Education: The Confluence of Curricular and Community Needs in the Instruction of Artificial Intelligence.

Ali, M. I., Feng, F., Liu, X., Min, W. K., & Shabir, M. (2009). On some new operations in soft set theory. *Computers & Mathematics with Applications (Oxford, England)*, 57(9), 1547–1553. DOI: 10.1016/j.camwa.2008.11.009

Alizadehsalehi, S., Hadavi, A., & Huang, J. C. (2021). Assessment of AEC students' performance using BIM-into-VR. *Applied Sciences (Basel, Switzerland)*, 11(7), 3225.

Alnasyan, B., Basheri, M., & Alassafi, M. (2024). The power of Deep Learning techniques for predicting student performance in Virtual Learning Environments: A systematic literature review. In *Computers and Education: Artificial Intelligence* (Vol. 6). Elsevier B.V. DOI: 10.1016/j.caeai.2024.100231

Alqahtani, F., Katsigiannis, S., & Ramzan, N. (2020). Using wearable physiological sensors for affect-aware intelligent tutoring systems. *IEEE Sensors Journal*, 21(3), 3366–3378.

Al-Samarraie, H., Shamsuddin, A., & Alzahrani, A. I. (2020). A flipped classroom model in higher education: A review of the evidence across disciplines. *Educational Technology Research and Development*, 68(3), 1017–1051. DOI: 10.1007/s11423-019-09718-8

Altawalbeh, K., & Irwanto, I. (2023). Game-Based Learning: The Impact of Kahoot On a Higher Education Online Classroom. *Journal of Educational Technology and Instruction*, 2(1), 30–49.

Altman, C., & Zapatrin, R. (2009). Backpropagation training in adaptive quantum networks. *International Journal of Theoretical Physics*, 49, 2991–2997.

Alvarez-Rodriguez, U., Lamata, L., Escandell-Montero, P., Martín-Guerrero, J. D., & Solano, E. (2016). Quantum machine learning without measurements. arXiv preprint arXiv:1612.05535.

Amado, J. A., Dayson, C. J. P., Gipaya, P. N., Hipos, A. M. G., Ortile, F. F., & Digo, G. S. (2024). Assessing the Impact of AI Generative Tools on Administrative and Supervisory Practices in Education. *Asia Pacific Journal of Management*, ●●●, 32–40.

Ambit, M. (2024). Artificial Intelligence Tools: Teachers' Pedagogical Adaptation in English Curriculum. *Nexus International Journal of Science and Education, 1*(2), 1–30. https://nijse.org/index.php/home/article/view/92

American Educational Research Association. (2011). Code of ethics. *Educational Researcher*, 40(3), 145–156. DOI: 10.3102/0013189X11410403

Amigoni, F., & Schiaffonati, V. (2007). The multi-agent technology and paradigm Within the Scientific discovery. *International Journal of Artificial Intelligence Tools*, 16(2), 219–242.

Aneesh, P. (2023). Developing an IoT-enabled smart classroom S3TH system. *Proceedings of ICIRCA 2023*. https://doi.org/DOI: 10.1109/icirca57980.2023.10220862

Ang, S. M. O., & Aragon, M. J. D. (2020). *Development of AI-Enhanced Information Technology Program: Preparing Today's Students in AI Era* (No. 4049). EasyChair. https://easychair.org/publications/preprint/dQmN

Angara, P., Stege, U., & MacLean, A. Quantum computing for high-school students an experience report. *2020 IEEE International Conference on Quantum Computing and Engineering (QCE)* pp. 323–329 (2020)

Angara, P., Stege, U., MacLean, A., M¨uller, H. A., & Markham, T. (2022). Teaching quantum computing to high-school-aged youth: A hands-on approach. *IEEE Transactions on Quantum Engineering*, 3, 1–15.

Anggriani, A., Sarwi, S., & Masturi, M. (2020). The effectiveness of guided discovery in distance learning to improve scientific literacy competencies of primary school students. *Journal of Primary Education*, 9(5), 454–462.

Ann Bautista, M. G., Roy Evangelista, I., Culaba, A., Concepcion, R., & Dadios, E. (2022). Technology Adoption of Augmented and Virtual Reality in a Progressive Philippines: A Socio-techno-economical Analysis. *2022 IEEE 14th International Conference on Humanoid, Nanotechnology, Information Technology, Communication and Control, Environment, and Management, HNICEM 2022*. https://doi.org/DOI: 10.1109/HNICEM57413.2022.10109429

Apicella, A., Arpaia, P., Frosolone, M., Improta, G., Moccaldi, N., & Pollastro, A. (2022). EEG-based measurement system for monitoring student engagement in learning 4.0. *Scientific Reports*, 12(1), 5857.

Aquino, J. M. D., & Sancon, R. J. S. The Philippine Legal Framework on the utilization of Artificial Intelligence (AI) in strengthening initiatives in combating climate change: an analysis on AI roles, opportunities and legal issues. UP Los Baños Journal, 20(2), 6.

Aquino, M. F. M., & Noroña, M. I. (2021, March). Enhancing cyber security in the Philippine academe: A risk-based IT project assessment approach. In *Proceedings of the international conference on industrial engineering and operations management* (pp. 5166-5179). http://dx.doi.org/DOI: 10.46254/AN11.20210878

Arango, F., Chang, C., Esche, S. K., & Chassapis, C. (2007, October). A scenario for collaborative learning in virtual engineering laboratories. In 2007 37th annual frontiers in education conference-global engineering: knowledge without borders, opportunities without passports (pp. F3G-7). IEEE.

Araujo, I. C., & Da Silva, A. J. (2020, July). Quantum ensemble of trained classifiers. In *2020 International Joint Conference on Neural Networks (IJCNN)* (pp. 1-8). IEEE.

Archibald, J., & Hare, J. (2017). *Learning, knowing, sharing: Celebrating successes in K-12 Aboriginal education in British Columbia*. Office of Indigenous Education/ Indigenous Education Institute of Canada, University of British Columbia.

Arias-Masa, J., Alonso-D'ıaz, L., Cubo-Delgado, S., Guti'errez-Esteban, P., & Yuste-Tosina, R. (2014). Assessment of the use of synchronous virtual classrooms in higher education. *The New Educational Review*.

Arnold, K., & Pistilli, M. D. (2012). Course Signals: Using Learning Analytics to Increase Student Success. *in Proceedings of the 2nd International Conference on Learning Analytics and Knowledge*, ACM, 267–270.

Artino, A. R.Jr, La Rochelle, J. S., Dezee, K. J., & Gehlbach, H. (2014). Developing questionnaires for educational research: AMEE Guide No. 87. *Medical Teacher*, 36(6), 463–474. DOI: 10.3109/0142159X.2014.889814 PMID: 24661014

Asif, R., Merceron, A., Ali, S. A., & Haider, N. G. (2017). Analyzing undergraduate students' performance using educational data mining. *Computers & Education*, 113, 177–194. DOI: 10.1016/j.compedu.2017.05.007

Association of African Universities. (2023). Artificial Intelligence in African Higher

August, S. E., & Tsaima, A. (2021). Artificial intelligence and machine learning: an instructor's exoskeleton in the future of education. Innovative Learning Environments in STEM Higher Education: Opportunities, Challenges, and Looking Forward, 79-105.

Auld, G., Snyder, I., & Henderson, M. (2012). Mobile phones are used as resources for literacy learning in a remote Indigenous community in Australia. *Language and Education*, 26(4), 279–296. DOI: 10.1080/09500782.2012.691512

Ávila-Herrera, S., & Guevara, C. (2021). Development of a Methodology for the Learning-Teaching Process Through Virtual and Augmented Reality. In Intelligent Human Systems Integration 2021: Proceedings of the 4th International Conference on Intelligent Human Systems Integration (IHSI 2021): Integrating People and Intelligent Systems, February 22-24, 2021, Palermo, Italy (pp. 651-656). Springer International Publishing.

Ayanwale, M. A., Adelana, O. P., Molefi, R. R., Adeeko, O., & Ishola, A. M. (2024). Examining artificial intelligence literacy among pre-service teachers for future classrooms. *Computers and Education Open*, 6, 100179. DOI: 10.1016/j.caeo.2024.100179

Azuma, R. T. (1997). A Survey of Augmented Reality. *Presence: Teleoperators and Virtual Environments/MIT Press*.

Bailey, T. R., Hughes, K. L., & Moore, D. T. (2003). *Working knowledge: Work-based learning and education reform*. Routledge. DOI: 10.4324/9780203463956

Bajaj, M. (2015). 'Pedagogies of resistance' and critical peace education praxis. *Journal of Peace Education*, 12(2), 154–166. DOI: 10.1080/17400201.2014.991914

Bajaj, M., & Hantzopoulos, M. (Eds.). (2016). *Peace education: International perspectives*. Bloomsbury Academic.

Baker, R. S. (2016). Big data and education: How analytics can transform learning and teaching. *Educational Data Mining Journal*, 8(2), 10–26. DOI: 10.1145/2895417

Baker, R. S., D'Mello, S. K., Rodrigo, M. M., & Graesser, A. C. (2010). Better to be frustrated than bored: The incidence, persistence, and impact of learners' emotions during interactions with three different computer-based learning environments. *International Journal of Human-Computer Studies*, 68(4), 223–241.

Baker, R. S., Esbenshade, L., Vitale, J., & Karumbaiah, S. (2022). Using demographic data as predictor variables: A questionable choice. DOI: 10.35542/osf.io/y4wvj

Baker, R. S., & Yacef, K. (2011). The state of educational data mining in 2009. *Proceedings of the 2nd International Conference on Educational Data Mining*, 3-16.

Bala, K., Colvin, A., Christiansen, M. H., Heinemann, A. W., Kreps, S., Levine, L., Liang, C., Mimno, D., Rush, S., Snyder, D., Tarlow, W. E., Thoemmes, F., Vanderlan, R., Stevenson Won, A., Zehnder, A., & Ziewitz, M. (2023). *Generative Artificial Intelligence for Education and Pedagogy*.

Balahadia, F. F., Miranda, J. P. P., & Hernandez, H. E. (2023, November). Teachers' and Students' Awareness on the Uses of ChatGPT: A Cross-Sectional Case Study. In *2023 IEEE 15th International Conference on Humanoid, Nanotechnology, Information Technology, Communication and Control, Environment, and Management (HNICEM)* (pp. 1-5). IEEE. https://doi.org/DOI: 10.1109/HNICEM60674.2023.10589186

Bala, P., Kulathuramaiyer, N., & Eng, T. (2022). *Digital socio-technical innovation and Indigenous knowledge*. IntechOpen., DOI: 10.5772/intechopen.101861

Bala, P., & Tan, C. (2021). Digital inclusion of the orang asli of peninsular Malaysia: Remote virtual mechanism for usability of telecentres amongst Indigenous peoples. *The Electronic Journal on Information Systems in Developing Countries*, 87(4). Advance online publication. DOI: 10.1002/isd2.12171

Balaquiao, E. C. (2024). Optimizing Students' Performance through Artificial Intelligence (AI) Technology: A Gamified Approach to Smart Learning Environment. *Journal of Pedagogy and Education Science*, 3(02), 104–114. DOI: 10.56741/jpes. v3i02.515

Bandura, A. (1977). *Social learning theory*. Prentice Hall.

Banham, D., Roder, D., Eckert, M., Howard, N., Canuto, K., & Brown, A. (2019). Cancer treatment and the risk of cancer death among aboriginal and non-aboriginal South Australians: Analysis of a matched cohort study. *BMC Health Services Research*, 19(1). Advance online publication. DOI: 10.1186/s12913-019-4534-y PMID: 31665005

Bansal, G., Rajgopal, K., Chamola, V., Xiong, Z., & Niyato, D. (2022). Healthcare in Metaverse: A Survey on Current Metaverse Applications in Healthcare. *IEEE Access: Practical Innovations, Open Solutions*, 10, 119914–119946. DOI: 10.1109/ACCESS.2022.3219845

Barajas, J. R., Sangil, M. J., Aspra, N., Gealone, P. J., Lucero, A., Ramos, M., Padua, O., & Oropesa, R. (2024, May). Exploratory Data Analysis of Artificial Intelligence Integration in Philippine Engineering Programs Offered by State Universities and Colleges: A Preliminary Assessment. In *2024 Systems and Information Engineering Design Symposium (SIEDS)* (pp. 360-365). IEEE. https://doi.org/DOI: 10.1109/SIEDS61124.2024.10534634

Barnett, T. P., Adam, J. C., & Lettenmaier, D. P. (2005). Potential impacts of a warming climate on water availability in snow-dominated regions. *Nature*, 438(7066), 303–309. DOI: 10.1038/nature04141 PMID: 16292301

Barnhardt, R., & Kawagley, A. O. (2005). Indigenous knowledge systems and Alaska Native ways of knowing. *Anthropology & Education Quarterly*, 36(1), 8–23. DOI: 10.1525/aeq.2005.36.1.008

Baron, J. V. (2024). A Double-Edged Sword: Examining the Link between Students' Dependence on Artificial Intelligence (AI) and their Psychosocial Maturity. *TWIST*, 19(3), 339–344. DOI: 10.5281/zenodo.10049652#236

Barrett, A., & Pack, A. (2023). Not quite eye to A.I.: Student and teacher perspectives on the use of generative artificial intelligence in the writing process. *International Journal of Educational Technology in Higher Education*, 20(1), 1–24. DOI: 10.1186/s41239-023-00427-0

Barron, B., & Darling-Hammond, L. (2008). *Teaching for Meaningful Learning: A Review of Research on Inquiry-Based and Cooperative Learning*. Book Excerpt. George Lucas Educational Foundation.

Barua, A., Mudunuri, L. S., & Kosheleva, O. (2013). Why trapezoidal and triangular membership functions work so well: Towards a theoretical explanation.

Bassey, B. A., Ubi, I. O., Anagbogu, G. E., & Owan, V. J. (2020). Permutation of UTME multiple-choice test items on performance in the use of English and mathematics among prospective higher education students. *The Journal of Social Sciences Research*, 6(4), 483–493.

Bates, B. C., Kundzewicz, Z. W., Wu, S., & Palutikof, J. P. (2008). *Climate change and water*. IPCC Secretariat.

Battiste, M. (2013). *Decolonizing education: Nourishing the learning spirit*. Purich Publishing Limited.

Batucan, G. B., Gonzales, G. G., Balbuena, M. G., Pasaol, K. R. B., Seno, D. N., & Gonzales, R. R. (2022). An extended UTAUT model to explain factors affecting online learning system amidst COVID-19 pandemic: The case of a developing economy. *Frontiers in Artificial Intelligence*, 5, 768831. DOI: 10.3389/frai.2022.768831 PMID: 35573898

Bawden, D. (2008). Origins and Concepts of Digital Literacy. In Lankshear, C., & Knobel, M. (Eds.), *Digital Literacies: Concepts*. Policies, and Practices.

Baxter, G., & Hainey, T. (2024). Using immersive technologies to enhance the student learning experience. *Interactive Technology and Smart Education*, 21(3), 403–425. DOI: 10.1108/ITSE-05-2023-0078

Beck, D. (2019). Special issue: Augmented and virtual reality in education: Immersive learning research. *Journal of Educational Computing Research*, 57, 1619–1625.

Becker, B. A., Denny, P., Finnie-Ansley, J., Luxton-Reilly, A., Prather, J., & Santos, E. A. (n.d.). *Programming Is Hard – Or at Least It Used to Be: Educational Opportunities And Challenges of AI Code Generation*.

Becker, A., & Bugmann, H. (2001). Global change and mountain regions: The Mountain Research Initiative. *Bioscience*, 51(8), 641–647.

Bedington, A., Halcomb, E. F., McKee, H. A., Sargent, T., & Smith, A. (2024). Writing with generative AI and human-machine teaming: Insights and recommendations from faculty and students. *Computers and Composition*, 71, 102833. Advance online publication. DOI: 10.1016/j.compcom.2024.102833

Beniston, M. (2003). Climatic change in mountain regions: A review of possible impacts. *Climatic Change*, 59(1-2), 5–31. DOI: 10.1023/A:1024458411589

Bermejo, B., Juiz, C., Cortes, D., Oskam, J., Moilanen, T., Loijas, J., Govender, P., Hussey, J., Schmidt, A. L., Burbach, R., King, D., O'Connor, C., & Dunlea, D. (2023). AR/VR Teaching-Learning Experiences in Higher Education Institutions (HEI): A Systematic Literature Review. *Informatics (MDPI)*, 10(2). Advance online publication. DOI: 10.3390/informatics10020045

Bernacki, M. L., Greene, M. J., & Lobczowski, N. G. (2021). A Systematic Review of Research on Personalized Learning: Personalized by Whom, to What, How, and for What Purpose(s)? *Educational Psychology Review*, 33(4), 1675–1715. DOI: 10.1007/S10648-021-09615-8

Bernardo, A. B., Cordel, M. O., Ricardo, J. G. E., Galanza, M. A. M. C., & Almonte-Acosta, S. (2022). Global citizenship competencies of Filipino students: Using machine learning to explore the structure of cognitive, affective, and behavioral competencies in the 2019 Southeast Asia Primary Learning Metrics. *Education Sciences*, 12(8), 547. DOI: 10.3390/educsci12080547

Biamonte, J., Wittek, P., Pancotti, N., Rebentrost, P., Wiebe, N., & Lloyd, S. (2016). Quantum machine learning. *Nature*, 549, 195–202. PMID: 28905917

Bianchini, S., Muller, M., and Pelletier, P. (2020). Deep Learning in Science, Papers 2009.01575, *arXiv.org, revised Sep 2020.*

Biddle, N., & Edwards, B. (2017). The characteristics and potential effects of the schools that Indigenous Australians attend. CAEPR Working Paper No. 119/2017. Centre for Aboriginal Economic Policy Research, Australian National University. https://doi.org/DOI: 10.25911/5c21c77718a8c

Biddle, N., & Markham, F. (2018). Indigenous population change in the 2016 Census. CAEPR 2016 Census Paper No. 1. Centre for Aboriginal Economic Policy Research, Australian National University. https://doi.org/DOI: 10.25911/5b4efd3bc2959

Biersteker, T. (2022). Quantum Pedagogy. Quantum International Relations: A Human Science for World Politics, 197.

Biggs, J., & Tang, C. (2011). *Teaching for quality learning at university* (4th ed.). Open University Press.

Biswas, P., Orero, P., Swaminathan, M., Krishnaswamy, K., & Robinson, P. (2021). Adaptive Accessible AR/VR Systems. *Conference on Human Factors in Computing Systems - Proceedings*. https://doi.org/DOI: 10.1145/3411763.3441324

Blau, I., Shamir-Inbal, T., & Avdiel, O. (2020). How does the pedagogical design of a technology-enhanced collaborative academic course promote digital literacies, self-regulation, and perceived learning of students? *The Internet and Higher Education*, 45, 100722. DOI: 10.1016/j.iheduc.2019.100722

Bloom, B. S. (1956). *Taxonomy of educational objectives: the classification of educational goals*. Susan Fauer Company.

Blumenstein, M. (2020). Synergies of learning analytics and learning design: A systematic review of student outcomes. *Journal of Learning Analytics*.

Bombay, A., Matheson, K., & Anisman, H. (2014). The intergenerational effects of Indian Residential Schools: Implications for the concept of historical trauma. *Transcultural Psychiatry*, 51(3), 320–338. DOI: 10.1177/1363461513503380 PMID: 24065606

Bonsay, J. O., Cruz, A. P., Firozi, H. C., & Camaro, P. J. C. (2021). Artificial Intelligence and Labor Productivity Paradox: The Economic Impact of AI in China, India, Japan, and Singapore. *Journal of Economics. Finance and Accounting Studies*, 3(2), 120–139. DOI: 10.32996/jefas.2021.3.2.13

Booc, N. B., Sobremisana, K. H. R. I. S. N. A., Ybañez, A. N. G. I. E., Tolosa, R. O. W. E. N. A., Ladroma, S. M., & Caparoso, K. M. (2023). Artificial intelligence-powered calculator application usage in mathematics summative assessments. *Iconic Research and Engineering Journal, 6*(10), 446-474. https://www.irejournals.com/paper-details/1704266

Borger, J. G. (2022, October). Getting to the CoRe of Collaborative Online International Learning (COIL). []. Frontiers Media SA.]. *Frontiers in Education, 7*, 987289.

Boulay, B., & Luckin, R. (2015). Modelling human teaching tactics and strategies for tutoring systems: 14 years on. *International Journal of Artificial Intelligence in Education*, 25(2), 1–12.

Brantmeier, E. J. (2013). Pedagogy of vulnerability: Definitions, assumptions, and applications. In Lin, J., Oxford, R. L., & Brantmeier, E. J. (Eds.), *Re-envisioning higher education: Embodied pathways to wisdom and social transformation* (pp. 95–106). Information Age Publishing.

Braun, V., & Clarke, V. (2006). Using thematic analysis in psychology. *Qualitative Research in Psychology*, 3(2), 77–101. DOI: 10.1191/1478088706qp063oa

Brayboy, B. M. J., & Maaka, M. J. (2015). K–12 Achievement for Indigenous Students. *Journal of American Indian Education*, 54(1), 63–98.

Bresciani, S., Ciampi, F., Meli, F., & Ferraris, A. (2021). Using big data for co-innovation processes: Mapping the field of data-driven innovation, proposing theoretical developments and providing a research agenda. *International Journal of Information Management*, 60, 102347. DOI: 10.1016/j.ijinfomgt.2021.102347

Bressane, A., Zwirn, D., Essiptchouk, A., Saraiva, A. C. V., Carvalho, F. L. de C., Formiga, J. K. S., Medeiros, L. C. de C., & Negri, R. G. (2024). Understanding the role of study strategies and learning disabilities on student academic performance to enhance educational approaches: A proposal using artificial intelligence. *Computers and Education: Artificial Intelligence*, 6, 100196. Advance online publication. DOI: 10.1016/j.caeai.2023.100196

Bryant, J., Heitz, C., Sanghvi, S., & Wagle, D. (2020, January 14). How artificial intelligence will impact K-12 teachers. McKinsey. https://www.mckinsey.com/industries/education/our-insights/how-artificial-intelligence-will-impact-k-12-teachers

Brynjolfsson, E. (2014). The second machine age: Work, progress, and prosperity in a time of brilliant technologies.

Brynjolfsson, E., & McAfee, A. (2014). *The second machine age: Work, progress, and prosperity in a time of brilliant technologies*. W. W. Norton & Company.

Bucea-Manea- oniş, R., Kuleto, V., Gudei, S. C. D., Lianu, C., Lianu, C., Ilić, M. P., & Păun, D. (2022). Artificial Intelligence Potential in Higher Education Institutions Enhanced Learning Environment in Romania and Serbia. *Sustainability (Switzerland)*, 14(10). Advance online publication. DOI: 10.3390/su14105842

Burchert, S., Alkneme, M., Bird, M., Carswell, K., Cuijpers, P., Hansen, P., & Knaevelsrud, C. (2019). User-centred app adaptation of a low-intensity e-mental health intervention for Syrian refugees. *Frontiers in Psychiatry*, 9. Advance online publication. DOI: 10.3389/fpsyt.2018.00663 PMID: 30740065

Bustos-Lopez, M., Cruz-Ramirez, N., Guerra-Hernandez, A., Sánchez-Morales, L. N., Cruz-Ramos, N. A., & Alor-Hernandez, G. (2022). Wearables for engagement detection in learning environments: A review. *Biosensors (Basel)*, 12(7), 509.

Byram, M., & Wagner, M. (2018). Making a difference: Language teaching for intercultural and international dialogue. *Foreign Language Annals*, 51(1), 140–151. DOI: 10.1111/flan.12319

Caccavale, F., Gargalo, C. L., Gernaey, K. V., & Krühne, U. (2024). Towards Education 4.0: The role of Large Language Models as virtual tutors in chemical engineering. *Education for Chemical Engineers*, 49, 1–11. DOI: 10.1016/j.ece.2024.07.002

Cadiz, M. C. D., Manuel, L. A. F., Reyes, M. M., & Natividad, L. R. (2024). Technology Integration in Philippine Higher Education: A Content-Based Bibliometric Analysis. *Jurnal Ilmiah Ilmu Terapan Universitas Jambi*, 8(1), 35–47. DOI: 10.22437/jiituj.v8i1.31807

Caffery, L., Bradford, N., Wickramasinghe, S., Hayman, N., & Smith, A. (2017). Outcomes of using telehealth for the provision of healthcare to Aboriginal and Torres Strait Islander people: A systematic review. *Australian and New Zealand Journal of Public Health*, 41(1), 48–53. DOI: 10.1111/1753-6405.12600 PMID: 27868300

Cajete, G. (1994). *Look to the mountain: An ecology of indigenous education.* Kivaki Press.

Cajete, G. (2015). *Indigenous community: Rekindling the teachings of the seventh fire.* Living Justice Press.

Caliskan, A., Brynjolfsson, E., & Mitchell, M. (2017). Semantics derived automatically from language corpora contain human-like biases. *Science*, 356(6334), 183–186. DOI: 10.1126/science.aal4230 PMID: 28408601

Calvet, L., Bourdin, P., & Prados, F. (2019). Immersive technologies in higher education: Applications, challenges, and good practices. *ACM International Conference Proceeding Series*, 95–99. https://doi.org/DOI: 10.1145/3371647.3371667

Canto, S., de Graaff, R., & Jauregi, K. (2014). Collaborative tasks for negotiation of intercultural meaning in virtual worlds and video-web communication. In *Technology-mediated TBLT* (pp. 183–212). John Benjamins.

Capone, R., & Lepore, M. (2020). Augmented reality to increase interaction and participation: A case study of undergraduate students in mathematics class. *Augmented Reality, Virtual Reality, and Computer Graphics: 7th International Conference, AVR 2020, Lecce, Italy, September 7–10, 2020. Proceedings*, 7(Part II), 185–204.

Carayannis, E. G., & Morawska, J. (2023). University and Education 5.0 for emerging trends, policies and practices in the concept of Industry 5.0 and Society 5.0,' in *Industry 5.0: Creative and Innovative Organizations*. Springer, (2023):1–25.

Cardona, M. A., Rodríguez, R. J., & Ishmael, K. (2023). *Artificial Intelligence and the Future of Teaching and Learning Insights and Recommendations Artificial Intelligence and the Future of Teaching and Learning*. https://tech.ed.gov

Carmigniani, J., Furht, B., Anisetti, M., Ceravolo, P., Damiani, E., & Ivkovic, M. (2011). Augmented reality technologies, systems and applications. *Multimedia Tools and Applications*, 51, 341–377.

Carpenter, J., Guerin, A., Kaczmarek, M., Lawson, G., Lawson, K., Nathan, L. P., & Turin, M. (2018). Digital language resource and database development in support of indigenous language revitalization in northeastern British Columbia. *Journal of Northern Studies*, 12(1), 37–56.

Carrascal, G., Barrio, A. D. D., & Botella, G. (2020). First experiences of teaching quantum computing. *The Journal of Supercomputing*, ●●●, 1–30.

Carroll, J., & McKendree, J. (1987). Interface design issues for advice-giving expert systems. *Communications of the ACM*, 30(1), 14–31.

Castagno, A. E., & Brayboy, B. M. J. (2008). Culturally responsive schooling for Indigenous youth: A review of the literature. *Review of Educational Research*, 78(4), 941–993. DOI: 10.3102/0034654308323036

Ceoca, O., & Dulf, E.-H. "Assistive Helmet for Visually Impaired Human Beings", *2024 IEEE International Conference on Automation, Quality and Testing, Robotics (AQTR)*, pp.1-6, 2024.

Chadwick, A., & Howard, P. N. (Eds.). (2009). *Routledge handbook of Internet politics*. Routledge.

Chamorro-Premuzic, T., Akhtar, R., Winsborough, D., & Sherman, R. A. (2017). The datafication of talent: How technology is advancing the science of human potential at work. *Current Opinion in Behavioral Sciences*, 18, 13–16. DOI: 10.1016/j.cobeha.2017.04.007

Chan, C. K. Y. (2023). A comprehensive AI policy education framework for university teaching and learning. *International Journal of Educational Technology in Higher Education*, 20(1), 38. Advance online publication. DOI: 10.1186/s41239-023-00408-3

Chang, Y. J., Chen, C. H., Huang, W. T., & Huang, W. S. (2011). Investigating students' perceived satisfaction, behavioral intention, and effectiveness of English learning using augmented reality. *Proceedings - IEEE International Conference on Multimedia and Expo*. https://doi.org/DOI: 10.1109/ICME.2011.6012177

Changa, W., Wang, H., Yan, G., & Liu, C. (2020). An EEG based familiar and unfamiliar person identification and classification system using feature extraction and directed functional brain network. *Expert Systems with Applications*, 158, 113448.

Chang, Q., Pan, X., Manikandan, N., & Ramesh, S. (2022). Artificial intelligence technologies for teaching and learning in higher education. *International Journal of Reliability Quality and Safety Engineering*.

Chang, Y. S. (2021). Applying the arcs motivation theory for the assessment of ar digital media design learning effectiveness. *Sustainability (Switzerland)*, 13(21), 12296. DOI: 10.3390/su132112296

Chan, V. S., Haron, H. N. H., Isham, M. I. B. M., & Mohamed, F. Bin. (2022). VR and AR virtual welding for psychomotor skills: A systematic review. *Multimedia Tools and Applications*, 81(9), 12459–12493. DOI: 10.1007/s11042-022-12293-5 PMID: 35221778

Charlton, P., & Avramides, K. (2016). Knowledge construction in computer science and engineering when learning through making. *IEEE Transactions on Learning Technologies*, 9, 379–390.

Chatti, M. A., Muslim, A., & Schroeder, U. (2019). Toward an open learning analytics ecosystem. In Ifenthaler, D., Mah, D. K., & Yau, J. Y. K. (Eds.), *Utilizing learning analytics to support study success* (pp. 195–212). Springer.

Chaudhuri, A., De, K., & Chatterjee, D. (2013). Solution of the decision making problems using fuzzy soft relations. arXiv preprint arXiv:1304.7238.

Chauncey, S. A., & McKenna, H. P. (2023). A framework and exemplars for ethical and responsible use of AI Chatbot technology to support teaching and learning. *Computers and Education: Artificial Intelligence*, 5, 100182. Advance online publication. DOI: 10.1016/j.caeai.2023.100182

Chavez, O. J., & Palaoag, T. (2024). AI-driven mobile application: unraveling students' motivational feature preferences for reading comprehension. *Journal of Research in Innovative Teaching & Learning*. Vol. ahead-of-print No. ahead-of-print. https://doi.org/DOI: 10.1108/JRIT-02-2024-0045

Cheng Chye Tan, M., Yen Leng Chye, S., & Shu Min Teng, K. (2022). "In the shoes of another": immersive technology for social and emotional learning. Grassini, S. (2023). Shaping the future of education: exploring the potential and consequences of AI and ChatGPT in educational settings. *Education Sciences*.

Chen, J. (2020). *Artificial intelligence: Foundations, theory, and applications.* Springer.

Chen, L., & Shi, J. (2024). Communication Technology and Environmental Communication: Challenges, Opportunities, and Emerging Agendas. *Environmental Communication*.

Chen, W. (2022). Research on the design of intelligent music teaching systems based on virtual reality technology. *Computational Intelligence and Neuroscience*.

Chen, X., Zou, D., Xie, H., Cheng, G., & Liu, C. (2022). Two Decades of Artificial Intelligence in Education: Contributors, Collaborations, Research Topics, Challenges, and Future Directions. *Journal of Educational Technology & Society*, 25(1), 28–47.

Chen, Y., Li, M., Huang, C., Cukurova, M., & Ma, Q. (2023). A Systematic Review of Research on Immersive Technology-enhanced writing education: The current state and a Research Agenda. *IEEE Transactions on Learning Technologies.*

Chen, Z., & Demmans, C. (2020). *Csclrec: Personalized recommendation of forum posts to support socio-collaborative learning.* International Educational Data Mining Society.

Childs, E., Mohammad, F., Stevens, L., Burbelo, H., Awoke, A., Rewkowski, N., & Manocha, D. (2021). An overview of enhancing distance learning through augmented and virtual reality technologies. *ArXiv Preprint ArXiv:2101.11000.*

Chiu, T. K. F., & Chai, C. (2020). *Sustainable Curriculum Planning for Artificial Intelligence Education: A Self-determination Theory Perspective.* Sustainability. MDPI.

Choi, D., Seo, S., Park, H., Hong, T., & Koo, C. (2023). Forecasting personal learning performance in virtual reality-based construction safety training using biometric responses. *Automation in Construction*, 156, 105115.

Choi, K. S., Deng, H., Laurat, J., & Kimble, H. (2007). Mapping photonic entanglement into and out of a quantum memory. *Nature*, 452, 67–71. PMID: 18322529

Choi, K. S., Goban, A., Papp, S., Enk, S. J., & Kimble, H. (2010). Entanglement of spin waves among four quantum memories. *Nature*, 468, 412–416. PMID: 21085175

Choi, Y., Ko, J., & Lee, S. (2019). Analyzing student participation in class discussions using speech recognition technology. *Journal of Educational Technology*, 15(3), 45–60.

Christensen, R. (1997). Effect of technology integration education on the attitudes of teachers and their students* (Doctoral dissertation). University of North Texas.

Chua, C. P., & Valencia, L. D. (2020). The Role of Artificial Intelligence in Education Amidst of the COVID-19 Pandemic. https://www.researchgate.net/publication/343691393_The_Role_of_Artificial_Intelligence_in_Education_Amidst_of_the_COVID-19_Pandemic

Ciloglu, T., & Ustun, A. B. (2023). The Effects of Mobile AR-based Biology Learning Experience on Students' Motivation, Self-Efficacy, and Attitudes in Online Learning. *Journal of Science Education and Technology*, 32(3), 309–337. DOI: 10.1007/s10956-023-10030-7 PMID: 36844360

Cipolla, R., Gal, Y., & Kendall, A. (2018). Multi-task Learning Using Uncertainty to Weigh Losses for Scene Geometry and Semantics. *2018 IEEE/CVF Conference on Computer Vision and Pattern Recognition.*

Clark, R. M., Kaw, A., & Delgado, E. (2018). Do Adaptive Lessons for Pre-class Experience Improve Flipped Learning? Proceedings of the ASEE Annual Conference & Exposition..

Clifford, P. L. R. (2024). AI in Higher Education: Faculty Perspective Towards Artificial Intelligence through UTAUT Approach. *Ho Chi Minh City Open University Journal of Science-Social Sciences*, 14(4), 3–21. DOI: 10.46223/HCMCOUJS.soci.en.14.4.2851.2024

Clow, D. (2013). An Overview of Learning Analytics. *Teaching in Higher Education*, 18(6), 683–695. DOI: 10.1080/13562517.2013.827653

Çoban, M., & Göksu, İ. (2022). Using virtual reality learning environments to motivate and socialize undergraduates in distance learning. *Participatory Educational Research*, 9(2), 199–218. DOI: 10.17275/per.22.36.9.2

Cochrane, T., Cook, S., Aiello, S., & Aguayo, C. (2017). Augmenting student engagement through AR/VR. *International Journal of Mobile and Blended Learning*, 9(1), 33–45. DOI: 10.4018/IJMBL.2017010103

Conati, C., & Maclaren, H. (2009). Empathic and affective tutoring systems. *International Journal of Artificial Intelligence in Education*, 19(1), 1–24.

Cook, M., & Lischer-Katz, Z. (2021). Practical steps for an effective virtual reality course integration. *College & Undergraduate Libraries*, 27(2–4), 210–226.

Coppola, N., Hiltz, S. R., & Rotter, N. (2002). Becoming a virtual professor: Pedagogical roles and asynchronous learning networks. *Journal of Management Information Systems*, 18, 169–189.

Copur-Gencturk, Y., Li, J., Cohen, A. S., & Orrill, C. H. (2024). The impact of an interactive, personalized computer-based teacher professional development program on student performance: A randomized controlled trial. *Computers & Education*, 210, 104963. Advance online publication. DOI: 10.1016/j.compedu.2023.104963

Córcoles, A. D., Takita, M., Inoue, K., Lekuch, S., Minev, Z. K., Chow, J. M., & Gambetta, J. M. (2021). Exploiting dynamic quantum circuits in a quantum algorithm with superconducting qubits. *Physical Review Letters*, 127(10), 100501.

Corpuz, J. C. G. (2023). Artificial intelligence (AI) and public health. *Journal of Public Health*, 45(4), e783–e784. DOI: 10.1093/pubmed/fdad074 PMID: 37309563

Cortez, P. M., Ong, A. K. S., Diaz, J. F. T., German, J. D., & Jagdeep, S. J. S. S. (2024). Analyzing Preceding factors affecting behavioral intention on communicational artificial intelligence as an educational tool. *Heliyon*, 10(3), E25896. Advance online publication. DOI: 10.1016/j.heliyon.2024.e25896 PMID: 38356557

Covington, M. V. (2000). Intrinsic versus extrinsic motivation in schools: A reconciliation. *Current Directions in Psychological Science*, 9(1), 22–25. DOI: 10.1111/1467-8721.00052

Creswell, J. W., & Plano Clark, V. L. (2017). *Designing and conducting mixed methods research* (3rd ed.). SAGE Publications.

Crompton, H., & Burke, D. (2023). Artificial intelligence in higher education: The state of the field. *International Journal of Educational Technology in Higher Education*, 20(1), 22. Advance online publication. DOI: 10.1186/s41239-023-00392-8

Cuhadar, E., & Kampf, R. (2014). Learning about conflict and negotiations through computer simulations: The case of PeaceMaker. *International Studies Perspectives*, 15(4), 509–524. DOI: 10.1111/insp.12076

Cummings, J., & Schrum, L. (2018). *Designing for the future: The role of technology in educational reform*. Routledge.

D'Mello, S. K., Lehman, B., & Pekrun, R. (2011). Emotion and learning. In *The Cambridge Handbook of the Learning Sciences* (pp. 324–340). Cambridge University Press.

Dahlstrom, E., Brooks, D. C., & Bichsel, J. (2014). The Current Ecosystem of Learning Management Systems in Higher Education: Student, Faculty, and IT Perspectives. *EDUCAUSE Review*. Retrieved https://www.educause.edu/ecar.2014

Dalalah, D., & Dalalah, O. M. A. (2023). The false positives and false negatives of generative AI detection tools in education and academic research: The case of ChatGPT. *International Journal of Management Education*, 21(2), 100822. DOI: 10.1016/j.ijme.2023.100822

Damasevicius, R., & Sidekerskiene, T. (2024). Ai as a teacher: A new educational dynamic for modern classrooms for personalized learning support. AI-Enhanced Teaching Methods. IGI Global Scientific Publishing.

Damaševičius, R., & Zailskaitė-Jakštė, L. (2023, November). From STEAM to STREAM: Integrating Research as a Part of STEAM Education. In International Conference on New Media Pedagogy (pp. 318-335). Cham: Springer Nature Switzerland.

Damasevicius, R., & Zailskaite-Jakste, L. (2024a). *Digital twin technology: Necessity of the future in education and beyond.* Automated Secure Computing for Next-Generation Systems. Wiley.

Daniel, B. (2015). Big Data and analytics in higher education: Opportunities and challenges. *British Journal of Educational Technology*, 46(5), 904–920. DOI: 10.1111/bjet.12230

Daniel, B. K. (2019). Big Data and data science: A critical review of issues for educational research. *British Journal of Educational Technology*, 50(1), 101–113. DOI: 10.1111/bjet.12595

Daniil Yaskevich, R.-o.-D. (2021). Digital Technologies, as a Factor in the Search for a New Quality of Inclusive Education. . 1-9.

Daron Cyr, J. W. (2022). Logics and the Orbit of Parent Engagement. *School Community Journal*, •••, 9–38.

Davies, R. S., Dean, D. L., & Ball, N. (2013). Flipping the classroom and instructional technology integration in a college-level information systems spreadsheet course. *Educational Technology Research and Development*, 61(4), 563–580. DOI: 10.1007/s11423-013-9305-6

de Jong, R. M., & Bus, D. (2023). Searching Scholarly Literature with Artificial Intelligence: An Introduction. *Research Software Community Leiden*, 12, 8–21.

De La Cruz, R. J. D. (2022). Science education in the Philippines. In *Science Education in Countries Along the Belt & Road: Future Insights and New Requirements* (pp. 331-345). Singapore: Springer Nature Singapore. https://doi.org/DOI: 10.1007/978-981-16-6955-2_20

de Leon, L. C. R., Flores, L. V., & Alomo, A. R. L. (2024). Artificial intelligence and Filipino academic librarians: Perceptions, challenges and opportunities. *Journal of the Australian library and information association, 73*(1), 66-83. https://doi.org/ DOI: 10.1080/24750158.2024.2305993

De Lorenzis, F., Prattic\`o, F. G., Repetto, M., Pons, E., & Lamberti, F. (2023). Immersive Virtual Reality for procedural training: Comparing traditional and learning by teaching approaches. *Computers in Industry*, 144. Advance online publication. DOI: 10.1016/j.compind.2022.103785

De Marsico, M., Sterbini, A., & Temperini, M. (2013). A framework to support social-collaborative personalized e-learning. In Human-Computer Interaction. Applications and Services: 15th International Conference, HCI International 2013, Las Vegas, NV, USA, July 21-26, 2013 [Springer Berlin Heidelberg.]. *Proceedings*, 15(Part II), 351–360.

de Moraes Rossetto, A. G., Martins, T. C., Silva, L. A., Leithardt, D. R. F., Bermejo-Gil, B. M., & Leithardt, V. R. Q. (2023). An analysis of the use of augmented reality and virtual reality as educational resources. *Computer Applications in Engineering Education*, 31(6), 1761–1775.

Debnath, S. (2021). Fuzzy hypersoft sets and its weightage operator for decision making. *Journal of Fuzzy Extension and Applications*, 2(2), 163–170.

Dec, G., Stadnicka, D., Paśko, Ł., Mądziel, M., & Figliè, R. (2022). Role of academics in Transferring knowledge and skills on artificial intelligence, the internet of things and edge computing. *Sensors (Basel)*. PMID: 35408110

Deci, E. L., & Ryan, R. M. (2012). Self-determination theory. *Handbook of Theories of Social Psychology, 1*(20), 416–436.

Dede, C. (2014). *The role of emerging technologies in transforming learning environments*. Harvard Education Press.

Deemer, A. D., Bradley, C. K., Ross, N. C., Natale, D. M., Itthipanichpong, R., Werblin, F. S., & Massof, R. W. (2018). Low Vision Enhancement with Head-mounted Video Display Systems: Are We There Yet?. *Optometry and vision science: official publication of the American Academy of Optometry, 95*(9), 694–703. https://doi.org/ DOI: 10.1097/OPX.0000000000001278

Dela Rosa, A. C. C., Dacuma, A. K. B., Ang, C. A. R., Nudalo, C. J. J., Cruz, L., & Vallespin, M. R. (2024). Assessing AI Adoption: Investigating Variances in AI Utilization Across Student Year Levels in Far Eastern University-Manila, Philippines. *International Journal of Current Science Research and Review*, 6, 1–8. DOI: 10.47191/ijcsrr/6-i00-00

Delgado, H. O. K., de Azevedo Fay, A., Sebastiany, M. J., & Silva, A. D. C. (2020). Artificial intelligence adaptive learning tools. *BELT-Brazilian English Language Teaching Journal*, 11(2), e38749–e38749.

Demmer, T. R., Kühnapfel, C., Fingerhut, J., & Pelowski, M. (2023). Does an emotional connection to art really require a human artist? Emotion and intentionality responses to AI- versus human-created art and impact on aesthetic experience. *Computers in Human Behavior*, 148, 107875. Advance online publication. DOI: 10.1016/j.chb.2023.107875

Dervojeda, K. (2021, 7). Education 5.0: Rehumanising Education in the Age of Machines. 1-8.

DesRoches, A. (2022). Harnessing the Power of Artificial Intelligence in Scholarly Publishing. *Editorial Office News*, 15, 9–11.

Devender, E.. (2023). IoT-enhanced learning environment optimization and student outcome. *International Journal on Recent and Innovation Trends in Computing and Communication*, 11(11). Advance online publication. DOI: 10.17762/ijritcc.v11i11.9954

DeVore, S., & Singh, C. (2016). Interactive learning tutorial on quantum key distribution. *Physical Review. Physics Education Research*.

Dewey, J., Montessori, M., Strzemiński, W., Piaget, J., Vygotsky, L., von Foerster, H., Bruner, J., Simon, H., Watzlawick, P., & von Glasersfeld, E. (1997). Constructivism (learning theory). *Journal of Social Sciences, Literature and Languages*, 9–16.

Dey, S. (2022). Phenomenon of Excess of Artificial Intelligence: Quantifying the Native AI, Its Leverages in 5G/6G and beyond. In *Radar and RF Front End System Designs for Wireless Systems* (pp. 245–274). IGI Global.

Diano, F., Jr., Kilag, O. K., Malbas, M., Catacutan, A., Tiongzon, B., & Abendan, C. F. (2023). Towards Global Competence: Innovations in the Philippine Curriculum for Addressing International Challenges. *Excellencia: International Multidisciplinary Journal of Education*, 1(4), 295-307. https://multijournals.org/index.php/excellencia-imje/article/view/66/71

Dillenbourg, P. (1999). What do you mean by collaborative learning?. Collaborative-learning: Cognitive and computational approaches., 1-19.

Dimitriadou, E., & Lanitis, A. (2023). A critical evaluation, challenges, and future perspectives of using artificial intelligence and emerging technologies in smart classrooms. *Smart Learning Environments*, 10(1), 1–26. DOI: 10.1186/s40561-023-00231-3

Dirnböck, T., Essl, F., & Rabitsch, W. (2011). Disproportional risk for habitat loss of high-altitude endemic species under climate change. *Global Change Biology*, 17(2), 990–996. DOI: 10.1111/j.1365-2486.2010.02266.x

Diseth, Å., Mathisen, F. K. S., & Samdal, O. (2020). A comparison of intrinsic and extrinsic motivation among lower and upper secondary school students. *Educational Psychology*, 40(8), 961–980. DOI: 10.1080/01443410.2020.1778640

Dobson, S., & Scaff, J. (2024). Qurio: QBit Learning, Quantum Pedagogy, and Agentive AI Tutors. Joint Mathematics Meetings, San Francisco, USA, January 3-6, 2024.

Doewes, A., & Pechenizkiy, M. (2021). On the limitations of human-computer agreement in automated essay scoring. In Proceedings of the 14th International Conference on Educational Data Mining (EDM21). https://educationaldatamining .org/EDM2021/virtual/static/pdf/EDM21_paper_243.pdf

Dombi, J. (1990). Membership function as an evaluation. *Fuzzy Sets and Systems*, 35(1), 1–21. DOI: 10.1016/0165-0114(90)90014-W

Domert, D., & Linder, C. (2005). Ingerman: Probability as a conceptual hurdle to understanding one-dimensional quantum scattering and tunnelling. *European Journal of Physics*, 26, 47–59.

Dong, D., Chen, C., Li, H. X., & Tarn, T. (2005). Quantum reinforcement learning. *IEEE Transactions on Systems, Man, and Cybernetics. Part B, Cybernetics*, 38, 1207–1220. PMID: 18784007

Donoghue, T., Voytek, B., & Ellis, S. E. (2021). Teaching creative and practical data science at scale. *Journal of Statistics and Data Science Education : An Official Journal of the of the American Statistical Association*, 29(1), S27–S39. DOI: 10.1080/10691898.2020.1860725

Dora, C., Waddington, C., & Edwards, S. (2020). Indoor air quality and student performance: A review of the evidence. *Environmental Research Letters*, 15(5), 055002.

Duan, S., & Zhao, Y. (2023). Knowledge graph analysis of artificial intelligence Application research in the nursing field based on visualization technology. *Alexandria Engineering Journal*.

Duman, M. Ç., & Akdemir, B. (2021). A study to determine the effects of industry 4.0 technology components on organizational performance. *Technological Forecasting and Social Change*, 167(6), 1–14.

Dupri, D., Candra, O., & Nazirun, N. (2021). The Implementation of Mini Volleyball in Physical Education to Increase Students' Creative Thinking Ability. *International Journal of Human Movement and Sports Sciences*, 9(4A), 89–93.

Duran, M., Simon, S., & Blasco, F. (2020, June). Science Education and Artificial Intelligence–A Chatbot on Magic and Quantum Computing as an Educational Tool. In EDEN Conference Proceedings (No. 1, pp. 137-142).

Dutta, U. (2019). Digital preservation of Indigenous culture and narratives from the global south: In search of an approach. *Humanities (Washington)*, 8(2), 68. DOI: 10.3390/h8020068

Education Data Security: 5 Things to Implement Now. (2023, August 11). Retrieved from https://computersnationwide.com/education-data-security-5-things-implement -now/

Ehrlich, J. R., Spaeth, G. L., Carlozzi, N. E., & Lee, P. P. (2017). Patient-Centered Outcome Measures to Assess Functioning in Randomized Controlled Trials of Low-Vision Rehabilitation: A Review. *Patient*, 10(1), 39–49. DOI: 10.1007/s40271-016-0189-5 PMID: 27495171

Ekman, P., & Friesen, W. V. (1971). *Constant variables in facial expressions of emotion*. Stanford University Press.

El Naqa, I., & Ten, R. (2016). SU-D-BRB-05: Quantum Learning for Knowledge-Based Response-Adaptive Radiotherapy. *Medical Physics*, 43(6Part4), 3338–3338.

Elias Carayannis, J. M. (2023). University and Education 5.0 for Emerging Trends, Policies and Practices in the Concept of Industry 5.0 and Society 5.0. 1-25.

Elias Ratinho, C. M. (2023). The role of gamified learning strategies in student's motivation in high school and higher education: A systematic review. *sciencedirect*.

Elisabeth, M. (2022). *Innovations in curriculum design: Trends and strategies*. Springer.

Ennis, R. H. (2011). The nature of critical thinking: An outline of critical thinking dispositions and abilities. *University of Illinois*, 2(4), 1–8.

Escolano, V. J. C., Caballero, A. R., Albina, E. M., Hernandez, A. A., & Juanatas, R. A. (2023, May). Acceptance of Mobile Application on Disaster Preparedness: Towards Decision Intelligence in Disaster Management. In *2023 8th International Conference on Business and Industrial Research (ICBIR)* (pp. 381-386). IEEE. https://doi.org/DOI: 10.1109/ICBIR57571.2023.10147638

Eslit, E. (2023). Thriving beyond the crisis: Teachers' reflections on literature and language education in the era of artificial intelligence (AI) and globalization. *Preprints*, 2023072151. https://doi.org/DOI: 10.20944/preprints202307.2151.v1

Eslit, E. R. (2023). Thriving Beyond the Crisis: Teachers' Reflections on Literature and Language Education in the Era of Artificial Intelligence (AI) and Globalization. *International Journal of Education and Teaching*, 3(1), 46–57. DOI: 10.51483/IJEDT.3.1.2023.46-57

Estrellado, C. J., & Miranda, J. C. (2023). Artificial intelligence in the Philippine educational context: Circumspection and future inquiries. *International Journal of Scientific and Research Publications*, 13(5), 16–22. DOI: 10.29322/IJSRP.13.04.2023.p13704

European Commission, Directorate-General for Education, Youth, Sport and Culture. (2022). Ethical guidelines on the use of artificial intelligence (AI) and data in teaching and learning for educators. Publications Office of the European Union. https://data.europa.eu/doi/10.2766/153756

Facione, P. A. (2011). Critical thinking: What it is and why it counts. Insight assessment, 1(1), 1-23.

Fainholc, B. (2016). Latin American present and future of teaching and learning in virtual environments related to university education. [RED]. *Journal of Distance Education*, 2(48).

Featherstone, D. (2017). The Aboriginal invention of broadband: How Yarnangu is using ICTs in the Ngaanyatjarra Lands of Western Australia. In Crouch, A., Rozentals, L., & Simovic, V. (Eds.), *Digital Participation through Social Living Labs* (pp. 299–316). Chandos Publishing., DOI: 10.1016/B978-0-08-102059-3.00016-6

Feng, F., Li, C., Davvaz, B., & Irfan Ali, M. (2010). Soft sets combined with fuzzy sets and rough sets: A tentative approach. *Soft Computing*, 14(9), 899–911. DOI: 10.1007/s00500-009-0465-6

Fenwick, T., & Edwards, R. (2016). Exploring the impact of digital technologies on professional responsibilities and education. *European Educational Research Journal*, 15(1), 117–131. DOI: 10.1177/1474904115608387

Fern'andez-Morante, C., Cebreiro-L'opez, B., Rodr'ıguez-Malmierca, M. J., & Casal-Otero, L. (2021). Adaptive learning supported by learning analytics for student teachers' personalized training during in-school practices. *Sustainability*.

Fernandes, C. W., Rafatirad, S., & Sayadi, H. (2023, June). Advancing personalized and adaptive learning experience in education with artificial intelligence. In 2023 32nd Annual Conference of the European Association for Education in Electrical and Information Engineering (EAEEIE) (pp. 1-6). IEEE.

Ferreira Mello, R., Freitas, E., Dwan Pereira, F., Cabral, L., Tedesco, P., & Ramalho, G. (2023). Education in the age of Generative AI: Context and Recent Developments.

Ferreira, G. (2023). Public policies for digital inclusion and indigenous peoples. *Revista Gênero E Interdisciplinaridade, 4(06)*, 500-520. https://doi.org/DOI: 10.51249/gei.v4i06.1766

Ferrier, B., Lee, J., Mbuli, A., & James, D. A. (2022). Translational Applications of Wearable Sensors in Education: Implementation and Efficacy. *Sensors (Basel)*, 22, 1675. DOI: 10.3390/s22041675 PMID: 35214578

Fingerhuth, M., Babej, T., & Wittek, P. (2018). Open source software in quantum computing. *PLoS One*, •••, 13. PMID: 30571700

Fish, J. (2023). "Inside of my home, I was getting a full dose of culture": Exploring the ecology of Indigenous peoples' development through stories. *The American Journal of Orthopsychiatry*, 93(6), 461–475. DOI: 10.1037/ort0000690 PMID: 37695347

Fitzpatrick, K., Ody, M., Goveas, D., Montesanti, S., Campbell, P., MacDonald, K., & Roach, P. (2022). Understanding virtual primary healthcare with Indigenous populations: A rapid evidence review. *Research Square*. https://doi.org/DOI: 10.21203/rs.3.rs-1953677/v1

Flood, M. (1951). *Report on a seminar on organizational science (P-7857)*. RAND Corporation.

Floridi, L., Cowls, J., Beltrametti, M., Chatila, R., Chazerand, P., Dignum, V., Luetge, C., Madelin, R., Pagallo, U., Rossi, F., Schafer, B., Valcke, P., & Vayena, E. (2018). AI4People—an ethical framework for a good AI society: Opportunities, risks, principles, and recommendations. *Minds and Machines*, 28(4), 689–707. DOI: 10.1007/s11023-018-9482-5 PMID: 30930541

Fontanilla, J. B., Bautista, K. H., Lactao, M.Jr, Villacorte, M. A., & Santos, R. (2023). Educators' Perspectives on the Impact of Artificial Intelligence on Writing Competence. *International Journal of Multidisciplinary Research and Publications*, 6(6), 29–34. https://www.researchgate.net/publication/375769974

Forawi, S. A., & Al Quraan, E. (2022). Status and Trends of STEM Education in the United Arab Emirates. *Status and Trends of STEM Education in Highly Competitive Countries: Country Reports and International Comparison.*

Forsyth, S., Dalton, B., Foster, E. H., Walsh, B., Smilack, J., & Yeh, T. (2021, May). Imagine a more ethical AI: Using stories to develop teens' awareness and understanding of artificial intelligence and its societal impacts. In *2021 Conference on Research in Equitable and Sustained Participation in Engineering, Computing, and Technology (RESPECT)*. IEEE. DOI: 10.1109/RESPECT51740.2021.9620549

Franco D'Souza, R., Mathew, M., Mishra, V., & Mohan Surapaneni, K. (2024). Twelve tips for addressing ethical concerns in the implementation of artificial intelligence in medical education.

Freericks, J. (2023). Focus on conceptual ideas in quantum mechanics for teacher training. *Journal of Physics: Conference Series*, ●●●, 2490.

Freire, P. (1970). Pedagogy of the oppressed. *Continuum : an Interdisciplinary Journal on Continuity of Care*.

Freire, P. (1996). *Pedagogy of the oppressed* (Rev. ed.). Penguin Books.

Friedman, L., Blair Black, N., Walker, E., & Roschelle, J. (2021, November 8). Safe AI in education needs you. Association for Computing Machinery Blog. https://cacm.acm.org/blogs/blog-cacm/256657-safe-ai-in-education-needs-you/fulltext

Gačić, M. (2009). Recommendation of the European Parliament and of the Council of 18 December 2006 on key competences for lifelong learning.

Galla, C. (2018). Digital realities of indigenous language revitalization: A look at Hawaiian language technology in the modern world. *Language and Literature*, 20(3), 100–120. DOI: 10.20360/langandlit29412

Galla, C. K. (2016). Indigenous language revitalization, promotion, and education: Function of digital technology. *Computer Assisted Language Learning*, 29(7), 1137–1151. DOI: 10.1080/09588221.2016.1166137

Galla, C. K. (2018). Digital realities of indigenous language revitalization: A look at Hawaiian language technology in the modern world. *Language and Education*, 32(3), 212–226. DOI: 10.1080/09500782.2018.1434097

Gamage, K. A. A., Dehideniya, S. C. P., Xu, Z., & Tang, X. (2023). ChatGPT and higher education assessments: More opportunities than concerns? *Journal of Applied Learning and Teaching*, 6(2), 358–369. DOI: 10.37074/jalt.2023.6.2.32

Gao, R., Merzdorf, H. E., Anwar, S., Hipwell, M. C., & Srinivasa, A. R. (2024). Automatic assessment of text-based responses in post-secondary education: A systematic review. In *Computers and Education: Artificial Intelligence* (Vol. 6). Elsevier B.V. DOI: 10.1016/j.caeai.2024.100206

Gao, Y., Chang, C., Yu, X., Pang, P., Xiong, N., & Huang, C. (2022). A VR-based volumetric medical image segmentation and visualization system with natural human interaction. *Virtual Reality (Waltham Cross)*, 26(2), 415–424. DOI: 10.1007/s10055-021-00577-4

Garcia, L. (2020). Strategic intelligence teaching to leverage professional success.

Garg, S., & Sharma, S. (2020). Impact of artificial intelligence in special need education to promote inclusive pedagogy. *International Journal of Information and Education Technology (IJIET)*, 10(7), 523–527.

Garrison, D. R. (1997). Self-directed learning: Toward a comprehensive model. *Adult Education Quarterly*, 48(1), 18–33. DOI: 10.1177/074171369704800103

Gartner. (n.d.). Gartner glossary: Augmented intelligence. Gartner. https://www.gartner.com/en/information-technology/glossary/augmented-intelligence

Gattullo, M., Laviola, E., Boccaccio, A., Evangelista, A., Fiorentino, M., Manghisi, V. M., & Uva, A. E. (2022). Design of a Mixed Reality Application for STEM Distance Education Laboratories. *Computers*, 11(4). Advance online publication. DOI: 10.3390/computers11040050

Gayed, J. M., Carlon, M. K. J., Oriola, A. M., & Cross, J. S. (2022). Exploring an AI-based writing Assistant's impact on English language learners. *Computers and Education: Artificial Intelligence*, 3, 100055. Advance online publication. DOI: 10.1016/j.caeai.2022.100055

Gay, G. (2018). *Culturally responsive teaching: Theory, research, and practice.* Teachers College Press.

Gee, J. P. (2003). What video games have to teach us about learning and literacy. Computers in entertainment (CIE), 1(1), 20-20.

Gelacio, B. A., Amodia, L., Cabaya, I. M., Toylo, K. J., & Dacula, J. (2024). Steering the Artificial Intelligence Landscape: Technological Readiness and Acceptance of Accountancy Students. *Psychology and Education: A Multidisciplinary Journal, 21*(1), 95-102. https://doi.org/DOI: 10.5281/zenodo.12191798

Genc, H., Aydin, S., & Erdal, H. (2021). Designing a virtual reality programming environment for quantum computers. *Computer Applications in Engineering Education*, 30, 690–707.

George, B., & Wooden, O. (2023). Managing the strategic transformation of higher education through artificial intelligence. *Administrative Sciences*.

Gerich, J., & Fellinger, J. (2012). Effects of social networks on the quality of life in an elder and middle-aged deaf community sample. *Journal of Deaf Studies and Deaf Education*, 17(1), 102–115. PMID: 21606089

Gerstein, J. (2014). *Moving from Education 1.0 Through Education 2.0 Towards Education 3.0*. Educational Technology Faculty Publications and Presentations. Boise State University Scholar Works.

Ghazinejad, M., Khoshnoud, F., & Porter, S. (2021). *Enhancing interactive learning in engineering classes by implementing virtual laboratories. In: 2021 IEEE Frontiers in Education Conference*. FIE.

Gibson, L., Roberts-Smith, J., Llewellyn, K. R., & Llewellyn, J. (2022). A New Approach to Virtual Reality in History Education: The Digital Oral Histories for Reconciliation Project (DOHR). *History Education in the Digital Age*, 103–121. https://doi.org/DOI: 10.1007/978-3-031-10743-6_6

Gil, Y., Greaves, M., Hendler, J., & Hirsh, H. (2014). Amplify scientific discovery with Artificial intelligence. *Science*, 346(6206), 171–172. PMID: 25301606

Gil, Y., & Hirsh, H. (2012). Discovery Informatics: AI opportunities in scientific Discovery. *AAAI Fall Symposium*.

GiveVision. (n.d.). https://www.givevision.net/en/sightplus

Glaser, B. G., & Strauss, A. L. (1967). *The discovery of grounded theory: Strategies for qualitative research*. Aldine.

Goli-Cruz, M. J. (2023). Perceptions of Higher Education Faculty Regarding the Use of Chat Generative Pre-Trained Transformer (ChatGPT) in Education. *International Journal on Open and Distance e-Learning, 9*(2). https://doi.org/DOI: 10.58887/ijodel.v9i2.249

Gonçalves, C., & Rua, O. (2022). *Learning Creativity and Students' Performance: The Academia Contributions. Developing Entrepreneurial Ecosystems*. IGI Global.

Gong, M. Y., Yuksel, T., Magana, A., & Bryan, L. (2015, June). Engineering and Physics Students' Perceptions about Learning Quantum Me-chanics via Computer Simulations. In *2015 ASEE Annual Conference and Exposition Proceedings* (Vol. 26, No. 1, p. 23952).

Gonta, I. (2021). Students' perspectives on online learning problems, opportunities and expectations. *ELearning and Software for Education Conference*, 157–161. https://doi.org/DOI: 10.12753/2066-026X-21-020

Gonzales, A. L. (2018). Technology maintenance: A new frame for studying poverty and marginalization. *Communication Theory*, 28(2), 129–148. DOI: 10.1093/ct/qtx009

González, L., Neyem, A., Contreras, I. and Molina, D. (2022). Improving learning Experiences in software Engineering capstone courses using artificial intelligence virtual assistants. *Computers in Engineering education. 30(2).*

Goodrich, G. L., & Kirby, J. (2001). A comparison of patient reading performance and preference: Optical devices, handheld CCTV (Innoventions Magni-Cam), or stand-mounted CCTV (Optelec Clearview or TSI Genie). *Optometry (St. Louis, Mo.)*, 72(8), 519–528. PMID: 11519714

Grant, E. K., & Humble, T. S. (2020). Adiabatic quantum computing and quantum annealing. In Oxford Research Encyclopedia of Physics.

Greenwood, D. A. (2013). A critical theory of place-conscious education. In Stevenson, R. B., Brody, M., Dillon, J., & Wals, A. E. J. (Eds.), *International handbook of research on environmental education* (pp. 93–100). Routledge.

Greller, W., & Drachsler, H. (2012). Translating Learning into Numbers: A Generic Framework for Learning Analytics. *Journal of Educational Technology & Society*, 15(3), 42–57.

Groh, A. (2016). The impact of mobile phones on indigenous social structures: A cross-cultural comparative study. *Journal of Communication*, 7(2), 344–356. DOI: 10.1080/0976691x.2016.11884917

Guan, B., Li, X., Luo, Z., & Liu, P. (2024). [Arouse You? The Impact of AI Services on Consumer Pro-Environmental Behavior. Journal of Hospitality & Tourism Research.]. *CANA*, •••, I.

Guetterman, T. C., Fetters, M. D., & Creswell, J. W. (2015). Integrating quantitative and qualitative results in health science mixed methods research through joint displays. *Annals of Family Medicine*, 13(6), 554–561. DOI: 10.1370/afm.1865 PMID: 26553895

Guilherme, A. (2014). Reflections on Buber's 'living-centre': Conceiving of the teacher as 'the builder' and teaching as a 'situational revelation.'. *Studies in Philosophy and Education*, 34(3), 245–262.

Guimond, E., Kerr, D., & Beaujot, R. (2014). Charting the growth of Canada's Aboriginal populations: Problems, options and implications. *Canadian Studies in Population*, 31(1), 55–82. DOI: 10.25336/P6HW3B

Gui, Q., Ruiz-Blondet, M., Laszlo, S., & Jin, Z. (2019). A survey on brain biometrics. *ACM Computing Surveys*, 51(6), 1–38.

Guo, S., Zeng, D., & Dong, S. (2020). Pedagogical data analysis via federated learning toward education 4.0. *American Journal of Education and Information Technology*, 4(2), 56–65.

Gupta, A. K., Aggarwal, V., Sharma, V., & Naved, M. (2024). *Education 4.0 and Web 3.0 Technologies Application for Enhancement of Distance Learning Management Systems in the COVID–19 Era*. Education Improvement.

Gupta, T., Shree, A., Chanda, P., & Banerjee, A. (2023). Online assessment techniques adopted by the university teachers amidst COVID-19 pandemic: A case study. *Social Sciences & Humanities Open*, 8(1), 100579. Advance online publication. DOI: 10.1016/j.ssaho.2023.100579 PMID: 37287633

Gurung, G., & Banskota, K. (2009). *Mountain tourism in Nepal: Developing responsible mountain tourism for sustainable development*. ICIMOD.

Guskey, T. R. (2002). Professional development and teacher change. *Teachers and Teaching*, 8(3), 381–391. DOI: 10.1080/135406002100000512

H. Sandhya, B. V. (2022). AI's Potential for Optimal Student Learning in Education: Ethical Implications.

Hagge, P. (2021). Student perceptions of semester-long in-class virtual reality: Effectively using "Google Earth VR" in a higher education classroom. *Journal of Geography in Higher Education*, 45(3), 342–360.

Hammerness, K., Darling-Hammond, L., & Bransford, J. (2005). *Preparing teachers for a changing world: What teachers should learn and be able to do*. Jossey-Bass.

Hammoud, S., Karam, R., Mourad, R., Saad, I., & Kurdi, M. (2019). Stress and Heart Rate Variability during University Final Examination among Lebanese Students. *Behavioral Sciences (Basel, Switzerland)*, 9(3). Advance online publication. DOI: 10.3390/bs9010003 PMID: 30591634

Hapsari, I. P., & Wu, T. (2022). AI chatbot learning model in English-speaking Skill: Alleviating speaking anxiety, boosting enjoyment, and fostering critical thinking. In Lecture Notes in Computer Science: 444–453.

Hara, M. (2024). Roles of artificial intelligence in education for sustainable development in Asia-Pacific contexts. *Global Journal of Business and Integral Security*, 1(2), 1–17. https://www.gbis.ch/index.php/gbis/article/view/350

Hargittai, E. (2002). Second-level digital divide: Differences in people's online skills. *First Monday*, 7(4). Advance online publication. DOI: 10.5210/fm.v7i4.942

Harper, K. C., Chen, K., & Yen, D. (2004). Distance learning, virtual classrooms, and teaching pedagogy in the internet environment. *Technology in Society*, 26, 585–598.

Harris, A., & Rea, T. (2018). Privacy and ethical concerns with emotion detection technologies. *Journal of Information Privacy and Security*, 14(2), 45–60.

Harris, I. M. (2004). Peace education theory. *Journal of Peace Education*, 1(1), 5–20. DOI: 10.1080/1740020032000178276

Harris, I. M., & Morrison, M. L. (2013). *Peace education* (3rd ed.). McFarland & Company.

Harrison, R., Bower, J., & Williams, K. (2017). The impact of classroom noise on student learning: A review of the literature. *Journal of Environmental Psychology*, 52, 1–10.

Hastie, M., Hung, I. C., & Chen, N. (2010). Kinshuk: A blended synchronous learning model for educational international collaboration. *Innovations in Education and Teaching International*, 47, 24–29.

Hatice Leblebic, A. T. (2021). Opinions of Teacher Candidates on Inclusive Education: A Parallel Mixed Method Study. *International Journal of Education and Literacy Studies*, 9(4), 32–44. DOI: 10.7575/aiac.ijels.v.9n.4p.32

Havl'ıcek, V., C'orcoles, A., Temme, K., Harrow, A., Kandala, A., Chow, J., & Gambetta, J. (2018a). Supervised learning with quantum-enhanced feature spaces. *Nature*, 567, 209–212. PMID: 30867609

Heese, R., Gerlach, T., M¨ucke, S., M¨uller, S., Jakobs, M., & Piatkowski, N. (2023). *Explainable quantum machine learning*. ArXiv.

Hefler, M., Kerrigan, V., Henryks, J., Freeman, B., & Thomas, D. (2018). Social media and health information sharing among Australian Indigenous people. *Health Promotion International*, 34(4), 706–715. DOI: 10.1093/heapro/day018 PMID: 29672684

Hein, G. E. (1991). Constructivist learning theory. *Institute for Inquiry. Available at:/*Http://Www. Exploratorium. Edu/Ifi/Resources/Constructivistlearning. *HtmlS*.

Hensel, J., Ellard, K., Koltek, M., Wilson, G., & Sareen, J. (2019). Digital health solutions for Indigenous mental well-being. *Current Psychiatry Reports*, 21(8). Advance online publication. DOI: 10.1007/s11920-019-1056-6 PMID: 31263971

Henson, C., Chapman, F., Shepherd, G., Carlson, B., Rambaldini, B., & Gwynne, K. (2023). How older Indigenous women living in high-income countries use digital health technology: Systematic review. *Journal of Medical Internet Research*, 25, e41984. DOI: 10.2196/41984 PMID: 37071466

Hentschel, A., & Sanders, B. C. (2010, April). Machine learning for adaptive quantum measurement. In *2010 Seventh International Conference on Information Technology: New Generations* (pp. 506-511). IEEE.

Hernandez, A. A., Caballero, A. R., Albina, E. M., Balmes, I. L., & Niguidula, J. D. (2023, May). Artificial Intelligence for Sustainability: Evidence from select Small and Medium Enterprises in the Philippines. In *2023 8th International Conference on Business and Industrial Research (ICBIR)* (pp. 818-823). IEEE. https://doi.org/ DOI: 10.1109/ICBIR57571.2023.10147579

Hernández-Mustieles, M. A., Lima-Carmona, Y. E., Pacheco-Ramírez, M. A., Mendoza-Armenta, A. A., Romero-Gómez, J. E., Cruz-Gómez, C. F., & Lozoya-Santos, J. D. J. (2024). Wearable Biosensor Technology in Education: A Systematic Review. *Sensors (Basel)*, 24(8), 2437.

Higher, T. B. (2014). [ITHET]. *Education + Training*, ●●●, 1–5.

Hill, R. J. (2017). Cultural and linguistic sensitivity in AI systems for education: Challenges and recommendations. *Journal of Educational Technology & Society*, 20(4), 22–31. DOI: 10.1016/j.edtech.2017.03.002

Hill, R. J. (2017). *Emerging technologies and the future of education*. Palgrave Macmillan.

Hobbs, R. (2010). Digital and Media Literacy: A Plan of Action. A White Paper on the Digital and Media Literacy Recommendations of the Knight Commission on the Information Needs of Communities in a Democracy. Aspen Institute. 1 Dupont Circle NW Suite 700, Washington, DC 20036.

Hollis, V., Arnaud, M., & Jun, Y. (2020). Ethical considerations for emotion recognition technology in educational settings. *Educational Technology Research and Development*, 68(1), 123–139. PMID: 33199950

Holmes, W., Luckin, R., Griffiths, M., & Forcier, L. B. (2019). Intelligence Unleashed: An Argument for AI in Education. Pearson. https://www.pearson.com/

Holmes, W., Bialik, M., & Fadel, C. (2019). *Artificial intelligence in education promises and implications for teaching and learning*. Center for Curriculum Redesign.

Holmes, W., Bialik, M., & Fadel, C. (2019). *Artificial intelligence in education: Promises and implications for teaching and learning.* Center for Curriculum Redesign.

Holmes, W., & Porayska-Pomsta, K. (Eds.). (2022). *The ethics of artificial intelligence in education.* Routledge. DOI: 10.4324/9780429329067

Holmes, W., Porayska-Pomsta, K., Holstein, K., Sutherland, E., Baker, T., Shum, S. B., Santos, O. C., Rodrigo, M. T., Cukurova, M., Bittencourt, I. I., & Koedinger, K. R. (2022, September). Ig, &, Bittencourt, I., & Koedinger, K. R. (2022). Ethics of AI in Education: Towards a Community-Wide Framework. *International Journal of Artificial Intelligence in Education,* 32(3), 504–526. Advance online publication. DOI: 10.1007/s40593-021-00239-1

Holotescu, C., & Grosseck, G. (2018). Towards a MOOC-related Strategy in Romania. *BRAIN. Broad Research in Artificial Intelligence and Neuroscience,* 9, 99–109.

Hornberger, N. H. (2019). Ethnography in language planning and policy research. In King, K. A., Lai, Y. J., & May, S. (Eds.), *Research Methods in Language and Education* (pp. 193–204). Springer., DOI: 10.1007/978-3-319-02249-9_15

Hsiao, T. C., Tai, K. Y., Huang, Y. M., Chung, Y. F., Wu, Y. C., Kurniati, T., & Chen, T. S. (2018). An Implementation of Efficient Hierarchical Access Control Method for VR/AR Platform. *ICETA 2018 - 16th IEEE International Conference on Emerging ELearning Technologies and Applications, Proceedings,* 206–208. https://doi.org/DOI: 10.1109/ICETA.2018.8572099

Huang, C., & Liu, R. (2019). IoT-based classroom environment monitoring and its impact on student performance. *International Journal of Computer Applications in Technology,* 60(3), 211–224.

Huang, S. (2021). Design and development of educational robot teaching resources using artificial intelligence technology. *Journal of Emerging Technologies in Learning,* Huang, X., Zou, D., Cheng, G., Chen, X., and Xie, H. (2023). Trends, research Issues and applications of artificial intelligence in language education. *Journal of Educational Technology & Society,* 26(1), 112–131.

Huang, S. P. (2018). Effects of using artificial intelligence teaching system for environmental education on environmental knowledge and attitude. *Eurasia Journal of Mathematics, Science and Technology Education,* 14(7), 3277–3284.

Hughes, C., Isaacson, J., Perry, A., Sun, R. F., & Turner, J. (2020). Teaching quantum computing to high school students. *The Physics Teacher.*

Hughes, M., & Dallwitz, J. (2007). Ara Irititja: Towards culturally appropriate IT best practice in remote Indigenous Australia. In Dyson, L. E., Hendriks, M., & Grant, S. (Eds.), *Information Technology and Indigenous People* (pp. 146–158). Information Science Publishing.

Humphreys, P., Kalb, N., Morits, J. P. J., Schouten, R., Vermeulen, R., Twitchen, D., Markham, M., & Hanson, R. (2017). Deterministic delivery of remote entanglement on a quantum network. *Nature*, 558, 268–273. PMID: 29899475

Hunasgi, S., Koneru, A., Rudraraju, A., Manvikar, V., & Vanishree, M. (2018). Stress recognition in dental students using smartphone sensor and a software: A pilot study. *Journal of Oral and Maxillofacial Pathology : JOMFP*. PMID: 30651673

Hung, J.-L., Rice, K., & Saba, A. (2012). An Educational Data Mining Model for Online Teaching and Learning. *Journal of Educational Technology Development and Exchange*, 5(2).

Hutahaean, B., Telaumbanua, S., Tamba, L., Hutabarat, R. G. N., & Sumani, S. (2024). Analysis of Innovative and Adaptive Higher Education Curriculum Development to Education 5.0 Based Challenges in Indonesia. International Journal of Learning. *Teaching and Educational Research*, 23(4), 76–98.

Hwang, G., & Tu, Y. (2021). Roles and Research Trends of Artificial Intelligence In Mathematics Education: A Bibliometric Mapping Analysis and Systematic Review. *Mathematics*, 2021, 9.

Hyman, A., Stacy, E., Mohsin, H., Atkinson, K., Stewart, K., Lauscher, H., & Ho, K. (2022). Barriers and facilitators to accessing digital health tools faced by South Asian Canadians in Surrey, British Columbia: Community-based participatory action exploration using photovoice. *Journal of Medical Internet Research*, 24(1), e25863. DOI: 10.2196/25863 PMID: 35023842

Hynsjö, D., & Damon, A. (2016). Bilingual education in Peru: Evidence on how Quechua-medium education affects indigenous children's academic achievement. *Economics of Education Review*, 53, 116–132. DOI: 10.1016/j.econedurev.2016.05.006

IEEE-USA Board of Directors. (2017, February 10). Artificial intelligence research, development and regulation. IEEE. http://globalpolicy.ieee.org/wp-content/uploads/2017/10/IEEE17003.pdf

Ilham, R., Muhammad, I., Aji, L. J., Rizal, S. U., & Özbilen, F. M. (2023). Artificial intelligence research in education: A bibliometric analysis. *Journal of Education Global*, 1(1), 45–55. https://penaeducentre.com/index.php/JEdG/article/view/25

Illahi, A. A. C., Culaba, A., & Dadios, E. P. (2019, November). Internet of Things in the Philippines: a review. In *2019 IEEE 11th International Conference on Humanoid, Nanotechnology, Information Technology, Communication and Control, Environment, and Management (HNICEM)* (pp. 1-6). IEEE. https://doi.org/DOI: 10.1109/HNICEM48295.2019.9072882

Illanes, P., Lund, S., Mourshed, M., Rutherford, S., & Tyreman, M. (2018). Retraining and reskilling workers in the age of automation. *McKinsey Global Institute*, 8(1), 1–8.

Immerzeel, W. W., Van Beek, L. P., & Bierkens, M. F. (2010). Climate change will affect the Asian water towers. *Science*, 328(5984), 1382–1385. DOI: 10.1126/science.1183188 PMID: 20538947

Ipsita, A., Patel, M., Unmesh, A., & Ramani, K. (2024). Authoring instructional flow in iVR learning units to promote outcome-oriented learning. *Computers & Education: X Reality, 5*, 100074.

Iqbal, N., Ahmed, H., & Azhar, K. A. (2022). EXPLORING TEACHERS' ATTITUDES TOWARDS USING CHATGPT. *Global Journal for Management and Administrative Sciences*, 3(4), 97–111. DOI: 10.46568/gjmas.v3i4.163

Isaksson-Daun, J., Jansson, T., & Nilsson, J. (2024). Using Portable Virtual Reality to Assess Mobility of Blind and Low-Vision Individuals With the Audomni Sensory Supplementation Feedback. *IEEE Access : Practical Innovations, Open Solutions*, 12, 26222–26241.

Iseke, J., & Moore, S. (2011). Community-based indigenous digital storytelling with elders and youth. *American Indian Culture and Research Journal*, 35(4), 19–38. DOI: 10.17953/aicr.35.4.4588445552858866

Ismail, N., & Yusof, U. K. (2023). A systematic literature review: Recent techniques of predicting STEM stream students. In *Computers and Education: Artificial Intelligence* (Vol. 5). Elsevier B.V. DOI: 10.1016/j.caeai.2023.100141

Ismaya, B., Perdana, I., Arifin, A., Fadjarajani, S., Anantadjaya, S. P .D., and Muhammadiah, M . (2021). Merdeka Belajar in the Point of View of Learning Technology in the Era of 4.0 and Society 5.0. *A l- Ishlah: Ju rnal Pendidikan.. 13 (3): 1777-1785.*

Jabar, M., Chiong-Javier, E., & Pradubmook Sherer, P. (2024). Qualitative ethical technology assessment of artificial intelligence (AI) and the internet of things (IoT) among Filipino Gen Z members: Implications for ethics education in higher learning institutions. *Asia Pacific Journal of Education*, ●●●, 1–15. DOI: 10.1080/02188791.2024.2303048

Jackson, S., & Panteli, N. (2023). Trust or mistrust in algorithmic grading? An embedded agency perspective. *International Journal of Information Management*, 69, 102555. Advance online publication. DOI: 10.1016/j.ijinfomgt.2022.102555

Jagušt, T., & Botički, I. (2019). Mobile learning system for enabling collaborative and adaptive pedagogies with modular digital learning contents. *Journal of Computers in Education*, 6(3), 335–362.

Jara, C., Her'ıas, F. A. C., Medina, F., Dormido, S., & Esquembre, F. (2012). Synchronous collaboration of virtual and remote laboratories. *Computer Applications in Engineering Education*, •••, 20.

Jiang, L., Yu, S., & Wang, C. (2020). Second language writing instructors' feedback practice in response to automated writing evaluation: A sociocultural perspective. *System*, 93, 102302. DOI: 10.1016/j.system.2020.102302

Johnson, R. B., Onwuegbuzie, A. J., & Turner, L. A. (2007). Toward a definition of mixed methods research. *Journal of Mixed Methods Research*, 1(2), 112–133. DOI: 10.1177/1558689806298224

Jonassen, D. H. (2010). *Learning to solve problems: A handbook for designing problem-solving learning environments*. Routledge. DOI: 10.4324/9780203847527

Jones, E., Peercy, M., Woods, J., Parker, S., Jackson, T., Mata, S., & Seely, E. (2015). Identifying postpartum intervention approaches to reduce cardiometabolic risk among American Indian women with prior gestational diabetes, Oklahoma, 2012–2013. *Preventing Chronic Disease*, 12. Advance online publication. DOI: 10.5888/pcd12.140566 PMID: 25837258

Jones, L., Jacklin, K., & O'Connell, M. (2017). Development and use of health-related technologies in indigenous communities: Critical review. *Journal of Medical Internet Research*, 19(7), e256. DOI: 10.2196/jmir.7520 PMID: 28729237

Jongbloed, K., Pearce, M., Thomas, V., Sharma, R., Pooyak, S., Demerais, L., & Spittal, P. (2020). The Cedar Project - mobile phone use and acceptability of mobile health among young Indigenous people who have used drugs in British Columbia, Canada: Mixed methods exploratory study. *JMIR mHealth and uHealth*, 8(7), e16783. DOI: 10.2196/16783 PMID: 32716311

Jose, J. A. C., Bandala, A. A., Culaba, A. B., Chu, T. S., & Dadios, E. P. (2022, December). Artificial Intelligence for Developing Countries: Philippine Context. In *2022 IEEE 14th International Conference on Humanoid, Nanotechnology, Information Technology, Communication and Control, Environment, and Management (HNICEM)* (pp. 1-5). IEEE. https://doi.org/DOI: 10.1109/HNICEM57413.2022.10109550

Judijanto, L., Ili, L., & Wardhana, M. G. (2024). Education 5.0: Collaboration and Creativity in improving students' digital intelligence. [INJOSEDU]. *The International Journal of Social Education*, 1(3), 682–693.

Julien, G. (2024). How Artificial Intelligence (AI) impacts inclusive education. *Educational Research Review*, 19(6), 95–103. DOI: 10.5897/ERR2024.4404

Jung, J. Y., & Lee, K. S. (2020). Improving classroom acoustics: The impact of sound level meters on student concentration and behavior. *Journal of Educational Research and Practice*, 10(2), 121–135.

Kabalisa, R., & Altmann, J. (2021). AI technologies and motives for AI adoption by countries and firms: a systematic literature review. In *Economics of Grids, Clouds, Systems, and Services: 18th International Conference, GECON 2021, Virtual Event, September 21–23, 2021, Proceedings 18* (pp. 39-51). Springer International Publishing. https://doi.org/DOI: 10.1007/978-3-030-92916-9_4

Kajiwara, Y., & Kawabata, K. (2024). AI literacy for ethical use of chatbot: Will students accept AI ethics? *Computers and Education: Artificial Intelligence*, 6, 100251. Advance online publication. DOI: 10.1016/j.caeai.2024.100251

Kaka'e, K., Taum, R. P., & Magee, L. (2019). Indigenous ways of assessing student learning: A Polynesian perspective. AlterNative. *An International Journal of Indigenous Peoples*, 15(1), 77–84. DOI: 10.1177/1177180119828769

Kamalov, F., Santandreu Calonge, D., & Gurrib, I. (2023). New era of artificial intelligence in education: Towards a sustainable multifaceted revolution. *Sustainability*, 15(16), 12451. DOI: 10.3390/su151612451

Kaul, D., Raju, H., & Tripathy, B. K. (2021). Quantum-Computing-Inspired Algorithms in Machine Learning. In Research Anthology on Artificial Intelligence Applications in Security (pp. 429-448). IGI Global.

Kearsley, G., & Shneiderman, B. (1998). Engagement theory: A framework for technology-based teaching and learning. *Educational Technology*, 38(5), 20–23.

Kee, K. (2017). Adoption and diffusion. *Encyclopedia of Communication*. https://doi.org/DOI: 10.1002/9781118955567.wbieoc058

Keegan, T. T., Mato, P., & Ruru, S. (2015). Using Twitter in an Indigenous language: An analysis of te reo Māori tweets. AlterNative. *An International Journal of Indigenous Peoples*, 11(1), 59–75. DOI: 10.1177/117718011501100105

Kell, D. B., & Oliver, S. G. (2004). Here is the evidence, now what is the Hypothesis? The complementary roles of inductive and hypothesis-driven science in the post-genomic era. *BioEssays*, 26, 99–105. PMID: 14696046

Kerr, P. (2016). Adaptive Learning. *ELT Journal*, 70(1), 88–93. DOI: 10.1093/elt/ccv055

Keskitalo, P., Frangou, S. M., & Chohan, I. (2019). Educational design research in collaboration with students: Using digital tools to learn about reindeer herding within a vocational Sámi pedagogical context. *Education in the North*, 26(2), 62–85. DOI: 10.26203/3jca-m555

Keskitalo, P., & Olsen, T. (2019). Historical and political perspectives on Sámi and inclusive school systems in Norway. In Petrovic, J., & Mitchell, R. (Eds.), *Indigenous Philosophies of Education Around the World* (pp. 177–198). Routledge., DOI: 10.4324/9781351069410-11

Kester, K., & Cremin, H. (2017). Peace education and peace education research: Toward a concept of poststructural violence and second-order reflexivity. *Educational Philosophy and Theory*, 49(14), 1415–1427. DOI: 10.1080/00131857.2017.1313715

Kharal, A., & Ahmad, B. (2009). Mappings on fuzzy soft classes. *Advances in Fuzzy Systems*, 2009(1), 1–6. DOI: 10.1155/2009/407890

Khattak, A. M., Khan, G. A., Ishfaq, M., & Jamal, F. (2017). Characterization of soft α-separation axioms and soft β-separation axioms in soft single point spaces and in soft ordinary spaces. *Journal of New Theory*, (19), 63–81.

Khosravi, S., Bailey, S. G., Parvizi, H., & Ghannam, R. (2022). Wearable Sensors for Learning Enhancement in Higher Education. *Sensors (Basel)*, 22, 7633. DOI: 10.3390/s22197633 PMID: 36236732

Kim, J., & Castillejos-Petalcorin, C. (2020). The role of government research & development in fostering innovation in Asia. *Asian Development Bank*. https://www.adb.org/documents/asian-development-outlook-2020-background-papers

Kim, Y., Soyata, T., and Behnagh, R.F. (2018). Towards emotionally aware AI Smart classroom: Current issues and directions for engineering and education, *IEEE Access*, (6) 5308_5331.

Kimble, H. (2008). The quantum internet. *Nature*, 453, 1023–1030. PMID: 18563153

King, R. D.. (2009). The Automation of Science. *Science*, 324(5923), 85–89. PMID: 19342587

Kirschner, P. A., & Karpinski, A. C. (2010). Effects of AI-powered tools on student learning outcomes: A review of the evidence. *Educational Technology Research and Development*, 58(4), 347–371. DOI: 10.1007/s11423-010-9183-4

Kiryakova, G., Angelova, N., & Yordanova, L. (2018). The potential of augmented reality to transform education into smart education. *TEM Journal*, 7(3), 556.

Kitano, H. (2016). Artificial Intelligence to Win the Nobel Prize and Beyond: Creating The Engine for Scientific Discovery. *AI Magazine*, 37(1), 39–49.

Kizilcec, R. F., Huber, E., Papanastasiou, E. C., Cram, A., Makridis, C. A., Smolansky, A., Zeivots, S., & Raduescu, C. (2024). Perceived impact of generative AI on assessments: Comparing educator and student perspectives in Australia, Cyprus, and the United States. *Computers and Education: Artificial Intelligence*, 7, 100269. DOI: 10.1016/j.caeai.2024.100269

Kizilcec, R. F., Piech, C., & Schneider, E. (2013, April). Deconstructing disengagement: analyzing learner subpopulations in massive open online courses. In *Proceedings of the third international conference on learning analytics and knowledge* (pp. 170-179). DOI: 10.1145/2460296.2460330

Klein, C., Lester, J., Rangwala, H., & Johri, A. (2019). Technological barriers and incentives to learning analytics adoption in higher education: Insights from users. *Journal of Computing in Higher Education*, 31(3), 604–625. DOI: 10.1007/s12528-019-09210-5

Klir, G. J., & Yuan, B. (1996). Fuzzy sets and fuzzy logic: Theory and applications. *Possibility Theory versus Probab.Theory*, 32(2), 207–208.

Koch, K. (2022). The territorial and socio-economic characteristics of the digital divide in Canada. *The Canadian Journal of Regional Science*, 45(2), 89–98. DOI: 10.7202/1092248ar

Koedinger, K. R., Corbett, A. T., & Perfetti, C. (2015). The knowledge component framework: A conceptual framework for describing students' knowledge. *International Journal of Artificial Intelligence in Education*, 25(3), 250–272.

Kohler, T., Wehrli, A., & Jurek, M. (2014). *Mountain ecosystems: Environmentally and socially sustainable development*. United Nations Environment Programme.

Kolb, D. A. (2014). Experiential learning: Experience as the source of learning and development. FT press.

Kose, U., & Ocak, M. A. (2020). Artificial Intelligence-Based Personalized Learning in Education. *Education and Information Technologies*, 25(4), 3335–3355. DOI: 10.1007/s10639-019-10088-4

Kostic, Z. O., Jevremovic, A. D., Markovic, D. S., & Popovic, R. M. (2011, October). Virtual educational system and communication. In 2011 10th International Conference on Telecommunication in Modern Satellite Cable and Broadcasting Services (TELSIKS) (Vol. 1, pp. 373-376). IEEE.

Kotecha, K. (2023). Employing multimodal co-learning to evaluate the robustness of sensor fusion for Industry 5.0 tasks. *Soft Computing*, 27(7), 4139–4155.

Kral, I. (2010). Plugged in: Remote Australian Indigenous youth and digital culture. Centre for Aboriginal Economic Policy Research, Working Paper No. 69/2010. https://doi.org/DOI: 10.25911/5d7bdbde8a9c5

Krauss, J. K., Lipsman, N., Aziz, T., Boutet, A., Brown, P., Chang, J. W., Davidson, B., Grill, W. M., Hariz, M. I., & Horn, A. (2021). Technology of deep brain stimulation: Current status and future directions. *Nature Reviews. Neurology*, 17(2), 75–87. PMID: 33244188

Kritt, D., & Winegar, L. (2007). *Education and technology: Critical perspectives, possible futures*. Lexington Books.

Krumhuber, E., & D'Angelo, S. (2024). *Facial expressions and emotion recognition: Advances and applications*. Cambridge University Press.

Krupa, V., Khapper, I., Issa, W. A., AlHmoud, G., Balakrishna, G., Islam, A. K., & Graves, C. A. (2024). A low-power IoT-based smart desk integrated with a classroom response system. *Proceedings of SoutheastCon*, 2024, 1591–1598. DOI: 10.1109/southeastcon52093.2024.10500186

Kshetri, N. (2021). Evolving uses of artificial intelligence in human resource management in emerging economies in the global South: Some preliminary evidence. *Management Research Review*, 44(7), 970–990. DOI: 10.1108/MRR-03-2020-0168

Kuhn, T. S. (1977). *The essential tension*. University of Chicago Press.

Kukutai, T., & Taylor, J. (2016). *Indigenous data sovereignty: Toward an agenda*. ANU Press., DOI: 10.22459/CAEPR38.11.2016

Kulik, J. A., & Fletcher, J. D. (2016). Effectiveness of intelligent tutoring systems: A meta-analytic review. *Review of Educational Research*, 86(1), 42–78. DOI: 10.3102/0034654315581420

Kulikova, T. A., & Poddubnaya, N. A. (2021). Training of future educators for the introduction of mobile applications, AR and VR technologies into the educational process. *CEUR Workshop Proceedings*, 4, 231–240.

Kumar, A., Nayyar, A., Sachan, R. K., & Jain, R. (Eds.). (2023). *AI-assisted special education for students with exceptional needs*. IGI Global.

Kumari, R. K. (2024). Artificial intelligence in special education. In Advances in educational technologies and instructional design book series (pp. 79–112). https://doi.org/DOI: 10.4018/979-8-3693-5538-1.ch003

Kumar, R., & Gupta, S. (2021). Adaptive learning systems with real-time feedback: A review of voice recognition and emotion detection technologies. *Educational Technology Review*, 39(4), 145–162.

Kuru-Çetin, S., Nayir, F., & Taşkın, P. (2020). Okul yöneticilerin eğitimde değişime ilişkin görüşleri. [MSKU Journal of Education]. *Muğla Sıtkı Koçman Üniversitesi Eğitim Fakültesi Dergisi*, 7(1), 12–23.

Kushimo, T., & Thacker, B. (2022). Investigating students' strengths and difficulties in quantum computing. arXiv preprint arXiv:2212.03726.

Labrague, L. J., Aguilar-Rosales, R., Yboa, B. C., & Sabio, J. B. (2023). Factors influencing student nurses' readiness to adopt artificial intelligence (AI) in their studies and their perceived barriers to accessing AI technology: A cross-sectional study. *Nurse Education Today*, 130, 105945. DOI: 10.1016/j.nedt.2023.105945 PMID: 37625351

Labrague, L. J., Aguilar-Rosales, R., Yboa, B. C., Sabio, J. B., & de Los Santos, J. A. (2023). Student nurses' attitudes, perceived utilization, and intention to adopt artificial intelligence (AI) technology in nursing practice: A cross-sectional study. *Nurse Education in Practice*, 73, 103815. DOI: 10.1016/j.nepr.2023.103815 PMID: 37922736

Lamichhane, S. K. (2012). Instructional design for student learning on quantum tunneling. *The Himalayan Physics*, 3, 27–34.

Lampou, R. (2023). The integration of artificial intelligence in education: Opportunities and challenges. *Review of Artificial Intelligence in Education*, 4, e15–e15.

Lampropoulos, G., Keramopoulos, E., Diamantaras, K., & Evangelidis, G. (2022). Augmented reality and gamification in education: A systematic literature review of research, applications, and empirical studies. *applied sciences, 12*(13), 6809.

Lampropoulos, G., & Sidiropoulos, A. (2024). Impact of Gamification on Students' Learning Outcomes and Academic Performance: A Longitudinal Study Comparing Online, Traditional, and Gamified Learning. *Education in Science*, 14(367). Advance online publication. DOI: 10.3390/educsci14040367

Langley, P. (2000). The computational support of scientific discovery. *International Journal of Human-Computer Studies*, 53, 393–410.

Laura, R. S., & Chapman, A. (2009). The technologisation of education: Philosophical reflections on being too plugged. *International Journal of Children's Spirituality*, 14(3), 289–298.

Lee, D., Arnold, M., Srivastava, A., Plastow, K., Strelan, P., Ploeckl, F., Lekkas, D., & Palmer, E. (2024). The impact of generative AI on higher education learning and teaching: A study of educators' perspectives. *Computers and Education: Artificial Intelligence*, 6, 100221. Advance online publication. DOI: 10.1016/j.caeai.2024.100221

Lee, J., Chen, M., & Kim, S. (2023). Socioeconomic disparities among students and their families: Implications for educational equity. *Educational Review*, 75(2), 208–226.

Lee, J., Surh, J., Choi, W., & You, B. (2021). Immersive virtual-reality-based streaming distance education system for solar dynamics observatory: A case study. *Applied Sciences (Switzerland)*, 11(19). Advance online publication. DOI: 10.3390/app11198932

Legaspi, J. B., Licuben, R. J. O., Legaspi, E. A., & Aguinaldo, J. (2024). Comparing AI detectors: Evaluating performance and efficiency. *International Journal of Science and Research Archive*, 12(2), 833–838. DOI: 10.30574/ijsra.2024.12.2.1276

Lehka, L. V., Shokaliuk, S. V., & Semerikov, S. O. (2023). Exploring the quantum frontier in school informatics: A pedagogical journey. *Educational Dimension*, 8, 112–142.

Lepper, M. R., & Woolverton, M. (2002). The wisdom of practice: Lessons learned from the study of highly effective tutors. In Aronson, J. M. (Ed.), *Improving academic achievement: Impact of psychological factors on education* (pp. 135–158). Academic Press.

Leymann, F., Barzen, J., Falkenthal, M., Vietz, D., Weder, B., & Wild, K. (2020). Quantum in the cloud: application potentials and research opportunities. arXiv preprint arXiv:2003.06256.

Li, X., & Heng, Q. *"Design of mobile learning resources based on new blended learning: a case study of superstar learning app,"* in 2021 IEEE 3rd International Conference on Computer Science and Educational Informatization (CSEI). IEEE, 2021, pp. 333–338. DOI: 10.1109/CSEI51395.2021.9477709

Liberati, N. (2016). Augmented reality and ubiquitous computing: The hidden potentialities of augmented reality. *AI & Society*, 31(1), 17–28. DOI: 10.1007/s00146-014-0543-x

Ligot, D. V., Melendres, R. L., Tayco, F. C., Vizmonte, E. J., Toledo, M., Gerlock-Barretto, A., Martinez, J. E., Benardo, G., Sindol-Ritualo, M., Neri, C., Nungcaras, J., & Pelayo, S. (2022). Philippines Data Analytics Sector Labor Market Intelligence Report. https://dx.doi.org/DOI: 10.2139/ssrn.4027384

Lim, J. Z., Mountstephens, J., & Teo, J. (2022). Eye-tracking Feature Extraction for Biometric Machine Learning. *Frontiers in Neurorobotics, 15.*

Lin, C. (2019). A review of the application of artificial intelligence in education. *Journal of Educational Technology Research and Development*, 67(4), 879–901. DOI: 10.1007/s11423-019-09648-0

Lin, N., Chen, B., Yang, M., Lu, F., & Deng, R. (2023). Low vision aids and age are associated with Müller-Lyer illusion in congenital visually impaired children. *Frontiers in Psychology*, 14. Advance online publication. DOI: 10.3389/fpsyg.2023.1278554 PMID: 38078226

Lin, X. P., & Li, B. Bin, Yao, Z. N., Yang, Z., & Zhang, M. (2024). The impact of virtual reality on student engagement in the classroom–a critical review of the literature. *Frontiers in Psychology*, 15. Advance online publication. DOI: 10.3389/fpsyg.2024.1360574 PMID: 38659670

Li, P., Fang, Z., & Jiang, T. (2022). Research Into improved Distance Learning Using VR Technology. *Frontiers in Education*, 7. Advance online publication. DOI: 10.3389/feduc.2022.757874

Li, S., & Rutab, N. M. P. (2023). An analysis of education problems in the post-pandemic era of COVID-19. *Adult Higher Educ.*, 5(1), 60–64.

Liu, J., Li, H., Zhu,H. Li, H, Zhang, X., Zhou, G., Lou, D, and Chen, Y. (2023).

Liu, D. Y. T., Bartimote-Aufflick, K., Pardo, A., & Bridgeman, A. (2017). Data-driven personalization of student learning support in higher education. In *Higher Education Learning Analytics: Navigating between Learning and the Digital Realm* (pp. 143–169). Springer.

Liu, S., Wang, Y., & Zheng, Y. (2020, June). Computational Intelligence in Science Education. In *Proceedings of the 6th International Conference on Frontiers of Educational Technologies* (pp. 34-38).

Liu, X., Zhao, Y., & Li, M. (2021). Privacy considerations in the use of voice recognition technology in education. *International Journal of Educational Technology*, 23(2), 89–102.

Li, W. (2023, April). Simulating Quantum Turing Machine in Augmented Reality. In *Proceedings of the 2023 8th International Conference on Multimedia and Image Processing* (pp. 107-112).

Li, X., Zhang, Y., Cheng, H., Li, M., & Yin, B. (2022). Student achievement prediction using deep neural network from multi-source campus data. *Complex & Intelligent Systems*, 8(6), 5143–5156.

Lockard, W., & De Maio, F. (2021). Digital inclusion initiatives in Aboriginal communities in Australia: A systematic review. *International Journal of Environmental Research and Public Health*, 18(6), 3080. DOI: 10.3390/ijerph18063080 PMID: 33802715

Lockard, W., & Huss, J. (2016). Learning to be Webbed: A Case Study of a Native American High School's Integration of Technology. *Journal of American Indian Education*, 55(2), 4–27.

Lock, J., & Duggleby, S. (2018). Exploring quality of life through an online international collaboration. *Technology, Pedagogy and Education*, 27, 533–548.

Lonchamp, J. (2006). Supporting synchronous collaborative learning: A generic, multi-dimensional model. *International Journal of Computer-Supported Collaborative Learning*, 1, 247–276.

Lotfi, A. (1965). Zadeh. Fuzzy sets. *Information and Control*, 8(3), 338–353. DOI: 10.1016/S0019-9958(65)90241-X

Lowe, K., & Yunkaporta, T. (2013). The inclusion of Aboriginal and Torres Strait Islander content in the Australian National Curriculum: A cultural, cognitive and socio-political evaluation. *Curriculum Perspectives*, 33(1), 1–14.

Luan, H., Geczy, P., Lai, H., Gobert, J., J. H. Yang, S., Ogata, H., Baltes, J., Guerra, R., Li, P., & Tsai, C. C. (2020). Challenges and Future Directions of Big Data and Artificial Intelligence in Education.

Luckin, R., Holmes, W., Griffiths, M., & Forcier, L. B. (2016). *Intelligence unleashed: An argument for AI in education.* Pearson.

Luckin, R., Holmes, W., Griffiths, M., & Forcier, L. B. (2016). *Intelligence Unleashed: An Argument for AI in Education.* Pearson.

Luo, G., & Pundlik, S. (2022). Usage patterns of Head-mounted vision assistance app as compared to handheld video Magnifier. In *Displays* (Vol. 75, p. 102303). Elsevier BV., DOI: 10.1016/j.displa.2022.102303

Lynn, N. D., & Emanuel, A. W. R. (2020). Using Data Mining Techniques to Predict Students' Performance. a Review. ICIMECE 2020 IOP Conf. Series: Materials Science and Engineering, 1096. DOI: 10.1088/1757-899X/1096/1/012083

Macchi, M. (2011). Framework for community-based climate vulnerability and capacity assessment in mountain areas. ICIMOD Working Paper 2011/13. International Centre for Integrated Mountain Development.

Machado, L. S. R., Frasseto, L. D. S., Bilessimo, S. M. S., Silva, J. B. D., & Silva, I. N. D. (2022, August). Pedagogical models focused on the integration of ICT in basic education: A systematic review. *International Journal of Advanced Engineering Research and Science. Jaipur.*, 9(8), 129–134.

Machine Learning Based Analysis of the Curriculum Standards and Textbooks of Middle School Biology Teaching. (2023). Case of "Curriculum Ideological and Political". *ICEKIM 2023. AHCS*, 13, 292–303.

Mageira, K., Pittou, D., Papasalouros, A., Kotis, K., Zangogianni, P., & Daradoumis, A. (2022). Educational AI chatbots for content and language integrated learning. *Applied Sciences (Basel, Switzerland)*, 12(7), 3239. DOI: 10.3390/app12073239

Maji, P. K., Biswas, R., & Ranjan Roy, A. (2003). Soft set theory. *Computers & Mathematics with Applications (Oxford, England)*, 45(4-5), 555–562. DOI: 10.1016/S0898-1221(03)00016-6

Maji, P. K., Roy, A. R., & Biswas, R. (2002). Akhil Ranjan Roy, and Ranjit Biswas. An application of soft sets in a decision making problem. *Computers & Mathematics with Applications (Oxford, England)*, 44(8-9), 1077–1083. DOI: 10.1016/S0898-1221(02)00216-X

Major, L., Francis, G. A., & Tsapali, M. (2021). The effectiveness of technology-supported personalised learning in low-and middle-income countries: A meta-analysis. *British Journal of Educational Technology*, 52(5), 1935–1964. DOI: 10.1111/bjet.13116

Majumdar, P., & Samanta, S. K. (2008). Similarity measure of soft sets. *New Mathematics and Natural Computation.*, 4, 1–12.

Majumdar, P., & Samanta, S. K. (2010). Generalised fuzzy soft sets. *Computers & Mathematics with Applications (Oxford, England)*, 59(4), 1425–1432. DOI: 10.1016/j.camwa.2009.12.006

Makarova, E. A., & Makarova, E. L. (2018). Blending pedagogy and digital technology to transform educational environment. International Journal of Cognitive Research in Science, Engineering and Education:(IJCRSEE), 6(2), 57-66.

Makrides, G. (2020). The evolution of Education 1.0 to Education 4.0: Is it an Evolution or a revolution? Anniversary Scientific Conference "Synergetics and Reflection in Mathematics Education", 16-18 October 2020, Pamporovo, Bulgaria.

Mallik, S. & Gangopadhyay, A. (2023). Proactive and Reactive Engagement of Artificial Intelligence Methods for Education: A Review. Schiff, D. (2021). Out of the laboratory and into the classroom: the future of artificial intelligence in education.

Mannocci, A., Salatino, A. A., Osborne, F., & Motta, E. (2017). 2100 AI: Reflections on the mechanisation of scientific discovery. In: Recoding Black Mirror @ ISWC '17, 21-25 Oct 2017, Wien, Austria.

Maqbool, M. A., Asif, M., Imran, M., Bibi, S., & Almusharraf, N. (2024a). Emerging E-learning trends: A study of faculty perceptions and impact of collaborative techniques using fuzzy interface system. *Social Sciences & Humanities Open*, 10, 101035. Advance online publication. DOI: 10.1016/j.ssaho.2024.101035

Marcial, D. E. (2020). Education 4.0: Disrupting education towards creativity, innovation, and commercialization. *International Journal of Scientific Engineering and Science*, 4(12), 25–33. https://ijses.com/volume-4-issue-12

Marougkas, A., Troussas, C., Krouska, A., & Sgouropoulou, C. (2023). Virtual Reality in Education: A Review of Learning Theories, Approaches and Methodologies for the Last Decade. *Electronics (Switzerland)*, 12(13). Advance online publication. DOI: 10.3390/electronics12132832

Marougkas, A., Troussas, C., Krouska, A., & Sgouropoulou, C. (2024). How personalized and effective is immersive virtual reality in education? A systematic literature review for the last decade. *Multimedia Tools and Applications*, 83(6), 18185–18233. DOI: 10.1007/s11042-023-15986-7

Mart'ınez-Cerd'a, J. F., Torrent-Sellens, J., & Gonz'alez-Gonz'alez, I. (2018). Promoting collaborative skills in online university: Comparing effects of games, mixed reality, social media, and other tools for ict-supported pedagogical practices. *Behaviour & Information Technology*.

Martin, F., Zhuang, M., & Schaefer, D. (2024). Systematic review of research on artificial intelligence in K-12 education (2017–2022). In *Computers and Education: Artificial Intelligence* (Vol. 6). Elsevier B.V. DOI: 10.1016/j.caeai.2023.100195

Marx, E., Leonhardt, T., & Bergner, N. (2023). Secondary school students' mental models and attitudes regarding artificial intelligence - A scoping review. In *Computers and Education: Artificial Intelligence* (Vol. 5). Elsevier B.V. DOI: 10.1016/j.caeai.2023.100169

Masala, R., & Monni, S. (2019). The social inclusion of indigenous peoples in Ecuador before and during the revolución ciudadana. *Development*, 62(1-4), 167–177. DOI: 10.1057/s41301-019-00219-y

Maslej, N., Fattorini, L., Brynjolfsson, E., Etchemendy, J., Ligett, K., Lyons, T., Manyika, J., Ngo, H., Niebles, J. C., Parli, V., Shoham, Y., Wald, R., Clark, J., & Perrault, R. (2023). The AI index 2023 annual report. Stanford University: AI Index Steering Committee, Institute for Human-Centered AI.

Masri, G., Al-Shargie, F., Tariq, U., Almughairbi, F., Babiloni, F., & Al-Nashash, H. (2023). Mental stress assessment in the workplace: A review. *IEEE Transactions on Affective Computing*.

Masri, G., & Member, G. S. (n.d.). Mental Stress Assessment in the Workplace. *RE:view*. Advance online publication. DOI: 10.1109/TAFFC.2023.3312762

Mathews, K. M. (2016). Transformative models in K-12 education: The impact of a blended universal design for learning intervention. An experimental mixed methods study (Doctoral dissertation, University of San Diego).

Mayer, R. E. (2012). Cognitive Theory of Multimedia Learning. *The Cambridge Handbook of Multimedia Learning*, 31–48. https://doi.org/DOI: 10.1017/cbo9780511816819.004

Mayer, J. D., Salovey, P., & Caruso, D. R. (2008). Emotional intelligence: New ability or eclectic traits? *The American Psychologist*, 63(6), 503–517. PMID: 18793038

McCarty, T. L., & Nicholas, S. E. (2014). Reclaiming Indigenous languages: A reconsideration of the roles and responsibilities of schools. *Review of Research in Education*, 38(1), 106–136. DOI: 10.3102/0091732X13507894

Mccloy, R., & Stone, R. (2001). Virtual reality in surgery. *BMJ (Clinical Research Ed.)*, 323(7318), 912–915. DOI: 10.1136/bmj.323.7318.912 PMID: 11668138

McCorduck, P. (1979). *Machines who think: A personal inquiry into the history and prospect of artificial intelligence*. W. H. Freeman.

McCorduck, P. (1985). *The universal machine: Confessions of a technological optimist*. McGraw-Hill.

McCorduck, P. (1988). Artificial intelligence: An aperçu. *Daedalus*, 177(1), 65–83.

McDaniel, P. N. (2022). Teaching, Learning, and Exploring the Geography of North America with Virtual Globes and Geovisual Narratives. *The Journal of Geography*, 121(4), 125–140. DOI: 10.1080/00221341.2022.2119597

McLachlan, C., Fleer, M., & Edwards, S. (2018). *Early childhood curriculum: Planning, assessment and implementation*. Cambridge University Press.

McLoughlin, C., & Lee, M. J. W. (2010). Personalised and self regulated learning in the web 2.0 era: International exemplars of innovative pedagogy using social software. *Australasian Journal of Educational Technology*.

McMahon, R. (2020). Co-developing digital inclusion policy and programming with indigenous partners: Interventions from Canada. *Internet Policy Review*, 9(2). Advance online publication. DOI: 10.14763/2020.2.1478

Melluso, N., Fareri, S., Fantoni, G., Bonaccorsi, A., Chiarello, F., Coli, E., Giordano, V., Manfredi, P., & Manafi, S. (2020). *Lights and shadows of COVID-19, Technology and Industry 4.0*. https://doi.org/DOI: 10.48550/ARXIV.2004.13457

Mena-Guacas, A. F., Urueña Rodríguez, J. A., Santana Trujillo, D. M., Gómez-Galán, J., & López-Meneses, E. (2023). Collaborative learning and skill development for the educational growth of artificial intelligence: A systematic review. *Contemporary Educational Technology*, 15(3), ep428.

Mendoza, J. R., Catapang, R. G., & Aquino, J. M. (2023). The Impact of Moodle-Cloud on Faculty and Graduate Students' User-Independence Engagement in a State University in the Philippines. *International Journal of Learning. Teaching and Educational Research*, 22(12), 299–325. DOI: 10.26803/ijlter.22.12.15

Mermin, N. (2002). From cbits to qbits: Teaching computer scientists quantum mechanics. *American Journal of Physics*, 71, 23–30.

Metila, R. A., Pradilla, L. A. S., & Williams, A. B. (2016). The challenge of implementing mother tongue education in linguistically diverse contexts: The case of the Philippines. *The Asia-Pacific Education Researcher*, 25(5-6), 781–789. DOI: 10.1007/s40299-016-0310-5

Meyer, A., Rose, D. H., & Gordon, D. (2014). *Universal design for learning: Theory and practice*. No Title.

Miao, F., Holmes, W., & Huang, R. (2021). AI and Education: Guidance for Policy-Makers. *UNESCO*.https://unesdoc.unesco.org/ark:/48223/pf0000376709

Michailidou, A., & Economides, A. (2003). Elearn: Towards a collaborative educational virtual environment. *Journal of Information Technology Education*, 2, 131–152.

Milgram, P., & Kishino, F. (1994). A taxonomy of mixed reality visual displays. *IEICE Transactions on Information and Systems*, 77(12), 1321–1329.

Militello, C., Rundo, L., Vitabile, S., & Conti, V. (2021). Fingerprint classification based on deep learning approaches: Experimental findings and comparisons. *Symmetry*, 13(5). Advance online publication. DOI: 10.3390/sym13050750

Miller, R., Smith, A., & Johnson, P. (2020). Enhancing classroom dynamics with real-time speech analysis: A case study. *Educational Technology Research and Development*, 68(4), 1157–1176.

Milloria, B. R. B., Marzon, A. M. D., & Derasin, L. M. C. (2024). Investigating AI-Integrated Instruction in Improving Academic Performance of Senior High School Students in the Philippines. *Journal of Harbin Engineering University*, 45(6), 61–66. https://www.researchgate.net/publication/382299009

Mills, K. A., Davis-Warra, J., Sewell, M., & Anderson, M. (2019). Indigenous ways with literacies: Transgenerational, multimodal, placed, and collective. *Language and Education*, 33(5), 400–420. DOI: 10.1080/09500782.2019.1629942

Mina, A., Tumanglao, M., & Bugarin, M. (2023). Enhancing clinical instructors' preparedness: A holistic approach to integrating artificial intelligence in nursing education. *Filipino Multidisciplinary Research Journal in Education*, 3(1), 1021. DOI: 10.5281/zenodo. 10777491

Mina, P. N. R., Solon, I. M., Sanchez, F. R., Delante, T. K., Villegas, J. K., Basay, F. J., Andales, J.-r., Pasko, F., Estrera, M. F. R., Samson, R.Jr, & Mutya, R. (2023). Leveraging Education through Artificial Intelligence Virtual Assistance: A Case Study of Visually Impaired Learners. *International Journal of Educational Innovation and Research*, 2(1), 10–22. DOI: 10.31949/ijeir.v2i1.3001

Mindajao, B. Y. (2023). Effectiveness of Chatbot as an innovative modality in grade reporting in the new normal. *European Journal of Education Studies*, 10(2), 244–252. DOI: 10.46827/ejes.v10i2.4686

Minglana, J., Tobias, R. R., & Roxas, R. E. (2021, December). Artificial intelligence applications in quality management system: a bibliometric study. In *TENCON 2021-2021 IEEE Region 10 Conference (TENCON)* (pp. 947-952). IEEE. https://doi.org/ DOI: 10.1109/TENCON54134.2021.9707340

Močkoř, J., & Hurtík, P. (2021). Jiˇ rˊ ı Moˇckoˇ r and Petr Hurtˊ ık. Approximations of fuzzy soft sets by fuzzy soft relations with image processing application. *Soft Computing*, 25(10), 6915–6925. DOI: 10.1007/s00500-021-05769-3

Mohamad Rasli, R., Md Norwawi, N., & Basir, N. (2016). Preliminary survey of educational simulations towards educational context.

Mohammed, F. H., Sharif, H., Rahman, M. A., Khan, A. A., Islam, M. M., & Habib, M. T. (2023). Design and development of SEMS - An IoT-based smart environment monitoring system. *Proceedings of I-SMAC 2023*. https://doi.org/DOI: 10.1109/i-smac58438.2023.10290331

Molenaar, I. (2022). Towards hybrid human-AI learning technologies. *European Journal of Education*, 00(4), 1–14. DOI: 10.1111/ejed.12527

Mollahosseini, A., Chan, D., & Mahoor, M. H. (2017). AffectNet: A dataset for facial expression, valence, and arousal computing in the wild. *IEEE Transactions on Affective Computing*, 10(1), 18–31.

Mollee Shultz, J. N. (2022). The role of epistemological beliefs in STEM pedagogy at Hispanic-Serving Institutions. *International Journal of STEM Education faculty's decisions to use culturally relevant*, 1-22.

Molodtsov, D. (1999). Soft set theory—First results. *Computers & Mathematics with Applications (Oxford, England)*, 37(4-5), 19–31. DOI: 10.1016/S0898-1221(99)00056-5

Montanaro, A. (2016). Quantum algorithms: an overview. npj Quantum Information, 2(1), 1-8.

Moorhouse, B. L., Yeo, M. A., & Wan, Y. (2023). Generative AI tools and assessment: Guidelines of the world's top-ranking universities. *Computers and Education Open*, 5, 100151. DOI: 10.1016/j.caeo.2023.100151

Moreno, F. G. (2023, July 13). AI readiness of Philippine Public Administration: A review of literature. https://doi.org/DOI: 10.31219/osf.io/kpzt6

Morgan, J. T., & Wittmann, M. C. (2006, February). Examining the evolution of student ideas about quantum tunneling. In *2005 Physics Education Research Conference* (Vol. 818, pp. 73-76).

Morgan, J., Wittmann, M. C., & Thompson, J. R. (2004). Student understanding of tunneling in quantum mechanics: Examining interview and survey results for clues to student reasoning. *University of Maine Physics Education Research Laboratory*, 720, 97–100.

Morley, J. (2020). *The impact of artificial intelligence on society: Exploring the future of work and ethics*. Routledge.

Moron, C. E., & Diokno, C. O. B. (2023). Level of readiness and adoption on the use of artificial intelligence technologies in the accounting profession. *Open Journal of Accounting*, 12(3), 37–54. DOI: 10.4236/ojacct.2023.123004

Moshtael, H., Aslam, T., Underwood, I., & Dhillon, B. (2015). High Tech Aids Low Vision: A Review of Image Processing for the Visually Impaired. *Translational Vision Science & Technology*, 4(4), 6. DOI: 10.1167/tvst.4.4.6 PMID: 26290777

Moundridou, M., Matzakos, N., & Doukakis, S. (2024). Generative AI tools as educators' assistants: Designing and implementing Inquiry-based lesson plans. *Computers and Education: Artificial Intelligence*, 100277, 100277. Advance online publication. DOI: 10.1016/j.caeai.2024.100277

Mu~niz, M. N., & Oliver-Hoyo, M. (2014). Investigating quantum mechanical tunneling at the nanoscale via analogy: Development and assessment of a teaching tool for upper-division chemistry. *Journal of Chemical Education*, 91, 1546–1556.

Mupaikwa, E. (2024). Artificial Intelligence-Driven Instruction and Its Impact on Heutagogy and Student Engagement. In *AI Algorithms and ChatGPT for Student Engagement in Online Learning* (pp. 101–123). IGI Global., DOI: 10.4018/979-8-3693-4268-8.ch007

Murumba, J., & Micheni, E. (2017). Big Data Analytics in Higher Education: A Review [IJES]. *The International Journal of Engineering and Science*, 6(6), 14–21. DOI: 10.9790/1813-0606021421

Muthmainnah, S., Ibna Seraj, P. M., Oteir, I., & Balakrishnan, B. (2022). Playing

Mykhailova, M. (2020, February). The Quantum Katas: Learning Quantum Computing Using Programming Exercises. In *Proceedings of the 51st ACM Technical Symposium on Computer Science Education* (pp. 1417-1417).

Mykhailova, M. (2021, March). Developing Programming Exercises for Teaching Quantum Computing. In *Proceedings of the 52nd ACM Technical Symposium on Computer Science Education* (pp. 1376-1376).

Mystakidis, S., Fragkaki, M., & Filippousis, G. (2021). Ready teacher one: Virtual and augmented reality online professional development for k-12 school teachers. *Computers*, 10(10). Advance online publication. DOI: 10.3390/computers10100134

Nakata, M., Nakata, V., & Day, A. (2020). Dreaming, knowing and knowledge sharing: Indigenous knowledges and higher education. In Frawley, J., Larkin, S., & Smith, J. A. (Eds.), *Indigenous Pathways, Transitions and Participation in Higher Education* (pp. 3–16). Springer., DOI: 10.1007/978-981-10-4062-7_1

National Center for Education Statistics. (2019). Digital technology use in rural and urban schools. U.S. Department of Education, Institute of Education Sciences. Retrieved from https://nces.ed.gov

National Research Council. (2000). *How people learn: Brain, mind, experience, and school.* The National Academies Press., DOI: 10.17226/9853National Academies of Sciences, Engineering, and Medicine. (2018). How people learn II: Learners, contexts, and cultures. The National Academies Press. DOI: 10.17226/24783

Naylor, R., Baik, C., Arkoudis, S., & Dabrowski, A. (2020). Exploring the experiences of Aboriginal and Torres Strait Islander students in higher education. In Frawley, J., Russell, G., & Sherwood, J. (Eds.), *Cultural Competence and the Higher Education Sector* (pp. 63–80). Springer., DOI: 10.1007/978-981-15-5362-2_4

Nazaretsky, T., Ariely, M., Cukurova, M., & Alexandron, G. (2022). Teachers' trust in AI-powered educational technology and a professional development program to improve it. *British Journal of Educational Technology*, 53(4), 914–931.

Nazaretsky, T., Bar, C., Walter, M., & Alexandron, G. (2022, March). Empowering teachers with AI: Co-designing a learning analytics tool for personalized instruction in the science classroom. In *LAK22: 12th International Learning Analytics and Knowledge Conference* (pp. 1-12).

Ngoenriang, N., Xu, M., Kang, J., Niyato, D., Yu, H., & Shen, X. (2023). Dqc ^2 o: Distributed quantum computing for collaborative optimization in future networks. *IEEE Communications Magazine*, 61(5), 188–194.

Nguyen, A., Gardner, L., & Sheridan, D. (2017). A MultiLayered Taxonomy of Learning Analytics Applications. *In Proceedings of the Pacific Asia Conference on Information Systems*, Article 54.

Nguyen, A., Ngan Ngo, H., Hong, Y., Dang, B., & Thi Nguyen, B. P. (2023). Ethical principles for artificial intelligence in education.

Nguyen, N. X., Weismann, M., & Trauzettel-Klosinski, S. (2009). Improvement of reading speed after providing of low vision aids in patients with age-related macular degeneration. In Acta Ophthalmologica (Vol. 87, Issue 8, pp. 849–853). Wiley. https://doi.org/DOI: 10.1111/j.1755-3768.2008.01423.x

Nguyen, A., Gardner, L. A., & Sheridan, D. (2018). A Framework for Applying Learning Analytics in Serious Games for People with Intellectual Disabilities. *British Journal of Educational Technology*, 49(4), 673–689. DOI: 10.1111/bjet.12625

Nguyen, A., Gardner, L., & Sheridan, D. (2020). Data analytics in higher education: An integrated view. *Journal of Information Systems Education*, 31(1), 61.

Nguyen, A., Gardner, L., & Sheridan, D. (2022). Artificial intelligence in education: Applications, benefits, and challenges. *International Journal of Educational Technology in Higher Education*, 19(1), 1–21. DOI: 10.1186/s41239-021-00309-1 PMID: 35013716

Nguyen, H. T., & Nguyen, L. T. (2019). Fingerprints classification through image analysis and machine learning method. *Algorithms*, 12(11), 241.

Nikum, K. (2022). Answers to the Societal Demands with Education 5.0:Indian Higher Education System. *Journal of Engineering Education Transformations,*, 115-127.

Nisha, N. B., & Varghese, R. R. (2021). Literature on information literacy: A review. *DESIDOC Journal of Library and Information Technology*, 41(4).

Nistor, N., & Hernández-Garcíac, Á. (2018). What Types of Data are used in Learning Analytics? An Overview of Six Cases. *Computers in Human Behavior*, 89, 335–338. DOI: 10.1016/j.chb.2018.07.038

Nita, L., Smith, L. M., Chancellor, N., & Cramman, H. (2020). The challenge and opportunities of quantum literacy for future education and transdisciplinary problem-solving. *Research in Science & Technological Education*, ●●●, 1–17.

Nitin Liladhar Rane, S. P. (2023). Education 4.0 and 5.0: integrating Artificial Intelligence (AI) for personalized and adaptive learning.

Noble, S. U. (2018). Algorithms of oppression: How search engines reinforce racism. In *Algorithms of oppression*. New York university press.

O'Lawrence, H. (2017). The workforce for the 21st century. *International Journal of Vocational Education & Training*, 24(1).

Obenza, B., Salvahan, A., Rios, A. N., Solo, A., Alburo, R. A., & Gabila, R. J. (2024). University Students' Perception and Use of ChatGPT: Generative Artificial Intelligence (AI) in Higher Education. *International Journal of Human-Computer Studies*, 5(12), 5–18. https://papers.ssrn.com/sol3/papers.cfm?abstract_id=4724968

Oberdörfer, S., Birnstiel, S., Latoschik, M. E., & Grafe, S. (2021). Mutual Benefits: Interdisciplinary Education of Pre-Service Teachers and HCI Students in VR/AR Learning Environment Design. *Frontiers in Education*, 6. Advance online publication. DOI: 10.3389/feduc.2021.693012

Odier-Guedj, C. C. (2022). Fostering Family–School–Community Partnership With Parents of Students With Developmental Disabilities: Participatory Action Research With the 3D Sunshine Model. *School Community Journal*, ●●●, 327–356.

Odule, T. J., Adesina, A. O., Abdullah, A. K. K., & Ogunyinka, P. I. (2020). Using Affiliation Rules-based Data Mining Technique in Referral System. *Iraqi Journal of Science*, 3095–3103.

OECD. (2015). *Students, computers, and learning: Making the connection*. OECD Publishing.

OECD. (2017). *Promising Practices in Supporting Success for Indigenous Students*. OECD Publishing., DOI: 10.1787/9789264279421-

OECD. (2024). *AI in education: Shaping the future of learning*. OECD Publishing.

Ofosu-Ampong, K. (2020). The shift to gamification in education: A review on dominant issues. *Journal of Educational Technology Systems*, 49(1), 113–137. DOI: 10.1177/0047239520917629

Okamoto, T. (2004). Collaborative technology and new e-pedagogy. In E-Learn: World Conference on E-Learning in Corporate, Government, Healthcare, and Higher Education (pp. 3064-3077). Association for the Advancement of Computing in Education (AACE).

Olsen-Reeder, V., Higgins, R., & Ratima, M. (2017). *Te Ahu o te Reo Māori: Reflecting on Research to Understand the Well-Being of Te Reo Māori*. Victoria University Press.

Oluyemisi, O. M. (2023). Impact of Artificial Intelligence in Curriculum Development in Nigerian Tertiary Education. *International Journal of Educational Research*, 12(2), 2023.

Oluyinka, S., & Cusipag, M. (2021). Trialability and purposefulness: Their role towards Google classroom acceptance following educational policy. *Acta Informatica Pragensia*, 10(2), 172–191. https://www.ceeol.com/search/article-detail?id=1020610

Omar Adil, M. (2015). Ali, Aous Y Ali, and Balasem Salem Sumait. Comparison between the effects of different types of membership functions on fuzzy logic controller performance. *International Journal (Toronto, Ont.)*, 76, 76–83.

Osorio, C. P. (2023). Regulating the Regulators: Economic Assessment of Philippine Electricity Regulation. *International Journal of Energy Economics and Policy*, 13(3), 191–196. DOI: 10.32479/ijeep.14213

Osuna, C. (2013). Educación intercultural y revolución educativa en Bolivia. Un análisis de procesos de (re) esencialización cultural. *Revista Española de Antropología Americana*, 43(2), 451–470. DOI: 10.5209/rev_REAA.2013.v43.n2.44020

Ouyang, F and Jiao, P. (2021). Artificial intelligence in education: The three

Ouyang, Y., Wong, C. K., & Luo, X. (2020). Assessing students' hazard identification ability in virtual reality using eye tracking devices. *27th International Workshop on Intelligent Computing in Engineering of the European Group for Intelligent Computing in Engineering (EG-ICE 2020)*, 12–21.

Ove, C. (2013). Virtual classroom in the cloud—Transnational scandinavian teaching with digital technology. *Journal of Literature and Art Studies*, 3, 669–676.

Oyewumi, A., Isaiah, O., & Adigun, O. (2015). *Influence of social networking on the psychological adjustment of adolescents with hearing impairment in Ibadan.*

Pagano, A., Angelelli, M., Calvano, M., Curci, A., & Piccinno, A. (2023, December). Quantum computing for learning analytics: an overview of challenges and integration strategies. In *Proceedings of the 2nd International Workshop on Quantum Programming for Software Engineering* (pp. 13-16).

Page, E. B. (1966). The imminence of grading essays by computer. *Phi Delta Kappan*, 47(5), 238–243.

Pahi, K., Hawlader, S., Hicks, E., Zaman, A., & Phan, V. (2024). Enhancing active learning through collaboration between human teachers and generative AI. *Computers and Education Open*, 6, 100183. DOI: 10.1016/j.caeo.2024.100183

Pahuriray, A. V., Basanta, J. D., Arroyo, J. C. T., & Delima, A. J. P. (2022). Flexible Learning Experience Analyzer (FLExA): Sentiment Analysis of College Students through Machine Learning Algorithms with Comparative Analysis using WEKA. *International Journal of Emerging Technology and Advanced Engineering*, 12, 1–15. DOI: 10.46338/ijetae1222_01

Palanivel, K. (2020). Emerging Technologies to Smart Education. *International Journal of Computer Trends and Technology*, (68), 5–16.

Panoy, J. F., Andrade, R., Febrer, L., & Ching, D. (2022). Perceived proficiency with technology and online learning expectations of students in the graduate program of one state university in the Philippines. *International Journal of Information and Education Technology (IJIET)*, 12(7), 615–624. DOI: 10.18178/ijiet.2022.12.7.1661

Pant, M., Krovi, H., Towsley, D., Tassiulas, L., Jiang, L., Basu, P., ... & Guha, S. (2019). Routing entanglement in the quantum internet. npj Quantum Information, 5(1), 25.

Paris, D., & Alim, H. S. (Eds.). (2017). *Culturally sustaining pedagogies: Teaching and learning for justice in a changing world*. Teachers College Press.

Patel, S., & Ragolane, M. (2024). The Implementation of Artificial Intelligence in South African Higher Education Institutions: Opportunities and Challenges. *Technium Education and Humanities*, (9), 51–65.

Patil, A., Thakur, K., Gandhi, K., Savale, V., & Sayyed, N. (2022). A review on Industry 5.0: The techno-social revolution. *Int. J. Mech. Eng.*, 7(5), 1–5.

Pattanayak, S. (2023, november 29). *HIGHER EDUCATION: Education 5.0 can address skill growth needed in evolving job market*. Retrieved from educationtimes. com: https://www.educationtimes.com/article/campus-beat-college-life/99734211/ higher-education-education-5-0-can-address-skill-growth-needed-in-evolving-job -market

Pauli, H., Gottfried, M., & Grabherr, G. (2012). Effects of climate change on the alpine and nival vegetation of the Alps. *Journal of Mountain Ecology*, 7, 9–12.

Pedersen, M. K., Skyum, B., Heck, R., Müller, R., Bason, M., Lieberoth, A., & Sherson, J. F. StudentResearcher-A virtual learning environment for interactive engagement with advanced quantum mechanics.

Peiris, D., Wright, L., News, M., Rogers, K., Redfern, J., Chow, C., & Thomas, D. (2019). A smartphone app to assist smoking cessation among Aboriginal Australians: Findings from a pilot randomized controlled trial. *JMIR mHealth and uHealth*, 7(4), e12745. DOI: 10.2196/12745 PMID: 30938691

Peng, H., Ma, S., & Spector, J. (2019). Personalized adaptive learning: An emerging pedagogical approach enabled by a smart learning environment. *Smart Learning Environments*, 6, 1–14.

Persson, A., Jonasson, H., Fredriksson, I., Wiklund, U., & Ahlström, C. (2021). Heart Rate Variability for Classification of Alert Versus Sleep Deprived Drivers in Real Road Driving Conditions. *IEEE Transactions on Intelligent Transportation Systems*, 22(6).

Petsch, M. (2019). How Do Non-Formal Environmental Education Experiences Shape Pro-. *Environment and Behavior.*

Pew Research Center. (2019). The state of digital access: A comprehensive analysis of technology availability and use. Pew Research Center. Retrieved from https://www.pewresearch.org

Phaengtan, K., Aimcharoen, N., & Suebsan, P. (2021). Partial averages of fuzzy soft sets in decision-making problems. *Journal of Interdisciplinary Mathematics,* 24(4), 1035–1052. DOI: 10.1080/09720502.2021.1881223

Piaget, J. (1970). *Piaget's theory* (Vol. 1). Wiley.

Picard, R. W., Vyzas, E., & Healey, J. (2001). Toward machine emotional intelligence: Analysis of affective states and affective computing. *IEEE Transactions on Pattern Analysis and Machine Intelligence,* 23(10), 1175–1191.

Picciano, A. G. (2009). *Blended learning: Research perspectives.* Routledge.

Picciano, A. G. (2012). The evolution of big data and learning analytics in American higher education. *Online Learning : the Official Journal of the Online Learning Consortium,* 16(3), 9–20. DOI: 10.24059/olj.v16i3.267

Pitshou Moleka. (2022). *Dispelling the Limitations of Education 5.0 and Outlining the Vision of Education 6.0.* Managing Research African Network.

Polizzi, N., & Beratan, D. (2015). Open-access, interactive explorations for teaching and learning quantum dynamics. *Journal of Chemical Education,* 92, 2161–2164.

Porayska-Pomsta, K. (2024). From Algorithm Worship to the Art of Human Learning: Insights from 50-year journey of AI in Education.

Prahani, B. K., Rizki, I. A., Jatmiko, B., Suprapto, N. and Amelia, T.(2022). Artificial Intelligence in Education Research During the Last Ten Years: A Review and Bibliometric Study. *iJET 17(08).*

Prakash Srinivasan, S. N. (2023). Education 5.0 Revolutionizing Learning for the Future (Vol.1). *reasearch gate.*

Prasolova-Førland, E., & Chang, T. W. (2007, July). Building a Babel Tower in 21st Century: Supporting Cross-Cultural Collaboration and Learning in a 3D CVE Spanning Three Continents. In *Seventh IEEE International Conference on Advanced Learning Technologies (ICALT 2007)* (pp. 295-299). IEEE.

Pratyusha, Y. B., & Varghese, B. (2024). Inclusive Educational Settings With Equity and Integration: Assessing Opportunities and Challenges. *Designing Equitable and Accessible Online Learning Environments*, 74-92.

Pulla, S. (2017). Mobile learning and indigenous education in Canada: A synthesis of new ways of learning. *International Journal of Mobile and Blended Learning*, 9(2), 39–60. DOI: 10.4018/IJMBL.2017040103

Pundlik, S., Shivshanker, P., & Luo, G. (2023). Impact of Apps as Assistive Devices for Visually Impaired Persons. In Annual Review of Vision Science (Vol. 9, Issue 1, pp. 111–130). Annual Reviews. https://doi.org/DOI: 10.1146/annurev-vision-111022-123837

Qiao, W., Sun, L., Wu, J., Wang, P., Li, J., & Zhao, M. (2024). EEG emotion recognition model based on attention and GAN. *IEEE Access : Practical Innovations, Open Solutions*.

Quinn, S., Hogan, M., Dwyer, C., Finn, P., & Fogarty, E. (2020). Development and Validation of the student-educator negotiated critical thinking dispositions scale (SENCTDS). *Thinking Skills and Creativity*, 38(4), 100710–100717.

Raharjana, I. K., Siahaan, D., & Fatichah, C. (2021). User stories and natural Language processing: A systematic literature review. *Institute of Electrical and Electronics Engineers Access*, 9(1), 53811–53826.

Rahimi, A. R., & Sevilla-Pavón, A. (2024). The role of ChatGPT readiness in shaping language teachers' language teaching innovation and meeting accountability: A bisymmetric approach. *Computers and Education: Artificial Intelligence*, 7, 100258. Advance online publication. DOI: 10.1016/j.caeai.2024.100258

Rahko-Ravantti, R. (2020). Sámi education in Finland: A multilayered context. In *Educational Equity* (pp. 109–124). Springer., DOI: 10.1007/978-981-15-4526-9_7

Rahman, M. S., Khan, A. R., & Alam, S. (2023). Inequitable distribution of resources and funding in education. *Journal of Education Policy*, 48(3), 355–374.

Raino, R., Kumari, N., Chandelkar, K., & Chetiwal, K. (2023). Role of artificial intelligence in psychological and mental well being: A quantitative investigation. *Journal for ReAttach Therapy and Developmental Diversities*, 6(2), 149–156.

Raja, R., & Raja, H. (2020). Assessment Methods of Cognitive Ability of Human Brains for Inborn Intelligence Potential Using Pattern Recognitions. DOI: 10.5772/intechopen.93268

Rane, N. L., Choudhary, S. P., & Rane, J. (2024). Education 4.0 and 5.0: Integrating Artificial Intelligence (AI) for personalized and adaptive learning. *Journal Of Artificial Intelligence And Robotics*, 1(1), 29–43.

Rane, N. T. (2024). ChatGPT and similar generative artificial intelligence (AI) for smart industry: Role, challenges, and opportunities for Industry 4.0, Industry 5.0, and Society 5.0. *Innovations In Business And Strategic Management*, 2(1), 10–17.

Rani, P. U., Angel, S., Janani, L., & Berista, S. (2024, March). Astute Assistance System for Blind and Visually Impaired People. In 2024 5th International Conference on Intelligent Communication Technologies and Virtual Mobile Networks (ICICV) (pp. 74-78). IEEE.

Rapaka, A., Dharmadhikari, S. C., Kasat, K., Mohan, C. R., Chouhan, K., & Gupta, M. (2025a). Revolutionizing learning – A journey into educational games with immersive and AI technologies. *Entertainment Computing*, 52, 100809. Advance online publication. DOI: 10.1016/j.entcom.2024.100809

Rasmani, K. A., & Shen, Q. (2006). Data-driven fuzzy rule generation and its application for student academic performance evaluation. *Applied Intelligence*, 25(3), 305–319. DOI: 10.1007/s10489-006-0109-9

Rawson, R., Okere, U., & Tooth, O. (2022). Using Low-immersive Virtual Reality in Online Learning: Field Notes from Environmental Management Education. *International Review of Research in Open and Distributed Learning*, 23(4), 211–221. DOI: 10.19173/irrodl.v23i4.6475

Razavy, M. (2013). *Quantum theory of tunneling*. World Scientific.

Reardon, B. (1988). *Comprehensive peace education: Educating for global responsibility*. Teachers College Press.

Regona, M., Yigitcanlar, T., Xia, B., & Li, R. Y. M. (2022). Opportunities and adoption challenges of AI in the construction industry: A PRISMA review. *Journal of Open Innovation*, 8(45), 45. Advance online publication. DOI: 10.3390/joitmc8010045

Reilly, R., Stephens, J., Micklem, J., Tufănaru, C., Harfield, S., Fisher, I., & Ward, J. (2020). Use and uptake of web-based therapeutic interventions amongst Indigenous populations in Australia, New Zealand, the United States of America, and Canada: A scoping review. *Systematic Reviews*, 9(1). Advance online publication. DOI: 10.1186/s13643-020-01374-x PMID: 32475342

Renkema, M., & Tursunbayeva, A. (2024). The future of work of academics in the age of Artificial Intelligence: State-of-the-art and a research roadmap. *Futures*, 163, 103453. DOI: 10.1016/j.futures.2024.103453

Rennie, E., Thomas, J., & Wilson, C. (2019). Aboriginal and Torres Strait Islander people and digital inclusion: What is the evidence and where is it? *Communication Research and Practice*, 5(2), 105–120. DOI: 10.1080/22041451.2019.1601148

Resta, P., & Laferrière, T. (2015). Digital equity and intercultural education. *Education and Information Technologies*, 20(4), 743–756. DOI: 10.1007/s10639-015-9419-z

Reynolds, C. R., & Suzuki, L. A. (2012). *Bias in psychological assessment: An empirical review and recommendations* (2nd ed.). Handbook of Psychology, DOI: 10.1002/9781118133880.hop210004

Ribble, M. (2015). *Digital citizenship in schools: Nine elements all students should know*. International Society for Technology in Education.

Rice, E., Haynes, E., Royce, P., & Thompson, S. (2016). Social media and digital technology use among Indigenous young people in Australia: A literature review. *International Journal for Equity in Health*, 15(1). Advance online publication. DOI: 10.1186/s12939-016-0366-0 PMID: 27225519

Rini, M., Lestari, A. D., & Muslim, M. A. (2024). IoT-integrated smart attendance and attention monitoring system for primary and secondary school classroom management. *Journal of Electronics Technology Exploration*, 2(1). Advance online publication. DOI: 10.52465/joetex.v2i1.381

Rita Vieira, J. O. (2023). Society 5.0 and Education 5.0: A Critical Reflection. *18th Iberian Conference on Information Systems and Technologies (CISTI)*. Aveiro, Portugal.

Roberts, T. S. (2008). Student plagiarism in an online world: An introduction. In *Student plagiarism in an online world: Problems and solutions* (pp. 1–9). IGI Global. DOI: 10.4018/978-1-59904-801-7.ch001

Robinson, G. M., Hardman, M., & Matley, R. J. (2021). Using games in geographical and planning-related teaching: Serious games, edutainment, board games and role-play. *Social Sciences & Humanities Open*, 4(1), 100208. Advance online publication. DOI: 10.1016/j.ssaho.2021.100208

Robledo, D. A. R., Zara, C. G., Montalbo, S. M., Gayeta, N. E., Gonzales, A. L., Escarez, M. G. A., & Maalihan, E. D. (2023). Development and Validation of a Survey Instrument on Knowledge, Attitude, and Practices (KAP) Regarding the Educational Use of ChatGPT among Preservice Teachers in the Philippines. *International Journal of Information and Education Technology (IJIET)*, 13(10), 1582–1590. DOI: 10.18178/ijiet.2023.13.10.1965

Rodr'ıguez-Triana, M., Mart'ınez-Mon'es, A., & Asensio-P'erez, J. I. (2011). Monitoring collaboration in flexible and personal learning environments. [s]. *Interaction Design and Architecture*, 11-12, 51–63.

Rodrigo Smiderle, S. J. (2020). The impact of gamification on students' learning, engagement and behavior based on their personality traits. *springeropen*.

Rodrigues, A. L. (2020). Digital technologies integration in teacher education: the active teacher training model. Journal of e-learning and knowledge society, 16(3), 24-33.

Rogers, J. (2023). Connecting in the gulf: Digital inclusion for aboriginal families on Mornington Island. *Visual Communication*, 23(2), 209–222. DOI: 10.1177/14703572231181598

Rogers, J. K. B., Mercado, T. C. R., & Decano, R. S. (2025). Moodle interactions and academic performance: Educational data mining in a Philippine university. [EduLearn]. *Journal of Education and Learning*, 19(1), 542–550. DOI: 10.11591/edulearn.v19i1.21549

Roll, I., & Wylie, R. (2016). Evolution and revolution in artificial intelligence in education. *International Journal of Artificial Intelligence in Education*, 26(2), 582–599. DOI: 10.1007/s40593-016-0110-3

Romanow, D., Napier, N. P., & Cline, M. K. (2020). Using active learning, group formation, and discussion to increase stu- dent learning: A business intelligence skills analysis. *Journal of Information Systems Education*, 31, 218–231.

Romero-Rodríguez, J. M., Ramírez-Montoya, M. S., Buenestado-Fernández, M., & Lara-Lara, F. (2023). Use of ChatGPT at University as a Tool for Complex Thinking: Students' Perceived Usefulness. *Journal of New Approaches in Educational Research*, 12(2), 323–339. DOI: 10.7821/naer.2023.7.1458

Rosales, M. A., Jo-ann, V. M., Palconit, M. G. B., Culaba, A. B., & Dadios, E. P. (2020, December). Artificial intelligence: the technology adoption and impact in the Philippines. In *2020 IEEE 12th International Conference on humanoid, nanotechnology, information technology, communication and control, environment, and management (HNICEM)* (pp. 1-6). IEEE. https://doi.org/DOI: 10.1109/HNICEM51456.2020.9400025

Ruiz-Rojas, L.I., Acosta-Vargas, P., De-Moreta-Llovet, J., and Gonzalez-Rodriguez, M. (2023). Empowering Education with Generative Artificial Intelligence

Russell, S. (2019). *Human compatible: Artificial intelligence and the problem of control*. Viking.

Rzheuskyi, A., Matsuik, H., Veretennikova, N., & Vaskiv, R. (Eds.). (2019).

Sabharwal, D., Verma, M., & Sood, R. (2022). Studying the Relationship between Artificial Intelligence and Digital Advertising in Marketing Strategy. Journal of Content. *Community & Communication*, 16, 118–126. DOI: 10.31620/JCCC.12.22/10

Saeidnia, H. (2023). Using ChatGPT as a digital/smart reference robot: how may ChatGPT impact digital reference services? *Information Matters, 2(5)*.

Saini, D. K., & Salim Al-Mamri, M. R. (2019). Investigation of Technological Tools used in Education System in Oman. *Social Sciences & Humanities Open*, 1(1), 100003. Advance online publication. DOI: 10.1016/j.ssaho.2019.100003

Salam, M. Y., Taman, M. M. and Mudinillah, A. (2023). Using Artificial Intelligence for Education in the Education 5.0 Era to Improve Reading Skills. *Arabiyat: Jurnal Pendidikan Bahasa Arab dan Kebahasaaraban. 10(2): 149-162.*

Salazar, J. F., Radoll, P., Cardoso-Castro, P., Rodrigues, R., & Dezuanni, M. (2020). Digital inclusion, indigenous peoples, and the Global South: A critical perspective from the margins. In Servaes, J. (Ed.), *Handbook of Communication for Development and Social Change* (pp. 1–19). Springer., DOI: 10.1007/978-981-15-2014-3_128

Salehi, O. (2020). Seskir, Z.C., Tepe, I.: A computer science-oriented approach to introduce quantum computing to a new audience. *IEEE Transactions on Education*, 65, 1–8.

Salman, A., & Rahim, S. (2012). From access to gratification: Towards an inclusive digital society. *Asian Social Science*, 8(5). Advance online publication. DOI: 10.5539/ass.v8n5p5

Samonte, M. J. C., & Ong, A. P. L. (2023, November). Analyzing the Impact of Artificial Intelligence in the Financial Industry. In *2023 IEEE 15th International Conference on Humanoid, Nanotechnology, Information Technology, Communication and Control, Environment, and Management (HNICEM)* (pp. 1–6). IEEE. https://doi.org/DOI: 10.1109/HNICEM60674.2023.10589026

Sánchez, J., Salinas, A., Sáenz, M., & de Benito, B. (2015). Computer-supported collaborative learning in a 1:1 laptop initiative in Chilean classrooms. In Spada, H., Rummel, N., & McLaren, B. M. (Eds.), *CSCL 2015 Proceedings* (pp. 409–416). International Society of the Learning Sciences.

Sandhya H., B. V. (2023). The Emerging Role of Innovative Teaching Practices in Tourism Education in the Post Covid Era. 1-15.

Santana-Mancilla, P. C., Garc'a-Ruiz, M. A., Acosta-Diaz, R., & Juárez, C. U. (2012). Service oriented architecture to support mexican secondary education through mobile augmented reality. *Procedia Computer Science*, 10, 721–727.

Santiago, C. S.Jr, Embang, S. I., Conlu, M. T. N., Acanto, R. B., Lausa, S. M., Ambojia, K. W. P., Laput, E. y., Aperocho, M. D. B., Malabag, B. A., Balilo, B. B.Jr, Paderes, J. J., Cahapin, E. L., & Romasanta, J. K. N. (2023). Utilization of writing assistance tools in research in selected higher learning institutions in the Philippines: A text mining analysis. *International Journal of Learning. Teaching and Educational Research*, 22(11), 259–284. DOI: 10.26803/ijlter.22.11.14

Santoro, N., Reid, J. A., Crawford, L., & Simpson, L. (2011). Teaching Indigenous children: Listening to and learning from Indigenous teachers. *The Australian Journal of Teacher Education*, 36(10), 65–80. DOI: 10.14221/ajte.2011v36n10.2

Santosh, J., Dzsotjan, D., & Ishimaru, S. (2023). Multimodal Assessment of Interest Levels in Reading: Integrating Eye-Tracking and Physiological Sensing. *IEEE Access : Practical Innovations, Open Solutions*, 11.

Santos, L., Escudeiro, P., & de Carvalho, C. V. (2013, September). Evaluating virtual experiential learning in engineering. In *2013 International Conference on Interactive Collaborative Learning (ICL)* (pp. 42-48). IEEE.

Sarra, C., Spillman, D., Jackson, C., Davis, J., & Bray, J. (2018). High-expectations relationships: A foundation for enacting high expectations in all Australian schools. *Australian Journal of Indigenous Education*, 47(1), 32–45. DOI: 10.1017/jie.2018.10

Sassirekha, M. S., & Vijayalakshmi, S. (2022). Predicting the academic progression in student's standpoint using machine learning. *Automatika Journal for Control, Measurement, Electronics, Computer Communications*, 63(4), 605–617.

Scavarelli, A., Arya, A., & Teather, R. J. (2019). Circles: exploring multi-platform accessible, socially scalable VR in the classroom. *2019 IEEE Games, Entertainment, Media Conference, GEM 2019, 2019-Janua.* https://doi.org/DOI: 10.1109/GEM.2019.8897532

Scherer, R., Siddiq, F., & Tondeur, J. (2019). The technology acceptance model (TAM): A meta-analytic structural equation modeling approach to explaining teachers' adoption of digital technology in education. *Computers & Education*, 128, 13–35. DOI: 10.1016/j.compedu.2018.09.009

Schrodt, P. A., Yilmaz, Ö., Gerner, D. J., & Hermrick, D. (2014). The CAMEO (Conflict and Mediation Event Observations) actor coding framework. *International Studies Perspectives*, 15(1), 145–161.

Schuld, M., Sinayskiy, I., & Petruccione, F. (2014). An introduction to quantum machine learning. *Contemporary Physics*, 56, 172–185.

Schwartz, D. L., Lin, X., Brophy, S., & Bransford, J. D. (2016). Toward the development of flexibly adaptive instructional designs. In Reigeluth, C. M. (Ed.), *Instructional-design theories and models: A new paradigm of instructional theory* (Vol. 2, pp. 183–213). Routledge.

Schwartzman, L. F., & Knobel, M. (2016). The Transformative Potential of Affirmative Action in Brazilian Higher Education. In Stevens, P. A. J., & Dworkin, A. G. (Eds.), *The Palgrave Handbook of Race and Ethnic Inequalities in Education* (pp. 247–290). Palgrave Macmillan., DOI: 10.1057/978-1-137-51944-1_8

Sebastian, S. (2023). Education 5.0: A Paradigm Shift in Learning.

Seegerer, S., Michaeli, T., & Romeike, R. (2021, October). Quantum computing as a topic in computer science education. In *Proceedings of the 16th Workshop in Primary and Secondary Computing Education* (pp. 1-6).

Seifert, K., & Sutton, R. (2019). The learning process. *Educational Psychology*.

Selwyn, N. (2019). *Should robots replace teachers? AI and the future of education.* Polity Press.

Seneff, S., & Wang, C. (2019). The challenges of facial expression recognition in diverse settings. *Journal of Computer Vision*, 136(1), 85–97.

Sengupta, U., Vieta, M., & McMurtry, J. (2015). Indigenous communities and social enterprise in Canada: Incorporating culture as an essential ingredient of entrepreneurship. *Canadian Journal of Nonprofit and Social Economy Research*, 6(1). Advance online publication. DOI: 10.22230/cjnser.2015v6n1a196

Seo, J., & Roll, K. (2021). Boosting AI knowledge among educators and students: Strategies and implications. *Journal of Educational Technology*, 18(2), 145–162. DOI: 10.1080/1475939X.2021.1896342

Seo, S. H., Kim, M. Y., & Kim, Y. (2024). A Design and Implementation of an Online Video Lecture System based on Facial Expression Recognition. *International Journal on Advanced Science, Engineering and Information Technology*, 14(3).

Seskir, Z. C., Migdał, P., Weidner, C., Anupam, A., Case, N., Davis, N., & Chiofalo, M. (2022). Quantum games and interactive tools for quantum technologies outreach and education. *Optical Engineering (Redondo Beach, Calif.)*, 61(8), 081809–081809.

Settles, B., & Meeder, B. (2016, August). A trainable spaced repetition model for language learning. In *Proceedings of the 54th annual meeting of the association for computational linguistics* (volume 1: long papers) (pp. 1848-1858). DOI: 10.18653/v1/P16-1174

Seyman Guray, T., & Kismet, B. (2023). Applicability of a digitalization model based on augmented reality for building construction education in architecture. *Construction Innovation*, 23(1), 193–212. DOI: 10.1108/CI-07-2021-0136

Sezgin, A., & Atagün, A. O. (2011). On operations of soft sets. *Computers & Mathematics with Applications (Oxford, England)*, 61(5), 1457–1467. DOI: 10.1016/j.camwa.2011.01.018

Shabir Ahmad, S. U. (2023). Education 5.0: Requirements, Enabling Technologies, and Future Directions. 1-24.

Shabir, M., & Naz, M. (2011). On soft topological spaces. *Computers & Mathematics with Applications (Oxford, England)*, 61(7), 1786–1799. DOI: 10.1016/j.camwa.2011.02.006

Shanta, S., & Wells, J. G. (2022). T/E design-based learning: Assessing student Critical thinking and problem-solving abilities. *International Journal of Technology and Design Education*, 32(1), 267–285.

Shao, Q., Sniffen, A., Blanchet, J., Hillis, M. E., Shi, X., Haris, T. K., & Balkcom, D. (2020). Teaching American sign language in mixed reality. *Proceedings of the ACM on Interactive, Mobile, Wearable and Ubiquitous Technologies*, 4(4), 1–27. DOI: 10.1145/3432211

Shibata, T. (2019). Virtual reality in education: How schools use VR in classrooms. *Advances in Intelligent Systems and Computing*, 827, 423–425. DOI: 10.1007/978-3-319-96059-3_48

Shinghal, K., & Saxena, A. (2020). Analysis of Entrepreneurial Mindset in Engineering Students. *International Journal of Advances in Engineering and Technology*, 13–23.

Shiri, A., Howard, D., & Farnel, S. (2021). Indigenous digital storytelling: Digital interfaces supporting cultural heritage preservation and access. *The International Information & Library Review*, 54(2), 93–114. DOI: 10.1080/10572317.2021.1946748

Shute, V., & Wang, L. (2016). Assessing and supporting hard-to-measure constructs in video games. The Wiley Handbook of Cognition and Assessment: Frameworks, Methodologies, and Applications, 535-562. DOI: 10.1002/9781118956588.ch22

Shute, V. J. (2008). Focus on formative feedback. *Review of Educational Research*, 78(1), 153–189. DOI: 10.3102/0034654307313795

Shwartz-Asher, D., Raviv, A., & Herscu-Kluska, R. (2022). Teaching and assessing active learning in online academic courses. *Social Sciences & Humanities Open*, 6(1), 100341. Advance online publication. DOI: 10.1016/j.ssaho.2022.100341

Siadaty, M., & Taghiyareh, F. (2007, July). PALS2: Pedagogically adaptive learning system based on learning styles. In *Seventh IEEE International Conference on Advanced Learning Technologies (ICALT 2007)* (pp. 616-618). IEEE.

Siahaan, J. H., Marson, F., & Forsyth, O. (2022). Transforming Primary School Science Education: The Quantum Teaching Revolution. Jurnal Ilmu Pendidikan dan Humaniora, 11(1), 35-51.

Siemens, G., & Long, P. (2011). Penetrating the fog: Analytics in learning and education. *EDUCAUSE Review*, 46(5), 30–40.

Silan, W., & Munkejord, M. (2023). Pinhkngyan: Paths taken to recognizing, doing, and developing indigenous methodologies. *Alternative, an International Journal of Indigenous Peoples, 19(2)*, 407-416. https://doi.org/DOI: 10.1177/11771801231167727

Silva, A. J., Ludermir, T. B., & de Oliveira, W. R.Jr. (2010, October). Superposition based learning algorithm. In *2010 Eleventh Brazilian Symposium on Neural Networks* (pp. 1-6). IEEE.

Silva, J. N. A., Southworth, M., Raptis, C., & Silva, J. (2018). Emerging applications of virtual reality in cardiovascular medicine. *JACC. Basic to Translational Science*, 3(3), 420–430. PMID: 30062228

Sim, S., Cao, Y., Romero, J., Johnson, P. D., & Aspuru-Guzik, A. A framework for algorithm deployment on cloud-based quantum computers. arXiv: Quantum Physics (2018)

Simon, C. (2017). Towards a global quantum network. *Nature Photonics*, 11, 678–680.

Singh, H., Chauhan, U., Chauhan, S. P. S., Saxena, A., & Kumari, P. (2024). Adaptive and Personalized Learning in Industry 5.0 Education. In Infrastructure Possibilities and Human-Centered Approaches With Industry 5.0 (pp. 1-19). IGI Global.

Singh, S., Keller, P. R., Busija, L., McMillan, P., Makrai, E., Lawrenson, J. G., Hull, C. C., & Downie, L. E. (2023). Blue-light filtering spectacle lenses for visual performance, sleep, and macular health in adults. *Cochrane Library, 2023*(8). https://doi.org/DOI: 10.1002/14651858.cd013244.pub2

Singleton, J., Straits, K. J. L., & Straits, K. (2015). Professional development for educators teaching in Indigenous contexts. In Reyhner, J., Martin, J., Lockard, L., & Gilbert, W. S. (Eds.), *Honoring our elders: Culturally appropriate approaches for teaching Indigenous students* (pp. 165–184). Northern Arizona University.

Sinti, M. E., Sánchez, F. M., & Vargas, R. C. (2021). Digital technologies for revitalizing indigenous languages: The case of the Kukama-Kukamiria people in the Peruvian Amazon. *International Journal of Educational Technology in Higher Education*, 18(1), 1–18. DOI: 10.1186/s41239-021-00244-3

Sisaye, S., & Birnberg, J. (2010). Organizational development and transformational learning approaches in process innovations. *Review of Accounting and Finance*, 9(4), 337–362. DOI: 10.1108/14757701011094562

Skutnabb-Kangas, T., & Dunbar, R. (2010). Indigenous children's education as linguistic genocide and a crime against humanity? A global view. Gáldu Čála – Journal of Indigenous Peoples Rights, 1, 1-128.

Smith, J., Green, H., & Roberts, K. (2018). Addressing challenges in voice recognition technology for educational settings. *Journal of Technology Education*, 32(1), 78–79.

Solmaz, S., Dominguez Alfaro, J. L., Santos, P., Van Puyvelde, P., & Van Gerven, T. (2021). A practical development of engineering simulation-assisted educational AR environments. *Education for Chemical Engineers*, 35, 81–93. DOI: 10.1016/j.ece.2021.01.007

Song, Y., Weisberg, L. R., Zhang, S., Tian, X., Boyer, K. E., & Israel, M. (2024). A framework for inclusive AI learning design for diverse learners. In *Computers and Education: Artificial Intelligence* (Vol. 6). Elsevier B.V. DOI: 10.1016/j.caeai.2024.100212

Squire, K., & Klopfer, E. (2007). Augmented reality simulations on handheld computers. *Journal of the Learning Sciences*, 16, 371–413.

Steele, J. L. (2023). To GPT or not GPT? Empowering our students to learn with AI. *Computers and Education: Artificial Intelligence*, 5, 100160. Advance online publication. DOI: 10.1016/j.caeai.2023.100160

Stoet, G., & Geary, D. C. (2018). The gender-equality paradox in science, technology, engineering, and mathematics education. *Psychological Science*, 29(4), 581–593. DOI: 10.1177/0956797617741719 PMID: 29442575

Struebig, M. J., Fischer, M., Gaveau, D. L., Meijaard, E., Wich, S. A., & Koh, L. P. (2015). The escalator to extinction: Emerging challenges for biodiversity conservation in tropical mountains. *Global Change Biology*, 21(8), 2829–2833. DOI: 10.1111/gcb.12843 PMID: 25846057

Strzelecki, A., & ElArabawy, S. (2024). Investigation of the moderation effect of gender and study level on the acceptance and use of generative AI by higher education students: Comparative evidence from Poland and Egypt. *British Journal of Educational Technology*, 55(3), 1209–1230. DOI: 10.1111/bjet.13425

Su, J., Zhong, Y., & Ng, D. T. K. (2022). A meta-review of literature on educational approaches for teaching AI at the K-12 levels in the Asia-Pacific region. In *Computers and Education: Artificial Intelligence* (Vol. 3). Elsevier B.V. DOI: 10.1016/j.caeai.2022.100065

Sue Stover, T. (2018). A Case Study of Teachers Implementing The Framework for 21st-Century Learning.

Sulasula, J. (2023). Towards Algorithmic University: Assessing the readiness of State Universities and Colleges (sucs) in Zamboanga Peninsula, the Philippines. https://dx.doi.org/DOI: 10.2139/ssrn.4505296

Sun, J. C.-Y., Ye, S.-L., Yu, S.-J., & Chiu, T. K. F. (2023). Effects of wearable hybrid AR/VR learning material on high school students' situational interest, engagement, and learning performance: The case of a physics laboratory learning environment. *Journal of Science Education and Technology*, 32(1), 1–12.

Sun, Z., Liu, R., Luo, L., Wu, M., & Shi, C. (2017). Exploring collaborative learning effect in blended learning environments. *Journal of Computer Assisted Learning*, 33, 575–587.

Su, P.-Y., Hsiao, P.-W., & Fan, K.-K. (2023). Investigating the Relationship between Users' Behavioral Intentions and Learning Effects of VR System for Sustainable Tourism Development. *Sustainability*, 15(9), 7277.

Surbhi, A. (2023). Artificial intelligence and education. *International Journal for Multidisciplinary Research*, 5(6), 2582–2160.

Suri, V. R., Ling, R., & Teo, C. L. (2019). Leveraging indigenous knowledge for sustainable development: A case study of the Bidayuh community in Sarawak, Malaysia. *Information Development*, 35(3), 447–466. DOI: 10.1177/0266666918754829

Suvrat, J. (2019). Role of artificial intelligence in higher education: An empirical investigation. *International Journal of Research and Analytical Reviews*, 6(2), 2349–5138.

Taer, A. N., & Taer, E. C. (2024). Transforming Philippine Agriculture Through Data-driven Innovation: A Quantitative Landscape Assessment to Prioritize Technological Solutions. https://doi.org/DOI: 10.21203/rs.3.rs-3943832/v1

Tan, Y., Xu, W., Li, S., & Chen, K. (2022). Augmented and virtual reality (AR/VR) for education and training in the AEC industry: A systematic review of research and applications. *Buildings*, 12(10), 1529.

Tapalova, O., & Zhiyenbayeva, N. (2022). Artificial intelligence in education: Aied for personalised learning pathways. *Electronic Journal of e-Learning*, 20(5), 639–653. DOI: 10.34190/ejel.20.5.2597

Teddlie, C., & Tashakkori, A. (2009). *Foundations of mixed methods research: Integrating quantitative and qualitative approaches in the social and behavioral sciences.* SAGE Publications.

Tekin, C., & van der Schaar, M. (2014). eTutor: Online Learning for Personalized Education.

Tene, T., Marcatoma Tixi, J. A., Palacios Robalino, M. D. L., Mendoza Salazar, M. J., Vacacela Gomez, C., & Bellucci, S. (2024, June). Integrating immersive technologies with STEM education: A systematic review. []. Frontiers Media SA.]. *Frontiers in Education*, 9, 1410163.

Tewari, V., Rahman, M., Mishra, A., Bajaj, K. K., & Shankar, A. U. (2023). Impact of Virtual Reality (Vr) and Augmented Reality (Ar) in Education. *Tuijin Jishu/Journal of Propulsion Technology, 44*(4), 1310–1318. https://doi.org/DOI: 10.52783/tjjpt.v44.i4.1014

Tham, J., McGrath, M., Duin, A. H., & Moses, J. (2018). Guest Editors' Introduction: Immersive Technologies and Writing Pedagogy. *Computers and Composition*, 50, 1–7. DOI: 10.1016/j.compcom.2018.08.001

Tharay, N., Nirmala, S. V. S. G., Bavikati, V. N., & Nuvvula, S. (2020). Dermatoglyphics as a Novel Method for Assessing Intelligence Quotient in Children Aged 5–11 Years: A Cross-sectional Study. *International Journal of Clinical Pediatric Dentistry*, 13(4), 355.

Theodore, R., Tustin, K., Kiro, C., Gollop, M., Taumoepeau, M., Taylor, N., Chee, K.-S., Hunter, J., & Poulton, R. (2016). Māori university graduates: Indigenous participation in higher education. *Higher Education Research & Development*, 35(3), 604–618. DOI: 10.1080/07294360.2015.1107883

This AI-powered backpack helps the visually impaired navigate world. (n.d.). IN-DIAai. https://indiaai.gov.in/case-study/this-ai-powered-backpack-helps-the-visually-impaired-navigate-world

Thorpe, K., Christen, K., Booker, L., & Galassi, M. (2021). Designing archival information systems through partnerships with indigenous communities. *AJIS. Australasian Journal of Information Systems*, 25. Advance online publication. DOI: 10.3127/ajis.v25i0.2917

Tiina Kivirand, Ä. L. (2021). Designing and Implementing an In-Service Training Course for School Teams on Inclusive Education: Reflections from Participants. *Education Sciences*, 11(4), 1–19. DOI: 10.3390/educsci11040166

Timms, C. (2016). *Creating the curriculum: A guide to effective curriculum design.* Routledge.

Tobias, R. R., Minglana, J., Hernandez, D. K., Mital, M. E., & Roxas, R. E. (2023). Artificial intelligence applications in quality management systems of Philippine higher education institutions. In *Intelligent Sustainable Systems: Selected Papers of WorldS4 2022, Volume 2* (pp. 159-172). Singapore: Springer Nature Singapore. https://doi.org/DOI: 10.1007/978-981-19-7663-6_16

Togo, M and Gandidzanwa, C. P. (2021). The role of Education 5.0 in accelerating

Tomandl, M., Mieling, T. B., Kroon, C. M. L. V., Hopf, M., & Arndt, M. (2015). Simulated interactive research experiments as educational tools for advanced science. *Scientific Reports*, ●●●, 5. PMID: 26370627

Topp, S., Edelman, A., & Taylor, S. (2018). "We are everything to everyone": A systematic review of factors influencing the accountability relationships of Aboriginal and Torres Strait Islander health workers (AHWs) in the Australian health system. *International Journal for Equity in Health*, 17(1). Advance online publication. DOI: 10.1186/s12939-018-0779-z PMID: 29848331

Tore Hoel, W. C. (2018). Privacy and data protection in learning analytics should be motivated by an educational maxim—Towards a proposal. *Research and Practice in Technology Enhanced Learning*. PMID: 30595748

Torre, L. D. L., Heradio, R., Jara, C., S'anchez, J., Dormido, S., Medina, F., & Her'ias, F. A. C. (2013). Providing collaborative support to virtual and remote laboratories. *IEEE Transactions on Learning Technologies*, 6, 312–323.

Toulouse, P. R. (2016). What matters in Indigenous education: Implementing a vision committed to holism, diversity and engagement. In Measuring What Matters, People for Education. Toronto: March, 2016.

Tran, C., Chen, J., Warschauer, M., Conley, A. M., & Dede, C. (2012). Applying Motivation Theories to the Design of Educational Technology.

Trivedi, D. R. (2023). *The Role of Industry 5.0 in Education 5.0 in Indian Perspective*. INTERNATIONAL JOURNAL OF INNOVATIVE RESEARCH IN TECHNOLOGY.

Tsai, S.-C. (2019). Computer Assisted Language Learning Using google translate in EFL drafts: A preliminary investigation. *Computer Assisted Language Learning*, 32(5-6), 510–526. Advance online publication. DOI: 10.1080/09588221.2018.1527361

Tsai, Y. S., Poquet, O., Gašević, D., Dawson, S., & Pardo, A. (2020). Complexity leadership in learning analytics: Drivers, challenges and opportunities. *British Journal of Educational Technology*, 51(6), 2304–2320. DOI: 10.1111/bjet.12846

Tsouktakou, N. A., Hamouroudis, N. A., & Horti, N. A. (2024). The use of artificial intelligence in the education of people with visual impairment. *World Journal of Advanced Engineering Technology and Sciences*, 13(1), 734–744. DOI: 10.30574/wjaets.2024.13.1.0481

Tuck, E., & McKenzie, M. (2015). *Place in research: Theory, methodology, and methods*. Routledge., DOI: 10.4324/9781315764849

Tuomi, I. (2018). The impact of artificial intelligence on learning, teaching, and education. *Journal of European Union*, 8(2), 1831–9424.

Tuominen, I. (2023). Protecting and accessing Indigenous peoples' digital cultural heritage through sustainable governance and IPR structures - The case of Sámi culture. *Arctic Review on Law and Politics*, 14. Advance online publication. DOI: 10.23865/arctic.v14.5809

Tuyen, P. T., Truong, A. T., Truong, D. P., Le, D. T., Pham, N. C., & Qui, N. C. (2023). Design and implementation of classroom environment monitoring system towards smart campus. *Proceedings of the 2023 International Conference on Smart Campus (ICSC)*. https://doi.org/DOI: 10.1145/3606150.3606177

U.S. Department of Education, Office of Educational Technology. (2024). *National education technology plan: Transforming teaching and learning with technology*. U.S. Department of Education.

Uhlig, R. P., Dey, P., Jawad, S., Sinha, B., & Amin, M. (2019). *Generating student interest in quantum computing. In: 2019 IEEE Frontiers in Education Conference*. FIE.

Umali, J. N. D. (2024). Artificial Intelligence Technology Management of Teachers, Learners Motivation and Challenges Encountered. *Educational Research*, 6(3), 821–880. https://www.ijmcer.com/volume-6-issue-3/

UNESCO. (2019). *Indigenous Peoples' Right to Education*. UNESCO.

United Nations. (2007). United Nations Declaration on the Rights of Indigenous Peoples. https://www.un.org/development/desa/indigenouspeoples/declaration-on -the-rights-of-indigenous-peoples.html

United Nations. (2020). Indigenous Peoples at the United Nations. https://www.un .org/development/desa/indigenouspeoples/about-us.html

Valerio, A. (2024). Anticipating the Impact of Artificial Intelligence in Higher Education: Student Awareness and Ethical Concerns in Zamboanga City, Philippines. *Cognizance Journal of Multidisciplinary Studies*, 4(6), 10–47760. DOI: 10.47760/ cognizance.2024.v04i06.024

Valladares Ríos, L., Acosta-Diaz, R., & Santana-Mancilla, P. C. (2023). Enhancing Self-Learning in Higher Education with Virtual and Augmented Reality Role Games: Students' Perceptions. *Virtual Worlds*, 2(4), 343–358. DOI: 10.3390/ virtualworlds2040020

Van Leeuwen, A., & Janssen, J. (2019). A systematic review of teacher guidance during collaborative learning in primary and secondary education. *Educational Research Review*, 27, 71–89. DOI: 10.1016/j.edurev.2019.02.001

Van Merriënboer, J. J. G., & Sweller, J. (2005). Cognitive load theory and complex learning: Recent developments and future directions. *Educational Psychology Review*, 17(2), 147–177. DOI: 10.1007/s10648-005-3951-0

VanLehn, K. (2011). The relative effectiveness of human tutoring, intelligent tutoring systems, and other tutoring systems. *Educational Psychologist*, 46(4), 197–221. DOI: 10.1080/00461520.2011.611369

Vasudevan, A. (2017). Slow learners – Causes, problems and educational programmes. *International Journal of Applied Research*, 3(12), 308–313.

Vats, S., & Joshi, R. (2023). The Impact of Virtual Reality in Education: A Comprehensive Research Study. *International Working Conference on Transfer and Diffusion of IT*, 126–136.

Vekiri, I., & Chronaki, A. (2008). Gender issues in technology use: Perceived social support, computer self-efficacy, and value beliefs, and computer use beyond school. *Computers & Education*, 51(3), 1392–1404.

Vellapandi, R., & Gunasekaran, S. (2020). A new decision making approach for winning strategy based on muti soft set logic. Journal of fuzzy extension and applications, 1(2), 112-121.

Verdote, R. J. M. (2019). The Philippines, Part 1: The University of Cordilleras and Its Place in Philippines Higher Education. In *The Global Phenomenon of Family-Owned or Managed Universities*. Brill., DOI: 10.1163/9789004423435_014

Verner, I., Cuperman, D., Perez-Villalobos, H., Polishuk, A., & Gamer, S. (2022). Augmented and Virtual Reality Experiences for Learning Robotics and Training Integrative Thinking Skills. *Robotics (Basel, Switzerland)*, 11(5). Advance online publication. DOI: 10.3390/robotics11050090

Vidal, J. (2022). Digital education: The approach of a modern teacher. *Jozac Academic Voice*, 71-76. https://doi.org/DOI: 10.57040/av.vi.246

Villanueva, A., Zhu, Z., Liu, Z., Peppler, K., Redick, T., & Ramani, K. (2020, April). Meta-AR-app: an authoring platform for collaborative augmented reality in STEM classrooms. In *Proceedings of the 2020 CHI conference on human factors in computing systems* (pp. 1-14).

Vinojini, M. & Anton Arulrajah, A. (2018). The Pro-Environmental Behaviour of Employee in an Apparel Manufacturing Organization in Nuwara-Eliya District of Sri Lanka.

Virgili, G., Acosta, R., Bentley, S. A., Giacomelli, G., Allcock, C., & Evans, J. R. (2018). Reading aids for adults with low vision. *Cochrane Library, 2018*(4). https://doi.org/DOI: 10.1002/14651858.cd003303.pub4

Virgili, G., Acosta, R., Grover, L. L., Bentley, S. A., & Giacomelli, G. (2013). Reading aids for adults with low vision. *Cochrane Database of Systematic Reviews*, 10(10), CD003303. Advance online publication. DOI: 10.1002/14651858.CD003303.pub3 PMID: 24154864

Viviroli, D., Weingartner, R., & Messerli, B. (2007). Assessing the hydrological significance of the world's mountains. *Mountain Research and Development*, 23(1), 32–40. DOI: 10.1659/0276-4741(2007)27[32:ATHSOT]2.0.CO;2

Volkova, L.V., Lizunova, L.R., Komarova, I.A.: (2021). Digital pedagogy. Revista on line de Polítíca e Gestˉao Educacional

von Garrel, J., & Mayer, J. (2023). Artificial Intelligence in studies—Use of ChatGPT and AI-based tools among students in Germany. *Humanities & Social Sciences Communications*, 10(1), 799. Advance online publication. DOI: 10.1057/s41599-023-02304-7

Vygotsky, L. S. (1978). *Mind in society: The development of higher psychological processes* (Vol. 86). Harvard university press.

Wade, A. D., & Wang, K. (2016). The Rise of Machines: Artificial Intelligence Meets scholarly content. *Learned Publishing*, 29, 201–205.

Wagner, A. R., Borenstein, J., & Howard, A. (2018, September). Overtrust in the robotics age. *Communications of the ACM*, 61(9), 22–24. DOI: 10.1145/3241365

Walker, R., Usher, K., Jackson, D., Reid, C., Hopkins, K., Shepherd, C., & Marriott, R. (2021). Addressing digital inequities in supporting the well-being of young Indigenous Australians in the wake of COVID-19. *International Journal of Environmental Research and Public Health*, 18(4), 2141. DOI: 10.3390/ijerph18042141 PMID: 33671737

Walle, H., Serres, B., Gilles, V., & De Runz, C. (2022). A Survey on Recent Advances in AI and Vision-Based Methods for Helping and Guiding Visually Impaired People. *Applied Sciences (Basel, Switzerland)*, 12(5), 2308. DOI: 10.3390/app12052308

Walter, S. L., & Dekker, D. E. (2011). Mother tongue instruction in Lubuagan: A case study from the Philippines. *International Review of Education*, 57(5-6), 667–683. DOI: 10.1007/s11159-011-9246-4

Walton Family Foundation. (2023, March 1). Teachers and students embrace ChatGPT for education. Walton Family Foundation. https://www.waltonfamilyfoundation.org/learning/teachers-and-students-embrace-chatgpt-for-education

Wang, Q., Kou, Z., Sun, X., Wang, S., Wang, X., Jing, H., & Lin, P. (2022). Predictive Analysis of the Pro-Environmental Behaviour of College Students Using a Decision-Tree Model.

Wang, Y., & Zhang, W. (2017). Factors Influencing the Adoption of Generative AI for Art Designing among Chinese Generation Z: A Structural equation modeling approach. *IEEE Access*. https://www.mendeley.com/reference-manager/reader-v2/91a8830d-70ac-34d3-a5c7-0743720fa9c1/6fc85f02-f390-2d55-11b9-4ff6473ab798

Wang'ang'a, A. W. (2024). Consequences of Artificial Intelligence on Teaching and Learning in Higher Education in Kenya: Literature Review East African. *Journal of Education Studies*, 7(1), 202–215.

Wang, C., Li, Z., & Bonk, C. (2024). Understanding self-directed learning in AI-Assisted writing: A mixed methods study of postsecondary learners. *Computers and Education: Artificial Intelligence*, 6, 100247. Advance online publication. DOI: 10.1016/j.caeai.2024.100247

Wang, J., Wang, S., & Zhang, Y. (2023). Artificial intelligence for visually impaired. *Displays*, 77(102391), 102391. DOI: 10.1016/j.displa.2023.102391

Wang, X., Li, Y., Zhang, H., & Chen, Z. (2023). Artificial intelligence in education: Current applications and future directions. *Journal of Educational Technology & Society*, 26(1), 12–27.

Wang, Y., Liu, C., & Tu, Y.-F. (2021). Factors affecting the adoption of AI-based Applications in higher education: An analysis of teachers perspectives using structural equation modelling. *Journal of Educational Technology & Society*, 24(3), 116–129.

Wang, Z., Liu, X., & Jiang, C. (2023). AI in higher education: The influence on student performance and teacher engagement. *Educational Technology Research and Development*, 71(1), 123–140. DOI: 10.1007/s11423-022-10167-6

Warschauer, M. (2003). *Technology and social inclusion: Rethinking the digital divide*. MIT Press.

Waskom, M. L. (2021). Seaborn: Statistical data visualization. *Journal of Open Source Software*, 6(60), 3021. DOI: 10.21105/joss.03021

Watson, A., & Duffield, L. (2015). From garamut to mobile phone: Communication change in rural Papua New Guinea. *Mobile Media & Communication*, 4(2), 270–287. DOI: 10.1177/2050157915622658

Wearable low vision glasses for visually impaired. IrisVision. (2024b, July 11). https://irisvision.com/esight-alternative/

Webb, A., & Radcliffe, S. (2016). Whitened geographies and education inequalities in southern Chile. *Journal of Intercultural Studies (Melbourne, Vic.)*, 37(3), 267–285. DOI: 10.1080/07256868.2016.1141757

Wei, S., Jing, B., Zhang, X., Liao, J., Yuan, C., Fan, B. Y., Lyu, C., Zhou, D., Wang, Y., Deng, G., Song, H., Oblak, D., Guo, G., & Zhou, Q. (2022). Towards real-world quantum networks: A review. *Laser & Photonics Reviews*, ●●●, 16.

Weng, X., & Chiu, T. K. F. (2023). Instructional design and learning outcomes of intelligent computer assisted language learning: Systematic review in the field. In *Computers and Education: Artificial Intelligence* (Vol. 4). Elsevier B.V. DOI: 10.1016/j.caeai.2022.100117

West, D. M. (2019). *The future of work: Robots, AI, and automation*. Brookings Institution Press.

Westfall, L., & Leider, A. (2019). Teaching quantum computing. In Proceedings of the Future Technologies Conference (FTC) 2018: Volume 2 (pp. 63-80). Springer International Publishing.

White House Office of Science and Technology Policy. (2022, October). Blueprint for an AI bill of rights: Making automated systems work for the American people. The White House Office of Science and Technology Policy. https://www.whitehouse .gov/ostp/ai-bill-of-rights/

Williamson, B. (2017). Moulding student emotions through computational psychology: affective learning technologies and algorithmic governance.

Williamson, B., & Eynon, R. (2020). Datafied Education: Privacy and Online Learning. *Learning, Media and Technology, 45*(1), 3-https://doi.org/DOI: 10.1080/17439884.2020.1694943

Winkler, R., & Söllner, M. (2018). Unleashing the potential of chatbots in education: A state-of-the-art analysis. In *Academy of Management Annual Meeting Proceedings* (Vol. 2018, No. 1, p. 15903). https://doi.org/DOI: 10.5465/AMBPP.2018.15903ab-stract

Woolf, B. P. (2010). *Building intelligent interactive tutors: Student-centered strategies for revolutionizing e-learning.* Morgan Kaufmann.

Woolf, B. P., Lane, H. C., Chaudhri, V., & Kolodner, J. (2013). AI grand challenges for education. *AI Magazine*, 34(4), 66–84. DOI: 10.1609/aimag.v34i4.2499

Wootton, J. R., Harkins, F., Bronn, N. T., Vazquez, A. C., Phan, A., & Asfaw, A. T. (2021, October). Teaching quantum computing with an interactive textbook. In *2021 IEEE International Conference on Quantum Computing and Engineering (QCE)* (pp. 385-391). IEEE.

World Bank. (2015). *Indigenous Latin America in the Twenty-First Century: The First Decade.* World Bank., DOI: 10.1596/978-1-4648-0325-9

Wu, B. (2019). Personalized Education for Graduate Students Driven by Artificial Intelligence and Big Data. *Teaching of Forestry Region*, (7).

Wu, Q., Zeng, Y., Zhang, C., Tong, L., & Yan, B. (2018). An EEG-Based Person Authentication System with Open-Set Capability Combining Eye Blinking Signals. *Sensors (Basel)*, 18(335). Advance online publication. DOI: 10.3390/s18020335 PMID: 29364848

Xia, C., Li, X., & Cao, S. (2023). Challenges for the government-controlled higher Education system in China. *International Journal of Educational Development*, (97), 102721.

Xiaolei, S., & Teng, M. F. (2024). Three-wave cross-lagged model on the correlations between critical thinking skills, self-directed learning competency and AI-assisted writing. *Thinking Skills and Creativity*, 52, 101524. Advance online publication. DOI: 10.1016/j.tsc.2024.101524

Xiao, Y., & Zhi, Y. (2023). An exploratory study of EFL learners' use of ChatGPT For language Learning tasks: Experience and perceptions. *Languages (Basel, Switzerland)*, 8(3), 1–12.

Xie, H., Chu, H.-C., Hwang, G.-J., & Wang, C.-C. (2019). *"Trends and development in technology-enhanced adaptive/personalized learning:"* A systematic review of journal publications from 2007 to 2017. *Computers & Education*, 140, 103599. DOI: 10.1016/j.compedu.2019.103599

Yufei, L., Saleh, S. Jiahui, H, Mohamad, S., and Abdullah,S. (2020). Review of The Application of Artificial Intelligence in Education. *International Journal of Innovation, Creativity and Change. 12(8).*

Yurtseven Avci, Z., Ergulec, F., Misirli, O., & Sural, I. (2022). Flipped learning in information technology courses: Benefits and challenges. *Journal of Further and Higher Education*, 46(5), 636–650. DOI: 10.1080/0309877X.2021.1986623

Zabala, C. (2023). Exploring the applicability of Artificial Intelligence in Local Government Units (LGUs) in Zamboanga Peninsula (Region IX), Philippines. https://dx.doi.org/DOI: 10.2139/ssrn.4506110

Zable, A., Hollenberg, L., Velloso, E., & Goncalves, J. (2020, November). Investigating immersive virtual reality as an educational tool for quantum computing. In *Proceedings of the 26th ACM Symposium on Virtual Reality Software and Technology* (pp. 1-11).

Zacamy, J., & Roschelle, J. (2022). Navigating the tensions: How could equity-relevant research also be agile, open, and scalable? Digital Promise. http://hdl.handle .net/20.500.12265/159

Zaraii Zavaraki, E. (2024). *Artificial Intelligence for People with Special Educational Needs*. IntechOpen., DOI: 10.5772/intechopen.1004158

Zastudil, C., Rogalska, M., Kapp, C., Vaughn, J., & MacNeil, S. (2023). Generative AI in Computing Education: Perspectives of Students and Instructors. *Human - Computer Interaction.* http://arxiv.org/abs/2308.04309

Zavaraki, E. Z., & Alimardani, F. (2023, July). The role of blended learning approach on interaction process of students with special educational needs. In EdMedia+ Innovate Learning (pp. 1243-1247). Association for the Advancement of Computing in Education (AACE).

Zavaraki, E., & Schneider, D. (2019). Blended learning approach for students with special educational needs: A systematic review. *Journal of Education & Social Policy.*, 6(3), 1–2.

Zawacki-Richter, O., Marín, V. I., Bond, M., & Gouverneur, F. (2019). Systematic review of research on artificial intelligence applications in higher education – where are the educators? *International Journal of Educational Technology in Higher Education*, 16(1), 39. DOI: 10.1186/s41239-019-0171-0

Zehui, Z. (2023). Pro-Environmental Behavior and Actions: Review of the literature and agenda for future research.

Zhai, X., & Jong, M. S. Y. (2021). Leveraging artificial intelligence to enhance educational practices: Challenges and opportunities. *Journal of Educational Technology & Society*, 24(1), 14–28. DOI: 10.1111/j.1468-0327.2021.01056.x

Zhang, C., Wang, X., Fang, S., & Shi, X. (2022). Construction and Application of VR-AR Teaching System in Coal-Based Energy Education. *Sustainability (Switzerland)*, 14(23). Advance online publication. DOI: 10.3390/su142316033

Zhang, H., Lee, I., Ali, S., DiPaola, D., Cheng, Y., & Breazeal, C. (2022). Integrating ethics and career futures with technical learning to promote AI literacy for middle school students: An exploratory study. *International Journal of Artificial Intelligence in Education*, •••, 1–35. DOI: 10.1007/s40593-022-00293-3 PMID: 35573722

Zhang, J., & Aslan, A. (2024). Teachers' perceptions of AI in education: Current use and future expectations. *British Journal of Educational Technology*, 55(3), 98–113. DOI: 10.1111/bjet.13242

Zhang, K., & Aslan, A. B. (2021). AI technologies for education: Recent research & future directions. *Computers and Education: Artificial Intelligence*, 2, 100025. DOI: 10.1016/j.caeai.2021.100025

Zhang, Y., & Li, X. (2022). Implementing smart classroom technologies: Benefits, challenges, and future directions. *Journal of Educational Technology Development and Exchange*, 15(1), 25–42.

Zhao, X., Ren, Y., & Cheah, K. S. L. (2023). Leading Virtual Reality (VR) and Augmented Reality (AR) in Education: Bibliometric and Content Analysis From the Web of Science (2018–2022). *SAGE Open*, 13(3). Advance online publication. DOI: 10.1177/21582440231190821

Zhao, Y., Wang, Y., & Li, H. (2016). Temperature regulation and student comfort in classroom environments: An IoT approach. *Building and Environment*, 104, 221–229.

Zheng, W. L., & Lu, B. L. (2017). A multimodal approach to estimating vigilance using EEG and forehead EOG. *Journal of Neural Engineering*, 14, 026017. DOI: 10.1088/1741-2552/aa5a98 PMID: 28102833

Zhou, L., Li, W., & Zhang, J. (2021). Ensuring equitable student engagement through voice recognition technology. *Journal of Educational Technology & Society*, 24(2), 123–136.

Zhou, L., Wang, Z., & Yang, F. (2020). Voice recognition for monitoring classroom participation: Benefits and limitations. *Journal of Classroom Interaction*, 55(1), 31–45.

Zou, Y., & Xiao, Z. (2008). Data analysis approaches of soft sets under incomplete information. *Knowledge-Based Systems*, 21(8), 941–945. DOI: 10.1016/j.knosys.2008.04.004

Zulehner, A., & Wille, R. (2017). Advanced simulation of quantum computations. *IEEE Transactions on Computer-Aided Design of Integrated Circuits and Systems*, 38, 848–859.

About the Contributors

Froilan Mobo is a Doctor of Public Administration graduate from the Urdaneta City University Class of 2016 and a graduate of the 2nd Doctorate Degree (Ph.D.) in Development Education program at the Central Luzon State University, Nueva Ecija, Philippines, Class of 2022. On March 11, 2024, Dr. Mobo was accredited and reclassified by the Commission on Higher Education (CHED) to the position of Professor II in the Philippine Merchant Marine Academy (PMMA), and this allowed him to work with different international research institutions, such as the Director and Research Consultant of the IKSAD Research Institute, Turkey. At present, he is in the process of finishing his 3rd master's degree, leading to social studies education at Bicol University. Recently, Dr. Mobo passed Batch 3—Certified Research Professional—and ranked in the top 5 in the National Examination and also passed the Certified Human Resource Associate (CHRA). He was appointed Editor-in-Chief of the International Journal of Multidisciplinary: Applied Business and Education Research, Malang, Indonesia, and appointed as a technical research evaluator by the Department of Science and Technology and Book Chapter Editor in IGI Global Publisher based in USA. He has published 109 research articles with 178 citations indexed in the Web of Science, Scopus, and ASEAN Citation Index

***

John Mark R. Asio currently works and designated as Research Director of the Research Development and Community Extension Services at Gordon College, Olongapo City. He does research in Higher Education, Educational Policy, Educational Management, Pedagogy, Social Sciences, Public Administration, and Organizational Management. He is also a Registered Nurse, Registered Midwife, Licensed Professional Teacher, and Civil Service Eligible (Professional).

Sreya Barik is a Diploma CSE student at Brainware University. Her research interests include AI, ML, and social networking, contributing significantly to advancements in her field.

Raino Bhatia is the Principal and Associate Professor of Akal College of Education, Eternal University, and holds an M.Phil. and Ph.D. in Education, along with the UGC-NET qualification. In 2009, she received the National Award and published the book, *The Quest for True Happiness*.

Saumendra Das presently working as an Associate Professor at the School of Management Studies, GIET University, Gunupur, Odisha. He has over 20 years of teaching, research, and industry experience. He has published more than 98 articles in national and international journals, conference proceedings, and book chapters. He also authored and edited 15 books of national repute. Dr Das has participated in and presented many papers at seminars, conferences, and workshops in India and abroad. He has organized many FDPs and seminars in his career. He is an academician, author, and editor. He has also published three patents. He is an active member of various professional bodies such as ICA, ISTE and RFI. In the year 2023, he was awarded as the best teacher by the Research Foundation India.

Arul Dayanand is an Assistant Professor at the Department of English and Foreign Languages (EFL) of the SRM Institute of Science and Technology, Kattankulathur. He has been guiding researchers and teaching communication skills for over a decade, with an extensive background in Linguistics and Educational Technology. He obtained his Doctoral degree from Bharathiar University, Coimbatore, and has published more than ten articles in accredited journals. His areas of research interest include Computer-Assisted Language Learning and Teaching, Teaching English as a Second Language, Linguistics, and Instructional Design.

Devaki V serves as an Assistant Professor at the Department of Education (SASHE), SASTRA Deemed to be University, Thanjavur. She holds Master of Science in Physics from Alagappa University, Karaikudi, graduating with the distinction of second rank in university. Additionally, she completed Master of Education at Sri Sarada College of Education, Salem, Tamil Nadu. She qualified for the position of Assistant Professor in Physics, having successfully cleared the Tamil Nadu State Eligibility Test and also passed in the Central Teacher Eligibility Test. She is currently pursuing her doctoral studies in the Department of Education at Bharathidasan University, Tiruchirappalli. Her research interests encompass metacognition, neurocognition, the pedagogy of science, and experiential learning.

Richa Joshi, is an assistant Professor in Education at Eternal University. She holds an M.Com. and M.Ed., complemented by her qualification in the UGC NET examination. She has participated in various Faculty Development Programs (FDPs) and seminars to enhance her skills and stay updated with the latest teaching methodologies.

Jagneet Kour is a research scholar in education and a gold medalist in postgraduate studies from Eternal University. She is currently pursuing her Ph.D. in Education, and previously earned degrees in B.Ed. and M.A. in Education, as well as qualifying UGC NET JRF on her first attempt and clearing the CTET examinations. Kour has published extensively in esteemed journals, such as *UGC CARE I* and other Scopus-indexed publications and is the editor of *Transforming Indian Education in the 21st Century*, centered on India's New Education Policy 2020.

S. Ramesh Kumar is an esteemed Assistant Professor in the English Department at Hainan University, China. He has over six years of experience in teaching Oral English at various universities across China. Furthermore, he has administered the Business English Examinations for Cambridge Assessment and imparted workplace communication skills to technical universities in India for five years. Dr. Ramesh Kumar's areas of expertise encompass English Language Teaching, and he holds a master's degree and a Ph.D. in Linguistics. He is also a certified Cambridge BEC Examiner, TESOL Certified by Arizona State University, and has completed the TEFL in China.

M Uma Devi is an Associate Professor in the Department of Computing Technologies. Her research interests include Data Mining, Information Retrieval, Language Digitization, and Computer Vision. Dr. Devi holds a Ph.D. and M.E. from the Sathyabama Institute of Science and Technology and a B.E. from N. I College of Engg, Manonmaniam Sundaranar University. Her academic and practical insights have made significant contributions to the field of computing, particularly in the areas of the Theory of Computation and Compiler Design.

Sunkesula Mahammad Ali has Multiple Master degrees in Philosophy, Physics, Telugu and Education from various universities of Andhra Pradesh. He has awarded Master of Philosophy in Education from Periyar University, Salem Tamilnadu. He has also received Doctoral research Degree in Philosophy of Education at the Dravidian university, Kuppam's CDLP department under the expert guidance of Prof. Balaganapathi Devarakonda. He has a rich and diverse experience in academic writing, teaching, translation, statistical analysis and research. He got opportunities to work as a Junior Linguist and Project Fellow in notable projects such as ILCI, UGC. This experience has enabled him to author, co-author, and edit 17 books/

reference materials and 10 research papers. He has also completed Post-Doctoral research at Dr. BR Ambedkar Open University, Hyderabad Telangana under Prof. MTV Nagaraju's guidance. Prior to his current role, he served as Assistant Professor and Principal in various education colleges across five Indian states. Currently, he is a PGT-Physics at AP Model School and Jr College, Amarapuram Sri Sathya Sai District -515 281, Andhra Pradesh.

Narayana Maharana, B.Sc., MBA, M.Com., is an Assistant Professor in the Department of Management Studies at GVP College of Engineering (Autonomous) in Visakhapatnam, Andhra Pradesh, India. Holding the prestigious UGC NET (JRF) in Management and UGC NET in Commerce, he showcases a deep understanding and mastery of these fields. With over eight years of dedicated teaching experience, He is committed to providing high-quality education in postgraduate courses in Management and related subjects. His passion for research is evident through his active participation in numerous Faculty Development Programmes and frequent presentations at national and international conferences. He has published over 20 articles in esteemed journals indexed in UGC CARE, Scopus, ABDC and Web of Science etc. He has also authored nine chapters in edited books. His scholarly contributions highlight his dedication to research and academia.

Debasis Pani has been working as an Assistant Professor in the Department of Business Administration at Gandhi Institute of Advanced Computer and Research in Rayagada, Odisha, India since last 17 years. He holds an MBA degree from Sambalpur University and MA in Economics from Andhra university. He also attended FDP entitled "Induction Training Programme in Management for Young Teachers" at Indian Institute of Management, Kozhikode. Holding the prestigious UGC-NET in Management reflects his deep understanding and mastery of these fields. Further, he was conferred with enthusiastic PhD degree in Management from Berhampur University. With over a decade of distinguished teaching experience and steadfast dedication to the teaching-learning profession, he is embarking on providing quality education in Management and related subjects. He has actively participated in many FDPs and presented research paper at national and international conferences. He has published over 10 articles in reputed journals indexed in UGC CARE, SCOPUS and Web of Science etc. His significant contribution in the in the research and academic odyssey is not only milestone but also testimonial of culmination of years of hard work and perseverance which lays foundation for his future endeavour.

Swetha Appaji Parivara is an Associate Professor at Presidency College (Autonomous), Bengaluru, with nearly two decades of experience in academia.

Her extensive career spans prestigious state universities and institutions, where she has made significant contributions to the field of finance and analytics. Dr. Swetha holds a Ph.D. in Finance and is a certified Data Science professional, with expertise in Python, R, and Tableau. Her scholarly work includes presenting and publishing research in national and international forums, including Scopus-indexed journals. In addition to her academic role, Dr. Swetha is a freelance Data Science professional and a corporate trainer, with a focus on finance and data science domains. Her diverse interests also extend to finance, accounting, and tourism, reflecting her multifaceted expertise.

Sunil Kumar Pradhan (b.1975) MBA, MFT, Ph.D, UGC NET(Management), is a distinguished Teacher having 25 years' experience in the field of Marketing & International Business. He has been conferred with his Ph.D degree by Berhampur University in 2009. He has published 35 research papers in different journals and magazines of National and International repute. He has participated and presented 40 papers in various National and international conferences, seminars, symposia and workshops. Under his able guidance, 6 Ph.D research scholars have been awarded and 4 research scholars pursuing their Ph.D degree. At present Dr. Pradhan is working as Assistant Professor- Stage-III, in the Dept. of Business Administration, Berhampur University since 2011.

Sutapa Sahu is a Diploma CSE student at Brainware University. Her research interests include AI, ML, and social networking, contributing significantly to advancements in her field.

Saptarshi Kumar Sarkar is an assistant professor at Brainware University. With a dedication to academic excellence, he brings a wealth of knowledge and his experience to students. His research interests include AI, ML, and social networking, contributing significantly to advancements in his field.

Kalyani Satone is a distinguished educator, researcher, and software expert whose journey in the realm of Computer Science and Engineering has been remarkable. With both a Bachelor's (B.E.) and Master's (M.E.) degree in Computer Science and Engineering from Govt. Engineering College Amravati, she laid the foundation for a thriving career filled with significant contributions to the field. She has amassed 19 years of total experience. Currently pursuing her Ph.D. from Amravati University, Kalyani's insatiable thirst for knowledge and passion for innovation continue to propel her forward. As an Assistant Professor in ST.Vincent Pallotti Colege of Enggineerinad and Technology, Nagpur Maharashtra, she plays a pivotal role in shaping the minds of aspiring young learners. She has authored several research papers presented and acclaimed at both national and international conferences. Kalyani has also penned four internationally published books: "Java Programming," "Excel for Managers," "Object-Oriented Modelling and Designing," and "Python Programming."

Sakshi Saxena has worked as an Assistant Professor of Finance with reputed Institutes in Bangalore, Delhi and NCR, India. She is PhD in Finance from Banasthali Vidyapith, Rajasthan, India. She holds a Master degree in Business Administration (MBA) and has also qualified NET exam conducted by UGC, India. She has a substantial expertise in teaching finance and management courses for more than a decade for both under graduates and post graduates. Her teaching experience is complemented by her research work, evident by having 20 plus research papers published in various Indexed journals like UGC Care, SCOPUS and ABDC Listed journals. She has also presented her research at various National and International conferences, some of which were conducted by premier Management Institutes of India such as IIM-Ahmedabad, IIM-Bangalore and IIM-Kolkata. She is actively reviewing manuscripts for various esteemed journals like Sage Publications. She also has a patent published to her credit.

Suresh Chinna received a PhD degree in Education from the Sri Venkateswara University, Tirupati, Andhra Pradesh, India, in 2018 and has an M.Sc. degree in Mathematics from Sri Krinshnadevaraya University, Anantapur, Andhra Pradesh, India, in 2010 and a. He works as an Assistant Professor at the Department of Education, School of Arts, Humanities, Sciences and Education, SASTRA Deemed to be University, Thanjavur, Tamilnadu-613401. His research interests include ICT in Education, Mathematics Pedagogy, Gender Studies, and Teaching Strategies.

Tran Minh Tung gains (his 1st Doctoral Degree) a Doctor of Business Administration (DBA Degree) in Marketing Management from University of Technology and Management (UITM), Poland and a Master of Science in Business Information Systems from Heilbronn University, German. He is currently Director FSB Danang - FPT School of Business and Technology (FSB) - FPT University cum Media and Business Lecturer. He has over 18 years of work experience and over 12 years in teaching and sharing at both over 40 Enterprises and over 22 Higher Educational Institutions in Vietnam. His research interests are in Social Media, PR, Marketing, Marketing in Higher Education, Innovation Teaching Methodology, Data Driven Marketing, Information Systems, Standards Based Curriculum, Experience Learning and Gamification in Education. Recently, he has completed and obtained (his 2nd and 3rd Doctoral Degree) EdD - Professional Doctorate in Educational Administration & Leadership and Doctor of Philosophy (Ph.D.) in Media and Communication from European International University, EIU-Paris, France, in

2023 which can assist him in his personal development plan (PDP) and professional career in current role.

Bindi Barghese has a Doctorate in Commerce, with 19 years of Academic experience;Currently, affiliated with Christ University, as an Associate Professor and is the Research Coordinator at School of Business and Management. Served as a national and international expert, and is working with Indian Tourism Congress (ITC) and is the honorary director at Kerala Development Society (KDS), New Delhi. The active researches undertaken include Impact Assessment Studies, Medical Tourism, Destination Management Organization and Ecological Studies. Dr. Bindi completed a major research project on the title "Strategic Intervention of Destination Management Organizations to Enhance Competitiveness of Tourism Destinations– A Model for Karnataka" funded by Christ University. Along with her academic expertise, she is also an Section editor for 'ATNA- Journal of Tourism Studies', published by Christ University, Bengaluru. She has authored one book; on Medical Tourism in India: and has edited a book on "Evolving Paradigms in Tourism and Hospitality in Developing Countries: A Case Study of India". The book is published by CRC Press, Taylor and Francis group - international publisher in US and released in 2018.

Yashwant Waykar is a dedicated educator and researcher at Dr. Babasaheb Ambedkar Marathwada University, specializing in Software Engineering, Machine Learning, Artificial Intelligence, and Learning Management Systems (LMS). With over 14 years of experience and a Ph.D., Dr. Waykar has authored 40+ publications in prestigious journals indexed in SCOPUS, UGC CARE, and Web of Science. Their research has earned accolades and includes several book chapters and four patents (3 granted, 1 filed) in LMS and AI. Dr. Waykar's teaching in AI, Web Development, and Software Testing is highly regarded, fostering a dynamic learning environment. They have completed three research projects funded by UGC and Dr. B.A.M.U. and have mentored 3 M.Phil and 2 Ph.D. students, guiding them in Machine Learning and LMS research.

Sucheta S. Yambal has been an Assistant Professor in the Department of Management Science of Dr. Babasaheb Ambedkar Marathwada University in Chhatrapati Sambhaji Nagar, Maharashtra since 2010. Her total teaching experience is 19 years, and she has about 16 years of research experience. She has taken on several significant duties as a member of the Board of Directors, organized multiple workshops, and given guest lectures at numerous universities. Dr. Yambal has supervised four M.Phil. and four Ph.D. research students at Dr. Babasaheb Ambedkar Marathwada University to date. She has also reviewed Ph.D. theses for

Tilak Maharastra Vidyapeeth, Pune. More than thirty national and international research papers have been published by her at prestigious institutes' international conferences, such as IIT Delhi and IIM Raipur. Her research has also been published in prestigious journals, such as SCOPUS and UGC- Care Listed. In November 2019, Dr. Yambal scored highly in the e-business course on the Nptel platform during an exam administered by IIT Kharagpur. She is deemed a "Women of Substance" 2018 Award which was organized at MGM, Chhtrapati Sambhaji Nagar. She had a stellar academic record from elementary school to the Dr. Babasaheb Ambedkar Marathwada University Ph.D. admission exam, where she received the best possible mark. Her areas of interest include employment, AI/ML, automation in industries, database management systems and data mining, modern and inclusive education, and employability.

Index

A

E

www.ingramcontent.com/pod-product-compliance
Ingram Content Group UK Ltd.
Pitfield, Milton Keynes, MK11 3LW, UK
UKHW052144050225
454711UK00006B/33

9 798369 381